NEW ZEALAND SOCIETY AT WAR
1914–1918

NEW ZEALAND SOCIETY AT WAR
1914–1918

Edited by Steven Loveridge

VICTORIA UNIVERSITY PRESS

TE WHARE WĀNANGA O TE ŪPOKO O TE IKA A MĀUI
VICTORIA
UNIVERSITY OF WELLINGTON

VICTORIA UNIVERSITY PRESS
Victoria University of Wellington
PO Box 600 Wellington
vup.victoria.ac.nz

First published 2016

National Library of New Zealand Cataloguing-in-Publication Data

New Zealand society at war 1914-1918 / edited by Steven Loveridge.
ISBN 978-1-77656-060-8
1. World War, 1914-1918—Social aspects—New Zealand.
2. World War, 1914-1918—New Zealand.
I. Loveridge, Steven,1985-
940.393—dc 23

creative nz
ARTS COUNCIL OF NEW ZEALAND *TOI AOTEAROA*

Printed by yourbooks.co.nz

Contents

Acknowledgements

The genesis of this book was a discussion between Professor Richard Hill and myself over a research project exploring the relationship between the New Zealand Police Force and New Zealand's war effort through 1914–1918. We were pondering the best site for this research when the ambition of locating it alongside similar investigations of other institutions, associations and groups arose. What followed was a venture to hitch specialists to this ambition.

The completion of this endeavour reflects generous contributions of time, labour and expertise from the contributors. I gratefully acknowledge their collegiality and commitment to advancing our scholarship and understanding of New Zealand society towards and through the years of the Great War.

Furthermore, I would like to give special thanks to Angela Clay, Dennis Hucker, Peter Cooke, Judy Malone, Jock Phillips, Malcolm McKinnon, Whairiri Ngata, Archives New Zealand and Statistics New Zealand, who aided in the accessing and securing of material, and to Hew Strachan, James Watson, Jim McAloon, Brian Johnson, Jan Hill, Carolin Marotzke and Kristina Marotzke, who volunteered assistance and advice in various parts of this book's production. I am indebted to Victoria University of Wellington, who provided a research grant supporting the original study of the New Zealand Police Force; the Stout Research Centre, where this book was edited; and Creative New Zealand, who supported research, editing and image investigation. Lastly, I thank Fergus Barrowman, Kyleigh Hodgson and the team at Victoria University Press for their work in preparing the text for publication.

Contemplating the complete text confronts us with the manners in which social elements responded to the cataclysm of war. Recognising the thoughts and forces within these responses might enrich our sense of the dynamics, convictions, passions, tensions, shortcomings and heartbreaks within a society at war.

Steven Loveridge
Wellington
January 2016

Illustrations

Foreword

New Zealand Society in the Great War

Hew Strachan

New Zealand's engagement with the history of the First World War has been reluctant and late, not least in the perception of its own historians. New Zealanders are understandably peeved when Anzac is used too often as a synonym for Australia, but that may be as much New Zealand's own fault as the product of Australian assertiveness. By common consent the interwar history of the New Zealand Expeditionary Force was poorly, and even woodenly, handled. Nor was the project to erect a great memorial in Wellington, fusing shrine and museum as in Canberra, fulfilled. Auckland did adapt its pre-war plan to build a museum for these purposes, but it commemorated the dead of the province, not of the nation. Only now, with the impetus of the centenary, have New Zealanders felt impelled to remedy these deficits.

In some respects, this gives today's historians of New Zealand an advantage not enjoyed by those of other belligerent nations. For many the memory of the war has been hijacked by myths. For them, patterns of commemoration reflect present needs more often than they mirror the complex, confusing and often contradictory realities of the events they mark. The first Australian narrative of the war was shaped by the war correspondent Charles Bean, the man who, more than any other – by dint of his work on Australia's official history and for the Australian War Memorial in Canberra – created the Anzac 'legend'. New Zealand had no equivalent of Bean, either during the war itself or in its immediate aftermath. Ian F. Grant's chapter in this book shows how inadequately the New Zealand press responded to the war. Poor reporting during the conflict itself may help to explain some of the corresponding gaps in the post-war legacy. But there is a gain in this loss: no legend means no myths, or at least not so many of them. The job that confronted Australia's historians as the centenary approached was to deconstruct Bean's legacy, to treat that legacy itself as part of history, and to move the debate from Gallipoli to other areas, both to France and back to Australia itself.

Because New Zealand did less building in the 1920s, it does not have so much deconstruction to do now.

By 2014 nothing illustrated the distinction more clearly than the manner in which the two countries elected to mark the centenary. Australia began planning for the Anzac centenary well in advance of most – if not all – other states. In 2011 it set up a centenary advisory board, which then recommended that the country should mark one hundred years of Anzac service, so explicitly linking past to present, and so also creating a continuity which glossed over political and strategic change. New Zealand entered the fray of centenary commemoration later, and when it did so it eschewed the idea of continuity. It opted to address the First World War as an isolated event, treating the conflict in its own right, so giving itself the opportunity to create the superstructure it had failed to erect in the 1920s and 30s. The first volumes of a new history of New Zealand's role in the war, edited by Glyn Harper, appeared in 2015, and the Great War Exhibition, designed by Peter Jackson, opened in the Dominion Museum building in Wellington on Anzac Day in the same year.

New Zealand Society at War should therefore be lauded, not for the usual reason for which important books are often praised – that they overthrow received wisdom – but for a much more significant quality. It goes into areas where there has been far too little wisdom to receive. It takes two jumps simultaneously – first in exposing the impact of the war on what, at least in Britain, came to be called 'the home front', and second, not least thanks to Steven Loveridge's perceptive introduction to the volume, putting that experience in a comparative context.

Lacking its own narrative, New Zealand has too readily taken Australia's as its own. The dawn service at Anzac Day makes sense for Australians because that was the time of day, at around 5.00 a.m., when the first troops of the Australian Imperial Force went ashore on 25 April 1915. The first New Zealanders did not land until after 10.00 a.m., and the main body even later, by which time Ottoman resistance was much more organised and determined. Today, however, New Zealand's commemoration apes Australia's customs rather than respects its own past. On Anzac Day New Zealanders get up as early as Australians when they don't actually need to; they didn't do that in the 1920s. More importantly, this sleight of hand enables another Australian narrative to cross the Tasman and establish a foothold in the land of the long white cloud. This says that modern Australia was born on the beach at Anzac Cove: it sees Australia before the First World War as British, and Australia after the war as not. It is an interpretation which does violence to Australia's own history; its migration to New Zealand does even more damage to New Zealanders' understanding of their own past.

The Commonwealth of Australia was established in 1901, not in 1915. Its independence from Britain was well in train before Gallipoli. Australia may not have had the power to formulate its own foreign policy, but it could decide how and to what extent it would take part in the war that Britain entered on 4 August 1914. Taking Gallipoli as the foundational story obscures not only the actual (and earlier) formation of Australia, but also the fact that it is the latter which makes the former – the Anzac legend – possible.

New Zealand has even more reason to reject such a simplified and inverted narrative. Its dominion status dates from 1907, and – as Steven Loveridge points out – it was 'born modern'. In 1914 Britain had a more restrictive suffrage than any European country except Hungary. Many of those British soldiers killed on the Western Front were not enfranchised, and not just by virtue of being under 21 years of age. If the obligation to undertake military service is the corollary of the rewards and rights of citizenship, as Jean-Jacques Rousseau and other luminaries of the eighteenth-century Enlightenment believed, the British soldier of the First World War was not a full citizen. By contrast, New Zealand had universal suffrage, both male and female. It introduced compulsory military training in 1909, while Britain was still debating the issue on the outbreak of war. New Zealand's modernity was not just constitutional and political, it was also social and economic. It introduced old age pensions in 1898; Britain only followed suit a decade later. Britain, the world's first industrialised nation, had passed the tipping point at which most of its workforce ceased to be employed on the land; most European countries in 1914 had yet to reach that stage of development, even Germany (second only to the United States as an industrial power) having only just done so. For all its status as a rural economy, New Zealand was more urbanised than its own pastoral self-image suggests. Under half of its workforce was employed on the land, and one third lived in its four major cities, even if many of their jobs (in the slaughterhouses and docks) depended directly or indirectly on agriculture.

Modernity did not translate into an assertive separation from Britain. New Zealanders in 1914 still identified themselves as British, and seem to have done so even more than did the white settlers of the other dominions. The effect of the war was not to rupture this link, but to intensify it – to make New Zealand more British, not less. For all New Zealand's distance from the principal theatres of war, and for all the consequent remoteness of the 'existential' threat posed by Germany, New Zealanders in 1914 neither doubted their Britishness nor disputed the legitimacy of Britain's war. They marched in step with London in embracing the 'big ideas' which underpinned the conflict from its outset – that this was a war for freedom, democracy and international law – and followed British examples in the major adaptations which the war effort required of the state.

The parallels are striking and significant. Britain went to war on the back of an implicit party truce, with the Conservatives committing themselves to support the Liberal government as it confronted the crisis of July 1914. In May 1915 the Prime Minister, H.H. Asquith, formed a coalition government. The fact that New Zealand held an election in December 1914 marked one substantial difference from Britain: Britain should have held an election in 1915 but did not, postponing the potential divisiveness of a campaign until after the war was over. But the outcome of the election in New Zealand was not dissimilar from the political outcome in London. William Massey's Reform Party won 40 of 80 seats, and so failed to secure an absolute majority. In 1915 he too formed a coalition, with Joseph Ward's Liberals. Thereafter, as the essays in *New Zealand Society at War* repeatedly show, Massey's government sought above all else to pursue consensus, so that New Zealand remained broadly united in its responses to the war's challenges. The government acted as a broker between employers and employees, between conscriptionists and their opponents, reading the public mood with adroitness, and marching in step with it rather than trying to force the pace.

Nowhere is this more striking than in its handling of wartime conscription. In 1916 Wellington watched London's moves in this direction with care, and like London did not proceed to conscription until the public mood decreed compulsion to be fairer than voluntary enlistment. Today the reputation of conscription – shaped by the memories of pacifists and conscientious objectors, not least in New Zealand through the testimony of Archibald Baxter – is one of inequity. But in both countries the government followed rather than anticipated the demand for conscription, and then set out to manage its implementation in ways that unified society more than fractured it. They sought simultaneously to meet the needs of both the wartime economy and the army. The big difference between New Zealand and Britain was the more centralised approach adopted by Wellington; the rules were applied unevenly in both countries, but that was particularly the case in Britain, where the tribunals were creatures of local government and so frequently reflected local priorities over national ones.

The story of wartime conscription exposes a cardinal difference between New Zealand and Australia. Australia held two referendums on the subject and rejected it both times. The determination of the

Prime Minister, Billy Hughes, proved abortive, and created deep splits in Australian society. He divided his own party, the Labour Party, for a generation. Not for nothing has Joan Beaumont called her recent magisterial history of Australia in the Great War *Broken Nation*. Here is the true counterpoint to the Gallipoli 'myth': the war divided Australia at home more than it forged it in the furnace of battle, at least in the short term. In New Zealand the trend was the other way. The Labour movement, defeated in the Great Strike of 1913, seemed divided and lost in 1914, but in 1916 it united to form its own political party. In Australia many Catholics were outraged by Britain's response to the Easter Rising in Dublin in 1916, and the Archbishop of Melbourne both supported Sinn Fein and spoke for a radicalised Australian working class. In New Zealand, by contrast, sectarian demagoguery was a preserve of the Protestants, as Brad Patterson's chapter shows. The ranting of the Reverend Howard Leslie Elliott of the Protestant Political Association now seems absurd (it is tempting to see Elliott as New Zealand's answer to Britain's Horatio Bottomley), but, crucially, it demanded greater support for the war effort. If he was subversive, it was because his demands for New Zealand to do even more were in danger of undermining the equilibrium sustained by the government, which had enabled it to do so much. The Catholics' response to Elliott's tirades against the Vatican was straightforward: to provide the evidence of their contribution, not to undermine the state.

The fact that New Zealand's press was less strident than others may have contributed to the creation of this cohesion. New Zealand society was less damaged by the war – at least comparatively – than were those of most belligerents. Prices rose but were more controlled than in Britain, not least because staples like food were never in short supply. Bank deposits rose during the war. Despite New Zealand's proportionately high losses on the battlefield, the exemptions from overseas service for single sons and married men with children cushioned families from some of the war's worst effects. Full-blown socialism and war weariness had less fertile ground in New Zealand than it did elsewhere.

To conclude that the war unified New Zealand more than it divided it would, as the chapters of this book show, fall into the trap of creating its own myth. The idea of national unity in 1914 remained a powerful trope in many countries during the war and after it. The use of the *Augusterlebnis* and the *Burgfrieden* of 1914 in the post-war nationalist rhetoric of Germany shows the dangers, as well as the over-simplification, inherent in such an approach. New Zealand experienced domestic discord as well as domestic unity. Unable to locate a real military danger close at hand, New Zealanders looked for one within; the anti-German movement in

New Zealand society created an enemy where there was none. The growth in bank deposits suggested war profiteering; Elliott's sectarianism proved alarmingly popular at the war's end; and the good story New Zealand liked to tell itself about Maori-Pakeha relationships was not unalloyed in the war. Resistance to the ballot was as evident among the Maori in Waikato as it was among some trade unionists. By-elections in 1918 were won by socialists, not by the parties in government, and pointed to incipient war weariness.

The story told by this book, important and pioneering as it is, ends in 1918. Self-evidently, as New Zealand's response to the centenary demonstrates, the country's engagement with the First World War had only just begun. How New Zealand would react to the Second World War was itself predicated on the experience of the First, and on the lessons both government and society had drawn from it. Of even greater importance for our own times is the outstanding question which the First World War poses not only for New Zealand but also for almost every nation which fought it. How did a war seen by so many in 1914 (including New Zealanders) as unequivocally just and necessary become transmogrified into a war without purpose? If we cannot answer that question coherently (and we still struggle to do so), then we also struggle to understand the stories of individuals and their complex motivations. How did a conscientious objector like Archibald Baxter make the journey from persecution and isolation to prominence and even renown? We tell the stories of war in overwhelmingly national terms, but those stories have a purchase which crosses frontiers, and whose comparative features illuminate both the experiences of other countries and the predicaments of our own times.

Introduction

A Small Land in a World War

Steven Loveridge

This book turns on the premise that the social history of First World War New Zealand is a multifaceted subject, the result of a conflict which, more or less, involved entire societies. Its chapters aim to contemplate the complexities arising from this rather straightforward premise through 18 investigations of particular social institutions, associations and groups. As well as exploring wartime experiences, each contributor outlines the historical context of their subject and what their perspective might add to our comprehension of New Zealand society at war. Together these investigations afford a novel opportunity to survey a mosaic of different, often interlocking, perspectives and experiences. Chapters range the social fabric (the rugby club, the pulpit, the union meeting, the voluntary association), visit both commanding heights (such as civilian and military leadership) and less autonomous realms (such as the world of children), and touch on the responses offered to the Great War.

In introducing the areas covered, this chapter provides some key historical and comparative context, charting the broad dynamics between belligerent societies and their war efforts. It does this under the rationale that there are mutual advantages to introducing New Zealand and Great War scholarship to one another. Certainly, the global boom in Great War social history over the last three decades is invaluable in remedying the observed need for more systematic study of New Zealand's home front; once described as 'a black hole of New Zealand historiography.'[1] Likewise, James Belich's argument that the 'grand themes of world history are often played out more rapidly, more separately, and therefore more discernibly, [in New Zealand] than elsewhere' is applicable to 1914–1918.[2] The country's population of some 1.1 million people provides a suitable scale to contemplate propositions raised in regard to other belligerents. This population included an indigenous people recovering from a demographic nadir and formulating various responses to an increasingly settled settler majority. Primarily, these settlers were some of the direct and descended results of the British Isles' shedding of some

22 million people between 1815 and 1914.[3] The arrival of peoples from beyond the British Isles adds another parameter, with some immigrants' backgrounds underwriting wartime 'enemy alien' statuses and unsettling even well-integrated citizens and residents.

New Zealand's social laboratory conditions likewise offer curious vantage points. The country stood as a leading liberal democracy with modern infrastructure and institutions, a civil society empowered by a universal franchise, universal primary education, near-universal levels of literacy, high average living standards and a populist disposition. The popular lyric 'it's a long, long way to Tipperary but my heart's right there' has a particular resonance, as distance saw New Zealanders described as 'from the uttermost ends of the earth', whilst emotional commitments bestowed an intense immediacy. This chapter represents some preliminary thoughts on what a small land and a world war can teach one another.

Modernisation

A fundamental approach to comprehending the world that went to war, and New Zealand's place within it, forms something of a challenge to the idea of 1914–1918 as a natural break point in the historical process.[4] Rather than terminating a static Edwardian condition, conflict erupted amidst a world in motion. At the dawn of the nineteenth century, European societies were principally agrarian, governed by landed aristocracies and historic dynasties resting varying portions of their political legitimacy upon established churches. A century later these configurations had either been substantially reworked or were in the midst of rapid transformation as the factory, the railway, the mass newspaper, the transoceanic cable, the nickelodeon, the suburb, growing franchises, expanding education systems and widening civil societies worked their creative destruction.

Then and now, this transformation has been seen as accompanied by shifting boundaries of belonging. This typically saw individuals deracinated from pre-modern networks, which were heavily based around kinship, face-to-face contact and mutual interdependence, into looser, more impersonal relationships. Modern life promoted a widening of horizons, a convergence of norms across regions and more broadly conceived collective identities. Diverse commentators recognised this phenomenon in descriptions of 'new nationalism', 'turning peasants into citizens' or an 'awakening proletarian consciousness'. The essential theme is the extension of identity and loyalties beyond immediate experiences to an 'imagined community' cited as binding unmet peoples together.[5]

However, in 1914, as in previous centuries, the bulk of the European population lived on the land and the rather unmodern figure of the peasant constituted a major demographic. Within some conservative visions, the peasantry were cast as sturdy patriots untouched by modern ideas of social change. However, distance from socialist doctrines could also reflect wider degrees of social or cultural detachment. Rural weights, measures, dialects and even currencies could vary from wider standardisations, and degrees of autonomy could see tax collectors or military recruiters perceived as alien interlopers.[6] Rural socialists voicing anti-war speeches may have been a rarity during the final days of peace, but the marches and patriotic songs witnessed in urban centres were also scarce.[7] This divide should not be presented as total; to varying extents, rural realms had been touched by wider metropolitan networks. Studies of the French and German peasantry around 1914 observe growing infrastructure, education, military service, mass politics and the mass market as breaching rural remoteness.[8] Conversely, Prime Minister Stolypin's designs to transform the communal plots of rural Russia into private holdings, worked by profit-minded, conservative-orientated farmers, largely failed.[9] Instead they were accompanied by fresh instances of rural unrest: in 1909, troops were deployed on 114,108 occasions to keep the peace in the countryside.[10] Needless to say, backwardness and an alienation between the state and some 85 per cent of the Russian population would place various constraints on the Russian war effort.[11]

As this suggests, the pace and precise manner of modernisation was extremely uneven, reflecting regional and cultural idiosyncrasies. In one sense New Zealand offers a prime example of coming modernity. A product of nineteenth-century colonisation, settler New Zealand has, along with Australia, been described as 'born modern': possessing social and political structures crafted by, or anticipating, the major technological, economic, and intellectual forces of the modern age.[12] Before the war, various visiting commentators advanced ideas of the country as the 'birthplace of the twentieth century', the 'political brain of the modern world' or the 'social laboratory from which the world should learn much'.[13] Certainly the second half of the nineteenth century had witnessed advancing modernisation reworking older patterns of Maori traditions, frontier existence and the natural landscape.[14]

Booming urban environments are a primary indicator of this reworking. By 1911 the urban population had overtaken the rural, and just under a third of the population resided in the four urban centres of Auckland, Wellington, Christchurch and Dunedin.[15] While nearly half the male workforce was employed on the land, many men, and increasingly unmarried women, laboured as factory and waterfront workers, on the railway, as shop assistants, as clerks, as public servants and within the professions.[16] The growth of a modern processing economy and an expanding white-collar sector was accompanied by rising levels of education and specialisation. Union membership, near 3,000 in 1888, blossomed to over 80,000 by 1919, with New Zealand being among the most unionised societies in the world.[17] Corresponding shifts in mass politics presented the Liberal Party with the predicament of being flanked on the right by the emergence of the Reform Party, under William Massey, and on the left by the potent looming force of political labour. Dampening labour's potency were divisions over ideals, goals and methods, as some elements within the movement sought to develop a socialist platform to be advanced via the political process, whilst a militant bloc (concentrated among maritime workers and miners) espoused syndicalism. All of these elements provide some context for the Great Strike of 1913, in which militant unionists and striking workers squared off against employers, farmers and the state. The resulting clash stands as one of the most disruptive affairs of modern New Zealand history.[18]

Development was not a phenomenon confined to the urban environment. A classic of New Zealand literature, John Mulgan's *Man Alone*, illustrates the imposition of farming on the landscape in the protagonist's description of 'seeing a new country open out like the raw edges of a wound.'[19] Other aspects of this rural world complement Mulgan's themes of modern alienation. Modernised agriculture is 'as much like working in a factory as anything else' and the perils and audacity of pioneering are presented as belonging to a vanished age overtaken by prevailing petty bourgeois ambitions.[20] W.H. Oliver once sketched pre-war New Zealand farmers with a comparable array of descriptions;

> something of a peasantry, but a peasantry sophisticated to the use of machines, devoted to a high standard of living . . . [and] suspicious of the townsman whether he was the banker who held an overdraft or the worker who struck for a rise . . . businessmen rather than husbandmen . . . a tier of North Island electorates was dominated by these people . . . and, in the twentieth century, a new political party emerged from its prosperity.[21]

Such descriptions hint at an insular and distinctive condition, but one economically and politically linked to wider society.

One significant force behind the widening horizons and shared experiences of this modern world is apparent in the modern newspaper. The 1877 integration of New Zealand's growing telegraph network into the wider imperial system permitted information to travel the length of the Empire in hours and distant events to become local news.[22] Mass circulation further empowered the press, with one pre-war commentator observing the newspaper as having 'a very high place in New Zealand. Everyone reads it, and there are few people ignorant or old-fashioned enough not to be interested in the news.'[23] The significance of the newspaper in modern life continued into 1914–1918, with the conflict claimed as 'the first media war' where mass media critically influenced mass participation, alongside mass spectatorship.[24] The social position of the press and its relationship with the cause thus begs consideration, with the matter pursued in Ian F. Grant's chapter.

As highlighted in regard to Europe's peasantry, metropolitan networks advanced with an uneven stride. The Maori population offers a fascinating case study, as iwi responded with varying strategies of engagement and disengagement.[25] Disengagements were underwritten by measures of economic autonomy, physical isolation, the enduring authority of tribal institutions and – notably in Taranaki, the King Country, Waikato and the Urewera – enduring bitterness around land confiscation and the legacies of the New Zealand Wars. However, by 1912 more Maori were attending public schools than native schools, a professional class of Maori schoolmasters, clergymen, nurses, solicitors and doctors had emerged and the Young Maori Party was working within the halls of power to improve Maori health and living standards.[26] The varying responses Maoridom gave regarding the war built on these idiosyncrasies. Some iwi, notably Ngapuhi, Ngati Porou and Te Arawa, actively sought involvement. Various commentators, Maori and non-Maori, would cast the 2,227 volunteers of the Maori Pioneer Battalion (bolstered by a further 500 Cook Islanders and 149 Niueans) as representing Maori martial excellence and solidarity with the Crown.[27] Apathy and dissent from other iwi saw Maori enlistment ultimately stand at proportionally half that of the Pakeha population, and over a quarter of Maori balloted either refused service or remained unlocated.[28] A chapter by Basil Keane and the editor further unpacks the complexities of the Maori relationship with the war.

The capacity for modernity to renegotiate space, time and potentially communal boundaries also reached beyond New Zealand. Thus the expansion of national infrastructure, the decline of the provincial system, the centralisation of political power and a developing sense of national identity developed alongside an increasing orientation towards the British metropole.[29] This is apparent in the expansion of transnational infrastructure, the growth of New Zealand–British trade, the dispatch of New Zealand troops to the wars of empire and the rise of Greater British nationalism within the sentiments of mass culture and mass politics.[30] This phenomenon is not unique to New Zealand and can be observed in Canada,

Australia, Newfoundland and, more problematically, in South Africa and Ireland. However, New Zealand has been tagged as 'the extreme case' and it has been noted as no coincidence that 'the smallest and most isolated of the white Dominions was also the most effusively loyal to Britain and the most determined to prove its worth to her.'[31] The economic, political and cultural links within this global system came into play during the war and the efforts made to protect it provide one stream of evidence for the claim that 'war for Europe meant war for the world.'[32] New Zealand demonstrated a particularly extensive commitment, producing some of the highest proportions of volunteers among the Dominions and enacting a system of conscription to make it *the* highest; South Africa enlisted 11.12 per cent of its men, Australia 13.43 per cent, Canada 13.48 per cent and New Zealand 19.35 per cent.[33]

Mobilisation

The war was also a product of this modernising world, with the technical possibilities and innovations of the industrial/scientific revolution turned from mass production towards mass destruction. Fritz Haber's chemical genius offers an acutely individual case. His work on synthesising atmospheric nitrogen broke constraints on food production, creating 'bread out of air', while his work weaponising poison gases saw him dubbed 'the father of chemical warfare'.[34]

Modernisation was also entwined with how effectively belligerents were able to mobilise for war, and an east–west gradient, correlating with broad understandings of modernisation, has been observed in regard to European belligerents.[35] Three dimensions of this phenomenon might be considered. The first is the state, which formed a critical centre for the vast bureaucratic, economic and social undertaking that war on this scale entailed. Those states possessing an effective interplay with mass society were better placed to take up the challenge of reorganising society for war, while traditional autocracies, where the relationship between rulers and ruled was domineering but detached, struggled in this endeavour.[36] Political order also became a factor as protracted war put a premium on public morale. States with established liberal-democratic traditions possessed greater reserves of popular legitimacy; assessing the collapse of eastern monarchies against French and British experiences, Roger Chickering notes it as 'more than incidental' that 'these two western European lands were home to much broader and more centralized parliamentary regimes, with traditions of civilian control over the military'.[37]

Indeed, despite the obvious power of centralised authority, the most effective efforts aligned committed societies alongside efficient governments, and the development of a broad sense of public purpose formed a second major site of mobilisation. In recent decades scholarship on how belligerents went to and stayed at war has decidedly modified older motifs of participation as representing lockstep jingoistic enthusiasm and mass manipulation.[38] Typically, reassessments do not inherently disregard that remarkable bursts of communal solidarity rallied diverse, sometimes vastly divided, social elements, or that party truces transcended chilly, sometimes toxic, political atmospheres, in various equivalents of the *Union Sacrée* or the *Burgfrieden*.[39] Rather, commitment is emphasised as reflecting an altogether more complex range of intellectual and emotional positions which, put concisely, were not uncontested, unconsidered or unconditional. This public mobilisation was empowered by established social networks, habits of co-operation and common moral obligations encapsulated in the term 'social capital'. The development gradient recurs here, with modernisation facilitating broader social networks and economies with higher numbers of intermediary positions – foremen, union leaders and farmers with enough land to require hired labour. Such networks proved essential in co-ordinating effective social organisation and influencing behaviour.[40] Indeed, as long as the war was perceived as legitimate, belligerents with healthy civil societies were able to augment their war efforts with higher degrees of co-operation and pursue them at more intimate levels. Ultimately belligerents poured their social, as well as their physical and human, capital into the war.

State and social efforts were both ultimately fuelled by individual commitments, making hearts and minds a third major site of mobilisation. Here too the east–west gradient has been observed in accounts identifying modern consciousness as being carried to war. Richard Vinen, for example, makes a critical distinction between how populations drawn from modern and undeveloped Europe perceived and fought the war:

> It was the bourgeoisie of western Europe that behaved in the most irrational way . . . continuing to obey orders even when such obedience was certain to bring their death. It was the 'primitive' peasant populations . . . who behaved most rationally – they deserted, allowed themselves to be taken prisoner, or mutinied.[41]

In some interpretations this distinction is taken as reflecting the capacity of modern institutions (the factory floor, the railway timetable, the school lesson, military training) to instil people with the greater predictability, efficiency and reliability demanded by modern life. Studies of British military discipline, for instance, have dwelled on the 'bedrock of social cohesion' instilled by the nature of British society and noted that the army's ranks were largely composed of 'probably the most highly disciplined industrial labour force in the world'.[42] This consciousness has also been considered to reflect socialisation within civil societies. A widely read novel of the 1920s, Scott Fitzgerald's *Tender is the Night*, articulates this understanding in a veteran's assertion that the capacity to accept the costs of the Western Front rested on intimately internalised devotions:

> This took religion and years of plenty and tremendous sureties and the exact relation that existed between the classes. The Russians and Italians weren't any good on this front. You had to have a whole-souled sentimental equipment going back further than you could remember . . . Why, this was a love battle.[43]

Assessing this passage, Jay Winter emphasises the sense that the war mobilised 'a degree of loyalty to community and nation, a commitment to defend what was, that could not have been created overnight. It took years, perhaps generations, to secure these bonds.'[44]

These sites of mobilisation offer some context for considering New Zealand's experiences. In regards to the state, William Pember Reeves once noted that 'In the colonies Governments are, rightly or wrongly, expected to be of use in a public emergency, and under the head of public emergency dull times are included.'[45] Certainly conceptions of active government had been established through state roles in migration, national development and social welfare, while drives to professionalise and rationalise state institutions augmented state authority and capacities for involvement in national life.[46] An example is seen in the sustained interest in military reforms from the 1890s, which saw the development of co-ordinated imperial defence, New Zealand's first overseas military deployment in the Boer War and the planning of an expeditionary force. This development is further explored in John Crawford's chapter on the Defence Department. However, the modernisation of the New Zealand state was accompanied by broadening accountability, meaning that the legitimacy to wield political authority increasingly rested on mass opinion and sanction. The development of the political franchise offers the clearest example of this and New Zealand stood in the vanguard of democratisation; the secret ballot was introduced after 1870, property qualifications were abolished after 1879, and the franchise expanded to include Maori men in 1867 and all women in 1893.[47]

The war vividly enhanced both aspects of political modernity, with unprecedented state efforts to rally and regulate the public body justified as acting in the interests of the national community. The repressive edge of these powers has often remained at the forefront of recollections and there is a basis for this. After sustained beatings, a conscientious objector incarcerated within Wanganui Barracks was taunted by the Commandant, 'I've got power to bury you here.'[48] Observations of New Zealand's war regulations note that the man who drafted them, the Solicitor-General Sir John Salmond, had a 'low threshold of pain' in balancing legality against expediency, and that regulations to suppress opposition emerged as 'a small industry'.[49] Examples across the following chapters attest to this and include intensified surveillance of public meetings and private correspondence, raids on union halls, 287 charges under sedition regulations (with 208 charges leading to convictions and 71 to incarcerations), a police operation in the Ureweras likened to a military expedition, and an experiment to ship 14 conscientious objectors to the front to coerce them into service. Simultaneously the enduring rhythms of party politics indicate how in New Zealand, as elsewhere, the harnessing of state political power was not unconditional. This point is impressed in James Watson's chapter on parliamentarians, where commitment to the war and (belated) coalition government did not avert fierce criticism of the administration by what was effectively a continuing Opposition. Furthermore, the links between the authorities and the wider public are evident in the shared costs of social mobilisation. Between them the 80 members of Parliament had 76 sons at the front and some, including Gordon Coates, Thomas Seddon, John Bird Hine, William Downie Stewart and William Henry Dillon Bell, enlisted themselves. Bell was killed in action on 31 July 1917, roughly a year before Salmond's own son.[50]

State influence was also channelled through institutions woven into the social fabric, and in this way the concept of 'civil society' can imply a misleadingly clear distinction between states and societies. The modern police force and schooling system, considered by Richard Hill's and Roger Openshaw's respective chapters, offer good examples. Neither can be properly understood as alien entities imposed on the social body; in practice constables and teachers were both agents of the state and members of their communities. These intermediary positions continued during wartime, offering insightful perspectives. Even the military, an institution which would seem to presume a clear divide and distinction from civilian society, was, in an age of citizen-soldiers, the *levée en masse* and martial spectacles, linked with national life and mythology. The intensified links with the wider population are most evident in the introduction of universal compulsory military training in 1909. In the original incarnation of the scheme, boys were enlisted at twelve in the Junior Cadets, graduated to the Senior Cadets at fourteen, were transferred to the General Training Section at eighteen, and were listed in the Reserve from twenty-one to thirty. The social presence of this scheme and the existence of the territorials is further explored in Peter Cooke's chapter.

Management of the war effort also formed new avenues for collaboration between state and society. David Littlewood's chapter on the Military Service Boards, established to hear appeals from balloted men, offers one example. Although serving in an official capacity, board members were appointed from public life in an effort to balance government social inputs. Likewise, the war enhanced the state's role as a broker in industrial matters, as the war effort made production and labour relations issues of strategic importance. A chapter by James Watson and the editor touches on officialdom's collaboration with those possessing the means of production, while Erik Olssen's chapter examines union experiences as the state pursued a cautious mix of conciliation, concession and coercion.[51]

With some caveats, the concept of an independent civil society remains meaningful and crucial in understanding how society mobilised. Enquiry upon New Zealand's historical levels of association and social capital received a burst from the popularisation of that concept in the 1990s and, more specifically, from responses to Miles Fairburn's 1989 evaluation of the foundations of modern New Zealand society. According to Fairburn, before 1880 New Zealand was characterised by 'atomised' weakly bonded communities, with isolation, transience and extreme individualism keeping social ties few and fleeting.[52] Towards the turn of the twentieth century, however, many observe a flourishing of communal engagement:

> Trade unions, friendly societies, cooperatives, mechanics institutes, sports clubs and a vast variety of hobby and interest groups proliferated. So too did business and professional associations. The better-off supported benevolent societies and hospitals for the poor. In the absence of an established church a great variety of Christian denominations fought for adherents in an increasingly skeptical populace.[53]

These networks bonded individuals into larger communal life and many formed decentralised sites for wartime 'self-mobilisation'.[54] The established places of local leaders, priests, newspaper editors, friends and family members in community and individual life, and the powerful and heartfelt meanings they could evoke, potentially granted them an enormous influence. The often difficult positions of associational life in wartime society are further explored in Peter Lineham's chapter on the relationship between organised religion and the war effort and Greg Ryan's investigation of organised sports, an activity various commentators have observed as another venerated part of New Zealand life.[55]

Another major aspect of the First World War was the mobilisation of gendered social activity, and popular memory often gravitates towards nurses and female war workers as feminine counterparts to the intensified connections between ideal masculinity and soldiering. Over 600 New Zealand women served as nurses, standing beside those less visible women who travelled overseas to take up semi-official and/or volunteer roles. The ten nurses killed when the troop transport *Marquette* was torpedoed represent the extreme example of the hardships and perils many faced.[56] Likewise, the paid female workforce experienced a modest expansion, mostly in the professional and primary sectors.[57] It has been the half-empty glass, however, that has often left a stronger impression. After her mid-1918 return from England, Dr Jessie Maddison reported her astonishment at the comparative scarcity of women in uniforms and in the workforce and proposed that New Zealand women should relieve male labour and take up auxiliary work.[58]

Perhaps the most significant avenue of womanpower was the mobilisation of wider conventions concerning female duties and roles in public life. These included a prerogative to set the moral pace regarding masculine behaviour and social propriety and to wield moral suasion in these tasks. Commentators as dissimilar as the Minister of Defence and the *Maoriland Worker* concurred that women formed the vanguard of anti-German activity, and similar observations have been made in regard to anti-shirker activity.[59] White feather distribution, though widely contested and condemned, stands as a particularly spiteful incarnation of this worldview.[60] More positively, womanpower also provided the muscle for a vast mobilisation of volunteer endeavours, pursuing a range of relief and support work. These organisations are estimated to have raised near £5,447,991 ($485 million in 2015 dollars) over the course of the war.[61] Even this fortune does not capture the thousands of hours of unpaid labour evident in, for example, the 64,126 knitted and sewn items received by the Red Cross in one six-month period.[62] Margaret Tennant investigates the mobilisation of organised aid work and its relationship with pre-war charities.

Our third site of mobilisation focuses on how New Zealanders as individuals were bonded and socialised within the customs and circumstances of these social structures. The formative experiences of those born between 1888 and 1895 are of particular interest as this was the age cohort constituting the bulk of New Zealand enlistees. While the processes that make people creatures of their time are punctuated by all manner of exceptions and idiosyncrasies, the broad outlooks, habits and norms instilled by New Zealand society might be glimpsed in wartime circumstances. Christopher Pugsley has noted the percentage of New

Zealand courts-martial of troops as less than one third of the Australian rate and half of the Canadian rate.[63] Similarly, balloted New Zealanders were less likely than Australians or Canadians to appeal for exemptions. This is despite Australian appeals being for exemptions to military training within Australia rather than overseas, and likely combat, service.[64] The continuation of this relationship between upbringing and war is explored in Jeanine Graham's chapter on children. Certainly the formative presence of wartime loomed over young witnesses and participants in various ways. Advertisements for girls and boys to work as machinists, bookbinders, confectioners or office workers indicate mobilisation of the young to replace enlisted labour, and children's letters to enlisted fathers and brothers poignantly express the disruptions to family life.[65] John Mulgan, near seven when the armistice was signed, later wrote that his generation felt the war's 'tragic waste and splendour' and grew up 'in the waste land that it produced.'[66]

Together these sites – state, communal life, and hearts and minds – produced an intense mobilisation effort. Consider New Zealand's enlistment machinery, the wheels of which were turned by government officials, representatives from local bodies and recruitment groups, military personnel and members of official boards established to assess medical states and exemption appeals. By November 1918, over 100,000 individuals had moved through the wheels of this machinery, appearing very small in a war of big numbers. Of 243,376 men deemed eligible by virtue of their sex and age, some 124,211 were enlisted and 100,444 embarked.[67] This represents roughly 10 per cent of the total population, 19.4 per cent of the male population, and nearly 51 per cent of the eligible population. As stated elsewhere, 'the reader, if male and between 20 and 45, might toss a coin to see whether or not he would have served; if the reader is not within that category they might toss for a loved one who is.'[68] Financing this effort entailed similarly massive investments. In 1921 the monetary cost of New Zealand's war was calculated as £81,538,570 ($7.237 billion in 2015 dollars).[69] To give that figure some context, by 1881 the public works development scheme of the Vogel era had borrowed some £21 million ($3.497 billion in 2015 dollars) to develop the country's transportation and communication networks, modernise economic infrastructure and entice migration.[70] Hypothetically, the money poured into the war effort could have afforded two Vogel-sized investments in social amenities and economic development whilst leaving a few hundred million dollars in change.

War on this scale required similarly immense emotional resources, and the investment of meaning was intimately entwined with commitments of blood and treasure. This cultural mobilisation was driven by decentralised support across civil society and buttressed by official regulation of information. Its results served to transform the war effort into a cause and to redeem suffering as sacrifice. It achieved this as effectively as it did by evoking heartfelt sentiments of what was felt to be worth fighting for. Significant examples came from regional/national/imperial patriotism, gendered/ethnic identities, martial values, personal relationships and theological traditions.[71] Much turned on the case that the war was a necessary and righteous struggle against an aggressive enemy. Sensationalist propaganda of 'Hunnish barbarities' represents a facet, not the total, of this case and pandered to the genuine outrage that actual German actions, atrocities and ambitions stirred.[72]

Upheaval and endurance

Paradoxically, wartime conditions demonstrated the potential both to rally societies and to fragment their material and moral bonds. At the turn of the twentieth century Ivan Bloch foresaw that a conflict between industrial powers possessing modern firepower would become a protracted process of grinding destruction and contemplated the array of physical, economic and emotional strains sustained commitment would entail: 'How long do you think your social fabric will remain stable under such circumstances?'[73]

The extent to which war conditions eroded stability varied immensely. By some measures French and British command economies wrought modest social improvements; elsewhere sustaining the war entailed mass deprivation.[74] Consider Germany, where the British blockade, the cessation of the Russian grain trade and the idiosyncrasies of German central planning saw rising affluence and living standards stall and reverse. The results included rising prices, shortages and products 'stretched' by all manner of unpalatable ingenuity. By the 'turnip winter' of 1916/1917, official rations were declining towards a July 1917 nadir of 1,100 calories per day (modern nutritionists suggest 2,500 calories as the standard for a healthy, full-grown man), some 11,000 *ersatz* (substitute) products were on sale and Berlin's food prices had risen some 178–400 per cent.[75] Such conditions made attrition profoundly personal. One 76.5-kilogram German weighed 57.5 kilograms after seven months of attempting to live on official rations without the crutch of the black market, and the average schoolchild of 1916/1917 was 2–3 centimetres shorter, 1.8–3.6 kilograms lighter and more susceptible to disease than their 1913 counterpart.[76]

Besides inducing malnutrition and lethargy, hunger was decisive in corroding social solidarity, political legitimacy and popular support for the war. In another paradox, declining morale fuelled two very different responses: weary disengagements and active, sometimes revolutionary, counter-mobilisations, with rhetoric linking 'peace' and 'bread' proving appetising.[77] Even belligerents with well-established traditions of civil order saw domestic discord escalate beyond well-tempered discontent. Fierce social/political division and industrial unrest in Australia has been cited as highlighting the extent to which the war divided society, and Canada's 1918 Easter riots have been described, with pardonable hyperbole, as the 'brink of civil war'.[78] More extreme radicalisations of state/subject relations are evident in rebellions in Ireland and South Africa, revolutions in Russia and Germany and extermination efforts in Armenia.[79]

Social upheavals also derived from external enemy action, and the Great War has been conceived as radicalising the conduct of war. One element of this dynamic was a broad conceptualisation of the enemy: 'the enemy was not merely the enemy army, but the enemy nation and the culture through which it defined itself.'[80] In Western Europe the German invasions of Belgium, Luxembourg and north-eastern France exposed non-combatants to atrocities (spontaneous and sanctioned), deliberate destruction of cultural heritage and a predatory occupation.[81] As the Western Front became entrenched, exchanges of violence were effectively confined to uniformed men, though U-boat campaigns and occasional bombardments (delivered by aviation, long-range artillery and warships) breached these restraints.[82] Beyond Europe, the seizure and establishment of rule over German colonial assets in Africa, Asia and the Pacific brought degrees of upheaval, violence and exploitation, as did the war in the Middle East.[83]

More extreme examples of the turmoil and physical destruction war could impose on social systems are evident in Eastern and South-Eastern Europe. In contrast to the entrenched west, the fluid Eastern Front was born with a Russian invasion of East Prussia, which saw mass atrocities against civilians, a German counter-offensive, which brought mass displacement, and a German military authority, *Ober Ost*, working to impose a new political order over a swath of Eastern Europe.[84] Eastern upheaval continued after the November Armistice as *the* war blurred into a plethora of civil, inter-state, revolutionary and counter-revolutionary wars. To the south, Austro-Hungary's invasion of Serbia brought irregular fighting, widespread atrocities and a heavy-handed occupation. This created conditions for social disintegration, mass starvation, epidemics and, consequently, the highest proportion of losses to population. By 1918 nearly 25 per cent of the 1914 Serbian population was dead and civilian deaths (650,000) outnumbered military deaths (450,000).[85] There is no basis to the apocryphal claim that New Zealand's per capita dead (1.6 per cent) represent 'a higher rate of loss than in any other combatant nation.'[86]

Post-war reflection on Bloch has focussed on his mistaken prediction that belligerents would be unable to sustain a war with enormous fiscal and human costs beyond a short duration. Indeed, in some circumstances, costs could galvanise convictions: reports of the Gallipoli landing casualties and the sinking of the *Lusitania* in May 1915 stimulated volunteering.[87] Wartime New Zealand offers a curious perspective on endurance and, compared with other belligerents, appears to be characterised by a relative stability. One trans-Tasman account observes the war as forming a unifying event in New Zealand but a dividing event in Australia.[88] A wider study of efforts to implement conscription across the English-speaking democracies observes New Zealand as bookending one end of the spectrum and encountering 'the least turmoil'.[89]

New Zealand's relative stability could be due to the country escaping some of the war's worst depredations. Continuous access to world trade and a secure food supply spared it the degree of deprivation seen elsewhere. While food prices increased some 48 per cent – higher than in South Africa (36 per cent) and equal with Australia, but significantly lower than Great Britain (116 per cent) or France (177 per cent) – state experimentation in price control sought, with mixed results, to promote equity.[90] In contrast to Germany's food nadir, a July 1917 union account listed the weekly expenses for a husband, wife and three children as including four pounds of sirloin steak, one pound of bacon, three pounds of stewing steak, two pounds of chops and one pound of sausages.[91] If hearts and minds are linked to stomachs then here is one basis of resilience. Furthermore, New Zealand was effectively spared the upheaval of enemy action. While German planners prepared a doctrine of 'ruthless warfare' to disrupt Australian and New Zealand trade and morale with coastal raids, the containment of the High Seas Fleet scuttled the implementation of such designs.[92] A minor exception is found in the raider *Wolf*, which captured, plundered and sank various vessels across the Atlantic, Indian and Pacific Oceans. Among the victims of these actions was the cargo ship *Wairuna*, sailing from Auckland to San Francisco, plundered and sunk on 2 June 1917. *Wolf* also laid a series of mines in New Zealand waters, resulting in the loss of 26 lives, the merchant ship *Port Kembla* off Cape Farewell on 18 September 1917 and the inter-colonial steamer *Wimmera* off North Cape on 26 June 1918.[93]

Within this relatively stable environment, the three sites of mobilisation previously outlined maintained a staggering commitment. Contrasting with other state mobilisations, where radical politicians and military strongmen (in the mould of Lloyd George, Georges Clemenceau, Billy

Hughes and Erich Ludendorff) seized power and instituted more far-reaching policies, New Zealand showed a greater degree of continuity. Whereas those leaders were eclipsed in the war's aftermath, William Massey retained office until his death in 1925, making him 'the only pre-War Prime Minister who carried on all through the War and into the period of reconstruction' and New Zealand's second longest serving prime minister to date.[94] In part this stability reflects how the formation of a coalition government and the postponement of elections restricted party and national politics. However the 1919 restoration of elections saw Massey's Reform Party seek political capital from wartime leadership and successfully retain power for a decade.[95] Public commitment likewise endured despite innocence and ignorance of the nature of the war being brutally chipped away. By 1917, troopship magazines dwelled, rather candidly, on 'what is in store for most of us . . . we cherish no illusions.' Yet this message remained devoted to the cause, asserting that 'mutilation', 'disease' and 'the Great Price' were sacrifices in a necessary war.[96] Despite this awareness, and the introduction of conscription, over 24,000 would volunteer for service between September 1916 and November 1918.[97] Some would continue to assert the war's legitimacy into the post-war world and for the remainder of their lives.[98]

However, while New Zealand was spared the manner and magnitude of upheaval witnessed elsewhere, the case for relative stability has its limits. Sustaining the war effort inherently entailed individuals and communities making an array of minor and major sacrifices rendered in physical, emotional and economic terms. Calculations of wartime increases to the cost of living range between 25 and 50 per cent; the official estimate stands at 39.35 per cent, and one investigation of wartime economics concludes, 'It is likely unskilled workers and their families lived pretty near the bone'.[99] Reduced access, via cost and availability, to certain commodities adds to assessments of a dark, chilly, threadbare austerity for some. Clothing prices rose 140 per cent over the course of the war and domestic use of coal became restricted.[100] Many experienced the human costs of protracted industrialised warfare as individual disfigurements and deaths rippled through social networks, diminishing other lives.[101] With the backbone of the army consisting of young, single men (the average age at enlistment was 27), many parents experienced the wartime inversion of surviving their children, and a 58 per cent casualty rate meant many others lived in fear of this possibility.[102] By the war's end New Zealand had sustained 59,483 casualties (18,166 of whom were dead) and many were left with the task of adjusting to new statuses: mourners, widows, fatherless children and repatriates with lasting physical and psychological injuries.[103]

Further tensions reflected not the absolute demands of the war but the equitable sharing of sacrifices. The centrality of frontline sacrifices in public culture underwrote a moral economy which made home front dissent less acceptable. That the lowest civilian wages were higher than a private's pay achieved a comparable effect in regards to industrial unrest. However, these dynamics also laid the ground for backlashes against any seeming to break with this accord, and the dramatic presence of 'shirker' antitypes in social and political expression is indicative of this.[104] Letters addressed to the Defence Minister contain numerous variations on calls for equality of sacrifice: 'It is high time some of the families with a big percentage of sons were tapped'; 'I consider it very unjust when there are so many family [sic] with 5 & 6 sons, all well to do, and none of these are called up'; 'my only two sons are gone . . . I think it is every young man's place to go . . . I would very much like this one [a neighbour's son] to be made to go.'[105]

A similar dynamic emerged in regard to the mixed consequences of the war economy. Not everyone lived 'near the bone' during the war. By some gauges, social affluence and the development of a consumer society continued apace or even accelerated during wartime. Indeed, access to relative luxuries such as beer, tobacco and sugar fluctuated around pre-war levels, money wagered at racecourses steadily increased, cinema attendance rapidly expanded, private bank deposits rose from £25.2 to £37.4 million. One furniture manufacturer noted unprecedented orders, often from working people, and often for 'astonishing costly articles such as chesterfields'.[106] Seeking to trace the varying effects of the wartime economy, the Government Statistician proposed that those living on returns from investments (who experienced enhanced returns), professionals (who often benefited from the enlistment of their competition) and those paid hourly (who gained higher wages, 'considerable overtime earnings' and the leverage of labour shortages) were the major economic winners and that those on fixed pay were the most severely affected.[107] Such disparate outcomes rattled communal cohesion, adding accusations of profiteering to wartime discourse.

As elsewhere, these strains, often building on existing fault lines, illustrate that social consent to the demands of mobilisation was neither unconditional nor uncontested. Some responses mixed criticism – sometimes fierce criticism – of the demands of the war effort with degrees of co-operation. Examples of conditional consent include the actions of the Second Division League and the Reductionist movement in negotiating the particulars of balloting.[108] Other critics called for improved pay for soldiers and the conscription of capital alongside men, or denounced conscription as reactionary militarism intended not 'to fight the Kaiser, but to fight Trade Unionism and the working classes'.[109] Consequent activism, unrest and emergence of an anti-conscription movement raised government fears of radicalisation, strikes and 'go-slows' in strategic industries. The 8 industrial disputes of 1915 (involving 295 workers) grew to 15 (involving 899) in 1916, 45 (involving 2,734) in 1917 and 40 (involving 4,056) in 1918.[110] While wages and hours were stated as the major cause, opposition to conscription was also cited: between November 1916 and February 1919, coal mine strikes against conscription saw an estimated 181 working days lost.[111]

In some places, conditional support blurred into direct dissent that rejected the cause as well as the conduct of the war. This manifested from diverse positions, ranging from non-ideological to complex mixes of pacifist, socialist, theological and identity politics. Elements of the labour movement denied the war's legitimacy, denouncing it as an imperialist/capitalist affair, and by 1916, some were calling for a negotiated peace.[112] Some saw degrees of friction between an ethnic identity and participation, as evidenced in Maori dismissal of a 'Pakeha war' or Irish rejection of an 'English war'.[113] Non-conformist creeds cited religious objections to war and feminist pacifists evoked a biological impulse against militarism.[114] David Grant's chapter considers the position of those motivated by an unconditional rejection of armed force and the challenges the peace movement faced during the war.

Lastly, some upheavals reflect how wartime emotions fragmented communal ties as boundaries of 'self' and 'other' were sharpened. Two major demonstrations include Catholic/Protestant tensions over the politics of sacrifice, and social reactions against those associated with enemy powers, with anti-Germanism forming the foremost occurrence.[115] Both saw associations emerge to denounce social elements, demonstrating that, just as human and physical capital can produce 'bread out of air' and chemical weapons, social capital can be put to various purposes. One account of European spy hysteria notes anxiety as greatest 'in places close to frontiers and with ethnically mixed populations.'[116] Two chapters explore how far these factors were stretched in distant and relatively homogenous New Zealand. A chapter by Rolf Brednich and the editor considers the wartime experiences of those associated with Germany via birth or ancestral links, focussing on the often dramatic undermining of social positions. This undermining extended to official citizenship, with aliens (those without British citizenship) and naturalised aliens (those who had obtained citizenship) transitioned to enemy alien statuses and hundreds interned under security measures.[117] Studying the activities and attitudes of the anti-German leagues, Graham Hucker's chapter offers an overview of the way those groups linked ethnicity with loyalty and endorsed suspicion and hostility towards individuals and objects associated with enemy powers. Brad Patterson considers the rise of an even greater wartime mass movement in the Protestant Political Association and contemplates the movement's stance and place within wider New Zealand history.

***

Comparing the universal and particular experiences of how belligerents entered, mobilised and endured the conflict during 1914–1918 offers a broad contextual basis for approaching New Zealand society at war. The following chapters pursue the specifics of this approach, expanding on the experiences and perspectives of distinct parts of the social body. Together, they convey some of the facets, complexities, dilemmas, characters and sentiments of a small land in a world war.

Chapter One

'Duty Well Done': The Defence Department at War: 1914–1918[1]

John Crawford

Between 1914 and 1918, New Zealand's immense war effort saw more than 9 per cent of the country's population serve in the New Zealand Expeditionary Force (NZEF), and directly led to a substantial expansion in the role of the state and in the powers of ministers and government departments.[2] This chapter outlines the central role New Zealand's Defence Department had within this war effort and how each of its major branches responded to the challenges presented by a total war. Particular attention is paid to those elements of the department which had the most important relationships with the public and, consequently, not all developments in the structure of the department are discussed.[3]

Contexts and circumstances

During the First World War the name 'Defence Department' generally referred to the New Zealand Military Forces and, in particular, to its headquarters in Wellington. This should not, however, mask the institution's wider scope. Between 1910 and 1914 New Zealand thoroughly reformed its military forces. Substantial quantities of new weapons and equipment were purchased, the number of regular military personnel was almost doubled, compulsory military training was introduced and a large citizen army, the Territorial Force, was created. On the eve of the war the military forces had 617 regular personnel, 81 civilian staff and a part-time Territorial Force with a strength of 25,684.[4] The principal role of the regular military personnel was to administer and support the Territorial Force and, to achieve this, a nationwide structure was designed. New Zealand was divided into four military districts with headquarters in Auckland, Palmerston North, Christchurch and Dunedin. Each district was divided into four or five sub-districts called Area Groups, which were in turn divided into Areas. The structure meant that the Defence Department had a permanent presence across the whole of New Zealand, from Bluff in the south to Waimate North in Northland. As pre-war planning had intended, this structure provided a good basis for raising and sustaining an expeditionary force.[5] By 1914 the Defence Department was in a much stronger position than it had been during the South African War of 1899–1902, when its administrative structures and systems had barely coped with the comparatively modest demands imposed upon them. The establishment of the NZEF was undertaken quickly and efficiently. Less than two months after the outbreak of war the force's 8,400-strong Main Body was ready to embark. From very early in the First World War there was, nevertheless, a clear recognition by senior officers that enhanced administrative systems and structures needed to be put in place for what was to be a much more taxing commitment.[6]

The military forces were commanded by the General Officer Commanding or Commandant. In August 1914, Major-General Sir Alexander Godley held this post. However, after being given command of the NZEF, Godley embarked in October 1914. Sailing with him were three of his immediate subordinates, 43 other officers and 167 other ranks of the regular forces. The departure of so many regular personnel was a major trial for the Defence Department. In meeting this challenge many of the remaining regular officers were moved to new appointments, and gaps in the establishment were filled with temporary appointments, mainly from the Territorial Force. Although there were some difficulties caused by less experienced citizen soldiers taking up positions formerly held by regulars, in general the temporary staff performed well.[7] Many of the regular military personnel who were required to remain in New Zealand to fill key staff and training roles were bitterly disappointed that they were not seeing active service. Captain David Cossgrove, who ran the recruiting branch of the Defence Department, went so far as to decline the award of an MBE in 1919. He wrote to the Governor-General that 'I cannot accept a reward for doing what little lay in my power on home service in the Dominion. No honour that can be conferred upon me will recompense me for the loss of seeing active service in the war.'[8]

After the departure of the Main Body, the headquarters of the military forces were reorganised along the lines recommended by the Inspector-General of the Overseas Forces after his tour in 1914. The new headquarters structure had three rather than five branches. Under the new arrangements Colonel (later Major-General Sir) Alfred Robin replaced Godley as General Officer Commanding; Lieutenant-Colonel (later Colonel) Charles Gibbon became Chief of the General Staff, with responsibility for all matters relating to the training and operations of the New Zealand Military Forces; and Lieutenant-Colonel Herbert

Pilkington was appointed Adjutant-General, with responsibility for discipline, personnel matters, support services and administrative functions. In May 1916 he was replaced by a senior Territorial officer, Colonel Robert Tate. Robin remained Quartermaster-General and, as such, continued to be responsible for financial matters and the equipment and supply of the forces. To effectively carry out both roles Robin had to work virtually every day of the week.[9] New Zealand's Minister of Defence throughout the war was James Allen, who was also Minister of Finance and Minister of Education until the formation of the coalition National administration in August 1915. Allen was a hard-working and effective minister, but until he was relieved of these additional portfolios he was greatly overtaxed. Allen worked closely and successfully with the senior officers of the Defence Department.[10] The department was an unusual organisation in that it was commanded by military officers, but included civilian public servants. This caused difficulties early in the war when the Public Service Commissioner questioned the need for extended working hours; a stand that prompted one NZEF officer in Egypt to comment that: 'This 9 to 5 and Saturday afternoon business is of course impossible in War time. Where would we be if the people we have with us took up the same attitude?'[11] During the war years these structures, systems and individuals faced the massive logistical challenges that recruiting, training, equipping, supplying, administrating and facilitating the NZEF entailed. The Defence Department's work and record in these tasks is outlined below.

Chief of the General Staff Branch: Censorship

Before the outbreak of war the Committee of Imperial Defence had undertaken detailed planning for the introduction of censorship. In the United Kingdom and right across the Empire censorship was quickly imposed after the outbreak of war.[12] In New Zealand preparations for putting censorship in place began at the end of July 1914. After war broke out regulations were passed under various acts of parliament placing the Chief of the General Staff in charge of all forms of censorship. Colonel Gibbon's heavy workload, along with his training and background, meant that this arrangement was far from ideal. Shortly after the outbreak of war, a senior Post Office official, H.W. Harrington, was appointed Deputy Chief Censor. He relieved Colonel Gibbon of most of the work associated with the censorship of cables. Harrington was based in Wellington and had a small team of assistants there and at the cable landing stations. A similar structure was put in place for postal censorship. A Deputy Chief Postal Censor was appointed who had assistant censors based in Auckland,

Wellington, Christchurch and Dunedin. All mail was liable to censorship, but only mail to European countries was examined on a routine basis.[13] The mail of New Zealanders who were seen as a threat to the Dominion's war effort was targeted by the censors and often stopped. In general, postal censorship became more pervasive and political from 1916.[14]

No deputy chief press censor was appointed, and throughout the war Colonel Gibbon had a much more direct role in this area of censorship. Although the government was pleased with his performance as Chief Censor, press censorship was rather ad hoc and unnecessarily heavy-handed, as was the censorship of news cables coming into New Zealand. Gibbon, in particular, was quite properly criticised for his order banning any mention in the New Zealand press of the escape of German prisoners of war from Motuihe Island late in 1917.[15]

NZEF Training Camps

The training of recruits brought the department similarly complex challenges. Rather than developing the four temporary mobilisation camps established for the Main Body of the NZEF, the Defence Department decided, late in 1914, to build a central training camp for reinforcements at Trentham, north of Wellington. Work began on developing the new camp, which was designed to accommodate up to 2,000 men, in October 1914. However, the upsurge in reinforcements being sent to the NZEF during 1915 led to serious overcrowding at the camp, with 7,000 men being accommodated in May 1915. This overcrowding, combined with major sanitation and drainage problems, led to serious outbreaks of infectious diseases resulting in the deaths of 26 soldiers during June and July 1915, which in turn led to a public outcry and widespread criticism of the administration of the camp. Certainly, the camp commandant and his staff, the senior officers of the military forces and the Minister of Defence all, at first, failed to appreciate the seriousness of the situation at Trentham. From early July 1915, however, decisive action was taken, including the removal of all fit recruits at Trentham to temporary camps in the Wellington region.

A commission established to enquire into the administration of Trentham Camp in July 1915 confirmed that the camp had been grossly overcrowded and that its facilities were seriously inadequate. By the time the commission completed its report, late in August 1915, significant progress had been made to upgrade Trentham Camp. By October it could house 4,200 men in improved huts with good drainage and other services, and when the development work was finished, Trentham, along with its satellite camps, could accommodate 7,150 men.[16]

However, it was apparent to the Defence Department that even an expanded and improved Trentham Camp could not cope with the numbers of reinforcements required. An even larger training camp was, therefore, developed near Featherston in the Wairarapa. Plans for the new camp incorporated all the lessons learnt from the problems at Trentham, and Featherston was widely regarded as a model camp. Construction began in August 1915 and, at its height, more than 1,000 men were working on the new camp, which eventually included accommodation for 4,500 men in huts and a further 2,500 men in tents. In addition, nearly 3,000 men could be accommodated in smaller satellite camps. The first men to be trained at Featherston entered the camp in January 1916.[17] In addition to the camps at Trentham and Featherston, smaller specialist training camps organised along similar lines were established at Narrow Neck on Auckland's North Shore for reinforcements for the Maori contingent and the New Zealand tunnelling company, and at Awapuni racecourse near Palmerston North for medical corps personnel.[18] The training camps were large, busy places, which in 1918 had a total staff of more than 2,000.[19] These numbers, the extent of construction and the mass of recruits being processed through the camp system give some indication of the scale of the task the department faced during the war years.

Quartermaster-General Branch: War Expenses

Once the decision had been taken to form an expeditionary force, it was realised that the Defence Department needed a new organisation to handle the financial matters relating to this force. On 8 August 1914, the War Expenses Branch was established, initially consisting of George Rodda, a capable public servant seconded from the Treasury, and one typist. The increasing scale and complexity of New Zealand's contribution to the British Empire's war effort led to the massive expansion of the branch to 400 staff by late 1918. A major part of the branch's work concerned the pay and allowances due to NZEF personnel and their families. All information about such matters was noted on the personal file of the individual concerned, which was held by Base Records.[20] Institutional expansion and the complexity of its work was also mirrored by the massive growth in defence expenditure. Between August 1914 and the end of March 1920, expenditure through the War Expenses Account, which was administered by the branch, totalled about £76.9 million (near $6.8 billion in 2015 dollars).[21]

Although the Defence Department was occasionally accused of wastefulness, it was in fact run in a rather parsimonious manner and great care was taken to account for public funds and property. This was sometimes carried to ridiculous extremes, as when a court of enquiry was held at Base Records into the loss of a rubber stamp.[22]

Munitions and Supplies Department

Supplying the NZEF brought another stream of work. Until the formation of the coalition National Government, the purchase of supplies and equipment for the New Zealand forces was in the hands of the Quartermaster-General's staff. The coalition agreement specified that there must be an equal number of Reform and Liberal cabinet ministers, which necessitated the transfer of a number of portfolios to former opposition politicians and provided the ideal opportunity to lighten Allen's workload. Responsibility for procuring supplies and munitions for the military forces, apart from those provided directly by the British to the NZEF, was passed to leading Liberal and successful Auckland businessman Arthur Myers. Under the new structure, the Defence Department specified the type and quantity of supplies needed and when they were required by and then passed responsibility for procuring the material to Myers's new organisation, which was initially called the Military Supplies Purchase Office, and later, after the scope of its activities was expanded, the Munitions and Supplies Department. The new ministry proved to be highly effective. By early 1917 it had 21 staff, led by a capable chief executive and supported by an expert committee of advisers. In response to new challenges posed by the war, the role of the department was later extended to include control over the coal trade, which was central to the life of New Zealand.[23]

Weapons and munitions, apart from small arms ammunition, were not produced in New Zealand. Large quantities of general supplies and items of uniform were, however, sourced from New Zealand producers. Military orders were particularly important to the footwear, textile and garment industries; for example, no less than 232,000 boots, 216,000 trousers and 120,000 greatcoats were purchased during the course of the war.[24] There were no cases of serious fraud of the kind that marked the activities of procurement organisations in other belligerent nations. Although there were problems with some items issued to New Zealand soldiers,[25] the Munitions and Supplies Department, which was closed down on 31 March 1919, succeeded in ensuring that supplies were purchased in a timely fashion and at reasonable prices.[26]

Works Directorate

In July 1915, Colonel Ernest Hiley, a senior Territorial Force officer who was also General Manager of the New Zealand Government Railways, was made Director of Barracks and Camp Construction, later Director of Works. He was charged with establishing an effective engineering and construction services organisation. The first major task Hiley was given was to oversee the complete upgrade of Trentham Camp. He was an extremely capable man and quickly established a serviceable directorate, which by late 1916 had an establishment of 99 personnel. The Works Directorate oversaw the design and construction of buildings for the Defence Department and undertook building maintenance work. The most important projects undertaken by the Works Directorate were the upgrade of Trentham Camp, the construction of Featherston Camp and the construction of a network of military hospitals and related facilities. Although Hiley undertook his Defence Department role on a part-time, unpaid basis, he did an excellent job. The Works Directorate was disestablished late in 1920.[27]

Adjutant-General Branch: Base Records

Before the outbreak of war the Defence Department had maintained personal files or other personnel records on regular and part-time members of the military forces. This important function greatly expanded after the establishment of the NZEF. The organisation responsible for the NZEF's records was originally called the Expeditionary Force Record Branch, but it soon became known as Base Records. It was described as 'a kind of brain centre for the collation of all particulars with regard to our military men.'[28] Base Records at first struggled with inadequate resources to develop an effective record system at a time when the NZEF was growing quickly. Once New Zealand troops were committed to action at Gallipoli, the flow of work, especially relating to casualties, vastly increased and serious problems developed. Delays in and mistakes with the way casualties were reported, in particular, caused great public concern.[29]

Robin recognised the need for comprehensive and well-organised personnel records and between August and December 1915 took action to put the records organisation on a sound footing. Major Norton Francis, a Territorial officer who was the manager of a substantial business and who had proved himself an effective staff officer, was appointed Director of Base Records. His staff was increased from fewer than 15 to about 80.[30] The structure of Base Records and its record-keeping procedures were also substantially improved. Base Records was divided into six and later as many as eleven sections. Each section dealt with a particular aspect of the office's work, including the records room, which held all the personal files and was responsible for tracking the files when they were being worked on, and the casualty section, which was responsible for casualty reporting.

Under standard procedure, an enlistment in the NZEF saw a file created in the Territorial Force Area Group from which the enlistee originated. This file was then forwarded to the camp where the recruit was undergoing their training. Personal information relating to matters such as medical problems, disciplinary matters, promotions and postings was added to these records. Once the soldier embarked, this file was transferred from the camp record office to Base Records, where all the NZEF personal files were arranged in alphabetical order. The files were updated whenever new information was received from NZEF record offices or other sources. A crucial innovation undertaken in late 1915 was the creation of a history sheet for each member of the NZEF that contained all the most important information about an individual. History sheets had a number of advantages and, in particular, made it easier to check and quickly issue casualty reports.

Indeed, the issuing of official casualty reports and lists was one of the key functions of Base Records and one that ensured it a very high profile with the New Zealand public. When a report was received that a New Zealand soldier had been killed or wounded or was seriously ill, no public list was issued for 24 hours. This ensured that the subject's next of kin could be contacted by telegram before the news was made public through lists issued to major post offices and New Zealand newspapers. From late 1915, Base Records did not have casualty telegrams delivered to families between the hours of 10 p.m. and 8 a.m., apparently so that they could get a decent night's sleep before receiving their distressing news.[31]

Base Records was originally housed in two rooms that a staff member described as a 'tiny little black hole'.[32] In 1916 it relocated to a large, temporary but purpose-built building in central Wellington. Throughout the course the war, staff numbers at Base Records increased to more than 300, most of whom were temporary female employees. Women clerks were considerably cheaper to employ than men and were considered to be highly efficient. From late 1915 the paid staff at Base Records was augmented by volunteers, of whom the most long-lasting and important were teams of women from the War League and later the Women's National Reserve.[33] They made a major contribution to the work of the organisation. As the director commented in 1916:

> He knew that to those who could not do battle for their country in the trenches it was a source of satisfaction to know that service could be rendered in another way. A certain pleasure was no doubt to be got from coming and doing the dull and monotonous work that the ladies had done, when they knew that it was done for the soldiers at the front, and for the Empire.[34]

Staff at Base Records often worked long hours to keep up with the flow of work. By early 1916, Base Records held approximately 35,000 files and was sending or receiving nearly 1,000 letters and telegrams each day. Three years later, in mid-1919, Base Records held about 110,000 files and was dealing daily with more than 4,000 items of correspondence.[35] Once the problems evident during the Gallipoli campaign were identified and addressed, there was an increasing appreciation of the effective way in which Base Records carried out its routine but vital role.[36]

Recruiting Branch

The Defence Department also took up increased tasks in recruitment for the NZEF. Initially recruitment for the NZEF was undertaken on a local basis by the personnel in the Area Groups, with the Chief of the General Staff's branch having a directing and co-ordinating role. As the demands for reinforcements increased and the number of volunteers coming forward decreased, the need for a more substantial recruiting organisation became apparent. To meet this requirement, the Adjutant-General (2) Branch, which was generally known as the Recruiting Branch, was established in July 1916. It took full control of recruiting for the NZEF on 25 September 1916, mirroring the larger trend towards more systematic management of the war effort. The new branch managed the process by which men entered the NZEF, tracking the progress of each volunteer and conscript until they entered camp. It was not responsible for disciplinary matters arising from conscription, the military service ballots that were undertaken by the Government Statistician, or the Military Service Boards that heard appeals by men who had been called up. The Recruiting Branch grew rapidly. By early 1918 it had a staff of 232 (88 military, 31 civilian males and 113 civilian females) and held some 165,000 files.[37] Although there were problems with the operation of conscription, when the branch was disestablished on 31 March 1919 it was recognised that it had generally performed satisfactorily.[38]

Personal Services

Handling the greatly increased number of disciplinary matters flowing from the introduction of conscription brought a further work stream. Consequently, the Adjutant-General (1) Branch was established early in 1917, headed by the Director of Personal Services, Major Osburne-Lilly, an experienced lawyer and Territorial officer. Although it was much smaller than Base Records and the Recruiting Branch, Personal Services, which had a staff of 22 (11 military and 11 female civilians) in early 1918, was an important component of the Defence Department.[39] Apart from certain complex or particularly important matters dealt with by the Solicitor-General, the branch managed virtually all legal questions concerning the Defence Department. The branch oversaw the conduct of courts martial, courts of enquiry and related matters; the work of the military police; and the operation of military detention barracks and internment camps. It was also responsible, in conjunction with the police, for identifying and tracking down military defaulters and deserters. The largest group of defaulters were men who had inadvertently failed to respond to their conscription papers, most commonly because they had moved from their recorded address. The branch had considerable success locating such accidental defaulters, but was much less successful locating men who were deliberately evading conscription.[40]

Before the outbreak of war, the imposition of military detention on men and youths who failed to meet their obligations under New Zealand's compulsory military training regime had been the cause of much controversy.[41] The Defence Department considered that detaining such people was 'an irksome and extraneous duty' for regular military personnel.[42] It pressed for such detention to be limited to offences actually committed by military personnel on duty and for all other cases to be dealt with by the civil courts. The government did not act on this advice and a small number of Territorials and Senior Cadets were subject to military detention during the war.[43] Furthermore, the enormous expansion of the military forces greatly increased the number of New Zealanders who were subject to the military justice system. Conscientious objectors, who refused to undertake military service and who had not been exempted by a Military Service Board, proved by far the most awkward group of offenders to deal with. Especially troublesome were those who refused to undertake any kind of military service. The department's general policy was to impose a short period of detention on conscientious objectors in an effort to break down their resistance and, if this failed, to put them before a court martial. When found guilty, such men were generally sentenced to between a year and two years' imprisonment with hard labour. By mid-1918, 188 conscientious objectors were serving sentences in New Zealand prisons.[44]

In its response to the problems posed by military defaulters, deserters and conscientious objectors, the department displayed a significant degree of flexibility in some areas and in general endeavoured to strike an appropriate balance between the resources devoted to dealing with these groups, public opinion and the likely outcome in terms of additional manpower.[45] The department's major failings in this area were the dispatch of 14 determined conscientious objectors to Europe, where they were subjected to brutal treatment by NZEF personnel, and its failure to prevent or quickly detect the abuse of conscientious objectors at its Wanganui detention barracks.[46]

The need to maintain order likewise saw an expansion in military policing. During the first years of the war New Zealand made do with rather ad hoc military policing arrangements, but in 1916 the increasing number of NZEF personnel in the country and the introduction of conscription led to military policing being put on a sound basis. Military police detachments were formed at the training camps and in each military district. These detachments were commanded by Assistant Provost-Marshals in each district, who reported to the Provost-Marshal at headquarters in Wellington. By late 1917, there were approximately 230 military police. They helped maintain discipline and dealt (in co-operation with the hard-pressed civil police) with offences by military personnel. They also worked with the civil police to arrest military defaulters and deserters.[47] Occasionally the military police were criticised for overbearing or unreasonable conduct.[48] Generally, however, the military police corps, which was disbanded in June 1919, was seen as doing a sometimes difficult and unpopular job effectively. The 1918 annual report of the military forces, for instance, attributed the markedly better behaviour of recruits on leave from NZEF camps 'to the presence and growing efficiency of the Military Police'.[49]

The Defence Department was also involved in a somewhat different form of regulation concerning enemy aliens. Shortly after the outbreak of war, substantial internment camps for citizens or former citizens of enemy powers and prisoners of war were established on Somes Island in Wellington Harbour and on Motuihe Island in the Hauraki Gulf. The administration of both camps was in certain respects unsatisfactory. On Somes Island internees were treated harshly and on some occasions physically abused. On Motuihe Island the lax regime at the camp was highlighted by the escape in December 1917 of a group of internees led by Count Felix von Luckner. The military personnel at both camps were inexperienced and in some cases unsuited to the role they had been given. Matters were made worse by the Defence Department's failure to provide adequate support for and supervision of the camps' staff.[50]

All of this additional work involved employment of numerous NZEF personnel in New Zealand, whether as internment camp guards, military police or clerks. Late in 1916, and in the context of increasing manpower difficulties, it was decided to formally establish a Home Service Section of the NZEF, constituted by volunteers who were unfit for overseas service and who could free up fit personnel. This new branch came into existence in June 1917. By the end of the war just over 7,000 men had served within it.[51]

Medical Services

The vast expansion of New Zealand's military forces and the terrible losses suffered by the NZEF meant that the provision of effective medical services both in New Zealand and overseas was of central importance. At the outbreak of war New Zealand's military medical organisation consisted of medical officers and the small medical units of the Territorial Force. In mid-1915, there were a number of significant developments. The Director of Medical Services, Colonel James Purdy, who had not responded well to the crisis at Trentham, was effectively demoted. Overall control of the medical services was passed to a specially recruited senior British Army medical officer, Colonel Robert Henderson, who was appointed to the newly created post of Director-General of Medical Services (DGMS) with the local rank of major-general. At the same time the return of increasingly large numbers of sick and wounded NZEF personnel made the need for the further development of New Zealand's medical arrangements clear. When casualties returned to New Zealand they were assessed by a medical board. Some were sent home to recuperate, others went to convalescent homes and those whose condition was more serious were sent for further hospital treatment.[52]

In August 1915 it was agreed, as part of the negotiations over the formation of the coalition government, that responsibility for the care of sick and wounded military personnel would be shared between the Defence and Public Health departments. The operation of this clumsy and impracticable dual control arrangement was made even more difficult by tensions between James Allen and George Russell, the Liberal Minister of Public Health. It was only in March 1918 that the dual control system was abandoned in favour of giving the Defence Department full control of the care and treatment of all invalids.[53]

New Zealand's military medical organisation developed greatly between 1915 and 1918. Two military hospitals were constructed, the King George V hospital at Rotorua, which opened in January 1916, and the Queen Mary Hospital, in Hanmer Springs, which opened in May 1916. These hospitals formed part of a complex network of institutions that stretched from Whangarei in the north to Invercargill in the south. In addition to these military hospitals and others that were established later, military wards were formed at public hospitals, and a range of specialist facilities created. The work of these institutions was supported by a defence medical store which was established in Wellington. The greatest challenge faced by the system was the influenza pandemic of 1918, which in less than 20 days claimed the lives of nearly 300 military personnel, including a nursing sister, five medical officers and at least 14 other members of the New Zealand Medical Corps. By the end of the war New Zealand had a sizeable military medical establishment. Even in mid-1920, there were more than 1,500 returned soldiers in hospital and a similar number who were outpatients. These men were cared for by 900 military medical personnel.[54]

Major-General Henderson proved to be a highly effective DGMS, and New Zealand's military medical system provided a good level of care to invalided military personnel. Before Henderson's return to the United Kingdom in mid-1919, Allen personally thanked him, writing:

> At the time of your arrival, the Dominion was face to face with many serious difficulties due to the rapid growth of its military forces and the consequent organisation of large training camps on a scale entirely without precedent in this country. Despite all difficulties, however, your wide knowledge and experience, combined with the unfailing tact and courtesy which have so endeared you to all, speedily produced results which have continued to bear fruit down to the present time.[55]

Conclusion

When the First World War ended, in November 1918, there were approximately 300 regular personnel in New Zealand, who were supported by a large number of mobilised Territorial Force personnel. There were 3,333 men serving in the Home Service Section of the NZEF and the civilian staff of the department had grown approximately tenfold, to a total of 764 in early 1918 (207 men and 557 women) and 879 in early 1919 (269 men and 610 women).[56] Such growth reflects the scale of the war effort the Defence Department was involved in.

Major assessments of the significance of this work began while the war was still being waged. In July 1918 the structure and operations of the Defence Department were subjected to careful, independent scrutiny in a Royal Commission on Defence Expenditure. Chaired by Australian businessman Sir Robert Anderson, the commissioners examined all aspects of the department's work in New Zealand and made a number of recommendations. These principally related to reorganising elements of the headquarters of the department in an effort to achieve greater efficiency; in some areas the commissioners found that the structures and systems put in place during the war were not optimal. In part they thought this was due to New Zealand slavishly following British Army arrangements, but they also recognised that the weaknesses they had uncovered were principally due to the rapid growth the department had to undertake in order to carry out a range of functions of unprecedented size and complexity.

From the evidence given to the commission and other sources, it is clear that the most important organisational challenge faced by the department during the war was the need to develop systems and structures to meet an unparalleled range of new or expanded demands while at the same time having to deal with urgent work relating to those demands. In this regard, comments made by a panel of senior public servants in a report prepared for the commission about the Recruiting Branch apply to the department as a whole:

> it is only right to point out that we are referring to organisations brought into existence to enable the country . . . to fulfil its obligations in regard to the war, and to carry out work of which no one had any previous experience. Hence, at various stages developments took place and systems were adopted in an honest endeavour to meet necessities of the time [that now] appear cumbersome and inefficient.[57]

The critical nature of many of the tasks carried out by the department meant that it could not afford a significant failure or breakdown in its operation, and this favoured incremental development. As Colonel Gibbon commented: 'in military organisations everything must be made certain. Early experience in Base Records and Recruiting showed that the country would not tolerate delay or mistakes.'[58]

Although most of the reservists and civilians brought in to fill posts performed creditably, the Defence Department's second most serious difficulty was attracting enough suitable staff. As Major-General Robin noted in his evidence to the commission, 'beggars cannot be choosers, and we have to get [staff] how and where we can'.[59] Finally, the department was handicapped by the difficulty it had obtaining or building suitable accommodation in Wellington for its rapidly expanding branches.[60]

In stark contrast to Anderson's scathing 1915 report on the financial operations of the Australian Department of Defence, the commissioners concluded their report with a strong endorsement of the Defence Department's performance. They noted that they had found no evidence of improper political influence, serious fraud or waste, that New Zealand's sick and wounded had received 'efficient and tender care' and, most significantly of all, that:

> An Army of 100,000 men excellently and fully equipped . . . [had been] carried to the other side of the world. A declaration by the most responsible public man four years ago that this could be done by New Zealand would have been described as 'rhetoric' – or worse.[61]

Besides being well merited, this praise is indicative of the place of the Defence Department's work in facilitating New Zealand's mobilisation. While mistakes were certainly made, the Defence Department successfully overcame many challenges and, in general, managed its greatly expanded size and role well. If it had not done so, the NZEF, New Zealand's most important contribution to the British Empire's war effort, could not have been so efficiently established, developed and maintained throughout the most costly struggle the world had ever seen.

Chapter Two

The Continuation of Politics: Parliamentarians and the Great War

James Watson

The First World War witnessed some dramatic political developments in New Zealand, including the formation of a coalition government, the repeated postponement of general elections and the effective deposition of an MP as a result of his imprisonment for disobeying a military command.[1] Viewed from a slightly different perspective, however, the war period saw a continuation of existing trends and the persistence of political issues and dynamics, if sometimes by different means and within a changed environment. The experiences of New Zealand MPs offer a frontline perspective on this wartime political arena.

This chapter examines how party politics dominated the first year of New Zealand's war and made the formation of a national government a fraught process. It then looks at how the lineaments of the Liberal-Labour alliance, with its stress on the concerns of working people, persisted throughout the war in what effectively, and sometimes explicitly, constituted the parliamentary opposition. It then proceeds to examine the circumstances and issues created by the strains of mobilisation and how they shaped and threatened the political consensus.

The political landscape and the outbreak of war

In the years immediately preceding the war, the Liberal alliance of rural and urban interests, which had governed since 1891, had decayed. The former had progressively deserted to the Reform Party led by William Ferguson Massey; in 1905 the Liberals held over two thirds of the seats classified by R.K. Newman as 'farmer' or 'rural', in 1908 they had less than half and in 1911 they had 14 out of 40.[2] There was also erosion of Liberal support in the cities as some of the working-class elements in the latter moved, more belatedly, to support various, ever-changing independent labour entities. In 1905 only one 'poor city' seat out of 11 was not held by the Liberals; in 1911 two out of 12 were held by Labour candidates and three by Reform.[3]

Despite lacking an overall majority, the Liberals had initially hung on to power. Ward was persuaded to relinquish leadership and his successor, Sir Thomas Mackenzie, narrowly won a confidence motion with support from three Labour MPs. However, desertions from the Liberal ranks meant the Mackenzie administration was defeated in July 1912. The subsequent Reform government under Massey held power with a small majority, while Sir Joseph Ward, not for the last time, was resurrected politically and once again led the Liberals. The violent end to the strike at the Waihi gold mine, the use of considerable force to defeat a strike on the waterfront, and land legislation that was widely seen as exposing Crown leasehold land to purchase by large landowners helped unite Liberal and Labour members in hostility to Massey and Reform. They had strong hopes of a joint victory in the election that had to be held by the end of 1914.

It was in the context of these historic changes and tumultuous times that the eighteenth parliament gathered to hear the reading of the declaration of war on the afternoon of 5 August 1914. This parliament was in its dying days and in view of the approaching election, Ward was anxious that the Liberals should not be seen as hampering the war effort. He had pledged the day before the declaration of war that '[t]he Opposition party of which I am the leader will co-operate in every way with the Government of the day in any action it may be necessary to take to preserve the integrity of the Empire'.[4] Most parliamentarians initially shared the widely held view that the war would be over by the time of the election. Even the normally cautious Massey declared that

> I hope and believe that the war which has just broken out will not last long, and I hope and believe that within a comparatively few months – to say weeks would be too much to expect – within a few months the Imperial authorities will be able to announce to us that peace with honour has come for the British Empire.[5]

Perhaps lulled by optimistic newspaper reports, or anxious to head off proposals for a postponement of the election, in mid-September the Prime Minister hoped 'that by the 1st December we will be able to say that the war will have very nearly reached its termination'.[6]

Unlike at the beginning of the Boer War, there was no suggestion from sitting politicians that entry into the First World War was misguided or that New Zealand should not send an expeditionary force to it. A week after the declaration of war, Paddy Webb, the Social Democratic MP for Grey, declared that '[s]ince the war started, we on this side of the House have fully recognized that this is no time for party contention and party wrangling' and he wanted New Zealand to follow the example of Australia, 'where the leader of the Opposition has been made practically a member of the Cabinet for the time being'.[7]

The continuation of party politics

Despite joining in declarations that party politics were no longer appropriate, the government declined to make major concessions to avoid conflict. Ward requested that presentation of the full Budget be postponed rather than plunge parliament into the 'cauldron of hot party politics', but Massey somewhat bluntly declined.[8] Consequently the opposition trooped out of the House when the Minister of Finance, James Allen, rose to present the Financial Statement, complete with reflections on the competency of previous Liberal administrations. However, the lion did briefly lie down with the lamb when Massey 'very courteously' agreed to an approach from the Labour grouping to exempt wage rates from any suspension of industrial awards under the sweeping Regulation of Trade and Commerce Bill.[9] On 14 August it was announced that six out of the ten men imprisoned for offences during the general strike would be released.[10] Parliament was also spared a potentially divisive debate when the Bible-in-Schools League withdrew its bill so that 'nothing should hinder the closest union between every section of the community'.[11]

Nevertheless, bickering across the floor of the House soon resumed, with accusations that opponents had resorted to 'party' becoming themselves a bone of contention.[12] The most heated of such exchanges came on 18 September, when the question, 'Is this a party speech?', directed at Francis Fisher, the Minister of Customs, led the latter to declare, 'Yes; I am sick of this rubbishy talk about party.'[13] The Liberal George Russell (Avon) responded fashionably that '[t]he honourable gentleman is a true German so far as his tactics in warfare are concerned'. Eventually Massey's quick temper was aroused in a display described shortly afterwards by another Christchurch Liberal: '[f]ancy the Premier, leaning over from his seat, shaking his fist, and shouting "I'm a better man than ever you were" to the member for Avon'.[14]

Shortly thereafter, representatives of the government and opposition conferred on whether the election should be postponed. Ward wanted it put off to March or June 1915.[15] Rather than opposing this on the grounds that the war would soon be over, Massey now argued that postponement was undesirable because it was unclear when the war would end, and he had Field-Marshal Kitchener's widely publicised estimate of the war lasting three years to suggest that any short postponement could well prove pointless.[16] Inevitably the government prevailed and the idea of a party truce became increasingly irrelevant. Far from being ring-fenced from party politics, issues surrounding the New Zealand Expeditionary Force (NZEF) became a focus of criticism, often with a strong element of class resentment. George Witty (Liberal, Riccarton) asked, regarding the departure from Lyttelton of a Canterbury contingent, 'Why were the officers' friends allowed on the wharf and the wives and sweethearts of the rank and file not allowed there?'[17] A Labour MP accused officers of eating all the chocolates donated to the Palmerston North camp.[18] More seriously, Harry Atmore (Liberal, Nelson) detected both political and social influences in the appointment of officers: 'it appears to me that fitness was not considered, but in some cases family connection and in other cases the amount of wealth the parents had'.[19]

The election of December 1914 was dominated by two developments. The first was the Great Strike in 1913, which had threatened to close the main ports and led to the mobilisation of special police to protect strike-breakers on the wharves. It appears to have brought a major influx of votes to the government, with Reform's share going from 33 per cent to 45 per cent.[20] The second development, an electoral arrangement between the Liberal Party and the Labour grouping not to stand candidates against each other, militated against the government, which lost some seats. Various local anomalies in the results and one case of improper practice led to appeals and by-elections and it was not until parliament met at the end of June 1915 that it was confirmed that Reform had been returned with the smallest possible majority.

The prolonged uncertainty as to the election's outcome meant that any moves to form a wartime coalition government foundered for several months on the question of who would lead such an administration. James Allen, who had borne the brunt of many political attacks as Minister of Defence, regretted that a coalition had not been formed at the start of the war and believed that the early formation of a coalition in the United Kingdom, combined with an imperial conference in London, might have done the trick.[21] As it was, back-channel suggestions from a Liberal politician as early as January 1915 that negotiations should commence were apparently based on the mistaken belief that Tau Henare (Northern Maori) was in the Liberal camp.[22]

The formation of a coalition in the United Kingdom in May 1915, not least in response to the disastrous campaign at the Dardanelles, finally presented an imperial example. More importantly, New Zealand's shocking losses in that ongoing campaign undoubtedly made many people feel that political bickering was, in Michael Bassett's phrase, akin to 'flatulence in church'.[23] The politicians were themselves affected by the brutal reality of war. The 1915 session began on a particularly sombre note, with Ward expressing his condolences to James Allen on the death of his son John on the peninsula, and many members on both sides of the House had relatives as well as constituents facing death or mutilation.[24] Furthermore, any opposition members who coveted ministerial office now had to accept that this could only be achieved through a coalition government. Both Massey and Ward were to make reference to the difficulty of ruling with a majority of one, which raises the possibility that if either had gained a clear majority at the election they might have persevered with a Reform or Liberal-Labour government, potentially setting New Zealand's politics on a very different trajectory, at least in the short-to-medium term.[25]

It took several weeks of unseemly haggling following Massey's first, decidedly meagre, offer before a coalition government was eventually formed on 12 August. Both Massey and Ward maintained that it had required the intervention of the Governor, Lord Liverpool, not hitherto renowned for his persuasive rhetoric, to achieve this.[26] While the Reform side was divided largely over how many seats in cabinet their opponents should have, the Liberal caucus wrestled with some more fundamental questions. Given that the Labour grouping had signalled that it would not join a coalition, entering government threatened to end the Liberal-Labour alliance. This displeased several radical, generally urban, Liberal MPs, doubtless because they found the alliance not uncongenial ideologically and it had sometimes assisted their own return at the recent election. One key to winning their acquiescence appears to have been agreement to the establishment of Board of Trade to do something effective about the cost of living. Even then, it proved necessary to create the largest cabinet the country had yet seen in order to augment support within the Liberal caucus. In the final distribution of spoils Massey remained Prime Minister, but Ward became Minister of Finance and Deputy-Prime Minister while rather incongruously remaining Leader of the Opposition. The Liberals had six cabinet ministers and Reform seven, including a non-voting Dr Maui Pomare.[27] There was also an arrangement that in any by-election in a government seat, the candidate selected by the party previously holding the seat would be supported by both parties.

The continuation of political opposition

As noted, this drive for political unity did not result in the absence of a parliamentary opposition, whose fires were overwhelmingly directed at Reform ministers. James Allen, who held the key post of Minister of Defence and was Acting Prime Minister during the long periods when Massey and Ward were in London attending imperial conferences, was the main target.

The Labour group was offered a member in the new cabinet, but it declined and formed its own caucus.[28] This did not represent a lessening of support for the war. In the Legislative Council the leading Labourite J.T. Paul declared, 'I recognize that in the case of every member of Parliament and of all the people of our country it is more than ever necessary for us to do everything possible to forward the interests of the Empire at this time of national crisis'.[29] Even Webb, the sole 'militant' member of the caucus, emphasised that Labour's non-participation was not because it disapproved of New Zealand's participation in the war: '[w]e do not want peace so long as Prussian militarism is over-running Flanders, or Belgium, or any part of France'.[30] It was simply refusing to be 'gagged', along with 'some of the more Radical members of the Liberal party'.

Within days, several Liberal MPs had indeed signalled their determination not to be silenced, when Tom Wilford (Hutt) described replies to him by James Allen as 'dirty' and declined to withdraw the remark unconditionally.[31] Wilford was probably disappointed at not having entered cabinet and may have been indicating to Ward and Massey that he could be a major nuisance outside it. However, in targeting Allen he would have known that he had the sympathy of several of his fellow Liberals and at least some Labour MPs. For all his administrative talents, dedication to duty and prodigious capacity for hard work, the patrician Allen was not the most accommodating individual. Despite his Christian faith, he was unprepared to follow St Paul's dictum and to suffer those he regarded as fools gladly, and many objected to what they saw as his supercilious attitude towards them. It was in this regard that John Hornsby (Liberal, Wairarapa) declared that 'the dignity of this Parliament will be much more effectively conserved if the Minister would not be so irascible – if he would not be so hard and harsh to members when he is replying to them'.[32]

The government, and Allen in particular, faced constant criticism for their alleged failure to control supposed enemy activity in New Zealand and to ensure that those believed to be sympathetic to the enemy did not join the expeditionary force.[33] In handling 'enemy aliens', Allen cleaved firmly to the principles laid down by the imperial government that only military reservists and those who gave definite indications of enemy sympathies should be interned. He was adamant that the New Zealand-born sons of German immigrants should not be excluded from enlistment. This stand, in which he was supported by Massey, put him at odds with much of the public and several MPs, principally from the Liberal party. John Payne (Grey Lynn), who had established himself before the war as the most vocal and combative of the Labour MPs in confronting the Massey government, became the parliamentary spokesman on behalf of the New Zealand Women's Anti-German League and made a habit of presenting Allen with a stream of questions regarding individuals with German names in the New Zealand Army.[34]

There was a considerable element of class feeling in the calls for further action against 'enemy aliens' and those regarded as unreliable because of their German descent, particularly in 1915, when a lot of the focus was on the continued employment of Professor von Zedlitz by Victoria University College. Robert Fletcher (Liberal, Wellington Central) declared of the academic that '[h]e might be a most worthy, amiable, and lovable man, but he felt that discrimination was being shown in this case simply because Professor von Zedlitz happened to be connected with the elite social circles in this town.'[35] Payne agreed that '[t]he whole crux of the position with regard to von Zedlitz was that he happened to be married to one of the *bon ton* of Wellington and that made all the difference in the world'.[36] Wilford claimed, 'I know a man who worked in one of the Government Departments in New Zealand for forty years – an ordinary working-man – and he is now on Somes Island. That is the discrimination I refer to.'[37] Class in the context of party politics was certainly an element in the outcry in 1916 over Lieutenant Grierson, a well-off English immigrant who had lived in Germany and had developed an admiration for German culture and business methods. He had worked in the German consulate in Wellington and assisted the American consul in Auckland with matters of German interest following the outbreak of war and before enlisting. Payne hounded Allen over Grierson's inclusion in the NZEF, while the working-class weekly *Truth* and the Wellington Liberal newspaper the *New Zealand Times* joined wholeheartedly in the pursuit.

Shortly after the 1916 parliamentary session opened, Payne and a posse of Liberal MPs launched an all-out attack on Allen. Payne emphasised alleged laxness with enemy aliens: 'We have in this country a very deplorable pro-German feeling. We have it on the one side from the extreme Socialists, and we have it on the other side from certain sections of the wealthy classes of this country.'[38] Wilford and other Liberals tended to focus on what they saw as the unresponsiveness of the government to the concerns they raised, not least in the interests of servicemen and their families. The Hutt MP was wounding: 'I believe the Minister of Defence is the hardest worker there is in this country . . . But he has no soul – he has no heart.'[39] Charles Poole (Liberal, Auckland West) supported Payne's bills 'if only for the reason that they may bring the Government to its bearings'.[40] His fellow Liberals George Witty, John Vigor Brown (Napier) and Henry Thacker (Christchurch East) also waded in, as did Paddy Webb and Bill Veitch (Wanganui) from the Labour caucus.

However, with Reform MPs, the Liberals in cabinet and most provincial Liberals unmoved, the attack petered out and the issue of conscription united most of parliament behind the government. Veitch supported the Military Service Bill and a couple of radical Liberals opposed it.[41] Leonard Isitt (Liberal, Christchurch North) fought hard to get a much wider religious exemption clause than the one that was eventually included. However, the fundamental issue of compulsion – which at this stage almost everyone considered (or at least hoped) would only actually be applied to single men – brought most MPs together. Certainly Allen believed that the agitation against conscription, largely outside parliament, served to unify the cabinet.[42] He had previously voiced concern at the frequent absences from cabinet of George Russell, the Minister of Health, and worried that he was busy building a political movement.[43] Given Russell's long-standing reputation as a radical within the Liberal Party, Allen presumably feared that he was preparing to revive the Liberal-Labour alliance. If Russell was indeed moving in that direction, the Military Service Bill seems to have brought him back to the fold.

The politics of sacrifice and the maintenance of political consensus

Despite the 1916 Parliamentary Elections Postponement Act, the rhythms of politics endured, and in some cases intensified, under the strains of the war effort. Taking many forms, these politics of sacrifice formed a potent and ongoing concern that threatened political consensus.

The rising cost of living was to be the greatest political issue of the war and its immediate aftermath. It has been questioned whether any efforts at controlling the cost of living could have been successful, but this was of little relevance politically – consumers generally seem to have believed that something could be done.[44] Despite assurances that 'exploitation' would be punished, and a readiness to undertake operations such as purchasing commodities overseas in order to dampen the market, Massey argued repeatedly that price increases in wartime were inevitable and that they were less in New Zealand than in other countries, even Australia, where governments were taking strong measures against them.[45]

The cost of living was an issue that tended to divide town and country. Items produced on local farms loomed large in the weekly budgets of New Zealand consumers. Hence efforts to control prices on those items threatened to reduce the returns to farmers. The exports of the country's main agricultural products – wool, meat and dairy products – were progressively 'commandeered', purchased by the government on behalf of the United Kingdom at prices substantially higher than before the war. However, there was a widespread awareness amongst farmers, echoed by their representatives in parliament, that the prices they were receiving were considerably below those now prevailing on world markets in wartime, principally in London.[46] While some farmers were embarrassed that their increased returns could be seen as 'blood money', arising from the slaughter of war, others believed they should get the market price. Furthermore, farmers faced a growing shortage of labour as young men enlisted, and rising prices of farm inputs.[47] In 1917, rates of land tax were increased and income tax, now at higher rates, was extended to farm profits. Although undoubtedly doing well out of the war, many farmers felt they were bearing at least as much of the burden as other sectors of society and refused to accept that they should make any further sacrifice in the interests of keeping the cost of living down for them.

On the other hand, most people in those other sectors – a substantial majority of the population – struggled to maintain their standards of living on their existing incomes, even with the addition of 'war bonuses' to some wages later in the war. Given that the task of making the household's income stretch to cover its accustomed standard of living was almost invariably the lot of the wife/mother, much of the pressure undoubtedly descended on women. It is unlikely that the Liberal Minister George Russell impressed many housewives in his electorate of Avon, or indeed the rest of the country, with his declaration that 'I believe that by reducing housekeeping to a scientific basis we would advance considerably, if only the people of New Zealand were instructed how to live at a maximum of comfort and yet economically'.[48] Representatives from the non-farming sectors were not slow to sheet much of the responsibility for the rise in the cost of living to the farmers. Brown declared that '[a]s a class they are, next to the woollen-factories, the greediest people in New Zealand'.[49]

When Massey and Ward departed for London at the end of 1916, the Liberal Minister of Agriculture, William Macdonald, replaced the Prime Minister as President of the Board of Trade. Massey may well have regretted agreeing to this. Allen, as Acting Prime Minister, proved less sensitive than his boss to the feelings of Reform's farming constituency while pursuing the national interest. Although Macdonald represented the largely rural seat of Bay of Plenty, he demonstrated a willingness to tackle items in the cost of living that related to farming. Particularly dramatic, and doubtless costly to the Liberal Party's rural seats in the long run, was his ushering in of a mechanism whereby the price of exported butter was 'skimmed' to subsidise its local price. Many dairy farmers were enraged by what they characterised as a 'class tax', and Massey apparently cabled Allen to express 'apprehension' over it, raising the possibility of the 'formation of a country party'.[50] The early 1917 opening of two state-owned butcheries in Auckland to compete with private enterprise was another of Macdonald's innovations and it was claimed these stores were saving customers £104,000 per annum (over $12.5 million in 2015 dollars).[51] Again Massey apparently conveyed concern over the initiative to Allen, who replied that 'I must confess I have been somewhat anxious about this procedure myself, but you know the difficulties, and how essential it is something [sic] to let the public see that we are making an honest endeavour to control the rise in food prices'.[52]

Reform MPs from dairying areas denounced the 'butter tax' unreservedly in parliament during the 1917 session. Massey had returned by then and issued an assurance that the question would be examined. It was announced shortly afterwards that the scheme would not be extended into the 1917–1918 season. Despite numerous calls from MPs for state meat-shops to be established in their electorates, the Auckland experiment remained an isolated one and early in 1918 Massey declared it 'not quite a success'.[53] It was replaced with sales of frozen meat through regular butcheries. Having appointed a commission of inquiry into the problem of the cost of living, chaired by the urban Reformer Charles Statham (Dunedin Central), the Prime Minister largely ignored its recommendations, which included the appointment of a Food Controller, as in the United Kingdom.

As parliamentarians prepared to return home, another urban Reformer, Alfred Newman (Wellington East), protested that the government was not taking enough interest in the cost of living and urged the appointment of a Food Controller.[54] Richard McCallum (Liberal, Wairau) then highlighted, as a 'country member' himself, what had become the crucial divide:

> Throughout this session I have never opened my lips on the question of the cost of living, and I doubt if a single member representing a country district has supported the town members in the manner they should . . . I do not think the country members have that sympathy with the town members that they should have.[55]

He rightly observed that this had implications in smaller centres as well: '[n]o doubt it affects many of our own people, because even in towns such as Oamaru and Blenheim there are a number of people who are affected by the food-prices'. Shortly afterwards Andrew Walker (Labour, Dunedin North) issued a prescient warning about the consequences of the rapidly rising cost of living for industrial relations, 'The labour world, though quiescent to a great extent, is much disturbed at the position of affairs'.[56]

Another burning public issue emerged when it became evident that at the current rate of reinforcement of the NZEF it would soon become necessary to conscript married men, essentially the 'Second Division' under the 1916 Military Service Act. This struck at a fundamental tenet of respectable New Zealand settler society: that the primary responsibility of a married man was to look after his wife and children. The entry into the war of the United States in April led to the belief that the young, unmarried men of that country should go to the front rather than New Zealand's husbands. The government's difficulties were compounded when it emerged that a build-up of reinforcements had enabled the creation of an additional New Zealand brigade. Many concluded that the government had been sending more troops than necessary.[57] Yet again, private Liberal MPs combined with their Labour counterparts to attack the government. A number of backbench Reform MPs also expressed their concern, although for the rural representatives amongst them this overlapped very much with discontent that the Military Service Boards had been unduly restrictive over exempting 'the last man on the farm'. A large and vocal Second Division League was formed to represent eligible married men and their wives, with particularly strong branches in towns.[58] Part of the debate centred on what would be adequate maintenance for wives and children while husbands/fathers were away, or in the event of their death or incapacity. This led to the government narrowly avoiding defeat in parliament when thirty MPs, largely Liberal and Labour, decided that the proposed limit on such provision was unduly niggardly.[59]

The session of 1917 might have been even more torrid, but in February the Liberal Minister of Justice, Robert McNab, had died and a number of individuals who might conceivably have replaced him appear to have been unaccustomedly quiet during the long and potentially turbulent session. Wilford, one of those individuals, got the nod after parliament had adjourned. Statham subsequently declared that '[t]he honourable member for Hutt having now been taken into the Ministry, we have lost the most critical leader of the Opposition'.[60] Nevertheless, the short session early in 1918 saw radical Liberals attacking the government on several fronts, particularly rising prices. Thacker declared that 'they have absolutely funked to do their duty in respect to the cost of living'.[61] Poole and Fletcher concurred.[62] Witty endorsed the attacks that had been made on the granting of exemptions from military service for men with high incomes: '[t]he wealthy men are left in the country while the poor ones have to go'.[63] Three Liberals and a Reformer joined with the Labour group (including Veitch) to try to prevent the direction of labour 'for private gain'.[64] A much larger number of Liberals revolted against the exemption of interest on government stock from income tax and the extension of the life of parliament to the end of 1919.[65] James McCombs (Labour,

Lyttelton) referred to where he sat as the 'Radical side of the House',[66] but with McCombs himself temporarily alienated over the liquor question, Veitch and Payne (the latter still the government's most trenchant critic) not members, and Webb in jail, it could hardly be said that the New Zealand Labour Party caucus, with a membership of two, was the backbone of the parliamentary opposition.

The continuation of mass politics

However, with the cost of living continuing to soar and the call-up of married men progressing, the political sky of 1918 was dark with electoral chickens coming home to roost. In February, Wellington North, hitherto solidly Reform, gave a third of its support to the 'Red Fed' Harry Holland in a by-election and the result was made surprisingly close by the leakage of 1,500 votes to independents, one of them a Liberal pledging to bring down Massey and force an election.[67] The influenza epidemic then led to a further flurry of by-elections.[68] The death of the radical Liberal and constant opponent of the National Government, Robert Fletcher, opened the way for Peter Fraser's victory in Wellington Central, while Robert Semple was returned in Wellington South after Labour's much more moderate leader Alfred Hindmarsh died. In October, S.G. Smith, an Independent Labour critic of the National Government with a strong Liberal pedigree, overturned a big Reform majority in New Plymouth following the death of Henry Okey.[69] A few weeks after the Armistice, Reform's J.A. Nash narrowly held the Palmerston North seat, with a large vote for an independent Liberal candidate and a low turnout putting the Labour candidate only 300 votes behind. Indeed, with the exception of New Plymouth, all of these by-elections were decided on very low turnouts, indicating the depth of antipathy to the National Government amongst electors who were not prepared to vote for the New Zealand Labour Party.

Earlier in the year the imprisonment of Webb had its sequel in a by-election in Grey with a somewhat different result. Apparently concluding that no non-Labour candidate stood a chance there, the Liberal leaders did not participate in the campaign and their candidate withdrew.[70] However, on polling day T.E. Coates, well-known to be a Reformer, came within 200 votes of taking the electorate, which had been solidly Liberal or Labour for decades. The Labour candidate, Holland once again, was not as personable as Webb and was not a coal miner, but he had agreed to stand aside when Webb returned and the main issue in the by-election was very much the latter's imprisonment. Webb was single, and one of the complaints of the Second Division League was that too many single men had been excused service and more (sometimes phrased as 'all') should be conscripted before the married were called upon. There was again a relatively low turnout, but this time it is possible many of the absentees were Labour voters who did not wish to endorse either Webb or the government.

The historical contingency of the influenza epidemic in terms of its timing and the parliamentarians it killed was certainly significant. It struck when popular exasperation with the government was at its height and caused two by-elections in Wellington, the city where a wartime boom had led to particularly sharp rises in the cost of living, especially in the area of rents, which had tended to stagnate elsewhere. As Barry Gustafson has pointed out, 'Had the by-elections occurred in Auckland, Christchurch, or Dunedin, instead of in Wellington and on the West Coast, it is probable that Labour would have won some of them but the new Labour members would have been drawn from the Party's more moderate wing'.[71] Certainly Hindmarsh was a much more moderate leader of the Labour Party than his successor, Holland. Furthermore, Robert Fletcher was a consistent critic of the coalition government and, like Thacker, he might well have survived the 1919 election. Certainly the election of three militants at this juncture, and the confirmation of Holland's leadership on the toss of a coin (surely the ultimate in historical contingency) at the end of 1918, made a Liberal-Labour electoral pact impossible for the upcoming election. It also meant that in 1922 the erstwhile Christchurch radical Liberals, Isitt and Witty, alienated by what they saw as Labour's extremism under Holland's leadership, would ensure that Massey could continue in government.

The resumption of national elections in 1919 saw Massey's wartime sensitivity to the concerns of farmers contribute greatly to Reform's breathtakingly disproportionate victory, in which it took 80 per cent of the 'farmer' or 'rural' seats. Meanwhile Labour candidates captured further city seats that had been radical Liberal strongholds. After that election they controlled half of Newman's 'poor city' seats. They had 10 out of 12 of them three years later, and generally held them through the Reform landslide of 1925 and the Liberal revival of 1928. Labour came out of the war period with a substantial base in the main centres, and Reform had expanded its base in rural areas, both at the expense of the Liberals. Indeed the wartime exacerbation of tensions between urban and rural interests, and the Liberals' efforts to meet the cost-of-living concerns of their urban wing, had hastened the alienation of their remaining supporters in the farming community. At the same time, those efforts were largely stymied in cabinet by Reform, leaving radical, largely urban Liberal MPs to rail helplessly against government inactivity alongside their Labour colleagues. While the war certainly did not deliver the *coup de grâce* to the Liberal

Party, it greatly accelerated its decay and the nation's movement towards a two-party system.

Conclusion

New Zealand's parliamentarians – Reform, Liberal and Labour – were united in their support for New Zealand's participation in the war in August 1914 and initially resolved to declare a 'party truce'. However, a belief that the conflict would be brief, the depth of differences over recent events in the country (particularly industrial disputes), and above all the imminence of the next general election comprehensively undermined that resolution. Then the prolonged uncertainty about the outcome of that election, which led to the leaders of both major parties nursing hopes of becoming prime minister, delayed moves to create a coalition government. Such a government was only formed at the beginning of August 1915 after lengthy negotiations and the intervention of the Governor.

Even then, previous political divisions continued, with radical Liberal and Labour MPs frequently united in attacking what they saw as government inaction on controlling the rising cost of living, which was a major concern of their generally working-class constituents. The same alliance was evident in criticism of the administration of New Zealand's war effort; this was particularly directed at James Allen as Minister of Defence, who was portrayed as haughtily unresponsive to public concerns. Unsupported by his colleagues, one Labour MP, John Payne, led several of the radical Liberals in denouncing the government for insufficient vigour in pursuing local enemy aliens and their alleged sympathisers, an issue that acquired overtones of class favouritism.

The war greatly exacerbated existing divisions between farming and other, especially urban, interests. These divisions were very evident in parliament, nowhere more so than over the cost of living, as high prices in wartime for food and fibre clearly benefited farmers while weighing heavily on urban consumers. Massey ensured that countermeasures that angered farmers – notably the 'butter tax' – did not survive long. The divide was also clear in the tendency of MPs with large numbers of farming constituents, most of them Reformers, to focus on keeping the 'last man on the farm' when tradesmen were being obliged to shut up their businesses on enlistment.

While MPs heavily supported the introduction of conscription itself in 1916, with only five Labour members and one Liberal implacably opposed, its extension to the married men of the Second Division the following year provoked a storm of criticism in the House of Representatives. Together with the seemingly inexorable rise in the cost of living, the issue made the government very unpopular during the last two years of the war. That unpopularity was made manifest in 1918 when a series of by-elections, most with low turnouts, saw it suffer defeats or near-defeats. Largely by chance, it also brought into parliament and to the leadership of the New Zealand Labour Party militants who were determined to displace the Liberals' radical wing rather than continue to make electoral arrangements with it. When the country as a whole was finally able to vote, in what was in large part a judgement on the politics of the war years, the existing trend of the Liberals losing rural seats to Reform and 'poor city' seats to Labour was strongly confirmed.

Chapter Three

'Priceless Worth': The Territorial Force and Senior Cadets in World War One

Peter Cooke

During the First World War, New Zealand's home defence forces were the poor cousin when compared to the New Zealand Expeditionary Force (NZEF), which was the stout son sent off to help protect the imperial family.[1] The poor cousin was deprived of funds and equipment and, with the job of resisting an invasion which did not eventuate, was finally drained of manpower to bolster the overseas force. This familial metaphor still holds largely true, but only in the context of military history. In regards to New Zealand's social life, the home defence forces were far more prominent. The Territorial Force was a permanent armed force and, despite being part-time, it had a tangible presence in most communities. Its social visibility in periodic encampments, parades, patriotic fundraisers and emergency call-outs was more pervasive than the fleeting appearances of NZEF drafts in training or upon departure. This social presence placed the Territorials beside other siblings in the home defence family: the National Reserve, the Rifle Clubs, and the Senior Cadets – which, while composed of 14- to 17-year-old boys, making it the youngest of the family, ultimately fed the Territorial Force and, indirectly, the Expeditionary Force.

These home defence forces had been created after a long review of the New Zealand Volunteer Force. The 'Volunteers' had over 50 years of tradition, but service in the force was not compulsory.[2] Standards of training and officer qualifications were imperfect, and appointment of officers was by popularity rather than proficiency.[3] A major burst of reform came in the 1909 Defence Act, which disestablished all volunteer units on 28 February 1910 and created the Territorial Force in their place. The regular New Zealand Permanent Force was replaced by the New Zealand Staff Corps for officers, and the New Zealand Permanent Staff for non-commissioned officers (NCOs) and others, whose job was to train Territorials (for whom service was made compulsory). The Act in its original form proposed training 12–14-year-old boys as Junior Cadets, though this did not find favour and the Junior Cadets were dropped in 1912. This meant boys were enlisted in the Senior Cadets at 14, graduated to the General Training Section at 18, and were included in the Reserve from age 25 to 30.

Though the Territorial Force was created only four and a half years before the war started, its component units were often far older. Units with origins dating back as far as the 1850s played a greater social role than the comparative youth of the force might suggest. Wellington's field artillery unit, D Battery, for example, dated from 1867.[4] It had some name changes but never a break in continuity of service. Auckland infantrymen traced their lineage back to 1858, but also identified with the Auckland volunteers who accompanied the British to fight Heke and Kawiti in Northland in 1845.[5] These units had formed when many first-generation settlers were still alive and when traditions from Britain strongly infused New Zealand society. Some early settlers would recall the ballots for militia service, which ended in Britain in 1829.[6] Even though Territorial service was compulsory, the volunteer spirit remained strong, with many units having quite enough volunteers clamouring for membership and not requiring unwilling conscripts. Most units worked to an 'establishment' – a formal listing of all the personnel, weapons and equipment needed to do their job. When the formation of a new field battery was announced in 1916, the media announced it as 'Good News for Waiting Recruits'.[7]

With their traditional nature, their prominent place in the social landscape and their role in the war effort, the home defence forces can offer useful insight on New Zealand society at war. Starting with an overview of the home defence forces' position in the war effort, this chapter proceeds to consider the experiences and perspectives of the constituent parts of the home defence system.

Home defences within the war effort

Activity in many parts of the country at the outbreak of the war affirmed the social presence of the Territorials and dispelled the misnomer of the Territorial as 'the peace soldier' who saw no active service.[8] The Garrison Artillery Territorial companies, for example, were mobilised to man the coastal forts, which remained on alert, mounting shifts for nine months.[9] Furthermore, fearing sabotage of vital places, the Post and Telegraph Territorials were mobilised to provide small parties to guard radio stations and cable-landing points, and for the first month of war every railway bridge and tunnel was guarded round the clock by mobilised men of the Railway Battalions.[10] The first service-related death for New Zealand in the war was a called-up Railway Battalion Territorial, Sapper Robert Hislop, who died on 19 August 1914 after falling from a rail bridge.[11]

Despite this presence, New Zealand's First World War era Territorials are, historiographically, very much overlooked. When enlistment figures are given, for instance, few actually mention the force to which such enlistments relate. Usually the NZEF is intended but this ignores the sizeable Territorial Force, whose scale rivals that of the NZEF. This reflects a broader confusion of figures relating to the strength of the NZEF. The number of men joining the NZEF over the course of the war is usually quoted as over 124,000. However, this figure is the number of enlistments, not individuals. Within the 124,000 figure are around 3,600 men who joined more than once, 11,300 men discharged before going overseas and around 10,000 still under training in New Zealand when the Armistice ended the flow of reinforcements.[12] Another 7,030 were for home service only, in a Home Service Section formed in November 1916.[13] These figures do not tally statistically (with some men in more than one group), but the number who served overseas in the NZEF is closer to 98,000.

Historical neglect of the Territorials is unfortunate as the Force has a direct relationship with the NZEF's performance. During the war 32,900 men or (27 per cent of the NZEF) were transferred from the Territorial Force to the Expeditionary Force.[14] But an additional category of men volunteered for the NZEF without being a *current* Territorial but who had *previous* military experience in it or the New Zealand Volunteer Force, Permanent Force, Royal New Zealand Artillery or HM Imperial Forces. Inclusion of this category boosts the figure to over 40,000.[15] Furthermore, about two thirds of the officers in the NZEF had previous military service. By the war's end 1,500 Territorial officers had joined the NZEF.[16] Lastly, of the 8,400 men in the Main Body, we know that 3,600 (42 per cent) were current Territorials and over 2,000 (23 per cent) had undergone previous military service.[17] This means 65 per cent of the Main Body were current or former soldiers. While this percentage dropped slightly over the course of the war, these two statistics explain how the New Zealand Division made such a good showing and why it was garlanded with elite status by the war's end. The Samoan Advance Party, moreover, was almost exclusively formed from Territorial soldiers, and was made up from their existing units – companies of Auckland and Wellington infantry, railway engineers, artillery, signallers and army service corps (ASC).[18] This background also shaped attitudes, with many voluntary Territorials believing, not surprisingly, that going to war was the ultimate reason for being in the force. Writing to his mother from Gallipoli, a Timaru Territorial, Sergeant Stanley Bowker, noted 'If this war is to be over quickly, we must have more men. The more we get, and the quicker we get them, the sooner will it be over.'[19]

The war saw a change in the scale of home defence. In 1914–1915 the size of the Territorial Force was constitutionally set at 30,000. Added to this were another 2,075 in the General Training Section (men not yet posted to units).[20] There were also 8,770 members of Defence Rifle Clubs, a formal part of the home defences.[21] Ensuring a ready flow of future manpower, 26,446 cadets were enrolled as Senior Cadets.[22] In 1915, former soldiers were invited to put their names on quasi-official registers such as the National Reserve or Citizens' Defence Corps, which peaked in strength at a few thousand.[23] Altogether, the size of the structured home forces in 1914–1915 stands at some 66,000. Lastly, each year added around 8,000–10,000 new enlistments, notably from the Senior Cadets.

So at least 60,000 men served in the Territorial Force during some part of the war. This means that these organisations rival the NZEF in terms of quantity: for every ten men who passed through the NZEF, six spent time in the Territorial Force. The scale of this rallying might be compared to what was occurring overseas. Once the New Zealand Division was formed in 1916, it and the New Zealand Mounted Rifles Brigade maintained around 23–24,000 fighting men in the field. The Territorial Force equalled or exceeded this number every year of the war.[24]

This numerical significance meant that the Territorial Force also suffered when the country hit its manpower brick wall. Always more ambitious than its numbers could support, New Zealand faced a personnel crisis mid-war.[25] The small size of the country's manpower pool is reflected by the fact that, at war's end, the categories of the First Division, New Zealand Reserve (over 80,000 single men) and Second Division (30,900 married men, 13,400 of whom were Class A 'without children' and 17,500 Class B 'with one child') 'were exhausted either by voluntary enlistments or by the operation of the ballot'.[26] Over 23,500 fathers with two children were called up, but very few who had not volunteered got to the front.

Facing these limits the government responded by reintroducing conscription (as first used in the 1860s–1870s), curtailing Senior Cadet and Territorial training and shortening the transfer pathway between the Territorials and the NZEF. In peacetime and for the first two years of war, men who entered the Territorials at age 18 had seven years of part-time training before being transferred, at 25, to a non-active reserve (for five years). After the pinch on manpower, Territorials could be transferred to the NZEF at age 20.[27] Their two-year service in the Territorial unit was now seen as giving them 'a satisfactory standard of discipline and individual efficiency' for service at the front.[28]

These strains on human capital meant Territorial officers were seen as a valuable, and limited, resource. The Force was used as a part-time labour exchange, with Territorial officers filling vacancies created when full-time NCOs and officers of the regular New Zealand Permanent Staff, New Zealand Staff Corps or Royal New Zealand Artillery went off in Expeditionary Force postings.[29] Examples include long-serving Territorial and headmaster of King's College, Charles Major, who took a full-time staff position during the war, and Territorial Colonel Joseph Cowie Nichols, who commanded the Otago Military District and Otago Mounted Rifles Brigade for the duration. Territorials were also favoured for many officer roles in the NZEF. When their numbers looked to be diminishing, an experiment of sending civilians to Trentham Camp for training as officers was attempted, but it was not successful.[30] To a certain extent, Territorial officers took over the training role within their own units from regular officers and NCOs who were called away to NZEF duties. Territorials, assisted by sage retired officers from the Reserve, also took on a greater role in training the Senior Cadets, until the cadet training was stopped in 1916 due to lack of resources.[31]

Wartime requirements for manpower meant that Territorials were also in demand at their normal places of work. Some employers expressed frustration at the annual two-week absences compulsory Territorial training demanded of their employees. In comparison with the total removal entailed by NZEF service, however, the Territorial scheme's impositions looked relatively trivial. Likewise, the authorities tried to hold the Territorial camps at times least inconvenient to employers, especially in rural areas or seasonal industries, whereas the NZEF camps worked to the rhythm of the insatiable need for reinforcements.[32] The 1916 introduction of conscription was even less popular with employers because it removed employees via the ballot, required employers to ascertain that their staff had registered for military service and exposed them to prosecutions for harbouring those who had not. Some large government departments were strongly represented in the Territorial Force (New Zealand Railways and the Post and Telegraph Departments offer primary examples) and wanted the impact of Territorial training on the public sector lessened. These departments did appeal at times, but often buckled when told their eligible non-essential staff had to be released. Social pressure came on private employers who might make the same appeal, with a Military Service Board saying of one employer it 'would begin to question his loyalty in that he would be placing his business before the wants of the country'.[33]

The physical infrastructure of the Territorials also faced wartime adjustments. Curtailing training from late 1917 saved money as well as reducing the demands on stretched instructors. Territorial Force encampments in country areas, or those incurring additional rental or other charges, were banned.[34] After this, appeals were made to patriotic land-owning bodies, such as jockey and racing clubs, industrial schools, A&P societies, farming groups or municipal councils, to lend paddocks for units to run annual cost-free camps. Other rented facilities, drill halls, stores and offices were closed to save funds and manpower.

The Territorials

That the Territorials weathered the strains of wartime mobilisation as well as they did reflects the relationship they possessed with wider society. Of New Zealand's one million people, 6 per cent donned a Territorial Force uniform – in terms of eligible manpower, the figure is closer to 10 per cent. The extensive nature of the force effectively meant that every suburban centre, rural crossroad, urban street, mainstream church, medium business or popular club included Territorials. The prominence of the Territorials within the social landscape was most evident in small-town New Zealand. Consider Kawakawa, a small Northland town with 386 ratepayers in 1914, which headquartered a company of infantry (A Company, 15th North Auckland Regiment), a portion of the North Auckland Mounted Rifles (D Squadron) and a body of Senior Cadets (65th Company).[35] When those regiments concentrated in annual camp, 780 men turned up. Likewise Hawera, with a population of 3,375 in 1916, hosted an infantry company and a mounted squadron but also had headquarters for both regiments, as well as the ubiquitous Senior Cadet company.[36] Paeroa, with a population of 1,705 in 1916, was headquarters to a regiment which took over 520 men into camp each year (on land lent by Mr Goonan on Mill Road).[37] It was also a Group headquarters, for which the Defence Department employed permanent staff and maintained office and drill-hall facilities. The same pattern is seen in Milton, Balclutha and a dozen other towns across New Zealand. Comparably, most big city suburbs fielded a troop, platoon, company, squadron or similar. With weekly parade nights or weekend training, uniforms and arms were a common sight on their streets.

This extensive presence reflects how Territorial Force recruiting and training infrastructure had been deliberately spread across the country – in 56 locations. These were managed by eighteen Group offices,[38] which in turn were responsible to the four Military District Headquarters (in Auckland, Palmerston North, Christchurch and Dunedin). Not only did this provide employment for many NCOs of the New Zealand Permanent Staff, but it also stimulated local economies through the hiring of offices, stores and halls as training facilities and the provisioning of local training concentrations. Alongside work, this institutional infrastructure also underwrote leisure; some facilities (particularly drill halls, which dated back to the Volunteer Force) functioned as social hubs, which became hives of activity during the war. While some units only had smaller clubrooms, these also provided sites for social interchange in drinking, games and general club life.[39] The nature of the events hosted varied widely, from formal dress military balls, to various patriotic and fund-raising events, and funerals for current and former soldiers.

However, Territorial units became societal institutions for reasons beyond their premises. Their reputation, culture and links to many parts of New Zealand society wove citizen forces into the social fabric. Membership of a unified service such as the Territorial Force offered society a ready means with which to assess the individual, and men of good character were recruited over those perceived to be vagrants, undesirables or shirkers. General Sir Ian Hamilton inspected them in 1914 and was impressed with the physical and intellectual calibre of the men. He saw in them 'human material second to none in the world'.[40] This sort of commendation gave social capital to the Territorial. The *Hawera & Normanby Star* said training had 'done much to improve their bearing and teach them the value of self-restraint and a proper recognition of authority'.[41] The Force also proved a site of broader socialisation. The Auckland College Rifles, for example, fostered a sporting culture which left their name synonymous with netball and rugby (almost exceeding their association with the military). Sports teams in Central Districts owe their identity to the Central Military District. Wellington Navals and the Star Boating Club – which both formed military units – left the capital not only adjacent landmark waterfront buildings, but also rowing sport traditions.[42] Some fire brigades formed from tired old units which had outlived their martial value. And the plethora of rifle ranges across the country is testimony to the marksmanship that many Territorial units claimed prowess in.

Furthermore, civic leadership in small-town New Zealand usually paid great heed to martial qualities and military service. Men who rose to lead their local Territorial sub-unit (or earlier volunteer corps) would come to notice and usually earn sufficient praise for them to adopt municipal or other leadership roles. Or, as demanded on the frontier, they were jacks of all trades, excelling at a range of activities. James Allen, a Minister of the Crown and a Territorial Colonel, is one example. Gordon Coates, a keen Territorial and Prime Minister during the mid to late 1920s, is another.[43] A lesser example is a Wanganui man, Herbert Harper, aged 56, who was noted in a 1918 article as 'well known in business circles, and a partner in the T.B. Williams auctioneering business'. He was a Territorial officer, and occupied the position of major as company commander in the 1st Battalion, 7th (Wellington West Coast) Regiment.[44]

Media descriptions of another former Territorial, Joseph Lennane, who was wounded at the front, allow the reader to imbue the subject with attractive qualities. He was described as 'an Otago Central boy', so clearly at one with his community and informal with it. He 'spent several years as a blacksmith', suggesting vigour, staying power and loyalty to a craft or employer. He 'was one of the most prominent backs' in a rugby football club, showing speed and agility – and also a sense of fashionable competitiveness. His outdoorsiness and patriotism is conveyed by the term 'a keen Territorial'. Other characteristics are that he 'is well known' in South Otago, suggesting sociability and good connections, and also that he 'took a prominent part in all social movements in Owaka', therefore an energetic leader who got on with everyone.[45] Not all Territorials were as skilled, or praised over such a broad spectrum, but being a Territorial was a good start to acceptability and upwards mobility.

The association between defence forces and society intensified during the war years and can be seen in the social phenomenon of the patriotic fundraiser. Such events occurred frequently in towns and cities, and often involved a parade, a series of events at a park to which the parade led, and a pageant of female virtues based around the Carnival Queen concept.[46] In these, several popular young women were nominated as 'queens' to various causes, whose supporters then feverishly promoted them and raised money (through 'two-penny votes'). The causes each queen stood for could be industry sectors, towns in a province, sports codes, or arms of His Majesty's Imperial Forces. The queen whose committee raised the most money would be the winner, and all money raised would go to the principal cause. This was usually the Belgian relief fund, wounded soldier funds, hospital ships, returned soldier clubs, ambulance purchases or other worthy charities. A Southland carnival in 1914 mixed up the causes, pitting the queens of Bluff and Gore against those for the 'Territorials', 'Athletic' sports club, 'Friendly Societies' and the 'Hospital'. The Gore Queen won, with the Territorial Queen coming third.[47]

While the war effort drew on these social networks, aspects of war regulations could also rattle their cohesion. For example, a January 1918 measure, building on the introduction of six o'clock closing for licensed premises in 1917, banned commissioned officers from drinking in hotel public bars. The reason given was that officers socialising with men of the lower ranks was 'detrimental to discipline'. The order was strengthened in

April to include all hotel bars, even the more salubrious lounge bars. No distinction was made as to which officers it applied to, so it would have included any regular, cadet or Territorial Force officer, as well as those with the NZEF.[48]

Lastly, and obviously, the Territorials' institutions and bonds with the community underwrote martial organisation and purpose. The significance of this is highlighted by the behaviour of the members of Auckland's College Rifles, who rallied at their Grafton Road rooms within fifteen hours of war being declared. Many then volunteered for the first expeditionary force, which went to Samoa, and for drafts going later to Europe. The home defence forces' presence in peacetime parades (for royal tours, provincial anniversaries, Empire Day, Dominion Day, visiting warships or visiting dignitaries) continued in farewells to reinforcement drafts. To send off Hawera's batch to the 9th Reinforcements, for instance, local Territorials marched with the Hawera Citizens' Band, National Reserve, Senior Cadets and Fire Brigade.[49] Scouts and women's groups were also usually present. The Territorials could also be a source of renewed bonds as returned men reacquainted themselves with their Territorial colleagues in clubrooms.[50] As social institutions, the Force kept faith with the family of soldiers they represented, counting the numbers who went to war and the smaller numbers who returned. They erected honours boards to the casualties[51] and published commemorations of their lives and deeds.

Rifle clubs, national reservists and the Senior Cadets

The Territorials, in turn, operated as part of the larger family of home defence. While the Territorial Force formed the first line, the Senior Cadets functioned as its nursery, and no discussion of New Zealand's home forces would be complete without mention of the second tier of armed defences – the rifle clubs and national reservists. The former were armed but not uniformed, and the latter badged but not armed.[52] Both were formally part of the defence scheme, though they operated with more autonomy than the Territorials. This independence was not unconditional; the quasi-official Citizens Defence Corps, for example, was assimilated into the National Reserve in 1916.[53] Defence rifle clubs had come under the wing of New Zealand Military Forces at the close of the South African War (when some were already four decades old), and were formally recognised as a second tier of the defence forces in 1912.[54] The Defence Amendment Act that year confirmed the relationship, laying down that no Territorial soldier could also be a member of a rifle club. Where fit men of soldierly age would be directed to Territorial units, unfit or older men would join the local rifle club. Attending rifle club parades was mandatory.[55]

Rifle clubs were as widespread as Territorial units: in 1915, 240 locations had a recognised rifle club, 35 of which had been formed since the outbreak of war.[56] Again, the place of communal associations is apparent. The Legion of Frontiersmen and the Farmers' Union, which helped oppose the Great Strike in 1913, formed defence rifle clubs, as did Scottish associations, school old boys, former volunteer corps, workingmen's clubs, veterans' associations, yachting clubs, large workplaces, local authorities, and many towns and suburbs.[57] Some took their role seriously, training in fieldwork for instance, but their enthusiasm was dampened when the supply of arms and ammunition temporarily abated.[58] The government imposed a maximum size of 100 members, which helped manage the demand for ammunition but also created waiting lists of prospective members. When a rifle club member joined the NZEF, the club was freed up to recruit another member.

Rifle shooting was tremendously popular as a sport, alongside other activities with similar frontier origins such as dog trialling, wood chopping, tug o' war, and agricultural and pastoral shows. A national championship was first shot in 1861 and is still going strong: the National Rifle Association claims the national championships to be the oldest in New Zealand.[59] Annual competitions had settled upon the long ranges at Trentham in the decade before the war, after previously roving around the country, and although formal national shoots were suspended during the war, club activities continued as much as the supply of ammunition allowed. Matches were social events, with men and women competing, and families enjoying the outings. Clubs also got involved in patriotic activities and fund-raising. This cemented in place an underlying acknowledgement that, in a frontier society (away from anyone else's help), every hand would be called on in one way or another if a true emergency arose. The idea of forming militias from these clubs was still being discussed in 1915 for mobilising men who were under no other obligation to become part of the defence scheme.[60]

The Senior Cadets were a leaping-off point in a larger training and service scheme. They had been around since the 1860s, having a similar vintage in New Zealand to volunteer corps and rifle clubs.[61] They also saw reform and expansion in the decade before the Great War, which formed the heyday of school-based military training. Under the 1909 reforms, the Cadets became a national, and compulsory, part of boys' education: two thirds of boys in public schools, and more in high schools, underwent military drill.[62] While most Senior Cadet companies were hosted by schools, other institutions could raise companies. During the war, Senior Cadets were formed into over 110 numbered companies. The New Zealand training ship *Amokura* raised a company, as did some scout and church groups (the Dunedin Christian Brothers, for instance). The keenest were the old public-school-type boys' colleges: Auckland Grammar, King's, Wellington, Christ's, Waitaki Boys', and other high schools in many middling towns. Auckland Grammar had ten companies but some others raised three or four.[63] Teaching staff were given Territorial commissions to lead and train these boys, or when this was not possible the local sub-area sergeant-major might visit periodically.

The soldier-nursery aspect of the scheme was quantified as equivalent to two or three months of basic training.[64] Senior Cadets were inured to the elementary disciplines of smart appearance, standing to attention, receiving instructions, marching, basic field and weapon craft and exposure to martial history and traditions. At major parades of armed forces, the Cadets would muster alongside aged veterans from Crimea, the Indian Mutiny and the Anglo-Afghan wars, and the South African 'contingenters', as well as men who fought in New Zealand's colonial conflicts.[65] They heard that when others mentioned the 'Great War' they were referring to the Napoleonic Wars, which gave them lessons in victory from Trafalgar, Leipzig, Borodino and Waterloo – and a century of central European peace thereafter in the Pax Britannica.[66] Furthermore, the Senior Cadets functioned as a feeder system to the armed forces. About 8,000–10,000 new Cadets were enrolled each year (aged 14) and roughly the same number were promoted to the Territorials each year upon reaching 18 years of age. The Territorial Force transferred about 10,000 men to the NZEF each year.[67] Between 1911 and 1918 almost 99,000 Senior Cadets were enrolled in the scheme, and by the war's end, the Territorial Force was composed largely of 18- and 19-year-olds.[68]

Besides military expediency, the scheme was also advocated on a wider social basis as a means to instil physical fitness and dutiful dispositions and defend against larrikinism.[69] It did not always achieve this ideal. For example, in March and September 1916, Karori School claimed that 'window breaking and forcing entry to classrooms and causing damage' was linked to Cadet drills.[70] From the start, a degree of opposition to the Cadets emerged from those who refused, on principle, to co-operate. Some were inspired by those who were imprisoned for refusing to pay fines imposed for failing to attend, particularly the 'Ripa Island Martyrs', who were briefly imprisoned on Fort Jervois, Ripapa Island, in Lyttelton Harbour.[71] Such prosecutions for non-attendance continued into the war years. In 1915, for example, 524 Cadets and 1,273 Territorials were convicted, mostly for non-attendance.[72] Similar numbers were reported each year of the war. Remembering that over 25,000 Cadets in 1915 were not prosecuted and did attend, it is clear that a large proportion of New Zealand society supported or tolerated the Senior Cadets in principle and/or in practice. Apart from the citizenship training, the scheme was perceived as having the same social benefits of the Territorials – i.e. as a way for young men to get ahead in a society favouring outdoors pursuits, active masculinity and communal involvement. As a bonus, Cadets also qualified for free rail travel when going to training.

As with the Territorials, the war brought challenges to the Senior Cadets. In 1915, 400 small-bore rifles (.22-inch calibre) had been imported specifically for Cadet use.[73] However, within a year, equipment shortages saw the Cadets requested to submit some of their equipment and arms to active Territorial units.[74] The keener schools stayed calm and carried on, even getting themselves attached to local regiments to maintain a sense of reality in their training. Likewise, Cadet artillery units attended the shell practices of their parent batteries.[75] This pattern of wartime strains and adjustments is also evident in terms of human resources. In 1915 there were 426 Cadet officers, all part of the order of battle. By 1916, though, the drain of personnel into the NZEF placed such a strain on teaching staff that Cadet training was suspended. Schools might continue a bit of drill on the rugby field, but Cadet camps and concentrations stopped.[76] Cadet training resumed after the war, and its legacy **is the universal programme of formal structured physical education which continues today.**[77]

Conclusion

Towards and during World War One much of New Zealand society sang to martial tunes. The country regimented its young, armed its menfolk and was confident in its ability to repel threats to its way of life. Territorial training embodied this ideal of the citizen-soldier defending and connected to the social body; those who donned uniforms and honed their martial skills were clerks, farmers, labourers, teachers, managers or professionals during their working hours.

New Zealand's war effort drew on this social resource, with military training and social networks coming into play. The home defences contributed directly, via being mobilised in their own right, and indirectly, by supporting the NZEF. Indeed, the General Officer Commanding's report in 1918 gives some idea of the significance of these institutions:

> The abolition of this system of training in 1914 would have meant an irredeemable loss to the Dominion of some forty-five thousand

> Territorials and over fifty thousand Cadets of an invaluable degree of military efficiency at a time when such training is of priceless worth . . . The efficiency and discipline inculcated in the ranks of the Cadet and Territorial Forces are directly contributory to the results obtained in the Expeditionary Force camps, and the splendid name created by the New Zealand Forces in the field.[78]

Chapter Four

'We could surely introduce . . .': The Impact of the Great War on New Zealand Education

Roger Openshaw

From the public primary school through to the University of New Zealand, the Dominion's education system was significantly affected by the First World War. This impact was truly multifaceted, sometimes introducing new considerations thrown up by wartime exigencies, but more often serving to accelerate trends already evident prior to 1914. Some trends that were still sharply in evidence during the immediate post-war period were soon to be challenged, and even reversed. Others were to continue and gain strength throughout the interwar years, eventually becoming conventional wisdom amongst later generations of educators.

The legacy

For much of the twentieth century, New Zealand's education system effectively comprised several discrete entities. By far the largest of these was the public primary school system, with 4,262 teachers and 172,168 students enrolled in 2,255 schools by the end of 1913, the majority of these being sole-charge.[1] Established nationally in 1877, the public primary schools were compulsory for non-Maori students who were British subjects. The public school system was complemented by the native school system established in 1869. However, even by 1914, native schools were losing students to the public school system; by the outbreak of war, there were only 4,521 enrolled in native schools as against 4,905 in public schools. This was and would continue to be the direct result of Maori leaders and Maori parents increasingly perceiving that the public primary schools offered an academically superior curriculum leading to better employment prospects in the growing towns.[2]

The relatively small but rapidly expanding secondary sector still consisted in 1914 of mainly fee-paying, highly academic high schools.

These had been originally intended for a small colonial elite. By 1914, however, the impact of the 1903 Secondary Schools Act compelling high schools to accept large numbers of government free-place pupils meant that far more of the student population were availing themselves of at least some secondary education.[3] There was also a network of technical high schools, providing specialist training for the trades, together with a handful of district high schools located mainly in the South Island.

Finally, there was the University of New Zealand. Although small by today's standards, the significance of this institution lies in the fact that the creation of universities in the British Empire was, in Tamson Pietsch's words: 'an essential marker of colonial development through which colonies could exert their own maturing identities, expand their elites and form the cadres that would be employed in and facilitate the emergence of the political, religious, institutional and educational institutions within their borders.'[4]

In 1914 the University of New Zealand consisted of four university colleges located in Auckland, Wellington, Christchurch and Dunedin. Whilst student numbers were increasing (including significant numbers of women), the university was still largely oriented to the needs of young men intending to enter the so-called black-coated professions, although like most high schools it steadfastly resisted explicit vocational and citizenship training. Moreover, whilst relatively 'new' subjects such as physics and chemistry were by then an accepted feature of the academic landscape, it was always on the tacit understanding that they remained a non-compulsory part of the traditional Bachelor of Arts structure.

In addition to the growth in student numbers throughout the education system as a whole, two further and often interrelated pre-war educational trends should be noted, although their impact across sectors was uneven. Perhaps the most significant of these was the increasing tendency towards centralised administration, leading to the Wellington-based educational bureaucracy represented by the New Zealand Department of Education assuming progressively greater power and control.[5] Centralisation was accelerated partially by teacher unionism, but perhaps even more by the growing public desire for greater participation in education's assumed benefits for a longer period than hitherto had been the norm, even if this were at the cost of a significant (if sometimes temporary) loss of family income.[6] However, there remained many contested areas, due partly to the fact that the passage of the colony's first national public education act in 1877 had been highly controversial, in effect precipitating an ongoing debate that was to endure for several decades. Thus John Mackey has observed that, in 1877, New Zealand's education system was still grappling with four fundamental problems: balancing central and local interests; specifying the sources of revenue; the issue of compulsion; and the protection of individual conscience in religious matters.[7] Although by 1914 some consensus was emerging regarding the latter two problems, the central versus local issue in particular was to remain contentious, resulting in considerable reluctance to effect major changes that might erode the 1877 settlement.[8]

As opponents of the original 1877 Education Bill maintained at the time, however, and as an increasing number of later critics maintained, the seeds of centralisation were already present in the opportunities educational expansion presented to the centralised bureaucracy. For instance in 1877, the Department of Education had but three staff (later cut back to two during the so-called Long Depression of the 1880s), but by 1914 it was well on the way to becoming the nationwide bureaucratised organisation familiar to later generations of educational critics (until its eventual demise in 1989 and replacement by a new Ministry of Education). Moreover, the creation of Teachers' Associations in Auckland (1873) and Canterbury (1874), together with the foundation of the primary teachers' union, the New Zealand Educational Institute (NZEI), in 1883, brought the Department of Education crucial allies in the years ahead.[9] Their respective memberships successfully fought for compulsory education and a centralised system of promotion, whilst opposing the powers wielded by local educational authorities such as education boards and school committees, which were claimed to hinder the development of teacher professionalism. Finally, in 1914, the school inspectorate was shifted from education board control to that of the Department of Education – a change that was to have implications both for the control of teachers through a comprehensive grading system, and for ongoing curriculum reform.

This latter process was to be particularly significant because the second educational trend which was noticeable prior to 1914 was indeed the growing pressure for curriculum reform. Initially, innovation was largely confined to the compulsory education sector and it was not until the interwar period that it was to have implications for high schools as well.[10] During the decade immediately prior to the outbreak of the First World War, educational reform received a major impetus under the leadership of the country's second Inspector-General of Education and later its first Director (1899–1915), George Hogben. Hogben was a strong believer in social efficiency and vocational education. Hence, the publication of the 1904 Syllabus of Instruction for public primary schools (reputedly written by Hogben himself) introduced a broader, less academic and more practically based curriculum, incorporating what Victoria's Director of Education, Frank Tate, termed at the time, 'the best of modern educational thought', and also including civics, moral instruction and elementary science.[11] The Hogben years also saw the beginnings of a comprehensive programme of physical education, replacing the former school cadet programme at primary school level.[12] Hogben's attempt to reform high schools and even technical schools along similar lines foundered, however, due to entrenched interests within the secondary sector.

The war years

The impact of the Great War upon the New Zealand education system as a whole was both immediate and urgent. From the very first days of the war the physical impact of this global conflict was to be highly visible as schools and university colleges alike suffered the loss of many male teachers and students, firstly through voluntary enlistment for overseas service, and later through conscription. Within a few months of the outbreak of war, large numbers of male teachers left for active service. In the public primary schools, the ratio of male teachers to female teachers steadily declined. In 1913, there had been 100 male teachers for every 166 female teachers, but by the beginning of 1915 the ratio was 100 to 193.[13] By the end of 1916, there were 650 primary school teachers enlisted, representing more than a third of all the male teachers employed in public primary schools in August 1914. Moreover, the Minister of Education, J.A. Hanan, noted that the remaining male teachers consisted almost entirely of men not then accepted for service, including many youths under the age of twenty, and older men well past military age who were often superannuitants.[14]

The loss of so many male teachers had a considerable impact upon school staffing at all levels, with most education boards experiencing dire shortages of suitably qualified staff. Most boards were obliged to effectively reverse the previous practice of denying employment to married women teachers. They also took back into the service those men who had previously retired on superannuation, although it was always on the tacit understanding that such measures were to last only for the duration of the conflict.[15]

Native schools, staffed overwhelmingly with European teachers, were similarly affected. Moreover, like their public school counterparts, native schools suffered the loss of many past students who would normally have contributed in various ways to the running of schools. The Maori Expeditionary Force, for example, was initially composed mainly of past native school students.[16]

By 1916 it was common for larger public primary schools and secondary schools to have retained only a single male teacher, and few boasted more than two. At secondary level, the situation was equally dire, and Hanan noted that in one all-boys school, six out of seven assistant teachers were women.[17] As far as past students were concerned, some of the most promising young men who had attended secondary school were soon to be killed. Janet Latchem, for example, has recently noted that out of 330 successful male candidates for Junior National Scholarships, no fewer than 56 were to die on active service, a casualty rate of 19 per cent.[18]

Whilst public primary schools, native schools, secondary schools and the University of New Zealand alike were to rapidly feel the effects of history's first 'total war', it was the public primary schools and the native schools that were to experience the most overt attempts to align them to the war effort. This was not in fact a difficult proposition for the authorities, given the degree of public enthusiasm for New Zealand's participation, at least initially. Writing within weeks of war having been declared, the native school inspectors reported that students attending the schools had displayed great interest in the war, with upwards of £200 being subscribed by children through various patriotic funds. One tribe donated a large block of land and many Maori students had provided gifts for soldiers at the front, often in considerable quantities. According to the inspectors, this clearly demonstrated that 'there [could] be no doubt that the native schools have played an important part in creating feelings of patriotism and loyalty in the young Maoris [sic] and that the policy of the Government in establishing a system of education for them has been a wise one.'[19]

The above observation illustrates the manner in which the education system had been used to promote patriotism and pride in the Empire. During the decade immediately prior to 1914, in both native schools and public schools, the *New Zealand School Journal* was a key element in this process. Following the outbreak of war, however, patriotic and imperial sentiment in the *School Journal* was, if anything, sharply increased. Moreover, it can be argued that after 1916 the tone of the *School Journal* became ever more poignant and urgent, stressing grim wartime realities to a far greater degree than hitherto. To the fore now were the imperatives of sacrifice, duty, conformity and the continuing urgency of imperial unity against a foe increasingly portrayed as both evil and contemptible.[20]

In June 1917 an article by the Earl of Meath, originally prepared for British children and subsequently reprinted in the *School Journal*, provided New Zealand children with four watchwords: duty, sympathy (for wounded Allied soldiers and bereaved families), responsibility and self-sacrifice. In the same issue, an article entitled 'Empire Day' informed students that even if they were themselves experiencing few personal hardships, this was only because the Empire remained strong enough to protect them.[21] In September 1918, amidst rumours that Germany might soon sue for peace, the *School Journal* featured a sobering article entitled 'The Fable of the Simple Potter and the Treacherous Serpent'.[22] This story related how a kindly but naïve potter had freed a snake from a trap, only to be killed for his act of charity by the serpent's own brood. A month later, in October 1918, an article entitled 'The Bell Ringer of Brunswick' related how 'old Hans', a triumphant veteran of Germany's victorious war against France in 1870–71, had suffered multiple bereavements as the war turned against Germany, eventually leading to the old man's death from hunger typhus.[23] As was the case in the wider society, there was scant sympathy for either old or young Germans in the *School Journal* as the war finally ground to an end in November 1918.

The University of New Zealand too had felt the impact of war almost immediately. As was the case elsewhere throughout the Dominion's education system, there was much disruption as students and staff were progressively engaged in the war effort. By early 1915 the University Senate heard that large numbers of students were already overseas and that many others were preparing to enlist. In order to accommodate this situation, special provisions were quickly made, one example being the development of special examinations in order for medical students to complete their studies earlier before transferring to the Ambulance Corps.[24]

The steady drain of university staff and students for the front line was to continue throughout the war. The commitment of the university as an institution, however, went beyond merely furnishing volunteers for the armed services. Pietsch has argued that the war both exploited and enhanced the academic connections between universities throughout the British Empire and the mother country. Hence, through '. . . mobilising the talents of many academics from the settler world and drawing them into the imperial capital, this conflict simultaneously strengthened the informal ties that linked British and settler scholars, creating expanded avenues for exchange in the interwar years'.[25]

As in the other Dominions, the services of New Zealand's university-based historians and other academics within the humanities were rapidly garnered to the Allied war effort. Professor Atkins, for instance, furnished two public lectures. The first, on the growth of Germany, alleged that the same aggressive spirit has been constant throughout German history. As a result, the German education system had been reorganised on scientific and technical grounds as an integral element of society.[26] Atkins' second lecture, entitled 'The Balkan Tangle', alleged German and Austrian complicity and, in an ironic reversal of late-Victorian foreign policy, suggested that future Russian gains in the Balkans were preferable to German ambitions.[27] As the war reached a crucial phase, other academics, doubtless from a mixture of both personal patriotism and public pressure to speak out, emphasised the need for societal unity. Thus in April 1917, Professor MacMillan Brown gave an address to the Overseas Club comparing the tactics and attitudes of the Industrial Workers of the World with Prussian militarism.[28]

University scientists too were quickly involved in the war effort. As in Australia and Canada, for instance, New Zealand's scientists were soon harnessed to the war effort to staff various military projects. Perhaps the most prominent of these was the physicist Ernest Rutherford, who was recruited from the University of Manchester to become chair of the Admiralty's Board of Invention, upon which sat a number of his Australian and Canadian colleagues, including William Bragg and Richard Threlfall. By the end of the conflict, Rutherford himself had played an essential role in the development of ASDIC, a key weapon in the anti-U-boat campaign.[29]

At home, science received an initial boost within the largely humanities-dominated university. In early 1916, University of New Zealand Senate member G.M. Thomson sent a blunt four-page letter to University Chancellor Sir Robert Stout, which was passed to the Senate for consideration.[30] In his letter, Thomson argued that the war was demonstrating the urgent need for radical curriculum changes within the university. In his view the university had for too long clung to the study of Greek and Latin, in spite of the fact that the war demonstrated the urgent need for scientific training. In contrast to the Allies, Germany had employed 'scientific knowledge in the production not only of every kind of deadly weapon and diabolical artifice . . .', but in order to develop substitutes for food, cotton, rubber, and various metals urgently required to continue fighting.[31] Thomson was particularly critical of the teaching of chemistry, biology and physics in New Zealand schools, slating it as academically inadequate, sterile and bookish. Consequently, the vision for the nation's educational future, in Thomson's view, had to come not from the schools but from the university and from New Zealand. As, 'one of the youngest of British communities', the Dominion should have the courage to lead the way because

> the greatest Renaissance the world has ever witnessed took place in a small and utterly condemned corner of the Roman Empire, and among a people who were looked on with supreme contempt and dislike by the rulers, and the first committee set up in connection with it consisted of but twelve ignorant men who were seeking for light.[32]

One hundred years later, these phrases seem somewhat high-flown, but Thomson's colleagues in the University Senate, enmeshed in the grim realities of total war, were sufficiently moved to set up a special committee to report on the whole question of the compulsory subjects necessary for a general pass degree. The committee's subsequent report recommended that the BA degree be arranged in three parts: Group A being languages, Group B being the sciences and mathematics, and Group C being education, history, ethics and philosophy. Students would be obliged to take two subjects from Group A, and one each from B and C. An amendment proposing that at least one science subject be compulsory in the BA prescription was narrowly lost.[33] A later meeting of the senate, however, advocated removing the clause in the BA regulations that did not allow students to keep terms unless they had passed in Matriculation Latin.

At the outset of war, as in the other Dominions, there were strenuous attempts by New Zealand academics to keep politics from eroding existing international academic contacts, especially with those scholars from nations with whom the Empire was now at war. However, despite the desire to keep the war effort free from personal and political suspicion and animosity, there were to be several notable exceptions, especially as the casualty lists began to mount. The most prominent of these was the case against Professor George von Zedlitz. Despite the steadfast support of the Victoria University College Council, backed by many staff and students, including those who would go on to serve in the war, continued public hostility made von Zedlitz's situation increasingly difficult, until finally the passage of the 1915 Alien Enemy Teachers Act forced him to resign his position. In the end the University Council reluctantly accepted the inevitable. As J.C. Beaglehole was to observe many years later, 'against the people of New Zealand it could stand indefinitely. Against the sovereign state it was bound to go down.'[34]

In fact, the entire education system was to be harnessed to the will of the state during the war years. This aim was aptly illustrated when, in a lengthy June 1916 policy statement, the Minister of Education, J.A. Hanan, provided a future blueprint for education as a vital vehicle for national reconstruction and regeneration both during and after the war. Hanan saw much merit in the current system of education, especially given the alacrity with which both young men and women had readily responded to the demands posed by the conflict. Nevertheless, the Minister also identified a serious weakness in what he regarded as

> an over-reliance on our resources, without appreciating the real need for system and control; an extreme deference to individual and local considerations; and the entrusting of expert and professional matters

> too much to lay administration . . . [hence] we could surely introduce more co-ordination and economy of effort, dependent on a wholesome amount of social and national discipline, without approaching the type of regimentation and autocracy against which we are fighting.[35]

Herein, however, lay a significant contradiction – and one that was to become significant after the war if not during the actual conflict – in that greater co-ordination and control was to be balanced by a desire to avoid the apparent excesses that many were now identifying in the hitherto much admired German education system that had prided itself on national co-ordination and efficiency.

In 1918, Hanan returned to the theme of what the New Zealand education system had learned after four long years of war. Turning to the question of morale, he singled out the human factor as being the most important in national reconstruction. The moral instruction and patriotism instilled by teachers during the war had, in the Minister's view, been exemplified by the performance of New Zealand servicemen overseas. 'If all curricula gave due recognition to subjects of real human interest and value,' Hanan claimed, 'many forms of study inflicted on pupils by mere tradition would give way to something better . . . .'[36]

As far as secondary school science teaching was concerned, however, Hanan took an opposite view to that of Thomson. He argued that both the war experience and contemporary university opinion indicated that the future lay in delaying the narrow specialisation that sometimes deterred students. Instead he spoke in favour of a general elementary science course that would serve as a foundation for later specialisation. Such an approach he deemed to be particularly important in the case of girls, in order to better fit them for marriage and future motherhood.[37] This latter argument had been largely conventional wisdom prior to 1914, but it would be wrong to dismiss Hanan's message as essentially conservative. For instance, the Minister also singled out what he saw as a lingering tendency amongst a few to see education merely a preparation for employment, reserving particular criticism for those who, in a country like New Zealand which prided itself on providing generous educational opportunities to all, still advocated that children of a certain social status should be discouraged from rising above certain types of occupations.[38] These contradictory strands were to be much in evidence during the post-war period.

After the armistice

The brutal experience of total war on a small, geographically isolated society was to exercise a signal impact across the education system in the immediate post-war years. The lasting consequences of social mobilisation were very much in evidence, especially during the first half of the 1920s. Anti-German sentiment in the *School Journal* continued unabated for several years. Weekly flag-saluting ceremonies in schools were officially encouraged and those who challenged this mood faced immediate consequences. In June 1921 for instance, Hedwig Weitzel, a young female student attending Wellington Training College, was convicted of distributing seditious literature under the 1920 War Regulations Continuance Act. Her German-sounding name, along with the fact that she was eventually intending to teach in a New Zealand public primary school, ensured widespread publicity for the case, and the subsequent public furore led to the passing of the 1921 Education Amendment Act. This made loyalty oaths for all teachers compulsory, and teachers who did not conform faced arbitrary dismissal.[39]

Such drastic measures, however, were soon to attract criticism as society quickly returned to peacetime conditions, and in education this sometimes led to a progressive reversal of wartime attitudes. The April 1921 issue of the *School Journal*, for example, featured both German and Turkish folk tales, a sure sign that ex-enemy nations were being gradually rehabilitated – and this occurred a mere month before the furore over the Weitzel case.[40] In July 1924, a *School Journal* article promoting the League of Nations argued that the recent war had begun from a small flame lit in the powder keg of European distrust. The article concluded that the development of weapons of mass destruction threatened to destroy whole nations unless a more peaceful solution to international differences could be found.[41] By 1929, the apparent success of the League of Nations, coupled with the growing influence of revisionist historians in North America and Europe, was encouraging a more critical attitude towards war in general and the Great War in particular. In the *School Journal* this was reflected, for example, in the publication of poems by anti-war poets such as Frederick Knowles.[42]

During the war, there had been a general recognition amongst New Zealand educators that the huge military effort then underway would inevitably have a detrimental impact upon post-war educational expenditure. Thus, the period from 1926 through 1935 was to see, as Murdoch pointed out, a strong demand for economy, which limited what could be achieved.[43] Nevertheless, some longer-term post-war educational trends were soon evident. First, a renewed debate over efficiency was to become a marked feature of the interwar years. This ensured that the pre-war trend towards greater centralisation of educational administration was to run even more strongly in favour of centralism in both the primary and secondary sectors. Thus, in his introduction to a history of New Zealand public education specially commissioned by the New Zealand Department of Education and published in 1930, A.G. Butchers reiterated the longstanding complaint of educational reformers and Wellington-based educational administrators alike – that the 1877 Act had been compromised by an undue deference to local interests. However, Butchers also noted with approval that the twentieth century had witnessed a more satisfactory outcome as successive governments, 'while paying lip-service to the sacred act proceeded to transform the education system from within to create . . . one of the most liberal systems in the world.'[44] Whilst the process was well underway during the decade immediately prior to the First World War, it was to be accelerated in the decade immediately following it.

High schools too were now to feel the pressure of centralisation and in particular the growing power and influence of the Department of Education. A Dominion-wide system of grading that included secondary teachers for the first time was instituted in 1920, being accompanied by an organised scale of salaries according to position. However, three discrete grading systems ensured that the primary, secondary and technical sectors remained distinct, with each sector retaining separate processes for appointing teachers and for receiving funding. Moreover, despite wartime statements regarding the value of female teachers, in all cases women's salaries were to remain lower than men's. Significantly for the secondary sector, however, the grading system gave much more power to the inspectorate and the department than hitherto had been the case, leading to an erosion of decision-making ability at the school level.[45]

Also during the 1920s, the department significantly increased its control over the secondary curriculum. By 1922, 93 per cent of students held government free places and these were tenable only if prescribed conditions were met. These included specified compulsory subjects and minimum requirements in optional subjects. Moreover, the establishment of junior high schools, later to become known as intermediate schools, further increased the pressure on high schools to reform their curriculum. Finally, the changing nature of the secondary sector clientele during the interwar years added considerable impetus to the reform process. Hitherto largely engaged in pre-professional training for a select group of students, secondary staff were increasingly confronted with the demands of parents, students, and secondary teachers themselves, for more specifically vocational training in the third and fourth forms, leading directly to opportunities for young men and women in the new industries.[46]

It is noteworthy that these changes were taking place in the context of an increasingly vigorous interwar debate concerning the shape of the entire secondary school sector. For instance, should high schools offer differentiated curricula depending on the type of institution and clientele, leading to different occupational destinations for students (the social efficiency argument)? Or should all secondary schools embrace the democratic principle that underlay a common core curriculum, whereby academic specialisation would be delayed until the upper secondary school? In fact, this debate was to rage throughout the 1920s and well into the 1930s, leading ultimately to the establishment of the comprehensive high school under the first Labour Government. It is noteworthy that, post-1945, the introduction of the so-called 'new' School Certificate examination in Form Five effected a convenient compromise that was to be a distinctive feature of the early post-Second World War era.[47]

The period between the two world wars was to witness an expansion of the pre-war notion of the school as a great moral force for good, but henceforth it was to incorporate a new message. Throughout the world, the war had shaken faith in the existing order, including education, leading to a growing sense of global unity and galvanising the intellectual foment that in 1921 led to the establishment of the New Education Fellowship (NEF) – an international organisation dedicated to educational reconstruction along progressive lines.[48] As a small nation that had made considerable wartime sacrifices, New Zealand was strongly influenced by these developments. Paul Adams has recently documented the post-war rise of NEF amongst New Zealand educators.[49] Examining the individual careers and intellectual networks of several educators broadly identified as educational progressives, and who later became influential educational leaders, Adams clearly documents the steady growth of home-grown progressivism during the interwar period. Whilst he cautions against seeing progressive education as the norm in a largely traditional, examination-dominated education system, Adams observes that the whole educational milieu during the interwar period was considerably more progressive than many previous scholars have thought.

Curriculum reform in the post-war era continued unabated. The 1919 Syllabus of Instruction for Public Schools gave teachers considerably more freedom to experiment. The 1929 Syllabus of Instruction went even further, attempting to balance the patriotic sentiment that had featured in the 1919 syllabus with an equally strong commitment to the League of Nations and to internationalism. Moreover, from the late 1920s on, many teachers, including some head teachers, were using the annual Anzac Day commemoration as an occasion to promote international understanding and anti-war feeling.[50] In 1936 the Proficiency Examination that had hitherto provided the gateway to secondary education was removed, and by the time the NEF Conference reconvened in New Zealand in 1937 with the backing of the Labour Government, the NEF message enjoyed a considerable degree of support both within and outside education.[51]

Native schools also experienced the results of a new, more critical post-war intellectual ferment. As early as the mid-1920s New Zealand's educators were beginning to view the previous policy of assimilation more critically than before.[52] In this fundamental reappraisal, they were strongly supported by Maori leaders such as Sir Apirana Ngata, who sought to strengthen and rejuvenate Maori culture in maraes and schools throughout the country. The Board of Maori Ethnological Research was created in 1923, the Maori Arts and Crafts Act was passed in 1926 and a School of Maori Arts and Crafts was created in 1927.[53] In 1930 a survey to evaluate the extent to which education had 'Europeanised' Maori revealed that, whilst a small but steadily increasing cohort of students went on to secondary education, some 96.6 per cent of Maori homes continued to speak Maori exclusively, resulting in many young Maori being reluctant to shift out of often impoverished rural areas to seek employment.[54]

The result of all this was that a new education policy of adaptation (later known as integration) was incorporated into native schools from 1931. Whilst the emphasis was on practical and vocational instruction related to the assumed needs of Maori students, there was also a new emphasis on instilling pride of race through the introduction of selected aspects of Maori culture. Fortuitously, this policy coincided with the influx of a more highly trained cohort of teachers into native schools as a result of the Great Depression, including many married women teachers previously dismissed by education boards. Moreover, from the mid-1930s on it was becoming increasingly apparent to the Maori leadership and to Pakeha policymakers that the Maori future lay in the towns. The stage was thus set for further changes in the post–World War Two era.[55]

The University of New Zealand was to be somewhat less affected by these post-war waves of reform. Notwithstanding the urgency of wartime demands for university studies to become more relevant to the needs of society in general, the reality was that, once the war ended, traditional rivalries and vested interests began to reassert themselves. For example, the role of science in creating a radically different student product for a brave new world of technology desired by some wartime commentators was not sustained. Moreover, although the war gave a temporary boost to exchanges between New Zealand, Britain and the other Dominions, in the longer term one should also note the growing influence of American philanthropy, which gave rise, for example, to the New Zealand Council of Educational Research in the 1930s. Anti-colonialist activists in the 1930s and, later, European refugee scholars, fleeing to New Zealand immediately prior to and after the Second World War, also served to broaden academic relationships, and consequently challenge more traditional imperial ties.[56]

Conclusion

The Great War had a profound impact upon the New Zealand education system at all levels, including those who taught or were taught within it, and the administrators and educational leaders who were to shape it over the coming decades. But when, with the benefit of hindsight, these influences are divided into those with a relatively short-term effect and those with longer-term effects, what stands out is not so much the continuation of wartime attitudes, prejudices and fears (profound as these were at the time), but in most cases their relatively short duration. In the longer term, the more significant effects were to be the impetus given to features at least partly in evidence prior to 1914, such as the onward march of centralisation and the continuing pressure for curriculum reform along more liberal lines. Arguably the most important of all effects for future generations of students, teachers and parents was the eventual triumph of progressive ideals. Whilst educational progressivism had exercised a relatively minor influence prior to the outbreak of war, the cumulative impact of war experience on a whole generation of educators greatly increased its attraction in a post-war world where established values and structures seemed increasingly less relevant for the future.

Chapter Five

State Servants and Social Beings: The Role of the New Zealand Police Force in the Great War

Richard Hill

This chapter aims to contribute to an incipient scholarly interest in wartime policing – itself part of an increasing pursuit of police history in general – by examining the interaction between police and civilians in New Zealand during the First World War. During the war years, as in any situation deemed to be a national emergency, the work of the New Zealand Police Force (NZPF) greatly intensified, not only through its exercise of much greater powers of surveillance and coercion but also through honing its capacities for persuasion. While special wartime regulatory measures were socially intrusive and often repressive, the state preferred persuasion to coercion in mobilising for, mediating social tension within and countering opposition to the war effort. This reflected the evolution of policing in the colony, with seeking social consent rather than wielding coercion having emerged as the prevalent mode of social control: by 1914 the police had secured a widespread legitimacy within society. Too great a reversion to more coercive modes of control would threaten to undermine such support, although harsher measures were readily resorted to when moral suasion or minimal force were seen to be failing. In such eventualities, sectors of society actively hindering (as opposed to showing little enthusiasm for) the government's chosen methods of social mobilisation felt the force that the relative benignity of modern policing often masked.[1] Taken together, both the coercive and the suasive functions of the force made the NZPF a crucial component of the Dominion's war effort.

The emergence of consent-based policing

By 1914, New Zealand's normative policing modes were quite different from those of fifty years before, a time when the colony's coercive forces were engaged in suppressing rebellion and widespread disorder. In this frontier environment, 'pacification' policing was central to the state's social-control imperatives. From 1867, the provincial police forces were supplemented by a mobile, centrally-controlled Armed Constabulary Force established, essentially, to surveil and suppress Maori. One of its expeditions in 1869, for example, brought some 620 armed constables (together with Pakeha militia and Maori allies) into the Urewera to conduct a scorched-earth campaign.[2] As Maori opposition to Crown sovereignty was increasingly suppressed, the constabulary could shed the more military of its functions and practices; it absorbed the provincial forces in 1877, and the internal balance within the new Constabulary Force became increasingly weighted in favour of civil policing.

Over and above the military and quasi-military suppression of dissident Maori tribes and communities – a process that underpinned the alienation of indigenous resources – growing numbers of Pakeha, freed from the complex control mechanisms operating in the 'Mother Country', also needed to be brought to order. Partly because of their pre-existing socialisation in the 'old world', however, such elements could be resocialised to colonial standards of order relatively quickly, even miners on the turbulent goldfields. Increasing numbers of the population, then, adapted to those behaviours and beliefs seen as necessary to underpin social peace and capitalist prosperity.

From the mid-1880s, accordingly, arrest rates declined, especially for the types of offending generally associated with a frontier milieu – brawling, homicide, assaults, drunkenness, and the like.[3] This development occurred against the background of an ongoing global phenomenon sometimes encapsulated in the term 'the modern era'. In New Zealand the watershed for this might be dated to 1886, the year the military function was split from that of the constabulary and the NZPF was established as an unarmed (at least for routine patrol purposes) body of men tailored to policing a quiet post-frontier society.[4] The processes of social 'settling down' were accompanied by the development of specialisation and professionalisation within state institutions, together with political developments based on increasing social quiescence – including among Maori, whose leaders increasingly sought rapprochement with the Crown as a survival and (ultimately) revival strategy. In the 1890s, social harmony became the proclaimed ideology of the Liberal government, which both promoted a corporatist partnership between state, capital and labour, and sought to channel labour relations within non-conflictual institutional parameters. New Zealand, now widely seen as the most peaceful of the British settler colonies, also became renowned as a social laboratory for progressive policies which amounted to a prototypal welfare state.[5]

There were relatively few post-frontier occasions when authorities needed to impose order with force: instances of Maori rebellion (as with the Hokianga Dog Tax Rebellion of 1898) or Pakeha working-class confrontations with employers and the state in the new century form such exceptions. It was in the context of a generally ordered society that ever more nuanced means of regulating behaviour could emerge, with constables instructed not only to use minimal force but also to act as role models within society. Such 'velvet glove' policing was summed up soon after the war by Police Commissioner John O'Donovan: 'We keep a baton, but seldom use it; when we do, its application should be scrupulously apportioned to the need.'[6] The authority possessed by constables to deter and detain was increasingly framed by the precept of 'policing by consent', whose principles were first elaborated when the London Metropolitan Police was established in 1829.[7] Coercion by the holder of the ancient office of constable was held to be legitimated not just by a state warrant but also by popular will, with public–police co-operation deemed essential to maximise social control.[8] By 1914, policing was geared to disciplining the untoward individual or small group rather than entire sectors of society, with unarmed patrols serving as both the first line of detection and deterrence and the apprehenders of those who did offend – assisted by the great majority of 'law-abiding' people.

With less violence and disorder to control, the ratio of police to population fell dramatically, from 1:944 in 1878 (when there also large numbers of quasi-police personnel) to 1:1,304 in 1914 (a time when there were very few auxiliaries assisting the force).[9] As the war approached, there were only 870 full-time personnel to police a population totalling 1.1 million, a force distributed across 324 stations, over two thirds of these manned by a single constable.[10] By this time, the occupation of policeman was increasingly being re-conceptualised as a calling in its own right, as opposed to an ephemeral job of decidedly military resonance. In 1898, New Zealand's first civil-police training depot was established at Mount Cook in Wellington, modelled along London Metropolitan Police lines. This was a major milestone on a long journey away from the founding methods of New Zealand policing (dominated by Royal Irish Constabulary and other overtly coercive policing modes) and towards the consent-based ethos of the 'British Bobby'.[11]

Such movement occurred in tandem with a quest for ever greater efficiency. Surveillance, detection and forensic techniques all benefited from methods imported from within and even beyond the British Empire. In 1903 New Zealand became one of the first countries to adopt a fingerprint-based classification system, and within a year there were 3,500 offenders' prints on file.[12] This resource would eventually become recognised as a successful mode of identification, detection and deterrence. The policing of the 1906–7 International Exhibition in Christchurch applied information-based detection strategies to identify 'undesirable' elements in advance and exclude or monitor them; the 23 weeks of the exhibition were 'practically crimeless'.[13]

However, while the trajectory from carbine-based to baton-based (or even suasion-based) policing was unmistakable by 1914, there were also many reminders that consent-seeking policing was underpinned by the 24-hour, seven-day potential for coercive deployment of police personnel. Constables continued to embody, both symbolically and actually, the full authority of the state, empowered to deter, detain and regulate the social body. The contemporary idiom of policing as an 'iron hand in a velvet glove' points to this dual character, the glove masking the hand's capacity to strike firmly whenever necessary – including with deadly force.

This coercive capacity is the sine qua non of policing. What became the normative, the 'coercion of some and co-operation of many', could change at any time, if circumstances required, to subjecting 'the many' to the harshest of state discipline. Thus, despite their 'demilitarisation' in 1886, the New Zealand police continued to suppress remaining pockets of Maori resistance, and ruthlessly subdued militant labour in the momentous industrial confrontations of 1890 and 1912–1913.[14] Initially, indeed, the NZPF was required to recruit only from the military, and when it did get to establish its own training system, the recruits learnt paramilitary drill as well as modern civil policing. Thereafter, constables retained the capacity to operate in conjunction with soldiers; conversely, the military could provide 'aid to the civil power' when called upon. Constables, then, embodied the strong arm of government, however benign they might appear when patrolling urban, suburban or rural locales armed only with a baton and handcuffs. The state needed police agents who could discipline and detain with as much force as needed in the interests of what the authorities called 'peace and good order'. Their uniforms continued to signify not just the generally respected authority of state but also its full might, which could quickly descend upon the normally respectful and respectable if the circumstances required.

In the event, the organisations and individuals opposing New Zealand's participation in or conduct during the Great War were unable to capitalise on popular disquiet to secure any significant change in official policy. Concomitantly, in its interactions with the majority of people – however disillusioned many of them might be – the NZPF could generally adhere to the consent-based methods it had been developing for decades. The Dominion, then, conformed to a common pattern on other home fronts during the conflict, with the great majority of the people at the very least acquiescing in intensified state regulation, coercion and even repression.

While the number and nature of policing tasks were undoubtedly enhanced and harshened in 1914–1918, therefore, a great deal of continuity with pre-war modes of control remained. In an overview of British policing since the eighteenth century, the doyen of British policing history, Clive Emsley, called his final chapter 'Everything Changes, Everything Stays the Same'.[15] This might aptly be taken to characterise New Zealand policing before, during and after the First World War. Wartime operational and policy changes, in other words, often involved deploying (and fine-tuning) established methods. There was consistency, for example, in the monitoring and arrest of both striking workers and opponents of compulsory military training before the war, and that of surveillance and suppression of public opposition to various aspects of wartime mobilisation, be it from pacifist, socialist, civil libertarian, industrial or other quarters. Both before and during the war, such transgressions were often framed as incitement to commit breaches of the peace, the easiest way of securing a conviction.[16] At the same time, the professionalising impulse within the police remained prominent, with the war effort requiring greater efficiency in recording, categorising, analysing and, where necessary, arresting or otherwise repressing social elements – including individuals who were generally regarded as law-abiding (such as those who violated regulations to curb alcohol consumption). And despite its duty to enforce numerous draconian wartime regulations, the NZPF continued to plan for the return of social peace.

'Servants of the public'

Since the beginning of the colony the police had been all-purpose agents of the state, and the demands of the war effort escalated their involvement in the government's requirements from its people. At the same time, wartime mobilisation complicated the horizontal relationships between constables and communities. The pre-existing general trend towards social acceptance of state legitimacy in both Pakeha and Maori communities (notwithstanding direct challenges to authority from time to time) was reinforced by a great patriotic upsurge at the beginning of the war, including among large sectors of the labour movement.[17] By some measures, the trajectory towards social cohesion and greater willingness to meet state requirements continued throughout the war, as reflected in part in a general overall decrease in rates of offending from 24.72 per 1,000 people in 1915 to 16.54 in 1918.[18] There were undoubtedly other factors in play, too, such as hard-pressed police ignoring petty offending, and the departure of young males to war theatres (although this latter needs to be offset by an increase in unruly behaviour when soldiers returned home).

Whatever the explanatory mix for the statistical 'improvement' in social behaviour, consent for policing seemed to increase in many quarters during the war, enhancing official portrayals of the policeman as servant of the public rather than agent of the state. Moreover, the official imagery of the constable embodying the 'rule of law' and answerable only to that law, and by extension of the police as guardians of civilised order, was boosted by the standard framing of the First World War as a struggle to preserve civilisation. Representations of the Kaiser as a bandit, or Germany as a brigand power needing to be brought to justice, contrasted with personified depictions of nations garbed in police uniforms, enforcing 'the law' and upholding the values of civilisation.[19]

The tasks of enforcing war-related laws and regulations and carrying out a raft of other routine and special measures aimed at 'keeping the peace' were made all the more difficult by a depletion in police numbers, with the government reluctant to to use young men of military age to replace those leaving the force.[20] While the decline in 'ordinary' crime did help the police to better focus on special wartime duties,[21] the charged emotional atmosphere of the period brought new problems. It was not just resisters to mobilisation – pacifists, socialists, militant workers, military 'defaulters' and many others – who created difficulties for the police. The enthusiasm of pro-war 'loyalists', too, could be counter-productive to order and hence to the war effort.

The activities of ultra-patriotic organisations, such as anti-German leagues and the rabble-rousing Protestant Political Association, injected greater tension into the horizontal links between the NZPF and the wider community. More broadly, huge numbers of individuals took it upon themselves to report the results of their own vigilance, resulting in much police energy needing to be expended in response to reports of people of German nationality or descent making unpatriotic remarks, undertaking disloyal activities, or engaging in sabotage or spying activities.[22] These allegations almost invariably proved groundless or inconsequential, but the investigations not only disrupted the lives of the accused but also led to rifts in the communities in which they lived. Constables also had to investigate threats to individual 'Germans', a catch-all term which could run to men of 'swarthy' complexion or people from Dalmatia or the Levant. More broadly still, a widely prevalent anti-German sentiment meant that war news could readily spark gatherings with the potential to threaten the peace – rioting in Wanganui, for example, after reports of the sinking of the *Lusitania* and casualties at Gallipoli, or rowdy protests elsewhere against alleged official softness towards 'enemy aliens'.[23]

Ultra-patriotic groups emphasised the notion of the police as servants of the public. They attempted to hold constables accountable to their own circles' imperatives, irrespective of the police obligation to uphold peace and good order, which included protecting people and property from vigilantist activity. In the face of much questioning of – and sometimes anger at – police containment and suppression of loyalist enthusiasm, the NZPF stressed that its role was to dispassionately enforce the law with 'neither fear nor favour'. Of course the majority of individual police, members of an essentially conservative organisation, shared 'loyalist' perspectives. But most were fully aware that if vigilante-generated disorder were to escalate, it might come to represent a serious challenge to government requirements for a peaceful, united and productive home front. On the other hand, police personnel were generally content to prosecute only a few readily identifiable offenders when anti-German sentiment produced disorder and riot. Records indicate that they made little effort to track down most of the rioters once an exemplary number had been charged. Typical police reports noted such items as: '[t]here was a man about 6 ft wearing no hat with very long curly hair parted in the centre [and while] I am sure he had a lot to do with last night's row', he could not be located; or, 'there was two maoris [sic] about twenty years of age who were throwing sausages at the police . . . I have not been able to obtain either of their names'.[24]

Yet local constables normally had little trouble identifying transgressors, partly because the small size of New Zealand communities meant that many an apprehension resulted from information received from the public. Even during wartime disorder, moreover, policemen used the communal links they had built up over time in order to procure a suitable quota of arrests – a few initiators of violence, together with some participants who were generally from working-class and marginalised sectors of society. Thus, in Wanganui a prostitute was sought for 'throwing missiles' at a shop, and a wharf labourer was identified as having thrown a stone through the window of Wohnsiedler's butchery and, 'acting like a madman', urging a loyalist crowd to wreak further havoc. The reported language of many rioters put them beyond the pale of the polite society from which many of the leaders of the anti-German organisations came, and made it easier for 'respectable' patriots to help the police make a suitable number of arrests. A man identified as an inciter to violence, for example, allegedly shouted: 'come, lets rush them, let us Britishers have our rights, fuck them.'[25] In an age when saying 'damn' or 'bugger' could lead to conviction, use of such language was well outside the bounds of tolerated behaviour.

Besides highlighting the difficulties police always faced in controlling unruly crowds and apprehending rioters, ultra-patriotic disorder points to some of the problems faced by the police in maintaining the notion of consent during times when communities became polarised. The police dilemma of facing criticism from sectors of society which normally supported them, and whose sentiments most of them generally shared, had surfaced early in the war. Even as the state quickly set about monitoring enemy aliens, and increasingly acquired powers to detain them and others on suspicion and at will, allegations of police softness towards Germans surfaced. Some accusers even alleged that there were enemy sympathisers within the police. 'A Britisher', for example, wrote to a Taranaki newspaper asking: 'is it not the duty of the Government to [intern] all Germans in the police' in view of 'the proved treachery' of even Germans who had been naturalised; 'why have not the Commissioner of Police and the Minister of Justice done their duty?'[26]

In such circumstances, however, the police generally drew support from significant sectors of the community which, however effusive in their patriotic fervour, were predisposed to assist the maintenance of order in all circumstances. After the Wanganui riot, and another in Gisborne, prominent locals helped identify individual 'ringleaders'. Social support for the police in times of disorder, moreover, had always been organised into auxiliary policing mechanisms whenever necessary. During occasions of mass protest, for example, such as the time of the 1913 Great Strike, large numbers of volunteers had been sworn in as special constables. When ultra-patriotic sentiments led to wartime rioting and destruction of property, often by elements considered to be dangerously anti-authority or just plain riff-raff, batons and identification badges were brought out of storage for use by 'specials'.[27] In the aftermath of such disorders, too, the police continued to mobilise public assistance so long as threats against citizens of German extraction and other tensions continued.[28]

However, swearing in special police whenever they were seen to be required was not sufficient for a number of groups and commentators, some of whom advocated that an auxiliary policing arrangement be established for the duration of the war. Senior police felt this to be unwise in view of the potential for untrained amateur police to prove counter-productive to the maintenance of order.[29] Women's organisations were among those particularly concerned that the police needed supplementing, with groups such as the South Invercargill branch of the Women's Christian Temperance Union urging the government to authorise 'women police patrols' to aid in 'guarding the morality of our military camps'.[30] This idea was an antipodean take-up of a campaign waged in Britain. It soon came to focus its activities on demands for all-purpose female patrols in urban areas, where they were to provide a force for moral suasion among both men and women. Not only were military recruits from the country seen to be at risk from prostitution and alcohol, but also 'innocent girls' needed to be saved from the perils of wartime: a widespread loosening of morals generally, and the predations of soldiers and city slickers in particular.[31]

Wartime temptations were deemed to so threaten the war effort that, from 1916, laws to prevent prostitution and the spread of venereal disease were tightened. But some campaigners saw the real problem as one of enforcement: although the police leadership (with the agreement of the politicians) continued to believe that their men could deal with any problems arising from loosening of public morality, the men on the beat had too little time to be moral exemplars and surveillers of petty offenders. Thus 'women patrol' advocates kept up their campaign: female patrollers would 'be of more use than the police. The men would be ashamed to go in to [brothels] if a decent woman was at the door.'[32] With official wariness about proselytising patrollers coming under sustained pressure, from 1917 compromise solutions were implemented. The Police Matrons in central city stations gained assistants who could be proactive in the communities if needed, and new 'social hygiene' legislation led to the establishment of Health Department female patrols. The departmental patrollers would both protect 'pure' women and prevent 'tainted' women from infecting would-be or actual soldiers with disease and despair.[33] But the idea of having sworn policewomen in the force remained off the agenda, and many moral campaigners remained unplacated.[34]

The refusal to contemplate women police, on the other hand, assisted the NZPF's continuing quest to secure consent from male sectors of the community, many of which opposed 'wowser' intrusions into their lives. The main opposition that police faced from male society in general at this time was incurred in enforcing liquor restrictions, excessive drinking being seen as a major impediment to the war effort. Even in peacetime there were endemic difficulties in enforcing liquor licencing laws among the many circles whose leisure focussed on drinking. The authorities did appreciate that access restrictions would garner resistance and have the potential to be counter-productive, and so resisted extreme demands from the powerful temperance movement. But restrictions gradually became more draconian, including the 1916 banning of 'treating' in pubs, and culminating with the introduction of 6 p.m. closing in drinking establishments the following year. As a consequence, while greater consent was gained among women in general and temperance circles in particular, tensions between police and the public were exacerbated in other quarters. While constables no longer had much opportunity to be as proactive in their moral exemplar role as before the war, they now had to patrol bars to ensure that rounds were not being bought and men were leaving after what became known as the 'six o'clock swill'. To help keep the 'drinking classes' on side, however, policemen often ignored all but the most flagrant breaches of licensing laws. All the same, it was hard to strike a balance, with 'wowser' groups, senior police and politicians alike vigilant in pointing to lax enforcement.[35]

The exigencies of war had quickly led to much social fragmentation, with a number of old communal bonds and links having being replaced by new alignments. These included notions of ethno-racial kinship and exclusion, which were legitimated by the political authorities equating Germanic background with security risk. Police Commissioner John Cullen, who worked closely with his Minister (Alexander Herdman) and whose default mode was adversarial, was inclined to conflate 'bloodlines' and national loyalty: 'I am satisfied that a German who goes through the form of getting naturalised does so merely to enable him to pose as a British subject so as to get employment, whilst he remains a German at heart just as much as he ever was.'[36] His men on the ground, however, often used their discretionary powers to categorise individual enemy aliens as loyal to community, country and empire, and in fact very few 'Germans' turned out to pose a threat to the war effort. All the same, draconian regulations had the potential to create fear and panic within 'Germanic' circles and the communities which hosted them. As a professional policeman, Cullen – for all his personal proclivities – appreciated the need to ensure community calm. In May 1915 he ordered his men to take 'energetic' steps to protect German and Austrian property and to 'do everything in [their] power to discourage violence towards persons and property or any incitement to rowdyism.' In October 1915, when the Commissioner ordered the internment of a number of 'unnaturalised enemy aliens', he specified that 'the arrests be effected as quietly as possible'. 'Care must be taken', he cautioned, 'that none of these men are arrested on or about the waterfront and that only two or three be arrested each day until they are all disposed of.'[37]

Despite official measures to dampen panic among enemy aliens and their circles, the possibility of internment – by the end of the war, there were well over 450 internees, including an entire German band whose enthusiastic rendering of British patriotic songs did not save them – highlighted the marginal social space inhabited by people linked in any way, however tangentially, with the German-speaking world.[38] With the police under social as well as political pressure, investigations of alleged disloyalty continued to arise throughout the war, diverting valuable manpower. In one not untypical example, a woman reported night-time lights flashing from a Wellington house that were similar to naval signalling operations she had observed in England. The investigating officer's report noted that the informant was hospitalised, 'very ill and somewhat eccentric', and could not see any houses from the bed to which she was confined.[39] Wellington's Superintendent, John O'Donovan, was speaking for many a policeman when his report on a 'signal light' that had turned out to be an evening picnic characterised the incident as 'a specimen of the will-o-wisps the police are frequently required to chase with much loss of time of men required for other really important duty'.[40]

Patriotic motivations for reporting on or persecuting suspected fifth-columnists in New Zealand society were often overlaid by – or excuses for – the pursuit of personal antagonisms or feuds. After investigating allegations that the President of the Women's National Reserve was a German, a constable concluded that these constituted nothing more than gossip emanating from jealousy of her status.[41] Another inquiry, centred on a demand that a Tauranga man be deported as an enemy alien, found that the accuser was 'taking advantage of the present intense feeling to try and vent his petty spite against an old man'.[42] However, while the evidence suggests that police tried to alleviate social tensions in their handling of accusations against suspected disloyal elements, in their capacity as 'servants of the public' they were not totally immune from emotions and tensions within society.

From the outbreak of war, many constables had wanted to join the New Zealand Expeditionary Force. When an embargo was placed on their enlisting, a number sought to resign in order to sign up – no light step with policing having become a semi-professional job with permanent career prospects. Many of the considerable numbers of military-age policemen who expressed a desire to enlist, however, were coerced or cajoled into staying on.[43] They could expect to be vilified in a number of quarters as 'shirkers', and their families might also be swept up in social expectations of equality of sacrifice. In 1916, complaints that a

Dunedin sergeant had five unmarried sons of military age in government employment were forwarded to the Minister of Defence. Although the allegations were essentially incorrect, the Minister's reply showed ambivalence: 'under the voluntary principle [of enlistment] I do not [k] now that we can take any action.'[44] Loyalist pressures on police and their families to enlist as soldiers continued until the end of the war.

Public accusations of lax investigation and enforcement also continued to surface, partly because of the links built up over time between local constables and sections of the community, including those of German descent. In Charleston, for example, Constable Richard Allan resisted an instruction to arrest a man of German origin who was 'a most loyal fellow', a stand that was unpopular with some. In the event this action proved successful because the constable secured support from significant parts of the local population.[45] The incident was but one of many which showed that police connections with communities, never taken for granted at the best of times, needed to be worked on especially assiduously amidst the tensions and emotions of wartime. In particular, as war weariness set in, policemen needed to devote increasing amounts of time to shoring up enthusiasm, using such means as managing the diffusion of official propaganda or boosting flagging rates of volunteering for military service.[46]

Constables, in short, built on their horizontal links with the community to enhance social stability and bolster the war effort. Despite periodic resurfacing of accusations of police shirking and softness towards enemy aliens, support from much of the general public continued strongly throughout the war's duration. A newspaper correspondent's riposte to the 'venomous tirade' of 'A Britisher' about alleged German fifth columnism within the NZPF encapsulated such endorsement:

> [The] well-known and highly popular police officer [of the] district . . . stands too high in the public esteem to be affected by this vicious attack. The fact of a man being of German descent does not always imply that he is a supporter of this swinish system of Prussian militarism which has brought misery to the world . . . So it would be well for 'a Britisher' to cease his petty attempt to oust from his position a [police]man whose only fault is his easy going nature and his consequent inactivity in attending to mischief-mongers and disturbers of the peace like 'a Britisher.'[47]

Agents of the state

Opposition to participation in the war, or to the state's methods of managing it, led to even greater community tension than that created by the activities of the ultra-patriots and vigilantists. Here too the police were integrally involved in mediating between opposing groups, but their priority was to administer the repressive regulations of wartime. By the very nature of the policing imperative, a close and potentially coercive watch was kept on individuals, organisations and movements refusing to rally fully behind the Crown and its requirements. The greater the numbers who declined to support aspects of the war effort, either through active opposition or through waning enthusiasm, the harder and more frequently the 'iron hand' was wielded against dissenters. As on other home fronts faced with similar problems, new sets of regulations continued to augment the state's power to control and repress – part of a systemic effort to buttress commitment, dampen social radicalisation and repress counter-mobilisations.[48] Their enforcement in New Zealand fell within the framework set by the 1914 War Regulations Act, which empowered the political executive to regulate all aspects of national life without reference to parliament, and permitted such regulations to supersede existing legislation. The Solicitor-General characterised this situation as 'a constitutional revolution': a 'despotic government' was necessary in a 'national emergency'.[49]

State-led mobilisation altered the police operating environment in ways that emphasised the NZPF's coercive powers against 'the enemy within', just as socially-driven mobilisation had ramifications for the way the police approached their essential tasks. The draconian powers embedded in the 1914 legislation prohibited actions deemed injurious to public safety, national defence or the effective conduct of military operations. Under the War Regulations Act, moreover, constables gained enhanced powers of arrest, including on grounds of 'reasonable suspicion'.[50] Subsequent wartime legislation built upon this coercive base.[51] The duty to enforce such legislation led to tension with significant sectors of society that were usually considered to be law-abiding, including broad sections of the labour movement and some churches. The police not only systematised surveillance and coercion of resisters to participation in the war, and of the much greater numbers who opposed aspects of the management of the war effort, but also kept a watching brief on those who took a detached position on social mobilisation or people believed to be shirking their legal or moral responsibilities. On the basis of its accumulated knowledge of the social condition, the NZPF could intervene with persuasion or coercion should this be needed. But the state's legitimating strategy was essentially to punish active rather than passive resisters, one which was broadly followed elsewhere among the Allies, including by the Britain and French authorities.[52]

At the beginning of the conflict, the police had moved fast to put systems in place to monitor potentially disruptive elements and politicised resistance. Stenographers, for example, routinely attended meetings on political and industrial matters, producing reports for police analysis.[53] The force strengthened its systems of surveillance and control as the social ramifications and costs of mobilisation became clearer and provoked greater dissent. Suppressing 'subversive' literature became a more central task as opposition to war measures grew, especially where such publications had potentially large markets in the labour and socialist movements. In 1915 the Industrial Workers of the World journal *Direct Action* was suppressed, and films that might have 'a demoralising tendency' were investigated; a 1916 raid on the *Maoriland Worker* seized some 3,000 copies of the Labour Party's peace manifesto; in the following year leaflets calling conscription the 'workers' hell' were deemed to be seditious.[54] As well as regulating information in the public arena, police worked with other agencies in investigating material gleaned from military interception and censorship of vast quantities of private mail.[55] Censorship of reading material and suppression of dissenting opinion impinged upon the civil liberties of large numbers of New Zealanders, including many who were not politically active against the war or its management. Even moderate trade unionists were alarmed that restrictions on literature had 'set back the wheels of progress'.[56] The police, at the front line of enforcement, found that consent among sectors of society for at least some of their activities had been withdrawn.

Despite many protests, the New Zealand authorities saw growing encroachments on civil liberties as a necessary way of preventing active war resisters from capitalising on a broader social disenchantment. Such potential disruption of the war effort, especially at a time when weariness at the conflict and its ramifications was setting in, led to police monitoring and intervention expanding into ever larger social sectors. Constables were ordered, among other things, to step up their surveillance of people of left-wing, Germanic or other suspect backgrounds working in 'sensitive' positions – chemists, for example, or waterfront workers.[57] Their reports on such people noted not just factual information, such as naturalisation status, home address and work location, but also comments and assessments gleaned from informants: 'an eccentric, having once been an inmate of Nelson Mental Hospital', 'son in Expeditionary Force', or 'no question of this man's loyalty'.[58] Job loss, or sometimes loss of liberty, might follow for those relatively few who were assessed as potentially or actually subversive.

As well as assessing numerous categories of civilians, from the beginning of the war intelligence was needed on large numbers of individuals potentially and actually enrolled in the armed forces. In the preceding years, police links with the military had increased as a result of the need to combat evasion of the compulsory military training introduced in 1909. By 1913, this had created so much work that payment to policemen for tracking down defaulters was being discussed.[59] The Defence Department was concerned, after war was declared, that 'persons of bad character' would enlist during the rush to mobilise. The police were obliged to furnish reports on enlistees considered undesirable: men who might 'contaminate' the others, prove to be unsuitable for military discipline, or be prone to desertion or cowardice. The military would consider the men's futures with constables' assessments in front of them. These noted many matters, including convictions (one sample of these ranged from breaking and entering to less major offences such as unlawful carnal knowledge and obscene language).[60] Enlistees who had slipped through the recruiting processes, only to change their mind and desert before embarking, also needed to be tracked down and handed to the military police.[61] Changes in recruitment mechanisms added immensely to police duties, especially the inauguration of a 'National Registration' system in August 1915 and the introduction of conscription a year later.[62] The considerable number of men evading registration and conscription (either through personal belief or shirking) meant that police needed to spend a lot of time tracking down defaulters laying low with relatives or friends or hiding within sympathetic and often remote communities such as West Coast mining towns. In some cases, such men or deserters from the military managed to leave the country.[63]

The need for surveillance, detection and detention of resisters, then, placed an ever greater wartime burden on police resources, adding to latent tensions between constables and communities. Locating defaulters and deserters was slow, arduous and socially intrusive work. In towns and cities, police searches were routinely launched in public venues and places of work, in addition to targeted raids based on tip-offs or the surveillance of relatives and associates of the missing. Such searches often took police out of their communities, with rural constables spending days at a time following up rumours of defaulters having 'gone bush': one police party tramped over 400 kilometres in three weeks to track down brothers who had been hiding out in a remote area of Fiordland.[64] At the end of August 1917, police were seeking 3,054 men.[65] These were large numbers for such a small force to track down, even with public and auxiliary-police assistance in many (but far from all) communities. But the search processes continued methodically, and a year later the number of missing actual or potential soldiers had reduced to 2,306.[66]

The power to track down and arrest such offenders against wartime regulations was but one of many ways police powers were enhanced by wartime needs. The foundational War Regulations Act contained provisions to convict:

> any person who commits, or attempts to commit, or does any act with intent to commit, or counsels, procures, aids, abets, or incites any other person to commit, or conspires with any other person (whether in New Zealand or elsewhere) to commit, any offence against a regulation made under this Act . . .[67]

Successive legislation extended the definition of seditious activity to include such matters as statements deemed to incite disaffection towards troop recruitment, training or discipline; disloyalty to the governments of the United Kingdom or New Zealand; and discouraging the prosecution of the war to a victorious conclusion.[68] The list of prohibitive regulations grew to cover many categories of spoken and published sentiments, and persons suspected of violating them were liable to be arrested without a warrant. Quite apart from increasing their penetration of the labour movement, and reporting back on those of its activities which specifically opposed aspects of the official war effort, police launched pre-emptive raids on union offices during industrial action in 1917–1918. These and other coercive interventions caused particular bitterness, especially after charges of sedition began to be laid under war regulations.[69]

Growing pacifist, anti-militarist and anti-conscription dissent and counter-mobilisations against the war effort within union, socialist, civil libertarian and other oppositional circles, along with rising social disillusionment, put ever greater pressure on constables already struggling to cope as a result of falling numbers of experienced policemen. The consent-based rhetoric of the new Police Commissioner from December 1916, John O'Donovan, could do little to alleviate their adversarial contact with widening elements of the public – which was sometimes harsher than it might have been if policemen had not been under such strain. The politicised dissent of organised labour most directly challenged the notion of the police as 'servants of the public'. Labour leaders dominated the ranks of those arrested for seditious utterances and activities, including men who would eventually become leading politicians when the Labour Party took office some twenty years later – among them the future Minister of Public Works, Robert Semple, and future Prime Minister, Peter Fraser.[70] Harry Holland, who would become leader of the Labour Party, recalled that by December 1916 'almost half the effective platform propagandists of the Labour Movement were placed behind prison bars'.[71] By the end of the war, 287 people had been charged with sedition or disloyalty under war regulations, with 208 of these having been convicted, including 71 imprisoned.[72]

Even greater repressive force was considered necessary from time to time, and some such occasions saw the NZPF revert to the paramilitary methods characteristic of frontier policing. In April 1916, Commissioner Cullen personally headed 60 policemen through the rugged Urewera mountains to repress a community led by the Maori prophet Rua Kenana, whose self-determinationist ambitions had been seen as subversive. This mission ended in a gun battle and the deaths of two of the prophet's closest followers (including his son) at his 'capital' of Maungapohatu. This invasion, which had been partly justified by Rua's reported pro-German utterances, has been aptly described as being 'conducted like a military operation'.[73] Legal niceties were cast aside during and after the operation, and Cullen orchestrated publicity to indicate that (in the words of the judge in the ensuing case), '[i]n every corner of the great Empire to which we belong the King's law can reach anyone who offends against him.' In some interpretations this police expedition is cast as the final action of the wars between the Crown and Maori.[74]

Less dramatic but equally suppressive measures were taken by the government, and hence by the police, against other Maori communities. All Maori had been exempted from conscription for a number of reasons, including enthusiastic volunteering from within pro-Crown tribes. The Waikato confederation of tribes, however, not only joined a number of other groupings in refusing to encourage the war effort but also launched a strong and successful campaign of resistance to enlistment amongst their young men – a consequence of their unaddressed historical grievances against the Crown. In 1917 conscription was imposed upon them, alone in Maoridom. This provided the police with yet another major new responsibility, a test of their human and financial resources as well as of their capacity as mediators in Crown–Maori relations. In the event, their efforts to persuade Waikato to co-operate or to force compliance upon its young men were not successful, and only a handful of the tribal war resisters were rounded up for military service.[75]

In its more coercive and suppressive manifestations, wartime policing might be seen as a regression within the NZPF's general evolution towards consent-based policing. Police imposition of firmer potential or actual social discipline was reinforced, in and near cities and military training camps, by military police responsible for regulation of order among enlisted soldiers. While there were some jurisdictional and professional difficulties,[76] both sets of police were engaged in essentially the same mission, with the work of each informed and complemented by that of the other. Regular police assisted their military colleagues to understand what could, and could not, be done in relation to such duties as enforcing liquor laws, cautioning them that internal military methods were not necessarily applicable to civil society. On the other hand, New Zealand policemen, in common with their counterparts in all parts of the world, had always operated outside legal boundaries to a greater or lesser degree. These traditional operational parameters helped reduce tensions with the military police – if not with affected members of the public.[77]

The heightened demands of wartime policing set up conflictual relationships with sectors of society, but this did not mean that the police could not cope, or that the majority of the population had turned against the pursuit or methods of the war effort. Nevertheless, the waning of social enthusiasm for the sacrifices demanded from waging war had seen the government launch remobilisation campaigns, and in these, too, the police were allocated prominent roles of persuasion. While their duties as both coercers and cajolers continued to prove onerous and strain their diminishing resources of experienced men, the active or passive assistance of the majority of the population allowed them to maintain an effective role in social mobilisation. This became more manageable as counter-mobilisations against the war effort lost momentum, especially when bad news from the military front in 1916–1917 made them appear more subversive than ever. By mid-1917, in fact, even conscription of labour for war service seemed resignedly accepted as inevitable, despite little corresponding indication of the major quid pro quo demanded by the oppositionists – a willingness to conscript capital as well as labour.[78] Government-orchestrated remobilisation, in which the overstretched but generally efficient NZPF had played a significant role, might therefore be seen as successful. While the solidarity of August 1914 could not be replicated, and active protest and its suppression continued, such resistance was insufficiently damaging to the war effort to require any endemic application of severely repressive measures.[79]

Conclusion

Located at the daily interface of state and society, the wartime NZPF was on the front line of official efforts to mobilise support for the war while at the same time attempting to maintain social stability. Straddling as it did officialdom and the public sphere, wartime policing, with its intricate mix of consent and coercion, provides insights for understanding the complications of war-effort mobilisations and counter-mobilisations on the home front. One set of such complexities, for example, emerges from the overarching (if uneven) shift towards broad social consent for policing at the same time as police personnel remained differentiated from other officials by their legitimated capacity to surveil and detain. The war years intensified the core police role as the state's 24/7 agency of surveillance and coercion, both its 'eyes and ears' and its 'iron hand'. But the authorities, seeking as wide a social legitimation as possible, sought to use no more state compulsion and coercion than necessary to underpin a maximal war effort.[80]

This strategy was essentially successful: while state controls and interventions were far more draconian than in peacetime, large sectors of the population gave general support to (or at least did not actively oppose) wartime regulations and their enforcement. As a result, most New Zealanders escaped the intensity of the scrutiny and intrusion experienced by targeted sectors of society – generally those on the left of the political spectrum or people with 'enemy bloodlines'. Yet even jingoistic supporters of the war effort could feel some disquiet when their friends and neighbours were investigated, or the local publican and his clientele were charged with breaches of restrictive drinking regulations. On the other hand, given the dearth of organised reaction within patriotic circles to such intrusions, it might be concluded that these were seen as a small price to pay for national and imperial security.

A policing perspective also sheds light on mobilisation as a social phenomenon at arm's length from the demands and aspirations of politicians and bureaucrats. The policeman's mediating position between public and state could lead to constables opting to reflect community-based wisdom rather than to apply the strict requirements of the law or follow the precise instructions of their superiors. This can be seen in their discretionary enforcement of liquor or moral regulations, for example. Sometimes, however, higher authorities saw their operational flexibility as threatening peace and good order or even endangering state security. In 1916, for example, the Defence Department complained that police had wrongly reported favourably on the loyalty of some enlistees of enemy alien parentage, and the Commissioner responded with a drastic threat to his constables: 'if any man of alien enemy parentage or descent is enabled to [join the expeditionary troops] on account of a favourable police report, and it is subsequently found that he harbours sentiments favourable to the enemy, the policeman who reported him favourably will be dismissed.'[81]

The heightening of both state direction and social mobilisation heaped upon the police many duties which had reversionary resonance, especially the application of significant degrees of coercion to whole sectors of society. With its dual function of coercing as well as encouraging social mobilisation, the NZPF held a central role in both the functioning and the security of state at the very time when its resources were under strain. Tight social control became more difficult when considerable numbers of police had left the force. While 'temporary regular Police' were appointed from late 1916 – men not normally eligible for reasons such as age, qualifications or disability – they received no specialist training (the training depot had closed) and were under the supervision of permanent members.[82] Such factors, combined with huge workload pressures, affected performance, as did a growing restiveness about longer working hours and deteriorating working conditions. All the same, the extant evidence indicates that the body of police, as a generality, performed the tasks they were set by their political masters with considerable effectiveness.[83] This relative efficiency was undoubtedly aided by the degree of consent they had obtained from most elements of society, even if this were sometimes eroded by wartime strains and circumstances.

While most wartime regulations were lifted relatively quickly after the conflict had ended, a number remained in place, complicating post-war attempts to fully reinstate consent-based policing.[84] But generally, post-war policing continued its long-term evolution towards modern, professional, 'velvet-glove' policing. One early manifestation of this trend was a commission of enquiry in 1919 that sought to systematise detection services and improve their efficiency.[85] The handover of the police commissionership to O'Donovan in late 1916 can be seen to mark the beginning of a retreat from the most repressive aspects of state-led mobilisation, those with which his predecessor Cullen – who had been a member of the Armed Constabulary – had felt most at home.[86]

This gradual wartime return to less severe social regulation was an uneven one, taking place as it did within policy parameters allowing heavy and intrusive social intervention into social sectors such as dissident labour or resistant tribes. But O'Donovan's propensity to seek the broadest possible social consent was further entrenched as a policy direction once Liberal MP Thomas Wilford took over ministerial responsibility for policing from February 1918. After the war, in fact, the overarching pre-war trajectory towards consensual policing resumed in a pronounced way: as a generally tranquil society re-emerged, policing could move in a benign direction.[87] But when workers struck, protesters marched or crowds rioted, and indeed on any occasions when the condition of public order or state security was potentially or actually challenged, the police and political authorities would readily re-employ the 'iron hand' – its use guided by the knowledge they had accumulated from the constables' ongoing surveillance of society. The capacity to use main force remained the function which, in the final analysis, characterised the work of the police force, however much consent it might be able to garner from the majority of the population.

Chapter Six

Striking a Balance: The Military Service Boards

David Littlewood

In December 1918, Howell Widdowson reflected on his experiences as chairman of the First Otago Military Service Board.[1] He wrote that determining appeals for exemption from conscription was a task 'of the most arduous character', but took comfort in the fact the members had always tried to do their duty to both 'the State and the appellants'. This nuanced approach had been driven by two underlying imperatives: accommodating government policy, and striking a balance between the needs of the army and the needs of New Zealand's wider war effort.[2]

Historians have usually claimed that only the first of these imperatives exercised a significant influence on the boards' collective outlook. John Martin and Gwen Parsons agree that they utilised the classification of industries when reaching verdicts, while James Belich implies a passive adoption of official instructions to exempt the 'strategic unions' and 'most farmers'.[3] Similarly, Len Richardson identifies no resistance to the government's attempts to manage the outcome of appeals from coal miners.[4] Paul Baker does suggest certain 'maverick' bodies refused to exempt farmers and Catholic seminarians, but maintains the boards as a whole 'generally welcomed' guidance.[5] In terms of how claims were treated, Sonia Inder, Lisa James and Kerry Stratton all contend rural appellants received little sympathy.[6] Parsons asserts the boards' members were 'cautious and even sceptical' about the evidence given to support cases, and Ian McGibbon finds they often regarded themselves 'as defenders of conscription'.[7] While Baker acknowledges that the appeal bodies became increasingly liberal, his figures still indicate they dismissed far more cases than they allowed.[8]

Yet there is strong evidence to suggest both of the imperatives cited by Widdowson were accorded considerable weight. As one MP predicted, the boards' verdicts became 'the pivot' on which the success or failure of conscription revolved.[9] By determining how many men would be available to the army and to the home front, they possessed the ability to derail any manpower initiative. However, this scenario never came close to occurring. Through legislation, regulation and instruction, the government configured the exemption system to allow for centralised control, and made sure the boards were well aware of its desire for a large number of exemptions to be granted. Appointed for their pliability and nuanced outlooks, the members in turn proved overwhelmingly receptive to official policy. Only by recognising this mutual desire to balance the various elements of New Zealand's war effort can we understand why large numbers of eligible men were exempted from conscription.

Structure of the boards

The Military Service Boards had an integral role in New Zealand's conscription mechanism. Passed on 1 August 1916, the Military Service Act assigned each Recruiting District a monthly quota to be met by volunteers, or by balloted conscripts if numbers were lacking. The Act intended that a First Division of all men aged 20 to 46 who were single, widowers without children, or married after 1 May 1915 was to be exhausted before the predominantly married men of the Second Division were called upon.[10] Every reservist, or his employer on his behalf, could appeal for exemption on the grounds of 'public interest', 'undue hardship', or religious objections.[11] Each case then came before a board, which, from the evidence produced, delivered one of several verdicts: dismissed, adjourned for rehearing at a set date, adjourned *sine die* (indefinitely), or allowed.[12]

Several of the Act's provisions indicate a desire for the boards to adopt a centralised and balanced approach. The appointment of their members was placed in the hands of the government, which also had the power to change a board's personnel for any reason it saw fit.[13] These prerogatives allowed the executive to choose individuals who could be relied upon to adopt the 'correct' attitude and who would be amenable to applying official instructions. The legislation's only concrete stipulation regarding the determination of appeals obliged the boards to exempt the sole surviving son of a family in which at least one other son had been killed.[14]

The government's intentions are also evident in a series of measures adopted before hearings commenced. Of particular significance was the decision to establish only four boards, one for each of the Military Districts: Auckland, Wellington, Canterbury and Otago. When justifying this decision, the Minister of Defence, James Allen, stressed the need for uniform procedures and verdicts.[15] Having such a small number of boards certainly made it easier to monitor their activities, both to determine if instructions were required and to ensure they were implemented in the desired manner. Furthermore, each board had to travel across a wide area and hold sittings in many different places. This meant the members often lacked familiarity, and a sense of connection, with the local conditions, thereby fostering an inclination to base verdicts on official policies. Although the high volume of appeals did necessitate the establishment of five more active boards in January 1917, nine was still a very small number to cover the whole Dominion.[16]

Further steps were taken to restrict the boards' discretion over occupational appeals. In October 1916, a regulation was gazetted stipulating that, when considering these cases, 'the Board shall, unless it sees good reason to the contrary, accept as sufficient [evidence] a certificate by the Minister of Defence'.[17] So strong was this wording that the Solicitor-General, John Salmond, claimed it created 'a serious risk of undermining public confidence in the impartiality, integrity, and fairness of the administration of the Military Service Act'.[18] Nevertheless, the government decided being able to protect essential workers made issuing the certificates worth the risk. Salmond was certainly correct to argue they amounted to a 'practical compulsion' of the boards, by applying considerable pressure to grant claims and creating an impression that the appellant deserved exemption before any testimony had been heard.[19] Indeed, Allen later stated he had 'no reason to believe that the Boards would not accept the certificate in every case'.[20]

The government then proceeded to issue additional directions. A list of those industries considered essential was set out by Allen to include coal mining, farming, shearing, freezing works, shipping, and leather and boot factories.[21] This list and its importance was further emphasised to the board chairmen at a conference called with the intention of achieving 'a uniform policy'.[22] Four days later, correspondence was sent to the appeal bodies that again outlined which industries were essential.[23] A desire to defuse potentially militant resistance to conscription also prompted the government to make special allowances for members of the 'strategic unions'. The boards were told to exempt all seamen with at least twelve months' experience, all *bona fide* slaughtermen who agreed to work in a similar occupation during the off-season and, with particular emphasis supported by an extensive use of the ministerial certificates, all coal miners.[24]

This promotion of a centralised and balanced approach is further evident in the choice of board members. All of the key decisions were made by the Recruiting Board, a body of three government ministers that had been established to co-ordinate enlistments.[25] Given that he was the senior government figure in the absence of Prime Minister William Massey and Deputy Prime Minister Sir Joseph Ward, it is safe to assume Allen took the lead.[26] On the one hand, he excluded anyone who might be reluctant to satisfy the army's needs. Members had to be over the eligible military age and not have sons who had failed to enlist when they could reasonably have been expected to do so. Allen also decided to avoid the appointment of elected figures, as their willingness to refuse appeals might be compromised by a desire to secure local favour and votes. Finally, candidates were vetoed if they had expressed any misgivings over the introduction of conscription.[27]

These stipulations ensured that all of the chosen individuals were firm believers in the need to win the war. Some of their 'official rhetoric' emphasised the defence of Britain and the Empire, supporting Keith Sinclair's contention that such prominent persons adhered to the concept of 'imperial federation, to imperialism'.[28] However, they just as frequently espoused the need to protect New Zealand from a brutal and authoritarian enemy.[29] The vast majority had sent at least one son to the front and several had lost family members killed in action.[30] Moreover, James Milton commanded the Christchurch Citizens' Defence Corps, while the government had supplied John McCaw with a car and a sergeant major in both 1914 and 1916 so he could 'go round the District and try to recruit as many [men] as possible'.[31] Even those members who were drawn from organised labour possessed decidedly pro-war views. Arthur Rosser's recruiting activities and involvement with the National Reserve had made him deeply unpopular in radical circles, but he chose to regard this criticism 'as a compliment to me as a Britisher'.[32] Likewise, Edward Kellett had sent two volunteer sons to the front, and, upon his election as Vice-President of the Dunedin Labour Representation Committee, promptly resigned the next day, stating that holding such a position was incompatible with his conscriptionist sentiments.[33]

Yet Allen also sought men who would adopt a nuanced outlook. The personnel of every board comprised a legal professional as chairman, accompanied by one member from a farming background, and one urban member who was either an employer or a 'moderate' trade unionist.[34] For example, the First Wellington Board was headed by Daniel Cooper, a stipendary magistrate and former deputy registrar of the Supreme Court.[35] Sitting alongside him were William Perry, a sheep farmer, justice of the peace and member of the Farmers' Union; and David McLaren, the Secretary of the Wellington Waterside Workers' Federation.[36] Allen claimed 'No man has been selected because he represents any particular section of the community'.[37] Nevertheless, the adoption of a balanced membership formula strongly contradicts this assertion. What the Recruiting Board actually appeared to do was to utilise the Arbitration Court, established by the Industrial Conciliation and Arbitration Act 1894, as a template. That court was designed to equitably represent the parties in an industrial dispute: one member was chosen by workers and one by employers, with a judge as an impartial president.[38] Before conscription, there had been a growing dispute between the rural and urban communities over their respective contribution to reinforcements.[39] The Recruiting Board seems to have recognised that the awarding of exemptions could exacerbate this conflict and configured the boards to ensure they could not be seen as biased.[40] In terms of their attitudes, members whose livelihoods depended on agricultural and industrial production were unlikely to support a wholesale loss of workers to the front. Moreover, Allen's willingness to appoint trade unionists, hardly the most militaristic group in society, demonstrates he did not want individuals who would focus solely on supplying the army.[41]

The boards and reinforcement rates

Official policy continued to encourage a balanced approach throughout the conscription period. Of great significance here was the declining rate of reinforcement for the New Zealand Expeditionary Force. After June 1917, when the rate peaked at 15 per cent, or approximately 2,200 men per month, several factors prompted a reassessment of the Dominion's commitments.[42] First was the imminent balloting of the Second Division, an event that would increase expenditure on separation allowances, disrupt family units and potentially cause unrest amongst men who were asked to leave their wives and children.[43] A second cause was the growing 'reductionist' movement. Although divided over its precise aims, this body of opinion argued that the costs of the war effort had become unjustified. Not only was New Zealand reinforcing at a relatively high rate, but the entry of the United States into the conflict also meant the Allies could call on millions of additional troops.[44] The final issue was a fear that current obligations would see the Dominion run out of men before the end of the war, forcing it into the embarrassing position of having to break up the New Zealand Division.[45]

These considerations acted as a strong incentive to reduce reinforcement. Allen approached the Army Council in July 1917 and negotiated a decrease to 12 per cent.[46] Yet this proved insufficient to halt the rising tide of reductionism.[47] In December, further pressure led to the rate being slashed to only 6.5 per cent, or 1,000 men per month.[48] While the defeats suffered by British forces in March and April 1918 necessitated a decision to raise reinforcement back to 13 per cent, it was quickly scaled down to 6.5 per cent again as soon as the German advance petered out.[49] These various reductions had a striking impact. The number of soldiers embarked for overseas service in 1918 was only half that of 1917.[50] Moreover, because the call up of the Second Division only reached married men with at least two children, approximately 16.7 per cent of eligible New Zealanders were never balloted.[51]

These reductions in the reinforcement rate meant the boards came under limited pressure to obtain recruits. During the early months of sittings, their activities were subject to a rarely stated intimation that men were more important than production.[52] However, this philosophy was swiftly contradicted by a number of directives that called for more exemptions to be granted.[53] Thereafter, the boards were told to adopt strict standards on only two occasions. The first came in July 1917, with instructions to review all the *sine die* adjournments granted to First Division reservists, and to award further time only where an individual was irreplaceable.[54] Although this measure was designed to reduce the number of exemptions, its import was mitigated by the fact the boards would not have granted relief in the first place if a man could be spared. The other instance of pressure was during the German Offensive in March 1918, when the boards were asked to reconsider all *sine die* exemptions and to rehear cases where men had been given periods of leave before they were required in camp. This was the one point during the appeal bodies' operations where they were told the needs of the army should override all other considerations.[55] Nonetheless, by May the government was stating that no more *sine die* men could be taken without significant economic dislocation. In June, the boards were informed that their priority was to maintain production 'at present standard' to enable the Dominion to meet its growing war expenditure.[56]

Limits of discretion

Although the boards were subject to few demands for soldiers, this did not mean they were granted a free hand in determining appeals. Instead, the government endeavoured to guarantee the exemption of certain occupational groups. Allen had obtained the Catholic Church's acquiescence to conscription by promising that its priests, teachers and theological students would receive certificates recommending their exemption, and a misunderstanding had given the impression the boards were obligated to accept these documents.[57] This provoked fury amongst the Catholic hierarchy when the Third Wellington Board dismissed the appeals of two theological students on 16 February 1917.[58] Accused of deception, Allen insisted the qualifier in the regulation, to grant exemption unless they saw 'good reason to the contrary', permitted the boards to reject a certificate.[59] Rather than accepting this explanation, the bishops viewed it as an incitement for other boards to follow suit in refusing the appeals of Catholic theological students.[60]

Allen was now caught at a crossroads. Had he been committed to preserving the boards' discretion he would have continued to defend their right to overrule the certificates. Instead, he endeavoured to have the decisions reversed. Mobilisation of the students was postponed so the Solicitor-General could draft regulations for a Final Appeal Board that would enable it to overturn verdicts.[61] The Recruiting Board then approached the Cabinet for approval to proceed, only to be rebuffed.[62] Allen's next move was to arrange a conference with the board chairmen in order to bring their 'decisions into line'.[63] On 27 April 1917, it was agreed that indefinite adjournments would be granted to all clergymen, all religious teachers whose schools would close in their absence and all theological students who were in the final four years of training.[64]

Yet the crisis did not end here. When awarding *sine die* exemptions, several boards signalled their intention to review these decisions before the calling of the Second Division. By June 1917, the imminence of this reassessment raised fears that more Catholic appeals might be dismissed, a concern given added impetus when another conference, including all of the boards' members, failed to ratify the April agreement.[65] The government now decided definite measures were required. The Expeditionary Forces Amendment Bill would have provided for the statutory exemption of ministers, men in holy orders and all teachers, but it was rejected by the Legislative Council.[66] With this failure, the government reverted back to directing the boards. In November 1917, a conference with their chairmen resulted in an agreement to grant *sine die* adjournments to all ministers and members of holy or religious orders.[67] While this meeting was again unable to define a policy over theological students, the chairmen did consent to suspend the hearings of these individuals after being informed that not one of their number had yet been required to mobilise.[68] The final acts in the Catholic exemption question came in May and August 1918, when the First and Second Wellington boards dismissed appeals from six more theological students.[69] In response, the Recruiting Board determined the men would not be taken into camp.[70]

Alongside the government's attempts to enforce the exemption of Catholics were its instructions to the boards regarding essential industries. A crucial move came during February 1917, when the National Efficiency Board was constituted to help develop policies for the maintenance of production.[71] In June, the government approved a classification prepared by the Efficiency Board that divided industries into 'most essential', 'essential', 'partially essential' and 'non-essential'.[72] This measure was taken further three months later, by grading the significance of different positions within each occupation.[73] These classifications were sent to the boards for their 'guidance'.[74] Nevertheless, in practice, the government insisted 'appeals should be considered strictly in accordance' with the classifications.[75] The Efficiency Board also conducted a constant review of the ability of industries to release men. Its findings were submitted to the government, which then forwarded them on to the boards, along with instructions to implement any necessary changes in their approach.[76]

The government also persisted in its efforts to protect the 'strategic unions'. Having directed the boards to exempt any seaman with twelve months' experience and all *bona fide* slaughtermen, the executive left these instructions in place for the remainder of conscription. Its only intervention came during January 1918, after the Second Wellington Board had dismissed the appeals of several slaughtermen.[77] Allen sent a letter stating that official policy had not changed and the men's union had been promised its members would be exempted. The board was ordered to rehear the appeals, with a firm intimation that it was expected to 'give effect to the Government's policy in this matter'.[78]

Official direction over coal miners was more proactive. During February 1917, Allen received evidence showing a recent downturn in output was due to a co-ordinated 'go-slow' action.[79] He wanted miners exempted to ensure adequate production, but could hardly justify their retention if they were not working to capacity.[80] Proceeding with caution, Allen instructed the boards to warn the men that a failure to increase output would forfeit their exemptions.[81] This game of brinkmanship continued until 24 April, when the crisis was apparently ended by an agreement that saw all of the unions end their 'go-slow'. However, two days later, miners at Runanga and Paparoa struck again over local economic issues.[82] Feeling he had been duped, Allen directed the First Canterbury Board to dismiss the appeals of all the men involved.[83] While this was a decisive action, it was one that Allen, fearing a renewed coal shortage, quickly regretted. The board was told first to halt the dismissal of men who had not been balloted at the time of the second strikes and then to stop refusing cases altogether. In addition, the appeal body was informed that men who had their claims turned down would be allowed to return to their occupation as 'soldier-miners'.[84] At this point the government's involvement largely ended. The only notable exception was an extension of the 'soldier-miner' provision to reservists whose cases were dismissed for low productivity.[85] By September

1918 there were around 100 'soldier-miners', a situation the Recruiting Board justified by stating it did 'not want to precipitate a coal crisis and would prefer to wink at evasions within limits'.[86]

The greatest volume of official direction concerned men engaged in working the land. During the early months of sittings, the executive came under sustained criticism over the boards' allegedly harsh treatment of these cases, with several organisations even demanding the automatic exemption of all farmers.[87] To try and stave off this criticism, Allen pressured the boards to act 'more circumspectly'.[88] On 16 March 1917, they were informed that it was no part of official policy to force men to give up their holdings; if there was any question over an individual's ability to obtain labour then he should be exempted.[89] The government also gave its sanction to the establishment of local trustee boards consisting of three farmers or businessmen. Over the next few months, the appeal bodies were repeatedly told that all doubtful cases, particularly those concerning the 'last man' on a farm, should be referred to the trustees for a report.[90]

Although these actions appeased some critics, they did not prevent the government coming under fire over the supposed willingness of several boards to flout its directives.[91] Allen dispatched a new memorandum on 12 October stating that 'in no case should the man who is doing the whole of the work on his own farm, or the last son on the farm of parents who are unable . . . to do the work themselves, or skilled agricultural labourers, be taken for military service, unless, with respect to the last named, efficient labour is available to replace them'.[92] A literal reading of this instruction would have required the exemption of the first two categories of men regardless of the circumstances. However, the government stated that, while the need to retain the 'last man' and keep up production should be adhered to, the boards could still investigate each case to prevent deliberate 'shirking'.[93] Except for the change during the March 1918 Offensive, this was the approach advocated in all future directives concerning farmers.[94]

Welcoming guidance

The boards were prepared to contest some of their official instructions. Although most clergymen, religious teachers and theological students were issued with certificates advocating their exemption, the appeal bodies did not accept these claims out of hand. The chairman of the Third Wellington Board defined the common attitude by asserting it was his body's duty to 'investigate every case which comes before us', as this was the only way they could satisfy themselves that exemption was justified.[95] Appeals from Catholic seminarians and teaching brothers were dismissed, and the board chairmen consistently refused to agree to the blanket exemption of theological students.[96] A second point of resistance was the claims of some men employed in essential industries. After beginning to act on Allen's directive to refuse all miners who had struck after the April 1917 agreement, the First Canterbury Board was dismayed by his subsequent climb down.[97] Despite repeated requests to halt the dismissals, the board continued rejecting the claims of 'second-strikers' over the following months.[98] Further discord occurred over the October 1917 memorandum regarding farmers. The chairman of the First Wellington Board lamented that this document 'wholly stultified' his body's independence, and would leave them unable to distinguish between genuine 'last men' and individuals who had only achieved this status by subdividing farms.[99] At a more general level, in March 1918 the Recruiting Board felt moved to remind the boards 'that appeals should be considered strictly in accordance' with the classification of industries.[100] A few months later, after complaints from the Efficiency Board that its scheme was still not being followed, Allen stated that 'he would see that the Military Service Boards were again warned upon that point'.[101]

Nonetheless, this opposition to government involvement was limited in both scope and extent. While the boards investigated all the Catholic appeals that came before them, most of these cases were ultimately successful. Outside of theological students, no clergymen and only one Marist Brother were refused exemption.[102] Within the essential industries, a handful of coal truckers and ship's pursers whose indispensability was in question at the beginning of conscription are the only reported instances of ministerial certificates being rejected.[103] Such responsiveness is even more evident over the appeals of seafarers. During their early sittings, several boards gave detailed consideration to these cases in order to ascertain the requirements of the mercantile marine.[104] Nevertheless, they quickly adopted the government's policy of exempting all seamen with twelve months' experience. Typical was the wording of Chairman Moorhouse, who indicated that his Third Wellington Board would 'take notice' of the directive 'except in case of special circumstances'.[105] A similar compliance is apparent in the boards' attitude to slaughtermen's appeals. Here an initial review was again conducted into the industry's requirements, while regular consultations were carried out with freezing works employers to see if any of their men could be spared.[106] Yet the boards were careful to state these appraisals were not a rejection of the government's directive; 'We only want to know whether these men are bona fide slaughtermen.'[107] That the executive was so quick to admonish the Second Wellington Board for dismissing a small number of appeals in early 1918 indicates how sensitive it was to the potential for industrial unrest. However, this criticism was seemingly both the first and last of its kind, suggesting the boards' approach was otherwise in accordance with official policy.

Further evidence contradicts the idea that some 'maverick' boards refused to follow the government's instructions regarding farmers.[108] In mid-1917, when criticism of the 'mavericks' was at its fiercest, Allen defended their conduct. He asserted that all of the boards were carrying out the government's wishes for 'last men' to be exempted if they could not be replaced. He also maintained that the supposedly renegade bodies were justified in refusing to exempt some who claimed to be 'last men', as the testimony showed they had only achieved that status by dividing a farm.[109] Of course, Allen might have felt compelled to reassure farmers they were not being victimised. Yet his assertions are probably genuine, as he repeated them in private correspondence with Massey, Ward and General Alexander Godley, where such circumspection was not required.[110] The boards certainly put forward no stated resistance to the government's policies prior to the October memorandum. In regard to that document, the First Wellington Board was alone in criticising the implications of its literal interpretation. The other boards either signalled their willingness to comply, or remained silent until the government clarified that only irreplaceable farmers and farm workers should be exempted.[111] With this guarantee of discretion, the First Wellington Board dropped its opposition, and there were few protests over 'last man' instructions for the remainder of conscription.

If the appeal bodies' relationship with the National Efficiency Board is analysed in its entirety, then co-operation again emerges as the dominant theme. Certainly the government reproved the boards over their perceived failure to make full use of the classification of industries. Yet this appears to have resulted from differing perceptions. The classification was never designed to be prescriptive; it explicitly stated 'each and every man' employed in the 'most essential' occupations should not automatically be regarded as entitled to exemption, but rather that relief should only be given to those who were irreplaceable.[112] While the boards adopted this philosophy, there were inevitably occasions when their notion of what amounted to irreplaceable differed from the government's.[113] However, the fact that the boards were admonished very infrequently suggests they followed the classification and reached acceptable decisions most of the time.[114] The appeal bodies also adapted their approach in line with the Efficiency Board's investigations. Allen outlined that reports on the ability of a range of industries to release men had been forwarded to the boards and that they had been 'acting on the recommendations'.[115] In most instances where a new type of claim came forward, the appeal bodies either adjourned cases to give the Efficiency Board time to investigate or arranged for a conference with its members.[116] These deliberations were then used as a guide for any future appeals, most notably when the chairman of the Second Canterbury Board stated 'In no case will this board go behind the Efficiency Board'.[117] During their valedictory reports, the board chairmen praised the Efficiency Board's efforts and commented on how useful its guidance had been.[118]

Even more striking is the fact that the boards made few complaints when men whose appeals they had dismissed were subsequently held back. The only exception concerned the First Canterbury Board. In November 1917, chairman Evans wrote to Allen to protest at the decision to retain Arthur Sparrow as a 'soldier-miner'. He explained that the appeal had been dismissed after Sparrow admitted leaving his farm for work as a coal trucker in a deliberate effort to avoid military service. Unhappy such a man was to be protected, Evans pointedly asked whether it was now the government's policy to retain all men who entered the mines 'ipso facto'.[119] In May 1918, another member of the board, James Milton, wrote to further call into question the executive's willingness to allow all dismissed men to become 'soldier-miners'. Citing individuals who had stopped work or taken unauthorised absences, he cautioned that his other colleague, Edgar Studholme, had threatened to resign unless defaulters were set to rights.[120] Although there is a lack of confirmation on whether the two events are linked, it is surely not a coincidence that Studholme left his position three weeks later.[121]

These actions were certainly notable protests, but their apparent strength was mitigated by a number of factors. No member of the board ever challenged the validity or justification of the 'soldier-miner' policy itself, only the way it was being applied.[122] Moreover, Studholme's threatened resignation was not designed to force a major change in the government's methodology. Instead, he simply asked that 'a few of the glaring cases shall be taken out of the mines'.[123] When Allen rather brazenly replied that the Recruiting Board preferred to allow recalcitrant men to evade their duties rather than running the risk of industrial unrest, Studholme was the only one who gave up his post.[124] Elsewhere, the boards proved considerably more acquiescent when their verdicts were nullified. No complaints followed the revelation that the military authorities had been directed to keep back all theological students and Marist Brothers, while the government's instruction to rehear the appeals of dismissed slaughtermen resulted in those individuals being granted exemption.[125] None of the boards ever refused to hold sittings, while Studholme was the only member who resigned for anything other than personal reasons.[126]

Rather than resisting the government's involvement, the boards regularly approached it for additional guidance. In the early months, the Third Wellington Board adjourned many appeals from the Railway Department to wait for an official policy on reducing services.[127] Similarly, the chairman of the First Otago Board requested the executive's views on how to deal with the numerous appeals the board received from medical students.[128] When the 'go-slow' crisis was in progress, the First Canterbury Board was in constant communication with Allen over how to handle the appeals of striking miners.[129] Chairman Evans emphasised his board's desire to know the 'mind and opinion of the Government' on the question and stressed they did not wish to act 'except in full concurrence with yourself'.[130] These three bodies also joined the others in requesting general advice on the approach they should adopt. During the March 1918 Offensive, the First Otago Board and both Auckland boards petitioned the government over how its directive that soldiers were now more important than production should affect the appeals of 'last men'.[131] Then, in May, Allen divulged that all of the boards had asked for 'a declaration of policy in regard to essential industries and exemptions'.[132]

A dual perspective

The board members' willingness to adopt a balanced approach is evident in their attitudes during appeal hearings. They insisted military requirements must be met in order to achieve victory, but also held that exemption should be granted if necessary. Chairman Day maintained his Second Otago Board wanted 'to determine how best men can serve their country', and the personnel of the Second Auckland Board signalled their intention 'To deal with appellants with due regard to the military demands of the State, while inflicting no undue hardship on the individual or imperilling food production'.[133] Every man would be given a 'fair chance' to state his claim, with the members asserting that their extensive questions were not motivated by a simple wish to fill reinforcement quotas, but by a need to reach informed decisions.[134] When replying to claims of excessive harshness, they frequently expressed disappointment that their earnest desire to balance the needs of the country and the appellant had not been recognised. One chairman stated 'scarcely a day passes that we do not hear anathemas passed upon [our] decisions, still we have to keep on and carry out our functions to the best of our abilities'.[135]

That these utterances were not mere self-justification can be illustrated statistically. By compiling all of the appeal verdicts reported in a range of urban and rural newspapers, a sample numbering more than 33,000 was obtained. Several types of verdict within this sample were then discounted from consideration. The first type was where claims were temporarily adjourned. Such a postponement certainly indicated a belief the case for exemption had not been fully substantiated, but it also pointed to a need to investigate the matter further, and the board might well have granted the appeal at a later date. Counting temporary adjournments against the percentage of appeals granted would ignore this later eventuality and effectively identify these decisions as refusals. A second category of excluded verdicts was instances where an appeal came up for hearing after the reservist had already been classed as medically unfit. Here the board's decision did not affect the individual's situation, as the state of his health had already afforded him a *de facto* exemption from overseas service.[136] The third point of omission was where the appellant failed to attend his hearing. The boards understandably felt compelled to dismiss these cases, as the man's absence made it impossible to assess his circumstances through questioning.[137] A final exclusion encompassed those claims that were withdrawn prior to a hearing taking place. Here the boards played no part in the outcome and were never given a chance to grant exemption.

Having made these various omissions, an analysis of the remaining 25,347 sample verdicts produces some striking findings. The most important is that the boards were more likely to grant a man's appeal than to order him into camp. Across the conscription period, 54.83 per cent of cases were either allowed or adjourned *sine die*. Moreover, even many of the negative verdicts still granted appellants a period of relief from military service. The boards possessed the ability to refuse a claim while simultaneously stipulating that the man would not be expected to mobilise before a certain date. Known as 'conditional dismissals', these decisions typically gave appellants between one and six months of unpaid leave to put their affairs in order.[138] Some 79.27 per cent of dismissals in the sample were conditional rather than unconditional. Therefore, when the positive verdicts and conditional dismissals are combined, it becomes apparent that 90.64 per cent of the boards' decisions granted at least a temporary reprieve from joining the army.

To what extent are these sample verdicts representative of all those delivered in New Zealand? Although it is impossible to provide a comprehensive answer, investigating two returns prepared by the Defence Department allows a conclusion to be drawn for 20 out of the 25 months that the boards held sittings. This methodology demonstrates a divergence regarding the two types of dismissal. The sample verdicts include 35.81 per cent conditional refusals and only 9.36 per cent unconditional refusals. In contrast, the overall figures indicate a much closer ratio: 24.93 per cent conditional dismissals against 18.97 per cent unconditional. Yet in terms of positive and negative verdicts, the two data sets are remarkably similar. In the sample, 54.83 per cent of appeals were allowed or adjourned *sine die*, compared to 56.1 per cent overall. Therefore, whichever of the figures is used, it is evident that the boards granted exemption in over half of their verdicts, and afforded at least some form of relief to the vast majority of men who came before them.

Conclusion

Most studies of the Military Service Boards have identified a responsiveness to central guidance, but without appreciating the impact this had on attitudes and verdicts. The government appointed members who shared particular traits and then sent them numerous instructions, all with the aim of encouraging a nuanced approach towards appeals. As the boards proved overwhelmingly receptive to official policy, they sought to balance the needs of the army against those of families, businesses and essential industries. This concern to satisfy the varied requirements of the war effort meant a large number of eligible New Zealanders were not conscripted for overseas service.

Chapter Seven

War a Daily Reminder, But Life Goes On: Newspapers during the First World War

Ian F. Grant

In early August 1914, newspapers were effectively the sole source of overseas information for New Zealanders when Britain's declaration of war against Germany automatically involved the furthest flung Dominion in the conflict.

Over the following years mass media proved essential in mobilising public support: scholarship has observed that 'a war effort . . . could not ignore mass opinion as it might have in an earlier age' and that 'newspapers and weekly journals helped shape a new national spirit'.[1] Generally, the country's newspapers, and the dailies in particular, willingly took up this role, supporting government decisions, applauding the dispatch of troop contingents, actively aiding patriotic fundraising, and demonising 'shirkers' and those who questioned the war. Newspapers both reflected and encouraged commitment to a war most New Zealanders believed to be necessary and just.

However, newspapers' positions within the war effort were complex, the result of multiple relationships and considerations. Christopher Clark neatly summarised the wartime relationship between press and government when he wrote: 'The press entered into the calculations of policymakers in many different ways. It was never under their control, and they were never under its control.'[2] Clark sees a situation in which there was 'constant interaction' and the press had 'semi-autonomy'.

The position of New Zealand papers was comparable. While the government desired enthusiastic press support, it was, with its strict censorship regime, very conscious of the risks involved when papers published stories, or printed soldiers' letters, that differed from the 'official' line. Newspapers, on the other hand, saw their primary role, in peace and in war, as providing their readers with news of importance and interest as soon as possible. This approach was inextricably coupled with the fact that newspapers were commercial businesses, and the most marketable news was up-to-the-moment, unvarnished information about campaigns, battles and casualties. Besides censorship, wartime circumstances threw up other hurdles. Supplies of newsprint, mainly from Canada, became less certain and, by one calculation, increased some 400 per cent in price over the war years.[3] Some, but by no means all, dailies compensated by printing smaller editions, and while advertising, essential to profitability, occupied as much space as before, there were definite declines in revenue.[4]

So, New Zealand newspapers were linked to the international and the local, were positioned between government and the public, and operated with regard to both extraordinary wartime measures and everyday concerns and interests.

Newspapers in the pre-war period

In 1914, New Zealand was entirely dependent on its newspapers for the northern hemisphere news so crucial to daily life and future prospects.[5] Radio was still at an experimental stage and television was not yet an idea forming in John Logie Baird's mind. This made newspapers the primary means of connecting the individual with the wider world, and there were an extraordinary number of newspapers in early colonial New Zealand. It has been estimated that in the four decades from 1860 to the beginning of the new century a total of 331 newspapers were launched.[6] It was an article of faith and a boost to survival for every new township, however small, to have its own newspaper providing essential community connection and carrying news from other provinces and faraway countries, albeit often long after the event.[7]

By 1911, when more New Zealanders lived in urban rather than rural environments, the growing strength of daily metropolitans, aided by better transportation, snuffed out a number of papers close to cities. Still, in August 1914 nearly all towns of any size had their own newspapers, publishing weekly or more frequently: 'in 1914 there were 63 daily newspapers which invariably carried columns of the same overseas news, as well as reports from other parts of the country, sent down the wire to them by the United Press Agency [UPA].'[8] A co-operative of largely daily newspapers established in 1880, the UPA formed another crucial part of the press system, distributing overseas and national news around the country.[9]

These papers were also increasingly connected to the wider world. For mainly economic reasons, New Zealand newspapers had been drawn into what has been called the 'imperial press system'.[10] For decades the network of undersea telegraph cables that by 1876 linked Britain with its colonial outposts was very expensive to use, and pre-war cable agreements were designed to provide international news as cheaply as possible. This news was British-orientated and, as Simon Potter notes,

> By the turn of the century almost all the cable news published in Australia and New Zealand was being filtered through one source, the *Argus* London office. There, staff drew directly and exclusively on news gathered by British concerns such as Reuters, the Central News Agency and various London papers.[11]

Though an Australian slant was added, the system had not been set up to provide New Zealand perspectives. New Zealanders were well-informed of European tensions, with newspapers receiving up-to-date cable news on the situation. In an April 1913 piece entitled 'The German Menace', for example, the *Wairarapa Age* noted:

> The details of the new German military proposals show clearly that Europe is confronted by a new war of armaments . . . This year the German Army is to be raised with all possible speed to a gigantic total in time of peace of 860,000 men, which means that it also is to be kept permanently mobilised.[12]

Papers also had established positions within the social/political landscape and were much more overtly politically aligned than their modern counterparts. In August 1914, most newspapers supported either William Massey's conservative Reform government or Sir Joseph Ward's Liberal opposition. Conservative papers like the *Dominion* and *Press* outnumbered those of more liberal persuasion like the *Lyttelton Times* and *New Zealand Times*. Weeklies like the *Otago Witness*, *Weekly Press* and *Auckland Weekly News*, with their substantial country readership, mirrored the views of their parent dailies. Independent weeklies like the *New Zealand Observer* and *New Zealand Free Lance* were often colourful and outspoken in their views and not dependent on the UPA daily news summaries. Two other weeklies – *Truth* and the *Maoriland Worker* – took a still more maverick stance. Proclaiming a populist solidarity with the common man, *Truth* ('Largest circulation throughout the Dominion' and sold throughout the country) stridently opposed 'militarism', 'wowserism', and 'Mr Fat' (the bloated representation of capitalism), and revelled in scandals. In the years prior to the war the paper had been increasingly radical, 'openly endorsing the FoL [Federation of Labour] and its platform of revolutionary socialism'.[13] The *Maoriland Worker*, the official organ of the United Federation of Labour since 1911, served as a still more entrenched critic of the social/political establishment and radical voice of the labour movement, its masthead declaring it a 'journal of industrial unionism, socialism and politics'.

Another feature of some publications were political cartoons, which often provided local perspectives and sometimes biting commentary.[14] Very little has been written about New Zealand editorial cartoons during this period, and some claims are lacking in accuracy. *Holding On To Home*, for example, claims that 'Political newspapers from all parts of the spectrum carried large topical cartoons, sometimes in colour'.[15] In fact, very few newspapers, and only one daily, carried cartoons during this period, only one was under 'political' control, and none published cartoons in colour. Tending to follow the editorial line of their newspapers and magazines to a greater degree than today, cartoons have been noted as 'represent[ing] an inherently local and especial reaction to national and international trends and developments'.[16] Certainly they were also particularly useful as propaganda for various purposes. They encapsulated the essence of complex issues – and simplifying these proved powerfully effective in wartime commentary.

When war did break out, the daily press *en masse* favoured British intervention and New Zealand's involvement.[17] The response of the *Poverty Bay Herald* was typical:

> Victory will not be won without much self-sacrifice and suffering but we feel sure that every loyal British subject will give this cheerfully in defence of all that is vital to his hearth and home. It is gratifying to know that New Zealand is doing its part speedily to assist the Empire.[18]

Even the *Grey River Argus*, which had given space to labour views before its 1919 purchase by West Coast trade unions, was fully supportive: 'Germany will find that she has not only to face England, for the whole Empire is standing alert and watchful, like a grim old lioness with her cubs.'[19]

Conversely, the *Maoriland Worker* and *Truth* forged a more critical and oppositional relationship with the cause. In its second wartime editorial, *Truth* asked whether 'there is another enemy deserving of more attention than even the braggart, bouncing German.' Sacrifices might be necessary but if this meant:

> the people of New Zealand, particularly the poorer and working classes, are to stand still and submit to highway robbery, by merchant trusts, tricky traders, the rich, bloated, greedy, mercenary middlemen, then the sacrifice will not be made, because then it will be seen what class loyalty and patriotism really means.[20]

Likewise, the *Maoriland Worker* saw no glory in participation. Just before war was declared, the weekly editorialised: 'Britain may . . . be dragged into the human maelstrom. The direct results . . . will then stretch to this country. Then will be utilised all the force and ingenuity of the capitalist class to arouse us into a state of frenzy, dubbed by them patriotism.'[21] Both weeklies would continue as major critical voices throughout the war.[22]

Life goes on

It is instructive to recognise and appreciate the place of the war within newspaper content. It is easy to assume that the war dominated life in New Zealand during the 1914–1918 period. In fact, the amount of newspaper space given to the conflict did not expand greatly over those four years.

Naturally, international news, which previously encompassed the world, now focussed on the war in its various theatres. But the claim that 'war topics came to dominate the content of local papers' is not true.[23] In fact, war news rarely ran to more than one or two pages an issue. A few metropolitan papers and the weeklies printed lengthier war reports, and there were more photographs and double-column headlines, but generally the emphasis remained strongly on the minutiae of local life – council meetings, church events, weddings, stock sales, sporting fixtures. With their advertising columns and local, everyday news, newspapers often portrayed a reassuring sense of normality to communities a world away from the actual fighting, and perhaps to soldiers receiving newspapers at the front. This recording of the normal and mundane would be in increasing juxtaposition to the lengthening casualty lists appearing several times a week, a constant reminder of the pain suffered by an increasing number of New Zealand families. Two weeklies were notable, later in the war, for running studio portraits of the dead, wounded and missing in action. 'The *Otago Witness* and the *Auckland Weekly News* ran pages of these images as an ongoing feature, cropped in the majority of cases from studio portraits taken before soldiers left New Zealand.'[24]

An analysis of ten New Zealand newspapers – across urban and rural regions and the North and South Islands in April 1915 – shows the war as a brooding presence but not one that dominated the routines and rhythms of everyday life.[25] The Dardanelles and Gallipoli Peninsula received only brief mention in all the papers, generally in reports from the British war correspondent Ellis Ashmead-Bartlett. The *Grey River Argus* and *Taranaki Daily News* carried the same report, telegraphed from a naval vessel off the Dardanelles, that it 'is essential that a powerful army be ready to occupy the Gallipoli Peninsula'.[26] In the *Wairarapa Daily Times*, Ashmead-Bartlett's report was given less space than another that began: 'One of the first effects of the Anglo-French attempts to force the Dardanelles was the lowering of wheat prices and, on the other hand, a small boom in oil shares'.[27] The *Dominion*'s attention was elsewhere, editorialising about the battle at Hill 60 that raged in Flanders on the Western Front through April–May: 'a thrilling glimpse of the battle clash in which full play is given to all the destructive forces which the men of science have placed at the disposal of the men of war'.[28]

The *Auckland Star* had the most room to devote to war news. A London message dated 26 April reported, in a combined Admiralty and War Office communiqué with a four-line headline over two columns, that the army had landed at various points on the Gallipoli Peninsula completely successfully with a large force established ashore before nightfall. The paper gave much more space to the municipal elections – and to the women standing. 'It would be difficult even for those who hold the more old-fashioned views of women's place in the world to raise any objection to the few women candidates who are offering themselves for election at the municipal polls tomorrow.'[29] The *Bay of Plenty Times*' editorial said: 'The interest which the municipal contests has aroused has perhaps . . . diverted public attention from the highly important matter of electing school committees for another year', and the *Thames Star* editorialised: 'It is to be regretted that the cult of true citizenship is not followed more enthusiastically at Thames'.[30]

Local news took most of the available editorial space, given that 50 per cent or more of each paper's column inches were filled by advertising ranging from double-column, line-block-illustrated sales pitches for Imperial Cygnia Corsets or the latest offerings from 'R. Hannah & Co (The Leading Shoeists)' to classifieds selling patent medicines at the bottom of news columns, and barely distinguishable as advertising at first glance. Increasingly, there was an emphasis on 'British made' products.[31] There were reports from sporting fixtures, the meetings of local bodies, and AGMs. The *Press* reported: 'At the fifteenth annual general meeting of the Christchurch Shorthand Writers' Association, [it was] stated that forty-one Pitman's speed certificates had been gained during the year for speeds ranging from 80 to 140 words per minute.'[32] Considerable space was given to detailed reporting of the latest film and stage entertainment. The *Poverty Bay Herald* gave particular attention to describing the 'serial drama photoplays' at Gisborne's World's Picture Theatre.[33] The *Dominion* noted that *Babes in the Wood* 'keeps the flag of merriment flying gaily at the Grand Opera House', while at His Majesty's Theatre 'Miss Florence West, a delightful soprano and one of that rare class which is always in tune, revived Sullivan's sweet old ballad "My Dearest Heart"'.[34]

The *Akaroa Mail* gave more attention to German Bay than to the Dardanelles, with questions about whether the bay should be renamed occupying many column inches. It first reported a meeting of residents to consider a name change in November 1914. 'It was thought that the name was an unfortunate one at the present time and might lead to their branded produce being treated roughly on wharves, etc.'[35] In May 1915, the paper reported a further meeting where 'it was unanimously decided to rename the bay Colonist's Bay'.[36] There was further disagreement about this and, finally, in late June, the original Maori name, Takamatua, was chosen.[37]

The wartime imperial press system

Another particularity of New Zealand newspapers' wartime position was their enduring reliance on the imperial press system and foreign sources. The Gallipoli campaign offers something of a case study of some of the effects of this dependence. Perhaps surprisingly, newspaper readers had heard about the Gallipoli Peninsula and its part in war plans some time before the landings there. There had been numerous stories about the projected Dardanelles campaign to open the way to Constantinople and more recently the Royal Navy's bombardment of Turkish gun positions, but there had been only the barest hint about the involvement of the New Zealand Expeditionary Force. The *Otago Daily Times* on 11 March reported: 'It is extremely probable that the Australasian Forces and others are now on the way to the Dardanelles . . . Most likely a part of the forces will be employed somewhere on the Gallipoli side'.[38] The *Northern Advocate* editorialised presciently the same day:

> there is something here of intimate gravity to us in New Zealand, if we are correct in our inference of the Prime Minister's utterances at Waiuku. Naturally Mr Massey could not be more explicit when he mentioned that probably a 'British' force would co-operate with the French, but we may easily perceive herein a transparent hint that the New Zealand troops will presently be in the thick of the fray.[39]

The *Bay of Plenty Times* quoted a London report of 19 March 1915: 'The *Daily Mail's* correspondent says that the most dangerous stage of forcing the Dardanelles is commencing', and an Athens one the same day: 'Forty thousand Turks are on the Gallipoli Peninsula, 30,000 in Turkey in Europe, and 110,000 south of the Dardanelles'.[40]

Generally, war news – short single-column items of one- or two-hundred words – was published in New Zealand the day after a raid, attack or sinking happened on the other side of the world. But not with the landings at Gallipoli after New Zealand troops struggled ashore on 25 April at what became known as Anzac Cove. New Zealanders read their newspapers on 27 April totally unaware of what had happened, and life went on very much as normal, with a number of articles that day giving information about the municipal and other local elections. Some accounts have claimed that the first general news about the Gallipoli landings was published in New Zealand on 29 April.[41] In fact, a story in the *Dominion* was typical of coverage that day in its dependence on rumour and surmise:

> Cheerful accounts by the Turks of successful defence at the Dardanelles admit of a simple explanation and are not necessarily wholly based on imagination. Their claim . . . is quite in keeping with British reports that the actual landings were accompanied by feints at other points . . . It is still probable that the operations on the Asiatic side are subsidiary, and that the main attack will be concentrated on the peninsula.[42]

The 29th of April also saw Australian Prime Minister Andrew Fisher announce that the Australian Expeditionary Force was in action on the Gallipoli Peninsula and 'the action is proceeding satisfactorily'.[43] With the report reaching New Zealand late that night, the government was forced to respond, and the Minister of Defence announced that 'about three weeks ago the New Zealand infantry left Egypt for the Dardanelles. The fact had been a profound secret until now'. It was also reported that 'since the receipt of the cablegram from the Secretary of State for the Colonies rumours have been in circulation to the effect that the New Zealanders had suffered severe casualties, and that the Government had received advice of the numbers.'[44] This was denied by the government.

With limited information, commentary hung on cable sources.[45] There were early reports of derring-do. Reuter's Cairo correspondent quoted one soldier: '"Nothing could stop us. Our big lads lifted the Turks at the end of their bayonets and hurled them over their heads. The Turks ran, screaming and howling in fear"'.[46] The *Waikato Times*'s editorial, for example, quoted from the Secretary of State's cablegram and its 'warmest congratulations on the splendid gallantry and magnificent achievements of your contingent in the successful progress of operations in the Dardanelles'. It waxed on: 'It testified in unmistakable terms that the sons of these far distant isles were Britons still; that they had been tried, and had proved that New Zealand's honour was in safe keeping.'[47] Even here, though, there was a sobering note: 'But the price? Wives, mothers, and sisters are anxiously waiting a reply to this question. It is hardly possible that our boys have escaped scathless, and the dreaded lists are awaited with fear and trembling.'[48] This wait was to continue. On 1 May, the *Otago Daily Times* noted: 'Our men are at the Dardanelles in force, and have borne themselves well. For the moment that is all we know; what is yet to tell we await with steady hearts.'[49]

The first Gallipoli casualty list from the Defence Department appeared in papers on 5 May and told a very different story. It listed 126 men wounded (19 of them officers) and 10 officers killed, but made no mention of deaths among the rest of the men.[50] The next day a Press Association message listed 150 men wounded.[51] After this there were almost daily tallies of numbers killed and wounded, and the casualty totals – 729 on 13 May,[52] and 1,007 on 17 May.[53] As late as 25 June, the Minister of Defence's response to questions concerning news delays on Gallipoli casualties was classic political-speak:

> I think that everything possible is being done to get the news of the casualties through at the earliest possible moment. The record office at Alexandria is doing exceedingly well and the people are being extremely well served. Never, in fact, have they been served so well in any previous war.[54]

It was soon obvious that, with almost all of UPA's copy coming from British and Australian sources, an authentic New Zealand voice was lacking. Some reports simply ignored the roles played by New Zealand soldiers. Ashmead-Bartlett, writing from a distant naval vessel about the 'storming' of the Dardanelles, seemed unaware of the involvement of New Zealand troops alongside the Australians: 'Major-General Alexander Godley wrote to [Defence Minister] Allen, noting that Ashmead-Bartlett never once used the words "New Zealand" or "New Zealanders" and that fortunately he had been able to see them inserted whenever necessary.'[55]

An effort was made to appoint New Zealand war correspondents. This, however, became a tortuous and messy business. From the late 1890s, four metropolitan dailies – not wanting to be entirely dependent on the UPA – had grouped together to fund the New Zealand Associated Press (NZAP) to provide additional international coverage from a London base. As Guy Scholefield, an experienced journalist and former member of the parliamentary press gallery, was writing for the *New Zealand Herald*, *Evening Post*, *Press* and *Otago Daily Times* at the outbreak of war, the NZAP sought and gained War Office approval for him to be accredited as a war correspondent on the Western Front. The New Zealand government's stipulation was that he supply all the country's papers, which the NZAP would not agree to. Consequently, Scholefield's war coverage was significantly restricted.

As Ron Palenski has written: 'The failure of the four newspapers which employed Scholefield to allow him to write for all, and the noticeable lack of interest by any other newspapers, or group of newspapers, to send a reporter to the war, led almost inevitably to the Government making the appointment itself.' [56] The appointment of Malcolm Ross as official war correspondent was controversial on several counts. It was thought he was too close to the Massey government and possibly too old (he was 52), and he wrote dispatches that were remote, detached and pedestrian. 'His most descriptive adjective appears to have been "interesting"!'[57] His dispatches were also lengthy – one early one was 5,500 words long – and, as Allison Oosterman noted, they 'were far too long for most New Zealand papers, even the biggest, the *NZ Herald*'.[58] Doubtless, this contributed to the decision forbidding him to cable his dispatches for a considerable period of time, on the grounds of excessive cost. The UPA supported the government's decision, with the result that the cables of other war correspondents and even soldiers' letters invariably arrived, and were published, before Ross's mailed dispatches. Perhaps inevitably, a number of papers preferred to run stories by Ashmead-Bartlett and Australian Charles Bean, so the intention to add a New Zealand perspective to the war coverage in local papers was largely unfulfilled.

Public commentary

Wartime newspapers also retained their role as public commentators, their relationship with their audience, and consequently their livelihood, resting on being in tune with their readers' interests, concerns, attitudes and prejudices. Besides previously mentioned everyday concerns, this relationship covered various 'home front' issues which arose from wartime circumstances. Here, press coverage was a heady mix of both detached reports and impassioned efforts to advance particular causes.

In those papers which supported the war effort, there was particular concern about the decline of volunteer rates into 1915 and subsequent editorial calls for the introduction of conscription to guarantee enlistments and push for an equitable distribution of sacrifice.[59] There were crude measures marking loyalty and disloyalty, with 'shirkers' becoming a particular target of newspapers and cartoonists. The *Bay of Plenty Times* wanted the death penalty for 'shirkers', noting that this penalty was meted out to disobedient frontline soldiers and should also apply to the 'home front'.[60] Conscientious objectors were denounced as 'shirkers' and sophisticated attempts to understand why some Maori, socialists, Irish and Christians refused to take up arms were in short supply. In this way 'propaganda was used to lionise those who served and demonise those who did not.'[61]

Anti-German material was prominent and reports of German setbacks and atrocities (real, sensationalised or fictional) were regular features and grist to the cartoonist's mill. However, the stirring of outrage could also extend to local enemy aliens. As Andrew Francis notes, 'the invasion of neutral Belgium gave newspaper editors, political commentators, cartoonists, and patriotic citizens at large, free rein to denounce all Germans as "Hunnish barbarians", regardless of where they were domiciled.'[62] As a result of anti-German sentiments, local companies and families changed their names and councils renamed streets. The Franz Joseph Glacier was in danger of disappearing from maps – for xenophobic rather than climatic reasons.[63]

The case of the German-born, English-raised George von Zedlitz is revealing. By 1914 von Zedlitz was the Professor of Modern Languages at Victoria University College and had been a Wellington resident for 13 years. However, he became the focus of an ongoing anti-German press campaign from the dailies and several weeklies, which largely underwrote the government's decision, in August 1915, to introduce the Alien Enemy Teachers Act that led to his dismissal. Francis observes the episode as highlighting 'the direct influence exerted by public opinion in the formulation of government policy' and emphasises the role of the media in shaping this opinion.[64]

Cartoon commentary offers another major example of how newspapers conveyed war-related material to the reading public. The popular tabloid-size weeklies, *New Zealand Observer* and *New Zealand Free Lance*, which focussed on the Auckland and Wellington markets respectively, made extensive use of cartoons for front-page spreads and internal illustrations. During the war these were often used to promote national and imperial unity, encourage recruitment, brand 'shirkers', push support for conscription and portray the enemy's malevolent nature.[65] The *Observer*'s cartoons were the preserve of part-owner William Blomfield ('Blo') while the *Free Lance*'s front-page spot provided opportunities for several cartoonists – W. MacBeth, K.M. Ballantyne, T. Ellis (aka Tom Glover), Brodie Mack, A.H. Messenger, Hank Portere – all of whom drew in a patriotic vein.[66] The *New Zealand Herald* ran wartime cartoons infrequently, usually in the paper's Saturday Supplement. Some were by Trevor Lloyd, who cartooned more for the *Auckland Weekly News*, and whose focus was invariably pro-Empire and very strongly anti-'Hun'. There was also the *Canterbury Times*, the weekly published by the *Lyttelton Times*, where David Low had earlier honed his skills. The paper's front-page cartoon, generally sympathetic to the war effort, was drawn by Jack Gilmour until the weekly closed in 1917.

The dynamics of public commentary are likewise evident in those papers with a dissenting or critical line regarding the war. The key example was the *Maoriland Worker*, which became a direct opponent of the war.

Besides questioning the morality and purpose of the war, the paper focussed on the war effort's social impacts and challenged the introduction of conscription. In these stances it presented itself as a voice of the working class and a guardian of traditional liberties: 'we venture to prophesy that the workers of New Zealand will meet any attempt to apply European Conscription here in a way that will do honour to every best tradition of British freedom and to every principle of human liberty.'[67] These messages were also conveyed visually and, until August 1917, the *Maoriland Worker* regularly ran anti-war page-one cartoons by Alsop and H. Mann, usually two columns wide across the eight-column broadsheet page.[68]

Truth, however, pursued a more complex editorial line, using its populism to present itself as a friend of the common soldier and critic of the war effort. A recent analysis notes that the paper 'found a way to keep patriotic readers and retain its anti-war principles' and 'became a tireless advocate of the average "boy in the trenches"' by reporting on soldiers' pay, pensions, appeal procedures and a number of other issues.[69] Moreover, the paper proved a strident anti-conscription critic, calling for wealth to be conscripted before people, and its editorials and cartoons continued to attack 'Mr Fat', now presented as profiting from the war and the sacrifice of the workingman.[70] *Truth* ran front-page cartoons across two columns, and sometimes more, of the paper's broadsheet page. Tom Glover cartooned for *Truth* throughout the war (except for a period he spent in the army in 1918) and until 1922. His excellent work led to an Australian career at the *Bulletin* in Melbourne and the *Sun* in Sydney.

Censorship and the news

The wartime position of newspapers was also shaped by the wartime regulation of information. Unquestionably, censorship was a major impediment to the New Zealand public learning as quickly as technically possible about the deployment of its troops and the casualties suffered. Very aware of newspapers' critical communications role, governments in Britain and New Zealand were quick to censor what appeared in their pages. With telegraphic cables now criss-crossing the oceans, there was a genuine fear that intelligence of military importance could be telegraphed to the enemy, as well as concern about public morale if military setbacks were published immediately or without a degree of positive nuancing. Almost immediately war was declared, Britain set up an official Press Bureau with military and civilian censors vetting all cables and telegrams. Newspapers were banned from publishing news about the movement of warships, troops, aircraft or war material without specific permission.[71] A very similar system was mirrored in New Zealand. To the growing frustration of New Zealand newspapers, cables to the UPA were censored in Britain and again in Australia (which was a lay-station in each cable's journey) before a third censorial scrutiny in New Zealand. The content of letters was more difficult to control.

Most newspapers accepted that censorship was necessary. The *Feilding Star* editorialised: 'every loyal journalist must, and does, consider his country first, second, and all the time'.[72] There were, however, limits to high-minded compliance. In cities where there were morning and evening dailies fighting their own circulation wars, gleaned military intelligence trumped local news, and pragmatism sometimes won over patriotism. For example, the Christchurch *Sun* provided its readers, and doubtless many *Press* regulars, with considerable detail about the expedition to capture the wireless station at Apia, German Samoa. It announced on 10 August that about 600 troops would leave from Wellington the next day. 'The details and composition of the force are a state secret, but as Samoa is not fortified its capture should present no difficulties.'[73] And the dispatch of the main Expeditionary Force in October 1914 was a temptation too much for the *Auckland Star*, the feisty evening competitor of the more stately *New Zealand Herald*. On 8 October the paper reported that naval ships were in the harbour and noted the names and ranks of officers as well as the number of troops and horses aboard.[74]

It was not until the passing of the War Regulations Act on 2 November 1914, and subsequent regulations, that there was clarity about what could be published and when.[75] Until then, papers ingeniously – or ingenuously – took advantage of loopholes. The authorities had decided newspapers could announce the departure of troops on or after 25 August and telegrammed them accordingly. It did not occur to anyone that a paper – the *Timaru Herald* – would publish the telegram the next day, buried as the eighth item in a 'Town and Country' column including weather reports, parish pump items and even classified advertisements for foot powder and pickled-egg preservative. It was a clear indication, without actually saying so, that the troops had already left, as they had on 16 August.[76]

News filtering back from the front, mainly in soldiers' letters that subsequently appeared in newspapers, was of particular embarrassment to the censors. New regulations prohibited the printing of any news on military or naval matters that was not passed by the telegraphic censor, already published in English papers, or specifically sanctioned by the local military, so newspaper editors welcomed letters offered by relatives about how New Zealand soldiers were actually faring for the insights and colour they provided. Much of the 'Diary of a Young Feildingite', published by the *Feilding Star*, was harmless enough: 'I was at church parade this morning, Captain Clarkson preached about ploughshares and reaping hooks being turned into swords and spears. No good to us! Even the officers have to carry rifle and bayonet and pack now, so there's nothing doing in the sword line'. But it also contained less innocuous observations: 'My, but ain't we glad we've got General Birdwood to keep our very own General Godley in hand! Things have been looking up ever since "Birdseed" took control'.[77] The editor responded to the sternly censorial rebuke he received with the claim that 'every paper in New Zealand has printed worse matter'.[78]

In 1916, censorship was tightened again. The April regulations forbade mention of a soldier's unit, summaries of casualties, and publication of uncensored soldiers' letters. The *Auckland Star* raised censorial blood pressures by printing the new 1916 regulations in full, adding: 'It is just as well that our readers should understand, in some degrees at all events, the difficulties under which the Press labour in this time of war'.[79] Later, 'sedition' for criticising conscription and the military was written into legislation. Likewise, any suggestion of British setbacks exercised the censors. The *Thames Star*, for example, ran details of the losses of British ships and seamen, which exceeded German losses, at the Battle of Jutland.[80] Subsequent histories have suggested there was no clear-cut winner in the last great high-seas battle, but at the time the report was labelled 'almost treasonable' in Parliament.[81]

As the war continued, newspapers continued to complain about, and sometimes ignore, censorship restrictions. There was no systematic monitoring by the censors and they generally responded, ineffectually and after the event, to complaints from rival newspapers. There was also a considerable legal and practical distance between the threat of prosecution and it actually happening. Editors and publishers were threatened with substantial fines and months in prison, but when prosecutions were taken the resulting fines were invariably very small. No editors or publishers went to prison; the *Maoriland Worker* suffered the greatest reaction, with its offices raided by police in 1916 to seize 'subversive' literature.[82] As R.B. O'Neill has written, 'censorship was just as clumsy, just as arbitrary, at the end'.[83] When an erroneous report of an armistice passed censorship, the government's response was to forbid any mention of the subject. This meant that cable messages reporting the actual Armistice signing, and end of the war on the Western Front, were suppressed until the next day. Records of the New Zealand Press Association state that 'New Zealand was about the last place in the whole world to hear the news'.[84]

Conclusion

Public opinion – and this was almost entirely expressed through the press during the war years – always modifies, and sometimes leads, democratic government decision-making. It mattered to the New Zealand government that the newspapers generally supported the war effort in a number of ways – and that they also, with their detailed coverage of everyday life and columns of advertising promoting familiar products, helped preserve a feeling of normalcy. The government also needed to maintain national morale and believed that this sometimes required managing, delaying or reinterpreting unpalatable information. It was in this area particularly that there was a real and continuing tension between the press and the government, one that reflected their respective roles and responsibilities, which sometimes merged and on occasion diverged.

Newspapers were commercial organisations: good news coverage sold copies and higher circulations lifted advertising percentages, which further boosted profits. Entwined with business concerns was a strong belief among newspaper proprietors, very much steeped in British traditions, that the press, as the Fourth Estate, had a quasi-constitutional role to keep the public fully informed about political, economic and social matters critical to the functioning of a democratic society. This role, which can sit uncomfortably alongside commercial imperatives, was generally observed by the New Zealand press. It helped, of course, that this commitment provided a service the public was prepared to pay for.

Despite its inherent tensions and challenges, the relationship between the press and government was an important component in New Zealand's social fabric during 1914–1918. Perhaps the press's greatest contribution to understanding New Zealand during the First World War was the day-to-day evidence that ordinary life – national and local politics, films and fairs, sport and the household products advertised – did go on, despite the stark reality of growing casualty lists.

Chapter Eight

Negotiating Conditions and Commitment: The Union Movement and the First World War

Erik Olssen

Through 1914–1918 the great majority of union members, like the majority of workers, strongly supported the New Zealand war effort. However, the most class-conscious unionists opposed the war, thus generating complex dynamics and developments. Part of this complexity reflected the ongoing influence of the tumultuous events of 1912–1913, the memory of which profoundly shaped the history of unions during 1914–1915, and continued to exert an influence throughout the last years of the war and the first years of the peace.[1] In the course of 1914–1915, however, the members of the defeated unions – miners, wharfies, seamen – established control of the new arbitration or 'scab' unions formed by their enemies to break the strike, built new national organisations, and exploited the favourable labour-market conditions created by the war to achieve significant improvements in conditions and wages. Most of the country's revolutionary socialists and industrial unionists belonged to these organisations and spearheaded opposition to the war and conscription. After a brief suspension of hostilities when the war began, the main body of unions – urban and skilled – also began to exploit the favourable labour-market conditions.

In 1914 the great majority of the 403 unions registered under the Industrial Conciliation and Arbitration Act seized control of the United Federation of Labour (UFL), created as a revolutionary industrial organisation in the aftermath of the Waihi strike of 1912, and turned it into the labour movement's parliament for the duration of the war.[2] Although the UFL never engaged in collective bargaining, it became the trade-union movement's voice on the issues of the day, especially conscription of men, and took the initiative in forming the New Zealand Labour Party in 1916. The UFL remained an important forum and advocate, and in 1918 led the opposition to industrial conscription, an issue which mobilised all unions into action. By the end of the war, however, the advocates of One Big [industrial] Union had captured the ideological initiative; seduced by the same vision, the UFL exited, not with a bang, but a whimper.

The unfolding story was always messier than this brief retrospect suggests, however. The impact of the war on the economy, no less than the labour markets, varied greatly from one region to another, between industries, and over time. How unions responded also differed, depending not only on the product and labour markets that they operated in, but also their size, their goals and the experience of their members. Most of these organisations, with an average size of around 180 members when war began, had to work hard to achieve agreement on many issues. Such complexities did not preclude either agreement or action, however. The overwhelming majority of union members, like the overwhelming majority of workers (most of whom were not unionised), supported the war.[3] Indeed the issues central to the war – playing by the rules, treating small and weak players fairly – resonated powerfully with most workers and union members. This doubtless helps to explain the virtual cessation of industrial conflict during the first three years of the war.[4]

The pre-war union movement and the outbreak of the war

War came at a bad time for the New Zealand labour movement, with the 'Red' Federation of Labour having just been routed in the Great Strike of 1913. Many of its leaders were still in jail, including Harry Holland, the dominant intellectual figure on the left, whose confrontation with the Chief Justice earlier in 1914 became legendary on both sides of the Tasman (for he had been a well-known revolutionary socialist in Australia before crossing 'the ditch'). Although Holland strongly opposed the war, he believed that it would 'end capitalism' and provide the chance to create a socialist republic if only the unions would unite. By contrast, E.J.B. Allen, Holland's successor as editor of the *Maoriland Worker* and arguably the most influential syndicalist in the Empire, strongly supported the war.[5] The British Socialist Party, founded and led by H.M. Hyndman, one of Allen's mentors, also strongly supported Britain's participation in the war against the 'Prussian military caste which controls the German state'.[6]

Because the revolutionaries – a disputatious gaggle of Wobblies and De Leonite socialists – had recently been blacklisted or had relocated to Australia, the anti-war position was more or less lost by default. Most of those blacklisted who stayed in New Zealand thinking the war an imperialist plot or the death throes of capitalism, prudently retreated to the more isolated work camps and coal mines, where their ideas were less out of favour. Not surprisingly, once Holland, on his release from prison, resumed his editorial duties and ousted Allen the revenue of the *Maoriland Worker* plummeted.[7] The government was more scared of the 30,000 members of the Passive Resisters' Union, a movement rooted in the Non-Conformist churches of the larger towns, which strenuously objected to compulsory military training.[8] Not only were opponents of the war without spokesmen, but the rout of 1913 had seen the more moderate sections of the labour movement assume control of the UFL.

Despite the totality of defeat, in those industries where the 'Red Feds' had proved most popular, the strike helped forge a new unity and resolve. Indeed the Massey Reform government's use of naval warships and armed special police – 'Massey's Cossacks' – to break the strike not only deeply angered the Red Feds but also acted to mobilise behind the strikers many unions that were hostile to Red Fed ideology. These included the so-called moderates of the skilled trades, who had never been attracted by the ideologies of direct action and class war and who disliked or even opposed strikes. Such men also disliked the revolutionaries' contempt for religion, their abuse of the King and their scorn for the British Empire.[9]

Following the defeat of 1913 those hostile to or suspicious of the revolutionaries quickly set out to reorganise the union movement. Early in 1914, at the request of a conference of arbitration unions convened by Arthur Rosser, the secretary of several Auckland unions, the UFL invited all unions to send delegates to discuss this matter.[10] Most unions were based in the main towns, rather than single-industry towns such as Blackball and Waihi, which had dominated the Red Federation, and the men who now came to the fore knew the range of views within the union movement and the wider working class. After a furious debate, the delegates exorcised the ghosts of revolutionary industrial unionism by deleting the revolutionary 'Preamble' from the constitution. They also threw out the industrial structure adopted in 1913, replacing the old Industrial Departments with District Councils. Symptomatic of the newly cautious mood, the central executive lost its power to call out all affiliates on strike, its power to levy affiliates in support of strikes in other industries was virtually removed, and considerable control over industrial issues was given back to the yet-to-be-formed district councils. Two well-known professional secretaries of craft unions, long detested by Red Fed activists, were elected President and Vice-President. Under these men – Dan Sullivan from Christchurch and Arthur Rosser from Auckland – the UFL became more akin to the old Dominion Trades and Labour Councils than to its own previous incarnation, although delegates did endorse the Social Democratic

Party (SDP) and assumed responsibility for the *Maoriland Worker*. The charismatic firebrand of the old 'Red' Federation, Bob Semple, was elected organiser; he resigned in disgust within three months.

Confusion remained, however. A few unions refused to send delegates, fearing that affiliation might involve them in strikes; some old Red Fed affiliates, notably the miners and the watersiders, refused to affiliate because they considered the new organisation gutless. For all that, the new leaders had skilfully created a new consensus, rejecting the old 'Lib-Lab' right, which had aligned itself with the Massey government during the Great Strike, and the 'Wobbly' left, which had scorned the Red Federation as nothing but a supine craft and sectional organisation.[11] Although the Wobbly leadership scattered far and wide throughout Australia, the Lib-Labs went nowhere.

The outbreak of the war added further complexities. Primarily, a burst of national solidarity saw the cry of 'country not class' become 'irresistible'.[12] Revolutionary socialists, revolutionary industrial unionists, and members of the Industrial Workers of the World undoubtedly opposed the war, as did some of the unions in which they had influence. However, the great majority of New Zealand's workers, like the great majority of Europe's workers, did not oppose mobilisation. Some rejoiced in heady mixes of jingoism, notions of war as a test of mettle, or less high-minded impulses for adventure. Others were convinced of the war's necessity or resigned themselves to playing a part in the drama.[13] Perhaps it was partly in response to this spirit that just a few months after the declaration of war, Massey's Cabinet authorised the release of all those imprisoned during the strike. The common belief that the war would be short and have little impact on New Zealand likely further influenced the responses of workers, as it did the public at large. Hundreds of unskilled and jobless young men rushed to enlist for fear of missing out. The Arbitration Court prudently decided to postpone hearings until the situation became clearer, and the largest union of the country's railway men, the Amalgamated Society of Railway Servants, dropped its pay claim. By and large, business continued as usual.[14]

The Labour movement divided. Most leaders of the SDP, founded in 1913 by the same Unity Conferences that established the UFL, opposed the war. Although the SDP was strong in Christchurch and the West Coast, in the most unionised towns – Wellington and Auckland – it had virtually no presence.[15] And even where the SDP had some presence, it had little influence over the local unions. The Trades and Labour Councils (T&LCs) and their Labour Representation Committees (LRCs), which were formed to contest the 1914 elections, strongly supported the war, and many of their leaders enlisted. The danger of allowing the Labour movement's quarrels to hand the election to Massey prompted an effort to unify. Everyone agreed to invite John Rigg, ex-president of the Wellington Trades Council and an outspoken pro-Labour legislative councillor, to visit the various towns and ensure that the SDP and the several LRCs did not both nominate candidates for the same seats. Where possible Rigg also brokered a deal with the Liberals in order to eliminate the danger of splitting the anti-Reform vote.[16]

Union reorganisation and conditional commitment

Still rent by recriminations over responsibility for the collapse of the strike, the UFL proved ineffectual in resisting Massey's introduction of measures designed to ensure that history could not repeat itself, notably an Industrial Disputes Investigation Act and amendments to the Arbitration Act. Early in 1915, however, delegates to the second annual conference of the UFL elected a tough, canny and widely respected coal miner, John Dowgray, as president. Under his guidance the UFL worked to bury enmities and focus on what needed to be done.[17] Such ongoing efforts to reorganise, and the altered social conditions the war effort created, highlight some of the conditional aspects of the unions' relationship with the war. That this process played out differently across unions also highlights the significance of variations across the movement.

Developments within political labour provide a particularly significant example. The war and the consequences of the 1913 strike dominated the elections of 1914. The morning newspapers in the four main towns portrayed the issue as 'Reds versus anti-Reds', with Reform and Liberal competing over which represented the anti-Reds more effectively. Sir Joseph Ward's Liberals tried to exorcise the ghosts of class conflict by spelling out a most progressive, not to say radical, programme, while Massey and Reform stood on their record as champions of law and order. The result was confusingly close. Pro-labour and socialist candidates won six seats, the Liberals 30 seats, and Reform 37 seats. Everything now hung on what Taurekareka Henare, the new representative for Northern Maori, would do, and he was in no hurry to say. Hammering the Red Feds had brought Reform no gains in urban seats, it seemed, but neither did Reform lose any ground. Nor had the Liberals recaptured their losses in 1911. It took another six months before it became completely clear that Reform had won a narrow majority.[18] It was overwhelmingly clear, however, that defeating Massey, if not achieving political power, had become a major goal for most of the country's trade unions. That it was not the goal for most of the country's workers, however, foreshadowed a major (if as yet unrecognised) problem for labour. Two major psephological studies have revealed that hostility towards such views was widespread and intense in non-unionised handicraft trades as well as in the union movement generally.[19]

While the election result remained unclear, Massey did not convene parliament and concentrated on recruiting. Matters, however, began to intrude. Although unions had been complaining about the rising cost of living since the early 1900s, it now began to rise sharply.[20] The imperial requisition of New Zealand's staple exports saw land prices soar and grain production fall. Consequently flour was in short supply and the price of bread rose markedly. Workers and their wives became increasingly disgruntled. Urban resentment of rural prosperity fuelled further discontent. The rapid rise in the cost of living became the main issue in union meetings (it remained a major issue for the duration).[21] In response the government pushed through the 1915 Cost of Living Act, which created a Board of Trade to investigate complaints about profiteering and recommend solutions. While the Arbitration Court did resume hearings in April 1915 and started granting 'war bonuses' a year later, it had no jurisdiction unless the union's previous award had expired.[22] By the end of 1915 the unions were blaming profiteering for the rising cost of living.[23]

The political situation changed late in 1915 when the Liberals and Reform agreed to form a National government. The six SDP–LRC MPs, five of whom had begun working together, refused to take part in the discussions and became, ipso facto, the opposition. This status proved a means of unity, clarifying a sense of 'us' and 'them'.[24] Furthermore, manpower shortages associated this fledgling Labour caucus with a critical issue, especially when the National Government agreed to provide a full division to the Western Front. In September 1915 a National Registration Act was passed to assess the country's capacities, and the executive of the UFL, accurately assessing the government's intentions, convened the first of its anti-conscription conferences in January 1916.[25] Although the UFL had only 72 affiliates with 10,000 members, another 10 unions representing another 8,500 workers also sent delegates to the anti-conscription conference.[26] This Open Conference, as it was called, proved so successful that the UFL organised one each year; in effect they became the labour movement's parliament, and at the same time akin to the annual 'party' conference for the labour caucus. Anti-war revolutionaries scared to speak their minds about the war now had an issue they could address. Several of the Red Federation's legendary firebrands, notably Bob Semple and Pat Hickey, were as if reborn. Although a majority of unionists favoured conscription, many also believed that men ought not to be conscripted without an equivalent conscription of wealth.[27]

Variations in how this negotiated commitment played out are evident in the shipping industries, on the waterfront and in the mines. In each of these industries, cadres of defeated revolutionaries campaigned to capture control of the arbitration unions set up by government and employers to defeat the Great Strike of 1913. Full employment and the government's fear of industrial unrest – for the flow of men into the New Zealand Division had become an imperial necessity – also helped. Equally important, however, was the attitude of the leaders of the Union Steam Ship Company, the largest in Australia or New Zealand, with substantial investments in coal mining and significant influence on the various Harbour Boards that owned and operated the country's wharves. The company's directors had learned, following the victory of 1890, that profitability depended not on screwing every humiliating advantage possible from their defeated workers, but from building a strong relationship with the union.[28]

The company's attitude doubtless helped the Federated Seamen's Union (hereafter the Seamen) reinstate its control over all ships in Wellington, now the headquarters for the national office. Although it took months to re-establish the national organisation (for the decision to strike and then to return to work had roused deep passions), every union member had a membership card which showed whether he was in good standing. Once the Seamen struck in 1913, every member had to have his membership card stamped and signed to indicate his loyalty. In 1914–1915 no seaman could get work in Wellington or its satellite ports, such as Patea, unless his membership card carried that stamp. After a few rounds of angry recrimination, Dunedin and Lyttelton swung into line. In Auckland, by contrast, the Northern Steam Ship Company led the campaign to ban ex-Red Feds from the ships and enjoyed considerable success until the 'bogus union' – the 'scab' arbitration union formed to break the strike and blacklist the strikers – sued for peace in January 1916.[29] During 1916–1917 the Seamen next proved that although it was illegal for any union registered under the Arbitration Act to strike, any well-organised union could still engage in collective bargaining and even go on strike without incurring any of the penalties prescribed in law.[30]

On the waterfront and in the mines, the battle for control was much more fierce. The Employers' Federation, the various Citizens' Committees, the Farmers' Union and the government had encouraged the formation of new arbitration unions – 'bogus unions' – when they reopened the wharves and mines. This situation, however, soon came under threat and Wellington's wharves became a decisive battleground. Led by a huge Irishman and gas stoker, 'Big Jim' Roberts, ably helped by Lou Glover (the secretary), the old Red Feds won control over the 'bogus union' and then expelled the 'scabs'.[31] A similar process took place in the mines. At one coal mine after another the defeated miners began attending meetings of the 'bogus union', and contested elections when they occurred. Despite the employers' attempt to blacklist all known activists, by the end of 1914 most of the newly formed arbitration unions in the coal mines of the Buller and the Grey had been captured by the Red Fed rank and file, although it took a terrible disaster at Huntly in the Waikato to give them a toehold. The miners did not get everything their own way: wages were pegged for two or three years and affiliation to national organisations was banned.[32]

In part this development reflects reorganisation. The defeat of 1913 drove miners and wharfies back into localism and sectionalism, but even when they had abandoned the old vision of One Big Union the old cadres of militants recognised the need for a wider alliance. In autumn 1915 Dowgray, who had enhanced his national standing during the strike, organised the New Zealand Coal Miners' Federation (CMF), the absence of the gold miners at Inangahua and Waihi reflecting the new mood of prudent sectionalism. The idea won overwhelming support from coal miners across the Coast.[33] In December 1915 Roberts took the lead in establishing a Waterside Workers' Federation (WWF), based in Wellington, to assist ex-strikers in other ports. In Auckland, where the Union Steam Ship Company's influence was much weaker and the Northern Steam Ship Company still had considerable clout, the blacklist proved highly effective and the Federation's help essential.[34] Both federations adopted a constitution that recognised the authority of the various local branches, but moved quickly to exploit their strategic advantage. In July 1915 the CMF demanded abolition of the contract system and a 20 per cent wage increase, and hotheads talked of striking. Dowgray denounced direct action, insisting that affiliates seek redress from the court. Semple, the WWF's agent in Wellington, echoed these sentiments.[35]

This development again shows how wartime pressures boosted unions' bargaining power. Quite apart from the loss of experienced men because of the blacklist, which was a major cause of the explosion at Huntly, the loss of young men to the front and the cessation of immigration meant there were fewer workers but no less work. Indeed, the wartime economy increased demands for the services of wharfies and miners and made disruptions in these areas matters of strategic concern.[36] In the autumn of 1916, although existing awards had at least two years to run, the government convinced the owners to negotiate for fear that the miners and wharfies might ally once again.[37] Cabinet ministers and senior public servants gave considerable thought to how best to ensure that such an alliance was not formed, and how to deal with it if it was.[38]

Furthermore, shortages of skilled labour, the virtual disappearance of a generation of potential apprentices, and no large reserve army of unemployed labour to call on offered the old Red Feds still more leverage. Disruptions took various forms.[39] Once hired, men could work to rule, 'go slow', hold stop-work meetings or initiate wild-cat strikes. Wharfies, hired by the day, could turn up late for the 'call', or not at all, without legal penalties, although they might forfeit future hires. Although the union's secretary usually co-ordinated these new forms of guerrilla warfare, as James Holt remarked, instructions were 'communicated to the rank and file by methods that were secret, ingenious, and therefore difficult to pin on union officials'.[40] By the end of the war, both the FSU and the WWF had achieved, in effect, a closed shop.[41]

Nor did blacklisted activists, some of whom suffered greatly, quietly fade away. Many of them sought revenge on the Farmers' Union for supplying 'scabs' to reopen the wharves, by organising farm labourers into a Rural Workers' Union. Some set out to organise public-works and railway-construction workers. Others organised freezing workers into a new national body.[42] When the Arbitration Court virtually destroyed the Shearers' Union in 1916, because it was recruiting workers from more than one industry, these cadres helped build a new and more aggressive organisation, influenced less by the moderate policies of old than by the syndicalist vision of One Big Union.[43] After the war it became the New Zealand Workers' Union, arguably the most voluble champion of revolutionary industrial unionism.

The 'craft' unions negotiated their relationship to the war effort somewhat differently. Labour historians have traditionally focussed almost exclusively on the so-called militant unions, dismissing the others – as the militants did at the time – as anachronistic survivors from the 'horse and buggy era'. This takes the militants at their own estimation, visits the condescension of history on the great majority of union members and ignores completely those working men and women who did not belong to unions (unless they entered the scene as strike breakers). Hence it is usually overlooked that no affiliate of the Red Federation in its heyday had more members than the largest craft-based union, the Amalgamated Society of Carpenters and Joiners (ASC&J), and that the largest general-purpose union, the Amalgamated Society of Railway Servants (ASRS), had more members than the entire Red Federation at its zenith. Although some crafts confronted the challenge of mechanisation, which allowed less skilled workers to do their jobs, or even extinction, as several crafts based around the horse did when supplanted by automated vehicles, it is a mistake to think that all crafts declined, or that craft skill became irrelevant to union organisation.[44] Indeed the so-called craft unions strenuously resisted 'dilution'.[45] It would also be a mistake to assume that their members opposed the war; far from it. Indeed at the Hillside railway workshops, Dunedin, the department's refusal to give ex-soldiers the day off on Anzac Day 1917 sparked an indignant uproar.[46]

Craft unions survived in good order or even expanded during these years, the membership of unions registered under the Industrial Conciliation and Arbitration Act increasing from 67,661 to 82,553 (a 22 per cent increase).[47] They also responded in much the same way as the so-called industrial unions (all of which retained autonomous local branches and a federal national structure). Take the two imperial organisations based on craft – the Amalgamated Society of Engineers (ASE) and the ASC&J. Although the processes began before 1914, both organisations sought to extract themselves from an Australasian district, established by the union's head office in England, and achieve local self-government. Although both unions grappled with how best to reconcile the requirements of the Arbitration Act with their benefit section, usually set up for the highest paid and most skilled men, they also sought to recruit less skilled men in related jobs, unite with other crafts in their industry, and find more effective means of negotiating directly with their employers.[48] The war accelerated these trends, bringing new members, often from less-skilled branches of the trade, who supported the campaign to seek a common front with other unions in their industry. Guild Socialism, with its vision of industries controlled and managed by their respective unions, together with the Workers' Educational Association provided both an ideology and a forum for achieving a wider unity.[49] Increasing frustration over the rising cost of living and the Arbitration Court's niggardly awards also saw most branches of both unions seek to affiliate with city-wide organisations and the UFL.[50]

Escalating tensions

As the war dragged on, the escalation of social strains had varying implications in regards to the union movement as well as to concessions won. In particular, the 1916 implementation of conscription galvanised sections of the labour movement as it became obvious that many were prospering while soldiers and their dependents suffered.[51] In a society predicated upon the central importance of fairness, the argument that wealth ought to be conscripted as well as citizens had considerable force.[52] While the big West Coast branches of the CMF talked of forcing the government to repeal conscription by striking – a policy Dowgray, now president of the UFL, strongly opposed – others saw different ways of exploiting the issue. Thwarted from challenging the 'boss class' and its political puppets on conscription, at least in New Zealand, many branches ramped up their campaign to abolish the contract system and obtain a 20 per cent pay increase.[53] Full employment had handed the initiative to the miners.

Meanwhile 'Big Jim' Roberts, long an advocate of 'One Big Union', the rallying cry of revolutionary industrial unionists around the world, spent the first six months of 1916 organising 5,000 wharfies in eighteen ports into an effective Waterside Workers' Federation. In May he approached other transport unions to establish a Transport Workers' Advisory Board, with a view to establishing a more tightly knit Transport Workers' Federation with a potential membership of 30,000. In June, delegates from the wharfies', drivers' and tramway unions sent delegates to a conference, which agreed to his proposal. To everyone's surprise two unions of state employees, the ASRS and the Locomotive Engine-drivers, Firemen's and Cleaners' Association, also sent delegates.[54] The conference also elected Roberts as the Board's secretary. The Seamen, although invited, did not send delegates. The UFL, although not invited, tried to muscle in, without success.[55]

The UFL had its own fish to fry, of course. Despite the CMF's decision to disaffiliate, following the success of its first anti-conscription conference the UFL's executive decided that the time had come to form a new political organisation to lead the charge.[56] Thanks to Harry Holland's diagnosis of the situation – he thought capitalism on the verge of collapse – a surprising consensus had formed in favour of political action.[57] The SDP, unable to attract union affiliates, or even get unionists to attend branch meetings outside of Christchurch, was also keen to seek a wider unity.[58] The UFL took the initiative and Dowgray chaired the meeting. All present in Easter 1916 agreed that the new organisation should be named the New Zealand Labour Party and that all unions and any branches of the SDP could affiliate through their local Labour Representation Committees. The new party's objective was 'The socialization of the means of production, distribution and exchange', the Second Socialist International's definition of socialism.[59] In the following week the conferences of the SDP and the UFL, both meeting in Wellington, approved all decisions. In adopting the socialist objective, the two conferences created a new and irreducible test of ideological position, a great psychological barrier between even the most radical Liberal and Labour's most moderate supporters. It also signalled the vast shift in the meaning of 'moderate' that had occurred since around 1905, with those who disliked the shift drifting away from the labour movement. In the elections of 1919 and 1922 several such men ran as independent labour candidates.[60]

Late in 1916 a series of events saw tensions escalate, unifying the union movement as never before and providing the fledgling Labour Party with its first triumphs. The growing sense that the war might end in stalemate, together with interminable casualty lists, helped sustain and diffuse those tensions. First, in November the Arbitration Court's niggardly award for the Drivers' Federation sparked a wave of industrial action that continued through the summer. The coal miners and the transport workers had begun secretly planning a general strike to achieve various industrial goals and repeal of conscription, but when that fell through, the miners implemented a go slow in the hope of extracting still further concessions from their employers. When that did not work, they resorted to illegal wild-cat strikes. Holt notes that before long, trouble also flared on the traditional hot spot of the Wellington waterfront and soon spread to other ports, notably Wanganui, Gisborne and Napier: 'A series of other issues soon emerged . . . and kept the ports of the lower North Island in a state of turmoil for several weeks.'[61]

The government inflamed the tensions by implementing conscription, holding the first ballot in November 1916. This, together with the defeat of the conscription referendum in Australia, reignited opposition.[62] Following another Open Conference of all unions in January 1917 to discuss how best to oppose conscription, convened by the UFL and chaired by Dowgray, the acting prime minister, James Allen, responded by authorising the arrest of several leading anti-conscriptionists, including several union leaders.[63] With the May 1917 arrest of Paddy Webb, the Labour MP for Grey, for (finally) opposing conscription, the government entrenched the longstanding conflict. When Semple was released in October, he launched a barnstorming tour of the coalfields, attacking, with all his now legendary wit and flair, the fact that Labour's leaders had been imprisoned without trial, unlike murderers and 'sexual perverts'. As ever, he was a smash hit.[64]

In terms of concessions, 1917 was a great year for organised labour. Labour shortages and the strategic importance of industrial peace continued to strengthen the bargaining position of organised workers. Rising living costs and the evidence that some were profiting from the war fuelled discontent.[65] While harrassing the labour movement's leaders the government also proved willing to force concessions to maintain harmony. Terrified by the prospect that the CMF and the WWF might ally and call a general strike, the government forced employers to concede a substantial pay increase to the miners and massive concessions to the wharfies, including penal rates for working in wet weather. Late in 1917 the Wellington Seamen struck, holding up coastal shipping for over six weeks; they refused to go before the Arbitration Court, and successfully insisted on direct negotiations with their employers.[66] The newly formed Public Service Association, together with many other unions, began establishing co-operatives (a device to restrain prices by eliminating the middle man).[67] Indeed, the government increasingly found itself more directly operating in a brokering role: 'Whether it was threatening strikers with prosecution, offering to arrange conferences between the parties, setting up special tribunals to settle disputes, or acting as an arbiter itself, cabinet found itself playing the role of industrial mediator, or adjudicator, or both.'[68] In the process it greatly weakened the authority of the Arbitration Court and legitimised the tactics of direct action and collective bargaining, while alienating almost everyone.

In 1917, anomalies generated by the implementation of conscription began to accumulate. In particular, the way in which the nine Military Service Boards interpreted one of the three criteria for exemption – the essential nature of one's work to the war effort – rapidly diverged.[69] All agreed that certain work was essential, but no consensus existed as to which specific industries or skills were essential. To address these issues and identify whether less skilled or even women workers might be substituted, the government established an Essential Industries Board and a National Efficiency Board. Allen and Massey refused to accept most of the Efficiency Board's recommendations, on the grounds that they would prove unacceptable to the unions, and upset their supporters by including among the essential occupations those reknowned for militancy: coal miners, shearers, railwaymen, sailors and slaughtermen.[70] It was not only conservative opinion that was outraged.

Paradoxically, success in gaining concessions and the inability to compel the government to repeal conscription threatened to erode the movement's momentum. The coal miners, who struck against conscription in 1917 and won a pay increase for their pains, began to focus on workplace issues.[71] Some other unionists became openly critical of the coal miners' sectional greed.[72] Other issues divided organised labour. 'White New Zealand' – an idea (borrowed from Australia) to exclude all non-whites from the country – sparked the most protracted and bitter debate at the UFL's 1917 conference. Although the revolutionaries carried the day, many were ambivalent and quite a few remained passionately committed to 'White New Zealand'.[73] More or less at the same time, the Labour Party, more akin to a 'millenarian cult' than a mass movement, almost tore itself apart over the 'Liquor Question' (prohibition being one of the most contentious issues of the era).[74] Most unionists regretted these divisions and awaited an issue that would unite them.

Oddly enough the government obliged. The Efficiency Board had recommended industrial conscription, but Massey and Ward refused. In early 1918, as the German counter-offensive on the Western Front appeared triumphant, government approved insertion of a clause in the Finance Act authorising it to direct the placement of all labour. Short of a military disaster, it had no intention of using this measure, but few unionists trusted the government, let alone Massey.[75] Auckland's most prominent champion of One Big Union and long that city's best-known revolutionary socialist, M.J. (Joe) Savage, quickly grabbed the issue.[76] He urged the UFL to damn the proposal but then agreed that the issue would best be addressed by the UFL's 1918 Open Conference (scheduled to meet immediately after the UFL's own annual conference). Savage, speaking for 50 Auckland unions, called for the complete rejection of industrial conscription and the introduction of public ownership (with the unions entrusted with management).[77] Scarcely a unionist in the country did not dislike and fear the idea of industrial conscription.[78] A well-attended meeting of the Hillside Branch of the ASRS, not known for radicalism let alone militancy, unanimously condemned industrial conscription 'for the benefit of private enterprise and profit'.[79] Although the matter requires more study, it may well be that the increased level of industrial conflict in late 1917 and 1918 reflected not only growing impatience with the failure to effectively address 'profiteering', but also a widespread conviction that industrial conscription would be the final straw.

At this point the UFL, long dismissed by militants and revolutionaries as weak and ineffectual, again rose to the challenge. Where many erstwhile revolutionary industrial unionists had retreated into a narrow sectionalism, looking after their own interests and ignoring the larger movement's interests, the UFL not only kept advocating for the larger labour movement but provided a forum for debating issues and forging a measure of common purpose, if not unity. Although the evidence is scanty, key figures in the UFL facilitated a new unity among the activists by adopting Guild Socialism, a distinctively English ideology which integrated industrial unionism, worker control of industry through guilds, and socialist political action.[80] The Dunedin gunsmith who had become a pivotal figure in brokering unity in Dunedin, Arthur McCarthy, appears to have been among the first to recognise Guild Socialism's potential as a coping stone for unity.[81] Even a well-known enemy of revolutionary socialism and industrial militancy, Dunedin's J.T. Paul, found in the new ideology a new basis for unity, and as the Labour Party's first president he proved invaluable.[82] In the main towns the rapid growth of the Workers' Educational Association (WEA) provided a forum where activists of various persuasions could meet and seriously debate the most complex issues of theory.[83] As Holland had foretold, the cost of conscription and war became so clear during 1918 that three firebrands of the old Red Federation – Holland, Fraser and Semple – won by-elections.[84] Holland told the House: 'We come proclaiming boldly . . . the Socialist objective of the labour movement throughout New Zealand; and we make no secret of the fact that we seek to rebuild society on a basis in which work and not wealth will be the measure of a man's worth'.[85]

Conclusion

Full employment and the government's fear of industrial unrest provided a secure foundation for a resurgent unionism during the war. From 1914 until 1919, union membership grew by more than 20 per cent until there were over 80,000 workers in unions registered under the Arbitration Act, perhaps another 30,000 registered under the Trade Union Act, almost 10,000 in the ASRS, and around 11,000 more in the Locomotive Engineers, Firemen and Cleaners' Association and the Post and Telegraph Employees' Association.[86] Although the proportion of the workforce in unions does not seem to have grown much, given the tens of thousands of pre-war union members who joined the army, this growth in absolute numbers of union members suggests that some non-unionised sections of the pre-war workforce came to accept the legitimacy of unions in protecting the interests of the workers. As the soldiers came home, union membership jumped by over 18 per cent.[87]

In January 1919 the UFL, conscious of the urgent need to bring the various federations of craft unions and the new syndicalist federations together, convened yet another of its invaluable conferences. The UFL's leaders had lost all confidence in the ideological legitimacy of the UFL's local and craft-based structure, however. Across the Western world progressive unions had adopted industrial unionism on a national basis. The success of the Bolsheviks in Russia in October 1917, and the wave of revolutions and strikes in Europe, not to mention a tsunami of industrial unrest in Australia and North America, discredited all but aggressively militant strategies and modes of organisation. Marxist study groups sprouted like mushrooms, especially on the West Coast. In Wellington, something of an ideological clearing house for the entire labour movement in 1917–1918, a new consensus emerged on the far left which eventually helped form the Communist Party.[88]

The delegates to the UFL's 1919 conference agreed to a new constitution for a new organisation, the National Industrial Alliance of Labour, predicated on the belief that all workers ought to organise themselves along industrial lines. The Transport Workers' Advisory Board, now supported by the Seamen and the CMF, also formed a new organisation named the New Zealand Alliance of Labour. Only national unions organised industrially could affiliate. The Alliance of Labour, led by firebrands like Jim Roberts and Arthur Cook, spearheaded a ripple of industrial unrest.[89] The so-called craft federations did not die, however. In 1920 the UFL met for the last time and terminated its own existence, recommending that its District Councils 'endeavour to get unions affiliated to organise industrially and nationally, so that they may become affiliated with the Alliance of Labour'.[90]

The willingness of the UFL's executive to subscribe to the rhetorical fiction and abdicate in favour of those who had assumed the right to lead the workers to the promised land ought not to obscure the substantial progress made by many of its affiliates. Indeed in some towns – Dunedin being the best documented – the various ideological factions had worked together to create a Central Labour Council, organised along industrial lines, which had enjoyed several notable successes. Despite ongoing recriminations among activists about the Council's decision to oppose conscription, in 1917–1919 the unions had grabbed their opportunities and achieved dramatic gains in membership.[91] At the national level these gains were also remarkable. Between 1915 and 1918 the membership of unions registered under the Arbitration Act increased by a mere 5.6 per cent, but in 1918–20 growth was explosive, at almost 35 per cent. Although this phenomenon has not received the attention it deserves, there can be little doubt that the war had heightened class feeling among many, and legitimised the role of unions and the Labour Party's campaign for a more fair society, while consolidating faith in democratic processes.

What the war had meant to workers, and union members in particular, had in large measure been determined by their pre-war experiences. Apart from opponents of the war, too scared or prudent to speak their minds, who constantly sought means to compel the government to repeal conscription, the great majority of workers and unions were unconditional in their support. However, they remained vigilant against exploitation. As far as we can tell, unions, backed by government, successfully resisted 'dilution'; they also established their right to be compensated for increases in the cost of living (which the government finally acknowledged in November 1918 by arming the Arbitration Court with the power to 'amend awards and agreements during their currency'); and full employment helped entrench these expectations among all workers, including the so-called unskilled in casual occupations.[92] As workers sensed victory in Europe, they clearly prepared to demand recompense for their war-time sacrifices.

The heady excitement born of the peace also saw the dream of creating a trans-Tasman, or even a trans-Pacific, organisation flourish.[93] It was not to be. Indeed most of the gains made by unions during the war became a battlefield as employers set out to claw back what they could, aided now by the return of unemployment. The employers were in for a battle, however, for full employment, no less than the government's willingness to make concessions in order to avoid conflict, had legitimised a new level of expectations, especially among the unskilled. Although the leaders of the country's unions found their power considerably less than they had enjoyed during the war, the rank and file had now mastered the techniques of industrial guerrilla warfare: reducing production, or threatening to; working to rule; taking seemingly impromptu industrial action, known as a stop-work meeting or a wildcat strike; and practises peculiar to particular industries, such as 'spelling' on the wharves. In some industries, almost certainly, a few die-hard revolutionaries practised tactical sabotage, known among insiders as 'wooden shoe philosophy'.[94] Often the employer had no idea who to blame. The wildcat strike became as common on the wharves as the 'go slow' was in the mines. The stop-work meeting became ubiquitous. The enforcers were hard men, usually pugilists. The unions no longer indicated their displeasure with arbitration by the formal and legal means of deregistering, as in the Red Fed years, but instead simply ignored the law and took industrial action in defiance of it.[95] E.J.B. Allen's text for industrial guerrilla warfare even armed non-unionised men with the techniques for controlling the job at the point of production. A new era, characterised by unprecedented levels of industrial conflict, at least for New Zealand, had dawned.

1. Calling for peace: a Society of Friends conference held over Easter 1914 adopts the motion that compulsory military training is an unjust encroachment 'on the liberties that are our Christian Heritage'. *Auckland Weekly News*, 23 April 1914, p.40.

2. Training for war: the Taranaki Rifles, commanded by William Malone, engage in field exercises in 1913. Malone Family Collection.

3. Going to war: a Wellington crowd gathers outside the Parliamentary Library to hear the announcement of a state of war between Germany and the British Empire. *Auckland Weekly News*, 13 August 1914, pp.46–47.

4. The war effort saw everyday settings become sites of mobilisation: an address to the New Zealand Engineering and Tunnelling Company from the Minister of Defence, James Allen, at the front of Auckland's Town Hall. Top: ATL, 1/1-008196-G. Bottom: *Auckland Weekly News*, 23 December 1915, pp.42–43.

5. Dunedinites listen to speeches delivered by civic leaders in the Queen's Gardens. *Otago Witness*, 24 February 1915, p.43.

6. The eighth reinforcement draft assembles at Lyttelton. *Auckland Weekly News*, 25 November 1915, p.38.

7. War infrastructure: Trentham Camp seen from the western hills. Besides the dormitories (aligned in neat rows in the centre of the picture), a Salvation Army institute and a saloon (in the upper right section of the camp) can be seen. From the left the three rifle ranges (in the foothills above the camp) are Collins Range, Somerville Range and Seddon Range. Thousands of recruits passed through the camp over the course of the war. Defence of NZ Study Group Collection.

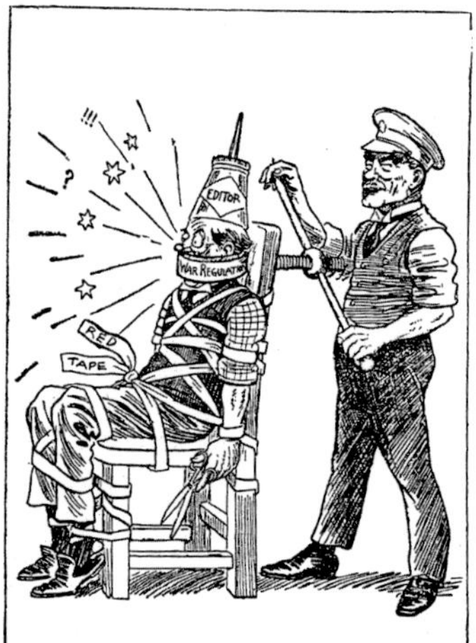

PUTTING ON THE SCREW

MORE AGONY FOR EDITORS.

Several New Zealand papers have been prosecuted for breaches of the War Regulations, and more prosecutions are in prospect. On top of this additional Regulations have been gazetted, which are of a particularly stringent nature. The lot of the poor editor is now a far from happy one.

Chairman of Appeal Board: You say that females have been tried as shepherdesses and proved a failure? Name a case.

Farmer: Little Bo-Peep.

8. War administration, such as the Military Service Boards (which heard exemption appeals) and censorship regulations, attracted various social commentary and critiques. Left: *Truth*, 7 April 1917, p.1. Right: *New Zealand Observer*, 24 August 1918, p.16.

9. Glimpses of enlistment bureaucracy showing reservist details being checked; the records room; ballots being loaded; and the Government Statistician (Malcolm Fraser) drawing a marble from the ballot box. *Auckland Weekly News*, 25 July 1918, p.39.

10. Two recruits at Featherston Camp. Military recruitment resulted in extensive surveying and documenting of the population. The man on the right is 6 ft, 8 in and weighs 95 kg. His companion is 4 ft, 11 in and weighs 44 kg. *Auckland Weekly News*, 6 December 1917, p.36.

11. Maori recruits 'at ease' at Narrow Neck Camp. *Auckland Weekly News*, 23 September 1915, p.47.

12. A Wellington troopship departure, illustrating the tradition of splitting streamers between those parting ways. In some cases, torn streamers formed souvenirs symbolising the hope of reunion. ATL, G-152620-1/2, Samuel Heath Head Collection, Alexander Turnbull Library.

13. Denis Malone's drawings, mailed to his father, who was killed in action at Gallipoli in August 1915. Malone Family Collection.

14. A Wellington crowd gathers at the corner of Willis and Mercer streets to watch the posting of the election results. *Auckland Weekly News*, 17 December 1914, p.40.

15. Seventy-five of the eighty parliamentarians elected in the 1914 election. The war years saw William Massey and Sir Joseph Ward (the two oval portraits) head a coalition government, several parliamentarians enlist (many more had sons in uniform) and Paddy Webb (top right) arrested and jailed for refusing military service. *Otago Witness*, 16 December 1914, pp.38–39.

16. Reporters of the news: a Christchurch street gathering contemplates the latest war news. ATL, 1/1-008414-G.

17. Presenters of the news: *Truth*'s depiction of the Kaiserschlacht. *Truth*, 6 April 1918, p.1.

18. Labour meetings in Dunedin's Triangle during the 1913 Great Strike and at the outbreak of the Great War. In early August 1914, the President of the Social Democratic Party observed: 'some little time ago there was trouble in this country . . . At that time my feeling was "My class right or wrong." This time . . . it is "My country right or wrong."' Top: *Auckland Weekly News*, 20 November 1913, p.50. Bottom: *Auckland Weekly News*, 20 August 1914, p.41.

19. The organising committee of a Dannevirke patriotic demonstration in which local Maori expressed 'their loyalty to the King'. A description of the demonstration read: 'Stalwart natives, clad with mats and with faces highly tattooed, preceded a lorry decked with ferns and national emblems, in which the wahines of the district in native attire were pleasingly grouped.' *Auckland Weekly News*, 20 August 1914, p.48.

20. Faces of charity: Gore's Queen Carnival fuses pageantry and fund-raising; wounded soldiers in a hat-trimming contest at Wellington's 'Gallipoli Day'; the Otago/Southland Red Cross headquarters organising skilled labour and practical efforts. Top: *Otago Witness*, 3 November 1915, p.36. Middle: *Auckland Weekly News*, 9 December 1915, p.36. Bottom: *Otago Witness*, 1 March 1916, p.41.

21. Like other major denominations, the Salvation Army took up a range of wartime activities, presenting them as applications of Christian teachings. *War Cry*, 18 September 1915, p.8.

22. Numerous businesses exploited war consciousness and identified a range of goods and services with the war. Left: *New Zealand Free Lance*, 18 January 1918, p.5. Right: *Thames Star*, 12 June 1916, p.3. Bottom: *Opinions on the War* (Auckland: George Hunt & Co., 1915), p.19.

23. School as a site of war work: Auckland children knit comforts for soldiers and for Belgium. *Auckland Weekly News*, 15 July 1915, p.37.

24. School as a site of war training: children of Richmond School undertaking cadet training, which became compulsory under the 1909 defence reforms. Defence of NZ Study Group Collection.

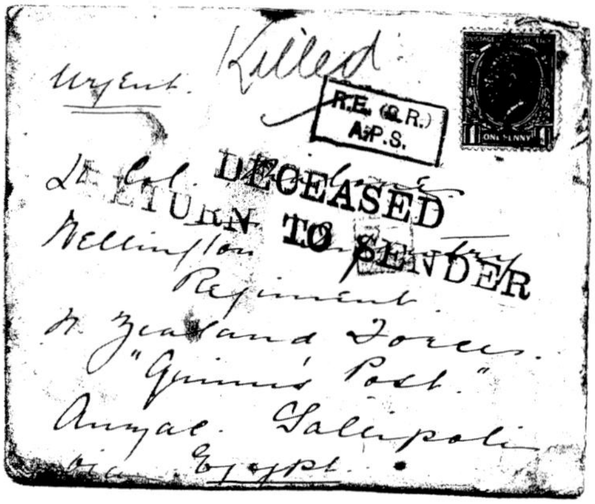

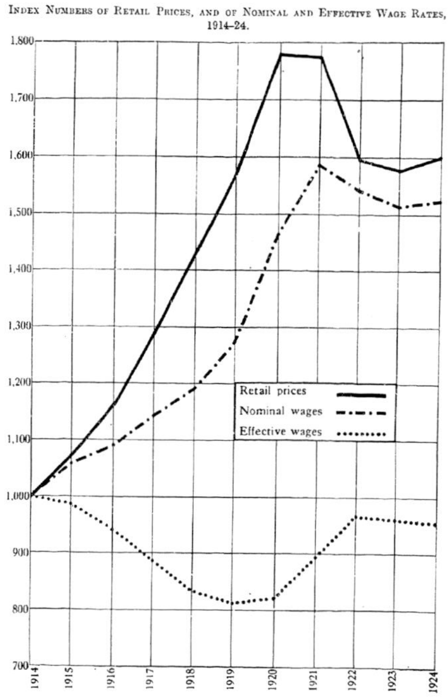

25. Sustaining the war effort inherently entailed sacrifice and strains on social stability. Men were removed, temporarily and permanently, from family, communal and economic structures, and the wartime economy saw a general decline in purchasing power. Above: Malone Family Collection. Right: *New Zealand Official Year-book*, 1926, p.753.

26. New Zealand society also showed a remarkable capacity to rally and endure in response to loss. A Christchurch crowd gathers in Cranmer Square on the first anniversary of the Gallipoli landings. *Auckland Weekly News*, 4 May 1916, p.35.

27. Sport presented as a preparation for war. *The Carnival Book: Cartoons and Sketches of the Queen Carnival, the Taking of Samoa and the Dardanelles* (Wellington, 1915), p.36.

28. Sport presented as a distraction from war. *Otago Witness*, 24 March 1915, p.42.

The Hope of His Side!

Though much has been made of the fact that under the Conscription Act every eligible man must take his chance at the ballot, so many callings are to be exempted that Conscription in New Zealand seems a misnomer. If many more stalwart tradesmen are exempted the country will have to depend on its sedentary pen-pushers, who, apparently, are about the only people not deemed indispensable.

Sing a song of conscripts
  Standing in a line,
When out rolled their marbles
  Wasn't there a shine!
Till the politicians,
  Quaking in their shoes,
Handed each a label
  Bearing better news.

Sing a song of "exempts"
  Smiling in a row,
At a little clerk bloke
  Who will have to go.
By Nature ne'er intended
  To do a fighting stunt,
As no one fears or wants him
  His place is at the front!

ROUND UP THE UNMARRIED SHIRKERS!

29. Differing conceptions of who was bearing, and shirking, the burdens of the war. Top left: *New Zealand Observer*, 18 December 1915, p.12. Middle left: *New Zealand Free Lance*, 18 May 1917, p.3. Top right: *Truth*, 9 December 1916, p.1. Bottom: *Maoriland Worker*, 25 August 1915, p.1.

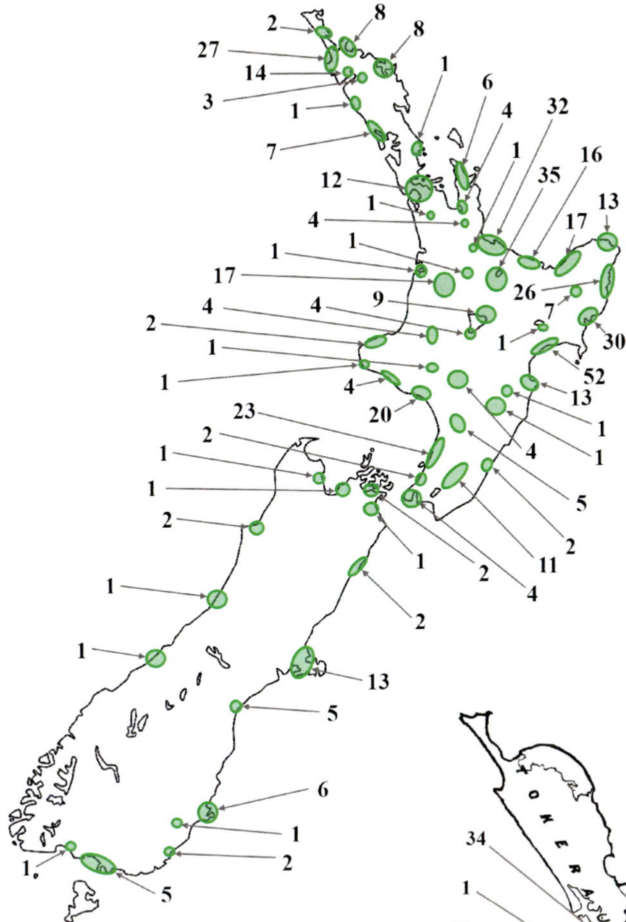

30. In September 1914, recruiting for the Maori Contingent began and saw enthusiastic volunteering from some of the Maori population. The approximate origins of 501 volunteers for the 515 ranks of the First Maori Contingent are displayed.

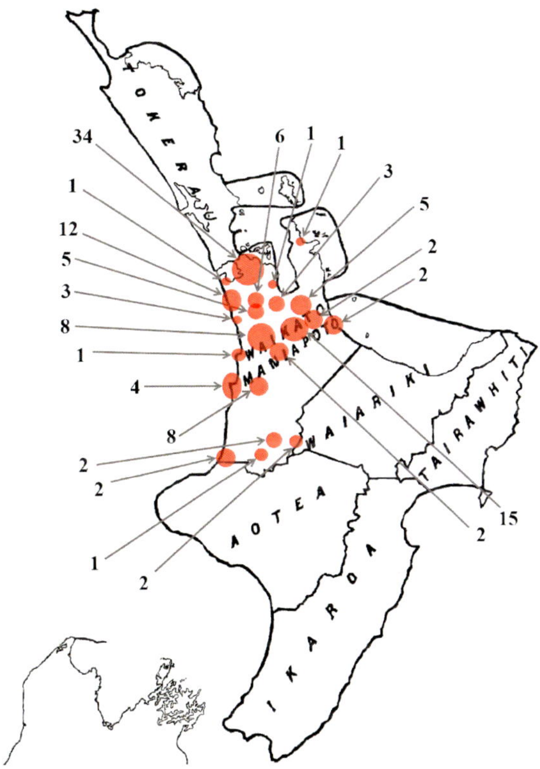

31. Conscription was extended to Maori in mid-1917, and in 1918 it was applied to the Waikato Maniapoto district; 552 Maori men were balloted by the end of the war. The approximate locations of those listed as defaulters in 1919 are marked.

"PEACE AT ANY PRICE."

The Freedom League Appeal Against Their Anti-recruiting Pamphlet Conviction.

32. The *New Zealand Observer* caricatures Egerton Gill and the Freedom League during court proceedings over what the editor regarded as their 'dissemination of poisonous twaddle'. *New Zealand Observer*, 29 April 1916, p.12.

Social Democratic Party

PEACE MANIFESTO

Two years ago Europe was plunged into War. The events which immediately preceded the outbreak would have been too trivial to produce such a gigantic catastrophe if the conditions favourable to war had not been in existence.

An examination of the Diplomatic Policies of the various European Powers, of the operations of the Balance of Power Policy, of the intrigues of the various national groups of capitalists, of concession hunters, of Armament Rings, inevitably brings the conclusion that, unless the policies of the nations had been altered considerably, warfare on a gigantic scale was inevitable sooner or later; and that the murder of the Austrian Heir Apparent, the tearing up of treaties, etc., were but the sparks which set the world ablaze. The material for the conflagration—clashing economic interests, and the suspicion, jealousy, and militarism engendered by such—were already on hand piled up. Alone among the peoples, the Socialists of the world realised this. They tried to point it out and to rouse the workers of all countries so that war could be rendered impossible. Before they could succeed the floodgates of bloodshed were opened and there was no time or opportunity for reason to be heard.

For two years War has raged. Millions of lives have been sacrificed. Millions of pounds have been wasted. Devastation, Disease, Death have swept over immense areas, and wrecked homes, ruined lives, maimed men, widows and orphans, misery, unhappiness, tears and distress have been its bitter fruits. Liberty of speech, thought, liberty of the most elementary kind, has been trampled underfoot, and Military Autocracy and despotism has acquired a new lease of life in every country involved in the struggle.

The War has settled nothing. It will settle nothing. Negotiations for Peace must take place sooner or later. Why not now?

Women's International League

NEW ZEALAND

OBJECTS:

To ensure that in future National differences shall be settled by some other means than war.

To demand that women shall have a direct voice in the affairs of the nation.

OUR HOPE—Universal Peace with Justice.

OUR AIM—To elevate and cement Sisterhood.

OUR EFFORT—To serve and uplift Humanity.

DO YOU WISH to win the war?
your country to be the land of freedom?
to avoid the national disgrace of national bankruptcy?
permanent peace in the future?
continued social progress?

THEN MAKE WAR ON CONSCRIPTION: and do not be misled by National Service agitators, fanatical militarists, or hypocritical Armament and Military Supplies profiteers.

Join the FREEDOM LEAGUE.

M. C. Irvine, M.A.
President,
Auckland Freedom League.

Secretary:
Egerton Gill,
16 Wyndham St,
Auckland.

Reliance Printery, 161, Albert Street.

LABOR'S PLIGHT

If the Massey-Ward Bill Succeeds

33. Pacifist, feminist, socialist and anti-militarist counter-mobilisations challenged the war effort's legitimacy, conduct and cause. Top left: Social Democratic Party, Peace Manifesto (Wellington, 1916). Top right: *Maoriland Worker*, 13 December 1916, p.12. Bottom left: Mazire Cheyne Irvine, Conscription (Auckland, 1916). Bottom right: *Maoriland Worker*, 7 June 1916, p.1.

34. Mobilisations against internal elements: In 1917 the Women's Anti-German League resolved to 'eliminate all traces of enemy interests from our social, political and economic life.' This copy of the resolution was posted to the Attorney-General, A.L. Herdman. [AAAB 478 12/ac] Archives New Zealand, The Department of Internal Affairs Te Tari Taiwhenua.

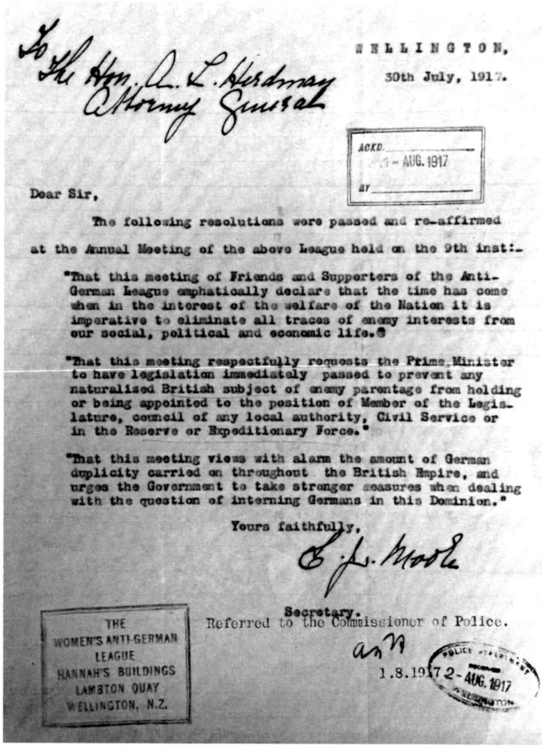

To The Hon. A. L. Herdman Attorney General

WELLINGTON,
30th July, 1917.

ACKD. 1 - AUG. 1917
BY

Dear Sir,

The following resolutions were passed and re-affirmed at the Annual Meeting of the above League held on the 9th inst:-

"That this meeting of Friends and Supporters of the Anti-German League emphatically declare that the time has come when in the interest of the welfare of the Nation it is imperative to eliminate all traces of enemy interests from our social, political and economic life."

"That this meeting respectfully requests the Prime Minister to have legislation immediately passed to prevent any naturalised British subject of enemy parentage from holding or being appointed to the position of Member of the Legislature, council of any local authority, Civil Service or in the Reserve or Expeditionary Force."

"That this meeting views with alarm the amount of German duplicity carried on throughout the British Empire, and urges the Government to take stronger measures when dealing with the question of interning Germans in this Dominion."

Yours faithfully,

E. J. Moore

Secretary.

THE WOMEN'S ANTI-GERMAN LEAGUE HANNAH'S BUILDINGS LAMBTON QUAY WELLINGTON, N.Z.

Referred to the Commissioner of Police.

1.8.1917

2 - AUG. 1917

35. The Protestant Political Association newsletter *The Nation* visualised a similar idea, with the Protestant vote cleansing the country of 'Wardism', 'Sinn Fein', 'anti-British' and 'pro-German' elements. *The Nation*, December 1919, p.1.

36. Friedrich Wohnsiedler's butchery in the aftermath of anti-German unrest over New Year's Eve 1914. The caption described this as 'Gisborne's adoption of "Kultur"'. *Auckland Weekly News*, 7 January 1915, p.50.

37. Enemy-aliens interned on Somes Island in Wellington Harbour. By the end of the war there were some 450 internees in New Zealand detention centres. ATL, 1/2-112282-F.

38. An armed police expeditionary party sent to arrest Rua Kenana at Maungapohatu. ATL, PA1-o-042-50-3.

39. An objector, Thomas Moynihan, undergoing forced drill at Wanganui Detention Barracks. Allegations of serious abuses at the barracks were raised in 1918. [AAYS 8638 738] Archives New Zealand, The Department of Internal Affairs Te Tari Taiwhenua.

40. Crowds celebrating the signing of the Armistice, at Princes Street and the Town Hall in Dunedin, and outside the Parliamentary Library in Wellington. Parades to honour the victory were held the following year as troops were repatriated. Top: *Otago Witness*, 13 November 1918, p.28; middle: *Otago Witness*, 20 November 1918, p.31. Bottom: *Auckland Weekly News*, 28 November 1918, p.45.

41. Sites of communal remembrance for parishioners, colleagues, Niue Islanders and ex-pupils. The 1920s and 1930s saw the building of more elaborate memorials and the entrenchment of remembrance rituals. Top left: *Auckland Weekly News*, 8 April 1920, p.32. Top right: *Otago Witness*, 11 November 1919, p.38. Bottom left: ATL, 6734. Bottom right: Defence of NZ Study Group Collection.

Chapter Nine

Economic Mobilisation: New Zealand Businesses and the Great War

Steven Loveridge and James Watson

The capacity to channel economic factors towards military ends has been identified as a major determinant in the course and outcome of the Great War.[1] Within New Zealand this economic mobilisation saw various businesses harness themselves to, and profit from, the massive economic and logistical challenges that the war effort represented. However, the war years also imposed a variety of destabilising strains and, in the words of one assessment, 'what is astonishing is not that some war economies broke down, but that others survived'.[2] Consequently the maintenance of effective mobilisation compelled increasingly systematic efforts to manage war production and to address wartime strains. This management inevitably entailed balancing competing demands from the business community and wider society that were often irreconcilable.[3] These dynamics mean that the relationship between business and the war effort can provide critical insight on the economic, political and social history of the war.

Within this chapter 'business' entails privately owned enterprises that were engaged in production, distribution or exchange. It therefore does not deal directly with the extensive activities of the state in those areas, through organisations like the Railways Department or the Post Office.[4] Privately owned enterprises varied in scale from large financial institutions, shipping companies and big sheep runs, down through substantial manufacturing enterprises and retail firms, to shops and farms operated by families or individuals.

New Zealand business towards 1914

In 1914 the New Zealand economy was largely modern, chiefly agricultural, semi-industrial and utterly reliant on the British market for its prosperity, and the coal, shipping, processing, handling, finance and marketing required to access it. These conditions reflected the revolutionary dynamics of late nineteenth-century capitalism, its innovations in production, transportation and communication, and the consequent expansion of global trade and mass markets it enabled.

Agriculture constituted the largest business sector, with sheep and cattle farming supporting extensive processing industries. Meat tended to be processed in large freezing works, often owned by businesses based in the United Kingdom that also had interests in other meat-producing countries. Conversely, almost all cheese and butter production took place in numerous small local factories that were mostly owned co-operatively by dairy suppliers. In drier areas of the country, principally in the South Island, large quantities of grain were grown in rotation with sheep. The most significant of these crops by value was wheat, which was almost entirely consumed within New Zealand. Yields varied considerably, partly due to variations in acreage sown as farmers estimated profitability, but mainly due to weather conditions.[5] Despite a high level of horse-drawn and steam-driven mechanisation, the labour involved in the cultivation and harvesting of grain was much greater than that in sheep farming, meaning that much more capital was invested into each crop.

Beyond the rural economy, the country's manufacturing and service sectors were developing; between 1877 and 1895 the number of new industries expanded by 260 per cent and capital investment doubled.[6] Sawmilling, gas works, grain milling, brewing and printing emerged as major manufacturing industries.[7] In 1910, more people were employed in the textile, clothing and footwear industries than in freezing works and dairy factories combined.[8]

Trans-oceanic trade was a crucial feature within the economic system; exploiting the modern capacity for mass transit, the fruits of pastoral and extraction enterprises were pumped into the world market while a range of industrial and consumer goods were sucked into the country.[9] A prime example of settler/dominion capitalism, this exchange was heavily entwined with Britain's global position as a hub of commercial and financial activity. One 1936 assessment asserted that 'the economic development of New Zealand may be regarded as part of the process of the industrialisation of Great Britain.'[10] By 1913 Britain was the destination of nearly 80 per cent of exports and the origin of 60 per cent of imports.[11]

The power dynamics of this economic edifice have formed a point of scholarly interest, with metropolitan capital, local business elements and the state nominated as nodes of influence. One influential interpretation has argued that dominion capitalism was dominated by 'a collaborating economic elite who clung to, and depended upon British power and British capital.'[12] Other accounts temper this, seeing a 'complex interplay of metropolitan and local forces'.[13] Certainly, the fact that these links were a major factor in New Zealand achieving a per capita GDP among the highest in the world indicates that internal operators were leveraging opportunities and prosperity from the structures of the British world.[14] One collective biography of the wealthy of Canterbury and Otago during the period towards 1914 notes them as originating from Britain's lower middle classes (64 per cent of farmers, 74 per cent of urban wealth-holders) and having made their fortunes in farming (50.9 per cent), trading and finance (13.5 per cent), the professions (9.7 per cent) or manufacturing (6.4 per cent).[15] A study of New Zealand's entrepreneurs through the period arrives at a similar conclusion and finds these businessmen as emerging from 'middle-class backgrounds, often where the father himself was an entrepreneur.'[16]

Consistent with their origins and attitudes, these men have been categorised as a fraction of the middle-class characterised by striving for self-advancement, strident work ethics and ongoing involvement in enterprise.[17] However, common origins and broadly shared values did not inevitably translate into lockstep solidarity, and sectional interests, such as those between rural producers and shipping interests, split the business community. Social/political issues like the prohibition debate further divided the community, as those advocating sober industry squared off against alcohol-related interests voicing their support for continuance. Neither were the values and attitudes of business detached from the wider social body. Indeed, they appear broadly in tune with a society in which prospects of economic and social advancement were cherished aspirations.[18]

While never constituting any manner of monopoly over a state swayed by competing interests and considerations, parts of the business community pursued political influence. For example, the Union Steam Ship Company – which by 1914 stood as the largest line in the southern hemisphere, the largest private-sector employer and the possessor of a monopoly over a crucial sector of the economy – is described as usually having 'the ear of government'.[19] Business associations were another avenue of influence, and many proved capable of effectively organising and lobbying, building political connections, and wielding influence and patronage.[20] For example, the Farmers' Union made a point of forwarding the resolutions of its annual conference to the Prime Minister and arguably incubated the Reform movement's advance into the parliamentary arena.[21] This interest was often returned. Prime Minister from 1906 to 1912 and Deputy Prime Minister from 1915 to 1918, Joseph Ward was a technocrat focussed on the business potential of new technologies, who argued that the state existed to support private enterprise.[22] Ward's chief political rival through this same period, William Massey, aka 'Farmer Bill', counted rural businesses among his closest political supporters. Legend has it that Massey entered politics when an invitation to stand for a seat was lifted, via a pitchfork, to his position atop a haystack.[23]

After the 1890s the business community's political and social positions reacted to rising populism, as landed wealth became a focus within political debate and sections of the labour movement centred on the capitalist caricature of 'Mr Fat' as a political antitype.[24] In response, the often liberal sensibilities (in the nineteenth-century sense) of the business community realigned towards a 'reinvented conservatism', advocating property rights, self-reliance and economic independence against socialism.[25] At times this went beyond talk. In 1912 the Employers' Federation established a defence fund 'to combat socialism, syndicalism and anarchy'.[26] In the face of the 1913 waterfront strike, the Federation pledged to keep the ports running, while the Farmers' Union organised rural men for service as police specials, aka 'Massey's Cossacks'.[27] Championing popular imperialism proved another aspect of this realignment, and the 1914 Farmers' Union annual conference, held in the final weeks of peace, discussed British naval supremacy as a critical factor in securing the sea lanes and thus New Zealand's economic livelihood.[28]

Observing such interests, one study has suggested that the financial links of business and empire distinguished and underwrote the 'pro-war' stance of an imperially engaged business elite.[29] Although the business community's emotional and intellectual responses to the war were, again, broadly in tune with wider society, some unique perspectives and engagements can certainly be identified. It did not take commerce long, for example, to brazenly associate everything – from clothing, photography and cigarettes, to chewing gum and toys – with the war. Supporters of protectionist policies argued that German economic power was the result of an exploitation of Britain's markets and concluded that only imperial protectionism could guarantee British power and victory.[30] Some manufacturers argued that war production offered an opportunity to broadcast the quality of local goods, and the president of the Wellington Provincial Industrial Association noted 'it may be that the war will teach a lesson even better than that taught by the holding of an exhibition.'[31]

The mobilisation of New Zealand's pastoral economy, processing industries and links with the global economic system offers a case study for the broader observation that Allied access to agrarian resources was decisive in a war that was of 'bread and potatoes' alongside 'steel and gold'.[32] These economic links also provide essential context for comprehending New Zealand's war effort. It has been noted that 'waging protracted industrial war required – one is tempted to say by definition – an established and well-articulated industrial base to supply huge quantities of essential military materials'.[33] Semi-industrial New Zealand was able to meet these requirements through its access to Britain's industrial base, in an exchange described as 'butter for guns'.[34]

Business prospects and constraints

The impact of the war on private business varied widely, depending on the sector of the economy that was involved and the region in which the enterprise was located. The outbreak of war was accompanied by a temporary paralysis in the centres of international trade, and the resulting economic uncertainty in New Zealand saw unemployment climb to the point that relief works were planned. Confidence recovered, however, as the containment of the German fleet and the rising demands of the British war effort underwrote trade stability and boosted production in numerous sectors. After mid-1915, demand for workers exceeded supply across most sectors.[35]

At the beginning of 1915, arrangements were secured for the British government to purchase the entirety of selected exports at fixed prices. In line with wartime market conditions the prices negotiated were much higher than those prevailing before the war. Frozen beef, mutton and lamb were included in this 'commandeer' system from March 1915 and other major goods were added over the war: cheese from November 1915, wool from November 1916 and butter from November 1917.[36] Considerable quantities of scheelite (tungsten ore), Glaxo (a milk powder product), canned rabbits, hides and skins were also purchased.[37] As well as building on New Zealand's established links with the British market, the commandeer was sensitive to existing business interests, with details arranged in conferences between Prime Minister Massey and representatives from the shipping industry, the freezing companies and the Board of Agriculture.[38]

These arrangements provided vital stability to the New Zealand economy and boosted associated businesses. Ten new freezing works, twenty new cheese factories and three new Glaxo factories opened between March 1915 and June 1917, and rural business enjoyed substantial increases in profits.[39] By the end of the war, the commandeer had earned New Zealand £96 million and by the time the system was terminated in 1921, earnings had risen to £160 million (respectively $981 million and $14 billion in 2015 dollars).[40] These arrangements give context to the £2 million rise in bank deposits over withdrawals in 1915 and the rise in deposits from £25.2 to £37.4 million over the war.[41] One marker of this prosperity was the expansion of rural vehicle ownership, and the motor industry was one of the rare industries in which importing seems to have expanded during the war. In 1918 Herbert Watson of Palmerston North disdainfully remarked that '[e]very little dairy farmer now has his car & although bad petrol is at 4/- the gallon they all do plenty of driving'.[42]

Beyond the rural sector, many manufacturers experienced comparable booms as government spending boosted demand. Woollen mills, clothing factories, bootmakers and tanneries were the notable beneficiaries of these orders and could experience significant growth in their share prices.[43] For example, between August 1914 and 30 June 1915, the firms of Abraham Levy, Sargood Son & Ewen, and Messrs Ross & Glendining secured contracts for uniform and kit items totalling near £75,000, £26,000 and £14,000 respectively ($10 million, $3.7 million and $2 million in 2015 dollars).[44] By 1916 an average of 2,500 recruits a month were being supplied with kit costing nearly £21 per man, and war-related expenses were estimated at nearly £1 million a month ($133 million in 2015 dollars).[45] Shipping, too, experienced 'extraordinary high profits' and between 1914 and 1917, investors in the Union Steam Ship Company saw their shares increase in value by 140 per cent.[46]

Government investment in war-related infrastructure brought further business prospects, and the decision to centralise troop training in the southern North Island had immense economic effects for Wellington and parts of its hinterland.[47] The Wairarapa, already benefiting from high prices for exports, enjoyed an economic boom after the establishment of military camps in the region. Several hundred men were employed for months in the construction of Featherston Camp and this workforce peaked at over a thousand in December 1915.[48] On completion, the main Featherston Camp and the adjacent Canvas Camp held up to 7,500 men, while nearby Tauherenikau could take 3,000 and Papawai, near Greytown, a further 500.[49] As Neil Frances notes, Featherston Camp represented by far the largest town in the Wairarapa.[50] This new population created massive demands for supplies and proved capable of devouring enough food to feed armies: in February 1916, Featherston was noted as requiring over 400,000 kilograms of meat and 150,000 litres of fresh milk every four months.[51] While a camp bakery was opened in August 1916 and the canteen was run by the military from November 1917, provisions were typically purchased from local businesses.[52] Wellington represented the nearest large centre for many of these demands and a number of businesses established branches at Trentham and Featherston to take advantage of soldiers' spending.

Both soaring exports and state borrowing (government debt doubled to £201 million – $20 billion in 2015 dollars – over the war) resulted in increased activity for the financial sector, and the Bank of New Zealand augmented its reserves.[53] However, these increases were under or around the rise in the cost of living, and the value of Bank of New Zealand shares grew at a much smaller rate than that of the shipping companies or even the woollen mills, rising by only about a quarter.[54] Some insurance companies appear to have done considerably better. South British Insurance saw a rise of about 63 per cent between the beginning of 1914 and October 1918, while New Zealand Insurance shares did better still, rising from 114 shillings to 214 shillings, or almost 88 per cent, between January 1914 and October 1918.[55]

However, the relationship between the war and business was riddled with complexities, with prospects and constraints standing side by side. The other side of the war economy's high demands was a deprioritising of civilian goods. Partially reflecting the strains on small retailers, enlistments and the shift to war-essential industries, the number of workplaces, which had grown every year since records began in the early 1890s, declined over 1915–1919.[56] Strains on shipping saw imported goods become more expensive and scarce, eroding importer prospects. While wartime circumstances benefited Wellington's economy, other regions were less fortunate. The disappearance of overseas markets for the kauri-gum industry, for example, adversely affected North Auckland. Similarly, a winding down of public works had a disproportionately negative impact on areas at the developmental frontier, compounded by the enlistment of the young, single men who predominated in such areas.

The experiences of particular businesses convey the disinvestment and belt-tightening experienced alongside wartime booms. For example, national trends of declining household formation and (with the great exception of Wellington) stagnating rental markets, saw a downturn in construction, which partly explains a very serious post-war housing shortage.[57] While no official construction statistics were compiled, between 1910–1911 and 1915–1916 the production of bricks declined by 23 per cent, planed timber by 26 per cent, and mouldings by a massive 63 per cent, and the numbers of men describing themselves as bricklayers or carpenters declined around 30 per cent.[58] Demands on labour, materials and capital also saw infrastructure projects increasingly shelved. In March 1917 the Auckland City Council's electricity engineer 'reported that he had continuously aimed at a reduction of extension work, and a great deal of it had been postponed until after the war'.[59] Lastly, the alcohol industry also dipped, although hotels within reach of the military camps experienced enhanced business. Demand was dampened by the departure of tens of thousands of men and the perceptions that liquor production and intoxication were inappropriate during wartime.[60] In 1917 the introduction of six o'clock closing saw the industry claim their sales had fallen by around a third.[61]

Social and economic strains

The relationship between business and war is also defined by the social and economic strains which wartime conditions and sustained mobilisation entailed, and the consequences this held for social cohesion. The experiences of some enterprises associated with enemy powers certainly attests to an altered business environment. War regulations suppressed trade and voided contracts with enemy powers, and New Zealand's relatively minor trade links with Germany (less than 2 per cent of the value of New Zealand's 1913 exports) withered to virtually nothing.[62] Beyond political regulation, certain public elements developed sensitive noses regarding enemy commerce, and suspect merchants were reported to Chambers of Commerce and the police.[63] Other, less civil, reactions included anti-German riots in which German businesses, and those suspected to be German, were vandalised and looted. In the aftermath of such riots in Wanganui, Hallenstein's Brothers took out advertising space to 'clear up any idea that the firm was a pro-German one.'[64] It was one of several companies to take such a step.[65]

However, public passions were not confined to those associated with enemy powers. Maintaining economic mobilisation entailed ongoing social and economic strains, with overtime hours stretched and more women, older men and children drawn into the workforce to compensate for labour shortages and crushing production schedules.[66] Wartime inflation drove up the cost of living and the first year of the war saw food bills for the average family rise by 16.5 per cent, only a little less than the increase over the previous twenty years.[67] At the end of the war the Government Statistician calculated that the food index had risen by 42 per cent between July 1914 and October 1918 in the four main centres, and that the weighted average for the whole dominion was only marginally lower.[68] Although wages also increased, many people experienced declining purchasing power.[69]

That these strains occurred while some were enjoying record profits generated friction, often along existing social divisions, and some of this discord became politicised. As with other belligerent nations, the image of the profiteer making money while others made sacrifices emerged as a core antitype.[70] Those newspapers appealing to socialism or left-wing populism, notably the *Maoriland Worker* and *Truth*, produced damning condemnations of 'Mr Fat', glutted with war profits.[71] Pre-war polemics attributing price rises to market manipulation by business rings intensified in condemnation of 'mutton magnates', 'wool kings', 'butter brigands' and 'beef barons'. In some cases protests saw the names and incomes of 'rich men made richer by the war' printed.[72] Likewise, radical Liberal MPs and their allies in the Labour grouping vocally condemned profiteering, with calls for the establishment of state-owned factories and the conscription of wealth.[73] A particularly curious rendition of this sense of an exploiting element betraying the greater good was Professor Bedford's argument that New Zealand's profiteering was bleeding Britain and making 'New Zealand the least patriotic part of the Empire.'[74]

Notions of profiteering and fair contributions played out within as well as against the business community. Indeed, the initial description of war-related profits as 'blood money' appears to have come from a prominent Manawatu farmer, Peter McHardy, who was one of several businessmen to adopt this terminology.[75] One response was generous sponsorship of war-related fund-raising and pledges to financially support or hold jobs for enlisted employees under notions of moral obligation. A Manawatu farmer, donating £1,000 ($145,000 in 2015 dollars) to Belgian relief, noted that 'the increased price of produce is, in my opinion, conscience money or ill-gotten gains.'[76] In some cases fortunes were donated: one landowner contributed £10,000 ($1.3 million in 2015 dollars) plus land to the Wounded Soldiers' Fund.[77]

Accusations of war profiteering also spurred parts of the business community to assert their contributions.[78] In an early-1916 Auckland town hall meeting, Alexander Herdman, the Attorney-General, was met with frequent applause when he proclaimed that British wealth and consequent ability to provide munitions and finance for the Allies was 'one of the chief reasons why Germany is not going to triumph.' This strength was, Herdman argued, the result of 'businessmen who had become wealthy through their energy, enterprise, and sound business principles . . . So that when a man talks about conscription of wealth, and the abolition of wealth, you should tell him he should be in Porirua [referring to a mental hospital].'[79] Likewise, in 1917, President Wilson of the Farmers' Union complained of 'biased writers' who 'flung contumely on the farmers for being unpatriotic; for not feeding the people with bread at less than cost price, and for asking a reasonable price for their produce.' He closed on the note that farmers deserved respect for their part in sustaining the Allies' armies and cause.[80] Besides the sense that businessmen should not be unfairly targeted and that their contributions should not be overlooked, this sensitivity likely reflected the deeply personal impacts of the war. In 1915 farmers were proportionally represented in enlistments and, as a speech to the 1915 New Zealand Farmers' Co-operative asserted, 'whatever might be said about farmers making money, those who had sons at the front would rather not make any money this year and have their sons back.'[81]

Go-slows, strikes and smouldering worker radicalism offered an outlet for this backlash. Thus the charge that profiteers represented a disloyal clique, which was outrageously exploiting the nation during its time of trial, was wielded against labour unrest. When the State Miners' Union threatened to greet the introduction of conscription with 'industrial revolt', the Greymouth Chamber of Commerce publicly denounced the 'enemy in our midst' as a 'nest of troublesome agitators who were being kept in occupation in the coal mines at great cost to the taxpayer'.[82] Employers' minutes in regard to waterfront disputes in 1917 reveal comparable attitudes, and the Employers' Federation Secretary recommended that disputing workers should be reduced to military pay and, if they refused work, imprisoned.[83]

Alongside these darkening antagonisms, protracted war placed crucial parts of the business world under increasing strains. Indeed, the profitability of many areas of farming faded considerably as production costs rose, tax burdens increased and labour shortages loomed (after November 1916 the rural workforce was depleted by nearly 18 per cent).[84] Taxation revenues expanded greatly (from £5.9 million in the year ending March 1914, to £13.8 million in the year ended March 1919 – $905 million to $1.3 billion in 2015 dollars) and many businesses reported record tax bills alongside record profits.[85] The Oamaru Woollen Factory Company, for example, paid £80 in taxes in 1913 and £6,707 in 1916 ($12,000 to $926,000 in 2015 dollars).[86] Some of these issues were becoming evident by the end of 1915, with the cost of placing produce in London having increased as much as 20 per cent in some cases, and many wheat growers struggled as grain prices dropped.[87] Furthermore, by 1917 many of the prices paid for requisitioned produce had fallen below market values. One calculation asserts that many farmers' real incomes declined past a 1915/1916 peak, with meat production slipping below the index of costs by 1918.[88]

Other crucial sectors experienced comparable dynamics. For example, responding to the stretched capacities of the country's textile mills to meet demands, an October 1915 conference saw arrangements made by which millers took on massive low-profit contracts and intense production schedules.[89] New Zealand's trade lifeline came under fire as Germany resumed unrestricted submarine warfare in February 1917. Among the ships lost were *Aotearoa*, *Aparima*, *Limerick*, *Roscommon*, *Waikawa*, *Waihemo* and *Waitemata*, while another, *Wairuna*, was claimed through the actions of the raider *Wolf*.[90] Access to the British market was further challenged as

British authorities increasingly favoured trans-Atlantic trade; a ship could return twice to Britain in the time it took to make one round trip on the Australasian route.[91] These strains in available shipping resulted in export stockpiles that threatened New Zealand's storage capacities and raised worries over financing, which was heavily dependent on clearing exports. Part of Massey's agenda at various imperial conferences was to secure sufficient shipping, and he made 'vigorous and emphatic representations to the controlling authorities at Home'.[92] Meanwhile the pre-war trend of ownership consolidation accelerated as a consequence of shipping interests buying up capital goods to avoid excess profit duties.[93] This led, in May 1917, to the British Peninsular and Oriental Steam Navigation Company taking over the Union Steamship Company.[94] Lastly, the coal supplies which fuelled this system were also threatened as shortages developed from 1916: 2,275,614 tons in 1914 fell to 2,068,419 in 1917 and 2,034,250 in 1918. This was the result of fewer miners – 4,734 employees in 1914 fell to 3,994 in 1918 – and growing unrest.[95]

Economic mobilisation and the state

As the scale and strains of the war effort expanded, the state took an increasingly systematic role in managing war production and mediating competing, sometimes irreconcilable, demands from business, labour and wider society. This work was typically guided by piecemeal responses, rather than any grand ideology, and built on the established concepts and apparatus of arbitration. Socialist theories and opposition status facilitated Labour MPs in calling for greater intervention. However, even Prime Minister Massey, who asserted that 'there were certain fixed economic laws, which it would be as foolish to tamper with as to try to interfere with the rotation of the earth', was obliged to act in a more pragmatic fashion.[96] Indeed, Massey's pledge that state bakeries would be opened if bread prices continued to rise earned him an editorial cartoon of a 'Red Fed' pondering if war had made a socialist of 'Farmer Bill'.[97]

State management of war production entailed various engagements between the state and those commanding essential sectors of the economy. The government empowered itself to fine suppliers who missed deadlines and to take possession of businesses that failed to meet contractual obligations. Six manufacturers were prosecuted under these powers for breaking contractual terms or for acting fraudulently.[98] Thus Abraham Levy and Company were charged with using inferior thread in uniform production, Scoullar and Company with supplying underweight mattresses and Hannah's with furnishing boots that were not properly standard screwed with brass wire.[99]

More nuanced collaboration can be seen in the appointment of Arthur Myers as Minister of Munitions ('munitions' here covered all military-relevant supplies) in August 1915. Coming from a background straddling business and politics, and carrying a reputation as an 'organising genius', Myers was accompanied by an advisory board staffed with business leaders and he habitually drew on expert advice from his professional connections.[100] He set about assessing the most practical application of New Zealand's economic resources. Among the first tasks of the department was registering workers skilled in the production of military goods and reviewing proposals for local munitions production beyond small-arms ammunition.[101] Initial investigations into the feasibility of securing necessary supplies and engineering skills were satisfactory, as were test grenades and machine guns.[102] The ambition to create a substantial armaments industry was ultimately rejected, however, after the British government noted that necessary machinery was unavailable and local engineers and experts returned an unfavourable report on the project.[103] Instead arrangements were made for Britain to supply New Zealand forces with munitions and the department focused on co-ordinating New Zealand manufactures with the needs of the Empire. In its three-and-a-half years of operation the department oversaw a build-up of primary and manufactured goods, including 10,840,000 pounds of meat, 4,150,000 pounds of butter, 3,469,000 pounds of jam, 364,000 tons of socks, 287,000 tons of underpants and 32,000 tons of boots.[104]

Myers, among others, stressed the need to better organise production and conserve essential workers and industries.[105] These urges led, in February 1917, to the establishment of a National Efficiency Board, whose members' backgrounds spanned farming, manufacturing, politics, engineering and management, to advise the government.[106] Major recommendations included tightening access to alcohol, bringing more women and retired men into the workforce and introducing a system of industrial conscription in which labour would be registered and directed. Low political will to implement any scheme of industrial conscription, and degrees of tension between Massey and the board, left the idea in limbo until interest revived in 1918 during the German Spring Offensives.[107] A clause was inserted into the 1918 Finance Act, empowering the government to prohibit or restrict any service, employment, occupation, business, work or industry, and to regulate remuneration.[108] Willingness to impose these measures remained low, however, and the changing tide in Europe saw them shelved until the Second World War.

Besides involvement in war production, efforts to counteract wartime economic strains saw the state increasingly act as a broker seeking to balance business and public interests. Increases in the cost of living were an ongoing concern and in 1914 the Regulation of Trade and Commerce Act was passed, allowing price controls, the regulation of exports and the suspension of employment awards and agreements.[109] By the year's end a commission of inquiry into price rises had banned the export of wheat and imposed price controls on wheat and flour.[110] The following year the Cost of Living Act established a Board of Trade, with powers of investigation and the authority to regulate prices.[111] By 1919 the Board of Trade controlled the price of 57 major grocery items, as well as a range of commodities including soap, sugar, candles, jams and matches.[112] More direct experimentation in economic intervention saw state attempts at shoe-making and running butcheries.[113]

The pattern of increased economic intervention and equity promotion also played out in efforts to finance the war. Taxation reforms centred on expanding the income tax base (which trebled from 14,000 to 43,000 taxpayers over 1914–1919).[114] Other measures were intended to target war-related wealth. For example, in October 1916 a butter-fat levy was introduced with the intention of 'providing a fund from which the sellers of butter for local consumption could be compensated in order to bring their returns to a parity with the price obtained by factories exporting on private account.' Between that date and June 1917, dairy exports were charged between 2.5 and 3.9 pence per pound of butter-fat in exported butter and cheese.[115] Likewise, an 'excess profits tax' intended to target war-related profits was introduced in 1916 but abandoned over difficulties in isolating such revenues. It was replaced in 1917 with a 'special war tax', which charged penal rates on taxpayers who did not make contributions to war loans proportional to their income.[116]

State success in managing strains was always relative and measures had to be balanced against competing concerns and interests. Thus taxation reforms stirred antagonism within the business community. The recurring theme within Farmers' Union commentary on taxation was that farmers were only 'too anxious to do their bit' but that 'class taxes', like the butter-fat levy or the excess profit tax, were 'cruel and unjust' for inequitably targeting the 'hardest worked portion of the community.'[117] Delegations to chambers of commerce similarly critiqued inequitable taxation and the president of the Auckland Chamber of Commerce complained that aspects of the excess profit tax made it 'most unpopular with the majority of the business people in Auckland.'[118]

Likewise, public sanction for conscription, introduced in the middle of 1916, rested on the principle that it would promote equitable sacrifice. This was not always easily reconciled with economic expediency and the need to preserve essential industries. The dilemma is apparent in the outcry around Auckland businessman Robert Laidlaw being granted an indefinite adjournment.[119] Balloted in early 1918, Laidlaw had appealed on the grounds that he was crucial to the continued running of Laidlaw Leeds (a mail-order business supplying the rural economy and employing some 189 employees) and that the closing of the business would be contrary to public interest. The outcome of his appeal saw various commentators evoke images of 'the small man doing the fighting for the big man'. *Truth* wondered 'how many would willingly go to do the fighting for Lucky Laidlaw and his profiteering business, when he himself will not fight in his own defence or that of his means of life?'[120]

Conclusion

Between 1914 and 1918 New Zealand's systems of production and distribution were harnessed towards the immense demands of the war. The means by which this economic mobilisation operated were complex, at times ad hoc, and meshed the business structures of market capitalism with a state which was already a significant actor in economic activity. They were relatively successful in meeting the economic challenges of the war years.

Certainly most farming prospered, sometimes handsomely, as did the industries and retailers associated with it, notably in the motor industry. The popular perception that woollen companies were doing very well out of the war appears to have been soundly based. Investors in shipping companies did even better. Parts of the finance sector, notably insurance, also found the war period boosted returns and the value of their shares. Likewise, the expenditure by the government of massive sums of largely borrowed money on the war effort created an environment that was generally beneficial to many businesses. The picture was considerably less healthy in other sectors, such as brewing and the myriad enterprises concerned with building and construction. The bulk of (often small) investors in rental property found their returns lagging far behind the increasing costs of living.

Despite shortages of labour, machinery and shipping squeezing and straining productivity, the economy displayed a remarkable resilience. As one 1918 assessment noted, 'perhaps the most salient feature of New Zealand agriculture during the year – a period comprising most of the fourth year of the Great War – has been its remarkable ability to "carry on" at a level of production but little below normal.'[121] Beyond stretching the workforce and prioritising essential industries, sustained production reflected efficiency gains from various technocratic thrusts and managerial reforms. By the end of the war various procedures had been reformed, practices standardised and facilities modernised. For instance, textile millers standardised cloth weights, pasteurisation expanded and cream-grading was introduced.[122]

While economic mobilisation inevitably wrought dislocations and strains, and while efforts to resolve these had proved intractable, they were, again, relatively successfully endured. A comparative survey of increases in food prices between July 1914 and March 1918 places New Zealand (30 per cent) well behind the United States (51 per cent), Britain (107 per cent) and Norway (195 per cent).[123] Comparative wartime stability might also be contrasted with some pre- and post-war disruptions. The country's lowest level of wartime coal production (2,034,250 tons) occurred in 1918, for example, but this output was still significantly higher than in 1913 (1,888,005 tons) or 1919 (1,847,848 tons).[124] The last year of the war was also the worst year of wartime industrial unrest, with 40 labour disputes involving 4,056 workers. Yet this was relatively restrained compared to the 77 disputes, involving 15,138 workers, that broke out in 1920.[125] In part, these post-war upheavals reflected suppressed tensions: 'many during the war had worked extremely long hours and not taken leave, on the understanding that it was for the national good. When peacetime did not bring redress, pent-up anger erupted.'[126]

The volatile circumstances wrought by the demobilisation of the war economy offer a further perspective on relative stability. Previously suppressed imports soared from £24 million in 1918/19 to £61.1 million in 1920 (a level not exceeded until 1937).[127] In late 1920 one commentator noted that people 'have never spent more on their amusements . . . The moving picture houses are crowded, and the race meetings have never been better attended.'[128] This coveting of normality and diversion was followed by 'the slump' of 1920–1921, as several war economies struggled to return to a peacetime footing. Britain's winding down of the commandeer between June 1920 and March 1921 saw stockpiled New Zealand meat and wool, plus normal annual production, dumped on the British market, bringing a collapse of prices.[129]

Furthermore, the business world stood at something of a crossroads in pondering how the wartime relationship of business and government sat with the future. Some spoke of restoring pre-war conditions.[130] Others, in a heady mix of socialistic ideals and commercial-minded pragmatism, argued the case for applying wartime principles to the post-war economy.[131] The record of central management certainly seemed to inspire some, and the winding down of the Department of Munitions and Supplies saw Arthur Myers receive numerous letters of commendation, with his administration described as 'probably the only department in the British Empire dealing with munitions that had not been the subject of some scandal.'[132]

In 1925 the Reform Party campaigned on the slogan 'more business in government; less government in business', and post-war Reform governments, in power until 1928, have been described as possessing a 'preoccupation' with implementing business methods in government.[133] However, they also maintained arrangements reminiscent of wartime state–business collaboration. Thus the National Efficiency Board contributed some planning to post-war economic adjustments, and elements of its work and rationale were echoed in other state planning endeavours.[134] The 1919 Board of Trade Act extended the mandate of that apparatus, giving it various regulatory powers over prices and industry.[135] A Meat Producers' Board was established in 1921 (a Dairy Board followed in 1923), which was intended to provide producer and government representation that could co-ordinate interests regarding market exports.[136] Thus elements of economic mobilisation continued in peacetime, with planning and collaboration between state and business perceived as means of national prosperity.

Chapter Ten

'The whole question bristles with difficulties': Sport and War

Greg Ryan

In a war which extensively mobilised societies, it was inevitable that sport would become keenly contested ground in New Zealand. In its myriad varieties, with rugby, cricket and horse racing to the fore, sport dominated leisure time and consumed thousands of column inches in the press. Many of its leading administrators were also prominent political, business and community figures in other contexts. The essential significance of sport is captured in the French geographer and critic André Siegfried's observations of Auckland at the turn of the twentieth century:

> Every Saturday in winter this ground is full of life; the stands are filled to overflowing, and the different teams begin Homeric struggles, before a public which follows the events of the game in the spirit of a connoisseur. In summer the crowd makes for the cricket field, magnificently equipped, where other teams play their interminable games before the same public, which never seems to get tired of looking on. A little further on is the racecourse, the classic meeting-place of Australasian cities, where few New Zealanders can resist the temptation to have a gamble . . . [A]n account of New Zealand life would be seriously incomplete if there were no mention of this love for physical exercise, which the Australasians have raised to the level of an institution.[1]

Underneath the cloak of popularity and between and within sporting codes, however, lurked class and other tensions. Those familiar with the middle-class athletic ideals of the British and New Zealand elite boys' schools promoted amateur sport, and the discipline and co-operation of team sport especially, as an ideal physical and moral training for the challenges of life, and sometimes as a bulwark against perceived foreign threats to the British Empire. Conversely, many of these proponents of sport, and others such as the increasingly vocal prohibitionist lobby, felt that working-class sport in particular was being drawn into the morally suspect world of pub culture and associated vices, such as gambling, and that strict controls needed to be put in place to contain rough male camaraderie. The first annual general meeting of the New Zealand Rugby Football Union (NZRFU) in 1893 set the tone with its determination to 'put down anything which may, in any way, detract from the standing of the game, to secure equal justice to players, while meting out just punishment to offenders, to secure uniformity of rules and practice; to discourage betting and lavish expenditure on the entertainment of teams'.[2] These tensions in turn intersected with broader divisions across New Zealand as to how the war effort should be managed and the sacrifices required for victory. Some regarded sport as an ideal preparation for combat, others saw it as a distraction and a luxury that should cease for the duration of the conflict. There were many views in between, and some sports, horse racing in particular, were subjected to extra scrutiny. Seeking to capture the complex relationship between sport and war, one commentator noted that 'the whole question bristles with difficulties.'[3]

Sport in the social landscape

The year 1914 was almost certainly the busiest for New Zealand sport to that point. In February and March a powerful Australian cricket team captivated all who saw them with scintillating batting performances. In July the All Blacks departed for an unbeaten tour of Australia, and shortly afterwards the All-England women's hockey team, the first international touring team in women's sport, arrived in New Zealand. The four main cities and larger provincial towns were the base for New Zealand sport. Most important were Saturday club competitions in the major team sports of rugby, cricket, soccer, hockey and rugby league. Secondary to these were mid-week competitions on a Wednesday or Thursday, depending on the preferred mid-week half-holiday for workers in various trades, shops and offices. Beyond the team competitions, there was a multitude of choice, both formal and informal, including athletics, bowls, boxing, cycling, golf, gymnastics, pigeon racing, polo, rifle shooting, rowing, swimming, tennis and yachting. As well as regular fixture lists and the activities of established clubs, the sporting columns abounded with reports of particular carnivals, championships, scratch matches and gatherings to mark important occasions – such as the regular cricket matches played by Pollard's Opera Company as they toured around New Zealand; or the range of Caledonian, Boxing Day, New Year's Day, lodge and other sports that were still popular, especially in provincial towns and rural districts. Underpinning all was an extensive calendar of race meetings, ranging from rough country courses to the opulence and tradition of the Canterbury

Jockey Club. Women's sport, hockey tourists notwithstanding, remained very much a peripheral activity, largely confined to elite girls' schools and their communities and constrained by objections and stereotypes as to what was morally and physically acceptable for the female form.[4]

While most sport was amateur, there were some opportunities for talented athletes to pursue handsome cash prizes in professional competitions in athletics, cycling and wood chopping, among other sports. Rugby union, which had greatly enhanced its profile through the success of the 1905 All Blacks, also perceived a threat from nominally professional rugby league, which had reached New Zealand in 1908.[5] Meanwhile, the respectable administrators of horse racing struggled with the pervasive influence of bookmakers and pushed the use of the totalisator to regulate betting, while a vociferous anti-gambling movement campaigned to remove betting altogether. Despite being banned in 1910, bookmakers maintained a strong and scarcely clandestine presence and punters found no shortage of opportunities to win and lose money.[6]

In a critique of the work of J.A. Mangan, Wray Vamplew argues that the claims for sport as a preparation for military service generally, and the Great War specifically, have been greatly exaggerated and misrepresented.[7] Nevertheless, it is evident that influential middle-class administrators and followers did regard sport as a moral and physical training ground for young men and, therefore, as a vital component of 'soldier-making'. Certainly, this understanding formed a dominant theme in press accounts of sport. War was frequently referred to as 'the greater game', as if the skills required to 'compete' were derived from sport. As Albert Devore, president of the Auckland Rugby Union, observed in April 1915, 'Sport had been one of the safeguards of the nation. The players of the game kept in the best physical condition and were used to obedience and discipline'.[8] On reporting the departure of a Taranaki golfer on active service, a columnist declared that:

> When golfers go into action against the Huns, they do not call 'Fore' but they 'play the game' as they did on the links. The lessons of the links will not be lost on the battlefield and in the trenches. The steady hand, the clear eye, the feeling of never knowing when one is beaten, all of which are gained and developed in the game, will play their part in the game of war.[9]

But most prominent of all were the sentiments expressed by James Allen, the Minister of Defence, in a speech at Milton on 6 April 1916:

> It is a great game, it is a greater game than your cricket, football and hockey. It is a great test of nationality, it is a great test of citizenship

> for every man who is a true sport. We are proud of our national games, and we deplore and hate this terrible war, but I venture to say that the man who is a true sport, the man who understands that the stakes are high, that the stakes are nationality, New Zealand or no New Zealand, will not hesitate to answer the call of his mates in the trenches and join in the great game.[10]

The extent to which such rhetoric was grasped by all ranks, and especially those not exposed to the athletic ideals of the elite secondary schools, can never be quantified. But at the very least there was an understanding that sports clubs, composed very largely of fit younger men, were ideal networks for recruitment.[11]

Sports and the war effort: concord

Echoing the common assumption that the war would not last long, sports clubs and associations initially emphasised the need to keep their activities in good shape for servicemen to return to. As volunteers initially came forward in sufficient numbers, the 1914–1915 summer season was relatively uninterrupted. The New Zealand Lawn Tennis Championships took place in Christchurch over New Year, the athletics equivalent was held in Wellington in mid-March and inter-provincial cricket continued exactly as before.[12] But following the Gallipoli landings, and the shift of the war from a rather abstract concept to something with very real consequences for New Zealanders, there was a marked change in focus during the 1915 winter season. One manifestation was that sporting bodies became determined to emphasise the numbers of their players who had volunteered and to explain the circumstances of those who had not. In May 1915, D. Williams of the Auckland Football Association cited the example of one club with 37 players on active service and added that most of those who remained were either cadets or territorials. The annual report of the Auckland Boxing Association for 1915 stated that there was not one eligible amateur boxer left in Auckland. In late 1916 the Napier Sailing Club announced that 47 of its 80 pre-war members had gone to the front, that two more had been accepted for the Motor Boat Patrol, that eight had been killed and many more had been wounded. The other members, it was noted, were either too old or too young, or had been rejected for medical reasons.[13] Even lawn bowls, where it was generally accepted that most of the active players were beyond military service age, emphasised that its participants were 'ardent National Reservists . . . [who were] doing their drill and marching work as keen as any young 'un'.[14] Although the claim from one rugby official that 10,000 players had enlisted by October 1915 is unlikely, it is equally true that the exact number of active sportsmen who enlisted can never be known.[15]

To further justify the continuation of sport, some administrators were quick to suggest that all active members of clubs should undergo military training. James Carlaw, president of the New Zealand Rugby Football League, said that a recommendation along these lines should be sent to every provincial league in New Zealand, while the Auckland Hockey Association proposed that players should give one Saturday afternoon each month and one evening each week to military drills. It was even suggested that they approach the Defence Department and ask for the assistance of instructors.[16] At a meeting of combined sports bodies in Wellington in late October, Dr Alfred Newman MP advocated the institution of weekly route marches by all sports bodies in the Dominion as an incentive to recruiting.[17] Such campaigns were augmented by an emphasis on the practical skills that sport could contribute to military service, and especially the apparent link between cricket and grenade throwing. A lengthy article on 'The Art of Bombthrowing' in the *Press* on 6 September 1915 concluded that Australian and British troops had particular prowess in this area because the throwing of bombs required a skill equivalent to overarm bowling, while:

> cricket and football players can easily gauge the flight of a bomb from the enemy's trench and easily escape its effects. For this reason probably the Germans dread the hand bombs more than the British troops, for they know nothing about cricket and football, and seem unable to gauge their own bombs correctly or those flung at them.[18]

Two months later, when the Otago and New Zealand wicketkeeper J.W. Condliffe returned from Gallipoli, having been 'dismissed leg before by a Turkish bullet', he reported that another Otago provincial cricketer, Tom Macfarlane, was making a name for himself as a bomb-thrower as 'his particularly fine fielding is apparently standing him in good stead in the trenches'.[19]

Many sports were actively involved in fund-raising for the war effort during 1915.. In mid-January 'Patriots' were urged to give their support to the annual gathering of the Kimbolton Sports Club, as all proceeds from its meeting were to be given to the Patriotic Fund.[20] A week later the Christchurch Polo Club decided to postpone its annual tournament on the basis that such expense could not be justified 'at the present time of world-wide financial stress and suffering', and the players were urged to give the money they would have spent to the Belgium Relief Fund. The New Zealand Polo Association had already postponed its Dominion tournament for similar reasons.[21] In Taranaki, a suggestion was made to the local Acclimatisation Society that the annual £1 charge for a fishing licence should be increased to £1.10s (near $160 in 2015 dollars)[22] and the difference donated to the War Relief Fund: 'The devotee of the gentle art of Isaak Walton would enjoy the sport of whipping the streams all the more in the thought that he was helping to make provision for those engaged in the gentle art of whipping his country's enemies.'[23] Towards the end of the year most amateur sports bodies combined to raise money to provide Christmas gifts and tobacco for the men at the front.[24]

Sports and the war effort: discord

As the lengthy casualty lists began to emerge from the Dardanelles, even the continuation of sport as a conduit for recruiting and fund-raising became harder to justify in the face of claims that it was a frivolous distraction from serious concerns.[25] In practical terms, many clubs and associations were struggling for active members and viable competitions as men volunteered. They were also weakened by declining subscriptions and gate revenue.[26] The most immediate impact was on inter-provincial fixtures and tournaments. The NZRFU annual report for 1915 declared that all tours would be postponed but that there was as yet no reason why club games should not continue as 'there is no dearth of younger players to fill the places of those who have gone to the front'.[27] Inter-union matches declined from 46 in 1914 to 13 in 1915 and none in 1916.[28] In late October 1915 the New Zealand Cricket Council suspended both Plunket Shield and Hawke Cup fixtures for the duration of war and also inter-provincial fixtures played for charitable purposes.[29] The New Zealand Football Association was quite explicit that its decision to suspend inter-provincial matches was to remove the temptation for players to stay at home – as if the provision of sporting spectacles and other entertainment would somehow be a defining factor in any decision to enlist.[30] Tennis and swimming were others among a growing list of national bodies to abandon championships.[31]

Rugby league was slower to curtail its activities during 1915 and soon felt the wrath of criticism. Apparently at the insistence of the New South Wales Rugby League, New Zealand was asked to adhere to its previously agreed tour to Australia in June 1915. But in an editorial widely circulated in New Zealand in late April, the Sydney *Daily Telegraph* caustically observed:

> There is a time for most things; the present is scarcely the hour to engage in sporting tours of such magnitude, even if no financial gain is attached to the expedition. If the tour eventuates the participants who enjoy it may discover the unenviable reputation of being the only

> players belonging to the countries vitally interested in the war who have found so much time in which to play.[32]

In response, James Carlaw insisted that New Zealand had asked for a postponement of the tour. But he also observed that as there were many men required to remain in New Zealand to maintain defence and industry, 'why should they be debarred from using the sporting fields for muscular development?'[33] Six weeks later, when the Canterbury Rugby League's efforts to develop the game on the West Coast were the subject of a heated public meeting organised by the West Coast Rugby Union, Henry Thacker MP, on behalf of the League, was reported as asking:

> Why not pull the blinds down and forbid the sun to shine while the war is on? It was not so at the front. The men indulged in games whenever they had the opportunity. At this time more than any other something was required to occupy the mind . . . All could not go to the front for the economic machine must go on.[34]

Carlaw and Thacker were both, perhaps deliberately, obscuring the point that, at this stage, it was not so much local club sport that was at issue, but touring.

Debate as to whether any sport should continue intensified from late 1915, and especially so in Christchurch, which tended to be regarded as the 'spiritual home' of New Zealand sport.[35] Those who looked to Australia or Britain for direction were met by both a lack of intervention from government and contrasting responses from sports bodies. Whereas the Football Association in England suspended its league competitions from 1915 and county cricket was not continued in 1915, there was an extensive programme of sport for the services, and horse racing continued relatively unabated.[36] At one extreme in New Zealand was the editor of the *North Otago Times*, who insisted in August 1915 that:

> It seems strangely incongruous that in one portion of the Empire, the people are indulging in their sports and pastimes as in the times of peace, while on the other side of the globe thousands of the bravest sons of the Empire – among them our brothers and sons – are fighting for their lives against an unscrupulous foe; fighting, too, alike for the liberties of the moral and the immoral, the patriots and the curs.

While he did not advocate that everybody should resign themselves to 'sackcloth and ashes' or that every patron of sport should be on active service, he maintained that there was 'an impropriety about the whole business'.[37] At the other end of the spectrum, Frederick Earl, president of the Auckland Cricket Association, felt that players had a 'sacred duty' to continue the game and 'should not worry too much over the sorrows and horrors of war'. He insisted that it was not the responsibility of sporting organisations to 'pry' into the motives of those who did not enlist.[38] This stance was echoed by the Canterbury Football Association, which concluded that eligibility for service was an issue for the government and for individual conscience.[39]

For the majority of sports and individual clubs, the compromise endured, albeit with sustained invective and eventually active restriction against any man deemed to be 'shirking' military obligations. Most telling of all were the condemnations from those sportsmen now overseas. In a letter to his family in September 1915, Gunner Archie Macdonald of the New Zealand Field Artillery, and a well-known Canterbury representative rugby player, remarked that it was with 'mingled feelings of pleasure and regret' that he read reports of his Christchurch club's success during the season.

> You know, when one is out here he can see there is a far bigger game than football to play, and we want a very large membership. On looking through the list of our senior team I can't help thinking that several of them could be here if they wished.[40]

Another Canterbury officer tersely observed:

> From the papers we see that at football and other sports meetings resolutions are carried on the grand work that our boys have achieved at the Dardanelles, with cheers, etc. The gallant boys out here, who are facing death the whole time practically, do not feel at all flattered by such resolutions, and are, if anything, very disgusted to think that able-bodied young fellows should be cheering in their club rooms at home when they ought to be doing it in a bayonet charge, and helping to defeat the enemy. The remarks of the men out here in this respect are anything but complimentary to the 'shirkers' who are staying at home. Every able-bodied man in New Zealand should be made to enlist, as thousands more will be required, and the more we have here the sooner the struggle will be ended.[41]

Such commentary reflects the shifts in the place and image of sport in the wartime social landscape. Conventional stereotypes of shirkers presented them as inactive, effeminate and lacking physical and moral strength – effectively the uncomplimentary antithesis of the masculine physicality and character of the soldier sportsman.[42] It is evident here that more specific shirker condemnations were emerging to refer to those unenlisted men who presented themselves as physically capable.

Certainly, as recruitment slowed from late 1915, there were prolonged discussions evoking the notion that those who were fit to play were fit to serve.[43] In response, clubs and governing bodies exhorted their members to enlist, and some took steps to shame supposed shirkers into doing so. In early December 1915 a widely reported meeting of the Sydenham Cricket Club in Christchurch unanimously passed a motion that 'any member of eligible age for enlistment, and single, shall be left out of any team, unless he gives sufficient reasons for not enlisting.'[44] The Otago Patriotic and Recruiting Committee immediately wrote to the Otago Cricket Association, urging them to follow suit, but the chairman of the association responded that he considered 'the cricketers of Otago had responded nobly to their country's call' and, although he was fully aware of the necessity for recruits, he did not think it necessary to take the action suggested. The letter was referred to clubs without any recommendation.[45]

For the winter of 1916 the Canterbury Rugby Football Union replaced its senior competition with two grades, under 19 and under 21. Its Auckland and Otago counterparts, and others in a variety of sports, soon took similar action.[46] But it is not always clear whether such moves were driven by patriotism or pragmatism. Declining numbers of available players forced many teams, and frequently whole clubs, to withdraw from local competitions. It was increasingly seen as practical to encourage junior sport rather than to persist with meagre and mediocre senior grades. In July 1916 the annual report of the New Zealand Football Association stated that it was now practically impossible to provide any competitions, except for players under twenty years of age. All of the country associations were practically non-existent and those in the four main centres were only surviving by shifting their main emphasis to schoolboys.[47]

Indeed, if there was any beneficiary from wartime conditions it was school sport. The editor of *The Taranakian*, the journal of New Plymouth Boys' High School, argued that whatever the fate of sport generally, it was essential to adhere to the routines of school games and 'the necessary training involved implies no ignorance of the seriousness of the present crisis, and no lack of sympathy with the awful sufferings and losses caused by the war'. To the contrary, sport was essential to develop those traits of character in boys that would be required to put the country back on a normal footing after the war. Moreover, it was better for young people to direct their leisure to 'wholesome sport than in moping about occupied with nothing but uneasy thoughts'.[48] In this context, annual matches between school XVs emerged as a focal point of community sporting interest and a number of fixtures were moved from schools to public grounds with a greater spectator capacity. Among these was the fixture between Christ's College and Christchurch Boys' High School, which was first played on Lancaster Park in July 1916, with the gate receipts going to various patriotic funds.[49] Swimming was another sport to follow this lead, emphasising 'juniors or nothing' and inaugurating a Dominion Schools' Championship in late 1917.[50]

It is perhaps surprising that women did not seem to benefit from this transformed sporting world as they did in Britain and Australia. There is no sign that they participated in the sort of charity fixtures that were evident in Western Australia and elsewhere. New Zealand also lacked the industrial infrastructure that produced thriving workplace teams and competitions in Europe.[51] To the contrary, there were some signs that during wartime women were expected to devote even more of their time to traditional civic and domestic roles, rather than to the apparently unfeminine arena of sport.[52] In response to a report that young ladies of St Andrews, South Canterbury, were proposing to form a hockey club, 'Patriotic' lamented to the *Timaru Herald*:

> I have no wish to bar anyone from legitimate pleasure, but would it not be better if instead of spending time and expense organising a new hockey club, the young ladies of that district formed a young ladies' guild and utilised their spare time in providing comforts and Red Cross necessities for our boys who have performed so gallantly? I am sure the young ladies would derive more pleasure from being employed in this way and would also have the satisfaction of thinking that although not able to personally offer their services they had made their sacrifice in giving up one kind of pleasure for another which in the end they recognise as better and more profitable.[53]

Two years later, from Greymouth, 'Mother of a Soldier' condemned both those men who were trying to avoid active service and those more generally who seemed preoccupied with sport: 'These people, ladies especially, are ready enough to talk patriotism, and to urge other fellows – your sons and mine – to go to the war, whilst they and their male friends and relatives live in ease at home.'[54] Of greater acceptability were the activities of the likes of the New Zealand Ladies' Golf Union, whose affiliated clubs raised £150 (near $21,500 in 2015) to be used by the Red Cross, or the Auckland Ladies' Hockey Association, which responded to a request from the Auckland Women's Patriotic League regarding preparation of gift parcels for the troops by asking member clubs to give the matter 'earnest consideration'.[55] But the dominant role for women in New Zealand sport was still to prepare the afternoon teas for male competitors.[56]

Racing's bristling difficulties

Of all sports, and noting that 1915 was one of the most financially successful years in its history, the continuation of horse racing was the most ferociously contested. Sir George Clifford, the president of the New Zealand Racing Conference, acted decisively in mid-1915 to emphasise the social and martial importance of racing. In a circular to all clubs shortly after the outbreak of war, and again in the 1915 annual report, he described the sport as a 'health-giving recreation' that was a 'beneficial antidote to gloom and depression' as well as a practical benefit to the preparation of artillery and cavalry horses: 'The thoroughbred horse is the foundation on which the stamina of the charger and the gunnery horse is built, and it behoves every country to see to it that a sufficient supply of such horses is available when required.' Clifford also stressed that, by mid-1915, racing clubs had contributed at least £15,000 (over $2,000,000 in 2015 dollars) to various war funds – a contribution that was preferable to forced taxation, which might cripple other institutions struggling because of the war. He estimated that racing contributed more than £100,000 (over $14,000,000 in 2015 dollars) in direct taxation.[57] H.F. Nicoll, on behalf of the New Zealand Trotting Association, added that they were taking a lead from Great Britain, where many 'responsible men', including the King, were still racing their horses: 'It could not be said that any of these men did not realise the war, or that they are apathetic or careless of the Empire's interests. Yet a reflection on New Zealand sportsmen must also be a reflection on his Majesty the King.'[58] This sentiment was reinforced by Canterbury official H.S. Bourn, who also stressed that racing was practically an essential industry since it provided a lot of employment, both in its own right and to supporting industries such as the railways, accommodation and food suppliers: 'These folks expected a harvest at race time, and their interests should be considered.'[59] It was also noted that most jockeys were under the height and weight requirements for the armed forces.[60]

Nevertheless, following the lead of other sports, the New Zealand Trotting Association resolved in April 1916 that no licence to train, ride, or drive would be granted to any single person who was eligible for recruiting, and that all clubs were to obtain from the local Recruiting Committee a certificate confirming that any applicant for a licence was not eligible.[61] There is no evidence that the Racing Conference did likewise.

Opponents were scathing in their response, none more so than Captain Donald Simson, a veteran of the Boer War and the Dardanelles, who delivered a 'fiery and straight from the shoulder speech', backed up by a parade of returned soldiers, after the third race at Riccarton on 13 November 1915. Simson first addressed the Canterbury Jockey Club stewards in the bird cage, including many prominent public figures, and reminded them that they 'were not only trustees of racing, but were also trustees of the young men and women in the country who were present at the races while the Empire was at the point of a crisis'. He claimed that New Zealand could not be said to be taking the war seriously while racing was allowed to continue, and that there was no substance to any belief that race meetings were aiding patriotic purposes when men were returning home maimed and with permanently damaged health. Turning to the outside enclosure, Simson labelled those present as 'shirkers' and 'rotters' who were indifferent to the call of the King, but said that in some respects he did not blame them for being at the races, as older men in the population should have given a better lead and told the government to stop racing. Turning finally to the ladies' enclosure, Simson said that their presence at the races showed that they had not considered the position seriously as they had encouraged men to attend: 'It is no good sheltering behind those men in mufti. They won't protect you from outrage. It is the men in uniform who will protect you, and them only.'[62]

Within the week, some racing officials, and most notably Dr C.F. Scott, president of the Gisborne Trotting Club, were recommending curtailment if not a wholesale suspension of racing. In response to the economic arguments of Clifford and Nicoll, others pointed out that during Cup Week in Christchurch £300,000 (near $42,000,000 in 2015 dollars) had been invested 'on the chances of the turf' and this reflected only a proportion of the total investment throughout New Zealand, including with illegal bookmakers.[63] The Wellington Central Auxiliary of the Baptist Union, encapsulating more than half a century of sustained religious and moral opposition to gambling in all forms, concluded its condemnation with the observation that 'racing exists for gambling, and gambling in all its forms is wholly evil'.[64] Others attacked the timing of race meetings. Although the Canterbury Jockey Club escaped most criticism by agreeing to postpone their Easter Tuesday meeting when it clashed with the first Anzac Day in 1916, their Auckland equivalent, via a motion from the Auckland Presbytery, was lambasted for holding a meeting at Ellerslie on the day the news of Lord Kitchener's death reached New Zealand.[65] In a letter to the *Dominion* at the end of 1916, Isaac Moses of Palmerston North echoed the sentiments of many when he asked, 'Why should not the jockeys, "guessors", touts, bookmakers, etc., who "prey seldom on their knees, but always on their neighbours" be made to go [to the front] like other citizens.'[66]

By early 1917 it was clear that racing would have to reduce its activities or the government would make the decision for them. Nevertheless, the Trotting Association petitioned the Minister of Internal Affairs, G.W. Russell, arguing that their activities should not be curtailed owing to their much smaller scale compared to the wider racing industry. But the claim was ignored and in early June, after debate in cabinet, it was decreed that the number of race meetings must be reduced by at least one third, spread equally across all racing districts.[67] At the end of July the report of the National Efficiency Board further emphasised that 'racing is non-essential, and that no man should be exempted from military service owing to his connection with or employment in racing or the breeding or handling of horses for racing purposes'. It was also recommended that the railways should not provide any special trains or other concessions for race meetings or the industry generally.[68] That the government was willing and able to intervene in this way, given that it did not do so in any other sporting context, is testimony to both the scale of racing and its financial dimensions, which could be seen to have a more tangible impact on the wartime economy than many other leisure activities.

Sports and conscription

Yet as racing was forced to retrench, other sports were gradually able to reassert themselves from mid-1917. The introduction of the 1916 Military Service Act and the first conscription ballot in November 1916 removed some of the pressure on sports bodies to defend the integrity of their participants. Many men were now better able to confirm that they were serving in New Zealand or unable to serve for medical or other reasons. There was also an increasing number of men returning to New Zealand now unfit for active service but still able to play sport in some form. Consequently the age and other competition restrictions of 1916 were largely removed in 1917 to allow sport for these groups, to sustain morale and to assist with fitness for those approaching military age.[69] Explaining the position of the Wellington Rugby Football Union at the beginning of the 1918 season, the *New Zealand Free Lance* noted,

> There is no question now of men playing the game who should be at the Front. If there are any that is the Government's business: the Rugby Union's sole concern is to provide the means whereby those who want to boot the ball about can do so under their auspices.[70]

Inter-provincial cricket and rugby re-emerged during 1917–1918, along with a number of fixtures involving Military Forces teams.[71] Certainly not everyone welcomed these developments. In April 1918 J.W. Poynton

SM was typical of an enduring hardline element when he argued that the country

> had an insufficiency of money for war loans, but plenty for racing; our land is going back for lack of labour, and yet thousands of able bodied men disport themselves on the racecourses; there is a serious shortage of benzine for industrial purposes, yet thousands of gallons are being used in hurrying north, south, east and west, in pursuit of sport and pleasure.[72]

But by the end of 1918 it was abundantly clear that returning soldiers, rather than being subdued by their exertions overseas, were determined to embrace their former clubs and teams and to ensure that sport was quickly returned to a normal footing.[73]

Conclusion

The legacy of the war years for New Zealand sport was necessarily varied. Most immediately, one could point to a missing or damaged generation of athletes. Among those who did not return were tennis maestro Anthony Wilding, promising New Zealand cricketer Rupert Hickmott, featherweight boxing champion Jimmy Hagerty, and thirteen All Blacks, including the 1905 captain Dave Gallaher, killed at Passchendaele in October 1917.[74] Indeed, rugby drew on its sacrifices, and especially Gallaher, to obscure its pre-war tensions and establish an enduring image in the public mind that it, above all others, was the game that shaped the qualities displayed on the battlefield. The quest for unity extended to the reinstatement of defectors to rugby league. For its part, league lacked the numbers, especially among schoolboys, to sustain public interest and meaningful competitions during the war in the way that rugby union did. The threat of a professional game that many had feared up to 1914 quickly shrank to a few small pockets. Rugby union was therefore able to emerge from the war with relative unity and increased respectability, and to secure by the early 1920s a much better claim to the title of 'national game' than could have been imagined earlier in the century.[75] Other team sports such as hockey and soccer also lost ground against rugby, and especially so outside the four main centres, as their smaller competitions struggled and frequently failed to survive the depletions of the war. The Taranaki, Horowhenua, West Coast and Buller hockey associations all disappeared during the war.[76]

Another, albeit short-lived, legacy of the war could be seen during the 1920s, when Returned Soldiers' Association (RSA) teams entered many local competitions in cricket, hockey, rugby and soccer as some men sought to retain the strength of wartime bonds rather than integrating back into local clubs. The Palmerston North RSA team won the local senior rugby competition in 1920.[77] At the same time, local branches of the RSA, and then the national body, began to lobby regional and national sports bodies to ban known conscientious objectors and military defaulters from all sporting competitions. Subsequent actions by sports bodies – including the Otago Rugby Football Union, which endorsed a ten-year ban from July 1922 – were largely if not wholly symbolic, in that the number of objectors was small and there is scant evidence of any individual actually being removed from sporting competition.[78] But the campaign is a potent expression of the intermingling of sport and wartime experiences: those who were unwilling to partake in crucial tests of manhood on the battlefield ought not to pursue them on the sports field.

Although the 'greater game' rhetoric of 1914 retreated during 1915–1916 amid sometimes bitter debates about the desired contribution of sport and sportsmen to the war effort, the relative resurgence of club and provincial sport from mid-1917 confirmed that even under the most difficult circumstances a degree of normality prevailed. Sport, such a pervasive component of pre-war New Zealand social life, was able to endure, adapt and emerge with its key structures largely in place and ready to seize post-war opportunities as the country sought a return to normality.

Chapter Eleven

The Rising Price of Rendering to Caesar: The Churches in World War One

Peter Lineham

When news arrived that Germany had declared war on Russia in the early evening of Sunday 2 August 1914, the local newspaper in Oamaru sent a runner to all the churches as they commenced their evening services. In that town the churches acted as both disseminators and interpreters of this news.[1] This episode offers a small glimpse at the churches' place in social life and hints at their coming role in mobilisation. Much social history of the war now emphasises the significance of parts of civil society as sites of communal 'self-mobilisation', and the roles and responses of New Zealand's churches provide a significant example of the phenomenon.[2] Indeed, particularly during the first two years of the conflict, the churches' contribution to civic initiatives in co-operative participation with a democratic state is striking. However, historiography has also come to observe increasingly systematic state management of the war effort over the duration. Again this is evident in regard to churches, for as the state increasingly seized the initiative, the churches were more obviously sidelined. The consequences of both phases were as distinctive and profound for churches as they were for other aspects of society. Inspired, anxious to participate, caught within complex polemics, churches felt the power of entanglement with the state and played some role in the shape that the wartime state assumed.

Churches, state and society, circa 1914

In 1914, the Anglican Church was planning a grand celebration of the centenary of Samuel Marsden's 1814 sermon as marking the introduction of Christianity to New Zealand. At this time the churches were playing an active and highly respected social role, contributing vociferously to the debate over how to reform the country. Protestants as a whole were keenly engaged in two great campaigns, one to add Bible instruction to the primary school syllabus, and the other to restrict the sale of alcohol. These two major causes gained extensive support from respectable parts of society, although Anglican support for prohibition was very limited in contrast to its support for the 'Bible in Schools' movement, where Canon David Garland of Queensland was made director of the campaign. A bill to hold a national referendum on Bible in Schools was before a select committee when the war broke out. At the war's end the temporary introduction of six o'clock closing was made permanent and a major referendum on prohibition was held.[3]

Although there was no established church, New Zealand's early-twentieth-century churches were privileged and protected (none more so than the Church of England), but this relationship was under challenge in various ways. The 1909 Defence Act's expansion of the Cadet scheme, for example, competed with church and other youth groups. Church leaders became critics of the scheme, successfully protesting its application to boys aged twelve (it was amended to fourteen) and the lack of a religious input in the training for older cadets.[4] This desire to participate in state provisions which went beyond churches' voluntary status illustrates what was to become a wartime theme. In some respects these aspirations backfired after the war.

The exact nature of the relationship churches forged with the war effort also reflects denominational differences. Broadly put, those churches that were more comfortable with their Protestant status were very prominent and united in support of the war, as they had been in the prohibition and Bible in Schools campaigns. Indeed, the Anglican Church sought to play a quasi-establishment role. This manifested in social organisation: at the outbreak of war the executive committee promptly decided to suspend fund-raising for the Marsden centenary, and offered the services of Rev. P.W. Clarkson, its organising secretary, to help with the Mayor's Patriotic Fund.[5] The Anglican clergy also sought to speak directly to the nation. Addressing the Mothers' Union on 3 December 1914, A.W. Averill, the Anglican Bishop of Auckland, argued that the church must not surrender its moral leadership and urged more engagement in politics: 'In New Zealand we are in danger of overlooking the only foundation upon which a true and abiding nation could be built, namely, national righteousness.'[6] Nevertheless, Bishop Averill was careful to maintain some distance in the church's stance – 'we cannot necessarily claim the sanction of God when brother fights brother, or lay the blame upon God'[7] – and balance the language of a church which sought to preserve its associations with the state while maintaining its independence from the state: 'We cannot say, "My Father" or "Our British Father," we can only pray as Christ has taught us.' He went on: 'Thank God, we have not rushed into the fray, or sought to involve our Empire in the horrors of war. Stern necessity has compelled us to unsheathe the sword.'

Presbyterians were also in a special position due to their established status in Scotland, and they were very comfortable about supporting the state, although they worried about 'the street-corner variety' of jingoism. The New Zealand branches of the English nonconformist churches (Methodist, Congregationalist and Baptist, in particular) were more sombre about the outbreak of war than the larger churches.[8] Yet their members were as influenced by patriotism as anyone else. Official Methodist statements recognised that there was a barbaric side to the war – 'It is a terrible anachronism that the foremost nations of the world should be engaged in a struggle that is essentially barbaric' – but their lay leaders were prominent in civic politics and wanted the denomination to enthuse about the war.[9]

The international stance of the Papacy placed the Catholic Church in a more difficult position from the outset (although the Pope was praised for his willingness to hold the Kaiser to account).[10] Nevertheless, the plight of little Belgium captured the Catholic imagination and, like most media, the Catholic press emphasised the barbarity of the invading German troops.[11] Much energy went into maintaining a high rate of Catholic volunteers in the first part of the war, as it did in Ireland, with the same hope that home rule would be the reward. Claims were made that the first Wellington contingent of the First Expeditionary Force had 500 Catholics out of 1,300 troops.[12] After the Easter Uprising in April 1916, the Catholic situation was more delicate. In Australia, Irish votes were essential in defeating the conscription referendums. In New Zealand, there were repeated accusations that the Catholic Church was not pulling its weight, which created the climate for emergence of the Protestant Political Association. In retaliation, James Kelly at the Catholic periodical *The Tablet* expressed a vehement support for Sinn Fein, and growing criticism of the war, but the episcopal hierarchy was very uncomfortable with this strategy.

The Salvation Army benefitted significantly from the war. It was, after all, already on a war footing. The Army was little troubled by theology and had a reformist and state-oriented focus which inclined it to seize the opportunities that the war afforded it.[13] In mid-1915 it was approached by the Minister of Defence to assist in the support of those in special need as a result of the war.[14] Five ambulances were sent to the front; chaplains and huts for soldiers were organised. It asked for £5,000 ($745,000 in 2015 dollars) from New Zealand supporters soon after the war began, and got away with separate fund-raising more easily than others.[15]

Lastly, small groups of more sectarian denominations, including Quakers, Plymouth Brethren (especially the Exclusive Brethren), Seventh-day Adventists, and the Two-by-Twos or Cooneyites, represent a very different church/war-effort relationship. Typically they were alarmed at the heightened pressure towards patriotism, which they regarded as subverting their loyalty to Christ. Their alarm turned to disobedience when conscription was introduced. The war marked a watershed for them too, as they, like others, observed the rising price of rendering to Caesar.

Mobilising support

With their weekly services and activism in communal life, churches were well placed to mobilise social support. The first two years of the war saw the major churches operate as a dynamic voluntary sector, undertaking supportive activities related to the war effort, often extending upon pre-war positions and roles. For example, a very striking feature of the first two years of the war was the success of church fund-raising campaigns. The variety of organisations in the church was not just at congregational level: it included children's and youth organisations within the church, brigades, ladies' guilds, men's groups – indeed, virtually all bodies within the church. Congregations organised informal events to raise money for patriotic causes. Churches right across the spectrum agreed to take up a collection for Belgians.[16] The government was eager to ensure that there was not a vast range of competing funds, and wished to avoid imposing a tax, if charity could produce the same effect. Interestingly, after a tour of the working-class town of Port Chalmers, Dunedin, its Anglican vicar noted that many housewives resented the demand for charitable donations to the Belgian cause, and therefore he saw a tax as a fairer method.[17]

Elements of this activity reflect denominational rivalries, and churches were quick to compare their levels of engagement. In Otago, claims were made that Catholics, Baptists and Methodists were doing well, and that Presbyterians and Anglicans were falling behind.[18] Of course, the larger Protestant churches had many nominal adherents and were therefore less able to inspire their members into action. Rivalries were also associated with establishing institutes at the rapidly formed training camps in New Zealand, and later at the front lines, which worked in association with the chaplains of their denomination. Anglicans and Catholics acted separately to establish their own institutes and spent much effort in raising money for them. Fr Thomas Siegrief explained that a denominational institution would give Catholics 'a just pride at being as good and as independent as any denomination in the camp'.[19] Indeed the Catholic Federation quickly conceived the idea of a Catholic Patriotic Fund to equip their chaplains and provide a marquee for masses.[20] Anglicans established a single fund and set targets for dioceses. Presbyterians co-operated with the smaller Protestant groups and with the YMCA to establish these institutes.

Recruiting proved another means by which the churches invested themselves in the war, and church involvement in local patriotic and recruiting committees played an important role in the volunteer-fuelled war effort. Anglican and Presbyterian clergy sometimes served on these committees, and ministers sometimes spoke at meetings encouraging enlistment.[21] The most notable of these was Dr Gibb, the very influential minister of St John's Presbyterian Church in Wellington, but there were many other clergy who urged their own youth to enlist, including W.E. Gillam and Jasper Calder at St Matthew's in Auckland. Calder gave five sermons on the message of the Allies, ending his final address with an ardent appeal for recruits.[22] Some clergy had a still more personal connection to the front. Bishops Sprott and Averill had enlisted sons, and Methodist records show that 26 of their ministers had one or more sons serving abroad.[23]

Initially, churches tripped over themselves to parade the proportion of the recruits from their denominations. The willingness of young men to enlist was often taken as a very positive sign by the churches, which were themselves so dependent on volunteers. In this light a strident sermon by the Anglican vicar of Oamaru in March 1915 reasoned that if the war was a holy cause against the powers of darkness, it was the Christian duty of every man to volunteer and, according to his calculations, New Zealand's rate of volunteering was vastly below Britain's.[24] *The Tablet* praised the level of volunteering, noting that 'Lip loyalty is cheap and easy, but the real thing is a matter of deeds rather than words'.[25] Catholics claimed a particularly high level of recruits, which may have had something to do with the Catholic working class being larger and freer of hindrances to volunteering. There was particular satisfaction when the cathedral in Christchurch was full of benches of young men preparing to volunteer.[26] There was also sensitivity to growing criticism that Catholics were shirking, which surfaced during 1915 and would become toxic in the latter years of the conflict.[27] Baptists similarly believed that the moral strength of the British cause lay in its dependence on a volunteer army, not a conscript one like the Germans had.[28]

As notions of a short war faded away and social commitment escalated, local churches continued as sites of mobilisation. Anglican churches were encouraged to follow the example of St Aidan's in Remuera and display on their doors the names of parish families who had volunteered a son for active service.[29] At a Te Aroha church parade of the Rifle Club and the

National Reserve, a strong urging was given to respond to the nation's need in the great war of right against wrong.[30] A Catholic spoke of 'the urgent necessity of making every sacrifice and putting every iron in the fire to bring about final victory and an assured peace.'[31] Methodists had begun to realise by early 1915 that greater sacrifices were needed and that perhaps the rate of volunteering was not high enough.[32] A resolution moved at the Methodist conference in 1915 insisted that Methodist levels of volunteering had been excellent.[33]

Even more directly, recruiting extended to the clergy, and from very early on various individual clergy offered to be chaplains. In a manner comparable to other sectors of society, chaplains who volunteered were great heroes in the eyes of their denominations.[34] Chaplains' letters were often reproduced in denominational periodicals, and presented part of the standard face of the church. The *Baptist* reported extensively on the work of their chaplain, the former popular minister of Mosgiel. Similarly, Catholics were proud of chaplain Fr James McMenamin. The role these chaplains played in maintaining public morale by offering reassurances and comfort to parents back home about their boys at the front should not be overlooked. Many Catholic parents, for example, were assured by Fr McMenamin from the camp that their sons attended mass, and were wonderfully fervent and brave because they were in a state of grace.[35]

Denominational provision of chaplains was organised according to the military district and was again subject to denominational rivalries.[36] Some watched the distribution of chaplains to the forces with some concern, perhaps fearing that the chaplains would convert for their own denominations; certainly Fr McMenamin wrote of how a Protestant soldier had converted and that the war was going to help the Catholic Church.[37] Anglicans demanded that their church provide 60 per cent of the chaplains (a figure which they derived from the denominations of the first volunteers),[38] and the Church of England Men's Society, which took responsibility for the Anglican presence at Trentham, urged the bishops to insist on separate Anglican chaplains.[39] The chaplains became a militant group in the church, and they enjoyed the status.[40] Methodists wanted a chaplain with every troopship, but accepted that their turn would be infrequent.[41] At the same time they were most anxious to have full access to the Featherston camp by home missionaries, even during the week.[42] According to *The Tablet*, disputes over chaplains were led by the hot-headed Dr Gibb.[43] Certainly, the Presbyterian Church under Dr Gibb fiercely complained when the hospital ship destined for the Dardenelles (funds for which had been raised by voluntary donations from many groups, including churches) included in its complement just two chaplains, one Anglican and one Catholic.[44] James Allen, Minister of Defence and himself an Anglican, replied in detail to the comments, insisting that the department was acting on the British government's regulations, and wishing that the churches could be more willing to co-operate at this time of national emergency. But he did concede the appointment of Rev. Daniel Dutton as a chaplain.[45] The issue kept reappearing, and Catholics too sought reassurance that they had been allowed their fair share of chaplains.[46]

By 1918, 130 ministers and priests had served as chaplains, while others served the forces in other capacities. This had a huge impact on the availability of clergy at home – in the case of the Methodist Church roughly one in four had served – and there were deep fears about how ministry was to be sustained at home. The Catholic Church became very sensitive on the issue of priests, but so too were other denominations.[47] Again these circumstances held potential for sectarian disputes.

Fund-raising and recruitment activities were accompanied by sermons, sometimes strident, speaking the language of commitment. The churches played an important role in advocating the war as a moral reckoning and commitment as embodying patriotism and worthy sacrifice. Much of this turned on ethical polemic against the German invasion and occupation of Belgium, with most denominations interpreting Germany's actions and Britain's intervention through biblical tenets and teachings.[48] Drawing on the words of Mary, in ways that she might not have conceived, the *Anglican* editor declared that 'We are called on to put down the mighty from their seat and to exalt the humble and meek.'[49] Similarly, in a lantern lecture at the Leys Institute in Ponsonby, Bishop Cleary dramatised the situation, calling on Auckland Anglicans 'to avenge the cruel wrongs inflicted on an inoffensive country which we have pledged ourselves to protect'.[50]

In articulating the nature of the conflict, many presented German autocracy and militarism as the root cause. The Catholic Dean of Invercargill, William Burke, expounded on the evils of the 'German creed' that might is right.[51] A sermon at St Matthew's called for New Zealand to send its best manhood 'to aid in the crushing of the animal spirit in Prussianised Germany'.[52] The Auckland Anglican paper expounded the faults of Germany's unrepresentative constitution.[53] The *New Zealand Baptist* denounced 'the ruthless schemes of Germany'.[54] Expatiating on this point, they condemned the German emperor:

> The blame for this swift uprush of savagery lies with the Kaiser and his war-lords . . . He has reckoned that he had the Almighty as an Ally in this ambitious purpose. He has induced his people to expend their resources to the fullest possible limit in building up an army and navy

> which might defy the world . . . He was consumed with an insensate ambition to 'bestride the world like a Colossus.[55]

The churches were by no means exceptional in this regard – expressions of outrage over Germany's actions and conduct were ubiquitous across the public sphere. But it hardly seems Christian for churches to have attacked German Kultur as some kind of primitive pagan force and assert that 'brutal German joy of battle' lay at the heart of the war.[56] A prime example was the March 1915 issue of the *New Zealand Baptist*, which contained two opposing editorials: one on the purity of the Allies' hatred of Germany's evil, and the other attacking the Germans for their focus on hate of the English![57]

There were more moderate and a few dissenting voices. Quakers maintained their rejection of war despite sarcasm in the press.[58] The Salvation Army was cautious of dwelling on devotions to national honour and of using 'Hun' language, and insisted that prayer and forgiveness towards Germans were appropriate.[59] Anglicans sought a Christian veneer to their concerns: they did initially provide congregations with a prayer for their enemies.[60] For one Methodist correspondent it was bewildering that there was a spirit of hatred towards the Germans, and no prayers for the Kaiser, and he felt this negated the claim that this was a Christian war.[61] Likewise, Baptists were horrified when German missionaries were interned, and requested that 'the whole missionary body should approach Government, asking it to state its reasons for the change of policy, and modify its rules of internment in the case of the missionaries'.[62] However, the civic role of the churches curbed these instincts. At an intercessory service in the Auckland Town Hall in mid-1915, one clergyman prayed eloquently about loving enemies and seeking peace, but there was a singular lack of Amens, and the speaker, the returned chaplain Rev. Guy Thornton, commented in his address that because Britain was fighting against devils this was not the time to pray to peace. The newspaper concluded that the appeal to love enemies was too tough for most of the audience.[63] In effect, anti-German sentiment led to crude behaviour, such as one amusing story of a parishioner cursing the Germans as he snoozed during the sermon, to the distaste of those who sat near him.[64]

The conviction that 'This war is for us a war of Right against Might' also advanced the sense of the war effort as a just cause.[65] *The Tablet* carefully surveyed the definition of 'just war' and found that World War I met two of the conditions of just war (just cause, just means), although it was not sure of the need to punish the infringer of rights. It saw the war as morally justified as a form of self-preservation.[66] Anglicans were told that it was legitimate to pray for victory because the cause was righteous.[67] Bishop Averill proclaimed that 'There are times when God calls us to fight His battles, and when His curse rests, as it rested on Meroz of old, on those who refuse His call.'[68] Elsewhere, in an important sermon, he insisted that war was a purgative for evil, so long as it was for righteousness, not for conquest, and this became an increasing theme in his wartime theology.[69] The Methodist conference approved without discussion Rev. Paul Fairclough's resolution that Britain was absolutely innocent of unleashing the dogs of war.[70]

This sense of the war's justice also manifested in impulses against a negotiated peace. At the outset of war there were many noble statements of the goal of peace but these often were complaisant with government decisions, 'happy in the conviction that the Empire is engaged in a noble cause', as a *Baptist* editorial put it.[71] There was a manifest lack of commentary on the conditions of peace: 'The Allies will know how to act magnanimously when the time comes to discuss terms of peace, but a premature pacification would be delusive, and only prelude a further outbreak of strife.'[72] Similarly, when the Anglican Church held a memorial service in the Town Hall during the Synod, the Bishop defended a military response to evil: 'It has been asked whether you can imagine Christ with a weapon of destruction in his own hand. But (said the Bishop) can you imagine him standing with folded hands while defenceless women and children were being done to death?'[73]

This offers some context for the 1916 introduction of conscription, which left little room for conscientious dissent from war. The 1916 Military Service Act recognised conscientious appeals if the appellant was a member of a religious body (and had been one before the war) whose doctrines held 'the bearing of arms and the performance of combatant service to be contrary to divine revelation.'[74] Quakers, Christadelphians and Seventh-day Adventists were recognised as meeting these stipulations. Others, like the Brethren and the Cooneyites, were probably not well understood because they did not operate as denominations but rather as movements. There were degrees of hesitation from more mainstream denominations: in 1915 the General of the Salvation Army insisted that fighting should be a decision left to each man's conscience, and the Catholic Church, though its views were muted in 1916, was very cautious about the decision to introduce conscription.[75] J.J. North, editor of the *Baptist*, registered a severe protest at the injustice to the individual religious conscience; and other church newspapers registered their concern as well, but were satisfied when provision was made for the Quakers.[76] The primary concern for most churches, however, was whether they would be able to retain their clerical muster at home. Several churches were mightily relieved that the decision was made in parliament, especially after they watched the sectarianism that the poll provoked in Australia.[77] The Women's Christian Temperance Union (WCTU) did consider the needs of conscientious objectors in 1917, but the motion was withdrawn because of the strong feelings on both sides.[78] In 1918 the WCTU rejected a resolution to protect the liberties of all (including conscientious objectors). It is little wonder that those concerned for conscientious objectors feared for the future of peace and international arbitration.[79]

The language of commitment was also heavily accented with imperial patriotism and, as a recent thesis has argued, 'in the minds of many, Church and Empire became welded into one unit'.[80] The sense was, as Canon Garland expressed it, that the churches needed to encourage national unity.[81] It was implied that without devoted help from volunteers, even in the Dominions, Britain would be defeated.[82] So there was a fair measure of duty and guilt involved in these outward displays of patriotism. When meeting in Wellington in November 1916, the Presbyterian General Assembly was chided by an unnamed critic for not singing the national anthem during proceedings.[83]

Anglican and Presbyterian voices were, not unexpectedly, very apparent in this jingoism. An important Anglican editorial issued an appeal: 'England, the mother of us all, calls us in her hour of need to maintain her honour'.[84] Declaring that 'the empire was noted for its colonising instinct and superabundant vitality', Bishop Averill borrowed the same imagery to say that 'the church existed for the sake of Empire-building, and that, therefore, there must always be a colonising instinct which must reproduce itself outside of its own borders.'[85] Consequently, he later urged a stronger sense of sacred statehood: 'Has the church fully realised the sacred nature of the nation, or its executive, the state?'[86] Likewise, in its 1915 resolution, the Auckland Synod voted:

> (a) that this synod while fearing that there is, apparent prospect of an early termination of the great war for liberty and righteousness in which the empire is engaged, desires to reaffirm its loyalty to the King and Empire and expresses its profound confidence that New Zealand is prepared to support the Empire to the very uttermost in this great struggle.
>
> (b) that this synod desires to express its pride and gratification in the heroic deeds done by our New Zealand soldiers in the Dardanelles, and assures them that the story of their self-sacrificing devotion to duty will be gratefully treasured in the hearts of their fellow-countrymen.[87]

Mixing with these sentiments, and hopes that the war would spur religious renewal, was a Protestant tendency to see the war in prophetic terms, as attested to in some very colourful literature.[88] When Guy Thornton, the first Baptist chaplain, spoke at the Baptist Tabernacle in Auckland prior to his embarkation with the First Expeditionary Force, his subject was 'The Present Crisis in the Light of Prophecy', and with a large Union Jack draped behind the pulpit, he predicted that the war was the harbinger of Christ's return to earth.[89]

Similar statements came from across the theological spectrum, with the Catholic voice striking an interesting tone. Claiming that there was little 'foolish jingoism' abroad (but rather 'the spirit of that nobler, saner type of imperialism'), they thought it was significant that people in every part of the Empire (including Ireland) were united.[90] Catholic chaplain Hackett claimed the British Empire was 'an empire under whose flag there was more freedom that in any other part of the world'.[91] Catholic commentators in the first two years of the war drew attention to Irish participation and argued that home rule should be granted to the Irish and the Dominions given more rights in return for their volunteers. This was a point drawn by *The Tablet* in particular.[92] Meanwhile, Baptists rejoiced that 'noble patriotism pulsates in the hearts of our Colonial youths': 'It is granted them to uphold the fair fame of the Dominion as well as to maintain the integrity of the Empire'.[93] Indeed, the magazine thought that war had a positive advantage in spurring a tighter empire and higher ideals in young people.[94]

Lastly, the sense of the war as a just and patriotic cause against a recognisable foe rendered losses as sacrifices, and some of those within the state church tradition took steps to sanctify the fallen soldier. At St Matthew's in Auckland the strident Rev. William Gillam (soon to be a chaplain), offered strong words to volunteers: 'If any of them fall in this most righteous struggle against tyranny and oppression, we shall feel that they have gone into the presence of God as martyrs.'[95] A prayer provided for Anglican memorial services intoned an aspiration that soldiers would be washed pure of all sins.[96] Bishop Averill compared the loss of parents to the loss of God the Father at the crucifixion.[97] However, churches sometimes differed sharply on finer points. Most Catholic priests and Protestant ministers were willing to apply the text 'greater love hath no man than this' to the soldiers' sacrifice but were cautious of going further.[98] Catholic commentators protested at viewing the soldiers' work as an atoning sacrifice.[99] The Salvation Army firmly rejected the notion that by fighting in the war people made atonement for their sins.[100] Baptist obituaries mostly sought comfort in accounts of the conversion of the fallen soldier.[101] When Rev. Percy Wainwright suggested that soldiers would be given an extra opportunity to respond to Christ in the hereafter, most Baptists rejected this.[102]

Changing relationships

Overall the church sought to position itself within a unified nation. However, it was increasingly evident in the latter half of the war that the strains of mobilisation spurred tensions in regards to churches' relationships with the state, society and one another.

Initially, a sense of national solidarity had made sectarianism less acceptable. Catholics, who felt particular pressure to prove that they were not sectarian, offer a good example. While the Catholic Federation continued to defend Catholic interests, its strategies worried other Catholics.[103] Also *The Tablet*, under its early wartime editor, emphasised that the Irish were loyal but ought to be given home rule; that the Catholic Federation and the Red Feds were able to work together; that the Pope could serve and lead the church throughout the world.[104] An early Catholic report of the military camp noted with pleasure the absence of sectarian bigotry there.[105]

Likewise, after the declaration of war the Protestant Bible in State Schools League announced the withdrawal of its bill (given public concern at such displays of sectarianism during a national emergency), and publicly supported early efforts to raise support for war needs.[106] The other much-debated issue, the prohibitionist no-licence campaign, was also deferred, out of churches' desire not to distract the public from the moral responsibility to war – though the results for the November 1914 election also showed that support for prohibition was not aided by war fever.[107] The prohibitionists announced that '[as] there is diversity of opinion amongst the people, we feel that even so great a cause as ours should be placed in the background until the present dangers to our Empire are overcome.'[108] Jews made few public statements but raised £935 (near $140,000 in 2015 dollars) in the first few months of the war, at the instigation of Sir Arthur Myers MP, to support the needs of Jewish refugees, and rabbis took their place on civic committees raising patriotic funds.[109]

In some sense, wartime conditions challenged the churches' social position. Civic committees played the key role, and churches and religious organisations generally placed their emphasis on participating in these efforts. How much they retained their own identity sometimes worried them. Tensions arose when the Bible in Schools Committee pledged to raise £1,000 (near $150,000 in 2015 dollars) for ambulance equipment but then found that some of its branches preferred to work directly with the Lady Liverpool Fund.[110] Likewise, the Anglican Church was aware that the national fervour undercut denominational special pleading. They were alarmed at the demand from soldiers for united services of worship: 'If the church will not assert herself she will be lost in the increasing tide of nonconformity'.[111] This heightened national solidarity also troubled New Zealand Methodists, who were not unmindful of German Methodists, while the Dublin rebellion raised questions about Catholic loyalties.[112]

Furthermore, hopes for religious renewal would clash with increasing exhaustion and longing for peace, especially in 1917 and 1918. While most denominational authorities kept on exhorting commitment, there were voices expressing degrees of doubt over the morality of continuing the war.[113] The theory of just war assessed the conduct of war as well as its causes, and it is surprising how rarely this issue was raised. Bishop Averill, for instance, had urged that the war not resort to 'fiendish methods', but did not comment when poison gas was deployed.[114] Yet people widely recognised the horrors of the war, and sermons throughout the war turned to addressing the concerns and implications it raised.[115] Thus at Ravensbourne Presbyterian Church in Dunedin, on the Sunday after the declaration of war, Rev. A. Gray addressed people's fears of soldiers being mangled in the battlefield, or a likely rise in the price of food.[116] The *Baptist* editor remarked on 'the fearful loss of life which modern warfare involves'. He went on to comment that 'It is supremely wicked and wasteful. And if the nations and their rulers are capable of learning anything, they may be expected to learn from this unprecedented conflict, that international disputes must be settled in a more rational way than by appeal to the sword.'[117] Similarly, the Salvationists spoke of the 'insensate folly' of war.[118] There was also plenty of attention paid to the morality of war in the magazines of the various denominations. The church newspapers from the evangelical churches focussed on the individual implications, idealising the spirit of self-sacrifice that they believed soldiers needed.[119] The evangelical churches and their chaplains were highly concerned with the morality of individual soldiers, and the resort to prostitution.[120] But here they were at odds with the permissiveness of officers. The YMCA at one point warned its Field Secretaries 'not to make public statements reflecting on the military authorities'.[121]

The erosion of social solidarity brought further strains. The decision to shelve potentially divisive issues was problematic, given the evocation of high principle, and suppressed issues often re-emerged and referenced wartime circumstances. During the war there was a widespread belief that sober people made better soldiers, and King George V's decision not to use alcohol during the war was just the sign that the Protestant churches were looking for as they sensed that alcohol consumption was growing.[122] But Anglicans generally counselled against the prohibition demands coming from the more Protestant churches.[123]

The politics of sacrifice also set the scene for a virulent re-emergence of sectarianism. In 1915 an Otago Presbyterian minister alleged that Catholics had contributed less to the Belgian relief cause than Protestants, and two priests responded before the editor closed the correspondence. This led *The Tablet* to make protestations that 'the Catholics of the Dominion are bearing their full share of sacrifice for the Empire'.[124] As the war, and its costs, rose, so did sectarian tensions.[125] There was the case of Laetitia Jane Hood, a Wellington dressmaker, who sent bitter letters to Catholic dignitaries and organisations criticising their values, under the pen name 'Gordon Andrew Martin, author of "Catholicism and Crime"'.[126] In 1916 the Dublin rebellion further aggravated tensions. The friendly reception given by Mayor Gunson of Auckland to the visiting Papal Legate, and the permission granted for the Domain to be used for an open-air mass, led to a letter of protest from the Orange Lodge. The Council, by resolution, 'express[ed] in the strongest terms its disgust at the bigotry and intolerance evidenced in this open letter'.[127] This did not stop the formation of the Protestant Political Association in 1917, for the tensions between the churches were reflective of a society which was moving more and more into total war.[128]

The war would also alter the churches' relationship with the state. Again, sentiments expressed early in the war seemed promising. The King's call for prayer was taken as a sign of the reciprocal relationship of the churches and the state, and perhaps helped in the call for loyalty.[129] As far as the political leaders were concerned, the responsibility of the church was to inspire people to be committed to the war. At an intercessory service in Wellington, the Anglican Bishop Sprott and Dr Gibb so inspired the congregation that the editor of the *Dominion* commented that the church could 'strike a deeper note than the politician. It can influence the very springs of conduct, and can render powerful help in the work of mobilising those spiritual forces which count for so much in days of peril.'[130] Similarly, the state was very aware of the importance of the churches, and the Governor wrote widely, including to the churches, thanking them for their contributions to the appeal to equip the hospital ship *Maheno* in 1915.[131] The visit of the Papal Legate early in 1916 enabled Catholics to give assurances at a public reception in the town hall, before no less a figure than James Gunson, Methodist mayor of Auckland, that their church would always support general projects for the well-being of all citizens.[132] The government (at the instigation of the King) asked the churches to host days of prayer, beginning on the first weekend of January 1915. There was another call for prayer after the drowning of Lord Kitchener and at frequent intervals thereafter, and churches took these up with alacrity, holding special services of intercession. British precedents were readily followed in the different situation of New Zealand.

However, this relationship, and the designation of churches in a therapeutic role, also threatened church autonomy. Chaplains, for example, were intended to have a strong role as propagandists, though Ormond Burton, for one, considered that compulsory church parades undermined their pastoral role.[133] In regard to chaplains, the state effectively co-opted the churches into the service, and they went willingly. Alfred North, the Baptist leader, insisted that church members should continue to serve and contribute to their church, unaffected by the heightened demands of the state.[134] But this was becoming an idealistic position, and only those sects like the Brethren and the Adventists, who rejected the idea of an appointed sphere for the state, resisted compliance to its demands.

These tensions were accompanied by a rising tone of moral criticism of the Dominion and the Empire, and whether it deserved to win. In July 1915 the WCTU persuaded the Christchurch Ministers' Association to attack the use of raffles to raise money for the war. Their statement provoked fierce criticism in the *Press* and a sharp division of opinion.[135] The state's craving for moral endorsement left it somewhat vulnerable to criticism. Some felt that the failure to build a righteous state by banning alcohol and introducing the Bible to schools had given New Zealand an uneasy moral status.[136] For example, T.H. Roseveare, the Presbyterian minister at St Andrew's in New Plymouth, gave a fervent discourse on the minor prophets and imperial sins in connection with the white slave trade and opium traffic, as well as the more familiar sins of the drink traffic and the desecration of Sunday.[137] The vicar of Takapuna, W.G. Monckton, a very popular speaker with a significant working-class following, likewise critiqued British moral standing: he noted notorious British and Belgian racism in regard to their colonies, and commercial greed dominating many businesses, who saw the war as an opportunity for profit.[138] Lastly, all sides were so caught up in the agonising task of ministering to the grieving that lofty sentiments were succeeded by grim realism and hopeful but nervous aspirations. But, as the Anglican Primate, S.T. Nevill, lamented to the General Synod of 1916, the war had not led to any return to religion.[139]

Conclusion

The churches felt their obligation to make a significant contribution to the war effort, and in the first few years of the war they did just that. In fund-raising, in prayer and in support for families, the churches made their presence known, although their strident patriotic tone came with a claim to moral authority which was repulsive to some. The second half of the war saw an increase in state intervention and the growth of sectarian divisions, and these undermined the moral prestige which the churches so desperately sought. Many soldiers did not return to church after the war. The League of Nations Union revivified religious visions for internationalism, and a therapeutic tone replaced Christian militancy. In retrospect, World War One represented a high-water mark for the churches in regards to political activism but, arguably, it also marked the beginning of the profound twentieth-century challenge to their place in society.

Chapter Twelve

Of Violets and Poppies: Charities in the Great War

Margaret Tennant

> Purple posies, cool and sweet,
> Spilling incense on the street,
> Call, ere yet your beauties die,
> 'Who helps England? Who will buy?'
>
> C.A. Marris, September 1914[1]

War is more usually associated with the carnage, chaos and stench of battle than with the delicate perfume and petals of violets. But as the military machinery was activated in 1914, September's 'Violet Day' symbolised civilian mobilisations and a reorientation of associational life in support of (and sometimes against) the war effort. It signalled a reconfiguration of charity that would involve another kind of 'battle'; one waged for public sympathies and donor largesse. And it was not the first organised effort in aid of those affected by the war that was escalating in Europe. Within two days of the declaration of war, the vice-regal consort Lady Liverpool had sought the assistance of the women of New Zealand in providing 'comforts' to soldiers. Within a week, Wellington women were reported as gathering to sew and knit, to make up 'Red Cross bandages' and doctors' overalls, and flannel shirts for soldiers. The communal rooms arranged for such activities were too small to hold all the eager volunteers, and those too ill to participate paid others to work on their behalf.[2] Industrial warfare was to have its gentler twin in the production-line charity of civilian life, in the pressures to participate and in the language of sacrifice, service and obligation.

Whether the Great War is seen as opening up a 'deluge' of change (as the title of Arthur Marwick's 1965 book suggested),[3] or 'business as usual', at best accelerated, depends upon the country in question and the area of concern. Distance from the physical battlefront, and established 'traditions, movements and dynamics'[4] shaped wartime responses and their post-war persistence. John Horne has argued that the 'pre-existing strength of the associative webs and mechanisms of national integration' were especially significant to the speed and success with which belligerents mobilised during the war.[5] Referring more specifically to charity, Peter Grant has put a case not only for its vast efflorescence in wartime Britain, but also that the strong and enduring social capital it represented gave Britain 'a distinct advantage over Germany' over the course of the war.[6] Here we examine the manifestations of war charity in a former British colony, far from the fighting front, which already had its own distinctive welfare arrangements and associational life.[7]

Welfare towards 1914

War charity built upon an existing welfare mix of state action, the voluntary sector, a small amount of private for-profit provision, and family support, which was calibrated differently according to national context.[8] In particular, the charity landscape which existed in New Zealand in 1914 brought the state, religious and voluntary organisations into a complementary relationship. Minimal military pensions had been in place since the New Zealand Wars of the 1860s. A civilian state pension system had come into being with the 1898 Old-age Pensions Act, men over 65 and women over 60 gaining pensions provided they met tight residency, asset and income-testing requirements prescribed by legislation. In 1911, widows with dependent children were the next social category to be admitted to the state pensions network. Pensions were linked to an older form of public welfare, the charitable aid system, by the moral assumptions embedded in their governing acts. Old-age pensioners were to be 'sober, moral and of good repute', which eliminated those who had recent prison terms or convictions for drunkenness and wife desertion, for example. Widows similarly had to prove good character and sober habits. 'Charitable aid', a New Zealand euphemism for the equivalent of a public poor law, was discretionary, and overseen by locally elected hospital and charitable aid boards and their officials. The boards provided relatively meagre assistance in grants, rent assistance and rations, and oversaw benevolent institutions which were essentially homes for the elderly and disabled.[9] On the eve of the First World War, pensions and charitable aid constituted the two main arms of public welfare; the first focussed on the 'deserving' pensioners in tightly defined categories, but with citizen entitlement under legislation; the second provided a discretionary, judgemental and very basic response to a wide variety of social need.

Although uneven, the voluntary sector was expanding and starting to generate its own 'social workers' – a term increasingly used to describe an assortment of religious deaconesses and nuns, city missioners and lay personnel, whose practical and often long-term engagement with the poor gave them knowledge of the social situations and personal shortcomings that beset their hapless clientele. They, and the mostly well-heeled volunteers who led voluntary sector committees, represented the interpersonal side of charity, variously presented as 'kindness in action', 'gushing philanthropy' or the officious policing of the lives of the poor and distressed.[10] Though theoretically independent of government, organisations within the voluntary sector often looked to the state for subsidies and other supports – I have argued previously that by international standards voluntary charity was slow to develop and modest in extent in New Zealand, with the state already the major force in welfare, broadly interpreted, by the 1900s.[11] Voluntary and state agencies all assumed that the family was the first resort of those in need, but many, especially immigrants, did not have a kin network at hand, or other family members able and willing to maintain them.

Whether public or private, in 1914 welfare was attuned to a society at peace, where economic inequality and personal misfortune interacted to produce demand for social services. War would test existing arrangements, introducing new dynamics, new outlets and new methods to the charity sector, the focus of this chapter. Organisations with a specific war focus supplemented (and occasionally supplanted) those already in existence, and both require attention in any discussion of wartime charity.

Shifting targets: sequencing and scale

Charles Marris's Violet Day poem goes on to invoke the 'gifts the gods have sent – Peace enduring, fond content' and to contrast New Zealand's serenity and plenitude with the bitter days ahead for England and her 'lowly folk'. 'Who helps England?': the answer was not in doubt. The Dominion would supply not only troops, but the proceeds of appeals such as Violet Day. 'Corps' of women, organised into 'contingents', were reported as 'commencing operations' in Christchurch at 8.45 a.m. on 4 September 1914 – military analogies started early.[12]

There was a sequencing of wartime charitable efforts. The destitute of Belgium and Ireland, as well as England, were embraced by the first Violet Day. Then, as reports came through of German atrocities, 'poor little Belgium' became a more distinct target for appeals and events, New Zealanders identifying with a small nation under siege.[13] Patriotic societies also provided 'comforts' – typically items such as underwear, pyjamas, socks, hold-alls, and 'housewives' (sewing kits) – for the men in training camps and then for those sent overseas as part of the Expeditionary

Force. An important focus for fund-raising and donations in kind over mid-1915 was the first New Zealand hospital ship *Maheno*, followed by the second, *Marama*. Once wounded soldiers returned from the Gallipoli campaign and hospital trains discharged their maimed human cargo up and down the main trunk line, 'Sick and Wounded' funds became more evident, as did attention to the needs of soldiers' families.[14] As in other parts of the Empire, the language of patriotism was increasingly tempered by the language of caring.[15] As a neutral body, the Red Cross was supposed to concern itself only with those taken out of combat by wounds and sickness, and it received a boost from 1915.[16] The visitation, entertainment and transport of wounded men soon provided opportunities for face-to-face engagement with the human consequences of war, and the needs of disabled veterans were to provide the basis of continued activity beyond it.[17] Soldiers' families could also seek assistance from the patriotic societies, and although the visitation they received could be inquisitorial, it was generally less moralistic than the public sector charitable aid system.[18]

From massive fund-raising efforts for those at a distance, to the making and packing of items for named and unnamed soldiers in camps or overseas, then the face-to-face care of returned servicemen – most of these activities were new and at first largely informal. Some groups remained little more than sewing circles and working bees over the duration of the war, while others transitioned from a spur-of-the-moment fund-raising activity into something more structured, with treasurer and committee. Branches of existing organisations like St John and the Victoria League added patriotic fund-raising to their existing activities soon after the war commenced, but there were also new formations, among them various patriotic associations and guilds, while at least one transnational organisation, the Red Cross, gained a national presence. It is difficult to quantify charitable activities even today, and for the First World War we are largely dependent upon official listings of registered patriotic funds. There were 529 such bodies reported in 1918, but other sources suggest closer to 1,000 if more localised groups which fed funds into larger centres are also taken into account.[19] The titles show that these forms of wartime voluntarism extended into the smallest of communities right across the country, and that some were general in focus while others had more specific targets – there were blind sailors' funds, pipe and tobacco funds, wounded animal funds, leather vest funds, and local relief funds for soldiers' families, to name just a few.[20] Local studies of the home front during the Great War confirm the deep penetration of war efforts into rural as well as urban communities.[21] It has been estimated that, by 1920, New Zealanders had raised £5.7 million (over $500 million in 2015 dollars) for patriotic purposes.[22] In a country where voluntary charities had mostly struggled for funds, and where philanthropy was very much an optional extra for the wealthy, this was a significant achievement, and one based heavily upon multitudinous small but intensive efforts. Even this amount did not represent the full extent of wartime charity, but it, and the copious newspaper references to voluntary activities, are testimony to an upsurge of voluntary effort on a scale never before experienced in New Zealand.

On the first Violet Day in 1914 it was noted that violets came from the 'humble little plot of ground that fronts the cottage of the labourer, the clerk, the factory hand', as well as the 'stately gardens surrounding the homes of wealth'.[23] Here the ubiquity of violets symbolised a cross-class effort, and leaders of patriotic societies often claimed social unity as the strength of the patriotic movement and war charities. Leonard Tripp's chapter on 'War Relief and the Patriotic Societies' in the 1923 book *The War Effort of New Zealand* even attributed victory to the 'splendid co-operation of all classes'.[24] But Tripp himself was a prominent lawyer and member of a South Island land-owning family, a noted imperialist, president of the national Federation of War Relief Societies and a dominant figure in the Red Cross. Social elites dominated the leadership of patriotic efforts and war charities, as they had dominated pre-war benevolent societies: there was little change here, except for the more overt trumpeting of 'Britishness' by those who had always been loyal to Empire and benefited socially, and often economically, from its reach.[25] Nonetheless, their constituency of fellow workers on the ground massively expanded over the war, driven by a more complicated mix of personal emotions and social pressures than any simple invocation of imperial zeal can capture.

The emotional force of wartime charity

'Knit-knit-knit! An army of women too!' went one of the verses in circulation during 1915, invoking a parallel mobilisation of female non-combatants alongside military recruitment.[26] Some 15 per cent of official patriotic funds identified themselves as ladies', women's or girls' groups, as branches of the Lady Liverpool Fund, or as knitting or sewing guilds,[27] but newspaper reports show that the role of women was far more extensive than this would indicate, especially at the informal and local level. The scale of activity was exceptional and the context different from women's pre-war voluntarism: Dorothy Page suggests that the war 'totally changed' the previously sedate style of women's organisations, sparking an unprecedented outpouring of energy.[28] Caroline Daley noted that in Taradale war efforts provided married women with an organised, secular and public role beyond the church for the first time.[29] Elsewhere, too, the town hall now supplemented the church hall as a site of voluntary organising and endeavour. And there was another important difference: in New Zealand, prior to the conflict, charitable giving and more direct involvement in helping those less fortunate had largely been an optional extra for those of means. Wartime expectations were much higher, the moral pressures less tolerant of non-involvement. Even women could be labelled 'shirkers' if they stood aside from the business: as Wellington's mayoress, Jacobina Luke, declared in 1915, 'Any woman who could use a needle, and who had a heart, was a coward who did not now "do her little bit" for the boys who went to the front'.[30]

Women first responded to a call by Lady Liverpool on 6 August 1914 for the formation of a network of local fund-raising bodies, which would feed money and goods to committees in the larger centres and thereby support the 'citizen army' being formed.[31] Mayoresses led efforts in local communities, but women gathered in countless homes and halls, in venues small and large, to plan, produce and pack as part of their voluntary contribution to the war effort. Bruce Scates and others have referred to the 'emotional labour' behind these activities, encapsulated in the image of female sock knitter.[32] Women had always provided the workforce behind charities, even when men provided leadership or controlled the finances, but war afforded new outlets and new drivers of activity. For women, and for men unable to 'go to war', involvement in charity provided an opportunity to participate in the excitement of war, to emulate sacrifice, and to divert patriotic outrage into constructive ends. For an Ashburton mother, the German sinking of the British ship *Lusitania* and shooting of nurse Edith Cavell made her so angry that she took after them in the only way she knew how: 'She cast about for a weapon. She couldn't find anything deadly that she could wield, but she could and did find something that demanded all her zeal. She flung herself into Red Cross work'.[33] Voluntary work provided a particularly important outlet for energy and outrage in New Zealand, since opportunities for employment in war industries were considerably less than in Britain, for example.

The emotional contours of war charity expanded beyond the compassion for others, Christian witness and aspirations to social control which are variously attributed to charity in the nineteenth century. Underpinning war charity was a volatile mix of other sentiments. Patriotic fervour was at first leavened by a certain amount of merriment and frivolity, most evident in the craze for fund-raising 'queen carnivals' all over the country during 1915.[34] Although the incongruity of high spirits amidst national emergency drew comment even at the time, the restless energy which underpinned it was also recognised and forgiven because it generated funds for the national cause and raised morale. Alongside the bazaars, parades, concerts, illuminations, sporting events, lotteries, balls and tableaux there were traditional elements of carnivalesque: mock courts where public figures were 'tried' for trivial offences, the sale of books in which politicians and others were caricatured, and cross-dressing, as 'khaki-clad maidens' paraded the streets (and others, in what would have been a particular transgression in peacetime, sold kisses to strangers in public). But the very public gaiety of the carnival was underwritten by the more sombre tones of grief and anticipated grief. As the Wellington *Carnival Book* recorded:

> It was a joyous, reckless, impudent, almost devil-may-care procession that yet managed, once or twice, to bring a lump into one's throat by a reminder that there were faraway battlefields where Queen Carnival did not reign, where New Zealand boys were fighting and dying very gloriously in order to subdue a grim and ugly monster born of those demons, Mad Militarism and Ill Faith. It was a procession that made much laughter and then put a price on it, for the citizen who smiled broadly usually found a collection box under his nose . . .[35]

There were some carnivals after 1915, but it may have become more difficult to justify their exuberance amidst bereavement and mourning. The quieter intimacies of the sewing circle and parcel-packing room were more compatible with shared grief and solace as more of those left behind faced, or anticipated, bereavement. As the *Red Cross Record* noted, the products of these gatherings were not simply material objects produced by women's labour: rather, they were 'tangible proof of myriads of kind thoughts towards [the soldiers] and aching desires to help them, sometimes, doubtless, with hopes and fears, dumb sorrow and poignant anxiety woven into every loop of sock and meshed muffler'.[36]

Those on the receiving end of philanthropy prior to the war had usually been constituted as 'other', as feckless and reckless, or at the very least as hapless victims distanced by class, location and circumstance from their benefactors, but those on whom patriotic efforts were lavished escaped such judgements. Soldiers were '*our* boys', geographically distanced once at the front, but imaginatively close to the collective heart of the home-front war effort. Historians have recently tended to downplay the notion of a fissure between the domestic and frontline experiences, pointing out the permeability of boundaries between the two, mitigated most of all by a constant flow of letters and the sending of 'comforts', the term itself imbued with cosy domesticity. Following Jay Winter's notion of 'adoptive kin', Rachel Patrick has emphasised the ways in which patriotic societies 'drew upon the language of kinship to stake a claim for patriotic women in the war effort'.[37] Even where the recipients of parcels were anonymous, patriotic organisations such as the Otago Soldiers' and Dependants' Welfare Committee drew upon familial imagery, while the press described the women volunteers as 'soldiers' mothers' tenderly producing kits and parcels, if not for their own, then for 'some other woman's "bairn"'.[38] Even an organisation could be become a substitute mother, endowed with qualities of tenderness and love: alongside the image of a monolithic nurse figure cradling a soldier, the Red Cross positioned itself as 'THE GREATEST MOTHER IN THE WORLD . . . ready and eager to comfort when comfort is most needed'.[39] Potential donors were asked to picture sons and husbands 'lying on beds of sickness in far distant lands, maimed, wasted, lonely', buoyed and cheered by one thing only: 'the sacred symbol of the Red Cross on a woman's breast'.[40] Familial discourses drew voluntary workers and the recipients of their efforts together in ways that had seldom informed pre-war charity. Webs of empathy, imagination and yearning sustained the increasingly efficient productivity of wartime voluntary effort.

'Organised kindness'

The emotional prompts which enabled activity on such a vast scale also necessitated its oversight and control. Violet Day and its successors represented other organisational dynamics of war charity: its increasing professionalisation, its regional and then national organisation, and the transnational sharing of fund-raising techniques.

In the early months of the war there were reports of inefficiency, duplication and the unsuitable nature of some goods supplied as 'comforts' to soldiers. Money was collected without clear accountabilities. Some men who went to camp were said to have been given multiple kits by patriotic committees, as well as their government issue, and unwanted items ended up in pawn shops. Other items were unsuitable to transport or to fit into soldiers' kits.[41] The Defence Department soon issued lists of supplementary items for supply by patriotic societies, and parcels of comforts became more standardised. At a meeting of women's patriotic funds convened by the Countess of Liverpool in March 1916, it was agreed that a uniform parcel be approved for distribution to the men at the front: it was to contain a selection of articles from a list which included sardines, anchovies, Bovril, extract of meat, curry powder, Glaxo powder, soup tablets, cocoa, cornflour, soap, writing paper and sanitary paper, to a total value of 2s 6d (nearly $20 in 2015 dollars).[42] Later in the year, the contents of Christmas gift parcels were similarly specified, with additional items including little luxuries such as chocolate, condensed milk and tobacco, alongside razor strops and insect powder. Soon there were regional quotas for parcels, a 'uniformity of cards [for insertion in the parcels] and stencilling', and specified dimensions for the boxes in which the parcels were dispatched.[43] At one stage, 24,000 dominion parcels were being dispatched per month.[44]

As more and more activity took place in the name of the Red Cross, its publication, the *New Zealand Red Cross Record*, revealed the increasingly systematic arrangements behind war charity. The *Record* quoted Sir Frederick Treves, one of the founders of the British Red Cross, on the need for kindness to be organised in time of stress: it was 'the primary business of the Red Cross societies to organise the generosity of the country, economise it, direct it into proper channels, and to prevent the waste of energy which is inevitable when no system of control exists'.[45] After a period of delayed and overlapping effort, the Red Cross established a central office in Wellington through which information about requirements was distributed to the depots in the four main military districts. This was then sent out to branches. The central office also arranged shipping space for the transmission of goods and a system to record the contents of each case sent, its value, source, destination and method of dispatch. It worked with the Department of Internal Affairs to ensure the safe transmission of funds to London.[46]

The Red Cross depots likewise co-ordinated the movement of goods and funds from their districts. All four centres oversaw busy and complex operations. The Canterbury depot in Christchurch's Cathedral Square had a sales department, from which cut-out garments and bandaging materials were sold to branches for processing; another department where returned products were checked, corrected and bundled up; a bandage-making and packing department; and a general packing department where boxes were finally nailed down 'by a male helper'. There was also a 'missing and wounded department', which worked with the International Red Cross to follow through on relatives' inquiries about missing men.[47] Instructions were circulated on the making of shirts, bed jackets, pyjamas, facecloths, dressing gowns, fomentation towels, handkerchiefs, nurses' overalls and hot-water bottle covers. The *Red Cross Record* printed precise dimensions for the making of specialised items such as rolled and triangular bandages and pneumonia jackets. Even knitters got their instructions, based, clearly, on previous deficiencies: rough wool should not be used on amputee stump socks; face holes in balaclavas were not to be more than three inches square; each sock in a pair should be stitched to the other.[48] Quantities were impressive: in July 1916, the Canterbury depot's 'bandage department' alone received 65,275 bandages, as well as thousands more swabs, operation sheets, limb pillows, fomentation cloths, dysentery pads and other specialist items – 138,000 articles in total.[49] This was production-line charity, linked with a wider international enterprise and its distribution networks. Industrial warfare generated semi-industrial charity. There were still inefficiencies, and by the end of the war British-based agencies placed more emphasis on the sending of money rather than goods, especially to supply prisoners of war.[50]

In other ways, too, charity became more highly organised and professional. While the sending of goods overseas drew heavily upon volunteers' donations of time, there was an increasing emphasis on donations of money to allow goods to be purchased closer to the front and to convalescent homes in the United Kingdom. Greater and greater ingenuity was required to separate members of the public from the contents of their purses, especially once a degree of donor fatigue crept in. The Great War saw the appearance of fund-raising techniques still current today. In some centres the Queen Carnivals were extravaganzas of such complexity and length that professional organisers made their appearance on a remunerated basis. A certain 'Professor' Owen Cardston, who claimed experience in organising carnivals throughout New Zealand and Western Australia, masterminded the Wellington and Auckland Queen Carnivals of 1915, while William Lints, whose speciality was organising stage entertainments, popped up in a number of centres, producing shows such as 'Our Reveille'.[51]

The Red Cross invoked imperial bonds when it joined in an Empire-wide 'Our Day' from 1916, claiming a dedicated collection day to raise funds for the sick and wounded. The use of a floral signifier also became more common from the First World War. Seasonally specific floral fetes and flower days had been used locally for charitable purposes prior to the war, and Violet Day was largely opportunistic, drawing upon a flower which happened to be in season and widely available in August and September 1914. Although held on different dates throughout the country, Violet Day continued as a fund-raiser for the sick and wounded even beyond the war. The Auckland Red Cross followed its British counterpart in promoting 'Alexandra Rose Day' in June 1918, the choice of a rose referencing England's national flower. Since roses were out of season, those sold were artificial blooms crafted by girls from the 'John Groom Crippleage' in England.[52] Roses and violets were eventually superseded by the remembrance poppy, inspired by lines in the famously evocative poem by Canadian John McCrae: 'In Flanders fields the poppies blow / Between the crosses, row on row'. The sale of poppies to assist veterans was a tradition started in the United States and taken up in New Zealand in 1922. War charity, like its peacetime equivalent, drew upon a transnational repertoire of fund-raising techniques, but these techniques had a more emotive pull when promoted as part of a vast imperial war effort.

As war charities attempted to become more standardised and efficient, they also came under government oversight. New Zealand had never had a charities commission of the kind which existed in England, but the 1915 War Funds Act drew voluntary ventures further into the web of total war, increasing the level of reporting and accountability required of groups that raised funds for patriotic purposes. Permits were required for patriotic collections and the monies raised were to be handled and dispersed by a limited number of officially recognised patriotic funds.[53] It was another sign that war-related charities were different from others, their scale and the unprecedented sums collected requiring government intervention.

Existing charities

Our focus has been on organisations and efforts linked to the war. What of those charities which existed prior to the conflict? For them, the impact of the war varied. Some were better placed than others to align themselves with the patriotic programme. The Plunket Society, formed by Frederic Truby King in 1907, consolidated its national presence and oversaw an expansion of branches during the war years. 'Saving babies' was presented as 'the most patriotic work anyone can undertake', newspaper articles helpfully pointing out that the high rejection rate for military service might have been obviated by earlier attention to infant welfare.[54] In the 1917 national 'Save the Babies Week' the link was particularly explicit. A Gisborne event was even advertised as supporting 'A National Necessity – the War Loan and "Save the Babies" Campaign'. (The prime attraction was a certain Miss Ray Raymond, who promised to sell kisses and perform 'fascinating dances' – a somewhat risqué linkage with a maternalist cause which would probably not have been acceptable in peacetime).[55]

On the other hand, the Auckland Ladies' Benevolent Society had long prided itself on doing good and doing it discreetly among a clientele dominated by 'old maiden ladies left stranded towards the eventide of life'.[56] It was hard pushed to maintain a presence amidst wartime distractions and the more public claims of young men who had placed their lives on the line in defending the Empire. The Society's already meagre subscription income fell from £722 (near $105,000 in 2015 dollars) in the 1914–1915 year to £166 (near $20,000 in 2015 dollars) in 1916–1917, the lowest in its 35-year history.[57] It was evidence of an 'unfortunate tendency on the part of the Auckland public to forget the needs of the poor, the sick and the aged, in wider claims made by the war'.[58] 'CHARITY V. PATRIOTISM' was an *Auckland Star* headline, linking the decline to the 'excitement of patriotic fervour', which had led people to redirect their giving.[59] Other organisations also found their donor bases disrupted by the war.

It was not only the redirection of money that had a distorting effect on charity. The giving of time had always been as important as the giving of money, and volunteers' energies were diverted from established causes. The Auckland Society for the Protection of Women and Children was one body which noted its members' involvement in patriotic work, the 1918 annual report anticipating that 'When the War is over we have no doubt that they will again be willing to help the Society in the necessary effort to extend its functions and activity'.[60] Some organisations had to share their experienced secretaries and social workers with patriotic societies: in Dunedin, for example, the Patients' and Prisoners' Aid Society allowed its agent, Francis Cummings, to devote almost all his time to the Otago Patriotic and General Welfare Association, while Effie Cardale, secretary-visitor of the Christchurch Society for the Protection of Women and Children, also became secretary of the Canterbury Patriotic Fund. Sister Hannah, from Auckland's Sisters of the Good Shepherd, became official visitor for the Auckland War Relief Association and spent most of the war assisting soldiers' wives.[61]

The patterning of need also showed the impact of war conditions. Charities involved in work with families noted rising demand for relief, attributing it to increases in the cost of living, most especially the price of basic foodstuffs. There was slackness of trade and unemployment, not least among women in domestic service as 'housewives, eager to show their patriotism' decided to do without household help and to apply the money saved to the various patriotic funds.[62] Soldiers' allotments to families were sometimes less than they had been earning in civilian life (but often more regular), and it became clear in soldiers' absence that many had responsibilities that extended beyond their nuclear families.[63] Some men were reported as joining the Expeditionary Force without providing for their families (or even informing them of an intended departure).[64] The Protection Society was active in pursuing individual cases and, eventually, in forcing the government to make such provision compulsory. On the other hand, war conditions forced the Society to temper its agitation for other legislative changes, such as the appointment of women jurors, justices and police.[65] Overall, existing charities tried to show their relevance and responsiveness to war conditions, but deferred, sometimes reluctantly, to the greater claims of the patriotic enterprise. Their members' ongoing dedication to clients whose situation lacked the emotive pull of wounded twenty-something soldiers was in itself heroic.

Conclusion

The social capital represented by war charities did not immediately dissipate upon the signing of the armistice. Geoffrey Rice has pointed out how it was mobilised in response to the influenza epidemic and, indeed, 'The existence of wartime fund-raising groups, patriotic societies and Red Cross branches enabled many towns to respond more quickly to the epidemic than if the disaster had occurred in peacetime'.[66] But many of the smaller patriotic groups soon faded, and donations to the patriotic funds similarly diminished after 1919. In its last issue of May 1919, the *Red Cross Record* gave a summary of Red Cross activity over the previous four years and ended on a prescient note: 'Goodbye – till the Next War'.[67]

On a personal level it is clear that many wartime charity workers retired, exhausted from the war effort, once peace was declared. Some faced the familial challenges of caring for returned men shattered in mind and body. But others took into the post-war era a sense of duty, the need to compensate for loss and to work for a better world. There were veterans such as Malcolm Galloway, who spent the rest of his life working for the Red Cross, which he blessed for his deliverance after being wounded on the Western Front.[68] There was Jacobina Luke, wartime mayoress of Wellington, whose leadership qualities, honed in the wartime packing room and fund-raising ventures, carried on in the Red Cross, St John, the YWCA, the Plunket Society, the Free Kindergarten Association, the National Council of Women and the McCarthy Trust Board, to name just a few of the bodies of which she was a highly active member.[69] There was Annie Herbert, a prominent Christchurch voluntary worker who, when asked why she worked so tirelessly helping the friendless, replied that 'it was when I lost my son Lester – our only child – in the Great War [that] I determined to devote myself to others in need'.[70] Narratives of social betterment and hope for a better world from the carnage of war often translated into social action.

On the organisational front, a cluster of war-related charities such as the provincial patriotic associations, the Red Cross and the Returned Soldiers' Association (RSA) continued after the war, broadening their mandate and augmenting the peacetime voluntary sector. Disabled returned heroes, at first relatively young, provided a new and 'deserving' constituency of need. Substantial amounts of war funds remained, and by legislation they needed to be applied to the objects for which they were raised – mostly the needs of returned soldiers, who became a distinctive group of beneficiaries. The Red Cross, for example, had responsibility for four convalescent homes for sick and wounded soldiers during the interwar period. But it also had branches which applied the discourse of battle to the fight against disease and natural disaster, carving out new niches in the post-war world. The RSA married service provision with advocacy for ongoing, and better, state provision for war veterans. The distinctive 'Anzac' poppy, forever associated with the battlefields of Europe, soon overtook the violet, a more subtle and diffuse fund-raising symbol.

There was no seismic shift overall in the existing trajectory of state–voluntary sector relations. If anything, the war and patriotic society interactions with soldiers' families disclosed families' inability to cope on existing wages even in peacetime.[71] The state remained the largest provider of social welfare, and wartime taxation and controls reinforced and accelerated the notion of state activism and intervention. Even amidst the vast mobilisation of civil society in support of the war effort, there had been firm statements about the obligation of the state to properly equip the Expeditionary Force and hospital ships out of taxation, to make provision for soldiers' dependants from the time of enlistment and to supply all necessities for the sick and wounded. The role of the patriotic societies was to provide additional comforts and to fill unforeseen gaps in state provision. Even though these gaps proved far more extensive than at first anticipated, the role of the voluntary sector was, and remained in peacetime, a supplementary one.[72] The government provision for returned servicemen and their dependants via pensions, health services and repatriation schemes provided a benchmark for civilian aspirations – in health care even more than in pensions. If the government's recompense to returned men for their sacrifice was less than perfect in its execution, this was because it built upon a pre-existing bundle of minimalism and moral judgement in public welfare provision.[73] But the state was still the larger player, and once the outburst of 'spontaneous voluntaryism'[74] associated with the war had subsided, the charity sector's role as supplementary and complementary to the state was even more apparent.

Chapter Thirteen

Where Were the Peacemongers? Pacifists in New Zealand during World War One

David Grant

This chapter narrates the story of pacifists in New Zealand during the First World War, defined as those who oppose all war at all times, regardless of the circumstances – an absolute rejection of armed force. It is not the story of the anti-militarists of many hues who were not necessarily pacifists but protested military conscription in this war for political, religious or personal ethical reasons, before and after the first ballots were cast in November 1916, and which, one would argue, is the most potent story of dissent during this war.

The energy and strength of the patriotic cause contrasted strongly with the insularity, yet the stubbornness, of the few who defied the jingoism that accompanied the war's outbreak. Days after Britain's entrance to the war, for example, the *New Zealand Herald* editorialised: 'War! There is no conception more inspiring, no condition nobler, no call that rings more gladly in the ears'.[1] In this atmosphere it is important to identify pacifists' moral courage in putting their hands up to resist this war, to record the enormous pressure they were under to abandon their stance, to observe what happened to them, and to suggest reasons why.

Considering New Zealand society's, and the government's, unwavering commitment to the war, who opposed this development? Very few it seemed. The country did have some history of anti-militarism before 1914, but this focus was mostly on opposing pre-war compulsory military training, introduced through the 1909 Defence Act. During the war this focus continued in those combating conscription. Pacifists were very thin on the ground indeed.

Pre-war anti-militarism

That was not the way it looked before the war, although it needs to be stressed that this activity was broadly anti-militarist rather than specifically pacifistic. In June 1910, Louis P. Christie, editor of the *Christian Herald*, founded an Anti-Militarist League to promote a socialist, anti-war credo: by the end of 1911 there were sixteen branches throughout New Zealand.[2] In June 1911, the wealthy Christchurch Baptist lay preacher Charles Mackie challenged his clergy's compliance with a government directive to collect the names of those within the congregations who would be eligible to be initiated into compulsory military training. When this compliance was not forthcoming, he founded a National Peace Council, an umbrella organisation comprising delegates from church, community and political groups, as well as the influential Women's Christian Temperance Union (WCTU) and the Women's Institute, the latter founded in 1892 to further international peace in the interests of women and children.[3] Other figures and ideas arrived from overseas. Perhaps the most outspoken figure was John Fletcher, a visiting English Quaker, who took the fight to the streets in an unrelenting campaign, during which he was arrested, fined and imprisoned.[4]

When the Anti-Militarist League formed an alliance with the National Peace Council in December 1912, they claimed a combined membership of 30,000.[5] Both groups, separately and together, pursued an active anti-war propaganda campaign by pamphlet, letter, public meeting, and rallies in Christchurch's Cathedral Square that attracted many hundreds of people. Indeed, Christchurch formed a centre of anti-militarist thought and activity and supplied two-thirds of New Zealand's objectors to compulsory military training.[6] Its radical 'British' non-conformity led one observer to describe it, not entirely unsympathetically, as a 'happy home of converts to fancy religions, cranky faddists, craven CO's and oblique visionaries of both sexes'.[7]

Anti-militarism had a complex relationship with the labour movement. This relationship was made more complicated by deep divisions within the labour movement in their attitude towards the war. The movement's history had been characterised by alternating competition and attempted conciliation between its two wings: the moderate majority, inheritors of the Liberal-Labour tradition of consensus, pragmatism and arbitrationist politics; and 'militants', whose war with capital was class-inspired and deeply influenced by Marxist ideology and International Workers of the World (aka 'Wobblies') tactics. The latter tended to be members of the Socialist Party and/or the Red Federation of Labour. Labour's defeat in strikes among miners in Waihi in 1912, and continuing industrial disruption, led to two 'Unity' conferences in 1913, the first of which, in January, saw the formation of a new party, the Social Democratic Party (SDP). As it was more 'militant' in essence than previous manifestations of Labour parties, one might have assumed it would oppose the forthcoming 'capitalist' war and form a bastion of anti-militarism.

That did not transpire. When it came to the crunch, the great bulk of SDP members and trade unionists, both militant and moderate, supported the war. The very few that did not did so on class grounds, asserting that war was simply a means by which capitalists exploited workers for undeserved profits while those from all countries were fighting each other and dying on the front line. Similarly, while some socialist union leaders – such as Fred Cooke, Ted Howard, Paddy Webb, Bob Semple, Peter Fraser and Jack McCullough, among others – had addressed Peace Council and Anti-Militarist League peace rallies in Christchurch and Auckland before the war, they kept their own counsel after its outbreak. Instead they channelled their angst towards vigorously opposing the introduction of conscription in 1916. In some respects, asserting universal workers' interests and solidarity became less politically tenable during the war. The reality, that New Zealand working-class men were being killed or grievously wounded in battle, was more horrific to union leaders of all hues than the fate of the enemy soldiers facing them. The extent to which the political landscape changed is glimpsed in the surge of social solidarity in August 1914: unions promised not to strike, the Arbitration Court was suspended and workers in essential industries began to win pay rises unheard of in peacetime, as labour was in short supply with workers leaving for the front line. In return, Prime Minister William Massey released those imprisoned after the 1913 strike. Temporarily, at least, the tumultuous events on the streets and waterfronts of the previous year seemed like a distant memory.[8]

This is comparable to the global reaction of mass anti-militarist movements. The war's outbreak proved international socialist solidarity to be much less powerful than national or imperial sentiment and loyalty. The European parties of the Second International, which, in a 1912 Congress in Basle, had unanimously resolved that in the event of war they would refuse service, quickly changed tack in August 1914, supporting the war efforts of their respective countries. In July 1914, the British Labour Party publicly reaffirmed allegiance to the Second International's principles, but by the end of the following month decided to support its government's recruiting campaign. This left a small rump of diehard socialist anti-war antagonists who, along with Christian pacifists, were roundly condemned by their fellows and the bulk of the British population. Those recalcitrants who continued to be vocal suffered the indignity of imprisonment for long periods.[9]

The history of peace movements in New Zealand, and their ability to oppose the war, likewise reflected the sharp shift in pre-war/wartime social attitudes. One such movement was the New Zealand Freedom League ('freedom' from war; 'freedom' from coercion to fight), founded in Auckland in March 1913 by Egerton Gill. It succeeded the short-lived New Zealand chapter of the International Arbitration and Peace Association. Gill, born in England in 1877, had immigrated to Auckland in 1902, setting up an accountancy practice. However, his occupation took second place as he thrust himself into League business.

The Freedom League was an umbrella group uniting a number of other small Auckland-based peace groups in a collective association. It was most concerned, after its first meeting, to have the compulsory clauses of the Defence Act repealed. By the outbreak of war in August 1914, the Freedom League had six branches and some 500 members in five different cities, although its strength remained in Auckland. It was here that it held meetings pronouncing the value of peace – near the wharf at the foot of Queen Street, or on street corners throughout the city during the day, and in the Royal Albert Hall and the Opera House in the evenings. With up to 40 members attending its fortnightly meetings, it was a vibrant, activist organisation and its leaders faced hecklers at their meetings with aplomb.[10] The printed word formed another avenue for distributing the League's philosophies. Secretary Gill, fellow accountant Ernest Wright and the first chairman, Methodist minister Reverend Richard Hall, among others, wrote court reports for compulsory military training dissenters, distributed anti-war leaflets and pamphlets (many from Great Britain, where the call for peace was strong), and wrote letters to newspaper editors, civic leaders and national politicians.

Gill was a Quaker, and his church's tenets include anti-war teachings. When the first Quakers (also known as the Religious Society of Friends) arrived in New Zealand in the 1840s, these tenets were tested as some refused to enlist in militia during the Land Wars of the 1860s; mostly, they were granted exemptions. At the first national Quaker conference in Wellington in May 1909, delegates passed a unanimous resolution calling on the government to adhere 'unswervingly to the principles of Peace' as all war was 'contrary to the authority of Christ'.[11] It is hard to argue that the Quaker Church was militant. Thomas Wright, clerk of the 1909 and 1910 conferences, wrote after the latter meeting that Friends worked hard to prove themselves 'loyal and faithful citizens and it is their readiness to serve their country that has mainly secured to them and others the many special exemptions where their conscientious scruples have been involved'.[12] In this sense, Gill was an exception.

Wright, in the genteel language that characterised the Society's pronouncements, wrote to Prime Minister Joseph Ward, 'deprecating the movement towards compulsory military training especially in our primary schools' (the original 1909 Defence Bill provided for military training for children as young as twelve; amendments raised the age to fourteen), 'believing that the combative tendency in our lads needs to restrained rather than encouraged'.[13] Initiating a meeting with the Society, Ward told the delegation early in 1912 that henceforth young Quakers would be exempt from compulsory military training on the grounds that the tenets of their religion forbade them to take up arms, provided they undertook non-combatant duties. These exemptions remained when a different, coalition, government enacted the regulations governing wartime conscription.[14]

The most dynamic pre-war anti-militarist group was the Passive Resisters' Union (PRU), established principally among young eligible conscripts forced to do military training under the Defence Act. This was strongest among working-class lads, particularly in Christchurch and largely based among apprentices at the Addington Railway Workshops, which employed many hundreds of workers. They pledged to 'resist coercion, conscription and military training and defy all penalties that may be imposed' and were remarkably successful.[15] By the end of 1913, a remarkable 7,030 potential military recruits refused to co-operate with the compulsory provisions of the Defence Act: 4,819 were convicted in court, and 849 who were convicted twice were sent to prison (while the PRU cannot, and did not, claim it was primarily responsible for this, it was able to spread the word widely through a well-researched journal, the *Repeal*).[16] These 'rebels' were hounded by officials, criticised by newspapers and abused by the public, sometimes physically by military conscripts and others. Some adolescents tried to avoid military training by disappearing into the bush or by moving to Australia. Nonetheless, it is hard to escape the conclusion that some resisters were adolescent rebels with scant political motivation, and that more than a few were influenced by peer pressure.

A 1913 episode boosted public attention and debate on compulsory training and anti-militarism. On the West Coast, five young resisters were arrested after they emerged from the bush to campaign for the socialist Paddy Webb in a by-election for the Grey seat. They were then marched through Christchurch under fixed bayonet and incarcerated in Fort Jervois on Ripa Island (aka Ripapa Island) in Lyttelton Harbour alongside another eight defaulters. Here they refused to clean guns or do semaphore and their leader, Reg Williams, led a hunger strike. When delegates at the Labour movement's July 1913 'Unity' conference in Wellington heard of this, hundreds marched to parliament in protest. The Social Democratic Party, which emerged from this conference, voted overwhelmingly that it would work towards a repeal of the Defence Act and create a volunteer 'citizen' army in its place.[17] The Minister of Defence, James Allen, was unsympathetic, retorting that the Defence Act was being 'violated by anarchists'.[18]

The government's inaction backfired in the face of increased adverse reaction from socialists, liberal Christians and civil libertarians. Having no wish to create martyrs, Allen backed down. On the island, conditions improved and the insubordination charges against the hunger strikers were dropped. When the resisters were released, they received an effusive reception at a public and very vocal gathering of 2,500 sympathisers, who unanimously called on the government to repeal the law. That did not happen; the dissent intensified. By August 1914, prosecutions of defaulters reached a high of 7,030, the courts were swamped and Friday, the day of judgement, was becoming known as 'Crucifixion Day'.[19]

Wartime pacifism

The street rallies and public meetings of the Peace Council and Freedom League and the PRU's militancy were the high-water mark of anti-militarist activity up until August 1914. After that everything changed. When the war broke out, anti-militarists of all hues fell away as activists felt the sharp bite of public opprobrium. On 19 September, just weeks after war was declared, the *Evening Post* reflected the public mood. 'The froth about anti-militarism has disappeared', it declared,

> a genuine spirit of manhood and patriotism stands revealed. It is, of course, war that has produced the remarkable difference. What is it that really protects our women and children, our homes and our properties from the outrages to which Belgium and France have had to submit? It is not the resolutions or the tracts of the Peace Society or even of the Churches but the armed forces of Britain, her dominions, and her allies. The blindest and least imaginative can realise the fact now, though a few weeks ago they were vapourising against militarism and asking us to trust 'international solidarity' and cosmopolitan benevolence as a sufficient protection. How foolish, how imbecile, these philanthropic sentiments appear in the light of concrete facts which have reported to us during the last six weeks.[20]

Those few who had the fortitude to continue were hounded in the street by neighbours, strangers, and even in some cases by 'fair-weather' friends. Cartoonists were vitriolic from the beginning. Fairly typical was Edward Brodie Mack, the young cartoonist for the *New Zealand Free Lance*, whose work often dominated the weekly's cover and highlighted the 'absurdity' of the pacifists' position as well as the threat 'that such traitorous and abominable sentiments represented to the empire'.[21] Indeed, those in every New Zealand community who were not seen to be fully and publicly behind the war, and involved with or vocally supportive of the patriotic groups that very quickly sprang up, were perceived as not being patriotic enough. Suspicions fed on each other, soon multiplying and descending even on those who were deemed not effusive enough in expressing their imperial loyalties. Despite this community anger, pacifists were not subject to official surveillance. Apart from those who were associated with Germany in some way, suspicion remained suspicion, in the early days anyway.[22]

In this inhospitable atmosphere, the Passive Resisters' Union dissolved in disarray. Some members fled overseas, mostly to Australia, to escape hostility and the potentiality of military conscription. A few, such as Reg Williams, continued to argue for peace. They would re-emerge more publicly to fight the introduction of conscription, and many were sent to prison. But most absorbed the propaganda that Germany was a military aggressor threatening traditional 'British' freedoms of speech and conscience. Their opposition to compulsory military training was now less important than defending New Zealand against a hostile power. Theirs had not been an argument against militarism *per se* but against compulsion. Members of the PRU now volunteered for the front line.[23] Likewise the Anti-Militarist League dissolved almost overnight, as its members slunk away in droves, intimidated by the forbidding atmosphere; some members even enlisted. Christie left for Australia and Fletcher went to the United States.

Only the National Peace Council and the Freedom League remained intact, but they retreated to quiet behind-door meetings. On 10 August, six days after New Zealand's entrance to the war, the League decided that it was unwise 'because of the existing state of war and consequent excitement, to continue with its propaganda work and meetings thereafter would be held fortnightly, not weekly'.[24] This was a necessary response to avoid breaching emergency war regulations around opposition to New Zealand's involvement in the war, which were enacted very quickly after the war broke out. The National Peace Council also lost much of its energy and membership. The government banned their outdoor meetings immediately as it reasoned they might lead to disorder.[25] In this 'new order' Mackie found it impossible to maintain the pre-war activity both for peace and protesting the compulsory clauses of the Defence Act. Not only did the Council fall away in all centres except Christchurch, but it also retreated into laager-like 'study groups', held sporadically. Mackie himself moved away from the 'militaristic' Baptists to the more sympathetic atmosphere of the Society of Friends. Such was his fear of prosecution under the war regulations that he refused to compose and distribute pamphlets under the Peace Council banner. Instead, he formed an alliance with the pacifist

Union of Democratic Control in London and surreptitiously distributed their propaganda, as well as other overseas material, some of which was intercepted and confiscated by police. Unlike the Freedom League, the Peace Council survived the war and operated under the gentlemanly Mackie's quiet direction until his death in 1943. However, the organisation was a shadow of its pre-1914 self. In regards to organised and visible pacifist activity, it was overtaken by a No More War Movement from 1928, and the Christian Pacifist Society from 1936.[26]

Even as it proclaimed itself as a 'pacifist' organisation, during the war the League was more concerned with what it felt were potentially achievable aims. Rather than stopping the war or calling for a negotiated solution, it primarily took up the role of a pressure group agitating for the repeal of the compulsory clauses of the 1909 Defence Act. The League also suffered from falling membership, with the hundreds on the mailing list, 35–40 of whom regularly attended meetings, declining to around 80 members and as few as 10–15 meeting attendees.[27] Numbers fell even further after Gallipoli. For the rest of the war they organised lectures, not all of which were 'pacifist' in spirit. Topics, as indicated in the organisation's minutes, included 'International Parliament', 'War and the National Character', and 'Psychology of War', all delivered by non-pacifist 'experts'. In July 1915, the League ran a six-week course with Auckland University law lecturer Ron Algie on 'International Relations'.[28]

The few pacifists who remained active did so surreptitiously, firstly to avoid state and public recrimination, and secondly to ensure that the propagandising that continued had at least some chance of reaching the ears of the curious. In March 1915, Egerton Gill ordered 2,000 copies of the British pamphlets *The End of the Armament Rings* by H.G. Wells and *Christianity and War* by Dr Alfred Salter, but how many were distributed is unknown. What is known is that Gill, after being caught handing out the Salter pamphlet, was fined £5 (near $700 in 2015 dollars) for, ironically, 'disturbing the peace'![29] Others did not get so far as receiving their pamphlets. In November of the same year, the Military Censor confiscated a carton of 500 leaflets from the British Stop The War Committee, addressed to Charles Mackie. By December that year, most of his mail, including Christmas cards, were being withheld and he told friends not to bother writing.[30] The press also helped to silence Mackie and Gill and their respective organisations by refusing to write about the activities of the Peace Council and Freedom League.

Gill repudiated silence. He promised 'determined' opposition to the 1915 National Registration Bill, which he saw, accurately, as a forerunner to conscription. He began by sending fellow Quakers a form with wording that could be used in completing their National Registration Cards. It read 'whilst registering as a citizen in conformity with the Government's demands, I could not for conscientious reasons take part in military service, in employment necessitating the taking of the military oath or in the production of materials the purpose of which is the taking of human life.'[31] This move coincided with a recruiting 'crisis' on 21 October 1915 and, on the state's command, a police raid on the Freedom League's Auckland offices, which seized the organisation's minute books and correspondence.[32] Gill was also arrested and fined for 'distributing a prohibited document', to wit, the aforementioned altered National Registration Card which he had distributed to members (mostly through the post), although it needs to be noted no law at the time had defined exactly what 'prohibited' entailed.[33] Sympathetic lawyers considered the penalty 'a gross travesty of justice' and 'out of all proportion to the offence', although most among the population probably would have agreed with the sentiments of the *Gisborne Times*, which wrote that 'unquestionably the authorities did the right thing'.[34]

That was certainly the view of the conservative weekly, the *New Zealand Observer*. In April 1916, before Gill had been arrested and fined, it castigated him as a 'fanatic':

> Many a fanatic, given a bath, a haircut and a suit of normal clothes would become innocuous. The Egerton Gills of society persist because people take notice of them. Egerton Gill and the New Zealand League of Freedom could never, under any circumstances, induce a man not to go for a soldier who was fit to be a soldier, but, by the dissemination of poisonous twaddle, the League can induce the authorities to make a Christian martyr of Egerton Gill, which, after all, is the main thing . . . The influence of such people is to be seen in the occasional 'conscientious objection' to soldiering of some adolescent youth. Such a conscientious objector is simply a lunatic shielding behind superior lunacy. He is the fruit of the seed planted by the Birds o' Freedom.[35]

What is remarkable is that the *New Zealand Observer* saw fit to ascribe to Gill, and the Freedom League, much more influence than they possessed. The League itself by this time was a very small organisation and Gill attracted media attention only because he continued to be arrested.

Gill's penalties always outweighed his 'crimes'. After the 1915 police raid on the Freedom League's Auckland offices Gill was fined £50 ($6,900 in 2015 dollars) under the War Regulations.[36] In January 1918, he was summoned to court for publishing a 'seditious' pamphlet, *The First Duty of a Citizen is to Obey the Law*. While it was satirical, the magistrate did not see the funny side and he was fined £20 (near $2,500 in 2015 dollars).[37] In February, the fine quadrupled when Gill was caught in public in possession of a British Christian Fellowship of Reconciliation pamphlet. The defence pointed out that the pamphlet made no allusion to the war but 'was written with the intention of encouraging citizens to examine the laws under which they are governed, and asserted the principle that where the law came into conflict with the individual conscience, the citizen had the right to ignore it'.[38] Yet such pronouncements were deemed to be a transgression of the War Regulations Act, and Magistrate F.V. Fraser, noting Gill's previous convictions, fined him a massive £80 (near $9,000 in 2015 dollars). On making this judgment, Fraser stated that inferences might be drawn from the pamphlet that could hinder recruiting and the prosecution of the war to a 'victorious conclusion'![39] Ignoring the heavy punishments, Gill refused to stop his campaign.

Gill was now firmly affixed on the state's radar as an undesirable malcontent. On 3 May 1918, aged 41 and with a 'gammy' leg, he was balloted for military service. Ignoring a medical examination, he protested on conscience grounds, was deemed 'insincere' and sent to nine months in Mount Eden Prison. This was despite the magistrate's comments that he was 'reluctant' to convict Gill as there was no doubt of his honesty of purpose, in that he belonged to the Society of Friends and the Freedom League. As a measure of the magistrate's respect, Gill was permitted a light in his cell so that he could study until nine p.m.[40] Other League members contented themselves with sitting at appeal board hearings to give moral support to men who resisted conscription. Some Quakers also joined these acts of solidarity, even though membership of their church allowed them exemption from combat service.[41]

Other opponents of the war were in no doubt as to where they stood in the unforgiving atmosphere. Christchurch anti-militarist and prominent trade union leader Jack McCullough chaired the original meeting of the National Peace Council and spoke at Council and Anti-Militarist League rallies against militarism. But he too was intimidated by the backlash that accompanied the war's outbreak, stating after the war that he had been 'afraid' to express his views because of their unpopularity and that he had been in 'a helpless and hopeless minority'.[42] In July 1915, when a lone Presbyterian minister tried to move a pacifist remit at a meeting of the Christchurch Presbytery, he failed to attract a seconder. 'It was a very hostile meeting,' he told Charles Mackie, 'and I feel deeply grieved'.[43] In September the same year, Christchurch Quaker Sarah Saunders Page, who would prove to be the staunchest of female pacifists, confessed to Mackie a 'feeling of hopelessness' in advancing her message.[44] When Auckland Methodist minister Reverend Percy Paris attempted to establish a New Zealand branch of the international Christian movement, the International

Fellowship for Reconciliation, in 1917, it soon disbanded through lack of support.[45] And late in 1915, when Hokianga-based anti-militarist Thomas Brocas wrote a letter to the local newspaper stating that all armies committed atrocities, he was so hounded by the local 'rabid, militaristic and jingoistic' crowd that he took temporary refuge in Tasmania, 'in a state', he wrote in his diary, 'of mental torment'.[46]

In small towns, dissenters like Brocas stood out like a sore thumb. Quaker and socialist Alfred Gregory was a draper in Dargaville who early in 1915 attracted an angry protest among townspeople for expressing anti-militarist views. Keeping such thoughts very quiet over the next months, he concentrated on 'civic' activity, which probably explained why he won a seat on the Dargaville Borough Council at the following local body election.[47] But loyalists were aghast. He had been asked to display in his shop window a poster advertising National Reserve Enrolment, in the sure knowledge he would refuse. When he did, he was convicted of a breach of the War Regulations, fined, and relieved of his council seat.[48] Declining to pay the fine, he was subjected to further backlash. Not only was he publicly vilified, his children were bullied at school and his shop was vandalised: windows were smashed, night soil was left outside the front door and slogans were splashed on his walls which read 'From Kiser (sic) to Alfred' and 'Gregory's Recruiting Centre. Boys Enlist Today'. He eventually lost so much custom that the shop had to be leased to another draper, and he and his family remained outcasts, living on charity from fellow Quakers for the rest of the war.[49]

Better known is the story of Timaru Unitarian minister James Chapple (the inspiration for Maurice Gee's novel *Plumb*), who preached against the war.[50] Fearing violence upon him and his family when angry crowds gathered outside his church, he soon took off with his wife and thirteen children to the then neutral United States, vowing not to return to New Zealand until 'democracy crushes militarism'.[51] When the United States joined the war, he returned, conducting services in his Christchurch church, which became noisy political meetings on subjects such as 'War Enables Profiteers to Stand on Velvet while the Poor Stand in Queues'. Hostile pressure from many among the local citizenry (who demonstrated outside the church on several occasions), the press and politicians (Defence Minister James Allen ordered an investigation) finally caused Chapple's lectures to be cancelled. Two speeches in Greymouth in March 1918, in which Chapple stated that patriotism and militarism were 'poisoning' New Zealand, led to him being arrested for sedition. In court, the magistrate rebuked him as 'dangerous' and sentenced him to eleven months' imprisonment.[52]

Very few other pacifists raised their heads above the parapet during the war, and those who did were hammered. When, for example, in August 1916 a 27-year-old Auckland secondary school teacher and Master of Arts English graduate, Harry Urquhart, wrote and distributed his pamphlet *Christianity and War*, a mild argument that advocated questioning the continuance of the war, he only just held onto his job at Seddon Memorial Technical College. Urquhart was a member of the British-based Christian Pacifist Fellowship of Reconciliation, which in 1916 formed an alliance with New Zealand's Freedom League.[53] Deeply religious, Urquhart had not always been a pacifist. Before the war, as a university student, he was attached to the Otago University Officers' Training Corps for two years and later held a captain's commission in the Auckland Cadet Corps, many of whom later fought and died at Gallipoli. But at a Student Christian Unity Conference at Woodville in January 1914, after listening to John Fletcher harangue selfish warmongers, he underwent an epiphany, resigned his commission and became an 'absolute' Christian pacifist.

Following *Christianity and War*, Urquhart wrote other anti-war pamphlets. In the 46-page booklet *Men and Marbles* he condemned military conscription as unchristian, and called upon the nations of the world to seek a negotiated peace based on the Christian principles of love and reconciliation. *Men and Marbles* began as an address to be given in Auckland's Globe Theatre on Christmas Eve in 1916 under the auspices of the Freedom League. But it was prohibited by the police at the eleventh hour. After protest, this ban was overturned by Auckland's Superintendent of Police and the address went ahead in the Globe on 28 January 1917. In it, Urquhart said that he had

> unbounded admiration for every man and woman who is willing to sacrifice everything for a principle which he deems noble and good. All I ask of you is to grant to others the right to live and if need be, die for that principle which they hold to be the truest and noblest within their mental and spiritual horizon.[54]

At that stage, police who were in the audience were seemingly happy with what he said.

However, when more senior police officers later examined his words, especially where he criticised versions of 'hatred' towards Germans as being 'unChristian', the speech was deemed to be seditious. Urquhart was arrested and put on trial. Magistrate Fraser, already noted for his intolerance of dissent, was unsympathetic and accused Urquhart of possessing an 'unbalanced mind'. He sentenced him to jail for eleven months with hard labour. Like Gill, within months of his release from Mount Eden, Urquhart was called up for military service, judged 'insincere' by the appeal board and sentenced to a further eleven months in prison as a 'military defaulter'. He spent much of his time in Waikeria Prison, weeding strawberries with other objectors.[55] Like others on the Military Defaulters List, Urquhart lost his citizenship rights for ten years after the war and was not allowed to teach again as he refused to take the oath of allegiance to the Crown (in case it conflicted with his Christian ethics). Urquhart became known as the 'father of Christian pacifism in New Zealand' and was an inspiration to Reverend Ormond Burton, a decorated soldier during World War One and New Zealand's most dynamic pacifist during the Second World War.[56]

Another strand of pacifist protest emerged from female activism. Historian Megan Hutching describes what she calls 'the biological argument' that many of these activists operated under: 'Their argument was generally couched in terms of women's inborn opposition to war because, as bearers of children, they had a natural interest in protecting life.'[57] Female anti-militarists had been active before the war, and many had sharpened their teeth protesting compulsory military training. In 1912, activist Christchurch women founded a Housewives' Union, which had pacifist tenets, and its dynamic leaders, Ada Wells and Sarah Saunders Page, wrote a pamphlet calling on all women to resist the Defence Act and to campaign for peace.[58] In Christchurch also, a young Quaker, Ida Bradley, founded a Children's Peace Society as a means of working with the Peace Council to deliver children from education of a 'military character'. The Society of Friends, the Christchurch Branch of the WCTU, and the Canterbury Women's Institute (CWI), founded in 1892 to further international peace and the interests of women and children, also publicly opposed war before August 1914.[59]

However, compared to those thousands who were involved to a greater or lesser extent in patriotic organisations, New Zealand women of peace were very few and far between after the war began. Being mostly middle-class and unworldly, they lacked influence over the body politic and appeared quite isolated from the international community as well. No New Zealand women attended a 'pacifistic' International Congress of Women held in The Hague in April 1915, the brainchild of Dutch doctor and suffragist Aletta Jacobs, though some would have read of it within the pages of the *Maoriland Worker*.[60] In Jacobs' words, this was not a peace conference, rather 'we simply assembled to protest against war and to suggest steps which may lead to war becoming an impossibility'.[61] The importance of this conference to New Zealand was that its steering committee called itself the International Committee of Women for Permanent Peace (ICWPP), which later evolved into the Women's International League for Peace and Freedom (WILPF), which did generate a local presence.[62] Similar to the CWI, the organisation maintained that disputes between nations needed to be settled by arbitration and conciliation, and argued that women needed to have a 'direct voice' in the affairs of the nation. In New Zealand, Marianne Jones and Annette D'Arcy Hamilton established a branch in Auckland, with others following in Wellington and Christchurch.[63] Their main activity was to keep in touch with their overseas branches in Great Britain, the United States and Europe.[64]

The WILPF did bring one anti-militarist to New Zealand for a series of peace lectures during the war. Adela Pankhurst (daughter of British suffragist leader Emmeline), a founder member of the Australian Communist Party who had spoken at peace rallies alongside the Yarra River in Melbourne, arrived in New Zealand in May 1916. She addressed mostly women audiences in town halls, some of which were packed. A *Truth* reporter covered her early meeting in the Auckland Town Hall and wrote of her 'slight, graceful figure', but noted that her voice was too weak to be heard clearly throughout the large hall and she spoke 'too quickly to be eloquent'. Nonetheless, he wrote that her speech was well-received.[65] Two thousand people crammed to hear her, reputedly the largest audience she had during her tour. Police monitored her later lectures, which largely focussed on the need to fight against the forthcoming imposition of military conscription. They took notes but no action was forthcoming.[66]

Conclusion

When New Zealand first entered the war, there were a variety of responses – from unabashed enthusiasm to deep anxiety about what lay ahead.[67] But most New Zealanders possessed a keen sense of imperialistic loyalty and duty towards the 'mother country' in her perceived time of need. This was fostered not only by politicians, the press (save for labour's *Maoriland Worker* and the leftist *Truth*) and the armed services, but also by the judiciary, the community, church leaders, patriotic groups, women (especially those with enlisted sons or husbands) and antagonistic public elements such as the Anti-German League and White Feather Societies. The handful of pacifists who remained true to their convictions stood beyond this broad social and political consensus, and both they and their message suffered because of it.

It is clear that the pacifist voice during this war was slight, sporadic and individualistic, and posed no threat to the body politic. There were few protests in public spaces or even behind closed doors. Those few who transgressed by publicly speaking, writing or even questioning New

Zealand's pursuit of the war were punished heavily under a variety of sanctions.

There was no 'militant' pacifist activity on the streets in New Zealand until late into the 1930s and during the early days of the Second World War, when activists belonging to the Christian Pacifist Society marched with poster parades and spoke at public rallies condemning the war and New Zealand's participation in it. These protests were often volatile, and by the early days of 1941 they had been ruthlessly stamped down by the police under tough 'Emergency Regulations', passed by an unsympathetic government. The activists were arrested and imprisoned, much like their predecessors from World War One.

Chapter Fourteen

'We stand for the Protestant religion, the (Protestant) King and the Empire': The Rise of the Protestant Political Association in World War One[1]

Brad Patterson

In mid-February 1918, following a political meeting in the Manawatu town of Feilding, the Reverend Thomas Miller (Presbyterian) and the Reverend F.H. Stockwell (Methodist) were set upon by up to a dozen men, thought to be employees of the local freezing works.[2] The well-attended meeting, called to form a branch of the newly established Protestant Political Association (PPA), had been addressed by the organisation's Dominion Organiser, Baptist minister the Reverend Howard Elliott, who delivered a sustained attack on the Roman Catholic Church and its adherents. Fearing trouble, the local organisers had smuggled Elliott out through a rear door, one of the unfortunate supporting clergymen then being mistaken for him.

Within days, a deputation from the PPA had waited upon the Minister of Justice, urging him to take strong action against 'the enemies at home'.[3] In nearby Wanganui, already a PPA stronghold, an indignation meeting was organised, while nationally Methodists and the Presbyterians recorded their strong disapproval of the attack. Also deploring the violence, the Catholic Federation nevertheless registered an emphatic protest against the Reverend Elliott being permitted to stir up religious strife 'at a time when the united efforts of the community are required to combat the common enemy'.[4] When arrests were made, the accused's Irish surnames were widely commented upon. Three were committed to trial in the Supreme Court on assault charges, two being subsequently discharged for lack of evidence; the third was sentenced to two months' imprisonment. Noting that this sentence was unusually light, an Auckland journalist pleaded for the community to recognise 'the evil of the religious strife, which, although we are fighting for our own and the world's freedom, is more acute in New Zealand today than at any time for many years'.[5]

Certainly the public mood was volatile. Hostilities had commenced in 1914 in an atmosphere streaked with optimism and enthusiasm, New Zealand's young men embarking for a grand overseas adventure. The losses at Gallipoli, then on the Western Front, brought a greater sense of reality and a search for a scapegoat. Beginning with anti-German demonstrations, by 1916 the witch-hunt had extended to other possible 'enemies within'. It was in this environment that a simmering broth of anti-Catholic feeling was brought to near boiling point.[6] Roman Catholics accounted for no more than one-seventh of the Dominion's population, with the vast majority of Irish extraction, and there were longstanding suspicions on both counts. There was also a class dimension in the strengthening prejudice, with a preponderance of Catholics being working-class. With the patriotism of militant labour also being questioned, a Catholic/Irish/socialist bogey took form. The tussle at Feilding in February 1918 was by no means unique. There were other physical confrontations, and the abuse freely tendered reached alarming proportions. In the words of Auckland's Catholic prelate Henry Cleary, it was as if New Zealand was caught in a 'cycle of sectarian epilepsy'.[7]

Sectarianism prior to World War One

Sectarianism was scarcely unknown in New Zealand. Religious animus, however, tended to be muted until Irish migrants began arriving in greater numbers in the 1860s and 1870s, Irish Catholics bringing with them religious commitments and political attitudes inculcated in the homeland.[8] Although they soon spread to all parts of the colony, tensions first became apparent where there were distinctive clusterings. On the South Island's West Coast there were a number of disturbances, while in Canterbury there was brawling following Orange Order marches on Boxing Day 1879.[9] The Protestant Irish had also landed with their own religious and cultural allegiances, and were soon joined by co-religionists. First introduced to New Zealand in the 1840s, the Loyal Orange Institution was flourishing by the 1870s.[10] Determined to limit Catholic influence in public affairs, Orangemen and other sympathising Protestants enthusiastically purveyed anti-Catholic literature, including prurient tales of religious life. Yet many clergy and lay leaders made it plain there was an aversion to rekindling old antagonisms.[11] In contrast to Ireland, New Zealand was an avowedly Protestant country, making it relatively easy for the Irish Protestants to merge with the predominantly Anglo-Scottish population. Conversely, the Catholic Irish tended to remain a clearly identifiable 'other'. Yet at no time did relations descend to the violence witnessed in Canada and, to a lesser extent, Australia.

The issues giving rise to the greatest friction between Catholics and Protestants prior to 1914 related to education.[12] As a result of early squabbles over denominational schools, the Education Act 1877 introduced a secular system of education. This was always a compromise. Fearing that non-sectarian religious education could well mean Protestant religious proselytisation, Catholic authorities made strenuous attempts to establish their own schooling network while conceding that such education would not be possible for all Catholic children; *ipso facto* all state schools should remain strictly secular.[13] This stance was unyielding and was soon matched by another demand. Between 1878 and 1891 at least four cases for funding of denominational schools were advanced through private member's bills.[14] Such propositions were staunchly opposed by most Protestant churches, who equally regularly lobbied for repeal of the secular clause, urging that Bible-based instruction be restored to classrooms by legislative means. From the mid-1890s several crusading Protestant groups emerged, which, along with other social reform campaigners such as the prohibitionists, futilely sought the passage of a General Referendum Bill, which would enable Bible in Schools to be put to a vote. Premier Richard Seddon, well aware that the churches were themselves divided as to the wisdom of Bible in Schools, listened but did nothing.

A number of other related issues assumed new prominence when, following the death of Seddon in June 1906, Sir Joseph Ward became Prime Minister, the first Irish Catholic to hold the office.[15] That Catholics were overrepresented in the public service had long been maintained by Protestant groups and politicians.[16] There had been strong charges in the 1890s that the Liberals under Seddon had endeavoured to secure Catholic votes through partiality. Ironically, a Royal Commission in 1909 suggested that, if anything, Catholics did less well under Ward than his predecessor.[17] Alongside this was the question of Irish Home Rule, a lively issue in the United Kingdom, but one previously confronted with relative indifference by most New Zealand Protestants, who conceived it as the conferral of a status already accorded New Zealand.[18] Visits by Irish Nationalist delegations from the 1880s had been civilly received, with Protestant opposition showing restraint. A less favourable response to a late-1906 delegation coincided with Ward's elevation to office: newspaper correspondence columns carried anti-Irish and anti-Catholic attacks, and anti-Home Rule meetings were called in several centres by the short-lived Protestant Defence Association, a front body first set up by Orange groups to protest the number of Catholics in public employment. Adding to Ward's difficulties, the papal *Ne Temere* decree of 1908 provoked an inchoate but ongoing Protestant response.[19] This decree ruled that marriages contracted by Catholics otherwise than before a priest were canonically invalid, as well as illicit. Construed by Protestants as an insult likely to give great pain to non-Catholic parties in mixed marriages, the decree legally did not challenge the law of the land, acknowledging that non-Catholics were not bound by Catholic canon law, but Protestant clergy were in no hurry to point this out. When agitation for protective local legislation failed to bring immediate action, some said it was because of the Prime Minister's beliefs.

The political landscape radically changed after the 1911 election, which eventually brought the first Reform government to power under William Ferguson Massey, an Ulster Protestant. In the lead-up to the election, the Bible-in-Schoolers had set up a combined Bible in State Schools League, primarily an Anglican and Presbyterian alliance, which embarked on a vigorous campaign for a referendum on the issue.[20] Opponents were attacked for doing all they could 'to obstruct the one thing needed to make the national schools system perfect'.[21] This new Protestant bellicosity, however, had an outcome they had not fully anticipated, as Catholics also organised, the objective being a Catholic Federation whose avowed aims were 'defence of the Catholic faith, the uplifting of Catholics generally, and the removal of religious bigotry'.[22] With a Dominion Council, diocesan councils and parish committees, the organisation was up and running by July 1913, and by early 1914 it claimed a membership of over 100,000.[23]

However, the recommencement of the Bible in Schools agitation also witnessed continuing aversions to the deepening antagonisms it caused. While the referendum advocates claimed a signed-up membership of 150,000, they failed to stir the grassroots within their churches and there were clear divisions both within and between Protestant churches.[24] Most New Zealand parliamentarians were similarly lukewarm. Preoccupied with combating industrial strife, the government exhibited little inclination to become involved, despite important Reform backers. With possible reluctance, in July 1914 Education Minister Hon. James Allen introduced a Bible in Schools Referendum Bill, but the select committee to which it was referred ultimately came down against any change in the existing secular education system. In August, war intervened and it was agreed that the matter should lapse. Even so, prior to the 1914 election, the Catholic Federation sought from all candidates their position on a referendum on Bible in Schools. Only 17 members were in favour; 11 failed to respond, while 48 believed no good purpose would be served.[25] The world of 1914 was not yet one which could give birth to and nourish an organisation such as the PPA.

The PPA in incubation

Following the inconclusive 1914 general election, New Zealand eyes turned fully towards the war. The level of sectarian tension perceptibly dropped, previous disagreements seemingly being put aside. Caught up in the wave of patriotic fervour, religious denominations almost universally endorsed support for the war effort. Thirty-five thousand New Zealanders had volunteered for service by October 1915.[26] Among them was a strong Catholic representation, *The New Zealand Tablet* boasting that while 'Catholics are about 14% of the population, yet they have contributed nearly 40% of the New Zealand fighting force . . . a splendid illustration of the practical character of Catholic loyalty'.[27] While a gross exaggeration (the proportion of New Zealand Catholic servicemen at that time was closer to 12 per cent), the sentiment was indicative of the Roman Catholic Church's stance at the commencement of the war. In a public lecture, Auckland's Bishop Dr Henry Cleary declared that Germany had badly miscalculated if it thought the Irish would not support the British war effort.[28]

While in no way dissenting from Cleary's position, the Catholic Federation saw no good reason to follow the Bible in State Schools League's decision to go into recess. It claimed responsibility for a number of social functions, including support for new immigrants and the provision of hostels for young Catholic women.[29] It lent its voice to the recruitment drive, supported patriotic fund-raising, provided comforts for troops and took responsibility for the erection of buildings 'for Catholic purposes' at the major military camps.[30] If the Federation had confined itself to these functions it could have attracted little serious criticism, but by late 1915 it was again taking up the cudgels in respect of support for church schools, as well as enjoining Catholic parishioners to elect suitable candidates to state school committees.[31] Representatives repeatedly hammered at the Minister of Education's door, raising bitter complaints that the National government was 'Sectarian and anti-Catholic'.[32] The Federation also launched sustained campaigns to remove 'obnoxious and anti-Catholic works' from libraries and bookshops, called for 'kinema film censorship', and issued terse denials to suggestions of disloyal elements in Ireland.[33] The Federation's assertive strain of Catholicism was to have unfortunate repercussions.

Renewed Catholic activism had been observed by gathering hard-line Protestants,[34] who were soon to find their leader and inspiration in the Reverend Howard Leslie Elliott, pastor at Mount Eden's Baptist Church.[35] Suspicion of Catholics was ingrained in Elliott, and from the outbreak of war he had been delivering sermons testifying to Vatican culpability.

Born in Victoria in 1877, from the time he entered the ministry, both in Tasmania and Queensland, he achieved 'no meagre notoriety for his Protestant zeal, and became the leader in strong conflict with the Romanists'.[36] In 1909 he accepted an invitation to guide one of Auckland's largest Baptist congregations, where he enthusiastically functioned as a watchdog of public propriety, delivering powerful denunciations of alcohol, brothel-keeping and general immorality. Concerned with contemporary social problems, for a time he flirted with the idea of launching a political party. When this fell through he turned his attention to a leadership role in the National Schools Defence League, co-operating, for perhaps the first and only time, with Catholic lobbyists in opposing a Bible in Schools referendum.[37]

It seems likely that Elliott's innate prejudices against 'the Catholic menace' were fed by a steady flow of 'no Popery' literature from the United Kingdom and the United States.[38] From the early months of 1915, his sermons focussed on the Anti-Christ and Romanist plots to subvert cherished Protestant liberties. Previously he had attacked drink, gambling and social wickedness with little success, now he fastened on blaming the war on the Roman Catholic Church. If the fiery rhetoric found willing listeners amongst Elliott's congregation, others in the local community were less enamoured, and his church buildings were subjected to vandalism.[39] Elliott's discourses and the destructive reaction to them were noticed by his local Orange lodge (Lodge 70, Martin Luther), and he was visited by Grand Master H.S. Bilby, who proposed common cause.[40] Lodge 70 was almost certainly Auckland's most militant, incorporating Ulster-born Protestant police officers and several aggressively anti-Catholic nonconformist ministers.[41] It was here that Elliott found his launch pad, becoming its leading personality and chief driving force in escalating anti-Catholic activities. Soon he was addressing other lodges across Auckland, with copies of his addresses distributed through New Zealand's Orange network.

Elliott and his Lodge 70 associates were especially active in early 1916. Expressions of approval from Presbyterian and Methodist elements had seen suggestions that a Protestant Association, 'representative of all the churches', might be formed.[42] A visit by the Papal Legate, Dr Bonaventura Cerretti, in February 1916, offered another stimulus. The Papacy's neutrality was condemned as pro-German, and Mayor Gunson's agreement that the Legate preach a mass in the Auckland Domain was condemned as a capitulation to 'idolatrous superstition'.[43] Contrary to evidence, Elliott claimed that Catholic clergy were actively discouraging recruitment and fund-raising, that Romanist Ireland was 'seething with sedition' and that

New Zealand's Catholic schools were 'seedbeds of disloyalty'.[44] These were themes that were to be constantly expounded by Elliott over the next three years. The Auckland City Council expressed 'in the strongest terms its disgust at the bigotry and intolerance evidenced', while newspaper columns registered lively protests.[45] For Elliott, this amounted to a call to arms. If the Orange Order was to serve as a vehicle for his objectives, the greater membership had to be stirred from apathy. The next step was to fully engage with the Lodge's leadership.

He found his chance at Easter 1916 as the Grand Lodge in New Zealand met for the eighth time, resolving 'to organise for Civic and Political action'.[46] Although a member of the institution for less than nine months, Elliott was acknowledged as its primary political spokesman and was at the fore of a special committee, drawn largely from the militant faction, tasked to bring recommendations to the gathering before it dispersed.[47] This committee recommended a further Wellington-based committee be appointed to deal with pressing and unexpected developments and to monitor politicians and public servants for unacceptable views. Increased funding for the Orange journal, *The Nation*, was sought alongside additional monies for the publication of propaganda. Most presciently, the appointment of 'a lecturer' (at £300 per annum – near $40,000 in 2015 dollars) to spread the message nationally was proposed, and there was little doubt as to who the appointee would be.[48] When the recommendations were agreed to, a further resolution directed that lodges throughout the country be asked to prepare for a campaign of action. While it is sometimes suggested that the PPA was a direct response to the Dublin uprising of Easter 1916, news of the uprising did not break in New Zealand until two days after proceedings concluded on 24 April.[49] However much events in Ireland contributed to the escalation in sectarian politics, the timing suggests that the foundations were already being laid.[50]

The emergence of the PPA

While sharing the militants' anti-Catholic sentiments, the traditional Grand Lodge leaders remained nervous about taking strong action in war conditions. The task of spearheading the formation of an ultra-Protestant political movement was instead embraced by an informal Auckland-based Orange group, drawn from Lodge 70, known as the Vigilance Committee.[51] Created early in 1916, during the Papal Legate's visit, this committee was small, tight-knit, centred round Elliott (with H.S. Bilby the nuts-and-bolts man) and quite independent of those set up at the 1916 conference.

Funded by Orange donations, the Vigilance Committee launched its own propaganda campaign in the closing months of 1916.[52] This campaign saw the expansion of Elliott's Auckland speaking circuit, moving to more public gatherings, as well as the mass distribution of pamphlet literature, sourced both locally and overseas. Much of the latter material consisted of extremely lurid accounts of clergy licentiousness, but even more damaging were publications such as *Rome's Hideous Guilt in the European Carnage*, over 20,000 copies of which were circulated.[53] Before long, such publications were brought before the Attorney-General (A.L. Herdman), and in December 1916 the Chief Military Censor was requested to scrutinise all printed matter passing through Lodge 70's postal box (Box 912), now shared by the Vigilance Committee.[54] That such action was contemplated when the subject matter differed little from earlier vintages indicates the growth of religious tensions.

In early 1917 the campaign took a new turn. Elliott, determined to further test his platform skills beyond the confines of Auckland, in January delivered addresses in Wellington, also visiting several small Taranaki towns.[55] On each occasion his discourse was on 'what caused the war', followed by the usual homilies on how Catholics were dominating the civil service, threatening the national education system, and – through the Catholic Federation – seeking to exercise undue influence over domestic, civil and political life. In Eltham and Stratford the response was subdued, with the small-town newspapers proving less than impressed. The *Eltham Argus* tartly observed that 'in this little village we would fain live at peace with one another . . . addresses such as last night make religious peace impossible'.[56] In a sense, however, Elliott achieved his aim, his statements drawing newspaper attention beyond Auckland. *The Tablet*, predictably, dismissed them as the rantings of 'A Prophet in Taranaki', urging the introduction of legislation curbing such attempted rabble rousing, but most critical was *Truth*, which roundly condemned 'the noisy little cleric from Auckland'.[57]

It took a hectic meeting in Hamilton at the end of February to really set the Protestant campaign alight.[58] Attended by around 900 people, it soon descended into uproar. Organised heckling of ferocious proportions bore out rumours that there would be an attempt by Catholics to break the meeting up. Before proceedings degenerated into complete chaos, however, Elliott succeeded in retelling his version of the war's causes, indicating that a range of literature was available for purchase, and urging good Protestants to join the Orange Institution. As the fiercely arguing attendees spilt onto the streets, only firm police intervention prevented physical violence. For the most part, press reaction was negative. The

New Zealand Herald felt that firm steps should be taken to prevent any repeat: 'during war time it is essential that . . . fanaticism should not be permitted to weaken national action by disturbing national harmony'.[59] The Catholic response was immediate and angry, Auckland officers of the Catholic Federation urging the Acting Prime Minister to take firm action.[60] Yet, beyond requesting the Auckland police to caution Elliott to be more circumspect, the government did nothing, with its unwillingness to act possibly interpreted as approval.[61]

With the Grand Lodge scheduled to meet again in Dunedin, the issues canvassed the previous year were certain to be readdressed.[62] Yet, with the Auckland Vigilance Committee having been far more proactive than the Orange leadership, the formation of a Protestant Political Association with Elliott as National Lecturer had already effectively been achieved. What was now important was conference endorsement and backing. When the delegates finally met, over 7–10 April, a resolution to form the PPA proceeded smoothly.[63] By the end of April 1917, Elliott had been appointed National Lecturer (soon Dominion Organiser) and his close associate Bilby, Dominion Secretary.[64] Preparations for the public launch of the PPA occupied a further three months, but by early July *The Nation* felt able to announce that the new organisation could already claim a membership of over 500.[65] The formal launch, in the Auckland Town Hall on 11 July 1917 (the date was deliberately selected to coincide with Protestant celebrations of the Battle of the Boyne), drew over 3,500 people, with large crowds milling outside.[66] Admissions were solely by ticket. Elliott whipped his audience into a fervour, speaking indignantly of the threat posed by the Catholic Federation, the privileges being sought, the extent of Catholic influence within the civil service, and the unholy alliance between Catholics and the burgeoning Labour movement.[67] At the height of the address he introduced a new accusation, claiming that mail intended for the Vigilance Committee had been intercepted and censored by Catholics in the Post Office. Inflaming emotions, he proceeded to read extracts, some explosive, from a selection of letters, purportedly from anxious Protestants. In one extract it was implied that a nun drowned at Taumarunui in the previous year may have been pregnant; in another, questions were raised about the body of a child supposedly buried in convent grounds. These allegations, although they were soon proved to be fabrications, ensured the PPA was launched in a full blaze of publicity.

The allegations of Post Office misdeeds prompted Postmaster-General Ward to initiate a judicial inquiry under Christchurch magistrate H.W. Bishop.[68] The inquiry, which opened in August 1917, heard evidence from 65 witnesses. It soon became clear that the Vigilance Committee and Box 912 had indeed been under surveillance for months. To test the system, Elliott had posted a number of letters under assumed names, including the inflammatory material presented at the Auckland launch. When Bishop's report was laid before parliament in September, Elliott's argument that the mail interceptions were a Catholic plot was completely dismissed. A reading from the fabricated letters by the Attorney-General shocked most members, Prime Minister Massey complaining that in all his years in the House he had never previously encountered statements more calculated to stir religious hatred.[69] A still stronger reaction came on 15 October, when Elliott was accosted by three men, knocked down and horsewhipped.[70] Their leader was a wounded returned serviceman and the brother of the drowned nun referred to at the PPA's launch. When the assailants were brought to court, they were discharged without penalty, and the presiding magistrate opined that the reverend gentleman had 'cast aside all considerations and pretence of ordinary decency'.[71] For some New Zealanders the PPA's tactics were viewed as unbecoming of committed Christians. Outraged, *Truth* labelled Elliott 'a slimy sectarian skunk'.[72] For Catholics, the lurid smearing of their religion engendered new levels of bitterness. An uncomfortably large, and growing, number of citizens, however, retained their faith in the seer.

The PPA in action

The growth of the PPA from mid-1917 was unprecedented in the history of New Zealand organisations. Under the slogan 'Equal rights for all, special privileges for none', by the end of 1917 the PPA claimed to have enrolled in the vicinity of 20,000 members, with more than 40 branches formed or in the process of formation, and there was a confident prediction that total membership would reach 100,000 within 12 months.[73] By April 1919 it was being claimed that the membership already topped 200,000, spread over 225 branches.[74] According to Elliott, growth continued into 1920, when a membership of over 250,000 was stated, amounting to just under 21 per cent of the European population of New Zealand.[75] With few records of the PPA having survived, the figures are now impossible to verify, but even allowing for considerable over-exaggeration there can be little doubt that a mass movement had been launched.[76]

The time spent planning before the PPA's formal Auckland launch was of considerable value in the recruiting drive, as was the solid organisational and financial support afforded by the district and local Orange lodges.[77] Its greatest asset, however, was its leader, who tirelessly stumped the country for several years and was rarely in his Wellington office. Tours and recruitment efforts advanced through the Waikato, Invercargill, Dunedin,

Christchurch, Wellington, Taranaki, Wanganui, the Manawatu and other southern North Island districts.[78] The strategy in each case was a preliminary meeting with identified sympathisers, often clergy and Orangemen, this being followed soon after by a public meeting. The success of this strategy is evident from the reported attendances. While large numbers, occasionally in the thousands, were to be expected in the main cities, in late 1917 it was possible to attract 1,000 in Gore and around 500 in Petone, early the following year 200 in tiny Leeston, twelve months later 500 in even tinier Otautau.[79]

This surge in support was accompanied by the usual exposés of Catholic machinations. Catholic plots were alleged to be evident in Rome's perfidy in international affairs and prospective alliances between Catholics and the labour unions. The Catholic Federation, a constant target, was described as 'a powerfully organised body which had a distinct effect upon the Government and the politicians' and its ongoing attempts to secure education concessions were depicted as sectionally selfish when the nation's priorities were necessarily elsewhere.[80] The perceived disproportion of Catholics in the public service was resurrected as 'an invasion of the citizenship rights of all other sections of the community'.[81] Catholic members of the police force were declared to be exercising their duties in a partial manner, their laxity at PPA meetings being cited.[82] The *Ne Temere* decree, 'which placed the law of the church above the law of the state', was repeatedly denounced.[83] Dismay continued to be expressed at the government prohibiting the admission and circulation of 'loyal and patriotic Protestant literature', this being seen as a 'sop to Catholic feeling'.[84] This proscription was bitterly contrasted with the freedom seemingly enjoyed by Catholic Church publications.

None of the complaints were new, but much more insidious were several issues directly related to the war effort. A recurring platform theme was Irish disloyalty, New Zealand Catholics and nationalist Irish being equated. In truth, news of the Easter Rising had come as much of a shock to New Zealand Catholics as to Protestants.[85] Catholic leaders were quick to denounce the rebels' actions, asserting loyalty to the Empire and claiming that the real Irish patriots were in the front lines.[86] Summary execution of the rebel leaders and the harsh military repression in Ireland which followed went some way towards modifying both prevailing New Zealand Catholic aspirations and Protestant thinking. If a growing number of Catholics were coming to the view that Home Rule would no longer be enough, some Protestants, further angered by writings in the *Green Ray* and *The Tablet*, now voiced strong doubts as to the wisdom of Home Rule. It was but a small step to accusations that Catholics were 'shirkers' in New Zealand

and the Empire's time of need, and that 'the Roman Catholic community should be compelled to take a share in the Empire's responsibility'.[87] In his Auckland launching address of July 1917 Elliott implied that Catholics were not enlisting in the hope that if there was an early election the overseas absence of patriotic Protestants might enable a takeover of government.[88]

The issue which more than any other afforded the PPA traction in 1917 and 1918 was conflict over the Catholic Church's objection to aspects of the operation of military conscription.[89] Like most, the Catholic hierarchy had welcomed the introduction of conscription, and when the first ballots were held in November 1916 no immediate difficulty was perceived in that Catholic religious constituted roughly 40 per cent of the clergy drawn for service.[90] Catholic bishops had made representations to ministers that they would strongly resist the conscription of clerics, seminarians and religious brothers, though a compromise had seemingly been found when Defence Minister Allen agreed that the Military Service Boards would be instructed to sympathetically deal with these appeals.[91] However, not all boards were inclined to simply fall into line, and while appeals from ordained clergy were uncontentious, seminarians and the teaching brothers courted controversy. By 1917, Protestant theological students had volunteered in such numbers that several of their colleges had closed and up to one third of male teachers in state schools were enlisted. When in February 1917 the appeals of two seminarians were dismissed, this occasioned a furious church response and, in turn, the issue became the centrepiece of PPA crusading.[92] Men with wives and families should not be called upon 'to take the places single men of the Marist and Christian Brothers should fill'.[93] Catholic schools should be required to make 'a sacrifice proportionate to that already made by public schools'.[94]

In regard to recruiting this was a minimal issue, centring on around 20 individuals. However, the strength of public ill-feeling is indicative of the sway the politics of sacrifice possessed, and state efforts to mediate these passions proved a difficult and thankless task. In the short term, the government sought to overcome the difficulty by deferring the call ups of those whose appeals had been dismissed. Meanwhile, it considered amendments to the Military Service Act to exempt the Brothers and remaining teachers in state schools; for almost the only time in his career Ward was willing to openly make a special case for Catholic interests. The measure passed narrowly in the House of Representatives, but when it was rejected in the Legislative Council a constitutional crisis threatened.[95] Politically, Ward was not prepared to push the matter further, but there was renewed pressure on the Military Service Boards to ensure that no Brothers or seminarians were forcibly inducted for military service.[96]

This result stoked PPA suspicions and while Ward was already well in the PPA sights, now Defence Minister Allen was continually accused of surrendering to the Catholic hierarchy.[97]

It would have been too much to expect that the Dominion's Catholics would simply accept such canards and wild accusations. The more moderate response was that adopted by members of the Catholic Federation and its clerical supporters, who approached ministers, issued statements and attempted to counter PPA charges in newspaper columns.[98] To be sure, protests were periodically lodged that government inaction permitted PPA speakers free rein, but for the most part the representations were privately made. Responses emphasised the extent of Catholic contributions to the cause and, when conscription was introduced, the Federation's Executive emphasised it was 'the law of the land, and members of the Catholic Federation as law abiding subjects will loyally conform to the legislation'.[99] Father Ainsworth's address in Auckland's St Patrick's Cathedral replied for those Catholics serving: 'the blood of Catholic and Protestant soldiers, a common family of loyal Britishers, was at present running in a common stream'.[100] That the PPA accusations were scarcely fair was easily proven. When New Zealand went to war the Catholic community had gone too, and with its church's blessing. By the end of July 1917, out of 77,283 men who had departed on active service, 9,731 were Catholic; at 12.6 per cent, this was only marginally less than the Catholic proportion of the New Zealand population.[101] It is possible there was some slowdown in Catholic recruitment, perhaps reflecting a fraying communal solidarity. According to a December 1917 return, 22.5 per cent of unapprehended defaulters from military service had Irish names and were therefore very probably Catholic (99 out of 440).[102] At a meeting in Otautau in March 1919, Elliott claimed that of 280 deserters from military camps in New Zealand, 111 (roughly 40 per cent) were Catholics.[103] The numbers, however, are small alongside those who served.[104]

Other Catholic reactions were less restrained. Following the 1916 uprising, a number of Irish clubs had been established, these federating into the Maoriland Irish Society in 1917.[105] The Society was a major disseminator of Irish republican sentiment until its paper the *Green Ray* was shut down in June 1918, with the editors jailed for sedition. Yet the most violent reactions came from a distinctly clerical source. From February 1917 *The Tablet* passed to the editorship of Wexford-born priest Dr James Kelly, nephew of the Archbishop of Sydney.[106] Kelly was an ardent Irish nationalist, who came to his post determined to return fire on those who had assailed Ireland, the Pope and Catholic loyalty. For him, Irish emancipation and support for Catholic schools were more important matters than the war with Germany. His command of invective was such that after only a few issues his writing came to the attention of the Solicitor-General, who advised that this journal too should be suppressed and its editor prosecuted for sedition.[107] That this did not occur reflected the government's concern that such action might further antagonise Catholics and reduce their support for the war. While undoubtedly Kelly enjoyed considerable clerical and lay support, even the bishops realised his tactics could be counterproductive. It was Bishop Cleary who attempted a more considered rebuttal strategy. In June 1918 he issued a direct challenge to the PPA, promising a substantial payment to the Red Cross if the organisation could disprove his statements of the Catholic position.[108] The response was at best feeble. In the following month Cleary launched his own journal, *The Month*, but Catholic counterassaults failed to significantly offset the progress of the PPA campaign.

By this point the PPA's campaigning front had already appreciably widened. The ultra-conservative elements forming the backbone of the organisation had long supported Massey's Reform Party. Ward, it was claimed, was in thrall to his co-religionists, carrying most of his fellow Liberals with him. There had been longstanding concern about the readiness of the Liberals to co-operate with representatives of the labour movement, but so long as the movement was splintered any danger was considered to be more potential than real. The formal establishment of the New Zealand Labour Party in July 1916, bringing together formerly competing factions, changed all that.[109] The critical stances parts of the labour movement took in regard to aspects or the total of the war, most evident in charges of sedition, were anathema to the PPA, and a fervent belief that the labour movement had been infiltrated by Catholics, who would exercise a controlling hand in Labour Party affairs, created an even greater 'Wardism-Romanism-Bolshevism' bogey.

With the launch of the PPA, all of Elliot's old pre-war prejudices of Catholic influences on organised labour had been revived. It was alleged that an 'unholy alliance' was being forged in which Catholics were seizing control of the unions.[110] True Protestant working men were urged to join the PPA and ensure that Catholics were barred from taking office.[111] There were stinging responses from Labour Party officials, who challenged Elliott to present proof, but nothing of any substance was forthcoming.[112] Further wild charges included that there was a preponderance of Irish names at the most recent Labour conferences, that priests were acting as organisers, and that not a single Labour member would hold his parliamentary seat 'in the face of Roman opposition'.[113] The exchanges continued throughout 1917 and into 1918.[114]

From the beginning, a proclaimed objective of the PPA was to 'secure the return of approved candidates to Parliament and to civil office'.[115] At elections, it would list tickets of candidates who were in accord with its views. Yet by September 1917 Elliott was speaking of the PPA 'nominating' candidates for every seat at the next general election, confidently predicting that the PPA could capture at least 40 seats, half of those in the House of Representatives.[116] Through early 1918 a more sophisticated organisational structure, one aligned to electorates, was developed, and following school committee elections in many parts of the country in April 1918, Elliott was able to report conspicuous success in the return of 'Protestant tickets'.[117] The November 1918 Wellington Central by-election provided the PPA with an opportunity to explore just how effectively it might bid for power in its own right.[118] With the major parties pledged not to contest with each other, there was no Reform candidate in the running. Government support for Liberal candidate W.H. Hildreth was lukewarm and there was PPA concern that the official Labour candidate, Scot Peter Fraser, 'an anti-conscription Bolshevik' and 'a Red Fed', might poll well.[119] Fraser personified all that the PPA disliked. The third serious candidate, Protestant M.J. Mack, was a conservative unionist who had been a hard-line member of a Military Service Board which had refused exemptions to seminarians. Eager to demonstrate the force of its influence, the PPA vigorously campaigned for Mack. Yet when the result was declared, Fraser was home by a long lead, attracting more than twice the votes of Mack in second place, with Hildreth a distant third.[120]

This reverse was a surprise for the PPA, Elliott predictably attributed the result to the 'sectarian and self-seeking interests of extreme Red Fedism, Liquor and Roman Catholicism'.[121] There was nevertheless a realisation that its support base was primarily drawn from the most conservative sections of the community, and that if the PPA chose to directly contest with Reform candidates there was every possibility the conservative vote could be split in key electorates, thus enabling Labour victories. With this being more than could be countenanced, the PPA abandoned all thought of putting up its own candidates, opting instead to act as a powerful conservative pressure group with an informal understanding with the Reform Party. It was fully involved in the lead up to the first post-war general election, scheduled for November 1919. Actively campaigning from the very beginning of the year, the PPA combined its usual anti-Catholic abuse with even more savage attacks on Labour, which it linked to 'the Industrial Workers of the World (IWW), controlled from Berlin'.[122] A major election issue was Protestantism versus Catholicism. Reform won the election hands down. It is impossible to determine precisely the impact of the PPA's campaigning, but in two seats their influence was significant. In Awarua, former prime minister Sir Joseph Ward was defeated, although other factors undoubtedly played a part, Ward having effectively been an absentee member for many years.[123] In the Bruce electorate Sir James Allan survived, but only just, his past willingness to consider Catholic views having been repeatedly vilified.[124] Probably the PPA's major achievements were to alter the size of some majorities and to impart a generally poisonous atmosphere to the practice of politics. Nevertheless, Elliott claimed that the PPA was now the most powerful political force in the country, that 70 per cent of the new parliament's members were pledged to uphold the Association's principles, and that around 40 members owed their seats directly to the Association's support.[125]

Conclusion

The PPA was an unruly and vindictive child of the stresses of war, and it flourished on fostered resentments. What made it stand head and shoulders above other dissonant New Zealand wartime organisations was both the extremism of its messages and the rapidity with which it transformed itself from a small, tight-knit, activist pressure group into a genuine mass movement, its growth from 1917 being unprecedented in the Dominion's history. Essentially, this burgeoning was made possible through the systematic exploitation of veins of religious bigotry long embedded in New Zealand society. Sectarian tensions tended to be curbed in normal conditions, but the increasing paranoia of a nerve-wracked and anxious community called for scapegoats. Giving voice to its anti-Catholic, and particularly anti-Irish Catholic, prejudices, the PPA was eager to assist in the search. From where was the PPA's supporting membership drawn? While this question remains to be more fully explored, that it was Protestant is axiomatic, with the strongest representation almost certainly from nonconformist churches. While birthed in the Orange Order, the PPA soon completely outgrew it, the greater part of the membership being from outside the lodges by early 1918. All indications are that the membership was weighted towards the lower middle and working classes and that it was equally spread in both urban and rural locations. Perhaps significantly, few individuals of acknowledged social standing chose to be closely associated with it.

The violent emotions that it had released were not easily constrained and took nearly a decade to ebb. Arguably, its influence was at its peak in the immediate post-war years, when it enjoyed almost unfettered access to Prime Minister Massey and his Reform cabinet, even if the nominated beneficiaries of its support were sometimes nervous of too open acknowledgement of the linkage. It soon won a number of concessions, including amendments to the education legislation restricting privileges to private schools; a controversial clause to the 1920 Marriage Amendment Act which made it an offence to question a lawful marriage; and, it was widely believed, influence over senior public service appointments.[126] For two further electoral cycles (1922 and 1925) the PPA remained a concerning, if diminishing, presence. The primary targets remained 'Romans and Reds', although it also forcefully advocated for 'a white New Zealand'.

However, as the community distress, which represented the lifeblood of the PPA, began to ebb, electorates and congregations began to tire of incessant invective. By the late 1920s the PPA was but a shadow of the force it had once been, as its leaders and supporters drifted away. The nadir was reached in November 1928, when Reform was swept from power by the newly formed United Party, with a rejuvenated Ward at its head. It is possible some wartime members came to regret their involvement and it may be indicative of a wider communal shift that Ward returned to power with a former senior member of the PPA alongside him in the United cabinet. Less than three months after Reform's defeat, Elliott resigned as Dominion Organiser, thereafter devoting himself to financial journalism and the spasmodic promotion of other conservative causes.[127] The organisation of which he had been the mainspring, in debt, hopelessly split, struggled on until 1933, when it was finally wound up.

Chapter Fifteen

'Bundling out the Hun': The Women's Anti-German League during the First World War

Graham Hucker*

From 1916 a small group of New Zealand women, under the banner of the Women's Anti-German League (WAGL), advanced ideas of internal enemies with intricate machinations and campaigned for uncompromising solutions to remedy this perceived threat. The Wellington-based WAGL were not the only anti-German activists to organise during the war; other groups were established in Hawke's Bay, Parnell and Wanganui.[1] However, the mentality, passions and actions of the WAGL represent a major example of wartime radicalisation and the divergent roles taken up in New Zealand wartime society.

The context of the League

New Zealand's involvement in the war created the basis for the sentiments and insecurities which fuelled the League's formation. As the war progressed, the sense of a German threat gained credence in the light of reports of atrocities – real, sensationalised and exaggerated – that filtered into the country. Consequently, attention turned to 'enemy aliens' residing within New Zealand, many of whom had been residents since before the turn of the twentieth century. Regardless, both official and unofficial attitudes towards them hardened as more ethnocentric and emotive concepts of belonging asserted pressure.[2] In November 1914, war regulations defined an enemy alien as 'any person who has been naturalised in New Zealand and who would have been an enemy alien had he not been so naturalised.'[3] Germans and Austrians represent the major examples of this phenomenon and within this chapter 'enemy alien' denotes these groups.[4]

* This chapter is adapted from an unpublished essay by Dr Hucker and is dedicated to his memory and contribution to historical scholarship. The editor gratefully acknowledges Angela Clay for her assistance and blessing in this endeavour.

Such a transfer of hate and suspicion is not difficult to comprehend. Germany was the foe, and resident Germans were seen as symbolic representations of the otherwise faraway enemy. Uneasy tolerance towards Germans in New Zealand continued to break down throughout 1915, and New Zealanders were called upon to identify destruction in Europe with their own circumstances: '[imagine] Queen Street, Ponsonby Road, Khyber Pass and every street that guns can reach carpeted by slaughtered innocents! Hamilton as Louvain; Takapuna as Liege; Whangarei and the furtherest farms given up to "frightfulness"!'[5] Nowhere was this retaliation more evident than in the spate of anti-German riots in early 1915.[6] On New Year's Eve 1914, a butcher's shop in Gisborne owned by Friedrich Wohnsiedler had its windows smashed and its interior ransacked. Further threats were made against German residents in Gisborne, with the effect that newspapers began to carry advertisements by threatened individuals denying German parentage. In May 1915, Heinhold's Butchery, Hallenstein's and the Bristol (Dresden) Piano Company in Wanganui were attacked by anti-German rioters. In New Plymouth, windows in the main street were smashed after a patriotic meeting.

Insecurities, centring on potential German spies and conspiracies, formed another part of this milieu. In Britain, 'the pre-war stereotype of the evil and ubiquitous enemy spy had been transferred to the entire German nation.'[7] The same may be said for New Zealand, where the early days of the war saw the growing belief that Germans were 'dirty, despicable, snaky spies.'[8] Again, individuals with foreign names or uncertain pasts came under the scrutiny of self-designated guardians of national security. In Ashburton, an alleged spy with a 'fierce and dark military moustache' was seen boarding a train carrying New Zealand soldiers.[9] It was later revealed that the alleged spy was an officer in the Expeditionary Force. Tensions were highlighted rather absurdly one dark morning when a sentry on duty at the Awanui wireless station fired a shot at a suspicious sound, killing a cow. A newspaper report noted that 'the only language the unfortunate creature could speak was suspiciously like German.'[10]

Concern was also expressed that spies were signalling and sending wireless transmissions to German vessels believed to be in New Zealand waters, and newspapers called for the government to undertake 'a systematic search of the whole Dominion for secret wireless plants.'[11] Tales of a dubious nature began circulating and from early in the war the police received exaggerated reports regarding secret wireless locations and signalling of a suspicious nature. In October 1914 the police received a report of mysterious lights, thought to be signalling, flashing between 8.30 and 8.45, with the reporter adding that a German named Wagner lived in the area. A few days later the informer noted that, on thinking the matter over, the light 'may have been that of some person bringing in their cows.'[12] This example proved typical and across the war such reports failed to yield anything substantial. Thus police investigation of alleged signalled messages from up in the hills at Mornington found the culprit to be a streetlamp partially obscured by trees, which looked as though it was emitting flashes when the branches swayed in the wind.[13] Suspicious lights on the coast near Waverley turned out to be lanterns carried by fishermen, and further mysterious lights at Karori were in fact women holding an evening picnic.[14]

The WAGL emerged against this backdrop of hate and suspicion, but it also reflected New Zealand women's involvement in the war effort. As the war effort intensified, more women took on a wider variety of jobs and roles. For some 600 nurses, alongside less visible volunteers, involvement entailed war-related duties beyond New Zealand.[15] Within New Zealand, women played an active role in fund-raising, advancing patriotic organisations and advocating for commitment.[16] Some undertakings were more specialised: protesting against conscription, campaigning to get women into the police force, and a small number seeking to protect the country from German spies and pro-German activities.

The League's campaign

The first meeting of the WAGL was on 10 January 1916 at Gamble and Creed's Tea-rooms in Wellington, and the League soon established itself in the first floor of the Hannah's Building on Lambton Quay, which served its headquarters for the duration of the war.[17] The League's objective was to foster an awareness of the 'enemy alien problem', and its concerted aims of protecting New Zealand welfare and advancing anti-German measures are apparent in the motto 'New Zealand for New Zealanders. No Germans Need Apply.'[18]

The executive committee included Anna Stout as president, Ida Boeufvé and Helen Lowry as vice-presidents, Beatrice Day as treasurer, E.J. Moore as secretary and Katherine Holmes as chairwoman.[19] These women were established social activists on welfare issues who possessed prominent social positions. The wife of Robert Stout (at various times the Premier and Chief Justice of New Zealand), Anna Stout was a leading voice in New Zealand's suffragette and temperance movements, president of the Women's Franchise League, vice president of the National Council of Women and an active supporter of British suffragettes.[20] Of Irish origins, Ida Boeufvé was the wife of M. Robert Boeufvé, the French Consul for New Zealand, and possessed influential family connections with the British establishment.[21] Helen Lowry was the daughter of James Watt, believed to be one of the richest men in New Zealand, and wife of Thomas Henry Lowry, the wealthy cricketer, racehorse breeder and farmer. Described as a 'formidable woman' and 'an inveterate traveler with wide connections', Lowry was generous in applying her means to philanthropic ventures, notably in regards to the Red Cross and the Order of St John; her work in wartime charities saw her awarded an OBE in 1918.[22]

These social connections proved a key source of patronage for the WAGL; on one occasion Thomas Henry Lowry donated £100 ($13,500 in 2015 dollars) to their campaign funds.[23] They also gained wider avenues of influence through the *New Zealand Times*, which rendered valuable service in the dissemination of the League's propaganda, and through their ally and supporter John Payne, the demagogic MP for Grey Lynn who was waging his own anti-German crusade in parliament.

The League's campaign revolved around the concern that Germans possessed undue and dangerous influence in New Zealand society, which required countermeasures. Within the League's manifesto, the foremost objective was to 'protest against the employment of Germans, sons of Germans and naturalised Germans in our army or in any position of trust where they can obtain information detrimental to our country's interest to impart to Germany.'[24] Secondly, the League appealed to women to purchase only New Zealand and British manufactured goods. Thirdly, the League expressed a desire to amend the laws pertaining to the naturalisation of enemy aliens; Anna Stout's comment 'once a German always a German' was 'a safe ground of reasoning to go upon' gives some idea of the mentality.[25] The League was particularly supportive of Napier MP John Vigor Brown's Naturalised Subjects Franchise Bill, which, if it had passed, would have disenfranchised naturalised subjects and prevented them from holding positions of responsibility. However, the bill was repeatedly introduced and thrown out from 1916 to 1919.

The start of the WAGL's campaign was met with an uneven public response including measures of criticism and mockery. The Reverend R.H. Hobday envisioned the WAGL as being 'a society calculated to incite people to vengeance and acts of cruelty', while others saw the League's anti-German agitation as 'pestering' and a 'persecution of genuine British subjects'.[26] Wider commentators concurred, claiming that the League's faulty rhetoric damaged its credibility and revealed it as seeking 'notoriety'.[27] The League was even accused of 'aiding the enemy' by failing to divulge information to the Defence Department.[28] Doubts about the accuracy of the WAGL's information and a belief that it might alienate the moderate section of the public persuaded May Hadfield to resign as early as February 1916.[29]

Similar attitudes are found within officialdom, and the League endured mockery from some politicians. When G.V. Pearce, MP for Patea, questioned the background of an alleged German, a colleague teasingly replied that 'they will think that you've joined the anti-German League.'[30] Similarly Charles Wilkinson, MP for Egmont, described the WAGL as 'a lot of hysterical women running hither and thither in Wellington . . . creating a disturbance where there is no justification.'[31] The police likewise struggled to take the WAGL seriously, insinuating that information supplied by the League was unreliable and that subsequent investigations diverted them from more pressing matters. Like other investigations of 'enemy signalling', the League's reports revealed misunderstandings of mundane circumstances. On one occasion Moore reported that a bright light had been seen glowing in the Grand Hotel every night from midnight until the early hours and noted that the light appeared before the troopships left Wellington. The subsequent police investigation revealed that two night porters required the light to carry out their work.[32] Similarly, an investigation into an accusation that jubilant Germans were celebrating the death of Earl Kitchener in an Auckland hotel in the presence of soldiers in uniform found that the men were prisoners from Motuihi Island, permitted to visit Auckland accompanied by their guards, who regularly dined at the hotel. The manager noted that while the table had ordered several bottles of hock, 'in the usual way', there was no unruly conduct and no remarks made in regard to the war.[33]

Other members defended the League's character and conduct. Responding to negative press, Vice-President Boeufvé described the League as 'persecuted and misrepresented' and subjected to harassment by disloyal elements.[34] Certainly, Boeufvé attracted hostility. In February 1916 she claimed to have received a death threat from a German woman residing in Wellington; in March 1916 a confrontation saw a German seize and shred a dozen of the League's leaflets whilst she was distributing them in Newton Park; and in August 1918 she claimed to have received word that an alleged German intended to murder her son, in retribution for Boeufvé supposedly ruining the former's army career.[35]

Clearly, these measures of scepticism and hostility towards the League reveal that they did not fully articulate the public view. This became more evident when the WAGL visited various North Island centres. In April 1916, Wellington members of the League travelled to Napier, Hastings and Palmerston North to speak on the enemy alien issue. At their opening meeting in Hastings, Boeufvé appealed to the women present to help put down the pro-German movement in New Zealand. What Boeufvé meant by the pro-German movement was not made altogether clear and she was perhaps trying to sensationalise her rhetoric by presenting apathetic citizens as being pro-German. At a second meeting in Hastings, Beatrice Day recited 'We Want a Hundred Thousand Men' and a League member named Hill sang 'La Marseillaise' and 'Keep the Home Fires Burning'. The meetings were characterised by a patriotic and vehement rhetoric designed to denigrate Germany. In Napier, Boeufvé dramatically told the audience that 'the hand of Germany is gripping New Zealand in its iron grasp. Let us stand together and free the country from this curse . . . For the sake of the living and the dead help us now and stand together. To be truly British we must be anti-German.'[36]

Upon arriving in Palmerston North the League found that their growing reputation had preceded them. One correspondent in the *Manawatu Daily Times* described their rhetoric as 'cock and bull stories'.[37] The writer attempted to qualify the statement by quoting a segment of the League's propaganda from their recent Hawke's Bay campaign, which claimed that 'the spread of infantile paralysis in New Zealand is due to German agents spreading microbes about.'[38] The editor commented on the League's presence as a 'somewhat unfortunate inspiration'.[39]

In Palmerston North the WAGL had been invited to participate in the first commemoration of the Dardanelles Campaign.[40] The service was supposed to witness the passing of eulogies in commemoration of those soldiers who had fallen at Gallipoli. Instead, the League used the service as a platform for the dissemination of their own brand of anti-German propaganda, at the forefront of which was the propagation of unqualified statements based on the ubiquitous German spy who was supposedly masquerading as the resident enemy alien. The League informed the audience that volunteering was waning in the far north because the men in that locality were afraid to leave their homes due to the presence there of 10,000 armed Austrians; that German firms in New Zealand were being allowed to wax fat on war profits; that there were a thousand Germans in different departments of New Zealand's government service; that there was evidence to show that New Zealand troopers at Gallipoli with German sympathies had altered the time fuses in the guns in such a way as to decimate the front line of Australian troopers; and that German sympathisers were habitually given military preferment and promotion by those in high places. These claims remained largely unsubstantiated, and the editorial in the *Manawatu Daily Times* reflected an air of doubt. Furthermore, it sounded a note of regret that the League had ever been invited, commenting 'we regret that these untoward disputations were allowed to superimpose themselves upon a function promoted for quite a different purpose.'[41]

Five months after its formation, the WAGL claimed 1,500 members, branches in Auckland and Napier, a total of £210 15s 6d (near $29,000 in 2015 dollars) raised in subscriptions and donations, distribution of 31,000 pamphlets, and a campaign expenditure of some £123 15s 9d ($16,500 in 2015 dollars).[42] In June 1916 the League attempted to spread the word further afield, with Boeufvé and Day departing Wellington bound for Great Britain. Here they aimed to affirm the League's imperial credentials and form an alliance between the various anti-German leagues throughout the Empire. The overarching theme was an expression of the Dominion's place within the British Empire and the unity of the British peoples in the common struggle against Germany. At the League's annual meeting in July 1917 it claimed membership stood at over 2,000, and at the June 1918 meeting it announced that membership had 'steadily increased'.[43]

Radicalisation

The WAGL campaigned on the belief that enemy aliens constituted a credible threat, that officials were failing to confront this threat and that more extensive solutions were required. Such beliefs and the manner in which they were advanced provide a case study of the radicalisation of part of wartime society.

By 1911 there were 4,015 Germans and 2,131 Austrians in New Zealand and, when war broke out, the government was quick to place restrictions on this population.[44] For example, the Enemy Contracts Act 1915 and the Enemy Alien Teachers Act 1915 cancelled business contracts with Germany and Austria and prohibited the employment of enemy aliens as teachers. Unnaturalised enemy aliens could not leave or enter the Dominion without the approval of James Allen, Minister of Defence.[45] While John Vigor Brown's bill never passed into law, the Revocation of Naturalisation Act 1917 allowed selective annulment of citizenship.[46] Further restrictions were placed on enemy aliens who wished to serve with the army. Only the sons of Germans who had been naturalised before their son's birth would be considered eligible, so long as there were no adverse reports about them.[47]

Internment was applied for enemy aliens considered dangerous or potential security risks and by June 1916, 271 aliens had been interned on Somes Island, 55 on Motuihi Island and 14 at Devonport Detention Barracks.[48] By May 1918, there were approximately 450 internees.[49] Those interned were predominantly young men who had been primarily engaged in labouring occupations, although representatives from the professions were also present. One mid-1916 survey, for instance, included two doctors, a customs official, three journalists, four teachers, a policeman, a postmaster, a government official and a professor.[50] There were a number of reasons why they had been interned. Of the 321 'aliens' still interned at the cessation of hostilities, 137 were alleged to be enemy reservists and 79 had been removed from ships, while others had been recommended for internment by the police and the Yugoslav Commissioner.[51] Amongst the others there was a 'lunatic', a wireless operator, an 'undesirable', an anti-militarist, one charged with sedition and two who had requested internment.[52]

From the WAGL's perspective, however, the government was not going far enough and was acting negligently in the face of a serious threat. The WAGL held with contempt and suspicion all enemy aliens, regardless of naturalisation, because of the persistent belief that they represented a concrete threat to the country's security. The 1913 Delbrück law exacerbated the matter, as it entitled Germans to retain their German citizenship.[53] This law was constantly referred to by the League and interpreted as a sign that Germans everywhere stood as servants of the Kaiser. Through this logic it maintained that there were some 21,000 enemy aliens in the country and consistently claimed that Germans or pro-German elements possessed influence in high places and were endangering national security.[54] In June 1916, Boeufvé told an audience that 'it is now fashionable to be pro-German in certain circles in Wellington. It is your duty to make this unfashionable and make your country too hot for Germans and pro-Germans.'[55] This sat beside wider notions of pro-German elements in the country. In June 1916 there had been an alleged pro-German celebration in Gore, and Charles Wilkinson had commented in the House on the pro-German feeling in Taranaki.[56]

The result was witch-hunt-like accusations linking enemy aliens with any mysterious setback. In March 1916, a member drew attention to the possibility of the enemy sabotaging the country's livestock, as had been reported in Britain, and darkly noted that outbreaks of paralysis amongst horses in Canterbury and a mysterious fire in Auckland which destroyed two hundred horses had 'never been explained'.[57] In April 1916, Boeufvé linked outbreaks of disease and German agents, stating 'I believe the way to get rid of spinal meningitis is to intern all Germans in New Zealand.'[58] A report in the *Dominion* of unexplained fires in Lyttelton and Wellington contemplated that 'the enemy in our midst' was responsible.[59]

Consistent with the broader mix of hatred with insecurity, at times discussion of the enemy alien presence transcended security issues, and

Germans were presented as a gross manifestation of everything that was brutal in life, who would contaminate New Zealand. In one address, for example, Boeufvé coloured her rhetoric with racist overtones: 'with this amount of cursed Hun blood in your country how can you keep your race pure?'[60] This led her further to assert that if something was not done about the enemy alien problem then New Zealand would become 'a country of hybrids – an unEnglish, spineless set of men neither flesh, fish nor good red herring.'[61] On another occasion the WAGL proclaimed 'the Germans who live in our midst have given us a moral anaesthetic and lulled us into a sense of false security just like the legendary vampire is supposed to send his victims to sleep before it sucks their blood.'[62]

To counteract this threat, urgent action was argued as necessary and on 30 July 1917, Moore wrote to the Attorney-General, A.L. Herdman, to forward the League's resolution that 'it is imperative to eliminate all traces of enemy interest from our social, political and economic life.'[63] This translated into calls for more extensive internment and denaturalisation policies, as the current practices, according to Anna Stout, 'did not go far enough'.[64] The WAGL was not alone in accusations that internment policies were lax. In January 1915, Auckland's Justices of the Peace had met to promote the internment of all enemy alien males, naturalised or not. Other calls for internment came from Colonel Wheeler's Anti-German League in Havelock North, the Women's Political League, the Napier Patriotic Society and John Mayo (mayor of Wairoa and a member of the Wellington Commercial Travellers' and Warehousemen's Association).[65] Similarly, the Christchurch Returned Soldiers' Association protested at the freedom enjoyed by enemy aliens, the National Executive of the Second Division League drew attention to aliens seizing the businesses and jobs of New Zealand soldiers while they were overseas, and the Market Gardeners' and Fruitgrowers' Association protested at aliens carrying on business as usual.[66]

Payne decried that enemy aliens were being pampered, raising inquiries over whether wealthy Germans and German colonial officials from Samoa were being interned on Motuihi Island instead of Somes Island, because a more congenial climate prevailed there.[67] Likewise, German prisoners and their guards observed wining and dining at an Auckland hotel prompted one correspondent to write that they 'could have called in the services of a man generally employed at hotels called "Boots" who could have shown that his name was not a misnomer.'[68] Such instances only served to strengthen the view, advanced by the WAGL, that the government was too liberal in dealing with enemy aliens and that, in order to promote security, internment had to be introduced for all.

If the government had wished to appease those calling for a 'clean sweep' and to 'intern them all' it would have been confronted with a series of unwanted logistical problems resulting from the locating, mustering, enclosing and maintaining thousands of enemy aliens. The task would disrupt family, communal and economic structures and represent a substantial financial burden on the state; the average cost per prisoner for April 1916 was £5 4s 6d (near $675 in 2015 dollars) on Somes Island and £15 6s 9 1/2d (near $2,025 in 2015 dollars) on Motuihi Island.[69]

In their quest to reveal the German 'hidden hand' in New Zealand, the League, working closely with Payne, attempted to expose as many Germans as possible. A particular area which the WAGL scrutinised for possible Germans was the army itself. The mere thought of an 'alien' or German descendant amongst the ranks of New Zealand soldiers was anathema to the League and the claim was made that 'no man of Austrian or German descent to four generations back should be entitled to serve.'[70] The crusade to 'root out the Hun Hog' from the ranks of the army saw lists of soldiers scanned, and any name that sounded remotely Germanic was conveyed to the Defence Department for investigation.[71] These included A.A. Flohr, who was appointed as Adjutant at Tauherenikau Camp, and the son of Eugene Langguth, the Austrian Consul, who was promoted to the rank of Captain. Similarly, Payne's periodical, the *New Zealand Philistine*, reported that a Captain Vosseller was in charge of plans of New Zealand's defence fortifications, that a man named Rockstrow was an officer on the General Staff who examined candidates for commissions and who had access to Defence Department correspondence, and that Arthur Otto von Keisenberg in the Health Department had access to information about hospital ship movements.

Perhaps the most famous case, however, was that of Lieutenant Alexander Hugh Grierson of the Twelfth Reinforcements. An Englishman who had migrated to New Zealand eight months before the outbreak of war, Grierson had been employed as a confidential clerk in the office of the German Consul in Wellington. On 23 March 1916 a Royal Commission of Inquiry to ascertain the loyalty of Grierson was opened by A.D. Thompson, the Assistant Public Service Commissioner, as a result of Boeufvé and Payne charging him with disloyalty to the King. Much of the case brought against Grierson was based on circumstantial evidence and hearsay; it was alleged by his landlord that on the King's birthday Grierson had queried the holiday and noted that he had an Emperor; fellow boarders considered Grierson to be decidedly pro-German; the police revealed ten confiscated postcards printed by the German Defence Society; and it was alleged he had a secret code in his possession.[72] Confident that the evidence was sufficient to remove Grierson from the army, the WAGL's hopes that the surrounding publicity would awaken the Dominion to the enemy alien danger were dashed as the Commission found Grierson innocent of all charges and free to join his regiment.

The WAGL failed to accept the decision and continued to agitate for Grierson's dismissal. A pamphlet entitled *The Truth about the Grierson Inquiry*, almost certainly written by the League, held the decision in contention and hinted at conspiracies. The pamphlet stated that:

> there is apparently more in this Grierson case than has been allowed to meet the eye. The setting up of a special commission is significant, the appointment of a Government employee as Commissioner is significant, the appearance of such a high legal officer as the Solicitor General as a special pleader for Grierson is significant and the rapid promotion that attended this recent arrival Grierson in his ascent to Lieutenancy is significant.[73]

Ultimately, the pamphlet asked, 'why did he [J.W. Salmond, the Solicitor-General] denounce the evidence against Grierson as flimsy and contemptible and the charges as foul and contemptible?'[74]

On 3 May 1916 the League pleaded their case to Allen, who rejected their assessment of the case. The WAGL then considered sending a petition to King George V asking for his intervention to remove Grierson from the army. These moves did not receive the support which the League had hoped for and the *Press* described the League as 'making mischief'.[75] More cutting was the *Manawatu Daily Times* editorial, which noted that the 'disgruntled females' and 'interfering dames' of that 'peculiar organisation' were 'bent on persecuting Lieutenant Grierson' and that their 'extravagant charges . . . fell to the ground when submitted to the cold light of reason.'[76]

However, the League continued to look at things from a different light, with the outcome of the Grierson inquiry reinforcing the League's belief that the government was failing to deal appropriately with enemy aliens and that Germans, or pro-Germans, held influence in New Zealand. This meant that Grierson was probably being protected by this influence. After all, what patriotic person would denounce the bringing to trial of an alleged pro-German, and spy for that matter, as foul and contemptible?

Other public figures were also alleged by the League to be part of a German conspiracy. Payne, angered at the outcome of the inquiry, even went so far as to declare parliament pro-German on the enemy alien issue.[77] This was a replay of earlier accusations, where Payne had stated in the House that 'the public are beginning to wonder whether or not we have Germans in the cabinet' and, singling out Alexander Herdman, asserted 'I have been told that the Minister of Justice is of German extraction – that he had a German mother.'[78] Similarly, in April 1918, the Minister of Munitions and Supplies, Arthur Mielziner Myers, was subject to victimisation by the League. Born in Australia in 1867, Myers was the son of German Jewish immigrants Louis Myers and Catherine Ehrenfried. Moving to New Zealand, Myers became involved in the family brewing business and entered public office, serving as the mayor of Auckland and within the Liberal Cabinet. From 1915 he served with distinction as the Minister in charge of Munitions and Supplies. Myers' episode with the League arose from a letter allegedly written some years prior in response to his being passed over for an invite to a party which Dr Solf, the former German Governor of Samoa, held for leading resident Germans in Auckland. In a mood of indignation, Myers letter allegedly declared that he was a pure German.[79] Furthermore, Myers was accused of abusing his position in regard to customs by importing whisky ahead of food, fencing wire and roofing material for farmers, which could not be imported for lack of shipping space.[80] No doubt the League interpreted this abuse of position as an indirect attempt to sabotage the country's war effort by undermining civilian morale and the war effort at home.

While accusations against Herdman and Myers were somewhat sporadic, those levelled at James Allen were more frequent. As the Minister of Defence, Allen was deemed ultimately responsible for enemy aliens being included in the army and positions of responsibility. The *Philistine* accused Allen, alongside Colonel Gibbon (Chief of the General Staff), of being responsible for 'the blackest piece of treachery ever recorded in British annals.'[81] This ultimately led to a call for Allen's dismissal by Payne and the WAGL. As late as October 1918, Allen was still being taken to task by the WAGL, and Anna Stout intimated that the mines laid off Cape Farewell by the German raider *Wolf* could have been laid by resident enemy aliens that the government had proved negligent in interning.[82] James Allen and Anna Stout later engaged in a spate of letter writing in a bid to validate their perspectives; the letters were published in the *Colonist* on 25 October 1918.[83]

Conclusion

On 20 March 1919, Katherine Holmes, now president of the League, convened a farewell afternoon tea for the League's supporters in the Pioneer Club rooms, which effectively brought to a close the League's activities. A brief reunion occurred in July that year when the members of the original executive (Stout, Boeufvé, Holmes, Lowry, Mormont,

M'Vicar and Moore) received medals and bouquets awarded by the Alliance Française in recognition of the WAGL's work.[84] The awards were presented by Sir Robert Stout, the Acting Governor-General and husband of Anna Stout, and were accompanied by speeches. Anna Stout reflected on the League's record, claiming that both indirectly and directly the WAGL had:

> prevented a great deal of harm being done by enemy aliens in our midst. The league had been confronted with many difficulties, and had had to fight against powerful influences. It had also had to work very quietly. Had not members dropped away from the society in the way they had much more work could have been accomplished.[85]

Miss Holmes hinted that activism would continue and that there was a need to induce a boycott of German goods and secure 'restrictive measures against the Germans in our midst'. She urged that Germans should be banned from becoming magistrates or Justices of the Peace, entering the civil service or holding seats in the House of Legislature. Touching on the contentious perception of the League's record, Mrs Moore's speech noted that she 'could not but remark upon the fact that recognition of the work done by the Women's Anti-German League came from a foreign country, an ally, but not from their own Government.'[86]

During the war the WAGL played an active part in the overall disorganised campaign of denigration towards Germany. The WAGL had attempted to convey that the average German was either 'a brutal bully or a low, sneaking, cringing, spying fraud', and spread the idea that beneath the cloak of every alien lurked an evil spy.[87] In attempting to mobilise and maintain animosity towards Germany, the League was relatively ineffective – the result of suspect rhetoric and a cause that uncovered nothing tangible in the way of pro-German machinations. No spies were ever caught or prosecuted and it was highly unlikely that spies were ever active in wartime New Zealand. Even in Great Britain, 'the Government did not prosecute because they could not find enough evidence to do so.'[88] With most enemy aliens being quite harmless, the League's extreme rhetoric damaged its credibility even among those resolutely committed to opposing Germany.

However, despite its overall ineffectiveness and shortcomings, the existence and dynamics of the WAGL should not be neglected and are important for three reasons. Firstly, the League was an indication of the divergent roles that New Zealanders pursued as part of the war effort. Secondly, the League's activities and philosophies give some clues about the war's impact on the popular mind. Thirdly, and perhaps most important of all, the WAGL offers a perspective of the impacts of anti-German activity on New Zealand society. The League provides us with an important view of the wartime expectation that members of society should labour, physically and emotionally, for the cause, whether by working as a soldier or a nurse, raising patriotic funds or knitting garments. The WAGL reflects a comparable, if radical, manifestation of this dynamic; its members were imbued with their own sense of patriotic duty and perceived their work as important to the war effort. Motivating sentiments of hatred, revenge, insecurity and helplessness should also be considered.[89] As one writer said, 'the propagandists were people gripped by war hysteria themselves who found a convenient scapegoat for the failure of the war in enemy aliens.'[90]

Chapter Sixteen

When Neighbours Became Alien Enemies: Germans in New Zealand during World War One

Steven Loveridge and Rolf W. Brednich

For many enemy-aliens in New Zealand, the First World War was a difficult time in which suspicion and hostility undercut established bonds. Those associated with Germany, whether through birth or descent, bore the brunt of this hostility; as one historian has put it, Germans were rapidly recast from 'proven worthy settlers' to 'lawless Hunnish brutes'.[1] This chapter sketches some of the contours of the human face of those confronted with the breakdown of communal bonds. It considers the context and mood in which this phenomenon occurred and the lives and fates of some of those observed, suspected, prosecuted, interned, beaten and expelled during and after the war.

German connections towards and into the war

From the arrival of the first German settler in 1843, settlers from German-speaking Europe worked to establish themselves in New Zealand. German settlements were established around Nelson, Westland, Marlborough, Canterbury, Otago, Southland, Puhoi, Taranaki, Hawke's Bay and Wellington, and in some regions, such as Manawatu and Rangitikei, German immigrants possessed a prominent presence.[2] While the numbers of immigrants from German-speaking Europe vary across investigations, in 1914, roughly 10,000 New Zealand residents were recorded as of German birth or extraction, constituting the largest migrant group after those from the British Isles.[3] The consensus is that these settlers were typically welcomed because of their expertise and (ironically, given what was to come) ideas of Anglo-Saxon–Teutonic kinship. In turn, these settlers were integrated into New Zealand life by way of friendship, communal links, professional commitments and marriage bonds. Days after the outbreak of the war, Wellington's *Evening Post* seemingly affirmed the hitherto favourable perception of German immigrants: 'New Zealand has a number of Germans who are good sturdy settlers; they have made their homes here; their interests are here; and they are regarded as New Zealanders by British friends who admire the manly qualities and the steady industry of their Teutonic cousins.'[4]

Many 'Teutonic cousins' seemed to share this sense of belonging, and among the most conspicuous reactions from local Germans in the first days of the war were pledges of loyalty and solidarity. Two days after New Zealand's entry into the war, a naturalised British subject, Carl Sauer, predicted that 'all Germans who had lived under the British flag and enjoyed the privileges of English territory in Australia and New Zealand would fight side by side with their fellow men to protect the honour and uphold the maintenance of these two countries.'[5] Even more explicit was the loyalty declaration drawn up by a patriotic meeting in Upper Moutere (a small town of prominent German heritage which changed its name from Sarau during the war): 'The application of "German" to any resident of Moutere refers only to language. There is not a single person of German extraction in the whole district who was not a naturalised British subject.' While some sentiment for the land of their birth was acknowledged, this was noted as irrelevant against their loyalty to New Zealand: 'the residents of German extraction . . . will stand shoulder to shoulder, man for man, with any other inhabitants of the colony . . . we unhesitatingly state that her foe is our foe'.[6] Referring to this declaration one commentator responded, 'with a declaration of such frankness, such reasonableness and such sweetness as that which our Moutere friends placed before the public eye, what risk now of their misunderstanding us, or any of us misunderstanding them?'[7]

At their worst, the forces the war unleashed would disregard 'frankness', 'reasonableness' and 'sweetness' and radically impact the perception, status and treatment that residents associated with Germany received. Across its course, the Great War saw the breakdown of social trust as established bonds of neighbourliness, personal networks, familial affection, friendship and legal status were eroded by suspicion and hysteria. This dynamic was not solely confined to Germans or those of German extraction. Croatian and Dalmatian gum-diggers also made public proclamations of their loyalty and grappled with wartime suspicions.[8] Germans would seem, however, to offer the most salient case study of this phenomenon.

Some complexities arose from the varying nature of German connections. For some residents this connection was a matter of ancestry or heritage. Some were born in Germany, or in lands that would unify into Germany in 1871, but had made a home in New Zealand – cemented by bonds of naturalisation, marriage, friendship, community, property and position. Conversely, German law meant that some – by expatriating, by ten-year absences, by acquiring foreign citizenship, by non-performance of military obligations, or (in the case of German women) by marrying a foreign husband – had forfeited their German citizenship.[9] In other cases, German connections were stronger and connections to New Zealand less established; consider the twelve members of a travelling German band who arrived in 1913 and who were subsequently arrested soon after the war began.[10] Some were unnaturalised, some retained a place on the German military reserves, and some even retained duties to Berlin; for example, German archival documents list Karl Seegner, the German consul in Auckland, as a spy tasked with gathering general and specific information for the German intelligence system.[11] Others held positions within the German state as consuls, colonial officials and members of the German military taken prisoner when New Zealand entered the war. Lastly, the boundaries of the Germanic could inflate, by way of ignorance and mistakes, to include other continental Europeans, sometimes with ironic results. Thus Johan Wielaert, a Dutchman with Belgian heritage, suffered an assault in a Hamilton hotel (his assailant refused to sit with a German) and one Polish immigrant ruefully noted 'at home we were persecuted by the Germans and now, here in New Zealand, we are regarded as Germans.'[12]

Against the backdrop of widespread outrage over Germany's actions in Europe, which was regularly inflamed by sensationalised reports and propaganda, were varying visions of local German elements.[13] Some drew a clear distinction between continental 'Huns' and locals of German descent, declaring that German communities in New Zealand 'all have so closely identified themselves with the Dominion's life and nationality that there can be no question of their fidelity to the country that has given them a far greater degree of prosperity than that which the Old World offered.'[14] Others agreed that the war was one against Prussian militarism, an interpretation which allowed a clear divorce between the German military and the wider German population: 'Our quarrel is not with the German people but with the German machine, the military machine, which, machine-like, is without a conscience, without a soul, without tenderness or feeling of any sort.'[15] Many applied this conception to distinguish between immigrants and German sympathisers. For example, in a parliamentary debate concerning security measures and foreigners, Prime Minister Massey stressed that a man should be 'known by his work' and that indiscriminate measures were unwarranted. While noting that there are undoubtedly 'a number of Germans whose sympathies are with their people and against us', he also observed that 'there are Germans in New Zealand who are old settlers, who are naturalised British subjects, and I have reason to believe that even in the present crisis their sympathies are with Britain.'[16] Some aligned this position with patriotic pride: 'We Britishers usually pride ourselves on . . . a love of fair play and justice . . . the ability to keep our heads and not get "panicky" in critical times. The letters of some of your correspondents on the subject of alien enemies seem to indicate a lack of these British characteristics.'[17] Another commentator, soon to be a soldier, noted his disappointment in recent anti-German activities directed towards local elements: 'I am proceeding very shortly to Trentham, but I hope to go with enmity towards the German nation and its ways, and not with a personal hatred of everyone German or of German extraction.'[18]

The interpretation these positions were arguing against was the sense that blood and loyalty ran the same way. This ethnocentric sense of loyalty and disloyalty flared during the war and forms a recurring point within Andrew Francis' recent study of wartime anti-Germanism; the titular quote 'To be truly British we must be anti-German' captures this dynamic.[19] Similarly, Steven Loveridge has argued that these wartime perceptions mobilised pre-war anti-alien prejudices, most notably ideas of an Asiatic 'yellow peril', in presenting the image of a 'Hunnish' enemy beyond the racial and cultural bounds of western civilisation.[20] Such an interpretation cast those in New Zealand with German connections – whether those connections were matters of political allegiance, sentimental attachments, birthplace or ancestry – as representing an internal enemy, and typically demanded a redefining of the community on grounds of blood-ties and racial stock. As one commentator put it, 'We all know that naturalisation is just a matter of convenience to get the franchise and advantages of citizenship. They are Germans first and naturalised British subjects after. ("Once a German, always a German.")'.[21] The consequent logic demanded that such threats be neutralised, with the apoplectic rhetoric of some public meetings and the anti-German leagues calling for deportation, or vowing to 'intern them all' and 'shoot them!'[22] And of course this worked the other way as well; such suspicions of enemy-aliens as loyal to an enemy power, and thus potential spies and traitors, possibly spurred those classed as, or associated with, enemy-aliens to suspect former neighbours and citizens as potential antagonists or informants.

Against this erosion of social trust, those with German connections faced uneasy circumstances, and they responded in various ways.[23] For some, seemingly atypical, individuals, identification with Germany was seemingly stoked by the war; this is probably indicative of their limited time in or links to New Zealand. While many reports of individuals openly flaunting their allegiance to the Kaiser or supporting a German victory reek of rumour and hearsay, others seem more credible.[24] Mrs Langguth, for example, had arrived in New Zealand six months before the outbreak of war and was noted as saying she was proud to be Prussian.[25] Some perhaps embraced a German identity that social ostracism had made them more aware of. It has been suggested that ostracism was a factor in the case of Private W.P. Nimot, a young man of naturalised German parents who, in 1916, deserted the NZEF to go over to enemy lines.[26]

More common were mixed strategies of keeping a low profile and burnishing patriotic credentials.[27] Attempts to blend in can be seen at varying levels. Some individuals anglicised their names or illegally changed them.[28] German associations made expressions of acquiescence, for example, the Wellington Liedertafel singing group renamed itself as the Wellington Male Voice Choir, and the Lutheran Church elected to hold its services in English so as to 'avoid any friction or misunderstanding with the worshippers' English fellow colonists.'[29] In some cases this occurred at a communal level; besides Sarau becoming Upper Moutere, Ranzau became Hope and German Bay in Akaroa became Takamatua Bay.[30] At times, nationwide examples are evident. The 1916 census revealed a distinct 'decline' in the country's German-born population (4,015 German-born in 1911 compared to 2,999 in 1916), while those claiming to be Russian-born almost doubled (658 Russian-born in 1911 compared to 1,242 in 1916).[31]

Others followed Upper Moutere's strategy of emphasising its pro-British position and pledging to support patriotic causes. Consider the successful import business Joosten & Murie. (The Joosten half of this venture was owned by Henry Joosten, born in 1871 in Schleswig-Holstein, who had immigrated to New Zealand aged 14 and been naturalised at age 22, renouncing his German citizenship.) With the declaration of war, the business offered assistance and subscribed to the war loans scheme, making a £1,000 donation (near $150,000 dollars in 2015 terms).[32]

Some articulate or forthright individuals put their voices to a comparable purpose. Friedrich Franz Wolter, for example, made a habit of publicly contesting notions that naturalised Germans retained loyalties to the Reich:

> By taking the oath of allegiance in New Zealand a German loses his nationality and he cannot, if he should return to the country of his birth, hold there any public position in time of peace, and he will be treated by the German authorities as an enemy subject in time of war. His own material interests are therefore indissolubly bound up with those of the country of which he became a citizen by free choice, and

> to suspect him of disloyalty towards the same amounts to supposing him capable of acting against his best interests.[33]

Born in Berlin in 1874, the academic vegetarian whose politics were orientated towards social democracy (braced with a 'supreme and unwavering contempt for "Kaiserdom" and "Junkerdom"') was a poor representation of bloodthirsty Prussian militarism.[34] By his own words, 'even while still in Germany I was never a German, according to the popular acceptance, having always been opposed to Kaiserism and to German militarism.'[35] Indeed, Wolter's time in the German Army, via compulsory service, had been terminated when he was sentenced by a military court to one year and seven months' imprisonment for impertinent remarks, contemptuous smiles and refusal to obey an officer. He later claimed his decision to immigrate to New Zealand in 1906 was based on the country's reputation as 'the most democratic country in the world'.[36] Naturalised in 1911, he took up a position in the Government Printing Office and, fluent in French and English and acquainted with the languages of Southern Europe, enrolled in Victoria College's Department of Modern Languages. By 1914 he had graduated with a BA Honours and an MA, been awarded the Jacob Joseph Scholarship[37] and submitted a doctoral thesis. His public ripostes were often accented with invocations of British liberty. In January 1915, for example, a large number of Justices of the Peace passed a resolution urging the internment of all male alien enemies, whether naturalised British subjects or unnaturalised, for the duration of the war. Wolter responded that such a scheme represented 'no less than an attack on one of the fundamental constitutional rights of British subjects, the right to personal liberty', as granted by the Magna Carta.[38]

Eroding social bonds

Though continuously critiqued, by some measures this redefining of communal boundaries advanced quite far over the course of the war. The erosion of formal citizenship forms one major metric, and several milestones are apparent. By November 1914, war regulations defined enemy-aliens as including 'any person who has been naturalised in New Zealand and who would have been an enemy alien had he not been so naturalised.'[39] From 2 May 1916, the wives of enemy-aliens, regardless of whether they were British-born citizens, were categorised as enemy-aliens. From 1917, measures within the Revocation of Naturalisation Act saw many naturalised aliens stripped of their citizenship.[40] However, this phenomenon cannot be fully perceived in regards to legislation, and recent research has emphasised the populist edge of anti-Germanism, noting it as 'often spontaneous, decentralized and capable of mobilizing mass popular support.'[41] Consequently, the redefining of communal boundaries is most evident in cracks and breaks in communal networks as German connections, or perceptions thereof, were deemed indicators of danger and disloyalty.

Security actions provide some of the earliest examples. Days after the outbreak of war, police took measures to prevent German and Austrian military reservists from leaving the country, and arrests of enemy reservists were reported across New Zealand.[42] Three days later the New Zealand government seized records held by all four German consulates. Over time, three of the four German consuls – all of whom were naturalised New Zealanders – were arrested. On 12 August 1914, some 90 Germans were marched from Alexandra Barracks, where they had been detained, to the wharves to be interned on Somes Island in Wellington Harbour.[43] Additional internment sites at Motuihi (aka Motuihe) Island, Ripapa (aka Ripa) Island, Devonport Barracks and Featherston Camp came into use, and other Germans were required to pay a £100 bond (near $15,000 in 2015 terms), supply character witnesses and report daily to the police.[44]

Fraying communal bonds similarly undermined other aspects of the lives of enemy-aliens and their dependents. After her German reservist husband was interned, one woman, 'a colonial of English parentage', noted that she had been left destitute.[45] Many German labourers found themselves unemployed, with new jobs difficult to find and channels of redress decidedly unsympathetic.[46] For example, when the captain of the steamer *Pakeha* took his crew to court for refusing to work alongside German members of the crew, the case was thrown out with the remark that 'no law-court would convict the men'.[47] Similar events occurred in the business world, such as the collapse of Eugene Langguth's kauri-gum business, due to gum diggers refusing to deal with him.[48] In academia, the von Zedlitz affair has become a familiar case study of a German individual whose life took a fatal turn from well-respected citizen to enemy-alien.[49] Born in Herrmannswaldau, a village in the Prussian province of Silesia, in 1871, George William von Zedlitz was the child of an English mother and a German father. He was educated at Oxford and immigrated to New Zealand in 1901 to take up a chair at Victoria College. Although he never naturalised, he tacitly relinquished his German citizenship by neglecting to return to Germany to undertake military service. By 1914 he had married into a prominent Wellington family and was a professor of modern languages, an official government translator, and a respected teacher, described as possessing 'not only urbanity, wit and oratorical gifts but also, in a remarkable sense, the civilised mind of Europe.'[50] The first stage of the affair, described as 'a stain on New Zealand history', occurred in early August when von Zedlitz visited the German consul and offered his services in a non-combatant role in the war that had just been declared between Germany and Russia.[51] Days later, when Britain entered the developing conflict, he abandoned the idea of serving Germany in any capacity. As anti-German sentiment grew, the allegation that von Zedlitz had sought to fight for the enemy joined broader accusations that an enemy-alien should not hold public employment, and that he was a German agent. These sentiments, as will be seen, escalated as the war endured.

From the start, hostility towards enemy-aliens extended into the threat and use of violence. Days after the outbreak of war, the windows of the German consul's office in Wellington were smashed. The offenders were reported to be 'a few irresponsible excited boys' and public donations repaired the damage.[52] In Bluff, a party of armed men called on a Mr Nichol demanding to know the whereabouts of his German gardener. When they were told to leave, they fired several shots at the gardener's cottage; fortunately there were no injuries, but one of the men was subsequently arrested.[53] The heights passions could reach are evident in the aftermath of the Rottmann trial. A 21-year-old former Wellington wharf worker, Arthur Rottmann, had taken up work on a dairy farm in Ruahine where, in late December 1914, he murdered his employer, his employer's wife and their baby while drunk.[54] While Rottmann was soon captured, tried, found guilty and hung, the case was read against developing ideas of inherent German brutality; an assessment which referenced the German military's disregard of international law, massacring of Belgian and French civilians and shelling of British coastal towns.[55] Under this argument some called for an equivalent suspension of restraints to restore security or justice. In Gisborne on New Year's Eve 1914, inspired at least in part by the Rottmann trial, some 2,000 citizens gathered and pillaged a butchery owned by Friedrich Wohnsiedler, a 35-year-old born in Eberbach, Germany, who had lived in New Zealand since 1902 and whose naturalisation papers were signed on 4 August 1914, the date Britain entered the war.[56] Other violence was self-inflicted. In Manawatu in early 1915 a 'quiet and retiring resident', believed to be of German extraction, committed suicide, with indications that this action was 'directly traceable to the war'.[57]

Escalating breakdowns

All of these reactions increased as the conflict became protracted, society became more intensely mobilised and the strains of war escalated. Val Burr notes that 'Being far from events in Europe, saw many New Zealanders express their pent-up anger towards those who were accessible.'[58] One manifestation was that security measures became more extensive and often reflected public concerns and pressures. Such tensions saw official inquiries into the parentage of officers against calls to 'eliminate all traces of enemy interests from our social, political and economic life.'[59] In 1917 the Registration of Aliens Act sought to create a database of the number, location and background of New Zealand's unnaturalised enemy-alien population.[60]

Internment also reflects these dynamics. In 1916, former German consuls were interned, as was the Austrian consul, Eugene Langguth, and the Danish consul, Paul Hansen (although he was Danish, his parents were from Schleswig, Germany). The exact rationale for this measure is unclear; when Langguth applied for naturalisation after the war the police seemed puzzled over the nature of his arrest.[61] Other examples similarly illustrate the sometimes offhand manner of internment procedures. In early 1918 a warrant was issued for Henry Joosten's arrest. Despite the police recommending against it, and various friends and associates vouching for his character, he was interned until July 1919. Similarly, Franz Wolter's reverence for British naturalisation, contempt for German militarism and scholarly achievements ultimately counted for little. Walking the Wellington waterfront in early 1916, Wolter visited the steamer SS *Manuka* (a passenger liner requisitioned for war service) and fell into conversation with some French reservists from Fiji; perhaps the eager language student wished to practise his French? Regardless of his motive, the Wellington waterfront was a sensitive site where questions, accented in German, were regarded as highly suspicious. Later commentary alleged that his questions 'indicated he wished to glean information he was not entitled to'.[62] An outbreak of suspicion and excitement saw him arrested and held for questioning at Mount Cook Barracks. Days later, without any legal procedure, he was moved to Somes Island and remained interned there until December 1919.

While interned on Somes Island, Paul Arnold composed sentiments recounting the broken bonds of work, friendship, love and liberty that internee status represented:

> *We Prisoners of War*
>
> Since every country calls its men
> Beneath the flags and colours,
> At least those men who freely can
> Now earn their fame through valours,
>
> It is for us a little bad
> Not that we care for fame,

But that we are prisoners without crime
Is going to make us tame.

Before the war we worked the land
In navvies' and bushman's graces,
We worked on stations, gave a hand
On flax and sawmill places,

We helped in England's merchant fleet
As firemen and sailors,
Made clothes, put shoes on many feet
As bootmakers and tailors.

We made us friends as Germans do
Amongst the country's people,
And many girls we loved to woo
Then our race is not feeble,

But since the war we have perhaps
Lost many friends in number,
Oh! May this wartime soon elapse
And soon succumb in slumber.[63]

By 1919 there were some 450 internees in New Zealand.[64]

Those who avoided these direct security measures could face social reactions which demonstrated more than an edge of moral panic. The criminologist Sarah Wright describes such phenomena as 'enacted melodramas',

> where everyday citizens experience the role of the suffering victims, where ordinary outsiders are shaped into extraordinary villains and where moral entrepreneurs 'step in' to become heroic . . . Melodramas depict their characters and their actions in highly exaggerated and emotional terms in order to clearly demarcate boundaries between good and evil, right and wrong.[65]

Such dramatic fury is notable in the escalation of the von Zedlitz affair during 1915. The central question, as one paper put it, was whether:

> an un-naturalised German, and therefore by law an 'enemy alien' be kept on in full and undisturbed enjoyment of his position and salary at a State-sided university whilst other un-naturalised Germans, not socially so high placed as this fortunate professor, have been dismissed, and very properly dismissed from the public service?[66]

Various colleagues rallied to von Zedlitz's defence. Professor Hunter, for example, argued that 'as we are fighting in this war on the basis of justice, we ought to be just.'[67] Some commentators rolled their eyes at 'the fuss and froth and fury' evident in the affair:

> It is curious that when two or three people are scandalised in New Zealand the scandal is allayed by as much political noise as can be got together in a short time . . . First of all, an enlightened community had to be told by somebody who had learned the German language that Von Zedlitz is a German name. Then the public fury had to be given time to grow, for the public neither knows nor cares who is educating its young men until somebody emits a 'Pro Bono Public' roar or a 'Father of Ten' scream or a 'Materfamilias' warning. Then some intrepid politician, who has to be loaded with the facts like a machine gun (politicians with an original idea are as rare as sovereigns in wartime), finds he has a chance of limelight, and he is scandalised horrified and hurt that a German professor is at work in Wellington. It matters to nobody that Dr. Von Zedlitz held his job for years before the war began and that nobody thought there was anything wrong about it. It mattered nothing that the learned person continued to carry on without the least interference when the Huns were torturing Belgium. Maybe the learned doctor is the sweetest flower that grows with a British heart and a hatred of Hunnism.[68]

These principled and irreverent stances ultimately proved ineffective. In 1915 the passage of the Alien Enemy Teachers' Act forbade the employment of enemy-aliens in teaching positions; it had been passed specifically with von Zedlitz in mind and he was the only individual in the country to which the law applied.[69] To adhere to the law, the College Council had no other option than to render the chair for modern languages vacant, though it expressed its regret, published a pamphlet setting out the events and voted that von Zedlitz receive a year's salary.

A broad consensus has stressed the play of social pressure in the von Zedlitz affair. Francis observes the episode as highlighting 'the direct influence exerted by public opinion in the formulation of government policy'.[70] Bernard John Foster notes that 'the Zedlitz case . . . is an excellent example of the folly of legislation in response to mass hysteria'.[71] Tim Beaglehole sees the College Council as 'defeated by patriotism of the worst sort'.[72] Rachel Barrowman astutely notes:

> It was an instance of official capitulation to the kind of popular paranoia that is not unexpected in wartime; but was also a chilling demonstration of the fragility of one of the more basic of those university ideals for which, in a different context, the reformers [to which von Zedlitz belonged] had recently been fighting – that of academic freedom.[73]

Published in 1963, von Zedlitz's autobiography gives scant clues on his personal thoughts and feelings about his circumstances.[74] His unpublished memoir notes, however, express the 'war depression' and economic hardship his forced retirement brought. A series of entries convey his situation and that of his wife Alice after his dismissal:

> 21 July 1918: the time when the war and the fate of humanity – or rather the fate during the rest of my lifetime of every ideal I value – was a constant source of oppression, seems almost like an old nightmare gone. Yet I am poorer daily, my prospect poorer, the outlook darker than ever after four years of war, and three years of living somehow on nothing a year.
>
> 25 April 1919: still incomeless until something turns up.
>
> 27 November 1919: Ill health, depression, poverty, fear of the future and the dullness of the present had dragged us both so low that we both realized that something must be done.
>
> 8 January 1920: On this day the Council of Victoria University College appointed Professor [Edwin Boyd-] Wilson to the chair occupied by me from 1902 to 1915 at the college. I suppose it could not be otherwise than that I should feel a considerable depression, though not, I hope, for long. Alice has always been convinced that this could happen and I have rarely doubted it. Still, it hurt when it happened.[75]

Past the early months of the war, tensions showed a capacity to flare into violent retaliation on little provocation. Consider Ernest Horne, a labouring man of German parentage, who in late 1915, after a few drinks in a Feilding hotel, boasted that Germany would win the war in three months. The resulting brawl pitched Horne against near one hundred men, in which the one soul who came to his aid was a soldier who failed to break up the mob.[76] At other places violence breached traditional restraints in regard to the sanctity of churches. In July 1917, Lutheran churches at Rongotea and Halcombe were destroyed by arsonists; Marton parishioners elected to keep a watch to guard their church from a similar fate.[77] In 1918, the bells of a Christchurch Lutheran church were hammered into oblivion and melted for scrap. Inscribed with the likeness of German royalty, the bells had been wrought in Berlin, with rumours incorrectly claiming that they were cast from French cannons captured during the Franco-Prussian War.[78]

In May 1915, Wanganui witnessed a second instance of mass anti-German unrest. Against news of casualties from Gallipoli and the 1,200 civilians drowned when a German U-boat torpedoed the *Lusitania*, an estimated 3,000 people vandalised and looted German-owned and suspected German-owned businesses.[79] The result severely taxed the town's capacity to restrain such hostilities, and estimates of damages started at £3,100 ($440,000 in 2015 dollars).[80] This local incarnation of the transnational outbreak of '*Lusitania* riots' was not nearly as destructive as elsewhere; London experienced 'the most widespread domestic disturbances in modern British history' and Johannesburg saw arson, mass destruction and much unrestrained looting.[81] However, while comparisons of relative destruction are meaningful, local targets did not experience the violence in relative terms. In the face of such volatile and uncertain circumstances, it is understandable that some sought out the relative security and stability of internment.[82]

However, conditions and experiences of internment varied. Parts of the record show internees roaming their island confines relatively freely, with diversions including sports, reading, letter writing, visits from 'the mainland', gardening, fishing and festivities, including celebrations of the Kaiser's birthday.[83] Interest groups, including an orchestra, were formed and some artisans honed their skills, passing the time and earning incomes by fashioning works of craft and art; some of the most striking of these creations are impressively fashioned jewellery boxes inlaid with paua shell.[84] Some internees possessed positions of trust and licence; the ex-wharfie Hans Hansen, for example, was allowed to make trips to Wellington to purchase supplies for his craft work.[85] Inspection visits from neutral nations noted internees as well-fed and living in clean quarters.[86] A constant theme of media commentary was that internees were being coddled.[87]

However, internment experiences also include complaints over conditions and allegations of abuse.[88] On Somes Island the commandant, Dugald Matheson, proved willing to respond to minor infractions with penalties intended to punish, humiliate and/or assert his authority.[89] Examples ranged from the withdrawal of visiting and letter-writing privileges, to corporal punishments, such as forcing an internee to sleep 26 nights on a concrete floor.[90] Enmity between the internees and guards, many of whom were former convicts, saw minor, needless brutalities and indecencies. Some of the intricately crafted boxes were stolen or smashed; some internees experienced vicious beatings administrated by guards at a secluded location, nicknamed 'Kultur Bay'; seven internees are noted as going mad; there were two attempted suicides; and several escape attempts, including Count Felix von Luckner's famous escapade at Motuihi, were inspired by abuses on Somes.[91] The internee Karl Joosten summarised that 'dispassionate historians' will find wartime internment as a 'black page in the book of this dominion's history.'[92]

Captivity was particularly physically and mentally demanding for Franz Wolter, who was convinced that his internment was the result of a scheme enacted by friends of von Zedlitz (whom he disliked) and underwent hunger strikes to protest his circumstances. Further misery came via beatings administered by the guards and ostracism from other internees who deemed him a traitor to the Fatherland; seemingly a consequence of Wolter asserting what has been described as a 'mystic reverence for his British nationality' and an 'anti-German fervour'.[93]

Conclusion

The experiences of the German community through 1914–1918 provide a case study of some of the social impacts of the war within New Zealand society. While many had argued that attempts to 'punish the continental "Huns" by persecuting local Germans' was 'a breach of the British code', the urge to distinguish between an enemy foreign power and the local German community was found wanting.[94] Given the scale and intensity of the war, it was inevitable that restraints of legality and humanity would be tested. The costs of these shifting perceptions and breakdown of social bonds were paid in the coinage of ostracism, hardship and violence.

The nature of the strains the war placed on some social bonds might be better understood by noting the unsteady demobilisation of wartime passions and attitudes. While many ex-enemy-aliens worked to repair frayed bonds and restore pre-war positions, they often laboured in an unfavourable climate. New Zealand's 1920s have been termed the 'xenophobic years', and the aftermath of the Great War heralded a new era of political and public debate concerning the boundaries of inclusion and exclusion.[95] Over 400 wartime internees left New Zealand on the *Willochra* in 1919.[96] These internees comprised both former prisoners of war being repatriated and former residents being deported. Some of the latter were accompanied by their families, representing a further severing of bonds. Consider, for example, a letter written by Helen Hansen – an Englishwoman married to a formerly naturalised German (who had lived in the country for 27 years), with a New Zealand-born son – to the Minister of Defence concerning the rumour of her husband's impending deportation:

> We should have to sacrifice the small amount of property we have accumulated as a provision for our old age, and to start again in an alien country with practically no capital, and past the prime of life to make a fresh living in an impoverished country, and under the deadly disadvantage of being considered English . . . To force an English woman and her child to live in such a place would be the refinement of cruelty.[97]

Some whose communal ties had been frayed during the war years experienced varying measures of success in rebinding them. Henry Joosten was paroled in 1919, refused to sign the Aliens' Register and began to enquire into the nature of his arrest and denaturalisation. Some 1,128 representatives, many from the academic, legal and business communities, petitioned with him, and the revocation of his naturalisation was annulled on 22 December 1920. However, having been unable to support his household during his internment, he had sold his share of Joosten & Murie, and shortly after the conclusion of this episode he departed for Hamburg.[98] Friedrich Wohnsiedler, whose butchery had been targeted in the Gisborne anti-German riot and whose naturalisation was overturned, was confirmed as a citizen in 1925. His occupation was recorded as 'farmer'.[99] Though von Zedlitz never resumed his old role as a professor of languages, in 1936 he was made Professor Emeritus at Victoria University College and elected to the Senate of the University of New Zealand. His portrait is displayed at Victoria University of Wellington and a university building has been named in his honour.[100]

Others were less fortunate. Franz Wolter was released from internment on parole in December 1919. Having lost his German citizenship, the revocation of his naturalisation meant he was now stateless.[101] Over the next three and a half years he endeavoured to rebuild a life in New Zealand; refusing to register as an enemy alien, he made sustained efforts, over 1920–22, to reinstate his naturalisation, and this was eventually enacted via an order of the Executive Council.[102] In 1922 the university office also announced that his doctoral thesis on 'Inductive Semantics' had been approved.[103] However, formal citizenship and academic achievements did not translate into community and livelihood.[104] Despite holding three university degrees and a prestigious scholarship, and winning the battle to be legally acknowledged as a New Zealander, Wolter never managed to secure a permanent position in his adopted country.[105] As L.H. Barber notes, 'Wolter's unjust treatment can in part be explained by the long lingering of anti-German feeling in the years following 1918.'[106] He repeatedly, fruitlessly, petitioned parliament and the League of Nations Union, seeking government service, and observed that 'as a result of the moral assassination I have suffered I cannot find employment, and am therefore unable to earn a living.'[107] In June 1924, government-supported emigration secured Wolter a passage to the United States. This concession was the result of an odd partnership between James Gibb, the anti-war Presbyterian minister of Wellington's St John's church, and the conservative prime minister Sir Francis Bell, who often proved sympathetic on issues of individual liberty and welfare.[108] Aged 50, Wolter departed the country he had arrived in some 18 years previously, and became an immigrant for the second time in his life.

Chapter Seventeen

Turangawaewae*: Maori Relationships with the Great War

Steven Loveridge and Basil Keane

Maori relationships with the Great War cover a spectrum from wholehearted commitment, through qualified support, to heartfelt opposition and some of the most stubborn and effective resistance in the country. Such variations are indicative of the complexities of the Maori position within the New Zealand society that went to war, and they possess implications for our understanding of that society. Maori experiences offer a markedly different study of wartime mobilisation, and comparison with Pakeha experiences brings both accounts into greater relief.[1] Furthermore, given increased consideration of 1914–1918 as a war between empires, Maori experiences provide further perspectives on the dynamics of the subjects of empires at war.[2] The Pakeha relationship with the British Empire has been described as centring around the idea of 'an association or partnership between Britain and the neo-Britains, held together by common culture and loyalties', and this association has been argued as forming a major basis of New Zealand's commitment to the war.[3] Maori standing in the British imperial edifice, in peace and war, was a more complex affair.

Towards 1914

In a broad sense, Maori responses to the war reflect the consequences set in motion by European expansion in New Zealand, with particular regard to events in the latter half of the nineteenth century. Traditional Maori social organisation centred on hapu and iwi kinship groups claiming descent from significant ancestors. Such organisation formed the obvious unit for interacting with the wider world, the basis for traditional rivalries and the foundation for collective rights to resources and territories used for

* Turangawaewae – literally turanga (standing place) and waewae (feet) – is often translated as 'a place to stand'. The term conveys the sense of belonging and possessing a place in the world.

cultivation, hunting and gathering. These rhythms of life were dramatically impacted by contact with Europe and the expansion of British power in New Zealand.

Though the country had formally come under British governance in 1840, British authority was, for a time, more aspirational than actual. Iwi actively manoeuvred for advantage, and their capacity for adaptation, trade and incorporation of European technologies and ideas were remarked upon by European observers from James Cook onward; major examples are evident in regard to Christianity, firearms, literacy and printing.[4] An agricultural revolution saw a rapid adoption and cultivation of introduced crops, with Maori foodstuffs providing significant supplies for expanding European settlements during the 1840s and 1850s, and some Maori men became active in trans-Tasman shipping as crew or even as captains.[5] It has become conventional to observe a weakening of the Maori position during and after the 1860s, as major wars over that decade challenged Maori military power. Changing demographics had made Maori a minority after 1857, the result of mass European immigration and a population decline brought about by introduced diseases and warfare; it is likely the Maori population fell from near 80,000 in 1840 to a nadir of near 41,000 by the start of the 1890s.[6] Maori enterprise struggled to adapt to a changing economy increasingly based around steam power, greater mechanisation and higher capital investment. The 1860s also saw a rapid alienation of Maori land, with a great deal being sold voluntarily, much under pressure and considerable amounts being confiscated in the aftermath of wars.[7]

Twentieth-century conditions, and ultimately Maori responses to the war effort, built on these circumstances. With a demographic recovery underway, the 1914 population was calculated at just under 50,000, with near 45,000 living in physically isolated areas, largely in the north of the North Island.[8] Many worked in the rural economy as casual labourers, or cultivating their own diminishing lands: 'Between 1912 and 1920 Maori holdings were further reduced from 2.8 million to 1.8 million hectares; and of that 1.8 million, 310,800 were unsuitable for development and 300,000 were already leased to Pakeha farmers.'[9]

Alongside physical isolation, tribal organisation, identity and authority remained strong and provided another basis for autonomy. However, to varying extents, Maori increasingly lived 'between two worlds', with their isolation breached and their tribal autonomy challenged by the infrastructure and dynamics of the modern era.[10] Some efforts to integrate Maori came from above, in the form of education and health measures and through the 1867 extension of the political franchise to Maori men.[11] Other networks came from advancing social institutions, notably missionary bodies.[12] Military service, which in other contexts of modernisation has been described as the 'school of the nation', likely played a comparable, if minor, role.[13] The 1909 introduction of universal military training had originally made no distinction between Maori and Pakeha, but subsequent amendments exempted Maori from compulsory provisions, with the exception of the Senior Cadets.[14] Even so, Maori could volunteer, and 488 were serving in the Territorials in August 1914.[15]

A major intent of these programmes was to assimilate Maori and produce what has been termed 'brown Britons'.[16] However, while infrastructure and institutional networks can knit peoples and regions together, community is not reducible to infrastructure and there is a rich record of Maori engaging with, subverting, challenging and disengaging from aspects of these advancing networks. Some individuals showed a particular adeptness for finding a place to stand in both worlds: Makereti Papakura – raised by an extended Maori family, 'one of New Zealand's first international media celebrities' and residing in a British manor when the war broke out – serves as an example of the extent to which this could be taken.[17]

At a broader level, responses might be plotted by iwi efforts to engage and disengage with the Pakeha state.[18] On one side, Maori leaders such as Apirana Ngata, Maui Pomare, Sir James Carroll, Te Rangi Hiroa (Peter Buck) and Paraire Tomoana – who were prominent members of the Young Maori Party – operated in collaboration with parliament. Their work to improve Maori living standards and social standing has been described as working 'to *combine* the technological, cultural and other benefits of European civilisation with preserving "the best" of Maori culture.'[19] Likewise, in a pattern comparable with other instances of British imperialism, the Crown had established and maintained working relationships with large iwi groups; Te Arawa and Ngati Porou offer key examples.[20] These iwi had established histories of partnership with the Crown, fighting with the government during the New Zealand Wars and offering troops during the Russian scare of 1885 and the South African ('Boer') War.

Other iwi attempted more autonomous existences, often reflecting enduring bitterness over the wars and land confiscations of the nineteenth century. Across the central North Island, disengagement found an expression in those Waikato, Maniapoto and Ngati Haua tribes which backed the pan-tribal Kingitanga movement to bring Maori under a unified sovereignty. Though pan-tribal legitimacy and independence had proved unobtainable, Te Rata, invested with kingship in 1912, headed an influential organisation and maintained a tradition of semi-splendid isolation.[21] Furthermore, significant parts of Tuhoe, and some of Ngati

Awa and Whakatohea, followed the prophet Rua Kenana. Claiming to be a successor of Te Kooti and citing a Bible-based pacifism, Kenana persuaded his followers to surrender their worldly goods, reject Pakeha authority and join his community of Maungapohatu, deep in the Ureweras.[22]

The jagged relationship between the Crown and the Kingitanga was highlighted in the months before the war. On 1 April 1914, some 5,000 politicians and dignitaries (including a small number of Maori and Pakeha veterans) gathered for the fiftieth anniversary of the battle of Orakau, unveiling a memorial to the most famous battle of the Waikato conflict. It was proclaimed that the battle marked 'the final acceptance of the British mana by a heroic and warlike native people', laying the ground for 'a just and generous reciprocity which is everywhere regarded as an example to the civilised world.'[23] However, this interpretation of Orakau and the Waikato War was challenged as Te Rata drew plans to travel to Britain and lay grievances before the British monarch as a partner under the Treaty of Waitangi.[24] He gained an audience with King George V on 4 June, and his delegation was still in England when the war broke out.

Pakeha racial attitudes were a final major element shaping Maori turangawaewae in wider society. These attitudes were a complex mix of romantic exoticism, sincere interest, protective (if patronising) paternalism and antagonising racism, with social expression varying immensely.[25] In 1909, children were taught that 'the good Maori stands as high as the good pakeha and the bad pakeha sinks as low as the bad Maori.'[26] Conversely, a respectable paper like the *New Zealand Herald* could candidly print that 'it is by no means evident that the world at large or humanity gains anything by the perpetuation of a race of lazy, half-civilised people, who do little for themselves, and nothing at all for anybody else.'[27] Such contradictory attitudes were also found in government. Various Maori parliamentarians gained respect and standing; Sir James Carroll would twice serve as Acting Prime Minister, in 1909 and 1911. Conversely, a physical confrontation, stopping just short of a brawl, came about when the demagogic MP John Payne responded to Maui Pomare's call to sit down with 'I do not take orders from a nigger.' Fortunately, the situation was de-escalated, with Payne apologising for 'a thoughtless moment'.[28]

Initial responses

August 1914 saw sectors of Maoridom show expressions of solidarity comparable to other instances of social unity at the war's outbreak. In the Bay of Plenty, Te Arawa, anticipating the British entrance into the war, sent a telegraph to the government on 3 August reading 'We of the Arawas, as our forefathers before us offer our services to our King and country in whatever clime and whenever you see fit to call us.'[29] A similar message from Ngapuhi read:

> As British subjects under the Treaty of Waitangi, we, the Ngapuhi people wish to convey through you to His Most Gracious Majesty, King George the Fifth, in this most trying epoch of his Empire, an assurance of our loyalty and devotion, and that we are ever ready and willing to in any way to assist in the defence of this Dominion against his enemies.[30]

Monty Soutar has observed this support as coming from 'iwi whose experiences with the Crown made them more amenable to notions of civic responsibility and service', arguing that 'they were motivated by ideals of patriotic service and the obligations of citizenship inherent in the Treaty of Waitangi.'[31] Pomare rendered such sentiments in unambiguous, conspicuous and not entirely accurate terms, asserting that 'the Maoris of the Dominion have expressed as with one voice unswerving loyalty to the British throne. They recognise that the British cause is their cause; that the British King is their King; that the God of the British is the God of the Maoris too.'[32]

For a month, however, Maori enthusiasm to participate was constrained by the Imperial Government's reluctance to deploy native troops against Europeans. This mirrored the situation some fifteen years earlier, when Maori had been officially barred from volunteering for the Boer War.[33] On both occasions, some men of Maori descent did manage to enlist and some departed with the NZEF in October 1914.[34] A broadened opportunity came in early September with London accepting 500 volunteers for a Maori Contingent, originally intended for garrison duty. Thus recruiting began for what became known as Te Hokowhitu-a-Tu (the seventy twice-told warriors of the war god Tu).

As with non-Maori, existing communal links and networks facilitated mobilisation. Many initial volunteers had connections to Anglican schools like Te Aute and St Stephen's, and forty students of Te Rau Maori Theological College volunteered.[35] The raising, and later reinforcing, of the Maori Contingent was heavily reliant on the emergent Native Contingent Committee (NCC), which agreed on recruitment quotas for each district, with men often attracted, trained and sent on a tribal basis, a process which 'left the recruits with the impression that they had been chosen as envoys of their tribes'.[36] A who's who of the Young Maori Party, the NCC had many prominent members, including Sir James Carroll, Apirana Ngata, Taare (Charles) Parata, Peter Buck and Maui Pomare, its chairman.

On 14 February 1915 the contingent departed, bound for Egypt. As with other reports of departing soldiers from this period, accounts described them as the flower of their generation. The majority were well educated, the result of church colleges. Aside from a few Boer War veterans, and some men with cadet training, most had no military experience.[37] The manner in which commentators, Maori and non-Maori alike, perceived these men as embodying the heritage of a 'martial race' has been well documented; the trope of comparing contemporary soldiers with past warriors and traditions, comparable to the mobilisation of chivalric imagery in the European context, quickly came into vogue.[38] Upon witnessing the contingent at work, a grey-haired chief accordingly proclaimed 'Oh! If I only had this army of men under me, I could conquer New Zealand.'[39]

This motif of Maori eminence in war was typically synchronised with the assertion of Maori turangawaewae within the Empire.[40] This is well evident in those assembled to farewell the contingent. Tureiti Te Heuheu, chief of Ngati Tuwharetoa, and Kingi Topia, of Whanganui, urged the men 'to be strong and of good courage, to face the foe without flinching, and to uphold the mana of the Great White King whom they had sworn to serve.'[41] Hari Wahanui, a chief from Otorohanga, comparably charged the contingent:

> Be truthful; be honourable. You carry the honour of the Maori race in your hands. Be brave, and remember the flag you have flying over your tents. With reference to your religious beliefs, don't forget that you aim for one heaven. Fear God, read and study your Bibles, and may the British reign over us for ever.[42]

Such sentiments were welcomed and mirrored by those Pakeha who cherished notions of racial harmony, or of Maori being uplifted under British governance. The *Evening Post* declared that 'time has enabled the Maori to give wonderful testimony to the British genius for colonisation and Government.'[43] The Prime Minister lent his support to a Maori unit, declaring that Maori 'are supposed to share with us all the privileges and benefits of British citizenship . . . I do not see why the Maoris should not have the privilege of fighting for the Empire'.[44] The Anglican Bishop of Auckland cited Maori volunteers, 'assembled and anxious to stand shoulder to shoulder with their European friends and fight the foes of England', as a milestone of social progress: 'We have every reason to marvel at such progress.'[45]

The confident nature of these sentiments belie some complexities. Firstly, commitment was not unconditional. After volunteering began, the Defence Department soon discovered that policies that transgressed tribal sensibilities resulted in elders threatening to withdraw recruits and support.[46] This dynamic was taken further when, after the contingent was deployed at Gallipoli, several Maori officers were dismissed on charges of incompetence and plans were aired to distribute the Maori Contingent across other battalions.[47] The result was the NCC noting 'it will no longer be possible to raise further contingents unless the race can be satisfied that no injustice has been done.'[48] The Defence Department was under no illusion concerning its ability to recruit without the support of the NCC, and by March 1916, Maori recruiting was pronounced 'absolutely dead'.[49] This impasse was overcome later that month, when the establishment of the New Zealand Division saw the Maori soldiers kept together as a Pioneer Battalion.

Secondly, commitment was not universal. Volunteering had varied across iwi, with many coming from Ngapuhi, Ngai Porou and Te Arawa, together with significant numbers from Ngati Kahungunu and South Island iwi.[50] Isolationist policy, political grievances and pacifism underwrote consistent indifference or hostility from other sectors of Maoridom. Rua Kenana discouraged, if not forbade, enlisting and, more broadly, the Ngai Tuhoe people appeared largely ambivalent towards the war. The East Coast-based Maori newspaper *Te Kopara*, which fused a Church of England and Ngati Porou focus, suggested that around 150 Tuhoe men had enlisted by September 1918, though contemporary research suggests the figure may be closer to 50.[51]

The Kingitanga formed another centre of non-commitment, officially claiming neutrality and declaring that Maori should enlist, or not, as they saw fit – though numerous accounts attest to key figures possessing less than neutral dispositions. *Te Paki o Matariki*, the official newspaper of the Kingitanga, observed that many belligerents had good reasons for involvement; King George V and Kaiser Wilhelm II were perceived as fighting over sovereignty, and France, Belgium and Russia were observed as being at war with Germany over land.[52] It was stated as 'right for those nations whose land is close to Germany to fight as they are fighting over their own land interests.' Conversely, the report noted that America and China (and, incorrectly, Japan) were not involved because they lacked land interests. Under this rationale it was concluded that Maori had no basis for involvement.[53] The emerging key figure of Waikato resistance, Te Puea Herangi, accented her objections with pacifism, citing King Tawhiao's symbolic laying down of arms in 1881 as the end of warfare in New Zealand, but she also evoked political and land grievances. Referring to recruiting posters, Te Puea quipped 'They tell us to fight for king and country, well that's all right. We've got a king. But we haven't got a country. That's been taken off us. Let them give us back our land and then maybe we'll think about it again.'[54] Despite the Waikato-Maniapoto region possessing some 1,306 eligible men (401 first division and 905 second division), Waikato presence in the first contingent was lacklustre, with only 1.8 per cent of recruits coming from the King Country.[55]

Thirdly, conceptions of 'martial races' stood beside more mixed perceptions of Maori soldiers. A paternalist assessment of the relationship between Maori and war, for example, is evident in a letter written by Charles Mackie of the National Peace Council to James Allen, the Minister of Defence:

> We believe that the principle involved in forcing the Maoris into such a conflict as this is extremely serious, especially in face of our past efforts to inculcate the spirit of goodwill among them. In actual practice we are belying our profession and the effect upon the Maori mind must be disastrous.[56]

An alternative representation of Maori that emerged in popular culture at the time was the stock character 'Private Puripeef' (bullybeef), typically a simple, happy-go-lucky joker who spoke a 'stage Maori' pidgin English. An extended example can be seen in James Fussell's tales of the wartime adventures of Corporal Henare Tikitanu, a fictional Waikato Maori who enlists to 'help Englan kick out te Sherman poaka [pig]'.[57] Across two books, his whirlwind adventures see him sustain his fellow soldiers with his good humour, outwit German guards, encounter a French nurse, earn promotion to 'Korpril', be awarded a Victoria Cross by King George V and dream of reunion with his sweetheart in 'Noo Zealan'.[58] His adventure concludes on a moral lesson:

> Bearing on his body the honourable scars of war, and on his breast the King's acknowledgement of his bravery and loyalty, Henare spent his days going in and out among the Waikatos and neighbouring tribes, telling them thrilling tales of Britain's might and honour; and showing them the terrible need there is for Pakeha and Maori alike to do and dare – for the sake of Britannia, the friend of Justice and Liberty.[59]

While Fussell's irreverence was intended as affectionate, other commentary portraying Maori as simple and unsophisticated could become openly disparaging:

> The prevailing Maori soldier will have to be attended to. He is often young, obstreperous, undisciplined and unclean . . . They become repeatedly drunk, offensive to sight and smell, and rude in speech. The vicinity of Narrow Neck Camp is now impossible for decent pakehas

> . . . At the end of Queen Street, the Maori soldier may be seen at the height of his offensiveness, odorous, unpleasant, undisciplined. He fills restaurants side by side with clean people and may be seen with his hands full of fish gobbling loudly . . . if Hone isn't cleaner and nicer, even his own officers may notice that he's one of Auckland's worst nuisances.[60]

Enduring commitment and resistance

Efforts to generate Maori military service became increasingly difficult as the war became protracted and obviously lethal. Of the 497 Maori deployed at Gallipoli on 3 July 1915, only 134 remained to be withdrawn in December.[61] Though the Pioneer Battalion was centrally employed in road and trench construction, it too experienced high casualties. Of the 2,227 Maori (and 458 Pacific Islanders) who served, 336 were killed and 734 wounded – a 48 per cent casualty rate.[62] Facing such enormous casualties throughout its forces, the British War Office pragmatically reassessed its position on non-white soldiers and, in May 1915, cabinet agreed to a request for a reinforcement rate of 250 Maori every three months.[63] However, enthusiasm had declined from its August 1914 peak, and many began to negotiate the terms of sacrifice. Ngapuhi petitioned for no more Maori to be sent; Frederick Bennett, an Anglican clergyman of Ngati Whakaue, proposed recruitment be capped at 1,000; a Maniapoto petition hinted that support might follow if its volunteers were guaranteed to be confined to garrison duty.[64] It was in this context that Apirana Ngata remarked that the pledges of August 1914 seemed as 'wind and words.'[65]

By the end of June 1915 the shortcomings in enlistment were becoming evident, with Allen expressing doubt over 'whether we shall be able to keep up the Maori Reinforcements.'[66] Though thirty reinforcement bodies followed the first contingent, maintaining a reliable reinforcement stream remained an enduring problem. By the end of the war, Maori, who comprised near 4.33 per cent of the population, constituted around 2 per cent of New Zealand enlistees, a proportional effort roughly half that of the Pakeha population.[67]

Between 1915 and 1918 there were ongoing attempts to boost Maori engagement, backed by expanded applications of state power.[68] The NCC remained a significant base of these attempts. During parliamentary debates concerning the introduction of conscription in mid-1916, members of the NCC proved resolute in asserting that Maori could play an equal role to Pakeha, reading a proclamation that 'the Maori should not be excluded.'[69] There was conviction backing this stance; Sir James Carroll and Apirana Ngata both had sons at the front and Peter Buck had volunteered as a medical officer. Indigenous leaders have been described as 'bridge people' between their cultures and Dominion political and social systems.[70] In regard to those Maori leaders seeking to maintain commitment to the war effort, the task became one of bridging divides in Maoridom; translating commitment at the top into mass support across tribal lines, and defusing resistance. Ultimately, this would prove unviable.[71]

As in other contexts, negotiations over sacrifice spurred increased accusations of shirking, support for compulsion and inflamed tribal rivalries. While recruitment had been low in Taranaki and Maniapoto, attention increasingly focussed on Waikato, King Country and Tuhoe. Some of this may have been useful for generating pressure. In March 1918, a Wairoa resolution sent to Allen noted:

> My hapus desire to inform you that all the tribes throughout the East Coast are responding to the call of our King and Empire, registering with enthusiasm, being noble of a fighting race, determined to carry out this war to a victorious conclusion and to maintaining the maximum effort by National Government in reinforcing the men who have shed and are still shedding their sacred blood for the cause of freedom and humanity.

The message signed off with the request that it be published to 'show Waikato the Patriotism of the East Coast tribes.'[72] That September, Reverend Wi Paraire Rangihau, the editor of *Te Kopara*, published an article entitled 'The obdurate refusal of Waikato', rebuking Waikato tribes: 'Waikato, do not let our people, the chiefly Maori people, a people held up high by the nations of the world, be brought low by you.' Further stoking tribal rivalries, the article compared Waikato and Tuhoe enlistments and noted that the assumption of Tuhoe as the least 'civilised' iwi was now being challenged: 'It can be seen now that Waikato has sent less people than Tuhoe.'[73]

However, intertribal pressure proved ineffective, as did a series of government missions to win support on the ground. In November 1916, Allen and Ngata visited Huntly Marae in the Waikato. Appealing to pride, Allen noted that 'the Maoris of old . . . were noted for their chivalry and their devotion to duty and he believed the same spirit remained in their descendants. Indeed, had it not already been well proven by all the tribes except the Waikatos?' He exhorted his audience to resist German militarism:

> United we stand, divided we fall . . . and if we fall what then? What for New Zealand and for the native race of New Zealand, as for the pakeha of New Zealand? The cruel fate of Belgium might well become the fate

> of New Zealand. Your women and children and babies might become the sport for German bayonets, your country ravaged by enemies who know not the meaning of mercy, and your strong men compelled at the point of the bayonet to work in the factories and mines of cruel foes . . . We hold out the hand to you, we who are fighting for country, for the peace to come, for justice, for the rights of those who have been wronged, for the weak, and for all that is good and holy. We would have you join in that fight. If you fail now you and your tribes can never rest in honour in the days that are coming.[74]

In early July 1917, Te Heuheu attended a hui involving Waikato, Ngati Maru, Ngapuhi and Ngati Paoa iwi. Arguing in support of conscription, he asserted that 'many of the best warriors had sprung from the Waikato tribe; let them, therefore, put all past grievances aside for the present and fight for the Empire of which they formed a part.'[75] Accompanying Pomare, Te Heuheu undertook another mission to Waikato in the winter of 1918. Rebutting Waikato resistance as 'untrue to the traditions and unfaithful to the sacred words of your great and illustrious dead', Pomare concluded his speech by asking the iwi to 'put aside the petty quarrels of the family, and take hold of the battles of the Nation.'[76]

These efforts to drum up commitment were unfruitful. Allen's speech, which King Te Rata and most eligible men had not attended, was met with a 'murmur of applause' and he was informed that no one was stopping men from enlisting. In a later meeting with Tupu Taingakawa, the uncle and tumuaki (a position comparable to a prime minister) of the King, Allen's call for unity was met with the response: 'Who will suffer? My people cannot suffer more than they have done in the loss of their lands and of their mana.'[77] Likewise, Te Heuheu's call for Maori to fight for the Empire was countered with the assertion that the Treaty of Waitangi, in its extension of royal protection, meant the government could not conscript Maori.[78] Finally, Pomare and Te Heuheu's 1918 mission to Waikato encountered conspicuous tribal enmity, with some seeing Pomare as seeking revenge on Waikato-Maniapoto for Taranaki's nineteenth-century defeats.[79] The two received abusive haka interspersed with the whakapohane (ritual baring of buttocks), followed by a poi dancer approaching the pair and exposing herself to them. While this was also a ritualised form of contempt, it came with a salient point: the woman asked what use were her private parts if Pomare was going to take her husband away.[80]

The ability of Maori leadership to resist volunteering has been noted as a 'lesson for the Crown in the power of Maori control mechanisms.'[81] In the aftermath of his 1916 Waikato mission, Allen noted that 'I am afraid it will take pressure, not talk, to bring them in.'[82] Events earlier that year indicate that the government was already willing to use power to send a message. In April 1916, an expedition of 67 armed police arrived at Maungapohatu to arrest Rua Kenana.[83] Although officially reacting to Kenana's non-appearance in court over charges of illegally trading alcohol, this move occurred against a background of escalating tensions, and numerous accounts have addressed the episode as one of asserting state sovereignty.[84] Kenana discouraged volunteering, and suspicious minds increasingly perceived malevolent intent in his millennial prophecies of the restoration of Maori rule and his alleged use of the (not uncommon) taunt that a German victory would see Maori regain their land. Such sentiments were perceived as seditious and Kenana was dubbed the 'Maori Kaiser'.[85] When the police reached Maungapohatu, confused circumstances resulted in a half-hour shootout in which Kenana's son and a follower were killed, and four policemen and an unknown number of Maori wounded. The aftermath saw the prophet put on trial and sentenced to a year's hard labour and 18 months' imprisonment.[86] The cost of the expedition and trial (£2,000 – nearly $265,000 in 2015 dollars) was charged to Maungapohatu, devastating the community.[87] The judge's verdict noted that 'the lesson that your people should learn from this trial' was that the law extended to 'every corner of the great Empire to which we belong.'[88]

In mid-1917, with efforts to persuade Waikato proving lacklustre, it was decided to register North Island Maori for conscription and to begin balloting the Waikato-Manipoto district (South Island Maori were deemed more integrated and able to enrol on European lines).[89] What followed was perhaps the war effort's greatest failure in regard to generating military power. The introductory chapter of this volume notes that effective war efforts aligned committed societies alongside efficient governments. Conversely, attempting conscription in the face of major gulfs between state and subjects, with ineffective governance and a lack of communal sanction, reveals some hard limits regarding mobilisation. Comparable crises highlighting the struggle or inability to introduce and operate conscription were witnessed in Australia, Russia, Canada and Great Britain (in regards to Ireland).[90]

Again the challenge was to translate designs at the top into results on the ground. Work at the top began in earnest: the North Island was divided into six Maori military districts, thousands of posters outlining the provisions of the Military Service Act were printed in Maori, registration cards were distributed and local police were briefed on the particulars of their duties.[91] On the ground, however, the project's limitations soon became evident.

Before 1913, Maori were not required to register births, and records were fragmented. The government, having illegally compiled 'confidential' information from the 1916 census to create a ballot register, suspected this, and subsequent registration efforts confirmed record gaps.[92] In a report dated 2 May 1918, a constable stationed at Te Awamutu described existing records as 'useless as a guide to the number of Natives, their ages and addresses in any of the Maori settlement in the Waipa, Waitoma [sic] and West Taupo Counties.' In regard to the latter it was noted that a third of the young men were not on the register.[93] Efforts to amend records were hampered by various forms of recalcitrance. In the Blenheim sub-district, a constable reported that only three Maori had registered, with the majority having no intention of joining them.[94] A Hawera officer claimed that local Maori 'absolutely refused to have anything to do with the signing of the enrolment card.'[95] Many exploited the police officers' lack of familiarity with the Maori community and gave false addresses and names, such as 'Henuwera Harry' (roughly translating as 'hot stuff').[96] Another officer noted that 'quite a large section of Maoris in these parts cannot read English, or speak it very much, and at the present time they make it convenient not to understand what I try to tell them.'[97] In other cases, even previously 'friendly' Maori became hostile or insulting, sometimes calling for a German victory. One police inspector concluded that 'to properly complete this work of registration with any degree of accuracy it will be necessary to employ a capable reliable Interpreter to visit each of the Settlements in order to get the correct names and information required.'[98]

By April 1918, however, Waikato-Maniapoto registration was deemed serviceable, and 209 names were balloted, including members of Te Rata's family. Just 68 reported.[99] Police set about apprehending defaulters, and these arrests proved another difficult task. Many, under Te Puea's influence, offered non-violent passive resistance. One balloted man, described as 'enormously fat', illustrates the point: 'He just lay on the ground. The police had much difficulty in carrying him to the motorcar. Of course no one would help them. We had to laugh, despite our tears.'[100] Given inadequate information and the lack of communal co-operation, identifying balloted men was difficult. Men were mistaken for their fathers, sons and brothers, and in October 1918 the commandant of Narrow Neck training camp complained that many of those sent to camp were ineligible by way of having dependents or by being underage.[101] Some claimed balloted men's identities in order to travel to Auckland before their deception could be discovered.[102] Many men went unlocated, and 120 warrants were outstanding in early 1919. Even when men were located and brought into camp, resistance could continue. In one case, 34 Waikato conscripts refused uniforms, and court-martials were brought against six of them.[103]

Such responses reflect conscription's lack of legitimacy in the Waikato. Indeed, the Military Service Act was dubbed *Te Ture Puruma* (literally the Broom or Sweeping Act), and *Te Kopara* printed correspondence elaborating on this theme:

> Listen to the voice of Allen who cries, Sweep! Sweep! Sweep the Maori people from the face of the earth . . . Why should I be taken by this broom, so that I may sit within the heat of battle? Maori people, is it correct that we should come under this law? . . . Each iwi has its own mana, its own tikanga and its own way of doing things. Therefore I shall not thoughtlessly tramp the heel of my foot on someone else's turangawaewae . . . As for the arrival of this broom to your door by this one or this one, it means we are adrift on the tides of the Pacific Ocean floating along, blown here and there by the wind.

Such commentary could also evoke tribal pride as a case against conscription:

> The Maori are a chiefly people, a people admired by Pakeha for fighting in the wars. A people who have developed expertise, at the arts of war, a brave and strong people when faced with battle. It is not appropriate to leave it to conscription to fetch them. I say to the iwi, my way of looking is that this belittles us the Maori people. The fame of bravery, the mana of your ancestors who have passed on to the neverending night.[104]

By the end of the war, 552 Maori had been balloted. Of these, 254 had been disqualified from service (161 unfit, 17 exempted, 76 ineligible); 150 had refused service (139 unlocated, 11 imprisoned); and 148 were being processed and trained.[105] At this time, conscription had failed to produce a single Maori conscript for frontline service. Ngata later reflected that 'as a device for securing men for the Maori contingent conscription was a dismal failure.'[106] With the war's end, the government cancelled unexecuted warrants, put arrested men on leave without pay and, in May 1919, discreetly released the eleven prisoners.[107]

Conclusion

The complexities that underwrote Maori relationships with the war effort endured as the guns fell silent. From March 1919 the Pioneer Battalion began to be repatriated, with officials and communities working to demobilise soldiers, to hang remembrance photographs in wharenui, to raise public memorials to Maori soldiers and respond to the traumas of the war.[108] This work was undertaken in trying circumstances, and the results were inevitably imperfect. Indeed the influenza pandemic proved more lethal than the war, and this was especially true for Maori: 2,160 Maori (nearly 4 per cent of the population) died during the pandemic, with the rate of Maori deaths (42.3 per thousand) over seven times higher than that of the Pakeha (5.5 per thousand).[109] Furthermore, repatriation initiatives for Maori veterans, which included efforts to offer practical educational lectures and land settlement, achieved limited results: the education scheme is described as 'not very successful' and only 1.8 per cent of Maori veterans (compared to near 10 per cent of Pakeha veterans) were assisted in land acquisition.[110]

The differences in post-war interpretations among Maori leaders further highlight the complexities regarding the meaning of the war for Maori. Pomare continued to espouse his ideal that military service had proved Maori as possessing an equal standing to Pakeha. Within the foreword of a 1926 history book, he proclaimed that Maori service was a statement of:

> the position of the Maori as a social and political entity in the life of New Zealand. Our people's voluntary service in the Great War gave a new and glorious tradition to the story of the Maori race. It gave the crowning touch to the sense of citizenship in the British commonwealth; it satisfied in the one fitting fashion the intense desire of the Maori to prove to the world that he was the equal of the pakeha in the fullest sense – physically, mentally and spiritually . . . Henceforth he was the racial peer of any man on earth.[111]

Though more nuanced, and written seventeen years after Pomare's foreword, Ngata's evaluation agreed that the Maori soldier 'came back with a straighter back and more assured mien' and that this was 'responsible for the broadening of the Maori outlook on the world.' However, he balanced this against a sense of unfulfilled potential: 'The role of the Maori in the last war was defined for him against his own inclination and the call of his warrior ancestry . . . The Maori soldier through the well-meant solicitude of his friends and mentors did not come of age at the end of the last war.'[112]

Conversely, in a new act of disengagement, many Maori backed the faith healer Tahupotiki Wiremu Ratana. Claiming to receive visions, Ratana cited the war as part of the need to seek redemption:

> I am the Holy Spirit, I have visited the scene of the war which has recently raged in Europe. In my travels I have found that the whole world has forgotten me. I have looked all over for some place to

> establish myself, and to ensure that God will again be truly known and accepted in the hearts of men. That is why I have come to you, the Maori people.[113]

Te Puea also set out on a post-war mission, raising funds and leveraging connections in the effort to build a settlement at Ngaruawahia. Besides safeguarding the welfare of Maori orphans of the influenza pandemic, this settlement was intended to help sustain the Kingitanga movement, for which the marae, named Turangawaewae, became a headquarters.[114]

As these positions suggest, patterns of Maori engagement and disengagement, alongside Pakeha attitudes, continued to shape the Maori position within interwar society. In various parts of life the 'colour bar' continued: in May 1919, three Maori veterans, two of whom were in uniform, entered a Wanganui hotel for a drink and were informed that 'no Maoris were served'.[115] Another veteran, Parekura Tureia, was, at the request of South Africa, barred from the touring New Zealand rugby team.[116] Furthermore, the grievances of the nineteenth century remained unresolved, and in 1924, a decade after Te Rata's journey, another Maori delegation planned to travel to England in an effort to present their grievances to King George V.[117]

At the same time, Monty Soutar's survey of Maori life in the interwar years observes general improvements in economic development and an increased emphasis on education among many iwi, with a few passing the Public Service exams and joining the Native Department.[118] The expansion of the English language and social networks helped foster a more integrated society. Influence in government also continued, with the careers and standing of many Maori ministers proceeding strongly. Pomare was knighted in 1920 and Ngata in 1927; Ngata went on to rank high in cabinet and serve as acting Deputy Prime Minister. The Reform government in the 1920s was observed as 'much more accommodating in Maori matters' than prior to the war, and efforts to address land questions in the 1920s and 1930s won an increased awareness of grievances.[119] These developments are undoubtedly linked to the smoother mobilisation of Maori during World War Two, which saw extensive iwi involvement in the war effort; even Te Puea offered support, if very much with a mind of her own.[120]

Chapter Eighteen

Enduring Mystery: New Zealand Children and the Great War

Jeanine Graham

Any foray into New Zealand children's experiences during the First World War is a slightly problematic mission, given the variables linked with ethnicity, gender, socio-economic circumstance; rural, urban, isolated or unsettled location; family and household composition, structure and dynamics; and age and education. Then, as now, each child's connection with the society in which he or she was growing up was unique, and personal evidence from children is at best fragmentary. So, initially, the relationship between the Great War and the lives of the country's youngest citizens might more readily be described in negative terms. No occupying forces. No physical destruction of homes, crops, landscape and cultural heritage. No forced dispossession or relocation. No targeting of civilians. Tamariki in the conflict zones of the North Island had experienced all of that half a century earlier. The scars were still apparent some five decades later, but not for children of the dominant Pakeha society.[1]

And just as the effects and outcomes of that colonial conflict lasted for generations, influencing the lives and attitudes of tamariki who grew up in its aftermath, so the children of early twentieth-century New Zealand would feel the impact of international conflict well beyond the period of military engagement. As Dorothy Butler, doyenne of children's literature, observed: 'Although the Great War, as we called it, had been over for seven years before I was born, it was still very much in our midst.' Butler was one of thousands who could describe the war's cost in personal terms. 'New Zealand was full of disabled men, war widows, and fatherless children – "all through sheer foolishness", our mother would tell us.'[2] And so it was during wartime, too. In a multitude of public and private contexts and to an extent determined largely by their age at the time, children variously listened, observed, participated, contributed and thought about what was happening in their daily lives. Not everything related to war, but that children should be part of the war effort was axiomatic. As a *New Zealand Herald* editorial proclaimed at the very start of the conflict:

> We shall ensure henceforth that every British boy grows fit to be a fighter and that every British girl grows fit to mother men . . . we shall teach them to be in peace as in war, helpful to one another, loyal and loving children of a world-wide Britain that can only live while for her they are glad to die.[3]

Central to this exploration is the very nature of childhood as an ongoing, developmental process. Children in this context are youngsters under the age of 15 since most of the country's youthful citizens, secondary school students generally excepted, were undertaking adult-style working roles once they left compulsory elementary schooling. Within that broad framework is a diversity of circumstance and experience, for children were variously cherished, cosseted, enjoyed, neglected, exploited, abused and abandoned. Charitable organisations had long been active on behalf of children and mothers in colonial society, and their endeavours, along with those of emergent state agencies, would continue throughout the war.[4] The difficult circumstances of many Maori children, gradually coming to more official attention through education and health initiatives, were exacerbated more by disease than war.[5]

Drawing on her examination of child and youth exposure and responses to the military and medical crises of 1914–1918, Charlotte Bennett has suggested the short-lived but devastating influenza pandemic that swept the country in November–December 1918 'created more disruption and instability in children's lives than the war ever did.'[6] That was certainly the case for tamariki in Maori communities hard-hit by the contagion. The loss of tribal elders, children, and men and women in their prime was a heavy blow for a people slowly recovering from the disease, conflict and dispossession of the colonial era.[7] Bennett's careful analysis also emphasises the influence of age and the importance of both the emotional and geographical proximity of youth to the crises of these years. Those whose lives were most directly disrupted by the war had a family member or relative involved. But the relative detachment of youth made possible by the conflict occurring overseas contrasted markedly with the sense of direct involvement generated when the influenza epidemic overwhelmed communities at home. This essay aims to complement Bennett's work and discern what insights can be gained from a focus on children's experiences during these years of crisis.

As shown through contemporary comment, such as the oft-cited correspondence to the children's pages of the *Otago Witness*, or through recollections expressed later in life, spoken and written evidence relating to this era suggests the Great War could have lasting effects on youthful consciousness, even if the memories were little more than random impressions.[8] In nuclear and extended families affected by military deaths, however, youngsters could become a means by which adults sought to come to terms with their own grief, a circumstance that might mean unwitting pressure being felt by such children as they grew older.

Pre-war childhoods

New Zealand's children were growing up in societies where childhood was viewed primarily as preparation for adulthood, a status that came early by modern standards. In legislative terms, 12 years had been the most commonly adopted age of demarcation in the late nineteenth century, though Liberal enactments tended towards making 14 years the threshold for transition.[9] Legislative inconsistencies remained, but with primary schooling compulsory for both Pakeha and Maori children between the ages of 5 and 14 years (from 1901 and 1903 respectively), the weight of officialdom was a powerful influence even on parents reluctant to send their children to school for so long.[10] Although there was provision for exemption from school attendance, from 1914 this could only apply to children who were over 13 years of age and who had attained their Certificate of Proficiency in Standard 6 (Year 8).[11] To attend secondary or technical schools was still the experience of a minority, albeit a growing one. Hence primary schools were the major forum through which both Maori and Pakeha children's minds and energies could be turned towards the war effort. Yet saluting the flag, knitting socks and scarves, reciting heroic poetry or rehearsing for patriotic performances could all be contained within the school day. What children did and experienced within their homes, neighbourhoods and communities was of equal if not more influence on their developing attitudes.

Most children of this era were raised within communities – those of family or whanau, nuclear and extended; and of neighbourhoods – physical and institutional.[12] Anonymity was uncommon, strangers and new arrivals conspicuous. The worlds of children were strongly influenced by cultural and personal values, socio-economic circumstance, exposure to education, authority and indoctrination, and societal expectations. Yet theirs were also worlds of physicality, of literal and imaginative adventure, of emotion and aspiration, and of activity. Idleness was not admired. Pre-war and wartime children were constantly on the move (periods of classroom or pew confinement excepted). They walked and they ran. Many skipped, some swam. Their occasional or regular use of public transport was limited to larger urban centres; travelling by car was only for the rich. 'Townies' might ride bikes; many 'country kids' had access to horses. The basic rhythm of outdoor/indoor life was governed by weather, season and daylight, though both farm children and boys trying to earn money through milk or paper rounds had working hours that began in or extended into darkness. Outdoor play, fishing or fort building was not always within adult view; pets, siblings and friends were the usual companions. Indoor personal space was limited and basically an alien concept for Maori and Pakeha youngsters alike. Beds and bedrooms or sleeping areas were shared. Most activity – in wage earner homes at least – took place at or around the (often) only table in the house and solitude, if sought, was likely to be short-lived, since a sibling's appearance or an adult's summons would wreck any reverie. Newspapers, children's annuals and books were the main means by which youngsters could transcend their day-to-day home environment but, religious tracts excepted, even the printed word was likely to be rationed or controlled for children living within state or charitable institutions.

In most communities, everyday life for children generally followed patterns and diets that were seasonal, adhered to routines that had both a daily and weekly rhythm, and involved children contributing time and energy to chores within their competence – such as bed-making, clothes washing, sibling care, food preparation and preservation, spring-cleaning, doing dishes, running errands, gathering firewood, collecting shellfish or seaweed, chopping kindling, gardening, feeding poultry, harvesting crops or helping neighbours.[13] The practical skills acquired in the process were both considerable and essential for everyday living. Only the most privileged or incapacitated were likely to grow up without in some way contributing to the daily functioning of their household.[14] Boredom might surface on a Sunday in worshipping households, should games, noise, rough and tumble play and laughter be unwelcome to adults, but even enforced quiet time could not last all day. For at least some of the Dominion's children, though, home life was difficult or downright miserable. Incessant economic hardship, inadequate food and clothing, poor hygiene, lack of basic health and dental care, erratic adult behaviour, harsh discipline, physical violence, even outright hostility from a caregiver could make up their lot. Despite the provisions and good intentions of the 1890 Children's Protection Act and subsequent legislation, children continued to suffer at the hands of the very people whose responsibility it was to nurture them.[15] For such youngsters the personal battle for survival was likely to take precedence over concern for any external conflict.

Children in wartime society

In the extensive visual record of the antipodean home front, children are a constant presence. They are to be seen at public and community occasions – street parades, station or dockside farewells, concerts, fund-raising carnivals and patriotic endeavours, and, from 1916, Anzac Day commemorations. Clusters of children feature in images relating to school, church and social group activity.[16] And they are prominent in more personal and intimate images, especially family portraits taken before a sibling or father departed for military training or service.[17] Yet, in exploring the impact of the war on children's lives, it is important to note that 95 per cent of men who served overseas classified themselves as unmarried. Melanie Nolan also records that married men comprised 6.9 per cent of volunteers to the end of 1915, and 7.6 per cent to June 1916. Only 796 childless married men and a small number of widowed, divorced or separated men without children actually reached Britain before the war ended. No married conscripts were deployed to the front line.[18] In terms of emotional or relational proximity, then, to use Bennett's term, it would seem that most children's personal awareness of the conflict was primarily through the involvement of brothers, uncles, cousins and close friends, with neighbourhood, school or community association forming a secondary sphere of contact.[19] Their practical mobilisation for the war effort came primarily through their schooling; their real emotional engagement was much closer to home.

Compulsory elementary schooling facilitated children's acquisition of literacy and numeracy skills. It also exposed them, from an early age, to prevailing ideas of patriotism and loyalty to Empire, ideas promulgated through both the curriculum content and the influential *School Journal*, founded in 1907. Carefully nuanced for readers in different standards, this publication was the most regular means by which pupils could access a world beyond the classroom and local community.[20] Notions of Duty, Responsibility, Sacrifice, Service and Loyalty propounded before and during the war may not always have been comprehended in full, but their repetition was an attempt, subtle at first but increasingly overt as the war progressed, to instil appropriate values in the future citizens of Empire. As Keith Scott has noted in his study of children's correspondence during 1914–1918, the war was both 'plucking away their pocket money' and 'playing about with their minds'.[21]

As detailed elsewhere, children were involved in a plethora of fund-raising endeavours from the earliest months of the war.[22] While the initial focus on Belgium was gradually replaced by the provision of support for New Zealand's soldiers, much of the fund-raising utilised skills and activities that were just part of children's normal lives. Collecting birds' eggs, scavenging for bones and bottles, gathering roadside cocksfoot and prairie grass seed: these typical means of earning pocket money were now undertaken for a patriotic cause. The Belgian Relief Fund, the French Orphans' Fund, the London Air Raid Fund, the Wounded Soldiers Fund, the Pocket Book Fund for Soldiers at the Front, the Soldiers' Hut Fund, a Plum Pudding Fund for Soldiers, various Patriotic Funds and copper (penny) trails for the Red Cross all benefited from children's efforts. Adult praise was possibly not an adequate substitute for a pocketful of sweets, but peer recognition of youthful sacrifice, facilitated through public correspondence, may have provided some compensation.

Enjoined to make sacrifices in the name of duty and love of country, youngsters were not necessarily willing conscripts to the cause. Older pupils especially might harbour some resentment that adult decisions deprived them of hard-won rewards, as happened when school prize money was donated to patriotic funds. That the affected students could be advised after the event, without any thought of consultation beforehand, simply reflected prevailing patterns of authority within schools and the widespread conviction that adults always knew what was best for children.

While primary schools generally served as one organisational centre for fund-raising efforts, harnessing a good deal of pupils' energy and commitment in the process, their integral relationship with their communities ensured that school-age children were frequent participants in public performances – singing, dancing, playing instruments (violins were less problematic than German-made pianos), delivering recitations. That significant involvement as performers reflected strong cultural traditions of family entertainment, for Maori and Pakeha alike, but only in communities with a strong Maori presence were Pakeha children likely to appreciate the richness and variety of waiata, poi dances and stick games in performance.

Organised fund-raising ventures designed to facilitate enjoyment along with donations to good causes fostered community interaction. Donkey rides could take on new significance once the role of the donkey in frontline rescue operations became acknowledged; target throwing at a symbolic Kaiser's head in the traditional coconut shy may have added to the side stall's appeal as the war progressed. As with annual picnics and other regular community festivities, children's presence and participation was automatic, unless illness or some exceptional circumstance intervened, and served to heighten a sense of communal endeavour.

The growing intensity of anti-German feeling had ramifications for children's play. Girls fortunate enough to possess a bisque (porcelain) doll were probably unaware of its origins: thousands were produced from factories in the Thuringia region of Germany during the 1900s. Nor were teddy bears free of 'enemy influence': German toymaker Richard Steiff's finely crafted models were soon supplanted by British-made bears once war broke out.[23] While parents may have chosen to ignore the issue of provenance in the case of their children's favourites, the front-room piano presented a more direct problem. The iron-framed instrument so central to public entertainment, childhood learning and family recreation was most likely to be of German manufacture. The saga of Foxton School's piano after the school was razed by an arsonist in September 1918 serves to illustrate how adult emotion could overwhelm reason under the guise of protecting children's interests. Despite many in the community owning and using German instruments, the school committee rejected one offer for a replacement on the grounds that 'It would be scandalous for the children to sing "God Save the King" accompanied by a German piano.' But the 'British' piano purchased in February 1920 was revealed by a piano tuner to contain German parts, whereupon three men of the school's committee entered a classroom while a singing lesson was under way and proceeded to pull the instrument apart, searching for the German bits. The dismembered piano was rendered useless.[24] **The children's reactions can only be imagined.**

As the treatment of 'enemy aliens', naturalised citizens included, became harsher, children were caught up in the consequences but not necessarily in the rhetoric. The families of men interned on Somes and Motuihe Islands, for instance, faced financial hardship as well as emotional upheaval when breadwinners were detained; and neighbourhood relations could deteriorate when those who were 'foreign' began to be harassed.[25] But where influential adults mediated hostility and ignorance, youngsters could sometimes critique practices that were manifestly unjust, such as the unfairness with which Dalmatian men were being treated.[26]

The Great War's impact on children's home life could be both gradual and abrupt. A brother's enthusiasm for enlisting, overheard snippets of adult conversation, parental comment on newspaper content, a mother's increased tension or anxiety: children with good hearing and sensitive antennae could be on the alert for change. The voluntary enlistment or, later, the conscription of a household member did not automatically signal overseas service, since many volunteers and conscripts alike were rejected for medical or other reasons, but even a temporary change in home dynamics might add to children's feelings of uncertainty. Letters became the principal means by which children could retain a tangible link to a parent or sibling in camp or overseas, and the communication was frequently two-way, with correspondence from the absent male likely to reinforce children's understanding of the roles and codes of conduct that boys in particular were expected to uphold. Those of provider and protector were paramount, though there could well have been some contrast between the peacetime domestic behaviour of the adult male writer and the ideals he expounded for younger siblings or sons to follow. Both in private correspondence and educational material, children were encouraged to be helpful and to do so in a cheerful manner: that was all part of their Duty and Responsibility in this time of national commitment to a greater cause. The published letters of Pakeha children indicate they took pride in what they were able to accomplish.[27]

Death entered children's lives abruptly and painfully. How each responded to the loss of a parent, older sibling or relative is largely a matter of conjecture but it seems likely that the grief of a bereaved mother would have compounded a child's sense of a personal world in turmoil. 'He is dead now [–] Daddy is dead now': the poignant note which young Norah Malone added to a letter received from her father, killed at Chunuk Bair in August 1915, expresses a finality, yet such losses triggered the start of major changes in children's lives, the effects of which could be compounded by social attitudes which did not always accommodate or recognise the impact of bereavement on children themselves.[28] Boys could be sensitive to the burden of responsibility that now lay upon them, one that other relatives or acquaintances could exacerbate with remarks about becoming 'the man of the house'. Adults could also be oblivious to the impact on children of well-intended comments made about them, in their hearing. Being described as 'poor little things' whose father was killed in the war could make youngsters feel different in ways they 'neither understood nor liked.'[29]

The influence of a dead father may have been even more powerful when children were old enough to have clear memories of their parent and were of an age to have written and received their own letters and developed their own relationship, as was the case of 12–13-year-old Leonard Norton, whose affectionate correspondence to his father usually began with the greeting 'Dear old Daddy Boy'. In March 1916, Harry wrote warmly to 'My dear son Lennie', applauding his good behaviour and encouraging him to continue being such a help to his mother and sister:

> Remember son, you have to take Daddy's place and you are the only man at home now. You will find it hard at times to keep right up, to do

> all your duties, but it is the man who sticks & perseveres & does his very best that is successful.

Nor were such qualities left undefined:

> Hard graft, being observant, holding fast, never despairing, keep smiling all the time and you must add helping others all you can to be happy. [If] you can do this you will win out & show the stuff you are made of . . . And if you work hard at school & at your music & in our home I will be so proud of you when I come home again. Remember to be obedient. We soldiers have to learn this too.[30]

Youngsters' letters were often acknowledged in ways that may have taken on special meaning if a father did not return. Noni, Jim and Wynn Smith were aged seven, five and three when their father, Wilfred, enlisted in October 1916. Two months after his embarkation in February 1917, another son, Athol, was born. Wilfred wrote frequently to his children, reminding them 'to help Mummie all you can' and leaving his family in no doubt about his changing outlook: 'Daddy is very tired of soldier life and wishes that he was home with you all again and once I do get home it will take a lot to persuade me to go to another war.' Wounded in action at Passchendaele, Smith died of his shrapnel wounds in October 1917. As both children and widow struggled to accept his death, references in the letters may have provided some comfort, if not immediately, perhaps in later years, for the older children especially. 'It brought tears to my eyes when I read about dear little Wynn in your letter', he had commented to his wife in September 1917, 'I still have the coin that you gave me for luck, and I also carry Noni's and Jim's letter.'[31] Such words were tangible reminders for the older children of what they had meant to their father. For the youngest in the family, the letters would also have revealed the values and attitudes which underpinned a father's decision to serve. The return of a dead soldier's correspondence and other personal effects could occasion further regrets. For young Leonard and Jean Norton there was the added poignancy that letters which they had formed so carefully during September and October 1916 were never read by him. Norton was killed in France on 15 September that year; the children's letters were returned unopened.[32] Harry's picture and war service medals were subsequently displayed, as if in a shrine, on the wall alongside the piano.[33] Whether or not Leonard became a competent musician, it seems unlikely he would have voiced too frequently the usual boyhood complaint about having to practise – or expressed a wish to give up one of the very pursuits his beloved father had endorsed. Upholding a deceased parent's precepts is not peculiar to wartime but it seems likely that such injunctions exerted a powerful influence in the lives of those who lost role models during the war.

Responses to the absence, injury, death or return of a soldier varied according to a child's age at the time and the nature of the relationship. Children too young to have a clear memory of a father who served and died overseas grew up with the parent of their imagination. Those youngsters whose perception of a father was shaped by maternal comment and wartime correspondence did not always find it easy to relate to the demobilised soldier. The physical and/or psychological effects of combat on soldiers also affected children and the quality of their family lives during the post-war decades. Pain and frustration could lead to sudden outbursts of anger; alcohol-induced oblivion rendered adult behaviour unpredictable. In such domestic environments, fear rather than affection could characterise child–parent relations. The length of service overseas and the age of a child at the time of separation could also affect the nature of the subsequent bond between child and returned parent, relative or sibling. Since any periods of leave for New Zealand's soldiers were normally spent in the northern hemisphere, separations were usually lengthy and could cover years that were particularly important in a child's development towards autonomy. The military emphasis on discipline could also affect relationships between two generations, especially if paternal absence had led to children exercising a degree of agency during the period. Having a 'problem' with one's dad was not an uncommon experience for boys in the aftermath of war. The children of returned servicemen were likely to have experienced a range of emotions – being unsettled, afraid, resentful, disillusioned or angry, particularly when a long-awaited reunification was marred by authoritarianism, financial struggle, frequent changes of rental accommodation, parental tension and marriage breakdown.[34]

Both during and after the war, children became aware of the human cost of the conflict, personified by the wounded soldiers invalided home and the damaged men who returned both before and after the armistice. They saw the contrast between the fit uniformed cadres of the farewell parades and the physically impaired servicemen whose future had been blighted by war injuries. They could be puzzled by silence, by the dearth of war stories from the very people in possession of them. The disjuncture between literature and life was all too apparent when the heroic and exciting adventures so prevalent in contemporary stories for children were not reinforced by personal narrative.[35] As actor Sam Neill's moving documentary, *Anzac: Tides of Blood*, made apparent, the conflict between private grief and public narrative was perpetuated for decades by the mythologising of the Gallipoli campaign. Neill spoke of an 'unarticulated absence' within his own family: that of his maternal grandfather killed in France in 1917, leaving a war widow and two young children. 'A soldier's daughter never cries' was firmly instilled as a family precept thereafter.[36] The 'enduring emptiness' felt by so many was real but there could be no questioning of the cause for which the sacrifice had been made.[37] To do so would invalidate the deaths and casualties.[38] Yet the rationale for war could still prove elusive for youngsters, and the very fact that it involved killing other people posed an ongoing ethical dilemma for children brought up to observe the Ten Commandments.

Dorothy Butler's awareness of being surrounded by legacies of World War One was the experience of many children born after the conflict ended. Another post-war child observed that she grew up 'very much in the aftermath of that war, where its influence and memories pervaded our lives. It was talked about, written about, and the people who had taken part in it were back there among us – or not back.' Her father's only brother had been killed by a sniper's bullet just weeks before the armistice. 'We knew the story . . . It became part of the family mythology.' Yet she still found it difficult to reconcile being raised with one set of moral values about the sanctity of life while family members had killed others and been commended for it. One of her earliest memories was of asking who had won the war and being told 'no one', a response which 'made war even more mysterious' and did nothing to satisfy her continuing curiosity.

> Anzac Day was of course the day of the year when war consciousness resurfaced, and the Anzac parade and service was the one event that everyone attended in our little town. It was a strict day of rest and presumably of remembrance . . . As children we watched all of those familiar men as they turned up with their medals, and solemnly paraded. We looked at them and tried to see those everyday people as men who had been *in the war*, who had actually been there *killing Germans*. I remember too at a picnic, as one of the men in the party undressed to swim, my sister and I couldn't stop gazing at his legs, at those great puckered scars where we knew he had been *wounded in the war*. All those years it was a continuing effort for us to reconcile the ordinary and the extraordinary, to find out more about the activity called War that grownups took part in, impelled as we were by a kind of fascinated horror.[39]

Public remembrance and commemoration involved entire communities. Every ceremony on a marae, whether for a hui or a tangihanga, involved a formal act of remembrance for those who had died, the mourning made all the more poignant because there was no repatriation of remains. Pakeha ceremonial observance came to revolve around Anzac Day and, in the immediate post-war years, there were buildings, archways and wrought-iron gates to be dedicated, Roll of Honour boards, statues and monuments to be unveiled.[40] Contemporary photographs and young people's letters to the newspapers reveal their presence on such occasions. Recollections penned years later convey both atmosphere and emotion. New Zealand-born Australian author Ruth Park grew up in a King Country township where there was a high degree of Maori and Pakeha interaction. 'Te Kuiti was the place for me', she wrote. 'But there were people who upset me, many of them, whom I could not bring myself to confront because I didn't know how.' Some were adults or children with physical deformities. Many were returned soldiers, 'lurching along on one leg, or with an empty coat sleeve pinned to a shoulder.' Their 'dreadfully scarred faces' seemed all the worse because most were men not yet in their thirties. 'Others were so mummified, so parched and yellow, they were like dead men walking. They had been gassed. These were not around for very long.' The memorial by the river often had flowers laid on its plinth, 'or sprigs of green leaves left by the Maori bereaved', she recalled:

> Amongst the Anzac Day crowd around the Memorial, I once saw a barefooted, shawled old woman stand and raise the tangi – the mourning cry. It echoed solitarily up and down the river, and well it might, for the pakeha people, dressed in their best, gloved, hatted, each with a sprig of rosemary on his or her breast, stood with their heads bowed, their hearts full of pain, but not a word out of their mouths . . . [T]he war was still a painful, raw memory in Te Kuiti.[41]

Conclusion

Conflict and ideology were two of the most dominant forces affecting children's lives globally in the twentieth century.[42] Disease, too, exacted a heavy toll. Yet the lives of young New Zealanders were also influenced by the changing concepts of childhood affecting child-related policies in the western world. Between the mid-nineteenth-century notion of child as chattel and the mid-twentieth-century recognition of child as psychological being was a transition period during which children gradually ceased to be regarded primarily as their parents' possessions and came to be valued as social capital, an asset to the state at large. Only later in the century would the concept of children's rights be enshrined in law.[43]

Reluctant though governments had been to interfere in the private world of the family, the scale of need exposed by child-saving charitable organisations in both the United States and Britain, in the latter decades of the nineteenth century especially, led to gradual changes in policy and increased state intervention on behalf of vulnerable children.[44] Within

New Zealand, where both voluntary and state agencies were actively involved, primarily but not exclusively with Pakeha children's welfare, both the reduction in family size, statistically apparent in the early twentieth century, and high infant death rates added further layers of concern for the future well-being of the young sons and daughters of empire.[45]

As Linda Bryder has demonstrated, the New Zealand Society for the Health of Women and Children, founded in 1907, would prove to be a highly influential voice for mothers and infants alike. Although still in its formative stage at the onset of war, the Plunket Society, as it was popularly known, became a powerful advocate for 'maternalist welfare' during the war and was well positioned to be in the forefront of moves to promote child welfare reform post war. The development of children's health camps and other important initiatives in child health and welfare were also given impetus as the human cost to New Zealand of both conflict and disease, 1914–1918, contributed to greater public acceptance of state support for the country's youngest citizens.[46]

Contributors

Rolf W. Brednich

Rolf graduated PhD from the University of Mainz and Dr. phil. habil. from the University of Freiburg. He is Professor Emeritus of Cultural Anthropology at Georg August University of Goettingen, Germany and was the 2001 Senior Honorary Research Fellow of the Stout Centre for New Zealand Studies, Victoria University of Wellington. He has published widely on traditional and contemporary fields of cultural anthropology, and is the general editor of the *Enzyklopaedie des Maerchens* and a co-editor of *Fabula. Journal of Folktale Studies* (both Berlin/Boston: de Gruyter).

Peter D.F. Cooke, BA (Hons)

Peter has long been interested in military history and his writing spans the subject. Under an interest in military technology and fortification he completed a two-volume history of home defences, *Defending New Zealand* (2000), a study of mine-proof vehicles in Africa and an examination of trophy guns, *Great Guns* (2013). His service histories include *Auckland Infantry* (2010), *The Territorials* (2011) and a study of the Royal New Zealand Artillery, *The Gunners* (2008). He has studied military communities in *All Formed Up* (2008), a study of the Wellington RSA, and in *Balls, Bullets & Boots* (2015), a study of Great War rugby. He provided research for Tolga Örnek's feature-length *Gallipoli* (2005), co-edited the Malone diaries, published as *No Better Death* (2005) and completed a ground-breaking study of Compulsory Military Training, *Fit to Fight* (2013). He is currently the Royal New Zealand Engineers' Corps historian and edits the journal *Forts & Works* for the Defence of NZ Study Group. He lives in Wellington with wife Carol Comber and two children, Arthur and Florence. He is actively engaged with his community and has lobbied hard for military heritage at risk (including the north Miramar defence reserve, saved in 2011).

John Crawford

John Crawford is the New Zealand Defence Force Historian. He is a member of the Governance Group of the Centennial History of New Zealand in the First World War and is currently working on a volume in the series dealing with the organisation of the New Zealand Expeditionary Force. John has written on many aspects of the history of the New Zealand Armed Forces and defence policy. His most recent publications include: a revised edition of *No Better Death: the Great War Diaries and Letters of William G Malone* (2014), and *The Great Adventure Ends: New Zealand and France on the Western Front* (2013), edited with Natalie Phillipe, Christopher Pugsley and Matthias Strohn.

Jeanine Graham

Jeanine Graham taught history at the University of Waikato for several decades, specialising in New Zealand history and developing a strong research interest in childhood history. Her publications include chapters in the *Oxford History of New Zealand*, edited by W.H. Oliver with B.R. Williams (1981), the *Oxford Illustrated History of New Zealand*, edited by Keith Sinclair (1990), *Children and War: A Historical Anthology*, edited by James Marten (2002), the *Encyclopedia of Children and Childhood in History*, edited by Paula Fass (2004) and *A Cultural History of Childhood and Family: Volume 6: in the Modern Age*, edited by Joseph Hawes and N. Ray Hiner (2010).

David Grant

Raised in Invercargill and a graduate of Canterbury and Auckland Universities, David Grant became a professional historian in 1991 after successful careers in newspaper journalism and secondary school teaching. He has written fourteen books, including three (*Out in the Cold*, *A Question of Faith* and *Field Punishment No. 1*) that cover pacifism and conscientious objectors in both world wars, as well as numerous essays for anthologies, encyclopedias, dictionaries, journals and magazines. His last major publication, *The Mighty Totara: The Life and Times of Norman Kirk*, was a finalist in the 2014 NZ Post Awards for general non-fiction. He was a founding executive member of PHANZA (Professional Historians' Association of New Zealand/Aotearoa), is a life member and former chairperson of the Labour History Project, is a trustee on the Archibald Baxter Memorial Trust and is a trustee and secretary of the Community Media Trust, a collective of prominent film-makers. He lives in Wellington.

Ian F. Grant

Ian F. Grant holds a political science degree from Victoria University of Wellington where he was a one-time editor of *Salient*. A long-time writer and publisher, he was a founding director/editor of *National Business Review*; is a partner, alongside his wife Diane, in boutique publisher Fraser Books;

and was awarded the Print Industry Outstanding Achievement Award at the 2012 Canon Media Awards. In 1992 he founded the New Zealand Cartoon Archive at Alexander Turnbull Library and is currently chair of the Guardians of the New Zealand Cartoon Archive. He is an Adjunct Scholar at the Alexander Turnbull Library, an Adjunct Research Associate at the Stout Research Centre and is currently working on his sixteenth book, a comprehensive history of New Zealand newspapers from 1840.

Richard Hill

Richard Hill is an historian of policing and social control in New Zealand and empire, and of Crown–Maori relations. He is a Professor of New Zealand Studies at the Stout Research Centre for New Zealand Studies at Victoria University of Wellington, where he is also Director of the Treaty of Waitangi Research Unit and the principal investigator for research on the history of state surveillance in New Zealand. He has written four books on the history of policing in New Zealand and two covering the history of the relationship between the state and indigeneity in twentieth-century New Zealand, along with other outputs on these and other subjects. He has held fellowships at the University of Cambridge and was recently appointed a Visiting Scholar at the Centre for Global History at the University of Oxford.

Graham Hucker

Much of Graham Hucker's research focused on rural New Zealand and the period towards the Great War. His PhD, 'The Rural Home Front' (2006), centred on the effects of the war on Taranaki, where he was born and lived until early adulthood. In the course of his career he served as Head of History at Palmerston North Boys' High School and lectured at Palmerston North Teachers' College and Massey University, where he was a Visiting Fellow. In 2009 he won a Fullbright Travel Award to America. He is remembered for his passion for education, love of the outdoors, running, photography, good food and wine. In his later years he turned to cycling and skiing with his partner Angela. He was close to his family in Taranaki and especially enjoyed the company of his young niece and nephew Emmy and Alan, encouraging them in similar pursuits. He passed away on 12 July 2010.

Basil Keane

Basil Keane's tribal affiliations are Ngati Kahungunu, Rangitane and Ngapuhi. He has an Honours degree in Maori Studies, a Master of Arts in History and is a licensed translator and interpreter. He has lectured in te reo and Maori society at the Eastern Institute of Technology and the Awatope campus of Te Whare Wananga o Awanuiarangi. For a decade he was in charge of Maori content on *Te Ara Encyclopedia of New Zealand*. His research focus is around kotahitanga movements and nineteenth-century Maori newspapers. He currently works as a senior researcher at the New Zealand Council for Educational Research.

Peter Lineham

Peter Lineham is Professor of History at Massey University's Albany Campus in Auckland. He is a member of the School of Humanities, and chairs the University Library Committee. He holds an MA from the University of Canterbury, a BD from the University of Otago and his PhD is from the University of Sussex. His early work was on religion in eighteenth- and nineteenth-century England, but most of his extensive range of publications focus on aspects of the history of religious movements in New Zealand. His papers and books range over Brethren, Anglicans, Adventists, Mormons and Methodists. He also frequently speaks and comments on trends in current religious movements.

David Littlewood

David Littlewood is a lecturer in history at Massey University's Palmerston North campus. His research focuses on the impacts of the First World War on New Zealand and British society, with particular reference to the implementation of conscription. He has been published in *War in History* and has presented his research at various specialist venues. His PhD, 'The Tool and Instrument of the Military?', examines Military Service Tribunals in British and New Zealand contexts and was included on the 2015 Massey University Dean's List of Exceptional Theses.

Steven Loveridge

Steven Loveridge graduated with a PhD in history from Victoria University of Wellington, works from the Stout Research Centre for New Zealand Studies and has researched, written and lectured on numerous aspects of the First World War. His work has been published in various scholarly journals, anthology works and in the international encyclopaedia 1914–1918 Online. His book *Calls to Arms: New Zealand Society and Commitment to the Great War* was published by Victoria University Press in 2014 and examines the social and cultural dynamics backing New Zealand's wartime commitment.

Erik Olssen, ONZM, PhD (Duke), FRSNZ & FNZAH

Erik Olssen taught at the University of Otago for 33 years and was Professor of History from 1984 until he retired in 2001. He has published over seventy articles and chapters on American and New Zealand history, including several comparative papers, and has also written several books, including *John A. Lee* (1977), *A History of Otago* (1984), *The Red Feds* (1988), *Building the New World* (1995), and most recently *Working Lives: A Photographic Essay* (2014). He has also edited and co-authored several books, most recently (with two co-authors) *An Accidental Utopia? The Social Origins of an Egalitarian Society* (2012), a comparative study of social mobility. For over twenty years he also directed the multi-disciplinary Caversham Project, the country's largest investigation of urban social structure (caversham.otago.ac.nz). He is currently completing a history of New Zealand.

Professor Emeritus Roger Openshaw

Roger Openshaw holds a Personal Chair in History of Education. He had six years' teaching experience in New Zealand primary and intermediate schools prior to gaining his doctorate in history from the University of Waikato, subsequently becoming a university researcher and teacher. His research interests include the history of school assessment practices, the evolution of educational reform, the history and politics of literacy in England and New Zealand, social studies and citizenship education, school curriculum policy and history, the politics of ethnicity, and the changing nature of educational theory and practice. He has written/co-written/edited/co-edited many national and international books, articles and book chapters. Currently retired, he remains research active and co-edits an international series entitled Palgrave Studies in Excellence and Equity in Global Education.

Brad Patterson

Brad Patterson is an Adjunct Research Fellow at the Stout Research Centre for New Zealand Studies, Victoria University of Wellington. He was formerly Director of the university's Irish-Scottish Studies Programme and, in 2010, held the W.F. Massey Fellowship at Massey University. His current research interests include Irish and Scottish migration to Australasia and the political economy of colonial settlement. The author or editor of ten books and numerous articles, his publications include *The Irish in New Zealand: Historical Contexts & Perspectives* (2002), *Ulster-New Zealand Migration and Cultural Transfers* (2004) and, most recently, the co-authored *Unpacking the Kists: The Scots in New Zealand* (2013).

Greg Ryan

Greg Ryan is Dean of the Faculty of Environment, Society and Design at Lincoln University. He has published various academic and popular press articles and chapters on sport in New Zealand, edited *Tackling Rugby Myths: Rugby and New Zealand Society 1854–2004* (2005) and *The Changing Face of Rugby: the union game and professionalism since 1995* (2008), and written three books – *The Contest for Rugby Supremacy: accounting for the 1905 All Blacks* (2005), *The Making of New Zealand Cricket 1832–1914* (2004) and *Forerunners of the All Blacks: The 1888–89 New Zealand Native Football Team in Britain, Australia and New Zealand* (1993).

Professor Sir Hew Strachan

Hew Strachan has been Professor of International Relations at the University of St Andrews since 2015. He is a Life Fellow of Corpus Christi College, Cambridge, where he taught from 1975 to 1992, and an Emeritus Fellow of All Souls College, Oxford. He was Professor of Modern History at Glasgow University 1992 to 2001, and Chichele Professor of the History of War at the University of Oxford 2002 to 2015. He is a Trustee of the Imperial War Museum, a Commonwealth War Graves Commissioner and member of the national committees for the centenary of the First World War of the United Kingdom, Scotland and France. In December 2012, *Foreign Policy* magazine included him in its list of top global thinkers for the year, and he was knighted in the 2013 New Year's Honours. His recent publications include *The Politics of the British Army* (1997), *The First World War: To Arms* (2001), *The First World War: a New Illustrated History* (2003) and *The Direction of War* (2013).

Margaret Tennant

Margaret Tennant is an Honorary Research Professor at Massey University. Her many publications in the areas of women's history and the history of social policy include *The Fabric of Welfare* (2007), along with articles on charity fund-raising, the voluntary sector in New Zealand, children's health camps and the social work of religious sisterhoods in New Zealand. Her most recent work, *Across the Street, Across the World* (2015), examines the history of the New Zealand Red Cross.

James Watson

James Watson is Associate Professor in History at the Palmerston North Campus of Massey University. His research interests are largely focussed on the relationship between New Zealand and the United Kingdom, particularly in the twentieth century, but also include rural history and the history of technology. His most recent book was *W.F. Massey: New Zealand* in the Haus Makers of the Modern World series on the Paris Peace Conference (2010). He also co-edited, with Lachy Paterson, *A Great New Zealand Prime Minister: Reappraising William Ferguson Massey* (2011). He is currently writing a book on the 'home front' in New Zealand during the First World War.

Notes

Introduction – A Small Land in a World War

1 John Crawford and Ian McGibbon, 'Introduction', in John Crawford and Ian McGibbon (eds), *New Zealand's Great War: New Zealand, the Allies and the First World War* (Auckland, 2007), pp.25–26. More recent assessments suggest this observation remains relevant. See Gwen Parsons, 'The New Zealand Home Front during World War One and World War Two', *History Compass*, 11/6 (2013), pp.419–428; Steven Loveridge, *Calls to Arms: New Zealand Society and Commitment to the Great War* (Wellington, 2014), pp.14–15.

2 James Belich, *Making Peoples: A History of the New Zealanders from Polynesian Settlement to the End of the Nineteenth Century* (Auckland, 1996), p.7.

3 John Darwin, *Unfinished Empire: The Global Expansion of Britain* (New York, 2012), p.90.

4 Eric Hobsbawm, *The Age of Extremes: A History of the World, 1914–1991* (New York, 1994).

5 Benedict Anderson, *Imagined Communities: Reflections on the Origin and Spread of Nationalism* (London, 2006).

6 Eugen Weber, *Peasants into Frenchmen: The Modernization of Rural France, 1870–1914* (Stanford, 1976), pp.30–33, 67–94; David Moon, *The Russian Peasantry, 1600–1930: The World The Peasants Made* (London, 1999), pp.237–281.

7 Alexander Watson, *Ring of Steel: Germany and Austria-Hungary at War, 1914–1918* (London, 2014), p.68. France, the only European country in which a general response to mobilisation was recorded, notes the overwhelming rural reaction as surprise and resigned acceptance. Clive Ponting, *Thirteen Days: The Road to the First World War* (London, 2002), p.259.

8 Weber; Peter Watson, *The German Genius: Europe's Third Renaissance, the Second Scientific Revolution and the Twentieth Century* (New York, 2010), pp.26–27.

9 Yanni Kotsonis, *Making Peasants Backward: Agricultural Cooperatives and the Agrarian Question in Russia, 1861–1914* (New York, 1999); Moon, 'Peasants into Russian Citizens?: A Comparative Perspective', *Revolutionary Russia*, 9 (1996), pp.43–81.

10 Norman Stone, *Europe Transformed 1878–1919* (London, 1983), p.244.

11 An overview of the 'peasant's succession' from economic mobilisation is provided in Stephen Broadberry and Mark Harrison, 'The Economics of World War I: An Overview', in Stephen Broadberry and Mark Harrison (eds), *The Economics of World War I* (Cambridge, 2005), pp.18–22. The effects of peasant illiteracy and unfamiliarity with technology on military efforts are considered in David R. Stone, *The Russian Army in the Great War: The Eastern Front, 1914–1917* (Lawrence, 2015), pp.32–34.

12 Nicholas Brown, 'Born Modern: Antipodean variations on a theme', *Historical Journal*, 48/4 (2005), pp.1139–1154.

13 The respective commentators were Frank Parsons, Henry Demarest Lloyd and Josiah Strong. See respectively *Ashburton Guardian*, 23 December 1904, p.3; *Oamaru Mail*, 17 December 1912, p.1; David Hackett Fischer, *Fairness and Freedom: A History of Two Open Societies New Zealand and the United States* (Oxford, 2012), p.312.

14 Erik Olssen, 'Towards a New Society', in W.H. Oliver with B.R. Williams (eds), *The Oxford History of New Zealand* (Wellington, 1981), pp.250–278.

15 Miles Fairburn, 'The Rural Myth and the New Urban Frontier: An Approach to New Zealand Social History, 1870–1940', *New Zealand Journal of History* (*NZJH*), 9/1 (April 1975), pp.3–21.

16 Belich, *Paradise Reforged: A History of the New Zealanders from the 1880s to the Year 2000* (Auckland, 2001), pp.126–146; Melanie Nolan, *Breadwinning: New Zealand Women and the State* (Christchurch, 2000).

17 Belich, *Paradise Reforged*, p.135; Olssen, 'Waging War: The Home Front 1914–1918', in Judith Binney, Judith Bassett and Erik Olssen (eds), *The People and the Land: Te Tangata Me Te Whenua: An Illustrated History of New Zealand, 1820–1920* (Wellington, 1990), p.311; Herbert Roth, *Trade Unions in New Zealand: Past and Present* (Wellington, 1973), p.169.

18 Olssen, *Red Feds: Revolutionary Industrial Unionism and the New Zealand Federation of Labour 1908–14* (Auckland, 1988).

19 John Mulgan, *Man Alone* (Hamilton, 1960), p.18. For further assessment on bush clearance, rural settlement and development see Rollo Arnold, *New Zealand's Burning: The Settlers' World in the Mid 1880s* (Wellington, 1994).

20 Mulgan, *Man Alone*, pp.19, 20–24. For further assessment on rural labour and the notion that 'a farm is in every sense a manufactory' see John E. Martin, *The Forgotten Worker: The Rural Wage Earner in Nineteenth-Century New Zealand* (Wellington, 1990), pp.97–136.

21 W.H. Oliver, *The Story of New Zealand* (London, 1960), pp.150–151. Likewise Siegfried noted that 'The peasant who has never been out of his district is an unknown type in Australasia.' André Siegfried, *Democracy in New Zealand*, translated by E.V. Burns (London, 1914), p.324.

22 Elisabeth Airey, *The Taming of Distance: New Zealand's First International Telecommunications* (Wellington, 2005); Simon Potter, *News and the British World: The Emergence of an Imperial Press System* (New York, 2003).

23 Siegfried, p.323.

24 Niall Ferguson, *The Pity of War* (New York, 1999), p.212.

25 Belich, *Paradise Reforged*, pp.194–215.

26 Michael Bassett, *The State in New Zealand, 1840–1984: Socialism Without Doctrines?* (Auckland, 1998), p.103; Richard S. Hill, *State Authority, Indigenous Autonomy: Crown-Māori Relations in New Zealand/Aotearoa 1900–1950* (Wellington, 2004), p.44.

27 Franchesca Walker, '"Descendants of a Warrior Race": The Maori Contingent, New Zealand Pioneer Battalion, and Martial Race Myth, 1914–19', *War & Society*, 31/1 (2012), pp.1–21; Kolokesa Mahina-Tuai, 'FIA (Forgotten in Action): Pacific Islanders in the New Zealand Armed Forces', in Sean Mallon, Kolokesa Mahina-Tuai and Damon Salesa (eds), *Tangata o le Moana: New Zealand and the People of the Pacific* (Wellington, 2012), pp.139–159; Margaret Pointer and Kalaisi Folau, *Tagi Tote A Loto Haaku: My Heart is Crying a Little: Niue Involvement in the Great War, 1914–1918* (Alofi, 2000).

28 Paul Baker, 'New Zealanders, Conscription, and the Great War' (PhD thesis, University of Auckland, 1986), p.498.

29 For the development of national infrastructure and political centralisation see Belich, *Making Peoples*, pp.437–446. For national identity see Ron Palenski, *The Making of New Zealanders* (Auckland, 2012).

30 For the tightening links between the British metropole and colonial peripheries see Belich, *Replenishing the Earth: The Settler Revolution and the Rise of the Anglo-World, 1783–1939* (Oxford, 2009). For New Zealand's collective identity within the British Empire see Felicity Barnes, *New Zealand's London: A Colony and its Metropolis* (Auckland, 2012) and Loveridge, *Calls to Arms*, pp.28–68.

31 Darwin, *The Empire Project: The Rise and Fall of the British World-System, 1830–1970* (Cambridge, 2009), p.168. Baker, p.5. In the interests of accuracy it should be noted that Newfoundland (a British Dominion from 1907 to 1949) was geographically and demographically smaller than New Zealand. Beyond this technical error, Baker's point remains insightful.

32 Hew Strachan, *The First World War: A New Illustrated History* (London, 2003), p.68.

33 Baker, p.299.

34 His institute was also involved in developing the predecessors to the cyanide gases later used in Nazi extermination camps. Daniel Charles, *Master Mind: The Rise and Fall of Fritz Haber, The Noble Laureate who Launched The Age of Chemical Warfare* (New York, 2005).

35 Roger Chickering, *Imperial Germany and the Great War, 1914–1918* (Cambridge, 2014), pp.221–222; John Horne, 'Remobilizing for "Total War": France and Britain, 1917–1918', in John Horne (ed.), *State, Society and Mobilization in Europe during the First World War* (Cambridge, 1997), pp.195–211.

36 Norman Stone's account of the Russian government's failure to introduce effective conscription is reflective of this point: 'Like most autocracies, its great strength was, not that it governed harshly, but that it governed less . . . real conscription was possible only where a partnership existed between people and administration.' Norman Stone, *The Eastern Front, 1914–1917* (London, 1975), p.214. See also David R. Stone.

37 Chickering, p.225; Horne, 'Remobilizing for "Total War"', pp.195–211.

38 For Britain see Adrian Gregory, *The Last Great War: British Society and the First World War* (Cambridge, 2008), pp.9–39; for France see Leonard V. Smith, Stéphane Audoin-Rouzeau and Annette Becker, *France and the Great War, 1914–1918* (New York, 2002), pp.27–29; for Germany see Jeffrey Verhey, *The Spirit of 1914: Militarism, Myth and Mobilization in Germany* (Cambridge, 2000), pp.231–236; for New Zealand see Graham Hucker, '"The Great Wave of Enthusiasm": New Zealand Reactions to the First World War in August 1914 – A Reassessment', *NZJH*, 43/1 (April 2009), pp.12–27.

39 For Germany see Watson, *Ring of Steel*, pp.78–89; for Britain see Gregory; for New Zealand see Baker, pp.12–22.

40 Pools of men with experience in management and leadership also conferred a bonus to the military, providing natural material for the non-commissioned ranks essential to effective discipline. David R. Stone, pp.40, 52.

41 Richard Vinen, *A History in Fragments: Europe in the Twentieth Century* (Cambridge, 2001), p.46.

42 Peter Simkins, 'Everyman at War: Recent Interpretations of the Front Line Experience', in B. Bond (ed.), *The First World War and British Military History* (Oxford, 1991), p.301; J.M. Winter, *The Experience of World War I* (London, 1988), p.159.

43 F. Scott Fitzgerald, *Tender is the Night* (London, 1985), pp.67–68. For further analysis in regards to New Zealand see Loveridge, *Calls to Arms*.

44 Winter, *Sites of Memory, Sites of Mourning: The Great War in European Cultural History* (Cambridge, 1995), p.201. In other contexts this sense of belonging, and its capacity to underwrite common purpose in the face of immense costs, was weaker. 'Russia's peasant soldiers did not particularly imagine themselves as Russian, but instead felt connection to their particular home region, their village, and their family . . . They had some awareness of events on a national scale, not simply local developments, and their loyalty to the Romanov dynasty and the Russian State was real, at least early in the war. This sense of belonging, however, and in particular the motivation to translate it into action, was far weaker than in Western Europe and would prove insufficient to overcome the burdens imposed by defeat after defeat.' David R. Stone, pp.34, 211.

45 W.P. Reeves, *State Experiments in Australia and New Zealand*, Volume One (New York, 1903), p.333.

46 For further reading see Michael Bassett.

47 Neill Atkinson, *Adventures in Democracy: A History of the Vote in New Zealand* (Dunedin, 2003).

48 Archives New Zealand (ANZ), R22429857-AAYS-8638-AD1-738-10/566-2, 'Territorial Force – Defaulters undergoing detention and imprisonment'. For an account of abuses at Wanganui see Baker, pp.425–431.

49 Alex Frame, *Salmond: Southern Jurist* (Wellington, 1995), p.168; Baker, p.80.

50 Frame, pp.178–179; Baker, p.73; W. Downie Stewart, *The Rt Hon Sir Francis Bell, P.C., G.C.M.G., K.C.: His Life and Times* (Wellington, 1937), p.109.

51 'Far from going out to bust the union movement, Reform made every effort to ensure that they did not antagonise the unions, even those like the miners that other unionists thought unacceptable.' Olssen, 'Towards a Reassessment of W.F. Massey: One of New Zealand's Greatest Prime Ministers (Arguably)', in James Watson and Lachy Paterson (eds), *A Great New Zealand Prime Minister?* (Dunedin, 2011), p.23.

52 Miles Fairburn, *The Ideal Society and Its Enemies: The Foundations of Modern New Zealand Society, 1850–1900* (Auckland, 1989). Several critiques of and responses to the atomisation thesis are collected in the October 1991 edition of the *NZJH*. See also Belich, *Making Peoples*, pp.412–414 and Chris Brickell, 'Men Alone, Men Entwined: Reconsidering Colonial Masculinity', *Journal of New Zealand Studies*, 13 (2012), pp.11–33.

53 Mark Lyons and Garth Nowland-Foreman, 'Civil Society and Social Capital in Australia and New Zealand', in Helmut K. Anheier and Stefan Toepler (eds), *International Encyclopedia of Civil Society* (New York, 2010), pp.213–218.

54 On self-mobilisation see Horne, 'Introduction: Mobilizing for "Total War"'.

55 For an example see Siegfried, p.249.

56 Peter Rees, *The Other Anzacs: Nurses at War, 1914–1918* (Crows Nest, 2008), p.xiii; John Meredith Smith, *Cloud over Marquette: The Epic Story of those Who Sailed in the Ill-fated Troopship Marquette* (Auckland, 1990).

57 Sarah Luxford, 'Passengers for the War: The Involvement of Women in Employment during the Great War 1914–1918' (MA thesis, Massey University, 2005); Melanie Nolan, '"Keeping the Home Fires Burning": Gender, Welfare and the First World War', in *New Zealand's Great War*, pp.493–515; Loveridge, *Calls to Arms*, pp.196–200.

58 *Auckland Star*, 26 June 1918, p.3.

59 ANZ, R22319674-ADBQ-16145-ALLEN1-9, 'Miscellaneous files and papers – Correspondence with Colonels Birdwood and Russell, December 1914 – April 1920 and copies of personal letters, 1920', letter from Allen to Birdwood dated 10 July

1916; *Maoriland Worker*, 21 August 1918, p.7. For examples of further observations see *Truth*, 6 March 1915, p.4; Belich, *Paradise Reforged*, p.100; Simon Johnson, 'The Home Front: Aspects of Civilian Patriotism in New Zealand during the First World War' (MA thesis, Massey University, 1975), p.110.

60 Loveridge, *Calls to Arms*, pp.187–189.

61 *Appendix to the Journals of the House of Representatives*, 1920, H-46, 'Patriotic Funds', p.1. All contemporary figures calculated using the Reserve Bank's Inflation Calculator, http://www.rbnz.govt.nz.

62 Heather Nicholson, *The Loving Stitch: A History of Knitting and Spinning in New Zealand* (Auckland, 1998), p.86.

63 Christopher Pugsley, *On the Fringe of Hell: New Zealanders and Military Discipline in the First World War* (Auckland, 1991), p.300.

64 David Littlewood, '"Should He Serve?" The Military Service Boards' Operation in the Wellington Provincial District, 1916–1918' (MA thesis, Massey University, 2010), pp.60–61.

65 Kate Hunter and Kirstie Ross, *Holding on to Home: New Zealand Stories and Objects of the First World War* (Wellington, 2014), p.143.

66 John Mulgan, *Report on Experience* (London, 1947), p.33.

67 Figures from Lieut-Colonel J.L. Sleeman, 'The Supply of Reinforcements During the War', in H.T.B. Drew (ed.), *The War Effort of New Zealand* (Auckland, 1923), p.11; *New Zealand Official Year-book* (NZOYB), 1919, p.257. These figures do not include those rejected on grounds of fitness: see Baker, p.563.

68 Loveridge, *Calls to Arms*, p.12.

69 Drew, 'War Finance', in *The War Effort of New Zealand*, p.243.

70 'Vogel's vision', http://www.nzhistory.net.nz/politics/the-vogel-era/vogels-vision (Ministry for Culture and Heritage), updated 17 July 2014 [accessed 20 February 2015].

71 For further analysis see Loveridge, 'Seeing Trauma as Sacrifice: The Link Between "Sentimental Equipment" and Endurance in New Zealand's War Effort', in David Monger, Sarah Murray and Katie Pickles (eds), *Endurance and the First World War: Experience and Legacies in New Zealand and Australia* (Cambridge, 2014), pp.49–63.

72 For further analysis on the links between atrocities, propaganda and the meanings layered on the war see Horne and Alan Kramer, *German Atrocities, 1914: A History of Denial* (New Haven, 2001), pp.227–261. For an analysis in the New Zealand context see Loveridge, 'A German is *Always* a German?: Representations of Enemies, Germans and Race in New Zealand circa 1890–1918', NZJH, 48/1 (April 2014), pp.51–77.

73 I.S. Bloch, *Is War Now Impossible?: Being an Abridgement of The War of the Future in its Technical, Economic and Political Relationships* (London, 1899), p.l.

74 For an introduction to literature on the topic see Winter and Antoine Prost, *The Great War in History: Debates and Controversies 1914 to the Present* (New York, 2005), pp.159–161.

75 For calorie intakes see Avner Offer, *The First World War, An Agrarian Interpretation* (New York, 1989), p.29. For *ersatz* products see Watson, *Ring of Steel*, p.334. For food prices see Thierry Bonzon and Belinda Davis, 'Feeding the Cities', in Jay Winter and Jean-Louis Robert (eds), *Capital Cities at War: Paris, London, Berlin, 1914–1919* (Cambridge, 1997), p.321.

76 Offer, p.33; Andrew Donson, *Youth in the Fatherless Land: War Pedagogy, Nationalism, and Authority in Germany, 1914–1918* (Cambridge, 2010), p.127.

77 Horne, 'Remobilizing for "Total War"'.

78 Joan Beaumont, 'The Politics of a Divided Society', in Joan Beaumont (ed.), *Australia's War, 1914–18* (St Leonards, 1995), pp.35–63; Martin F. Auger, 'On the Brink of Civil War: The Canadian Government and the Suppression of the 1918 Quebec Easter Riots', *Canadian Historical Review*, 89/4 (2008), pp.503–540.

79 On the relationship between the war and the radicalisation of political life see Richard Bessel, 'Revolution', in Winter (ed.), *The Cambridge History of the First World War, Volume II: The State* (New York, 2014), pp.126–144.

80 Alan Kramer, *Dynamic of Destruction: Culture and Mass Killing in the First World War* (Oxford, 2007), p.31.

81 Horne and Kramer; Kramer, pp.6–30.

82 For details on the German, French, British, Russian and Italian militaries' experimentation with doctrines/campaigns of strategic aviation bombing see Rodney Madison, 'Air Warfare, Strategic Bombing', in Spencer C. Tucker and Priscilla Roberts (eds), *The Encyclopedia of World War I: A Political, Social, and Military History* (Santa Barbara, 2005), p.46. For the German Navy's bombardment of British coastal towns and sinking of merchant and passenger shipping see Robert K. Massie, *Castles of Steel: Britain, Germany and the Winning of the Great War at Sea* (New York, 2003), pp.309–360, 528–552, 685–714. For the German military's shelling of Paris with long-range artillery see David T. Zabecki 'Paris Gun', *The Encyclopedia of World War I*, p.900.

83 For Africa see Anne Samson, *World War I in Africa: The Forgotten Conflict Among the European Powers* (London, 2013). For Asia see Guoqi Xu, 'Asia', in Winter (ed.) *The Cambridge History of The First World War, Volume I: Global War* (Cambridge, 2014), pp.479–510. For the Pacific see Hermann Hiery, *The Neglected War: The German South Pacific and the Influence of World War I* (Honolulu, 1995); for upheaval relating to New Zealand's administration in Samoa see pp.154–182. For the Middle East see Eugene Rogan, *The Fall of the Ottomans: The Great War in the Middle East* (New York, 2015) and Leila Tarazi Fawaz, *A Land of Aching Hearts: The Middle East in the Great War* (Cambridge, Massachusetts, 2014).

84 Watson, '"Unheard of Brutality": Russian Atrocities against Civilians in East Prussia, 1914–1915', *The Journal of Modern History*, 86/4 (December 2014), pp.780–825; Peter Gatrell, *A Whole Empire Walking: Refugees in Russia during World War I* (Bloomington, 2005); Vejas Gabriel Liulevicious, *War Land on the Eastern Front: Culture, National Identity and German Occupation in World War I* (Cambridge, 2000).

85 Andrej Mitrović, *Serbia's Great War 1914–1918* (London, 2007); http://www.nzhistory.net.nz/war/world-at-war.

86 For the quoted example of this recurring claim see Fischer, p.417. For the record, New Zealand's per capita deaths are also lower than France (3.5 per cent), Germany (3.0 per cent) and Austria-Hungary (2.5 per cent), and broadly comparable with Great Britain's (1.5 per cent). These figures are calculated with data from http://www.nzhistory.net.nz/war/world-at-war. Given variations in death statistics, the broad pattern should be regarded as more significant than the exact figures.

87 Baker, pp.35–38.

88 James Bennett, *'Rats and Revolutionaries': The Labour Movement in Australia and New Zealand 1890–1940* (Dunedin, 2004), p.73.

89 Margaret Levi, 'The Institution of Conscription', *Social Science History*, 20/1 (1996), p.141.

90 ANZ, R22319764-ADBQ-16145-ALLEN1-5-M2/61/2, 'Ministerial Files – Cost of living taxation and fixing prices, etc'. For a critical account of wartime economic

regulation see Alan Everton, 'Government Intervention in the New Zealand Economy 1914–1918: Its Aims and Effectiveness' (MA thesis, Victoria University of Wellington, 1995).

91 Barry Gustafson, *Labour's Path to Political Independence* (Auckland, 1980), p.96.

92 Jürgen Tampke (ed.), *'Ruthless Warfare': German Military Planning and Surveillance in the Australia–New Zealand Region before the Great War* (Canberra, 1998).

93 McGibbon, *Blue-Water Rationale: The Naval Defence of New Zealand, 1914–1942* (Wellington, 1981), pp.29–31; Robin Bromby, *German Raiders of the South Seas* (Sydney, 1985), pp.126–159.

94 Stewart, p.105.

95 New Zealand Political Reform League, *General Election Campaign 1919* (Wellington, 1919).

96 J.P. Thornton, Thos. E. McMillan and H.L. Rhodes (eds), *Te Karere, The Message* (1917), p.2.

97 Baker, p.563.

98 For further reading see Loveridge, 'Not so Quiet on the New Zealand Front: *All Quiet on the Western Front* and New Zealand Memories of First World War', *Journal of New Zealand Studies*, 18 (2014), pp.23–40 and Scott Worthy, '"Light and Shade": The New Zealand Written Remembrance of the Great War, 1915–1939', *War & Society*, 22/1 (2004), pp.19–40.

99 Everton, p.420; M.F. Lloyd Prichard, *An Economic History of New Zealand to 1939* (Auckland, 1970), p.266. For an analysis on wages and working hours see G.W. Clinkard, 'Wages and Working Hours in New Zealand, 1897–1919' in NZOYB, 1919, pp.860–935.

100 Malcolm Fraser, *An Inquiry into Prices in New Zealand 1891–1919* (Wellington, 1920), p.127. For regulations on coal and coal consumption see Everton, pp.371–373 and ANZ, R22319765, 'Ministerial Files – Coal – General file'.

101 For an overview see Rachel Patrick, 'Bereavement and Mourning (New Zealand)', *1914–1918-Online: International Encyclopedia of the First World War*, URL: http://dx.doi.org/10.15463/ie1418.10557 [accessed 1 April 2015].

102 Loveridge, *Calls to Arms*, p.176.

103 McGibbon, 'Casualties', in McGibbon (ed.), *The Oxford Companion to New Zealand Military History* (Auckland, 2000), p.80. In regard to repatriates' experiences see Elizabeth Anne Walker, '"The Living Death": The Repatriation Experience of New Zealand's Disabled Great War Servicemen' (MA thesis, Victoria University of Wellington, 2013).

104 Loveridge, *Calls to Arms*, pp.136–170.

105 ANZ, R22429678-AAYS-8638-AD1-731-10/284/53, 'Territorial Force – Shirkers – Forwarding Names of A.E. and H. Syme'; ANZ, R10075045-AAYS-8698-AD82-8-62, 'Section 35 Military Service Act, August 1916 – March 1917'; ANZ, R22429657-AAYS-8638-AD1-731-10/284/15, 'Territorial Force – Shirkers – Gisborne District'.

106 Everton, pp.395, 425–426; Prichard, pp.252, 260; G.T. Bloomfield, *New Zealand, A Handbook of Historical Statistics* (Boston, 1984), pp.416–417; ANZ, R22319764, 'Ministerial Files – Cost of living taxation and fixing prices'.

107 ANZ, R22319764, 'Ministerial Files – Cost of living taxation and fixing prices'.

108 See Baker, pp.284–299, 309–331.

109 *New Zealand Herald*, 13 December 1916, p.11.

110 NZOYB, 1921–22, p.529. The number of disputes continued to grow after 1918. In 1920 there were 75 disputes involving 9,612 workers.

111 ANZ, R22319765-ADBQ-16145-ALLEN1-5-M2/61/5, 'Ministerial Files – Coal – General file'. Other grievances resulted in the loss of 246 working days; losses due to 'go slow' actions remain unestimated.

112 Social Democratic Party (New Zealand), *Peace Manifesto* (Wellington, 1916).

113 For further analysis see Baker, pp.373, 469–492 and Harry Holland, *Armageddon or Calvary: The Conscientious Objectors of New Zealand and 'The Process of Their Conversion'* (Wellington, 1919).

114 Megan Hutching, 'The Moloch of War: New Zealand Women who Opposed the War', in *New Zealand's Great War*, pp.85–95.

115 P.S. O'Connor, 'Sectarian Conflict in New Zealand, 1911–1920', *Political Science*, 19/1 (1967), pp.3–16. For further examples of wartime anti-alienism see Judith Bassett, 'Colonial Justice: The Treatment of Dalmatians in New Zealand during the First World War', *NZJH*, 33/2 (October 1999), pp.155–79; Andrew Trlin, *Now Respected, Once Despised: Yugoslavs in New Zealand* (Palmerston North, 1979).

116 Watson, *Ring of Steel*, p.76.

117 War regulations defined enemy aliens as including 'any person who has been naturalised in New Zealand and who would have been an enemy alien had he not been so naturalised.' *New Zealand Gazette*, 10 November 1914, p.4022. In some cases this went further, with the revocation of or suspension of citizenship rights under the 1917 Revocation of Naturalisation Act. For an overview of internment experiences see Andrew Francis, *'To Be Truly British We Must Be Anti-German': New Zealand, Enemy Aliens and the Great War Experience, 1914–1919* (New York, 2012), pp.113–152.

Chapter One – 'Duty Well Done': The Defence Department at War: 1914–1918

1 *Evening Post* (EP), 11 June 1919, p.7. This quotation refers to the work of Colonel Gibbon, but the epithet can equally well be applied to the Defence Department.

2 *New Zealand Statutes*, 1914, No.38, pp.128–129; *Otago Daily Times* (ODT), 24 October 1914, p.12; *Northern Advocate*, 11 November 1914, p.5; Michael Bassett, *The State in New Zealand 1840–1984* (Auckland, 1998), pp.123–146.

3 *New Zealand Gazette* (NZG), 7 June 1917, pp.2283–2310; *Appendices to the Journals of the House of Representatives* (AJHR), 1918, H-19, 'Defence Forces of New Zealand', p.20.

4 AJHR, 1909, H-19 'Defence Forces of New Zealand'; AJHR, 1914, H-19 'Defence Forces of New Zealand', pp. 3–5, 12–13.

5 AJHR, 1914, H-19, 'Defence Forces of New Zealand', pp.1–2, 32–33, 39–40; AJHR, 1914, H-19a, 'Military Forces of New Zealand', pp.1, 9–13, 30–33; Peter Cooke and John Crawford, *The Territorials: the History of the Territorial and Volunteer Forces of New Zealand* (Auckland, 2011), pp.150–189.

6 Archives New Zealand (ANZ), WA231/2 (Retrieved Manually), 'Fitting out of Troop Transports July–September 1914', Godley to Nash, 5 September 1914; AJHR, 1902, B-20 'Imperial War Office Expenditure'; AJHR, 1902, 'Defence Forces of New Zealand', p.1; John Crawford, '"Should we 'be drawn into a maelstrom of war": New Zealand Military Policy on the Eve of the First World War', in Peter Dennis and Jeffrey Grey (eds), *1911 Preliminary Moves: The 2011 Chief of Army History Conference* (Canberra, 2011), pp.126–129.

7 AJHR, 1915, H-19, 'Defence Forces of New Zealand', p.1; AJHR, 1917, H-19, 'Defence Forces of New Zealand', p.11.

8 *New Zealand Herald* (NZH), 7 June 1919, p.8; *Press*, 22 March 1918, p.6.

9 *The Quarterly Army Lists of the New Zealand Forces for April 1914 and October 1914* (Wellington, 1914), pp.2–4; *New Zealand Expeditionary Force (Europe), 1914 War Diary* (Wellington, 1915), p.clxviii; AJHR, 1915, H-19, 'Defence Forces of New Zealand', pp.1, 9–10, 29; *Dominion*, 27 November 1914, p.6; *Dominion*, 12 May 1916, p.4; EP, 10 May 1918, p.7.

10 ANZ, R24048325-ACID-25038-WA252-1/[2], '[Correspondence between] General Sir Alexander Godley [Commander New Zealand Expeditionary Force] and Colonel Hon. [Honourable] Sir James Allen, Minister of Defence, 2 April – 18 December 1915', Allen to Godley, 11 May 1915; ANZ, R24048327-ACID-25038-WA252-1/[4], '[Correspondence between] General Sir Alexander Godley [Commander New Zealand Expeditionary Force] and Colonel Hon. [Honourable] Sir James Allen, Minister of Defence, 6 January – 28 December 1917', Allen to Godley, 27 November 1917; Hocken Library, AG-458-8, Dixon to Charles Allen, 30 August 1944; *Auckland Star*, 4 August 1917, p.10; EP, 11 June 1919, p.7; Ian McGibbon, 'James Allen', in *The Dictionary of New Zealand Biography* (DNZB), Vol.3, 1901–1920 (Auckland, 1996), pp.10-11; John Crawford, '"I Get Blamed for Everything": Enduring the Burdens of Office, James Allen as Minister of Defence in 1915', in David Monger, Sarah Murray and Katie Pickles (eds), *Endurance and the First World War: Experiences and Legacies in New Zealand and Australia* (Newcastle Upon Tyne, 2014), pp.14–30.

11 ANZ, R22432290-AAYS-8638-AD1-893-39/223, 'Reports by Colonel J.J. Esson on NZEF abroad', Esson to Robin, 5 June 1915.

12 ANZ, R24533922-ACHK-8604-G1-194-1915/1686, 'Date: 21 May 1915 Subject: Censorship and Press Bureau', Liverpool to Prime Minister 15 July 1915, Army: Memorandum on the Censorship, Cd. 7679, 1915, p.3; ANZ, R19162368-ACHK-16604-G49-20/47, 'Report on Cable Censorship during the Great War'; John Anderson, 'Military Censorship in World War I: Its Use and Abuse in New Zealand' (MA thesis, Victoria University College, 1952), pp. 37–42.

13 ANZ, R22432692-AAYS-8638-AD1-913-43/584/6, 'Miscellaneous – Deputy Chief Censor Wellington – Appointment of', Moorhouse to Chief of the General Staff (CGS), 1 August 1914 and related papers; ANZ, R22430468-AAYS-8638-AD1-23-8, 'Administration and Miscellaneous-Censorship-Regulations Postal', Deputy Chief Postal Censor, 'Postal Censorship in New Zealand', nd but probably 1918 or 1919; ANZ, R19162368-ACHK-16604-G49-20/47, 'Report on Cable Censorship during the Great War', pp.239–40; ANZ, R19162367-ACHK-16604-G49-20/46, 'Report on Postal Censorship during the Great War', pp.232, 235, 256; Anderson, pp.43–57.

14 Anderson, pp.9, 100–132; Steven Eldred-Grigg, *The Great Wrong War: New Zealand Society in WWI* (Auckland, 2010), pp.231–232, 327.

15 ANZ, WA230/22 (Retrieved Manually), 'Organisational Chart, Defence Headquarters General Staff Branch Feb 1919', CGS Branch organizational chart, nd but late First World War; ANZ, R3885399-AAYS-8647-AD10-10-19/21, 'Rules for the censorship of the press, September 1918 – May 1919', Thompson to CGS, 29 October 1918; ANZ, R22428950-AAYS-8638-AD1-704-8/19/35, 'Communications – Censorship Otago Daily Times – 23/9/1916 – 26/10/1918', Editor ODT to CGS, 14 December 1917; *Press*, 3 April 1917, p.6; *North Otago Times* (NOT), 28 November 1918, p.2; EP, 11 June 1919, p.7; *The Press 1861–1961: The Story of a Newspaper* (Christchurch, 1963), pp.152–153.

16 ANZ, R24048325-ACID-25038-WA252-1/[2], '[Correspondence between]

General Sir Alexander Godley [Commander New Zealand Expeditionary Force] and Colonel Hon. [Honourable] Sir James Allen, Minister of Defence, 2 April – 18 December 1915', Allen to Godley, 17 July 1915; ANZ, R15420172-ADRK-17391-T1-185-12/285, 'History of Works Branch, Defence Department from inception', New Zealand Military Forces: Branch of the Director of Works – History of from Inception to Handing over to Ordinance Branch in January 1919, nd but June 1919; AJHR, 1915, H-19b, 'Trentham Camp Commission', pp.xxvi–xxxix; Imelda Bargas and Tim Shoebridge, *New Zealand's First World War Heritage* (Auckland, 2015), pp.38–48, 54.

17 Neil Frances, *Safe Haven: The Untold Story of New Zealand's Largest Ever Military Camp: Featherston: 1916–1919* (Masterton, 2012), pp.1–35; Tim Shoebridge, *Featherston Military Training Camp and the First World War, 1915–27* (Wellington, 2011), pp.11–18, 27–34.

18 Bargas and Shoebridge, pp.53, 58.

19 Bargas and Shoebridge, p.70.

20 ANZ, R15419630-ADRK-17391-T1-162-1/90, 'War Expenses Account (1915)', Jones to Public Service Commissioner, 24 December 1914; ANZ, R10701485-AAYS-8694-AD78-8-23/10/3, 'Returns – History of War Expenses Branch'; AJHR, 1915, H-19, 'Defence Forces of New Zealand', p.21; AJHR, 1919, H-19, 'Defence Forces of New Zealand', pp.22–23.

21 NZH, 5 January 1916, p.8; *New Zealand Official Yearbook*, 1920, p.85; AJHR, 1920, H-19a, 'War Expenses Account', p.9. All contemporary figures calculated using the Reserve Bank's Inflation Calculator, http://www.rbnz.govt.nz

22 ANZ, R15419630-ADRK-17391-T1-162-1/90, 'War Expenses Account (1915)', Jones to Public Service Commissioner, 24 December 1914; ANZ, R15419696-ADRK-17391-T1-165-1/158/1, 'War Expenses Division – Defence Department – Col. Esson's report re general organisation and administration', Esson to Treasury Secretary, 9 August 1916, Circular Memorandum by Robin, 9 November 1916 and related papers; ANZ, R11741829-ADAV-16028-A5-217-26/1, 'War Expenses Audit – Programme of Work and Instructions to Audit Staff', Report of Work and Instructions of Audit of War Expenses, nd, but probably in 1917 or 1918; AJHR, 1917, H-19, 'Defence Forces of New Zealand', p.18; AJHR, 1918, H-19c, 'Royal Commission on Defence Department Expenditure, 1918', pp.11–15, 63; AJHR, 1919, H-19, 'Defence Forces of New Zealand', p.1; *Horowhenua Chronicle*, 4 February 1919, p.1.

23 AJHR, 1916, H-24; AJHR, 1917, H-24, 'Military Supplies and Munitions'; Paul Goldsmith and Michael Bassett, *The Myers* (Auckland, 2007), pp.115–116.

24 AJHR, 1919, H-24, 'Military Supplies and Munitions', p.1.

25 Steven Loveridge, 'Not Quiet on the Tasman Front? The Trans-Tasman Rivalry in New Zealand's Great War Cartoons', *European Journal of Humour Research*, 2/4, pp.108–125.

26 AJHR, 1916, H-24, 'Military Supplies and Munitions'; AJHR, 1919, H-24, 'Military Supplies and Munitions', *New Zealand Observer*, 12 April 1919, p.4; *New Zealand Parliamentary Debates* (NZPD), Vol.183, 4 December 1918, p.730.

27 ANZ, R15420172-ADRK-17391-T1-185-12/285, 'History of Works Branch, Defence Department from inception'; ANZ, R3898783-AAYS-8697-AD81-1-1/14, 'Colonel E.H. Hiley – Director Defence Works', Allen to Robin, 22 July 1915; ANZ, R22432655-AAYS-8638-AD1-911-43/460, 'Staff, miscellaneous – Staff – Director of Railways and Works – Appointment of', 30 October 1916, Richardson to Public Service Commissioner, 6 September 1920; ANZ, R23513682-AABK-

18805-W5674-1-425133-D.2/1571, 'Territorial Force – Sir Ernest Haviland Hiley, KBE, CBE', Allen to Hiley, 19 May 1919.

28 NZH, 5 January 1916, p.8.

29 *Poverty Bay Herald*, 29 June 1915, p.3; *Colonist*, 20 October 1915, p.4.

30 ANZ, R22432458-AAYS-8638-AD1-898-39/394, 'Reports – Reports progress – Base records', report by Captain Vine on Base Records Office, 27 August 1915 and related papers; ANZ, R22432408-AAYS-8638-AD1-896-39/310/18, 'Report Annual Base records', Kelly to Hilley 15 September 1915; ODT, 1 March 1916, p.3.

31 NZH, 5 January 1916, p.8; ANZ, R22432458-AAYS-8638-AD1-898-39/394, 'Reports – Reports progress – Base records', CGS to Robin, 2 August 1915, marginalia by Robin, 2 August 1915, Officer in Charge Expeditionary Force Records to Adjutant-General (AG), 5 August 1915, report by Captain Vine on Base Records Office, 27 August 1915; *Wairarapa Age*, 10 September 1915, p.5; ODT, 1 March 1916, p.3; EP, 8 March 1916, p.3; *Press*, 6 May 1919, p.2; Will Lawson, *Historic Trentham: 1914–1917* (Wellington, 1918), pp.28–31.

32 *Dominion*, 24 February 1919, p.4.

33 *Dominion*, 24 February 1919, p.4; Secretary Public Service Commissioner to Permanent Heads, 5 October 1915 and related papers, T1 23/102, ANZ, R15420742-ADRK-17391-T1-209-23/102, 'Re Voluntary Assistance rendered to Defence Department by Officers', Secretary Public Service Commissioner to Permanent Heads, 5 October 1915 and related papers; ANZ, R22433698-AAYS-8638-AD1-830-29/252/8, 'Establishments and Recruitment – Establishment – Home service sections – Base records', Francis to AG, 1 March 1918; ANZ, R22432408-AAYS-8638-AD1-896-39/310/18, 'Reports – Report annual base records', Director of Base Records Annual Report for the Year Ending 31 May 1918; AJHR, 1918, H-19c, 'Royal Commission on Defence Expenditure', p.58; EP, 2 November 1915, p.3; EP, 24 January 1918, p.9.

34 *Dominion*, 27 June 1916, p.7.

35 ANZ, R22430522-AAYS-8638-AD1-774-23/112, 'Administration and Miscellaneous – Base records – Organisation', Francis to Esson, November 1916; ODT, 1 March 1916, p.3; EP, 8 March 1916, p.3; *Press*, 6 May 1919, p.2.

36 ODT, 1 March 1916, p.3.

37 AJHR, 1918, H-19c, 'Royal Commission on Defence Expenditure', pp.68, 11; ANZ, WA230/20 (Retrieved Manually), 'Report on Recruiting NZEF by Director of Recruiting, Mar 1919', New Zealand Expeditionary Force 1914–1918, Recruiting 1916–1918 Report by the Director of Recruiting New Zealand Military Forces, 31 March 1919.

38 *Dominion*, 2 April 1919, p.8.

39 ANZ, WA231/23 (Retrieved Manually), 'Development of the Adjutant General of the Forces Branch of the Director of Personal Services, report of work, n.d.'

40 ANZ, WA231/23 (Retrieved Manually), 'Development of the Adjutant General of the Forces Branch of the Director of Personal Services, report of work, n.d.'; Paul Baker, *King and Country Call: New Zealanders, Conscription and the Great War* (Auckland, 1988), pp.202–206; *Alex Frame, Salmond: Southern Jurist* (Wellington, 1995), pp.165–173.

41 For further background see Loveridge, *Calls to Arms: New Zealand Society and Commitment to the Great War* (Wellington, 2015), pp.115–117.

42 AJHR, 1916, H-19, 'Defence Forces of New Zealand', p.11.

43 AJHR, 1918, H-19, 'Defence Forces of New Zealand', p.15.

44 Baker, pp.162–178.

45 ANZ, WA231/23 (Retrieved Manually), 'Development of the Adjutant General of the Forces Branch of the Director of Personal Services, report of work, n.d.', Personal Services; Baker, pp.165, 173–175, 209.

46 ANZ, WA230/20 (Retrieved Manually), 'Report on Recruiting NZEF by Director of Recruiting, Mar 1919', Recruiting 1916–1918, p.32; ANZ, R22436164-AAYS-8638-AD1-1038-64/7, 'Returns – Defaulters – Under Military Service Act', DPS to AG, 17 July 1917, Robin to Allen, 9 February 1918; ANZ, R22319675-ADBQ-16145-ALLEN1-9, 'Miscellanous files and papers – Correspondence between J Allen and WF Massey, 1st September 1916 – 1st August 1919 [Loose papers]', Allen to Massey, 12 and 24 June 1918; Baker, pp.178–201.

47 ANZ, R22431347-AAYS-8638-AD1-779-24/109, 'Personnel – Police (Military) Christchurch – Appointment during war', Officer Commanding Canterbury District to HQ New Zealand Military Forces, 6 December 1915; ANZ, R22432397-AAYS-8638-AD1-896-39/282, 'Reports – Reports Assistant Provost Marshal HQ [Headquarters] Wellington', Provost-Marshal to AG, 19 November 1918; New Zealand Military Forces General Orders, No.87, 1916 and No.597, 1917, Defence Library, Headquarters New Zealand Defence Force, Wellington; NZH, 6 February 1917, p.9; Lawson, pp.109–110.

48 *New Zealand Truth* (NZT), 28 December 1918, p.5; NZT, 16 February, 1918, p.5; EP, 19 April 1918, p.7.

49 AJHR, 1918, H-19, 'Defence Forces of New Zealand', p.15; NOT, 31 May 1918, p.1.

50 ANZ, R22319675-ADBQ-16145-ALLEN1-9, 'Miscellanous files and papers – Correspondence between J Allen and WF Massey, 1st September 1916 – 1st August 1919 [Loose papers]', Allen to Massey, 24 June 1918; *Dominion*, 13 February 1918, p.6; Val Burr, 'Somes Island Internment Camp for Enemy Aliens during the First World War: an Historical Enquiry' (MA thesis, Massey University, 1998), pp.181–187; Andrew Francis, *'To Be Truly British We Must Be Anti-German': New Zealand, Enemy Aliens and the Great War Experience, 1914–1919* (Oxford, 2012), pp.114–129, 143–150; David McGill, *Island of Secrets: Matiu/Somes Island in Wellington Harbour* (Wellington, 2001), pp.44–67; James Bade, *Sea Devil: Count Felix von Luckner in New Zealand and the Pacific* (Wellington, 2006), pp.50–93, 143–147.

51 ANZ, R22436117-AAYS-8638-AD1-1036-62/46-1, 'Formation of Corps – Home Service Section – NZEF', Robin to Allen, 14 November 1916; *War, 1914–1918: New Zealand Expeditionary Force, Its Provision and Maintenance* (Wellington, 1919), p.47; *Poverty Bay Herald*, 10 June 1918, p.4.

52 ANZ, R24048325-ACID-25038-WA252-1/[2], '[Correspondence between] General Sir Alexander Godley [Commander New Zealand Expeditionary Force] and Colonel Hon. [Honourable] Sir James Allen, Minister of Defence, 2 April – 18 December 1915', Allen to Godley, 17 July 1915; A.D. Carbery, *The New Zealand Medical Service in the Great War 1914–1918* (Auckland, 1924), pp.7–13, 137–138, 262.

53 Hocken Library, Downie Stewart Papers, MS-985-2/3, Allen to Downie Stewart, 7 July 1916; AJHR 1918, H-19c, 'Royal Commission on Defence Department Expenditure, 1918', p.51; *Provision and Maintenance*, p.51; *Press*, 11 March 1918, p.6; ANZ, R22429947-AAYS-8638-AD1-743-12/139, 'Camps – Camps and hospitals (military) – List of', Tate to Auditor-General , May 1917 and related papers; Carbery, pp.503–504, 548; Bargas and Shoebridge, pp.198–200.

54 AJHR, 1917, H-19, 'Defence Forces of New Zealand', pp.9–10; Bargas and Shoebridge, pp.198–206; Carbery, pp.507–514, 548.

55 R23513676, ANZ, R23513676-AABK-18805-W5674-1-425127-D. 1/563, 'New Zealand Permanent Staff – Robert Samuel Findlay Henderson CB, MB, KHP', Allen to Henderson, 28 April 1919; Carbery, pp.504–517.

56 AJHR, 1918, H-19, 'Defence Forces of New Zealand', pp.4, 8–9; *New Zealand Army List 1918* (Wellington, 1918); AJHR 1918, H-14, 'Public Service Commissioner', p.7; AJHR, 1919, H-14, 'Public Service Commissioner', p.21; *Provision and Maintenance*, p.46.

57 AJHR, 1918, H-19c, 'Royal Commission on Defence Department Expenditure, 1918', pp.63–68; ANZ, R22429251-AAYS-8638-AD1-720-9/318, 'Expeditionary Force – Appreciation of work of Defence Department and Military Forces – General file', Liverpool to Allen, 30 April 1915.

58 ANZ, R22436369-AAYS-8638-AD1-1047-73/8/4, 'Commissions – Defence expenditure – Evidence by Chief of General Staff', Gibbon to Robin, 22 June 1918; ANZ, R22436377-AAYS-8638-AD1-1048-73/8/7, 'Commissions – Defence expenditure – Evidence by General Officer Commanding', Transcript evidence given by Robin, 10 May 1918, p.4.

59 ANZ, R22436377-AAYS-8638-AD1-1048-73/8/7, 'Commissions – Defence expenditure – Evidence by General Officer Commanding'.

60 ANZ, R22436377-AAYS-8638-AD1-1048-73/8/7, 'Commissions – Defence expenditure – Evidence by General Officer Commanding', Transcript of evidence given by Robin, 10 May 1918, pp.9, 41, 51; ANZ, R22436369-AAYS-8638-AD1-1047-73/8/4, 'Commissions – Defence expenditure – Evidence by Chief of General Staff', 'Transfer Branches of Director of Recruiting and Director Personal Services to Government Statistician', nd but mid-1918; AJHR, 1918, H-19c, 'Royal Commission on Defence Department Expenditure, 1918', pp.63–67; AJHR, 1919, H-19, 'Defence Forces of New Zealand', p.7.

61 AJHR, 1918, H-19c, 'Royal Commission on Defence Department Expenditure, 1918', pp.67, 66; Clipping 'High Praise', EP, 28 June 1919 in Allen1, M20/90, ANZ, R22319767-ADBQ-16145-ALLEN1-5-M2/90, 'Ministerial Files – Letters of appreciation'; Eric Andrews, *The Department of Defence* (Melbourne, 2001), pp.46–58.

Chapter Two – The Continuation of Politics: Parliamentarians and the Great War

1 Labour's Paddy Webb (Grey) was the MP involved. The House of Representatives declined to give him leave of absence.

2 R.K. Newman, 'Liberal Policy and the Left Wing, 1908–1911' (MA thesis, University of Auckland, 1965), pp.397–403.

3 However, there wasn't a further swing of votes in rural seats to Reform in 1911, with the party's increased proportion of the vote that year coming from city, mining or timber-milling seats. Miles Fairburn and S.J. Haslett, 'Who Voted for Massey, 1908–1914', in James Watson and Lachy Paterson (eds), *A Great New Zealand Prime Minister?: Reappraising William Ferguson Massey* (Dunedin, 2011), pp.64–65.

4 *New Zealand Parliamentary Debates* (NZPD), Vol.169, 4 August 1914, p.381.

5 NZPD, Vol.169, 5 August 1914, p.399.

6 NZPD, Vol.169, 15 September 1914, p.867.

7 NZPD, Vol.169, 11 August 1914, p.509.

8 NZPD, Vol.169, 6 August 1914, pp.403–406. The Liberal L.M. Isitt (Christchurch North) explained his party's dilemma: 'If we criticize we shall be told we are hampering you.'

9 The words were those of James McCombs. NZPD, Vol.169, 6 August 1914, p.484.

10 NZPD, Vol.169, 14 August 1914, p.566.

11 NZPD, Vol.169, 7 August 1914, p.467. The League's hopes were not fulfilled. In 1917, attempts by the government to grant exemption from conscription for the celibate but not ordained Marist Brothers caused considerable division in parliament, while the Protestant Political Association fomented great religious disunion in the community more broadly.

12 See for example the prolonged and rather acerbic debate less than a fortnight after the outbreak of war on whether parties were continuing to hold public meetings. NZPD, Vol.169, 27 August 1914, pp.626–641.

13 NZPD, Vol.170, 18 September 1914, p.64.

14 NZPD, Vol.170, 18 September 1914, p.69.

15 NZPD, Vol.170, 22 September 1914, p.100.

16 NZPD, Vol.170, 22 September 1914, p.100.

17 NZPD, Vol.170, 29 September 1914, p.187.

18 NZPD, Vol.170, 29 September 1914, p.168.

19 NZPD, Vol.171, 4 November 1914, p.873.

20 Michael Bassett, *Three Party Politics in New Zealand 1911–1931* (Auckland, 1982), p.66.

21 Archives New Zealand (ANZ), R22319706-ADBQ-16145-ALLEN1-12, 'Miscellaneous files and papers – Miscellaneous correspondence and papers [Loose papers]', James Allen to Lionel Curtis, 9 June 1915.

22 ANZ, R22319723-ADBQ-16145-ALLEN1-1-M1/3-1 'Ministerial Files – Correspondence with WH Triggs (Press Editor)', Triggs to Allen, 8 January 1915.

23 Bassett, p.20.

24 For further details see John Crawford, '"I Get Blamed For Everything": Enduring the Burdens of Office, James Allen as Minister of Defence in 1915', in *Endurance and the First World War: Experiences and Legacies in New Zealand and Australia* (Newcastle upon Tyne, 2014), pp.14–30.

25 Some Reform newspapers had argued that Massey should persist with a one-party government. Antony Wood, 'The Origins of the First National Government: A Study in New Zealand Wartime Politics, 1914–15' (MA thesis, University of Canterbury, 1963), pp.176–177.

26 NZPD, Vol.172, 4 August 1915, pp.651–652. See also Gavin McLean, *The Governors: New Zealand's Governors and Governors-General* (Dunedin, 2006), p.178.

27 G.A. Wood, *Ministers and Members in the New Zealand Parliament* (Dunedin, 1992), p.5.

28 John Payne (Labour, Grey Lynn) declined to join. He later stated that he had decided to support the new government 'because the Liberal side of it was pledged to see to it that the question of the cost of living was fairly dealt with'. NZPD, Vol.177, 4 August 1916, p.814.

29 NZPD, Vol.173, 19 August 1915, p.3.

30 NZPD, Vol.174, 23 September 1915, p.146. Gustafson sees Webb as the only member who was not a 'moderate'. Barry Gustafson, *Labour's Path to Political Independence: The Origins and Establishment of the New Zealand Labour Party, 1900–19* (Auckland, 1980), p.89.

31 NZPD, Vol.174, 28 September 1915, p.262.

32 NZPD, Vol.174, 28 September 1915, p.264. The recent death of Allen's son and the tremendous administrative burden he was carrying also no doubt further reduced the Defence Minister's patience.

33 The Yugoslavs working on the kauri gum-fields of the Far North occupied a peculiar position in this dispute. The Reform MPs for the local electorates of Bay of Islands and Northern Maori did join calls for greater control over this population, but at the same time the main defenders of the 'Dalmatians' were Reform ministers. A lot of the resentment towards the Yugoslavs on the part of the 'British' and Maori was linked to competition in gum-digging, an occupation open to people with little or no capital.

34 Despite his grotesque distrust and persecution of those of 'German blood', Payne's contributions to parliamentary debates were generally quite cogent. He was the first to raise in parliament the problem of venereal disease amongst troops and strongly advocated prophylactic measures. Barry Gustafson has understandably described him as '[a] witty and well-informed debater and one of the most flamboyant figures in the history of New Zealand politics'. Gustafson, p.164. While Payne did not join the New Zealand Labour Party, Gustafson is wrong to describe him as 'pro-conscription'. Gustafson, pp.89, 164. Payne voted against passage of the 1916 Military Service Bill, having described it as an 'iniquitous measure'. NZPD, Vol.175, 31 May 1916, p.577. Payne moved for Webb to be given leave of absence.

35 NZPD, Vol.173, 25 August 1915, p.129.

36 NZPD, Vol.173, 25 August 1915, p.137.

37 NZPD, Vol.174, 6 October 1915, p.707. One of the three internment camps in New Zealand for enemy aliens was on Somes Island in Wellington Harbour.

38 NZPD, Vol.175, 10 May 1916, p.18. A von Zedlitz Grant Restoration Bill, aimed at retrieving the £700 (near $100,000 in 2015 dollars) that Victoria University College had given to its former Professor of German, was one of a flock of bills that Payne introduced. All contemporary figures calculated using the Reserve Bank's Inflation Calculator, http://www.rbnz.govt.nz.

39 NZPD, Vol.175, 10 May 1916, p.26.

40 NZPD, Vol 175, 11 May 1916, p.28.

41 Fletcher and Thacker. However, Thacker reversed his vote on the Third Reading. NZPD, Vol.175, 31 May 1916, p.577; NZPD, Vol.175, 9 June 1916, p.786.

42 ANZ, R22319675-ADBQ-16145-ALLEN1-9, 'Miscellanous files and papers – Correspondence between J Allen and WF Massey, 1st September 1916 – 1st August 1919 [Loose papers]', Allen to Massey, 22 November 1916.

43 Bassett, *Sir Joseph Ward: A Political Biography* (Auckland, 1993), p.227.

44 For a critical account of the government's interventions in the economy see Alan Everton, 'Government Intervention in the New Zealand Economy 1914–1918: Its Aims and Effectiveness' (MA thesis, Victoria University of Wellington, 1995).

45 For examples see NZPD, Vol.178, 2 August 1916, p.629; NZPD, Vol.182, 15 April 1918, p.251.

46 George Pearce (Reform, Patea) claimed as early as September 1915 that £1.5 million (near $210 million in 2015 dollars) extra would have been received at prevailing world prices. NZPD, Vol.173, 2 September 1915, p.309.

47 For further reading see Watson, 'Patriotism, Profits and Problems: New Zealand farming during the Great War', in John Crawford and Ian McGibbon (eds), *New Zealand's Great War: New Zealand, the Allies, and the First World War* (Auckland, 2007), pp.534–549.

48 NZPD, Vol.177, 2 August 1917, p.666.

49 NZPD, Vol.178, 12 July 1917, pp.351–352.

50 This is referred to in ANZ, R22319675-ADBQ-16145-ALLEN1-9, 'Miscellanous files and papers – Correspondence between J Allen and WF Massey, 1st September 1916 – 1st August 1919 [Loose papers]', Allen to Massey, 28 October 1916.

51 *Ashburton Guardian*, 10 July 1917, p.7. All contemporary figures calculated using the Reserve Bank's Inflation Calculator, http://www.rbnz.govt.nz.
52 ANZ, R22319675-ADBQ-16145-ALLEN1-9, 'Miscellanous files and papers – Correspondence between J Allen and WF Massey, 1st September 1916 – 1st August 1919 [Loose papers]', Allen to Massey, 2 February 1917.
53 NZPD, Vol.182, 15 April 1918, p.254.
54 NZPD, Vol.181, 31 October 1917, pp.674–675.
55 NZPD, Vol.181, 31 October 1917, pp.675–677.
56 NZPD, Vol.181, 31 October 1917, p.694.
57 For further reading see Paul Baker, *King and Country Call: New Zealanders, Conscription and the Great War* (Auckland, 1988), pp.132–138.
58 For further reading see Baker, pp.142–152.
59 NZPD, Vol.180, 2 October 1917, p.578.
60 NZPD, Vol.182, 10 April 1918, p.54.
61 NZPD, Vol.182, 10 April 1918, pp.39, 54.
62 NZPD, Vol.182, 10 April 1918, p.39; NZPD, Vol.182, 12 April 1918, p.154.
63 NZPD, Vol.182, 11 April 1918, 71. Albert Glover (Liberal, Auckland Central) made a similar attack. NZPD, Vol.182, 12 April 1918, p.167.
64 NZPD, Vol.182, 15 April 1918, p.239.
65 NZPD, Vol.182, 13 April 1918, pp.178, 199–200.
66 NZPD, Vol.182, 15 April 1918, p.227.
67 *Evening Post*, 22 February 1918, p.3. This by-election, which was clearly politically inconvenient for the government, was occasioned by the decision of Alexander Herdman to use his powers as Attorney-General to appoint himself a Supreme Court Judge. Susan Butterworth, 'Herdman, Alexander Lawrence', *The Dictionary of New Zealand Biography*, Vol. 3 (Auckland, 1996), p.212.
68 Gustafson, pp.136–137.
69 Allen certainly did not see this defeat coming, writing earlier that 'I do not think there can be any doubt about the result. Connett [the Reform candidate] ought to win by a large majority'. ANZ, R22319675-ADBQ-16145-ALLEN1-9, 'Miscellanous files and papers – Correspondence between J Allen and WF Massey, 1st September 1916 – 1st August 1919 [Loose papers]', Allen to Massey, 19 September 1918. Okey does not appear to have died from influenza. NZPD, Vol.183, 25 October 1918, p.14.
70 ANZ, R22319675-ADBQ-16145-ALLEN1-9, 'Miscellanous files and papers – Correspondence between J Allen and WF Massey, 1st September 1916 – 1st August 1919 [Loose papers]', Allen to Massey, 14 May 1918.
71 Gustafson, p.136–137.

Chapter Three – 'Priceless Worth': The Territorial Force and Senior Cadets in World War One

1 Peter Cooke, 'The Poor Cousin: New Zealand's Home Defence', in John Crawford and Ian McGibbon (eds), *New Zealand's Great War: New Zealand, The Allies and The First World War* (Auckland, 2007), pp.426–446.
2 For a general history see Peter Cooke and John Crawford, *The Territorials: The History of the Territorial and Volunteer Forces of New Zealand* (Auckland, 2011).
3 Ian McGibbon, *The Path to Gallipoli: Defending New Zealand 1840–1915* (Wellington, 1991), pp.85–105.
4 Brig L.F. Brooker, *New Zealand Army Historical Records, Vol 1: Volunteers and Territorial Units, Part 1: 1800–1937* (Wellington, 1986?), p1.030201.

5 Peter Cooke, John H. Gray and Ken Stead, *Auckland Infantry: The Story of the Auckland (Countess of Ranfurly's Own) and North Auckland Regiments and of the Citizen Soldiers Who Served New Zealand* (Auckland, 2010), p.38.
6 Peter Cooke, *Fit to Fight: Compulsory Military Training and National Service in New Zealand 1949–72* (David Ling, 2013), p.14.
7 *Press*, 23 August 1916, p.6.
8 *Dominion*, 27 June 1918, p.6.
9 *Appendices to the Journals of the House of Representatives* (AJHR), 1915, H-19, 'Defence Forces of New Zealand', p.4.
10 AJHR, 1915, H-19, 'Defence Forces of New Zealand', p.4.
11 *Dominion Post*, 14 August 2014, p.A4.
12 John Studholme, *Some Records of the NZ Expeditionary Force Unofficial, But Compiled From Official Sources* (Wellington, 1928); Appendices Table 'Strength of NZEF Overseas by Monthly Total. . .'; New Zealand Military Forces, *War, 1914–1918: The New Zealand Expeditionary Force, Its Provision and Maintenance* (Wellington, 1919), Table XXX, p.50; Table XVIII, p.45.
13 *War, 1914–1918*, Table XXIV, p.47.
14 *War, 1914–1918*, Table XXVIII, pp.47–48.
15 AJHR, 1919, H-19, 'Defence Forces of New Zealand', p.7.
16 AJHR, 1919, H-19, 'Defence Forces of New Zealand', p.7.
17 Cooke and Crawford, p.196. Military experience included membership of a Defence Rifle Club.
18 *Dominion*, 27 June 1918, p.6.
19 *Press*, 15 September 1915, p.4. Bowker of the South Canterbury MR was killed in action before his letter was published.
20 The General Training Section was disestablished in 1916 and its men absorbed into the substantive Territorial Force.
21 For further reading see Cooke, 'The Poor Cousin', pp.435–446.
22 AJHR, 1915, H-19, 'Defence Forces of New Zealand', p.9. The figure is in regards to 30 April 1914.
23 Barry O'Sullivan, 'The National Reserve of World War One and Canterbury's Contribution', *The Volunteers: The Journal of the N.Z. Military Historical Society*, 40/3 (March 2015), p.47.
24 Figures for the Territorial Force are available within AJHR, H-19, for each year. Figures for the NZEF are available in *War, 1914–1918*, Tables III and XXVIII.
25 Paul Baker, *King and Country Call: New Zealanders, Conscription and the Great War* (Auckland, 1988), pp.58–63.
26 AJHR, 1919, H-19, 'Defence Forces of New Zealand', p.14.
27 AJHR, 1917, H-19, 'Defence Forces of New Zealand', p.3; AJHR, 1918, H-19, 'Defence Forces of New Zealand', p.7.
28 AJHR, 1918, H-19, 'Defence Forces of New Zealand', p.3.
29 AJHR, 1915, H-19, 'Defence Forces of New Zealand', p.9.
30 AJHR, 1915, H-19E, 'Expeditionary Force', p.7.
31 AJHR, 1915, H-19, 'Defence Forces of New Zealand', p.3.
32 For instance the HQ Wellington district got in touch with Chambers of Commerce, Farmers Unions, A&P Associations, Employers Federal branches, Labour unions, and employers generally, 'with the object of ascertaining their views as to the suitability of the times when the camps were held last year'. *Poverty Bay Herald*, 19 October 1918, p.2.

33 *Otago Daily Times*, 13 January 1917, p.10. The piece references Invercargill's Military Service Board.
34 AJHR, 1918, H-19, 'Defence Forces of New Zealand', p.17.
35 *Northern Advocate*, 23 March 1914, p.4.
36 *Hawera & Normanby Star*, 21 November 1916, p.4.
37 For population see *Thames Star*, 7 November 1916, p.4; for camps AJHR, 1915, H-19, 'Defence Forces of New Zealand', Appendix B, p.24.
38 Whangarei, Auckland, Paeroa, Hamilton, Hawera, Napier, Masterton, Palmerston North, Wellington, Nelson, Kaiapoi, Greymouth, Christchurch, Timaru, Oamaru, Dunedin, Milton, Invercargill. These grew to 21 under the 1916 Military Service Act.
39 Paul Neazor, *100 Years of College Rifles 1879–1997* (Celebrity Books, 1997), p.39.
40 Cooke and Crawford, p.189.
41 *Hawera & Normanby Star*, 25 February 1916, p.3.
42 Frank L. Lewis, *The Star Boating Club – One Hundred Years of Rowing* (Upper Hutt, 1966).
43 Michael Bassett, *Coates of Kaipara* (Auckland, 1995), p.25.
44 *Ashburton Guardian*, 20 August 1918, p.4. The paper gave his age as 66 but he was 56 when he died. *The Quarterly Army List of the New Zealand Forces for June 1915* (Wellington, 1915), column 101.
45 *Clutha Leader*, 18 May 1915, p.5.
46 For further details see Margaret Tennant, 'Fun and Fundraising: The Selling of Charity in New Zealand's Past', *Social History*, 38/1 (2013), pp.46–65.
47 *Inangahua Times*, 3 August 1914, p.2.
48 NZ Defence Forces, General Order 34/1918, published in *NZ General Orders* No.1, 8 January 1918, p.23; General Order 180/1918 published in *NZ General Orders* No.4, 2 April 1918, p.27.
49 *Hawera & Normanby Star*, 12 October 1915, p.4.
50 Paul Neazor, *100 Years of College Rifles 1879–1997* (Celebrity Books, 1997), p.39.
51 Some honours boards, such as that for the Karori Borough Council, claimed to name all staff members who served, but in fact only named those who served overseas. This reflected a pecking order of service, in which the 'returned man' gained pre-eminence (sometimes way out of proportion to the quality or duration of his service) over the long-suffering home service Territorial. Arguments for recognising the service of Territorials or the deaths of men in New Zealand-based training from unheroic causes (such as disease, accident or suicide) usually fell on deaf ears. 'WWI Honours Board, Karori', *The Stockade* No.26, Karori Historical Society.
52 O'Sullivan, p.47.
53 *Press*, 19 June 1916, p.10.
54 Archives New Zealand, 'Rifle Meetings – Dominion Rifle Association – General file', R22433999-AAYS-8638-AD1-1011-54/9, GOC to Minster of Defence, 31 March 1914.
55 William O. Ludlow went before the courts for failing to attend a rifle club parade. *Clutha Leader*, 20 April 1917, p.2.
56 AJHR, 1915, H-19, 'Defence Forces of New Zealand', p.6.
57 *The Quarterly Army List of the New Zealand Forces for April 1916* (Wellington, 1916), column 275.
58 AJHR, 1915, H-19, 'Defence Forces of New Zealand', p.5.
59 Amy Hatcher and Karyn Flanagan, *National Rifle Association of New Zealand, Fullbore Rifle Shooting* (Wellington, 2014).

60 AJHR, 1915, H-19, 'Defence Forces of New Zealand', p.12.
61 McGibbon, 'Cadets', in McGibbon (ed.), *The Oxford Companion to New Zealand Military History* (Auckland, 2000), pp.76–77.
62 Roger Openshaw, 'Patriot Band: The School Cadets From Their Evolution to the Great War', (MA thesis, Massey University, 1973), p.5.
63 *The Quarterly Army List of the New Zealand Forces for June 1915* (Wellington, 1916), column 157.
64 Cooke and Crawford, p.169.
65 At the Taranaki review for General Sir Ian Hamilton, 120 such veterans paraded alongside hundreds of cadets – 'who are being trained to take their place in the battle grounds of the future'. *Taranaki Daily News*, 21 May 1914, p.4.
66 For an example of the term 'Great War' referring to the Napoleonic Wars see *New Zealand Spectator & Cook's Strait Guardian*, 16 October 1850, p.3. For the legacy of Napoleon's battles see *Auckland Star*, 17 October 1903, p.3. See also Jan Morris, *Pax Britannica*, 3 volumes (London, 1992).
67 AJHR, 1919, H-19, 'Defence Forces of New Zealand', p.7.
68 AJHR, 1919, H-19, 'Defence Forces of New Zealand', p.12.
69 Openshaw, p.9. Steven Loveridge, *Calls to Arms: New Zealand Society and Commitment to the Great War* (Wellington, 2014), pp.148–150.
70 Will Chapman, 'A School in Wartime – Karori School during WWI', *The Stockade*, Journal of the Karori Historical Society, (2001), 34, p.15.
71 See *Grey River Argus*, 3 July 1913, p.5; R. L. Weitzel, 'Pacifists and Anti-militarists in New Zealand, 1909–1914', *New Zealand Journal of History*, 7/2 (1973), pp.128–147.
72 AJHR, 1915, H-19, 'Defence Forces of New Zealand', Appendix E, p.30.
73 AJHR, 1915, H-19, 'Defence Forces of New Zealand', p.5.
74 AJHR, 1916, H-19, 'Defence Forces of New Zealand', p.10.
75 AJHR, 1916, H-19, 'Defence Forces of New Zealand', p.3.
76 AJHR, 1916, H-19, 'Defence Forces of New Zealand', p.5.
77 AJHR, 1913, H-19, 'Defence Forces of New Zealand', p.6.
78 AJHR, 1918, H-19, 'Defence Forces of New Zealand', p.7. In the original 'contributory' was spelt 'contributary'.

Chapter Four – 'We could surely introduce . . .': The Impact of the Great War on New Zealand Education

1 *Appendices to the Journals of the House of Representatives* (AJHR), 1914, E-2, 'Education: Primary Education', p.11.
2 AJHR, 1915, E-3, 'Education: Native Schools', p.4.
3 I.A. McLaren, 'The Politics of Secondary Education in Victorian New Zealand', in R. Openshaw and D. McKenzie (eds), *Reinterpreting the Educational Past: Essays in the History of New Zealand Education* (Wellington, 1987), pp.64–81.
4 John. M. McKenzie, General Editor's introduction to T. Pietsch, *Empire of Scholars: Universities, Networks and the British Academic World 1850–1939* (Manchester & New York, 2013), p.vii.
5 For a comprehensive discussion of centralisation in this period see A.E. Campbell, *Educating New Zealand* (Wellington, 1941), especially chapter 2, pp.24–73.
6 D. McKenzie, H. Lee and G. Lee, *Scholars or Dollars? Selected Historical Case Studies of Opportunity Costs in New Zealand Education* (Palmerston North, 1996).
7 J. Mackey, *The Making of a State Education System: The Passing of the New Zealand Education Act, 1877* (London, 1967), p.178.

8 L.C. Webb, *The Control of Education in New Zealand* (Wellington, 1937), p.130.
9 R. Openshaw, G. Lee and H. Lee, *Challenging the Myths: Rethinking New Zealand's Educational History* (Palmerston North, 1993), p.95.
10 Openshaw, Lee and Lee, pp.145–151.
11 Campbell, p.95. See also, H. Roth, *George Hogben: A Biography* (Wellington, 1952) for a detailed examination of the 1904 Syllabus and its subsequent reception.
12 Those particularly interested in this period should consult the 1912 Royal Commission on Education [the Cohen Commission]. This primary source (AJHR, 1912, E-12 'Education Commission', pp.1–744) furnishes a comprehensive snapshot of attitudes towards and issues in New Zealand education immediately prior to the outbreak of war.
13 AHJR, 1916, E-1, 'Thirty-ninth Annual Report of the Minister of Education', p.16.
14 AHJR, 1916, E-1, 'Thirty-ninth Annual Report of the Minister of Education', p.16.
15 See for instance, AJHR, 1916, E-2, Appendix A 'Report of the Auckland Education Board'. It should be noted, however, that this was not a formal policy until the passing of the Married Women (Lecturers and Teachers) Act 1932, as a Depression measure.
16 AJHR, 1915, E-3, 'Education: Native Schools', p.11.
17 AJHR, 1917, E-1, 'Education: Fortieth Annual Report of the Minister of Education', p.5.
18 J. Latchem, 'A Generation of Promise; The 1908 Junior Scholarship Candidates – Education, Occupation and the First World War', *Journal of New Zealand Studies*, 18 (2014), p.74.
19 AJHR, 1915, E-3, 'Education: Native Schools' p.11.
20 See for instance, R. Openshaw, 'Patriotism and the New Zealand Primary School: The Decisive Years of the Twenties' (PhD dissertation, University of Waikato, 1978). See also D.R. Jenkins, 'Social, Civic and Moral Attitudes in the New Zealand School Journal' (MA dissertation, Victoria University College, 1937); E.P. Malone, The New Zealand School Journal and the Imperial Ideology', *New Zealand Journal of History*, 7/1 (April 1973), pp.12–27.
21 Openshaw, 'Patriotism and the New Zealand Primary School', pp.21–22.
22 'The Fable of the Simple Potter and the Treacherous Serpent', *School Journal*, 12, part 3 (September 1918), pp.213–217.
23 H. Brighouse, 'A War Story: The Bellringer of Brunswick', *School Journal*, 12, part 3 (October 1918), pp.284–287.
24 Archives New Zealand (ANZ), R12485392-AAMJ-W3119-457, 'University of New Zealand Senate Minutes', 'The effect of the war on our university', Minutes of Proceedings of Forty-Fifth Annual Session and Special Sessions of the Senate of the University of New Zealand. Christchurch: January 1915; Wellington: April 1915, June 1915, p.2.
25 Pietsch, p.8.
26 ANZ, R24007972-ACID-24945-WA250-1/35, 'Training papers – Lectures on the growth of Germany and the growth of Russia by Professor Atkins', 'Lecture 1: The Growth of Germany'.
27 ANZ, R24007972, 'Training papers', 'Lecture 2: The Balkan Tangle'.
28 See '"Red Feds and Prussianism: Startling Similarities", Address by Professor MacMillan Brown' in *North Otago Times*, 16 April 1917, p.1.
29 Pietsch, pp.132, 138.
30 ANZ, R12485392, 'University of New Zealand Senate Minutes', G.M. Thomson. Letter to Sir Robert Stout, Chancellor, University of New Zealand, Minutes of Proceedings of the New Zealand University Senate, 31 January 1916, pp.33–36.

31 ANZ, R12485392, 'University of New Zealand Senate Minutes', Minutes of Proceedings of the New Zealand University Senate, 31 January 1916, p.35.
32 ANZ, R12485392, 'University of New Zealand Senate Minutes', Minutes of Proceedings of the New Zealand University Senate, 31 January 1916, p.36.
33 ANZ, R12485392, 'University of New Zealand Senate Minutes', Minutes of Proceedings of the New Zealand University Senate, 31 January 1916, p.40.
34 J.C. Beaglehole, *Victoria University College: An Essay Towards a History* (Wellington, 1949), p.172.
35 AJHR, 1916, E-1A, 'Educational Progress', p.2.
36 AJHR, 1918, E-1, 'Report of the Minister of Education', p.6.
37 AJHR, 1918, E-1, 'Report of the Minister of Education', p.6.
38 AJHR, 1918, E-1, 'Report of the Minister of Education', p.9.
39 R. Openshaw, '"A Spirit of Bolshevism": The Weitzel Case of 1921 and its Impact on the New Zealand Educational System', *Political Science*, 33/2, 1981, pp.127–139.
40 See *New Zealand School Journal*, vol.15, part 1 (April 1921), pp.54–57.
41 Article entitled 'The League of Nations', *New Zealand School Journal*, vol.18, part 3 (July 1924), p.24. No author given.
42 Openshaw, 'Patriotism and the New Zealand Primary School', pp.206–207.
43 J.H. Murdoch, *The High Schools of New Zealand: A Critical Survey* (Whitcombe & Tombs/New Zealand Council for Educational Research, Educational Research Series No.19, 1944), p.61.
44 A.G. Butchers, *Education in New Zealand: An Historical Survey* (Dunedin, 1930), p.8.
45 Murdoch, *The High Schools of New Zealand*, pp.58–60.
46 Murdoch, pp.56–58.
47 Openshaw, Lee and Lee, pp.215–240.
48 W. Boyd and W. Rawson, *The Story of the New Education* (London, 1965).
49 P.J. Adams, '"The End of the Beginning?": An Examination of the 'New Education Fellowship (NEF) in New Zealand in the Interwar Period (1919–1938) with Particular Reference to the NEF Conference 1937' (PhD dissertation, Massey University, 2013).
50 R. Openshaw, 'New Zealand State Primary Schools and the Growth of Internationalism and Anti-war Feeling, 1929–1934', *Australian New Zealand History of Education Journal*, 19/1 (1980), pp.1–14.
51 Adams, pp.334–335.
52 Openshaw, Lee and Lee, p.58.
53 J.M. Barrington, 'Maori Schools Policy: A View from the Schools', *New Zealand Journal of Educational Studies*, 20/2 (1985), p.151.
54 Openshaw, Lee and Lee, pp.58–59.
55 Openshaw, Lee and Lee, pp.60–65.
56 See for example, J.N. Bade, *Out of the Shadow of War: The German Connection with New Zealand in the Twentieth Century* (Melbourne, 1998).

Chapter Five – State Servants and Social Beings: The Role of the New Zealand Police Force in the Great War

1 For an international model of such developments see John Horne, 'Remobilizing for "Total War"': France and Britain, 1917–1918', in John Horne (ed.), *State, Society and Mobilization in Europe during the First World War* (New York, 1997), pp.195–211.
2 James Belich, *The New Zealand Wars and the Victorian Interpretation of Racial Conflict* (Auckland, 1986), pp.277–288; Judith Binney, *Encircled Lands: Te Urewera, 1820–1921* (Wellington, 2009), pp.148–159.

3 Graeme Dunstall, 'Frontier and/or Cultural Fragment? Interpretations of Violence in Colonial New Zealand', *Social History*, 29/1 (2004), pp.59–83.

4 For the development of policing in New Zealand until the beginnings of the modern period, see Richard Hill, *Policing the Colonial Frontier: The Theory and Practice of Coercive Social and Racial Control in New Zealand, 1767–1867* (Wellington, 1986); *The Colonial Frontier Tamed: New Zealand Policing in Transition, 1867–1886* (Wellington, 1989); *The Iron Hand in the Velvet Glove: The Modernisation of Policing in New Zealand 1886–1917* (Wellington, 1995).

5 For the latest coverage of the Liberal period, see T. Brooking, *Richard Seddon: King of God's Own* (Auckland, 2014).

6 J. O'Donovan, 'Address to the New Zealand Police Force', in *The Police Force Act, 1913, Police Force Amendment Act, 1919, and Regulations Made Thereunder for the Guidance of the Police Force of New Zealand* (Wellington, 1920), p.v. See too Richard Hill, 'Policing in New Zealand – A Short History', in Sherwood Young (ed.), *With Confidence and Pride: Policing the Wellington Region, 1840–1992* (Wellington, 1994), p.17.

7 Clive Emsley, *The Great British Bobby: A History of British Policing from the 18th Century to the Present* (London, 2009).

8 See Emsley. As another text puts it, '[t]he challenge the police face in getting information is that there must be some level of trust for citizens to cooperate with the police.': Victor E. Kappeler and Larry K. Gaines, *Community Policing: A Contemporary Perspective*, 4th ed. (Newark, 2005), p.8.

9 *Appendices to the Journals of the House of Representatives* (AJHR), 1918, H-16, 'The Police Force of the Dominion', p.6.

10 AJHR, 1914, H-16, 'The Police Force of the Dominion', pp.1, 15–18. In addition, in 1914, there were 23 District and Native Constables not included in the 870 total.

11 The two were not mutually exclusive: see, for example, Richard Hill, 'Policing Ireland, Policing Colonies: The Irish Constabulary "Model"', in Angela McCarthy (ed.), *Ireland in the World: Comparative, Transnational, and Personal Perspectives* (New York and London, 2015).

12 AJHR, 1914, H-16, 'The Police Force of the Dominion', p.5.

13 Archives New Zealand [ANZ], R24474130, ACIS-17627-P1-278-1906/666, 'From: Commissioner of Police, Wellington Date: 27 September 1907 Subject: Christchurch Exhibition'.

14 Melanie Nolan (ed.), *Revolution: The 1913 Great Strike in New Zealand* (Wellington, 2005); Hill, *The Iron Hand in the Velvet Glove*, pp.271–323.

15 Emsley, pp.257ff.

16 Hill, *The Iron Hand in the Velvet Glove*, pp.346–352; Michael Bassett (with Michael King), *Tomorrow Comes the Song: A Life of Peter Fraser* (Auckland, 2000), pp.61–62, 72.

17 Ian McGibbon, 'The Shaping of New Zealand's War Effort, August–October 1914', in John Crawford and Ian McGibbon (eds), *New Zealand's Great War: New Zealand, the Allies and the First World War* (Auckland, 2007), p.51.

18 G.T. Bloomfield, *New Zealand: A Handbook of Historical Statistics* (Boston, 1984), p.369.

19 For examples see *Auckland Weekly News*, 25 May 1916, p.43; *New Zealand Free Lance*, 2 June 1915, p.3; *New Zealand Free Lance*, 19 November 1915, p.3.

20 Hill, *The Iron Hand in the Velvet Glove*, pp.355–357.

21 Police 'diaries of duties and occurrences' and other records during the war mostly record minor criminal offending; see, e.g., Constable W.H. Almond's documents, in author's possession.

22 For further reading see Andrew Francis, *'To Be Truly British We Must be Anti-German': New Zealand, Enemy Aliens and the Great War Experience, 1914–1919* (New York, 2012).

23 An analysis by the author in December 2015 of a number of records relating to police history (held at the Stout Research Centre for New Zealand Studies) indicated very clear such patterns.

24 ANZ, R21371890-AAAB-478-12/aq, 'Riot, Wanganui'.

25 ANZ, R21371890-AAAB-478-12/aq, 'Riot, Wanganui'.

26 ANZ, R21371635-AAAB-478-5/c, 'Germans in police force'. Allegations of police sympathy with 'the enemy' were not uncommon in times perceived as national emergencies. Numbers of policemen during the 1913 Great Strike, for example, were accused of being on the side of militant labour: Hill, *The Iron Hand in the Velvet Glove*, pp.320–321.

27 This, for example, was the case in Wanganui: ANZ, R21371425-AAAB-478-11/ag, 'Wanganui riot'.

28 ANZ, R21371640-AAAB-478-12/aq, 'Gisborne Anti-German riot'.

29 This phenomenon had been experienced in the 1913 Great Strike, to the chagrin of many police, although in this instance the use of specials was in the context of a political showdown with organised labour: Hill, *The Iron Hand in the Velvet Glove*, pp.309–314.

30 ANZ, R22430661-AAYS-8638-AD1-779-24/83, 'Personnel – Police – Employment of women as'.

31 For Great Britain's wartime use of female police officers see Emsley, p.178; the New Zealand debate was informed by this and developments elsewhere.

32 ANZ, R22430661-AAYS-8638-AD1-779-24/83, 'Personnel – Police – Employment of women as'. See too Bronwyn Dalley, '"Come Back With Honour": Prostitution and the New Zealand Soldier, at Home and Abroad', in Crawford and McGibbon (eds), *New Zealand's Great War*, pp.364–377; and Katherine Sanders, '"The Sensational Scandal which has Worried Wellington": The Kelburn Raid, Sex, and the Law in First World War New Zealand', *New Zealand Journal of History*, 48/2 (October 2014), pp.91–118.

33 Hill, *The Iron Hand in the Velvet Glove*, pp.403–406.

34 For women police in New Zealand, see Valerie P. Redshaw, *Tact and Tenacity: New Zealand Women in Policing* (Wellington, 2006).

35 Hill, *The Iron Hand in the Velvet Glove*, pp.341–345; Richard Hill, interview with former wartime constables C.S. Chesnutt and Arnold Butterworth, 1979. Butterworth noted that 'the police found it impossible to enforce [anti-treating regulations] so just ignored them.'

36 Richard Hill, 'Cullen, John, 1850?–1939', *The Dictionary of New Zealand Biography*, Vol. 3 (Wellington, 1996), pp.125–127; ANZ, R21371431-AAAB-478-11/am, 'Wellington: Wharves: Aliens'.

37 New Zealand Police, Circulars and Memoranda Book, 1877–1926, Hampden Police Station; ANZ, R21371431-AAAB-478-11/am, 'Wellington: Wharves: Aliens'.

38 AJHR, 1919, H-33, 'Prisoners of War on Somes Island', p.2.

39 ANZ, R21371956-AAAB-478-10/t, 'Signalling, Wellington Hospital'.

40 ANZ, R21371956-AAAB-478-10/t, 'Signalling, Karori'.

41 ANZ, R21371770-AAAB-478-6/I, 'Lockwood, Mrs'.

42 Simon Johnson, 'The Home Front: Aspects of Civilian Patriotism in New Zealand during the First World War' (MA thesis, Massey University, 1975), pp.96–97.

43 Hill, *The Iron Hand in the Velvet Glove*, pp.355–356.

44 ANZ, R22429670-AAYS-8638-AD1-731-10/284/32, 'Territorial Force – Shirkers – Six Sons of Sgt. McKeefry – Police Force – Dunedin'. As it turned out, only two of the sons were of military age and they were negotiating to travel to England to join the Air Services.
45 Hill, *The Iron Hand in the Velvet Glove*, p.350.
46 ANZ, R21371538-AAAB-478-2/c, 'Censorship of correspondence'.
47 ANZ, R21371635-AAAB-478-5/c, 'Germans in police force'.
48 Horne, 'Remobilizing for "Total War"'
49 Alex Frame, *Salmond: Southern Jurist* (Wellington, 1995), p.167.
50 *New Zealand Statutes*, 1914, No.38, pp.128–129.
51 For some key examples see *Manual of the War Legislation of New Zealand Comprising Acts of Parliament, Proclamations, Orders in Council, and other Instruments passed, issued, and made in consequence of the War, and in Force on 30th September, 1916* (Wellington, 1916), p.v.
52 Horne, 'Remobilizing for "Total War"'.
53 Bassett, pp.71–72.
54 Hill, *The Iron Hand in the Velvet Glove*, p.353; Bassett, p.73; Commissioner J. Cullen to Superintendent A. Wright, Dunedin, 2 September, 1915, and Commissioner J. O'Donovan to Wright, 19 February 1917, both copied into New Zealand Police, Circulars and Memoranda Book, 1877–1926, Hampden Police Station.
55 Jared Davidson, 'Censored: Letters of the First World War', draft chapters for forthcoming book, kindly supplied by the author, January 2015.
56 Canterbury Museum Archives, 'Diary of J.A. McCullough, Feb 16, 1915 to Feb 10, 1917, vol. 5'; entry for 14 October 1915. For McCullough, a pacifist but also a workers' representative on the Arbitration Court, see Melanie Nolan, *Kin: A Collective Biography of a Working-Class New Zealand Family* (Christchurch, 2005).
57 ANZ, R21371539-AAAB-478-2/d, 'Chemists, Enemy'; ANZ, R21371431-AAAB-478-11/am, 'Wellington: Wharves: Aliens'; ANZ, R3885352-AAYS-8647-AD10-9-17/7, 'Police inquiries re aliens on wharves, April'.
58 ANZ, R21371539-AAAB-478-2/d, 'Chemists, Enemy'; ANZ, R21371431-AAAB-478-11/am, 'Wellington: Wharves: Aliens'.
59 ANZ, R22429370-AAYS-8638-AD1-724-10/13, 'Territorial Force – Reward – Payment of to Police for Arrest and Conviction of Defaulters under Defence Act'. The system of paying rewards to the police for obtaining convictions was discontinued in 1926 'as a general principle considered objectionable'.
60 ANZ, R21371600-AAAB-478-3/s, 'Expeditionary Force: bad characters'.
61 ANZ, R21371603, AAAB-478-3/v, 'EF [Expeditionary Force]: deserters'.
62 National registration required men between 17 and 60 to signal their willingness or otherwise to serve. These and later regulations involved much registration enforcement work for the police, as did related duties such as monitoring all steamer departures to ensure that any men on the National Register had permission to leave. See Hill, *The Iron Hand in the Velvet Glove*, p.349.
63 Belich, *Paradise Reforged: A History of the New Zealanders from the 1880s to the Year 2000* (Auckland, 2001), p.102; Paul Baker, *King and Country Call: New Zealanders, Conscription and the Great War* (Auckland, 1988), pp.202–209.
64 Baker, pp.207–208.
65 Hill, *The Iron Hand in the Velvet Glove*, p.352.
66 ANZ, R22430678, AAYS-8638-AD1-780-24/188/2, 'Personnel – Military defaulters list – General file'; AJHR 1920, Session I, H-19, 'Defence Forces of New Zealand', p.11.

67 *War Regulations Act, 1914, and Regulations Made Thereunder* (Wellington, 1915), sec.4, p.2.
68 Bassett, p.72.
69 James Holt, *Compulsory Arbitration in New Zealand: The First Forty Years* (Auckland, 1986), pp.128–132; Hill, *The Iron Hand in the Velvet Glove*, p.360; Bassett, p.72.
70 For an account see Bassett, pp.72–73.
71 Harry Holland, *Armageddon or Calvary: The Conscientious Objectors of New Zealand and 'the Process of Their Conversion'* (Brooklyn, 1919), p.14.
72 David Grant, *Field Punishment No. 1: Archibald Baxter, Mark Briggs and New Zealand's Anti-Militarist Tradition* (Wellington, 2008), p.36.
73 Peter Webster, *Rua and the Maori Millennium* (Wellington, 1979), p.243
74 *Wairarapa Daily Times*, 4 August 1916, p.4; James Belich, 'The East Coast Wars', in *The New Zealand Wars*, episode 5, directed by Tainui Stevens (Auckland, 1998); Hill, *The Iron Hand in the Velvet Glove*, p.388.
75 For the background to these events, see Michael King, *Te Puea: A Biography* (Auckland, 1977); tension between Waikato and the state remained in place for decades thereafter, perhaps eventually resolved by the settlement of Waikato-Tainui's historical claims over confiscated land and other issues in 1995.
76 There was tension, for example, when the military accused police of lack of rigour when assessing volunteers' suitability for war service: Hill, *The Iron Hand in the Velvet Glove*, p.350.
77 Hill, *The Iron Hand in the Velvet Glove*, pp.348–349, 355; ANZ, R21371601-AAAB-478-3/t, 'Exped Fce [Expeditionary Force]: breaches of discipline in Addington Camp'; ANZ, R22431358-AAYS-8638-AD1-779-24/152, 'Personnel – Police – Military – Featherston'.
78 For a discussion of such issues: Peter Clayworth, '"Lucky Laidlaw" and "Worried Webb": The Robert Laidlaw Exemption Case and Public Attitudes to Conscription in 1918', *Journal of New Zealand Studies*, NS20 (2015), pp.72–86.
79 Hill, *The Iron Hand in the Velvet Glove*, p.352; Horne, 'Remobilizing for "Total War"', p.210.
80 For an overtly revisionist perspective on this, and many other wartime issues, see Stevan Eldred-Grigg, *The Great Wrong War: New Zealand Society in WWI* (Auckland, 2010).
81 ANZ, R21371604-AAAB-478-3/w, 'EF [Expeditionary Force]: disloyalty'.
82 New Zealand Police, Circulars and Memoranda Book, 1877–1926, Hampden Police Station, Commissioner O'Donovan to Superintendent A.H. Wright, Dunedin, 5 February, 1917.
83 Graeme Dunstall, *A Policeman's Paradise?: Policing a Stable Society 1918–1945* (Wellington, 1999), p.42.
84 Over 2,000 defaulters remained at large by the end of June 1920, for example: ANZ, R22430678, AAYS-8638-AD1-780-24/188/2, 'Personnel – Military defaulters list – General file'; AJHR 1920, Session I, H-19, 'Defence Forces of New Zealand', p.11.
85 New Zealand Police Force, 'Minutes of Evidence Taken at the Police Commission' (Wellington, 1919: typescript in author's possession).
86 Cullen went on to become Commissioner of Aliens with the Defence Department, where his capacity for ruthlessness was again manifested: Hill, 'Cullen'.
87 Dunstall, *A Policeman's Paradise?*

Chapter Six – Striking a Balance: The Military Service Boards

1 This chapter is based on research conducted for the author's PhD thesis: David Littlewood, '"The Tool and Instrument of the Military"? The Operations of the Military Service Tribunals in the East Central Division of the West Riding of Yorkshire and those of the Military Service Boards in New Zealand, 1916–1918' (PhD Thesis, Massey University, 2015).

2 Archives New Zealand (ANZ), R10075058-AAYS-8698-AD82-2-1/11/2, 'Military Service Boards – General, October 1917 – December 1918', Widdowson to Allen, 13 December 1918.

3 John E. Martin, 'Blueprint for the Future? "National Efficiency" and the First World War', in John Crawford and Ian McGibbon (eds), *New Zealand's Great War: New Zealand, the Allies and the First World War* (Auckland, 2007), pp.522–523; Gwen A. Parsons, '"The Many Derelicts of the War"? Repatriation and Great War Veterans in Dunedin and Ashburton, 1918 to 1928' (PhD thesis, University of Otago, 2008), p.44; James Belich, *Paradise Reforged: A History of the New Zealanders from the 1880s to the Year 2000* (Auckland, 2001), p.101.

4 Len Richardson, *Coal, Class & Community: The United Mineworkers of New Zealand, 1880–1960* (Auckland, 1995), pp.171–173.

5 Paul Baker, *King and Country Call: New Zealanders, Conscription and the Great War* (Auckland, 1988), pp.122–129, 162–164.

6 Sonia Inder, 'Middlemarch, 1914–1918' (Research Essay, University of Otago, 1992), p.36; Lisa James, 'Doing Their Duty: The Impact of Conscription on Farming Families in New Zealand during the Great War' (Research Essay, Victoria University of Wellington, 2006), p.21; Kerry Stratton, '"Doing Their Bit": The Impact of the First World War on the Inhabitants of Tuapeka County' (Research Essay, University of Otago, 1992), pp.102–103.

7 Parsons, p.48; Ian McGibbon, 'Conscription', in Ian McGibbon (ed.), *The Oxford Companion to New Zealand Military History* (Auckland, 2000), p.118.

8 Paul Baker, 'New Zealanders, the Great War, and Conscription' (PhD Thesis, University of Auckland, 1986), p.258.

9 Wilford, *New Zealand Parliamentary Debates* (NZPD), Vol.178, 25 July 1917, p.717.

10 *New Zealand Statutes* (NZS), Military Service Act, 1916, No.8, sections 2–4.

11 NZS, Military Service Act, 1916, section 18.

12 NZS, Military Service Act, 1916, sections 25–28.

13 NZS, Military Service Act, 1916, section 19(3).

14 NZS, Military Service Act, 1916, section 18(3).

15 *New Zealand Herald* (NZH), 25 September 1916, p.7.

16 ANZ, R22430446-AAYS-8638-AD1-769-22/151, 'Courts Martial and Courts of Inquiry – Boards (Medical and Military Service) – Formation of Additional Boards', Robin to Allen, 16 January 1917. For example, while the Third Wellington Board largely remained in Wellington City, the First Wellington Board heard appeals across the Manawatu, Wanganui and Taranaki Recruiting Districts, and the Second Wellington Board worked the whole of Hawke's Bay, Poverty Bay and the Wairarapa.

17 *New Zealand Gazette* (NZG), 10 October 1916, p.3208.

18 ANZ, R10075002-AAYS-8698-AD82-7-30/1, 'Exemption – General, July 1916 – December 1918', Salmond to Gray, 1 December 1916.

19 ANZ, R10075002-AAYS-8698-AD82-7-30/1, 'Exemption – General, July 1916 – December 1918', Salmond to Gray, 1 December 1916.

20 ANZ, R10075075-AAYS-8698-AD82-4-5/1, 'Roman Catholic priests and Marist Brothers, November 1916 – July 1918', Allen to Coffey, 21 March 1917.
21 NZH, 24 November 1916, p.8.
22 ANZ, R10075033-AAYS-8698-82-8-74, 'Shearers and slaughtermen, November 1916 – March 1918', Allen to Reardon, 9 December 1916.
23 ANZ, R22319675-ADBQ-16145-ALLEN1-9, 'Miscellanous files and papers – Correspondence between J. Allen and W.F. Massey, 1st September 1916 – 1st August 1919', Allen to Massey, 19 December 1916.
24 *Evening Post* (EP), 14 February 1917, p.8; ANZ, R10075033-AAYS-8698-82-8-74, 'Shearers and slaughtermen, November 1916 – March 1918', Allen to Niall, 16 January 1918; ANZ, R10074998-AAYS-8698-AD82-7-28/1, 'General – Coalminers, September 1916 – October 1918', Allen to Webb, 2 September 1916.
25 ANZ, R22429092-AAYS-8638-AD1-712-9/169-2, 'Expeditionary Force – Recruiting organisation', Recruiting 1916–1918: Report by Director of Recruiting, 31 March 1919.
26 ANZ, R10075057-AAYS-8698-AD82-2-1/11/1, 'Military Service Boards – General, August 1916 – October 1917', Gray to Fraser, 11 September 1916.
27 EP, 14 September 1916, p.8; EP, 27 September 1916, p.3.
28 Keith Sinclair, *A Destiny Apart: New Zealand's Search for National Identity* (Wellington, 1986), p.173. For examples see NZH, 23 February 1917, p.8; EP, 14 June 1917, p.2; *Wairarapa Daily Times* (WDT), 22 December 1917, p.4.
29 For examples see WDT, 13 December 1916, p.2; *Timaru Herald*, 6 February 1917, p.5; *Dannevirke Evening News*, 20 March 1917, p.3.
30 *Ohinemuri Gazette*, 29 September 1916, p.2; *Ashburton Guardian* (AG), 13 May 1918, p.4; *Otago Daily Times* (ODT), 19 September 1918, p.5.
31 ANZ, R10075057-AAYS-8698-AD82-2-1/11/1, 'Military Service Boards – General, August 1916 – October 1917', Gray to Fraser, 11 September 1916; Alexander Turnbull Library (ATL), MS-1164, McCaw, John, 1849–1930, 'Biography of my life for the benefit of my children', 1929.
32 ANZ, R22430442-AAYS-8638-AD1-769-22/117, 'Courts Martial and Courts of Inquiry – Boards (military service) proposals', Rosser to Allen, 12 September 1916.
33 ATL, MS-Papers-6164-046, 'Edward Kellett', Roth, Herbert Otto, 1917–1994: Papers (MS-Group-0314); *Maoriland Worker*, 29 November 1916, p.3.
34 NZG, 26 September 1916, p.3125.
35 G.H. Scholefield, *Who's Who in New Zealand and the Western Pacific, 1925* (Napier, 1924), p.51.
36 Scholefield, p.176; Barry Gustafson, *Labour's Path to Political Independence: The Origins and Establishment of the New Zealand Labour Party, 1900–19*, (Auckland, 1980), p.161.
37 EP, 27 September 1916, p.3.
38 James Holt, *Compulsory Arbitration in New Zealand: The First Forty Years* (Auckland, 1986), p.28.
39 Baker, *King and Country*, pp.54–56; James Watson, 'Patriotism, Profits and Problems: New Zealand Farming during the Great War', in *New Zealand's Great War*, pp.535–536.
40 ANZ, R22429092-AAYS-8638-AD1-712-9/169-2, 'Expeditionary Force – Recruiting organisation', Recruiting 1916–1918: Report by Director of Recruiting, 31 March 1919.
41 David Littlewood, '"Should He Serve?": The Military Service Boards' Operations in the Wellington Provincial District, 1916–1918' (MA thesis, Massey University, 2010), p.16.

42 ANZ, R22319700-ADBQ-16145-ALLEN1-2-M1/15-4, 'Ministerial Files – Correspondence with General Godley', Allen to Godley, 6 February 1917.

43 Baker, *King and Country*, p.142; John Crawford, '"New Zealand is Being Bled to Death": The Formation, Operations and Disbandment of the Fourth Brigade', in *New Zealand's Great War*, p.263.

44 ANZ, R22319700-ADBQ-16145-ALLEN1-2-M1/15-4, 'Ministerial Files – Correspondence with General Godley', Allen to Birdwood, 31 July 1917; ANZ, R22319700-ADBQ-16145- ALLEN1-2-M1/15-4, 'Ministerial Files – Correspondence with General Godley', Allen to Godley, 7 August 1917.

45 ANZ, R22319700-ADBQ-16145-ALLEN1-2-M1/15-4, 'Ministerial Files – Correspondence with General Godley', Allen to Godley, 23 July 1917.

46 ANZ, R22336788-ADBQ-16145-ALLEN1-3-M1/57-2, 'Ministerial Files – Correspondence with Governor General', Liverpool to Bonar Law, 17 July 1917 and 17 August 1917.

47 ANZ, R22319674-ADBQ-16145-ALLEN1-9, 'Miscellanous files and papers – Correspondence with Colonels Birdwood and Russell, December 1914 – April 1920 and copies of personal letters, 1920', Allen to Russell, 29 January 1918.

48 ANZ, R22319674-ADBQ-16145-ALLEN1-9, 'Miscellanous files and papers – Correspondence with Colonels Birdwood and Russell, December 1914 – April 1920 and copies of personal letters, 1920', Allen to Birdwood, 10 April 1918.

49 ANZ, R22319674-ADBQ-16145-ALLEN1-9, 'Miscellanous files and papers – Correspondence with Colonels Birdwood and Russell, December 1914 – April 1920 and copies of personal letters, 1920', Allen to Birdwood, 10 April 1918; Massey, NZPD, Vol.182, 11 April 1918, p.65.

50 This information regarding embarkations is drawn from the Auckland War Memorial Museum's Online Cenotaph (http://www.aucklandmuseum.com/war-memorial/online-cenotaph).

51 Baker, 'New Zealanders', Appendix 25.

52 *Akaroa Mail and Banks Peninsula Advertiser* (AMBPA), 14 April 1917, p.2; M.J. Kelly, *Military Board Appeals: Otago Witness, March 1917 to July 1917* (Auckland, 1994), pp.27–28.

53 ANZ, R10075057-AAYS-8698-AD82-2-1/11/1, 'Military Service Boards – General, August 1916 – October 1917', Gray to Military Representatives, 16 March 1917; ANZ, R22319675-ADBQ-16145-ALLEN1-9, 'Miscellanous files and papers – Correspondence between J. Allen and W.F. Massey, 1st September 1916 – 1st August 1919', Allen to Massey, 17 March 1917.

54 ANZ, R10075057-AAYS-8698-AD82-2-1/11/1, 'Military Service Boards – General, August 1916 – October 1917', Gray to Military Service Board Chairmen, 10 July 1917.

55 ANZ, R10075057-AAYS-8698-AD82-2-1/11/1, 'Military Service Boards – General, August 1916 – October 1917', Gray to Military Service Board Chairmen, 17 April 1918.

56 ANZ, R22429828-AAYS-8638-AD1-736-10/512, 'Territorial Force – Exemption – Reservists under Military Service Act', Gray to Allen, 20 May 1918; ANZ, R10075057-AAYS-8698-AD82-2-1/11/1, 'Military Service Boards – General, August 1916 – October 1917', Gray to Military Service Board Chairmen, 12 June 1918.

57 ANZ, R22319675-ADBQ-16145-ALLEN1-9, 'Miscellanous files and papers – Correspondence between J. Allen and W.F. Massey, 1st September 1916 – 1st August 1919', Allen to Massey, 19 December 1916; ANZ, R10075075-AAYS-

8698-AD82-4-5/1, 'Roman Catholic priests and Marist Brothers, November 1916 – July 1918', Allen to Coffey, 21 March 1917.

58 ANZ, R10075075-AAYS-8698-AD82-4-5/1, 'Roman Catholic priests and Marist Brothers, November 1916 – July 1918', O'Shea to Allen, 17 February; EP, 17 February 1917, pp.5, 9.

59 ANZ, R10075075-AAYS-8698-AD82-4-5/1, 'Roman Catholic priests and Marist Brothers, November 1916 – July 1918', Allen to O'Shea, 26 February 1917.

60 ANZ, R10075075-AAYS-8698-AD82-4-5/1, 'Roman Catholic priests and Marist Brothers, November 1916 – July 1918', Coffey to Allen, 16 March 1917.

61 ANZ, R10075075-AAYS-8698-AD82-4-5/1, 'Roman Catholic priests and Marist Brothers, November 1916 – July 1918', Gray to Allen, 30 March 1917.

62 ANZ, R10075075-AAYS-8698-AD82-4-5/1, 'Roman Catholic priests and Marist Brothers, November 1916 – July 1918', Gray to Tate, 27 March 1917.

63 ANZ, R22319675-ADBQ-16145-ALLEN1-9, 'Miscellanous files and papers – Correspondence between J. Allen and W.F. Massey, 1st September 1916 – 1st August 1919', Allen to Massey, 28 April 1917.

64 ANZ, R22430349-AAYS-8638-AD1-765-20/43, 'Conferences – Conference – Chairmen Military Service Boards', 27 April 1917.

65 P.S. O'Connor, 'Storm Over the Clergy – New Zealand, 1917', *Journal of Religious History*, 4/2 (1966), p.140; ANZ, R10075011-AAYS-8698-AD82-7-46/7, 'Chairmen of MS [Military Service] Boards, July – August 1917', Conference of Military Service Boards: 2 August 1917.

66 Ward, NZPD, Vol.181, 11 October 1917, pp.46–48; NZPD, Vol.181, 25 October 1917, pp.496–497; NZPD, Vol.181, 30 October 1917, p.652.

67 ANZ, R10075005-AAYS-8698-AD82-7-46/1, 'Chairmen of MS [Military Service] Boards, 29 November 1917', Conference of Military Service Boards, 29 November 1917.

68 ANZ, R10075005-AAYS-8698-AD82-7-46/1, 'Chairmen of MS [Military Service] Boards, 29 November 1917', Conference of Military Service Boards, 29 November 1917; ANZ, R10075075-AAYS-8698-AD82-4-5/1, 'Roman Catholic priests and Marist Brothers, November 1916 – July 1918', Gray to Cosgrove, 10 June 1918.

69 *Dominion*, 17 May 1918, p.7; EP, 7 August 1918, p.3.

70 ANZ, R10075075-AAYS-8698-AD82-4-5/1, 'Roman Catholic priests and Marist Brothers, November 1916 – July 1918', Gray to Cosgrove.

71 *Appendices to the Journal of the House of Representatives* (AJHR), 1917, H-34, 'Proposals for the Organization of Industries in New Zealand, during the War and Afterwards'.

72 AJHR, 1917, H-43-B, 'Classification of Industries, Professions, and Occupations, as Approved by Government'.

73 ANZ, R22319695-ADBQ-16145-ALLEN1-11, 'Miscellaneous files and papers – National Efficiency Board, miscellaneous papers', Allen to Massey, 18 September 1917.

74 ANZ, R10075057-AAYS-8698-AD82-2-1/11/1, 'Military Service Boards – General, August 1916 – October 1917', Gray to Military Service Board Chairmen, 30 July 1917.

75 ANZ, R10075058-AAYS-8698-AD82-2-1/11/2, 'Military Service Boards – General, October 1917 – December 1918', Gray to Military Service Board Chairmen, 5 March 1918.

76 See correspondence in ANZ, R10075057-AAYS-8698-AD82-2-1/11/1, 'Military Service Boards – General, August 1916 – October 1917' and ANZ, R10075058-AAYS-8698-AD82-2-1/11/2, 'Military Service Boards – General, October 1917 – December 1918'.

77 ANZ, R10075033-AAYS-8698-AD82-8-74, 'Shearers and slaughtermen, November 1916 – March 1918', Poynton to Moss, 28 November 1917; WDT, 22 December 1917, p.4.
78 ANZ, R10075025-AAYS-8698-AD82-1-1/4, '2nd Wellington MS [Military Service] Board – General, January 1917 – November 1918', Gray to Poynton, 15 January 1918.
79 R10074998-AAYS-8698-AD82-7-28/1, 'General – Coalminers, September 1916 – October 1918', Evans to Gray, 16 February 1917.
80 Len Richardson, 'Politics and War: Coal Miners and Conscription, 1914–18', in Philip Ross May (ed.), *Miners and Militants: Politics in Westland, 1865–1918* (Christchurch, 1975), pp.140–141.
81 ANZ, R10074998-AAYS-8698-AD82-7-28/1, 'General – Coalminers, September 1916 – October 1918', Gray to Evans, 17 February 1917.
82 Len Richardson, 'The Workers and Grey District Politics during Wartime, 1914–1918' (MA thesis, University of Canterbury, 1968), p.143.
83 R10074998-AAYS-8698-AD82-7-28/1, 'General – Coalminers, September 1916 – October 1918', Gray to Evans, 30 April 1917 and 1 May 1917.
84 R10074998-AAYS-8698-AD82-7-28/1, 'General – Coalminers, September 1916 – October 1918', Gray to Evans, 14 May 1917 and 25 June 1917; ANZ, R22429816-AAYS-8638-AD1-736-10/483, 'Territorial Force – Coalminers and Military Service Act', Gray to Commandant, 6 July 1917.
85 R10074998-AAYS-8698-AD82-7-28/1, 'General – Coalminers, September 1916 – October 1918', Milton to Gray, 22 May 1918.
86 ANZ, R22429816-AAYS-8638-AD1-736-10/483, 'Territorial Force – Coalminers and Military Service Act', Tate to General Officer Commanding, 2 September 1918; R10074998-AAYS-8698-AD82-7-28/1, 'General – Coalminers, September 1916 – October 1918', Gray to Milton, 6 June 1918.
87 *Farmers' Union Advocate*, 9 December 1916, p.5; *Auckland Star*, 12 January 1917, p.4 and 7 March 1917, p.8.
88 ANZ, R22319675-ADBQ-16145-ALLEN1-9, 'Miscellanous files and papers – Correspondence between J. Allen and W.F. Massey, 1st September 1916 – 1st August 1919', Allen to Massey, 17 March 1917.
89 ANZ, R10075057-AAYS-8698-AD82-2-1/11/1, 'Military Service Boards – General, August 1916 – October 1917', Gray to Military Representatives, 16 March 1917.
90 ANZ, R10075057-AAYS-8698-AD82-2-1/11/1, 'Military Service Boards – General, August 1916 – October 1917', Gray to Military Service Board Chairmen, 23 March 1917, 31 March 1917 and 5 May 1917.
91 Anstey, NZPD, Vol.178, 18 July 1917, p.480; Wilkinson, NZPD, Vol.179, 24 August 1917, p.614.
92 ANZ, R10075057-AAYS-8698-AD82-2-1/11/1, 'Military Service Boards – General, August 1916 – October 1917', Gray to Military Service Board Chairmen, 12 October 1917.
93 ANZ, R10075064-AAYS-8698-AD82-1-1/3, '1st Wellington MS [Military Service] Board – General, September 1916 – December 1918', Gray to Cooper, 26 October 1917.
94 ANZ, R10075058-AAYS-8698-AD82-2-1/11/2, 'Military Service Boards – General, October 1917 – December 1918', Gray to Military Service Board Chairmen, 12 June 1918; WDT, 22 June 1918, p.6 and 5 July 1918, p.5.
95 EP, 20 March 1917, p.7.
96 ANZ, R10075011-AAYS-8698-AD82-7-46/7, 'Chairmen of MS [Military Service] Boards, July – August 1917', Conference of Military Service Boards, 2 August

1917; ANZ, R10075005-AAYS-8698-AD82-7-46/1, 'Chairmen of MS [Military Service] Boards, 29 November 1917', Conference of Military Service Boards, 29 November 1917.

97 ANZ, R10074998-AAYS-8698-AD82-7-28/1, 'General – Coalminers, September 1916 – October 1918', Evans to Gray, 2 May 1917.

98 ANZ, R10074998-AAYS-8698-AD82-7-28/1, 'General – Coalminers, September 1916 – October 1918', Gray to Evans, 14 May 1917 and 25 June 1917; *Grey River Argus* (GRA), 19 June 1917, p.3; GRA, 18 July 1917, p.3; GRA, 15 August 1917, p.4.

99 ANZ, R10075064-AAYS-8698-AD82-1-1/3, '1st Wellington MS [Military Service] Board – General, September 1916 – December 1918', Cooper to Gray, 15 October 1917.

100 ANZ, R10075058-AAYS-8698-AD82-2-1/11/2, 'Military Service Boards – General, October 1917 – December 1918', Gray to Military Service Board Chairmen, 5 March 1918.

101 ANZ, R3091131-ADRE-17315-NEB1-16-703, 'Report of Second Military Service Board's Conference', Ferguson to Gray, 4 August 1918.

102 EP, 27 July 1917, p.7; ANZ, R10075075-AAYS-8698-AD82-4-5/1, 'Roman Catholic priests and Marist Brothers, November 1916 – July 1918', Gray to Allen, 9 November 1917.

103 ANZ, R10074998-AAYS-8698-AD82-7-28/1, 'General – Coalminers, September 1916 – October 1918', Myers to Cabinet, 11 January 1917; Baker, *King and Country*, p.119.

104 EP, 30 December 1916, p.6; EP, 31 January 1917, p.7; EP, 18 April 1917, p.8.

105 EP, 14 February 1917, p.8.

106 *New Zealand Times*, 20 April 1917, p.7; ANZ, R10075033-AAYS-8698-AD82-8-74, 'Shearers and slaughtermen, November 1916 – March 1918', Conference re Freezing Industry Employees and Military Service, 6 October 1917.

107 EP, 20 April 1917, p.7.

108 Baker, 'New Zealanders', pp.258–262.

109 Allen, NZPD, Vol.178, 18 July 1917, pp.480, 482; NZPD, Vol.178, 27 July 1917, p.824; NZPD, Vol.178, 31 July 1917, p., 833; Allen, NZPD, Vol.180, 21 September 1917, p.314.

110 ANZ, R22319675-ADBQ-16145-ALLEN1-9, 'Miscellaneous files and papers – Correspondence between J. Allen and W.F. Massey, 1st September 1916 – 1st August 1919', Allen to Massey; ANZ, R10075057-AAYS-8698-AD82-2-1/11/1, 'Military Service Boards – General, August 1916 – October 1917', Allen to Ward; ANZ, R22319700-ADBQ-16145- ALLEN1-2-M1/15-4, 'Ministerial Files – Correspondence with General Godley', Allen to Godley, 27 March 1917.

111 *Hawera & Normanby Star*, 23 October 1917, p.4; ODT, 31 October 1917, pp.2–3; *Southland Times* (ST), 7 December 1917, p.4.

112 AJHR, 1917, H-43-B, 'Classification of Industries, Professions, and Occupations, as Approved by Government'.

113 EP, 11 May 1917, p.2; ANZ, R3091131-ADRE-17315-NEB1-16-703, 'Report of Second Military Service Board's Conference', Gray to Ferguson, 8 August 1917.

114 ANZ, R22429092-AAYS-8638-AD1-712-9/169-2, 'Expeditionary Force – Recruiting organisation', Recruiting 1916–1918: Report by Director of Recruiting, 31 March 1919.

115 Allen, NZPD, Vol. 178, 31 July 1917, pp.833–834.

116 ODT, 9 June 1917, p.11; ODT, 28 June 1917, p.2; GRA, 6 December 1917, p.4; GRA, 20 March 1918, p.4.

117 AG, 8 October 1918, p.4.
118 ANZ, R10075068-AAYS-8698-AD82-3-1/22, 'Report of Wellington MS [Military Service] Board, December 1918', Cooper to Gray, 10 December 1918; ANZ, R3091131-ADRE-17315-NEB1-16-703, 'Report of Second Military Service Board's Conference', Day to Ferguson, 29 August 1917; ANZ, R10075058-AAYS-8698-AD82-2-1/11/2, 'Military Service Boards – General, October 1917 – December 1918', Burgess to Gray, 5 December 1918.
119 ANZ, R10074998-AAYS-8698-AD82-7-28/1, 'General – Coalminers, September 1916 – October 1918', Evans to Gray, 16 November 1917.
120 ANZ, R10074998-AAYS-8698-AD82-7-28/1, 'General – Coalminers, September 1916 – October 1918', Milton to Gray, 28 May 1918 and 4 June 1918.
121 ANZ, R10075057-AAYS-8698-AD82-2-1/11/1, 'Military Service Boards – General, August 1916 – October 1917', Return of Military Service Boards, undated.
122 ANZ, R10074998-AAYS-8698-AD82-7-28/1, 'General – Coalminers, September 1916 – October 1918', Evans to Gray, 2 July 1917.
123 ANZ, R10074998-AAYS-8698-AD82-7-28/1, 'General – Coalminers, September 1916 – October 1918', Milton to Gray, 4 June 1918.
124 ANZ, R10074998-AAYS-8698-AD82-7-28/1, 'General – Coalminers, September 1916 – October 1918', Gray to Milton, 6 June 1918.
125 ANZ, R10075005-AAYS-8698-AD82-7-46/1, 'Chairmen of MS [Military Service] Boards, 29 November 1917', Conference of Military Service Boards, 29 November 1917; ANZ, R10075075-AAYS-8698-AD82-4-5/1, 'Roman Catholic priests and Marist Brothers, November 1916 – July 1918', Gray to Cosgrove, 10 June 1918; WDT, 7 June 1918, p.6.
126 ANZ, R10075057-AAYS-8698-AD82-2-1/11/1, 'Military Service Boards – General, August 1916 – October 1917', Return of Military Service Boards, undated.
127 EP, 17 February 1917, p.5; EP, 17 March 1917, p.6.
128 M.J. Kelly, *Military Board Appeals: Otago Witness, Dec 1916 to Feb 1917* (Auckland, 1993), pp.47–48.
129 ANZ, R10074998-AAYS-8698-AD82-7-28/1, 'General – Coalminers, September 1916 – October 1918', Evans to Gray, 16 February 1917 and 28 April 1917.
130 ANZ, R10074998-AAYS-8698-AD82-7-28/1, 'General – Coalminers, September 1916 – October 1918', Evans to Allen, 13 March 1917.
131 ANZ, R22429828-AAYS-8638-AD1-736-10/512, 'Territorial Force – Exemption – Reservists under Military Service Act', Gray to Allen, 20 May 1918 and Burgess and Earl to Gray, 27 May 1918.
132 EP, 23 May 1918, p.8.
133 ST, 14 March 1917, p.5; NZH, 21 May 1917, p.7.
134 ANZ, R10075057-AAYS-8698-AD82-2-1/11/1, 'Military Service Boards – General, August 1916 – October 1917', Evans to Gray, 9 December 1918 and Widdowson to Allen, 13 December 1918; *Press*, 13 January 1917, p.13.
135 ANZ, R3091131-ADRE-17315-NEB1-16-703, 'Report of Second Military Service Board's Conference', Cooper to Ferguson, 27 August 1917.
136 ANZ, R10075057-AAYS-8698-AD82-2-1/11/1, 'Military Service Boards – General, August 1916 – October 1917', Tendall to Gray, 14 September 1917.
137 EP, 28 February 1917, p.7.
138 ANZ, R22429092-AAYS-8638-AD1-712-9/169-2, 'Expeditionary Force – Recruiting organisation', Recruiting 1916–1918: Report by Director of Recruiting, 31 March 1919.

Chapter Seven – War a Daily Reminder, But Life Goes On: Newspapers during the First World War

1 Steven Loveridge, '"Sentimental Equipment": New Zealand, the Great War and Cultural Mobilisation' (PhD thesis, Victoria University of Wellington, 2013), p.287; Andrew Francis, 'Anti-Alienism in New Zealand during the Great War: The von Zedlitz Affair, 1915', *Immigrants & Minorities*, 24/3 (November 2006), p.255.
2 Christopher Clark, *The Sleepwalkers: How Europe Went To War in 1914* (New York, 2013), p.238.
3 *New Zealand Free Lance* (NZFL), 28 March 1918, p.6.
4 *Truth*, for example, cut its page numbers and noted that 'small type has been resorted to'. *Truth*, 15 August 1914, p.4.
5 For further reading on New Zealand newspapers see David Hastings, *Extra! Extra!: How the People Made the News* (Auckland, 2013); Guy Scholefield, *Newspapers in New Zealand* (Wellington, 1958).
6 Scholefield, p.6.
7 For further reading on nineteenth-century newspapers see Ross Harvey, 'Economic Aspects of Nineteenth-Century New Zealand Newspapers', *Bibliographical Society of Australia and New Zealand*, 17/2 (1993), pp.55–78 and Harvey, 'The Power of the Press in Colonial New Zealand: More Imagined than Real?', *BSANZ Bulletin*, 20/2 (1996), pp.130–145.
8 Ian F. Grant, 'The News in New Zealand Newspapers during World War One', *Turnbull Library Record* (2014), p.27.
9 Alongside its London arrangements, the UPA had an office in Sydney to organise dispatches across the Tasman.
10 Simon J. Potter, 'Communication and Integration: The British and Dominions Press and the British World, c. 1876–1914', in Carl Bridger and Kent Fedorowich (eds), *The British World: Diaspora, Culture and Identity* (London, 2003), p.197.
11 Potter, p.197.
12 *Wairarapa Age* (WA), 17 April 1913, p.4.
13 Redmer Yska, *Truth: The Rise and Fall of the People's Paper* (Nelson, 2010), p.40.
14 Though several papers also reproduced overseas cartoons.
15 Kate Hunter and Kirstie Ross, *Holding On To Home: New Zealand Stories and Objects of the First World War* (Wellington, 2014), p.101.
16 Sarah Murray, *A Cartoon War: The Cartoons of the New Zealand Free Lance and New Zealand Observer as Historical Sources, August 1914–November 1918*, New Zealand Cartoon Archive Monograph Series No.1 (Wellington, 2012), p.3.
17 Though there has been some questioning of the relationship between these reports and public mood: 'The announcement [of war] generated excitement according to newspaper reports, but there is evidence to suggest that not everyone was enthusiastic about the news.' Graham Hucker, '"The Great Wave of Enthusiasm": New Zealand Reactions to the First World War in August 1914 – a Reassessment', *New Zealand Journal of History* (NZJH), 43/1 (April 2009), p.61.
18 *Poverty Bay Herald* (PBH), 6 August 1914, p.2.
19 *Grey River Argus* (GRA), 5 August 1914, p.4.
20 *Truth*, 15 August 1914, p.1.
21 *Maoriland Worker* (MW), 5 August 1914, p.4.
22 Possibly, Gwen Parsons goes too far when she suggests that 'support for the war was class-divided' – the elites and middle class generally in favour and the labour movement and its supporters against. This might have been so for a small number

of political activists of the right and left, but it is also true that the peace movement had middle-class roots and there is no doubt that the working classes provided, willingly in the beginning, a clear majority of military volunteers. Gwen Parsons, 'Debating The War: The Discourses of War in the Christchurch Community', in John Crawford and Ian McGibbon (eds), *New Zealand's Great War: New Zealand, the Allies and the First World War* (Auckland, 2007), p.550. A survey in the *Christchurch Star*, prompted by a reader's comment, analysed the composition of the Canterbury mounted section of the 4th Reinforcements, which consisted of 106 officers and men. The figures were as follows: 20 labourers, 4 shepherds, 4 blacksmiths, 4 farm hands, 4 bushmen, 3 butchers, 3 miners, 3 drapers, 2 sawmillers, 2 shearers, 2 ploughmen, a baker, a stockman, a groom, a coachman, a carter, a cleaner, a cook and a porter – or 62 drawn from what were termed the working classes. There were also 29 farmers, leaving 15 from the 'professional' classes. *Christchurch Star*, 26 May 1915, p.4.

23 Hunter and Ross, p.100.

24 Sandra Callister, '*Stabat mater dolorosa*: Death, Photography and Collective Mourning', NZJH, 41/1 (April 2007), p.13.

25 In March 1915, there had been heady press optimism that Germany would soon be defeated. A *Feilding Star* item was typical of stories New Zealand papers ran: '"At the end of three months' war, definite victory awaits us." These words are reported as coming from Field-Marshal Sir John French in an interview. The end of the war by the end of June! Well, why not? The steel girder binds the enemy closer every day and the Allies are on the eve of coming out of their trenches for the forward movement.' *Feilding Star* (FS), 25 March 1915, p.2.

26 GRA, 27 April 1915, p.5; *Taranaki Daily News*, 27 April 1915, p.5.

27 *Wairarapa Daily Times* (WDT), 27 April 1915, p.4.

28 *Dominion*, 27 April 1915, p.4.

29 *Auckland Star* (AS), 27 April 1915, p.4.

30 *Bay of Plenty Times* (BPT), 27 April 1915, p.2; *Thames Star* (TS), 27 April 1915, p.4.

31 For further analysis of commercial patriotism see Francis, '*To Be Truly British We Must Be Anti-German': New Zealand, Enemy Aliens and the Great War Experience, 1914–1919* (New York, 2012), pp.181–213.

32 *Press*, 27 April 1915, p.4.

33 PBH, 27 April 1915, p.5.

34 *Dominion*, 27 April 1915, p.7.

35 *Akaroa Mail* (AM), 6 November 1914, p.2.

36 AM, 25 May 1915, p.2.

37 AM, 29 June 1915, p.3.

38 *Otago Daily Times* (ODT), 11 March 1915, p.6.

39 *Northern Advocate*, 11 March 1915, p.4.

40 BPT, 20 March 1915, p.3.

41 For example, *New Zealand Listener*, 2 May 2015, p.7.

42 *Dominion*, 29 April 1915, p.4.

43 *Waikato Times* (WT), 30 April 1915, p.5.

44 WT, 30 April 1915, p.5.

45 The significance of Britain's media network was exploited by Charles Masterman's London-based War Propaganda Bureau, which began disseminating a wide array of media material intended to effectively portray the British/Allied cause. C. Roetter, *Psychological Warfare* (London, 1974), pp.33–35.

46 FS, 6 May 1915, p.3.

47 WT, 30 April 1915, p.5.

48 WT, 30 April 1915, p.5.
49 ODT, 1 May 1915, p.7.
50 WA, 5 May 1915, p.5.
51 AS, 6 May 1915, p.5.
52 AS, 13 May 1915, p.5.
53 WDT, 17 May 1915, p.5.
54 *Wanganui Chronicle*, 25 June 1915, p.4.
55 Loveridge, *Calls to Arms: New Zealand Society and Commitment to the Great War* (Wellington, 2014), p.103.
56 Ron Palenski, 'Malcolm Ross: A Forgotten Casualty of the Great War' (MA thesis, University of Otago, 2008), p.117. See also Palenski, 'Malcolm Ross: A New Zealand Failure in the Great War', *Australian Historical Studies*, 1 (2008), pp.19–35.
57 Allison Oosterman, 'Covering Gallipoli: A New Zealand war correspondent in the age of empires', *Politics, Media, History: Australian Media Traditions* conference, University of Canberra, 2005, p.18.
58 Oosterman, p.8. Ross's war journalism was also the basis of a book. See Malcolm Ross and Noel Ross, *Light and Shade in War* (London, 1916).
59 Paul Baker, *King and Country Call: New Zealanders, Conscription and the Great War* (Auckland, 1988), pp.42–58. Unsurprisingly, there were very few newspaper stories concerning Australian referendums rejecting conscription.
60 BPT, 3 August 1915, p.2.
61 Loveridge, 'Soldiers and Shirkers: An Analysis of the Dominant Ideas of Service and Conscientious Objection in New Zealand during the Great War' (MA thesis, University of Waikato, 2009), p.71.
62 Francis, 'Anti-Alienism in New Zealand during the Great War', p.255.
63 NZFL, 22 October 1915, p.8.
64 Francis, *To Be Truly British*, pp.153–154.
65 For extensive examples and analysis see Murray.
66 Ian F. Grant, *The Unauthorized Version: A Cartoon History of New Zealand* (Auckland, 1980), p.81.
67 MW, 1 September 1915, p.4.
68 The *Maoriland Worker*'s income appears to have suffered during the war. Jack Vowles, 'Ideology and the Formation of the New Zealand Labour Party: Some New Evidence', NZJH, 16/1 (April 1982), pp.46–47.
69 Yska, *Truth*, p.55. See also Yska, 'The First World War and Truth', in Charles Ferrall and Harry Ricketts (eds), *How We Remember: New Zealanders and the First World War* (Wellington, 2014), pp.147–159.
70 Seren Wendelken, 'Visual Constructs of Wealth' in *The Maoriland Worker*, 1911–12: Cartoon and Intertext', in Miles Fairburn and Erik Olssen (eds), *Class, Gender and the Vote: Historical Perspectives from New Zealand* (Dunedin, 2005), pp.193–216.
71 Archives New Zealand collects records of censor rebukes against various newspapers who breached censorship regulations. See records under AAYS-8638-AD1-(Box/Item 702-706).
72 FS, 10 August 1914, p.2.
73 John Anderson, 'Military Censorship in World War 1: Its Use and Abuse in New Zealand' (MA thesis, Victoria University College, Wellington, 1952), p.169.
74 AS, 8 October 1914, pp.4–6.
75 *New Zealand Statutes*, 1914, No.38, pp.28–29.
76 *Timaru Herald*, 20 August 1914, p.6.
77 FS, 4 March 1915, p.1.

78 Anderson, p.194.
79 AS, 4 April 1916, p.8.
80 TS, 9 June 1916, p.5.
81 Anderson, p.200.
82 Michael Bassett and Michael King, *Tomorrow Comes the Song: A Life of Peter Fraser* (Auckland, 2000), p.73.
83 R.B. O'Neill, *The Press, 1861–1961: The Story of a Newspaper* (Christchurch, 1963), p.154.
84 O'Neill, p.154.

Chapter Eight – Negotiating Conditions and Commitment: The Union Movement and the First World War

1 For the Waihi and waterfront strikes of 1912–13 see Erik Olssen, *The Red Feds: Revolutionary Industrial Unionism and the New Zealand Federation of Labour 1908–14* (Auckland, 1988), pp.148–160 (for Waihi), 180–197 (for 1913).
2 Throughout this chapter figures relating to the numbers of unions registered under the Industrial Conciliation and Arbitration Act and their membership are from *Appendices to the Journal of the House of Representatives* (AJHR), H-11A, 1901 onwards. For the UFL's foundation see Erik Olssen, *The Red Feds*, pp. 163–179.
3 The most incisive analysis of the figures relating to union membership remains Miles Fairburn, 'Why Did the New Zealand Labour Party Fail to Win Office until 1935?', *Political Science*, 37 (December 1985), pp.101–124 and Fairburn and Stephen Haslett, 'Cleavage Within the Working Class? The Working Class Vote for the Labour Party in New Zealand, 1911–51', *Labour History*, 88 (May 2005), pp.183–214.
4 Herbert Roth, *Trade Unions in New Zealand: Past and Present* (Wellington, 1973), Table 4, p.171.
5 Allen was assistant editor of the *Maoriland Worker* and took over on Holland's arrest, although, because of his views, he did not last long. For Holland's views, see P.J. O'Farrell, *Harry Holland: Militant Socialist* (Canberra, 1964), pp.65–67; for Allen's views see Olssen, 'W.T. Mills, E.J.B. Allen, J.A. Lee and Socialism in New Zealand', *New Zealand Journal of History* (NZJH), 10/2 (October 1976), p.119.
6 Cited by Julius Braunthal, *History of the International 1914–1943*, translated by John Clark, London, 1967, pp. 29–30.
7 For the plumetting revenue, see Jack Vowles, 'Ideology and the Formation of the New Zealand Labour Party: Some New Evidence', NZJH, 16/1 (April 1982), pp.46–47.
8 The movement was strongest in Christchurch. See Jim McAloon, 'Radical Christchurch', in John Cookson and Graeme Dunstall (eds), *Southern Capital: Christchurch, Towards a City Biography 1850–2000* (Christchurch, 2000), pp.176–78 and Melanie Nolan, *Kin: A Collective Biography of a New Zealand Working-class Family* (Christchurch, 2005), pp.74–76.
9 This aspect of some branches of the socialist movement often gets overlooked. Olssen *The Red Feds*, pp.113–115, 128–130, 133–134 and Jared Davidson, *Sewing Freedom: Philip Josephs, Transnationalism & Early New Zealand Anarchism* (Oakland and Edinburgh, 2013), pp.51–77.
10 The *Maoriland Worker* provided full coverage of this conference. For an extended discussion see Olssen and Len Richardson, 'The New Zealand Labour Movement, 1880–1920', in Eric Fry (ed.), *Common Cause* (Wellington and Sydney, 1986), pp.13–15.

11 The Industrial Workers of the World ('Wobblies'), founded in the United States in 1905 and powerful on the West Coast of North America, enjoyed considerable influence throughout New Zealand in 1912–13. See Olssen, *The Red Feds*, passim.

12 R.C.J. Stone, 'The Unions and the Arbitration System, 1900–1937', in Robert Chapman and Keith Sinclair (eds.), *Studies of a Small Democracy: Essays in Honour of Willis Airey* (Auckland, 1963), p.207.

13 H. Stuart Hughes, *Consciousness and Society* (New York, 1958); Eric Hobsbawm, *Nations and Nationalism since 1780: Programme, Myth, Reality*, 2nd ed. (Cambridge, 1992), pp.101–130.

14 Others feared that any disruption to external trade would cause business failures and unemployment. James Holt, *Compulsory Arbitration in New Zealand: The First Forty Years* (Auckland, 1986), pp.119–120.

15 For the changing regional strength of the union movement see Olssen, 'The Origins of the Labour Party: A Reconsideration', NZJH, 21/1 (April 1987), pp.84–85. For an excellent case study of the SDP in Christchurch, see Libby Plumridge, 'The Necessary But Not Sufficient Condition: Christchurch Labour and Working-Class Culture', NZJH, 19/2 (October 1985), pp.130–150.

16 These moves are well documented. See B.S. Gustafson, *Labour's Path to Political Independence: The Origins and Establishment of the New Zealand Labour Party 1900–19* (Auckland, 1980), pp.82–84.

17 Roth, p.41.

18 See Michael Bassett, *Three Party Politics in New Zealand 1911–1931* (Te Atatu North, 1982), pp.15–20 and Bassett and Michael King, *Tomorrow Comes the Song: A Life of Peter Fraser* (Auckland, 2000), pp.64–67.

19 For a study based on ten provincial towns, see Miles Fairburn and Stephen Haslett, 'Cleavage Within the Working Class? The Working-Class Vote for the Labour Party in New Zealand, 1911–1951', *Labour History*, 88 (May 2005), pp.183–214 and 'How Far Did Class Determine Voting in New Zealand General Elections, 1911–1951?', NZJH, 39/2 (October 2005), pp.215–242. For a case study which reaches the same conclusions see Olssen and Bruce Scates, 'Class Formation and Political Change: A Trans-Tasman Dialogue', *Labour History*, 95 (November 2008), pp.3–14.

20 Holt, p.120 summarises the evidence.

21 See for instance the reports of the many branches of the Amalgamated Society of Railway Servants (ASRS) in that union's monthly, *Railway Review*.

22 Holt, p.121.

23 Gustafson, *Labour's Path*, pp.95–104 provides the most balanced account.

24 The best study of the negotiations and the establishment of the National government remains Anthony Wood, 'The Origins of the First National Government: A Study in New Zealand Wartime Politics, 1914–15' (MA thesis, University of Canterbury, 1963).

25 While there has never been a careful analysis of this anti-conscription campaign, it almost certainly drew on the pre-war Non-Conformist campaign against compulsory military training. In pre-war Christchurch, Dissent and Non-Conformity were influential within the union movement and Baptists and Methodists throughout the country played prominent roles in many of the skilled unions and within the local Trades and Labour Councils. For further reading on the anti-conscription movement see Paul Baker, *King and Country Call: New Zealanders, Conscription and the Great War* (Auckland, 1988), pp.58–63.

26 As Baker points out, apart from the 380 unions representing almost 73 per cent of

all union members that did not send delegates, there were usually sizeable minorities in these unions that supported conscription. Baker, p.72.

27 Baker, pp.64–78, provides the fullest analysis.

28 The company's role is explored more fully in Olssen, *The Red Feds*, pp.213–214.

29 Conrad Bollinger, *Against the Wind: The Story of the New Zealand Seamen's Union* (Wellington, 1968), pp.114–118 and Olssen, *The Red Feds*, pp.213–214.

30 Holt, pp.128–129.

31 P.N. Pettit, *The Wellington Watersiders: The Story of Their Industrial Organisation* (Wellington, 1948), pp.66–70 and Olssen, *The Red Feds*, pp.213–217.

32 For the mining towns on the West Coast, see Richardson, *Coal, Class & Community: The United Mineworkers of New Zealand 1880–1960* (Auckland, 1995), pp.158–161. Unfortunately there are no good studies of the mines where the Red Feds were most powerful, the Huntly coal mine and the Waihi gold mine; for a brief account of events at Huntly see Richardson, *Coal, Class & Community*, pp.156–158, 165.

33 Dowgray was elected vice-president of the UFL at its founding conference and became acting president during the strike when Tom Young of the Seamen, the first president, was arrested. See Richardson, 'Dowgray, John', *Dictionary of New Zealand Biography, Te Ara – the Encyclopedia of New Zealand*, http://www.teara.govt.nz/en/biographies/3d14/dowgray-john.

34 Pettit, pp.66–69, 73–75. See also Olssen, *The Red Feds*, pp.214–216.

35 Richardson, *Coal, Class & Community*, pp.164–166.

36 For an excellent and succinct sketch of the situation with regard to coal, see Richardson, *Coal, Class & Community*, p.155.

37 Holt, pp.127–128. See Richardson, 'Politics and War', in Philip Ross May (ed.), *Miners and Militants: Politics in Westland* (Christchurch, 1975), pp.132–134, for a sensitive analysis of the interplay between government, employers and unions. See also Richardson's definitive account in *Coal, Class & Community*, pp.161–166.

38 For further reading see Archives New Zealand, R3794970-ACHK-16581-G26-8, 'Confidential Outwards Despatches to the Secretary of State – 3 April – 14 December 1916', Alexander Herdman to the Governor General, Lord Liverpool, 10 June 1916.

39 Pettit, pp.78–79.

40 Pettit, pp.72–73 and for the quotation Holt, p.128.

41 Olssen, *The Red Feds*, pp.216–217. For the ingenious means of communicating and co-ordinating action, see Pettit, pp.72–73.

42 Edward Hunter, *The Road the Men Came Home* (London and Manchester, 1921), pp.70, 112. See also Roth pp.44–45.

43 D.T. McNaughton, 'The New Zealand Shearers' Union and the Crisis in the Shearing Industry, 11910-1916', *Auckland Historical Society Annual* (1971) and Olssen, *Red Feds*, p. 217.

44 Olssen and Maureen Hickey, *Class and Occupation: The New Zealand Reality* (Dunedin, 2005) provides the fullest account of the New Zealand occupational structure and stratification system in these years.

45 Olssen, *Building the New World: Work, Politics and Society in Caversham, 1880s–1920s* (Auckland, 1994), pp.147–148.

46 Not only did the Hillside Railway Workshops' branch of the ASRS strongly favour conscription of men, but by July 1916 some 134 men had volunteered. *Railway Review*, 28 July 1916, p.315. Fopr the furore see *Railway Review*, 1 June 1917, p.231.

47 Roth, Table 2, pp.169–170.

48 After the Supreme Court ruled in 1915 that unions registered under the Arbitration Act were only permitted to do what the Act specified, i.e. seek awards, a new

structure had to be invented. See Holt, pp.125–126 and Shaun F. Ryan, 'Men of Metal: The Amalgamated Society of Engineers in Dunedin c. 1874–1923' (MA thesis, University of Otago, 1997), pp.148–150.

49 Ryan, 'Men of Metal', pp.161–166.

50 This paragraph draws on my own research into the history of the ASC&J and Ryan, 'Men of Metal', pp.122–179.

51 Baker, pp.67–70 reviews the arguments against conscription. Gustafson, *Labour's Path*, especially pp.109–116, reveals how the issue became central despite deep divisions within the labour movement.

52 For the centrality of fairness see David Hackett Fischer, *Fairness and Freedom: A History of Two Open Societies – New Zealand and the United States* (New York, 2012).

53 Richardson, *Coal, Class & Community*, pp.166–169.

54 For the proceedings, see 'Report of Conference of Transport Workers' Unions . . .', *Railway Review*, 2 June 1916, pp.1–20. The fullest discussion of this organisation remains Stone, pp.207–209. See also Michelle Slade, 'Industrial Unionism in New Zealand, 1916–1925: A Study of the Transport Workers' Advisory Board and the Alliance of Labour, 1916–1925' (MA thesis, University of Auckland, 1983). The only in-depth study of any railway workers in this period remains my study of the men of the Hillside railway workshops. See Olssen, *Building the New World*, pp.123–154.

55 Roth, p.43.

56 The CMF's decision appears to have been more tactical than anything else, for Dowgray, the CMF's president at the time, had become the UFL's president.

57 For Holland's sophisticated reasoning see O'Farrell, *Harry Holland*, pp.65–84 and his earlier article, 'The Formation of the New Zealand Labour Party', *Historical Studies: Australia and New Zealand*, 10 (May 1962), pp.190–202.

58 For the SDP's plight, see Bassett and King, pp.70–71 (Fraser was the SDP Secretary). The party's strength reflected the fact that Paddy Webb and James McCombs, who both won by-elections in 1913 (in Grey and Lyttelton, respectively), represented the SDP.

59 See 'Linking up Labour's Political Units', *Maoriland Worker*, 12 July 1916, p.5 and 'John Glover (Secretary of the NZLP) to all Branches and Unions', Social Democratic Party Circular, 14 July 1916, McCarthy Arthur P. Papers, ARC-0446, Vol.3, Hocken Collections.

60 Bruce Brown', *The Rise of New Zealand Labour: A History of the New Zealand Labour Party* (Wellington, 1962), pp.23–26 provides a succinct chronicle and Gustafson, *Labour's Path* (especially pp.89–94) places it in its larger national context. See also Vowles, 'Ideology and the Formation', pp.39–42, for an analysis of the historiography.

61 For the secret plan see Baker, pp.157–162. See also Richardson, *Coal, Class & Community*, pp.169–175; Pettit, pp.76–79; and Holt, pp.127–129 (the quoted sentence is from p.128).

62 See Baker, p.155.

63 The second anti-conscription conference was less well attended than the first. See Baker, pp.157–158. For the arrests, see Bassett and King, pp.71–73 (Fraser himself was arrested, needless to say).

64 Richardson, *Coal, Class & Community*, pp.174–175 (for Webb and Semple), pp.171–180 (for the complex interplay of issues and negotiations).

65 For many years historians assumed that Labour's critique was fair and accurate, but for a more balanced appraisal see Olssen, 'Towards a Reassessment of W.F. Massey: One of New Zealand's Greatest Prime Ministers (Arguably)', in James Watson and

Lachy Paterson (eds), *A Great New Zealand Prime Minister? Reappraising William Ferguson Massey* (Dunedin, 2011), pp.15–30.

66 Richardson, *Coal, Class & Community*, pp.171–173; Pettit, pp.78–79; and Holt, pp.127–129. Baker, pp.157–169, provides a sound analysis of the government's story.

67 *Railway Review* ran many articles on co-operatives in 1917–18. For example see 4 May 1917, pp.199–203; 23 August 1918, pp.427–429; and for the PSA's campaign see 28 June 1918, p.292.

68 For brief but deft analysis of the government's predicament see Holt, pp.129–134 (and p.133 for the quotation).

69 For further reading on the Military Service Boards and their work see Baker, pp.109–110, 115–124 and David Littlewood, '"Willing and Eager to Go in Their Turn"? Appeals for Exemption from Military Service in New Zealand and Great Britain, 1916–1918', *War in History*, 21/3 (2014), pp.338–354.

70 There is no thorough study of the implementation of conscription, but in his chapter on 'New Zealand in the World War' for the *Cambridge History of New Zealand* (Cambridge, 1933), Sir James Allen devoted a section to the Efficiency Board, his idea, although he said nothing about industrial relations, doubtless a source of sleepless nights. For the fullest account of the Board's work see Olssen and Hickey, pp.85–87 and John E. Martin, 'Blueprint for the Future: National Efficiency and the First World War', in John Crawford and Ian McGibbon (eds), *New Zealand's Great War: New Zealand, the Allies and the Great War* (Auckland, 2007), pp.516–533.

71 Richardson, *Coal, Class & Community*, pp.175–178.

72 See the editorial in *Railway Review*, 4 May 1917, p.183.

73 G. Warburton, 'The Attitudes and Policies of the New Zealand Labour Movement Towards Non-European Immigration, 1878–1928' (MA thesis, University of Canterbury, 1982), especially pp.120–124. Although he includes Warburton in his bibliography, James Bennett, *'Rats and Revolutionaries': The Labour Movement in Australia and New Zealand 1890–1940* (Dunedin, 2004), largely ignores this debate.

74 Gustafson, *Labour's Path*, pp.120–123 and Shaun F. Ryan, 'The Politics of Pragmatism: J.T. Paul and the New Zealand Labour Movement 1916–1922' (BA Hons dissertation, University of Otago, 1993), pp.28–35. For the phrase see Bassett and King, p.74.

75 Baker, pp.138–142.

76 Gustafson, *Cradle to Grave*, Chs. 4 and 5 and Olssen, *Red Feds*, Ch. 9 for Savage's Auckland background.

77 Gustafson, *Cradle to Grave*, pp.100–101.

78 It was not that socialists opposed state control of industry, for the government was not proposing to do that. Rather the 'left' opposed state control of labour, an issue that had become a major grievance in Britain. Unlike the United Kingdom and the United States, the New Zealand government already owned most utilities and had no plans to nationalise any other sector. Instead government used various techniques for ensuring that prices remained reasonable. For further analysis see W.B. Sutch, *Price fixing in New Zealand* (New York, 1932).

79 *Railway Review*, 28 June 1918, p.317.

80 The key text was A.R. Orage and S.G. Hobson, *National Guilds* (London, 1914). See also S.T. Glass, *The Responsible Society* (London, 1966).

81 For Guild Socialism's importance, see Vowles, 'Ideology and the Formation' and Vowles, 'From Socialism to Guild Socialism: Some Neglected Aspects of the Ideology of the Labour Movement, 1914–1923', in John E. Martin and Kerry Taylor (eds), *Culture and the Labour Movement: Essays in New Zealand Labour History* (Palmerston North, 1991), pp.283–303.

82 Erik Olssen, 'Paul, John Thomas . . .', *The Dictionary of New Zealand Biography* (DNZB), Vol. 3, pp.390–392.

83 Within a year some 20 unions in Christchurch affiliated to the WEA; by 1920 the number had risen to 26. The best local study of the WEA remains Jean Sharfe, 'The Canterbury Workers' Educational Association. The Origins and Development, 1915–1947: A Working Class Organisation?' (MA thesis, University of Canterbury, 1990), pp.50–52.

84 Gustafson, *Labour's Path*, pp.133–136.

85 Cited in Bassett and King, p.86.

86 Leslie Lipson, *The Politics of Equality: New Zealand's Adventures in Democracy* (Chicago, 1948), Table 18, p.369 provides figures on the total number of workers involved in the public service and calculates that they comprised around 12 per cent of the total workforce (declining from 13.7 per cent in 1916 to 11.6 per cent in 1936). Over the same period the proportion of local government employees doubled, the percentage increasing from 4.8 to 9.2 per cent. For the breakdown by industrial sector in 1909, see Lipson, Table 20, p.432. For the membership of unions registered under the Arbitration Act I have relied on Roth, Table 2, p.169. The Department of Labour did not give figures for unions registered under the Industrial Disputes Act, but indicated in its annual report that four unions in the Auckland district were currently engaged in a dispute; AJHR, 1920, H-11.

87 For the size of the workforce, see Olssen and Hickey, pp.101–102 and for unions registered under the Arbitration Act, an underestimate, see Roth, Table 2, p.169.

88 Taylor, pp.160–177. For the impact of the Bolshevik Revolution locally, see O'Farrell, 'The Russian Revolution and the Labour Movements of Australia and New Zealand, 1917–1922', *International Review of Social History*, 8 (1963), pp.177–197 and Bennett, pp.78–80.

89 According to the Department of Labour, in 1918–19 some 82 strikes and three lockouts occurred, involving 8,086 workers (less than 3.7 per cent of the working class and 9.8 per cent of all unionists registered under the Arbitration Act); Roth, Table 4, p.171.

90 *Report of [UFL] Conference, July 1920*, p.8, cited in Roth, p.45.

91 The Otago Labour Council and its Central Labour Office, which instituted a universal clearance card, awaits its historian, but see Richard Tubbs, 'Mark Silverstone and the Dunedin Labour Movement with particular reference to the years 1912–1920' (BA Hons dissertation, University of Otago, 1981) and Olssen, 'Paul, John Thomas . . .', DNZB, Vol. 3, p. 392.

92 For the Court's new power, see Holt, p. 134.

93 Gustafson, *Savage*, p.115 and Bennett, pp.88–89.

94 Most of these tactics had been outlined by Allen in *Revolutionary Unionism*. For the phrase 'wooden shoe philosophy' see *Direct Action*, 1 May 1914, p.1.

95 Holt, pp.127–128.

Chapter Nine – Economic Mobilisation: New Zealand Businesses and the Great War

1 Hew Strachan, 'Economic Mobilisation', in Strachan (ed.), *The Oxford Illustrated History of the First World War* (New York, 1998), pp.134–149; Avner Offer, *The First World War: An Agrarian Interpretation* (New York, 1989); Stephen Broadberry and Mark Harrison, 'The Economics of World War I: An Overview' in Broadberry and Harrison (eds), *The Economics of World War I* (Cambridge, 2005), pp.3–40.

2 Jay Winter and John Horne, 'Introduction to Part III', in Winter (ed.), *The Cambridge History of the First World War, Volume II: The State* (New York, 2014), p.293.

3 Horne, 'Remobilizing for "Total War": France and Britain, 1917–1918', in Horne (ed.), *State, Society and Mobilization in Europe during the First World War* (Cambridge, 1997), pp.195–211.

4 For an assessment of the place of the state in the New Zealand economy see Michael Bassett, *The State in New Zealand, 1840–1984: Socialism Without Doctrines?* (Auckland, 1998).

5 Prices were also highly dependent on growing conditions in Australia. A drought across the Tasman could boost returns dramatically, while an excellent season could depress them severely.

6 Ian Hunter, *The Age of Enterprise: Rediscovering the New Zealand Entrepreneur, 1880–1910* (Auckland, 2007), p.48.

7 Hunter, p.45.

8 In 1910 a total of 3,978 workers were employed in meat preserving and freezing works, while 5,019 were employed in clothing, waterproof, and boot and shoe factories. Butter, cheese and condensed-milk factories employed 1,560 people, while 1,410 worked in woollen mills. *Census*, 1911, Table XIV, 'Occupations – Arranged Alphabetically'.

9 A key focus of this linkage of New Zealand and British producers and consumers has been the growth of New Zealand's 'protein industry' of refrigerated meat and dairy exports after 1880, a subject often associated with James Belich's idea of 'recolonisation'. This phenomenon is a leitmotif within his general history of New Zealand and the subject of a transnational study. See James Belich, *Paradise Reforged: A History of the New Zealanders From the 1880s to the Year 2000* (Hawaii, 2001) and *Replenishing the Earth: The Settler Revolution and the Rise of the Anglo-World, 1783–1939* (Oxford, 2009).

10 J.B. Condliffe, *New Zealand in the Making: A Study of Economic and Political Development* (London, 1936), p.57. On settler/dominion capitalism see Donald Denoon, *Settler Capitalism: The Dynamics of Dependent Development in the Southern Hemisphere* (Oxford, 1983) and Jim McAloon, 'Resource frontiers, environment and settler capitalism', in Eric Pawson and Tom Brooking (eds), *Making a New Land: Environmental Histories of New Zealand* (Dunedin, 2013), pp.70–85.

11 M.F. Lloyd Prichard, *An Economic History of New Zealand to 1939* (Auckland, 1970), p.209.

12 P.J. Cain and A.G. Hopkins, *British Imperialism: Innovation and Expansion, 1688–1914* (New York, 1993), p.265.

13 McAloon, 'The New Zealand Economy, 1792–1914', in Giselle Byrnes (ed.), *The New Oxford History of New Zealand* (Melbourne, 2009), p.198.

14 David Greasley and Les Oxley, 'Refrigeration and Distribution: New Zealand Land Prices and Real Wages 1873–1939', *Australian Economic Review*, 45/1 (March 2005), pp.23–44. Margaret Galt, 'Wealth and Income in New Zealand c. 1870 to c. 1939' (PhD thesis, Victoria University of Wellington, 1985).

15 Hunter; McAloon, *No Idle Rich: The Wealthy in Canterbury and Otago, 1840–1914* (Dunedin, 2002), pp.20–21.

16 Hunter, p.86.

17 McAloon, *No Idle Rich*. This characterisation rejects the 'gentry' label of Stevan Eldred-Grigg's interpretation of landed wealth. See Stevan Eldred-Grigg, *A Southern Gentry: New Zealanders who Inherited the Earth* (Wellington, 1980). For further studies on New Zealand wealth see Graeme Hunt, *The Rich List: Wealth*

and Enterprise in New Zealand 1820–2000 (Auckland, 2000) and Belich, *Paradise Reforged*, pp.127–133.

18 For studies assessing how these values played out in mass politics see Miles Fairburn and Stephen Haslett, 'Cleavage within the Working Class? The Working-Class Vote for the Labour Party in New Zealand, 1911–1951', *Labour History*, 88 (2005), pp.183–214 and Fairburn and Haslett 'Who Voted for Massey 1908–1914?', in James Watson and Lachy Paterson (eds), *A Great New Zealand Prime Minister? Reappraising William Ferguson Massey* (Dunedin, 2011), pp.61–76.

19 Gavin McLean, *The Southern Octopus: The Rise of a Shipping Empire* (Wellington, 1990). See also Gordon McLauchlan, *The Line that Dared: A History of the Union Steam Ship Company 1875–1975* (Mission Bay, 1987).

20 McAloon, *No Idle Rich*, pp.124, 176–177; Les Cleveland, *The Anatomy of Influence: Pressure Groups and Politics in New Zealand* (Wellington, 1972), p.99. For further studies see Selwyn Parker, *Wealthmakers: A History of the Northern Employers' and Manufacturers' Associations* (Auckland, 2005); J. Halket Millar, *The Merchants Paved the Way: The First Hundred Years of the Wellington Chamber of Commerce* (Wellington, 1956).

21 Leicester Chisholm Webb, 'The Rise of the Reform Party: A History of Party Politics in New Zealand between 1910 and 1920 (Honours thesis, University of New Zealand, 1928). See also McAloon, 'The Making of the New Zealand Ruling Class', in Melanie Nolan (ed.), *Revolution: The Great Strike in New Zealand*, (Christchurch, 2006), pp.217–236.

22 Michael Bassett, *Sir Joseph Ward: A Political Biography* (Auckland, 1993).

23 Watson, *W.F. Massey: New Zealand* (London, 2010), p.29.

24 Belich, *Paradise Reforged*, pp.38–46. Erik Olssen, *The Red Feds: Revolutionary Industrial Unionism and the New Zealand Federation of Labour* (Auckland, 1988).

25 McAloon, *No Idle Rich*, pp.113–124.

26 New Zealand Employers' Federation Circular no .67, (Wellington, 1912). Collected with *Report of Proceedings of the New Zealand Employers' Federation 1903–1908* in Alexander Turnbull Library (ATL). See also New Zealand Employers' Federation, *Organising and Defence Fund Schemes: A Plea for the Complete Industrial Organisation of all Employers of Labour in New Zealand* (Wellington, 1912).

27 *New Zealand Herald* (NZH), 31 October 1913, p.8; NZH, 1 November 1913, p.8; NZH, 3 November 1913, p.8.

28 *Farmers' Union Annual Dominion Conference*, 1914, p.3. Rather portentously, when the troubles of balancing the requirements of compulsory military training against the needs of farmers were raised, Mr J. M'Queen replied 'this country is worth making sacrifices for. If the sacrifices were more than had been anticipated they should not shirk them.' *Farmers' Union Annual Dominion Conference*, 1914, p.6.

29 Gwen Parsons, 'Debating the War: The Discourses of War in the Christchurch Community', in John Crawford and Ian McGibbon (eds), *New Zealand's Great War: New Zealand, the Allies and the First World War* (Auckland, 2007), pp.551–552.

30 Andrew Francis, *'To Be Truly British We Must Be Anti-German': New Zealand Enemy Aliens and the Great War Experience, 1914–1919* (New York, 2012), pp.181–213. For examples see *The Empire's Task: Germans vs British Trade* (Christchurch, 1918); 'Anti-German Trade Campaign', *War Pictures and Their Obvious Lesson* (Christchurch, 1915); W.F. Massey, *Post-war Policy: Some Aspects of Imperial Preference* (Wellington, 1920).

31 Parker, p.64.

32 Offer, p.1.

33 Roger Chickering, *Imperial Germany and the Great War, 1914–1918* (Cambridge, 2014), p.221.

34 Steven Loveridge, *Calls to Arms: New Zealand Society and Commitment to the Great War* (Wellington, 2014), p.38.

35 The effect of war on the sea lanes was something of a preoccupation for the Farmers' Union. See, for example, *Farmers' Union Advocate* (FUA), 8 August 1914, pp.5–6; John E. Martin, *Holding the Balance: A History of New Zealand's Department of Labour 1891–1995* (Christchurch, 1996), p.123; *Appendices to the Journals of the House of Representatives* (AJHR), 1915, H-11, 'Department of Labour', p.3.

36 AJHR, 1919, B-6, 'Financial Statement', pp.xxvi–xxviii.

37 Martin, 'War Economy', in Ian McGibbon (ed.), *The Oxford Companion to New Zealand Military History* (Auckland, 2000), p.582.

38 AJHR, 1918, H-38, 'Department of Imperial Government Supplies', p.1.

39 H.G Philpott, *A History of the Dairy Industry, 1840–1935* (Wellington, 1937), p.161; AJHR, 1917, H-38, 'Department of Imperial Government Supplies', pp.4–5; Julia Millen, *Glaxo: From Joseph Nathan to Glaxo Wellcome: The History of Glaxo in New Zealand* (Wellington, 1997), pp.50–51; Tod Simpson, 'The Origins of Statutory Producer Control Legislation in New Zealand Agriculture, 1914–1925' (MCA thesis, Victoria University of Wellington, 1991), pp.34–38.

40 Alan Everton, 'Government intervention in the New Zealand Economy, 1914–18: Its Aims and Effectiveness' (MA thesis, Victoria University of Wellington, 1995), pp.17, 408; Martin, 'War Economy', p.582.

41 *Dominion*, 8 December 1915, p.8; Prichard, p.260.

42 While British motor imports were stifled, American makes, often regarded as suited for New Zealand's rural roads, remained readily available. Herbert Watson found that 'Sunbeam or any other English cars are unprocurable here, except 2nd or 3rd hand ones at prices far beyond what they cost when new. Bell Bayly & Co. Ltd (chiefly Strangs I believe) have been selling about 2 Buicks per week for the last couple of years & as they probably make £100 on each they are doing good business.' ATL, MS-Papers-5714-017, 'Letters from Herbert Watson', Herbert Watson to Daniel Riddiford, 4 December 1918.

43 A number of less obvious enterprises, such as jewellers who made badges, also benefited. Archives New Zealand (ANZ), R3885211-AAYS-8647-AD10-2-4/1, 'Commission of enquiry – Defence stores 1915, June–August'. The rise of woollen companies' profits during the war was reflected in share prices. At the beginning of 1914, ordinary shares in the Wellington Woollen Company sold at 80 shillings, compared to 125 shillings in early 1918: a near 56 per cent rise. Comparably, the Kaiapoi Woollen Company saw its share price grow from 103 shillings in early 1914 to 158 shillings in October 1918. *Otago Daily Times* (ODT), 4 January 1915, p.3; *Dominion*, 28 February 1918, p.8.

44 ANZ, R3898751-AAYS-8696-AD80-8-285, 'Return of expenditure furnished to Defence Stores Commission [Commission of Inquiry re Defence Stores], August 1915'.

45 ANZ, R3898752-AAYS-8696-AD10-8-290, 'New Zealand's part in the war, March 1917 – September 1919'; H.T.B. Drew, 'War Finance', in Drew (ed.), *The War Effort of New Zealand* (Auckland, 1923), p.237. All contemporary figures calculated using the Reserve Bank's Inflation Calculator, http://www.rbnz.govt.nz.

46 At the beginning of 1914, Union Steam Ship Company ordinary shares stood at 24.75 shillings; each ordinary share was valued at 'something over 60' shillings in the takeover by the P. and O. Company. ODT, 4 January 1915, p.3; *Auckland Star*

(AS), 4 June 1917, p.7. This pattern is also evident in the Huddart-Parker Company, a major player in the trans-Tasman trade, whose shares increased by around 90 per cent between early 1914 and October 1918. *Sun*, 18 February 1914, p.8; *Press*, 19 October 1918, p.7. Ordinary shares in the New Zealand Shipping Company increased over 83 per cent in value between the beginning of 1914 and September 1916, when the P. and O. Company purchased them in another takeover. ODT, 4 January 1915, p.3; *Press*, 16 August 1916, p.2. See also McLean, 'The Fourth Service: The Merchant Marine's War', *New Zealand's Great War*, p.418.

47 Additional camps were established at Awapuni in Palmerston North and at Narrow Neck on Auckland's North Shore.

48 Neil Frances, *Safe Haven: The Untold Story of New Zealand's Largest Ever Military Camp: Featherston: 1916–1919* (Masterton, 2012), pp.19–21.

49 Frances, pp.viii–ix.

50 Frances, p.viii.

51 Frances, p.64.

52 There were a number of private shops inside and outside the camp perimeter, including clothing stores, laundries, watchmakers/jewellers, photographers and, until the service was militarised in November 1917, hairdressers. Furthermore, soldiers frequently headed for other Wairarapa towns by taxi during local leaves, spreading the benefit of their spending and making the local taxi industry very profitable.

53 NZOYB, 1921–22, p.259. The Bank of New Zealand had a net profit of £336,607 in 1918, down on the £365,489 of the previous year, but well up on the £308,490 of 1914. The Bank's reserve fund had increased from £1,601,608 to £2,200,000. ODT, 15 June 1915, p.3; ODT, 21 June 1918, p.2.

54 ODT, 4 January 1915, p.3; *Dominion*, 22 October 1918, p.8.

55 ODT, 4 January 1915; ODT, 23 October 1918, p.6.

56 Martin, *Holding the Balance*, p.378.

57 One consequence of the port of Wellington serving as the point of departure for most troops was the mass arrival of family members wishing to farewell soldiers. In 1916 Dr A.K. Newman (Reform, Wellington North) complained of the overcrowding 'due entirely to the fact that there was a great rush of people to the city'. Likewise, Massey claimed that the introduction of a War Legislation Amendment Act with provision to control rents was because of the situation in Wellington. *New Zealand Parliamentary Debates* (NZPD), Vol.176, 7 July 1916, p.592; NZPD, Vol.177, 25 July 1916, p.394.

58 *Census*, 1916, Appendix D, pp.lxi, lxvi. Calculated from *Census*, 1911, Table XIV, 'Occupations – Arranged Alphabetically' and *Census*, 1916, 'Occupations – Alphabetical List'.

59 AS, 23 March 1917, p.2. Likewise, the following month the engineer and manager of the Wanganui City Council's Tramway Department stated that '[t]he new plant contracted for more than a year ago is not yet to hand, and probably will not be delivered until after the war.' *Wanganui Chronicle* (WC), 18 April 1917, p.2.

60 For examples see Arthur Mee and J. Stuart Holden, *Defeat or Victory? The Truth about the Betrayal of Britain* (Dunedin, 1917); Mee, *The Fiddlers: Drink in the Witness Box; with Official NZ Facts and Figures* (Dunedin, 1917).

61 Giving evidence in the Canterbury Hotel Employees' dispute in December 1917, hotel proprietors variously stated that their takings had decreased by 39 per cent, approximately 30 per cent, 37.5 per cent and 34.5 per cent. *Press*, 17 December 1917, p.4.

62 *New Zealand Statutes* (NZS), 1914, No.40, pp.132–133; *New Zealand Official Year Book* (NZOYB), 1919, p.399.
63 For examples see ANZ, R21371634-AAAB-478-5/g, 'German sweets' and ANZ, R21371715-AAAB-478-7/x, 'Kirkcaldie and Stains'.
64 *Evening Post* (EP), 21 May 1915, p.10.
65 For other examples see EP, 2 January 1915, p.9; EP, 30 June 1915, p.2; *New Zealand Observer* (NZO), 29 August 1914, p.7. Ambiguities around 'alien firms' are well illustrated in the case of the Swiss transnational Nestlé, with inquiries raised concerning the company's operation. ANZ R3898763-AAYS-8696-AD80-9-427, 'Alien firms in New Zealand, September 1916 – July 1917'.
66 Olssen, 'Waging War: The Home Front', in Judith Binney, Judith Bassett and Erik Olssen (eds), *The People and the Land Te Tangata Me Te Whenua: An Illustrated History of New Zealand, 1820–1920* (Wellington, 1990), pp.308–309; Watson, 'Patriotism, Profits and Problems: New Zealand Farming During the Great War', *New Zealand's Great War*, pp.534–549.
67 Barry Gustafson, *Labour's Path to Political Independence* (Auckland, 1980), p.96.
68 ANZ, R22319764-ADBQ-16145-ALLEN1-5-M2/61/2, 'Ministerial Files – Cost of living taxation and fixing prices, etc'.
69 NZOYB, 1919, p.786. For an in-depth study see G.W. Clinkard, 'Wages and Working Hours in New Zealand, 1897–1919' in NZOYB, 1919, pp.860–935.
70 Jean-Louis Robert, 'The Image of the Profiteer', in Winter and Robert (eds), *Capital Cities at War: Paris, London, Berlin 1914–1919* (Cambridge, 1997), pp.104–132.
71 Seren Wendelken, 'Visual Constructs of Wealth in *The Maoriland Worker*, 1911–12: Cartoon and Intertext', in Fairburn and Olssen (eds), *Class, Gender and the Vote: Historical Perspectives from New Zealand* (Dunedin, 2005), pp.193–216.
72 *Maoriland Worker*, 8 December 1915, p.1.
73 For examples see NZPD, Vol.173, 8 September 1915, p.481; NZPD, Vol.173, 7 September 1915, p.432; NZPD, Vol.178, 12 July 1917, pp.351–352; NZPD, Vol.174, 20 September 1915, p.3.
74 H.D. Bedford, *Cost of Living in New Zealand: War Profit, War Finance* (Dunedin, 1916).
75 NZPD, Vol.172, 6 July 1915, pp.143–144. For further examples see EP, 30 August 1915, p.8. See also *Northern Advocate*, 30 August 1915, p.2; AS, 30 August 1915, p.6; *Waikato Times*, 30 August 1915, p.4; *Dominion*, 31 August 1915, p.7; *Wairarapa Daily Times*, 31 August 1915, p.4; NZPD, Vol.175, 12 May 1916, p.95; ATL, MS-Papers-5714-017, 'Letters from Herbert Watson', Herbert Watson to Daniel Riddiford, 4 December 1918; http://www.teara.govt.nz/en/biographies/3g5/gibbons-hopeful.
76 EP, 17 March 1915, p.8; *Thames Star*, 20 February 1918, p.1; NZH, 19 February 1918, p.6; NZH, 22 August 1914, p.7.
77 *Wairarapa Age*, 17 March 1916, p.4. Many such acts of charity continued after the war: 2,600 sheep owners, for example, funded the establishment of 'Flock House', near the town of Bulls, to offer agricultural training to the children of British seamen who had lost their lives or been wounded during the war. *Hawera & Normanby Star* (HNS), 19 July 1924, p.5.
78 Some of the sentiments of the president of the Employers' Federation towards the end of 1915 also hint at this growing discord. See *New Zealand Employers' Federation: Address Delivered by the President, T. Shailer Weston, Esq., at the Annual Meeting of the Federation held in Wellington on Wednesday September 15th, 1915* (Wellington, 1915).
79 EP, 24 February 1916, p.4.

80 HNS, 24 July 1917, p.4.
81 Watson, 'Patriotism, Profit and Problems: New Zealand Farming During the Great War', *New Zealand's Great War*, p.536; *Dominion*, 8 December 1915, p.8.
82 Len Richardson, 'Politics and War: Coal Miners and Conscription, 1914–18', in P.R. May (ed.), *Miners and Militants, Politics in Westland 1865–1918* (Christchurch, 1975), p.134.
83 ATL, MS-Papers-11367-192, 'New Zealand Employers' Federation – Minute book of 1917 dispute'. Paul Baker, *King and Country Call: New Zealanders, Conscription and the Great War* (Auckland, 1988), p.139.
84 Baker, p.141; EP, 24 July 1917, p.2; Watson, 'Patriotism, Profits and Problems', pp.534–549.
85 NZOYB, 1921–22, p.259.
86 McLean, *Spinning Yarns: A Centennial History of Alliance Textiles Limited and its Predecessors 1881–1981* (Dunedin, 1981), p.34.
87 *Dominion*, 8 December 1915, p.8.
88 Simpson, pp.34–45; Everton, pp.416–418.
89 ANZ, R3898752-AAYS-8696-AD10-8-290, 'New Zealand's part in the war, March 1917 – September 1919'.
90 McLean, 'The Fourth Service', p.418; McLean, *The Southern Octopus*, p.182.
91 EP, 2 April 1917, p.8.
92 FUA, 12 January 1918, p.3; Drew, p.236. For further analysis on Massey and trade see Watson, '"The Greatest Commercial Traveller in the Empire": Massey and Trade', *A Great New Zealand Prime Minister?*, pp.121–128.
93 McLean, 'The Fourth Service', p.418.
94 McLean, 'The Fourth Service', p.422.
95 Some of the shortfall was made up by coal imports from Australia, the United States and the Admiralty, although strains on shipping and coal shortages in Australia made this relief sporadic. For coal production over the period see NZOYB, 1919, p.591.
96 WC, 23 June 1915, p.8.
97 NZO, 27 March 1915, p.1. For further assessment of Massey's attitudes to economic intervention see Everton, pp.144–145.
98 ANZ, R3898752-AAYS-8696-AD10-8-290, 'New Zealand's part in the war, March 1917 – September 1919'.
99 ANZ, R3898757-AAYS-8696-AD80-8-331/1, 'Prosecution of A. Levy, Esq., April 1916 – October 1917'; AS, 26 October 1916, p.2; *Dominion*, 14 March 1917, p.8.
100 *New Zealand Free Lance*, 13 August 1915, p.5. For further background see Paul Goldsmith and Michael Bassett, *The Myers* (Auckland, 2007).
101 Arrangements were made for the supply of small-arms ammunition through the Auckland Colonial Ammunition Company. For the supply contract see AJHR, 1915, H-19d, 'The Ammunition Contract 1915', pp.1–4.
102 NZPD, Vol.174, 11 October 1915, pp.883–884.
103 ANZ, R22428909, AAYS-8638-AD1-700-6/114, 'Ammunition and Explosives – Munitions manufacture in New Zealand – 4/5/1915 – September 1915'.
104 AJHR, 1919, H-24, 'Munitions and Supplies Department', p.1.
105 ANZ, R3898711-AAYS-8696-AD80-4-112, 'Register of skilled workers, August 1915 – March 1917'.
106 For accounts of the Efficiency Board see Martin, 'Blueprint for the Future? "National Efficiency" and the First World War', *New Zealand's Great War*, pp.516–533 and Baker, pp.138–142.

107 Martin, 'Blueprint for the Future?', pp.525–527.
108 NZS, 1918, No.2, pp.5–18.
109 NZS, 1914, No.6, pp.12–18.
110 Everton, pp.41–45.
111 NZS, 1915, No.69, pp.444–447. For further assessment of the Board of Trade see Bassett, *The State in New Zealand*, pp.130–132.
112 AJHR, 1919, H-44, 'Board of Trade', p.1.
113 Everton, pp.242, 283–306.
114 Malcolm McKinnon, *Treasury: The New Zealand Treasury, 1840–2000* (Auckland, 2003), p.85; Everton, p.419.
115 AJHR, 1919, H-38, 'Department of Imperial Government Supplies', pp.11–12.
116 NZS, 1917, No.9, pp.24–58. EP, 2 August 1917, p.8.
117 HNS, 18 November 1916, p.4. For further examples see FUA, 4 December 1915, p.5; FUA, 23 September 1916, p.5; FUA, 19 May 1917, p.23.
118 NZH, 11 July 1916, p.5.
119 For a recent account of the case see Peter Clayworth, '"Lucky Laidlaw and Worried Webb": The Robert Laidlaw Exemption Case and Public Attitudes to Conscription in 1918', *Journal of New Zealand Studies*, 20 (2015), pp.78–79. For a biography of Robert Laidlaw see http://www.teara.govt.nz/en/biographies/3l2/laidlaw-robert-alexander-crookston.
120 *Truth*, 16 March 1918, p.2.
121 AJHR, 1918, H-29, 'Department of Agriculture Industries and Commerce', p.1. This puts New Zealand on one side of a general comparison one study makes on agricultural mobilisation; 'in richer countries the government paid *more* to the food producers, and this worked, but in poorer countries . . . the government wanted to pay *less* and this had entirely predictable results.' Broadberry and Harrison, p.19.
122 AJHR, 1917, H-38, 'Department of Imperial Government Supplies', pp.4–5.
123 AJHR, 1918, H-44, 'Board of Trade', p.15.
124 NZOYB, 1921–1922, p.591.
125 Martin, *Holding the Balance*, p.384.
126 McKinnon, 'Post-war Economies (New Zealand)', in Ute Daniel, Peter Gatrell, Oliver Janz, Heather Jones, Jennifer Keene, Alan Kramer and Bill Nasson (eds), *1914–1918 Online: International Encyclopedia of the First World War*, issued by Freie Universität Berlin, Berlin 2015-02-17, doi: 10.15463/ie1418.10556.
127 McKinnon, 'Post-war Economies'.
128 *Manawatu Times*, 6 December 1920, p.5.
129 Simpson, p.18.
130 Certainly business groups lobbied to normalise taxes, and achieved some successes. Custom duties, which constituted 60 per cent of taxation revenues in 1914, had fallen in significance over the war (reaching 29 per cent in 1918). By 1925 they had crept back to forming the most significant source of taxation, at 50.39 per cent. NZOYB, 1921–22, p.259; NZOYB, 1927, p.606; McKinnon, 'Post-war Economies'.
131 Bassett, *The State*, p.130. In 1932 William Sutch completed a PhD thesis in favour of the ambitions of the Board of Trade's endeavours. This was later published as W.B. Sutch, *Price Fixing in New Zealand* (New York, 1968).
132 ANZ, R3898752-AAYS-8696-AD10-8-290, 'New Zealand's part in the war, March 1917 – September 1919'; R.J. Stone, 'Myers, Arthur Mielziner', *Dictionary of New Zealand Biography, Te Ara – the Encyclopaedia of New Zealand*, http://www.teara.govt.nz/en/biographies/3m66/myers-arthur-mielziner. NZPD, Vol. 183, 4 December 1918, p.730.

133 The slogan was borrowed from the United States Republican Party. Bassett, *The State*, p.151; McKinnon, *Treasury*, p.89.
134 Martin, 'Blueprint for the Future?', pp.530–531.
135 NZS, 1919, No.15, pp.46–55.
136 NZS, 1921, No.73, pp.648–654; NZS, 1923, No.28, pp.168–175.

Chapter Ten – 'The Whole Question Bristles with Difficulties': Sport and War

1 André Siegfried, *Democracy in New Zealand*, 2nd ed. (Wellington, 1982), p.249.
2 A.C. Swan, *The New Zealand Rugby Football Union 1892–1967* (Wellington, 1967), pp.16–21; Jock Phillips, *A Man's Country? The image of the Pakeha Male: A History* (Auckland, 1987), pp.96–97.
3 *Hawera & Normanby Star* (HNS), 11 December 1915, p.6.
4 See for example, Greg Ryan, *The Making of New Zealand Cricket 1832–1914*, (London, 2003), pp.53–80; Carolyn J. Mincham, 'Horseracing in the New Zealand Colonial Community, 1841–1911' (MA thesis, Massey University, 2001); M.A.E. Hammer, 'Something Else in the World to Live for: Sport and the Physical Emancipation of Women in Auckland, 1880–1920' (MA thesis, University of Auckland, 1990).
5 See for example, Geoffrey T. Vincent and Greg Ryan, '"A Small Knot of Muscular Friends": Class and athletic clubs in colonial Canterbury, 1870–1890', *Journal of New Zealand Studies*, 8 (2009), pp.121–44; Ryan, '"The Axe is the Pioneer of Civilisation": Competitive wood chopping and New Zealand sporting culture 1890–1914', *Turnbull Library Record*, 45 (2013), pp.44–57.
6 David Grant, *On a Roll: A History of Gambling & Lotteries in New Zealand* (Wellington, 1994), pp.49–55.
7 Wray Vamplew, 'Exploding the Myths of Sport and the Great War: A First Salvo', *International Journal of the History of Sport* (IJHS), 31/18 (2014), pp.2297–2312.
8 *New Zealand Herald* (NZH), 24 April 1915, p.6.
9 HNS, 24 June 1916, p.6. See also *New Zealand Free Lance* (NZFL), 8 October 1915, p.20.
10 *Press*, 7 April 1916, p.9.
11 Fiona Hall, '"The Greater Game": Sport and Society in Christchurch During the First World War 1914–18' (MA thesis, University of Canterbury, 1989), pp.15–32; Steven Loveridge, 'Soldiers and Shirkers: Modernity and New Zealand Masculinity during the Great War', *New Zealand Journal of History*, 47/1 (2013), p.65.
12 Hall, pp.10, 55.
13 NZH, 21 May 1915, p.8; NZH, 26 April 1916, p.5; NZFL, 3 November 1916, p.25.
14 NZFL, 16 April 1915, p.24.
15 NZFL, 8 October 1915, p.20.
16 NZH, 21 May 1915, p.8.
17 *Press*, 23 October 1915, p.10.
18 *Press*, 6 September 1915, p.10. See also *Press*, 23 August 1916, p.8.
19 *Press*, 1 November 1915, p.8; HNS, 13 November 1915, p.6.
20 *Feilding Star*, 19 January 1915, p.2.
21 *Sun*, 25 January 1915, p.2.
22 All contemporary figures calculated using the Reserve Bank's Inflation Calculator, http://www.rbnz.govt.nz.
23 *Taranaki Daily News*, 9 September 1915, p.6.
24 *Evening Post* (EP), 2 November 1915, p.2.

25 For further analysis on this dynamic see Loveridge, *Calls to Arms: New Zealand Society and Commitment to the Great War* (Wellington, 2014), pp.221–231.
26 Hall, p.11.
27 *Press*, 11 May 1915, p.8.
28 Swan, *History of New Zealand Rugby Football 1870–1945* (Wellington, 1946), pp.170–173.
29 EP, 1 November 1915, p.4.
30 NZH, 21 May 1915, p.8.
31 Hall, pp.78–79, 84.
32 *Grey River Argus* (GRA), 22 April 1915, p.7. For further criticism from the *Daily Telegraph* see *Otago Daily Times* (ODT), 24 April 1915, p.10. See also Rodney Noonan, 'Offside: Rugby League, the Great War and Australian Patriotism', IJHS, 26/15 (2009), pp.2201–2218.
33 EP, 23 April 1915, p.8.
34 GRA, 17 June 1915, pp.6, 8.
35 Ryan, 'Sport in Christchurch', in J.E. Cookson and G.C. Dunstall (eds), *Southern Capital: Christchurch: Towards a City Biography, 1850–2000* (Christchurch, 2000), pp.325–352.
36 EP, 26 June 1915, p.17. See also Michael McKernan, 'Sport, War and Society: Australia, 1914–1918', in Richard Cashman and Michael McKernan (eds), *Sport in History* (St Lucia, 1979), pp.1–20.; John M. Osborne, '"To keep the life of the Nation on the old lines": The Athletic News and the First World War', *Journal of Sport History*, 14/2 (1987), p.144.
37 *North Otago Times*, 17 August 1915, p.4.
38 NZH, 13 October 1916, p.6.
39 *Press*, 31 March 1916, p.8.
40 *Press*, 3 September 1915, p.9.
41 *Press*, 31 October 1915, p.7. See also *Press*, 4 October 1915, p.5.
42 Loveridge, 'Soldiers and Shirkers', pp.69–71.
43 Hall, pp.33–43. See also, among many examples, *Ohinemuri Gazette*, 29 September 1916, p.3; EP, 11 December 1915, p.14; EP, 27 December 1915, p.2.
44 *Press*, 4 December 1915, p.11. Among many other examples see *Wanganui Chronicle*, 6 December 1915, p.5; *Taranaki Daily News*, 11 December 1915, p.11.
45 ODT, 3 February 1916, p.8.
46 *Press*, 24 February 1916, p.7; *Press*, 16 March 1916, p.9; *Auckland Star* (AS), 7 April 1916, p.2.
47 EP, 11 July 1916, p.5. Among many other examples, see *Wanganui Chronicle*, 22 May 1916, p.6.
48 *HNS*, 9 October 1915, p.6.
49 See Ryan, 'A Dragon With Claws That Feeds on the Young: The Reaction Against Rugby in the New Zealand Secondary Schools 1920–30', *History of Education Review*, 28/1 (1999), pp.49–63.
50 *Press*, 23 November 1917, p.6.
51 See for example Rob Hess, 'Playing With "Patriotic Fire": Women and Football in the Antipodes during the Great War', IJHS, 28/10 (2011), pp.1388–1408; Hess, 'Missing in Action? New Perspectives on the Origins and Diffusion of Women's Football in Australia during the Great War', IJHS, 31/18 (2014), pp.2326–2344; Ali Melling, 'Wartime Opportunities: Ladies' Football and the First World War Factories', in J.A. Mangan (ed.), *Militarism, Sport, Europe: War Without Weapons* (London, 2004), pp.120–141.

52 Loveridge, *Calls to Arms*, pp.171–204.
53 *Timaru Herald*, 7 May 1915, p.2.
54 GRA, 8 March 1917, p.3.
55 HNS, 11 September 1915, p.3; HNS, 6 May 1916, p.6.
56 For example, *Ohinemuri Gazette*, 17 May 1918, p.3.
57 J. Costello and P. Finnegan, *Tapestry of Turf: The History of New Zealand Racing 1840–1987* (Auckland, 1988), p.145; EP, 16 July 1915, p.10.
58 *Sun*, 1 December 1915, p.10.
59 *Colonist*, 3 April 1917, p.2.
60 Hall, p.199.
61 AS, 6 April 1916, p.2.
62 *Star*, 13 November 1915, p.9.
63 *Poverty Bay Herald*, 18 November 1915, p.4.
64 EP, 7 April 1917, p.5. See also Grant, *On a Roll*, pp.61–63, 88–89, 99–106.
65 *Press*, 15 April 1916, p.8; NZH, 14 June 1916, p.9.
66 *Dominion*, 12 December 1916, p.6.
67 *Dominion*, 16 March 1917, p.4; NZH, 6 June 1917, p.6; EP, 8 June 1917, p.8; Costello and Finnegan, p.147.
68 *Appendix to the Journals of the House of Representatives*, 1917, H-43, 'National Efficiency Board (Report of)', p.11; EP, 31 July 1917, p.8.
69 Hall, pp.70, 103–106, 117, 226–231; ODT, 5 March 1918, p.6.
70 NZFL, 2 May 1918, p.20.
71 Swan, *History of New Zealand Rugby Football*, pp.170–173; T.W. Reese, *New Zealand Cricket: 1914–33* (Christchurch, 1936), pp.206–211.
72 *Wairarapa Age*, 20 April 1918, p.4.
73 See for example *Press*, 30 December 1918, p.3.
74 Hall, p.47.
75 Len Richardson, 'The Invention of a National Game: The Struggle for Control', *History Now*, 1/1 (1995), pp.7–8.
76 AS, 12 May 1917, p.17.
77 Stephen Clarke, 'Return, Repatriation, Remembrance and the Returned Soldier's Association 1916–22', in John Crawford and Ian McGibbon (eds), *New Zealand's Great War: New Zealand, the Allies and the First World War* (Auckland, 2007), pp.157–181.
78 Ryan, 'Men Who Defaulted in the Greatest Game of All: Sport, Conscientious Objectors and Military Defaulters in New Zealand 1916–1923', IJHS, 31/18, (2014), pp.2375–2387.

Chapter Eleven – The Rising Price of Rendering to Caesar: The Churches in World War One

1 *Oamaru Mail* (OM), 3 August 1914, p.3.
2 John Horne (ed.), *State, Society and Mobilization in Europe during the First World War* (Cambridge, 1997).
3 *War Cry* (WC), Vol. 35, No. 43 (17 July 1915), p.3.
4 Megan Hutching, 'Turning Back This Tide of Barbarism: New Zealand Women Who Were Opposed to War, 1896–1918' (MA thesis, University of Auckland, 1990), pp.79–69; *New Zealand Baptist* (NZB), Vol. 31, No. 375 (March 1914), p.43; NZB, Vol. 31, No. 376 (April 1914), p.73; NZB, Vol. 31, No. 278 (June 1914), p.133.

5 *Church Gazette* (CG), Vol. 44, No. 9 (September 1914), p.155.
6 CG, Vol. 45, No. 1 (January 1915), pp.4–5.
7 CG, Vol. 44, No. 9 (September 1914), p.163.
8 OM, 3 August 1914, p.3. For further reading in regard to the Methodist Church see Ross Malcolm Anderson, 'New Zealand Methodism and World War 1: Crisis in a Liberal Church' (MA thesis, University of Canterbury, 1983).
9 *New Zealand Methodist Times* (NZMT), Vol. 5, No. 12 (3 October 1914), p.1. See also the editorial, 'Two sides of the war cloud', NZMT, Vol. 6, No. 2 (15 May 1915), p.8. Note in the same issue, p.3, that three quarters of the mayors of the cities were Methodist.
10 *New Zealand Tablet* (NZT), Vol. 42, No. 22 (3 June 1915), p.22.
11 For examples see *Hastings Standard*, 17 August 1914, p.3 and NZT, Vol. 42, No. 19 (13 May 1915), p.34.
12 *Sun*, 17 August 1914, p.8.
13 WC, Vol. 34, No. 8 (14 November 1914), pp.4, 5.
14 WC, Vol. 35, No. 37 (5 June 1915), p.4.
15 *Evening Post* (EP), 22 December 1914, p.4. All contemporary figures calculated using the Reserve Bank's Inflation Calculator, http://www.rbnz.govt.nz.
16 NZT, Vol. 41, No. 35 (3 September 1914), p.34. The Anglican Bishop of Christchurch wrote to other dioceses to initiate collections for needy people in Belgium and Britain as a result of the war. CG, Vol. 44, No. 10 (October 1914), p.175.
17 *Otago Daily Times* (ODT), 1 May 1915, p.4.
18 NZT, Vol. 42, No. 20 (20 May 1915) p.34.
19 NZT, Vol. 43, No. 8 (24 February 1916), p.29.
20 NZT, Vol. 41, No. 36 (10 September 1914), p.35.
21 For an example see Rev. Fitchett on the Dunedin committee in ODT, 15 December 1914, p.7. For the report of the meeting see ODT, 27 November 1914, p.6, where the clergy speaker was Rev. G.H. Balfour.
22 CG, Vol. 46, No. 1 (January 1916), p.6.
23 *Nelson Diocesan Magazine*, 2/11 (November 1915), pp.11–13. On Gibb, see Lawrence H. Barber, *The Very Rev. James Gibb: Patriot into Pacifist* (Dunedin, 1973); NZMT, Vol. 6, No. 2 (19 February 1916), p.9.
24 *Press*, 5 March 1915, p.6.
25 NZT, Vol. 41, No. 33 (20 August 1914), p.34.
26 NZT, Vol. 41, No. 34 (27 August 1914), p.23.
27 NZT, Vol. 42, No. 25 (24 June 1915), p.45.
28 NZB, Vol. 32, No. 378 (June 1915), p.98.
29 CG, Vol. 45, No. 6 (June 1915), p.91.
30 CG, Vol. 45, No. 7 (July 1915), p.107.
31 NZT, Vol. 42, No. 20 (20 May 1915), p.22.
32 NZMT, Vol. 5, No. 19 (9 January 1915), p.8.
33 NZMT, Vol. 5, No. 24 (20 March 1915), p.3.
34 See, for example, NZT, Vol. 41, No. 36 (10 September 1914), p.51.
35 NZT, Vol. 43, Vol. 4 (27 January 1916), p.15.
36 For the Presbyterian approach see *Timaru Herald*, 2 June 1915, p.3.
37 NZT, Vol. 42, No. 20 (20 May 1915), pp.18–19.
38 CG, Vol. 45, No. 12 (December 1915), Synod Supplement, p.xviii.
39 CG, Vol. 44, No. 11 (November 1914), p.198.
40 This is the tone in CG, Vol. 46, No. 7 (July 1916), pp.100–107.
41 NZMT, Vol. 5, No. 24 (20 March 1915), p.6.

42 NZMT, Vol. 5, No. 24 (20 March 1915), pp.5–6.
43 NZT, Vol. 42, No. 25 (24 June 1915), p.22.
44 EP, 12 June 1915, p.6.
45 *Dominion*, 15 June 1915, p.6.
46 NZT, Vol. 43, No. 4 (27 January 1916), pp.42–43.
47 For figures see J. Bryant Haigh, *Men of Faith and Courage: The Official History of New Zealand's Army Chaplains* (Auckland, 1983), p.46. For the impact on ministry see, for example, NZMT, Vol. 7, No. 18 (6 January 1917), p.2, and W.J. Williams, *Centenary Sketches of New Zealand Methodism* (Christchurch, 1922), p.288, which includes home missionaries and probationers. Allan Davidson, in a forthcoming book on World War One chaplains, has identified 18 chaplains who served overseas out of about 96 ministers (18.75 per cent of the ministers), and a further 35 ministers, probationers, theological students and home missionaries who served overseas in the army or with the YMCA. On my count, in 1919 there were 96 ministers, 24 probationers, 29 home missionaries, and 13 home mission probationers: a total of 162 church workers. In addition to the chaplains who served overseas, a further 36 ministers are listed as Territorial chaplains in 1919; see *Methodist Annual Conference Minutes* (Christchurch, 1919), pp. 8, 13, 14, 98, 111–112.
48 CG, Vol. 44, No. 10 (October 1914), p.182.
49 CG, Vol. 44, No. 10 (October 1914), p.182.
50 NZT, Vol. 41, No. 36 (10 September 1914), p.33.
51 NZT, Vol. 42, No. 19 (13 May 1915), p.31.
52 Taken from Gillam's sermon at St Matthew's before he left as a chaplain, CG, Vol. 45, No. 8 (August 1915), p.122.
53 CG, Vol. 44, No. 10 (October 1914), p.182.
54 NZB, Vol. 32 [i.e.31], No. 369 (September 1914), p.161. Some issues of volume 32 of NZB were called volume 31 by the printer.
55 NZB, Vol. 32, No. 369 (September 1914), p.172.
56 NZB, Vol. 32, No. 374 (January 1915), p.22. See also NZB, Vol. 32, No. 373 (January 1915), p.27, which suggests that W.S. Rollings may have written this.
57 NZB, Vol. 32, No. 375 (March 1915), pp.51–52.
58 *Press*, 27 July 1915, p.6; *Auckland Star* (AS), 7 August 1915, p.18.
59 WC, Vol. 36, No. 5 (23 October 1915), p.2; WC, Vol. 36, No. 20 (5 February 1916), p.4.
60 CG, Vol. 44, No. 9 (September 1914), p.156. See also CG, Vol. 45, No. 3 (March 1915), p.37.
61 NZMT, Vol. 5, No. 23 (20 February 1915), p.7.
62 NZB, Vol. 32, No. 375 (March 1915), p.44.
63 *New Zealand Observer* (NZO), 19 June 1915, p.16.
64 NZO, 19 June 1915, p.16.
65 CG, Vol. 44, No. 12 (December 1914), p.216.
66 NZT, Vol. 41, No. 33 (20 August 1914), pp.33–34.
67 CG, Vol. 46, No. 4 (April 1916), p.50.
68 CG, Vol. 44, No. 10 (October 1914), p.182.
69 CG, Vol. 45, No. 9 (September 1915), pp.146–148. For further examples see CG, Vol. 45, No. 12 (December 1915), Synod Supplement, pp.viii–ix.
70 NZMT, Vol. 5, No. 24 (20 March 1915), p.3.
71 NZB, Vol. 32, No. 373 (January 1915), p.11.
72 NZB, Vol. 32, No. 373 (January 1915), p.15.
73 CG, Vol. 46, No. 11 (November 1916), p.171. See also Geoffrey M. Troughton,

'Jesus and the ideal of the manly man in New Zealand after World War One', *Journal of Religious History*, 30/1 (February 2006), pp.45–60.

74 *New Zealand Statutes*, 1916, No.8, Section 18 (1) e.

75 WC, Vol. 35, No. 49 (28 August 1915), p.5. For an example see the address by Fr Groggan in NZT, Vol. 43, No. 11 (16 March 1916), p.55.

76 NZB, Vol. 33, No. 392 (August 1916), pp.141–142, 150–152. NZMT, Vol. 7, No. 6 (22 July 1916), p.1; NZMT, Vol. 7, No. 7 (5 August 1916) p.1.

77 See the comment by 'Limelight' in the *Truth*, 20 May 1916, p.8 on the Anglican General Synod's stance, and the similar letter in the *Star*, 15 May 1916, p.5.

78 Alexander Turnbull Library (ATL), 79–057, 'New Zealand Women's Christian Temperance Union: Records', Convention Minutes, 23 March 1917.

79 ATL, 79-057, 'New Zealand Women's Christian Temperance Union: Records', Convention Minutes, 20 March 1918.

80 Dickon John Milnes, 'The Church Militant: Dunedin Churches and Society during World War One' (PhD thesis, University of Otago, 2015), p.136.

81 CG, Vol. 44, 9 (September 1914), p.162.

82 NZB, Vol. 32, No. 370 (October 1914), p.181.

83 AS, 29 November 1916, p.4.

84 CG, Vol. 44, No. 10 (October 1914), pp.182–183.

85 CG, Vol. 45, No. 6 (June 1915), p.87.

86 CG, Vol. 46, No. 6 (June 1916), p.93.

87 CG, Vol. 45, No. 12 (December 1915), Synod Supplement, p.xvii.

88 AS, 13 February 1915, p.14.

89 NZB, Vol. 32, No. 370 (October 1914), p.185.

90 NZT, Vol. 41, No. 33 (20 August 1914), p.33.

91 NZT, Vol. 41, No. 34 (28 August 1914), p.25.

92 NZT, Vol. 41, No. 36 (10 September 1914), p.22.

93 NZB, Vol. 32, No. 369 (September 1914), p.161. See also 'Sursum Corda', NZB, Vol. 32, No. 381 (September 1915), pp.177–178.

94 NZB, Vol. 32, No. 369 (September 1914), p.172.

95 CG, Vol. 44, No. 11 (November 1914), p.194.

96 CG, Vol. 45, No. 7 (July 1915), p.100.

97 CG, Vol. 46, No. 11 (November 1916), p.171.

98 NZT, Vol. 43, No. 26 (1 July 1915) p.29.

99 NZT 42, No. 17 (29 April 1915), p.21.

100 WC, Vol. 35, No. 39 (19 June 1915), p.4.

101 For an example see William S. Currie, Waikino, in NZB, Vol. 32, No. 370 (October 1915), p.182.

102 NZB, Vol. 32, No. 370 (October 1915), pp.187–188.

103 NZT, Vol. 43, No. 5 (3 February 1916), pp.11–15.

104 For an example see NZT, Vol. 43, No. 17 (29 April 1915), pp.26–27, 33; NZT, Vol. 43, No. 18 (6 May 1915), p.13; NZT, Vol. 43, No. 22 (6 June 1915), pp.27, 34.

105 NZT, Vol. 41, No. 36 (10 September 1914), p.51.

106 See NZT, Vol. 41, No. 32 (13 August 1914), pp.25–26; NZMT, Vol. 5, No. 20 (23 January 1915), pp.3–4; CG, Vol. 44, No. 9 (September 1914), p.162.

107 NZB, Vol. 32, No. 371 (November 1914), p.201; NZMT, Vol. 5, No. 19 (9 January 1915), p.7.

108 CG, Vol. 44, No. 9 (September 1914), p.162.

109 *Dominion*, 18 August 1914, p.6; ODT, 19 August 1914, p.6; *Star* (Christchurch), 4 November 1914, p.4; *Dominion*, 23 May 1917, p.4.

110 *Sun*, 13 August 1914, p.7.
111 CG, Vol. 45, No. 11 (November 1915), p.184.
112 NZMT, Vol. 6, No. 1 (1 May 1915), p.1.
113 NZMT, Vol. 7, No. 18 (6 January 1917), p.1; NZT, Vol. 45, No. 5 (31 January 1918), p.13.
114 CG, Vol. 45, No. 9 (September 1915), p.148.
115 ODT, 10 August 1914, p.5.
116 ODT, 11 August 1914, p.2.
117 NZB, Vol. 32, No. 373 (January 1915), p.11.
118 WC, Vol. 36, No. 7 (6 November 1915), p.3.
119 NZB, Vol. 32, No. 369 (September 1914), p.173; WC, Vol. 35, No. 52 (18 September 1915), p.4.
120 WC, Vol. 35, No. 21 (13 February 1915), p.4; see also WC, Vol. 35, No. 22 (20 February 1915), pp.2–4.
121 ATL, 95-017-01/4, 'YMCA and World War One – Miscellaneous papers', YMCA Minutes of Exec 1916–18; Field Secretaries conference, 26 June 1917.
122 NZMT, Vol. 5, No. 26 (17 April 1915), p.1.
123 For an example see CG, Vol. 46, No. 9 (September 1916), p.132.
124 *Otautau Standard* (OS), 20 April 1915, p.4; OS, 4 May 1915, p.5; OS, 11 May 1915, p.5; NZT, Vol. 42, No. 18 (6 May 1915), p.34.
125 For an example see, *Manawatu Times*, 4 August 1914, p.6.
126 NZT, Vol. 42, No. 25 (24 June 1915), p.31; EP, 18 June 1915, p.8.
127 NZT, Vol. 43, No. 18 (4 May 1916), pp.17–18.
128 See H.S. Moores, 'The Rise of the Protestant Political Association: Sectarianism in New Zealand Politics during World War I (MA thesis, University of Auckland, 1966); P.S. O'Connor, 'Sectarian Conflict in New Zealand, 1911–20', *Political Science*, 19/1 (1967), pp.3–16; Max Satchell, 'Pulpit Politics: The Protestant Political Association in Dunedin from 1917 to 1922' (BA Hons, University of Otago, 1983).
129 For an example see NZMT, Vol. 5, No. 19 (9 January 1915), p.9.
130 *Dominion*, 10 August 1915, p.4.
131 NZB, Vol. 32, No. 368 (August 1915), p.148.
132 NZT, Vol. 43, No. 9 (2 March 1916), p.17.
133 Ormond Burton, *The Auckland Regiment* (Christchurch, 1922), pp.217–218.
134 NZB, Vol. 32, No. 370 (October 1914), p.194.
135 *Press*, 21 July 1915, p.8; *Press*, 23 July 1915, pp.2, 6.
136 For an example see Rev. S. Robertson Orr at Tokomairiro, reported in full in *Bruce Herald*, 20 August 1914, p.5.
137 *Taranaki Daily News*, 12 August 1914, p.6.
138 *Colonist*, 7 January 1915, p.2.
139 *Proceedings of the General Synod* (Christchurch, 1916), pp.4–5.

Chapter Twelve – Of Violets and Poppies: Charities in the Great War

1 From Charles Marris, 'Who Will Buy? Specially written for the *Sun*', *Sun* 4 September 1914, p.6.
2 *Evening Post* (EP), 10 August 1914, p.9.
3 Arthur Marwick, *The Deluge: British Society and the First World War* (London, 1965).
4 For an account emphasising continuities within New Zealand's wartime experiences see Steven Loveridge, *Calls to Arms: New Zealand Society and Commitment to the Great War* (Wellington, 2014), p.244.

5 John Horne, 'Introduction: Mobilizing for "Total War", 1914–1918', in Horne (ed.), *State, Society and Mobilization in Europe During the First World War* (Cambridge, 1997), p.7.

6 Peter Grant, 'Voluntarism and the impact of the First World War', in Matthew Hilton and James McKay (eds), *The Ages of Voluntarism: How We Got to the Big Society* (Oxford, 2011), p.46. For an earlier description of the varieties of war charity in Britain see Simon Fowler, 'War Charity Begins at Home', *History Today*, 49/9 (September 1999), pp.17–23.

7 For a broad discussion of the non-profit sector in New Zealand see Margaret Tennant, Mike O'Brien and Jackie Sanders, *The History of the Non-profit Sector in New Zealand* (Wellington, 2008). I have discussed welfare more specifically in Tennant, *The Fabric of Welfare: Voluntary Organisations, Government and Welfare in New Zealand, 1840–2005* (Wellington, 2007).

8 The notion of a 'mixed economy of welfare' was elaborated most fully from the 1990s, especially in the United Kingdom. For examples see Geoffrey Finlayson, *Citizen, State and Social Welfare in Britain, 1830–1990* (Oxford, 1990).

9 See Tennant, *Paupers and Providers: Charitable Aid in New Zealand* (Wellington, 1989).

10 Tennant, The *Fabric of Welfare*, pp.22, 40, 62.

11 Tennant, *The Fabric of Welfare*, pp.21–65.

12 *Press*, 4 September 1914, p.8.

13 *Papers Past* shows that the phrase 'poor little Belgium' appeared constantly in newspapers from late 1914. For examples of contexts see, *Auckland Star* (AS), 19 November 1914, p.2; *Hawera & Normanby Star* (HNS), 9 November 1914, p.3; *Truth*, 19 December 1914, p.5; *Mt Ida Chronicle*, 20 August 1915, p.1.

14 For the responses of patriotic societies to the needs of soldiers' families see Melanie Nolan, '"Keeping New Zealand Home Fires Burning": Gender, Welfare and the First World War', in John Crawford and Ian McGibbon (eds), *New Zealand's Great War: New Zealand, the Allies and the First World War* (Auckland, 2007), pp.493–515; Rachel Patrick, 'An Unbroken Connection? New Zealand Families, Duty and the First World War' (PhD thesis, Victoria University of Wellington, 2014), pp.141–169.

15 Sarah Glassford, 'Marching as to War: The Canadian Red Cross Society, 1885–1939' (PhD thesis, York University, 2007), p.263.

16 The wartime establishment of the Red Cross in New Zealand is covered in more detail in Margaret Tennant, *Across the Street, Across the World: The Red Cross in New Zealand 1915–2015* (Wellington, 2015), pp.29–54.

17 For overviews of patriotic activity see nzhistory.net: 'Who were the volunteers?', URL: http://www.nzhistory.net.nz/war/supporting-war-effort/the-volunteers (Ministry for Culture and Heritage), updated 19 December 2014; 'What were the causes?', URL: http://www.nzhistory.net.nz/war/supporting-war-effort/wartime-causes (Ministry for Culture and Heritage), updated 2 February 2015.

18 Nolan, p.507.

19 See Dorothy Page, 'Service Organisations', in Anne Else (ed.), *Women Together: A History of Women's Organisations in New Zealand. Ngā Rōpu Wāhine o Te Motu* (Wellington, 1993), p.292; 'Supporting the war effort, 1914–1919', URL: http://www.nzhistory.net.nz/war/supporting-war-effort (Ministry for Culture and Heritage), updated 22 December 2014.

20 A gap between the official list of reported patriotic funds and the wider voluntary effort is suggested by the total of 64 funds associated with the Canterbury Military District in 1918 and the claim of the Red Cross's alone to at least 150 branches and

sub-branches in the same area. *New Zealand Red Cross Record* (NZRC), 15 February 1917, p.16.

21 Graham Hucker, 'The Rural Home Front: A New Zealand Region and the Great War 1914–26' (PhD thesis, Massey University, 2006); Sarah Luxford, '"Partners in the Welfare of the Nation": The Involvement of Cambridge Women in Local Patriotic Organisations during the Great War' (BA Hons research exercise, Massey University, 2002); Sarah Jane Piesse, 'A History of the Otago Patriotic and General Welfare Association 1914–1950 and the Otago Provincial Patriotic Council 1939–' (MA thesis, University of Otago, 1981); Simon Johnson, 'The Home Front: Aspects of Civilian Patriotism in New Zealand During the First World War' (MA thesis, Massey University, 1975).

22 'Supporting the war effort, 1914–1919', URL: http://www.nzhistory.net.nz/war/supporting-war-effort, (Ministry for Culture and Heritage), updated 22 December 2014. All contemporary figures calculated using the Reserve Bank's Inflation Calculator, http://www.rbnz.govt.nz.

23 *Sun*, 3 September 1914, p.6.

24 L.O.H. Tripp, 'War Relief and Patriotic Societies', in H.T.B. Drew (ed.), *The War Effort of New Zealand* (Auckland, 1923), p.176.

25 Piesse, pp.63–64; Gwen Parsons, 'Debating the War: The Discourses of War in the Christchurch Community', in *New Zealand's Great War*, pp.550–555; Stevan Eldred-Grigg, *The Great Wrong War: New Zealand Society in WWI* (Auckland, 2010), pp.86–71, 106, 242 and *passim*.

26 *New Zealand Farmer*, September 1915, p.1215, quoted in Johnson, p.48.

27 *Appendices to the Journal of the House of Representatives*, 1918, H-46, 'Patriotic Funds', pp.4–15.

28 Page, p.292.

29 Caroline Daley, *Girls and Women, Men and Boys: Gender in Taradale 1886–1930* (Auckland, 1999), pp.117–118.

30 EP, 1 May 1915, p.9.

31 HNS, 7 August 1914, p.5.

32 Bruce Scates, 'The Unknown Sock Knitter: Voluntary Work, Emotional Labour, Bereavement and the Great War', *Labour History*, 81 (November 2001), pp.29–49; Joy Damousi, *The Labour of Loss: Mourning, Memory and Wartime Bereavement in Australia* (Cambridge, 1999).

33 Hucker, pp.80–81.

34 Johnson, pp.50–53; Tennant, 'Fun and Fundraising: the Selling of Charity in New Zealand's Past', *Social History*, 38/1 (February 2013), pp.46–65.

35 *The Carnival Book Wellington 1915: Cartoons and Sketches of the Queen Carnival* (Wellington, 1915), p.8.

36 NZRC, 27 July 1918, p.19.

37 Patrick, p.26.

38 *Otago Witness*, 23 September 1914, p.43, quoted in Patrick, p.53.

39 *Pukekohe & Waiuku Times*, 21 June 1918, p.2.

40 *NZRC*, 27 August, 1918, p.7, *NZRC*, 16 October 1918, p.3.

41 *Otago Daily Times*, 28 January 1915, p.2; *Poverty Bay Herald* (PBH), 13 March 1915, p.4.

42 *Dominion*, 10 March 1916, p.2.

43 *Otautau Standard and Wallace County Chronicle*, 6 June 1916, p.1; *Colonist*, 28 August 1916, p.2; *Sun*, 20 July 1917, p.4,

44 Page, p.293.

45 *NZRC*, 26 April 1917, p.3.
46 *NZRC*, 17 August 1916, p.11, *NZRC*, 15 January 1917, pp.3–4.
47 *NZRC*, 15 May 1916, p.17.
48 *NZRC*, 27 August 1918, p. 18.
49 *NZRC*, 17 August 1916, p. 26.
50 New Zealand High Commission, *A Short Sketch of the New Zealand Prisoners of War Department, London and of Other Undertakings Connected with the War* (London, 1917), p.25.
51 Johnson, pp.51–52; EP, 3 June 1915, p.62.
52 *New Zealand Herald* (NZH), 20 June 1918, p.7.
53 Tripp, p.179.
54 See, for example, *Sun*, 4 July 1917, p.11; *Sun*, 30 May 1917, p.4.
55 PBH, 31 August 1917, p.4.
56 AS, 10 February 1916, p.2.
57 NZH, 26 June 1917, p.8.
58 NZH, 26 June 1917, p.7.
59 AS, 10 February 1915, p.2.
60 *Annual Report, Society for the Protection of Women and Children (Auckland Branch), 1917–18*, p.8.
61 Tennant, *The Fabric of Welfare*, p.86; Margaret McClure, *Saving the City: The History of the Order of the Good Shepherd and the Community of the Holy Name in Auckland, 1894–2000* (Auckland, 2002), pp.65–66.
62 NZH, 5 July 1915, p.5.
63 Nolan, p.507.
64 Tennant, *Paupers and Providers: Charitable Aid in New Zealand* (Wellington, 1989), p.109.
65 See, for example, *Annual Report, Society for the Protection of Women and Children (Wellington Branch), 1915–16*, pp.5, 7. See also Nolan, pp.502–503.
66 Geoffrey Rice with assistance from Linda Bryder, *Black November: The 1918 Influenza Pandemic in New Zealand*, 2nd ed. (Christchurch, 2005), p.151.
67 *NZRC*, May 1919, p.3.
68 Tennant, *Across the Street*, p.86.
69 EP, 15 March 1937, p.16.
70 *New Zealand Life*, September/October 1929, p.22.
71 Nolan, pp.509–511.
72 Piesse, pp.85–95; Archives New Zealand, R17489929-ADBO-16141-W2756-SS7W2756-63-11/2/38, 'War Pensions – General – Patriotic societies and war relief funds', Conference of Patriotic Societies, 17–18 February 1916.
73 I have discussed the longer-term impact of war in Tennant, *The Fabric of Welfare*, pp.86–87, 100. See also an extended discussion by Parsons, 'Challenging Enduring Home Front Myths: Jingoistic Civilians and Neglected Soldiers', in David Monger, Sarah Murray and Katie Pickles (eds), *Endurance and the First World War: Experiences and Legacies in New Zealand and Australia* (Newcastle upon Tyne, 2014), pp.66–85.
74 This phrase was in *Federation of New Zealand Patriotic War Relief Societies*, quoted in Piesse, p.26.

Chapter Thirteen – Where Were The Peacemongers? Pacifists in New Zealand During World War One

1 *New Zealand Herald* (NZH), 8 August 1914, p.1.

2 R.L. Weitzel, 'Pacifists and Anti-Militarists in New Zealand, 1909–1914', *New Zealand Journal of History* (NZJH), 7/2 (October 1973), p.130.

3 Born in 1869, Mackie was the son of a sheep farmer, also named Charles, who belonged to one of the original runholding families in Canterbury. In 1884, Charles senior sold his share in the run for £10,043 and returned to England; his son was able to live on the largesse and devote himself fulltime to peace work, as well as the Workers' Educational Association, the New Zealand Society for the Protection of Women and Children and the New Zealand Howard League for Prison Reform. See J.E. Cookson, 'Mackie, Charles Robert Norris', *Dictionary of New Zealand Biography, Te Ara – the Encyclopaedia of New Zealand*, www.teara.govt.nz/en/biographies/3m20/mackie-charles-robert-norris.

4 David Grant, *Field Punishment No 1: Archibald Baxter, Mark Briggs and New Zealand's anti-militarist tradition* (Wellington, 2008), p. 26.

5 Grant, *Out in the Cold: Pacifists and Conscientious Objectors in New Zealand during World War II* (Wellington, 1986), p.15.

6 Grant, *Field Punishment*, p.26. See also Weitzel.

7 P.S. O'Connor, 'The Awkward Ones – Dealing with Conscience, 1916–1918', NZJH, 8/2 (October 1974), p.24.

8 Grant, *Field Punishment*, pp.28–29.

9 Elsie Locke, *Peace People: A History of Peace Activities in New Zealand* (Christchurch, 1992), pp.48–49.

10 This information is gleaned from the Freedom League's Minute Books across March 1913 – July 1914. See Alexander Turnbull Library (ATL), MS-Papers-2531-1, 'New Zealand Freedom League: Minute Books' and MS-Papers-2531-2, 'New Zealand Freedom League: Minute Books'.

11 Penelope A. Dunkley (ed.), *In the Beginning: Minutes of the First and Second Conferences of the New Zealand Society of Friends held in 1909 in Wellington and in 1910 in Auckland, with some Associated Papers* (Wellington 2003), pp.13–14.

12 Dunkley, p.42.

13 Wright added in his letter: 'we believe that all war is contrary to the authority of Christ and that righteousness exults a nation whilst the war spirit tends to its destruction'. Minute 13 of the General Conference of New Zealand Friends held in the Druids Hall, Wellington, over 10–12 May 1909. Cited in Dunkley, pp.13–14.

14 Dunkley, pp.14, 35. K.R. Adams records in some detail the Quaker opposition to the 1909 Defence Act, the church's anti-militarist activities during the First World War – particularly in response to the military conscription legislation – and some of the experiences of Quakers jailed after they lost their appeals against military service and refused to undertake non-combatant service; see K.R. Adams, 'The Growth and Development of the Society of Friends in New Zealand, 1840–1920' (MA thesis, University of Canterbury, 1986), pp.155–185.

15 *Repeal*, 31 March 1913, p.4.

16 *Repeal* was so-called because these young agitators wanted to repeal the Defence Act. Grant, *Field Punishment*, p.24.

17 Yet protesting compulsory military training was still a minority issue and many thousands of young New Zealand men were trained as soldiers in this fashion. Moreover, it is likely that some resisters were rebels with scant political motivation. Grant, *Field Punishment*, pp.24–25.

18 See Herbert Roth, 'The Prisoners of Ripa Island', *Here and Now*, (1954), pp.16–18 and Weitzel.

19 Grant, *Field Punishment*, p.26.

20 *Evening Post* (EP), 19 September 1914, p.6.
21 Despite being of military age, Mack never served in the war. Sarah Murray, *The Cartoon War: The Cartoons of the New Zealand Free Lance and New Zealand Observer as Historical Sources. August 1914–November 1918* (Wellington, 2012), p.22.
22 Grant, *Field Punishment*, p.27.
23 Grant, *Field Punishment*, pp.26–27. Locke, p.49.
24 ATL, MS-Papers-2531-4, 'New Zealand Freedom League: Minute Books', 10 August 1914.
25 Paul Baker, *King and Country Call: New Zealanders, Conscription and the Great War* (Auckland, 1988), p.75.
26 Cookson. The Christian Pacifist Society was led by Reverend Ormond Burton, a decorated World War One soldier and war historian, and Archibald Barrington. It ran street protests and held public meetings in Wellington through late 1939 and 1940 until its activists were arrested and imprisoned. See Grant, *Out in the Cold*, pp.36–41 and Grant, *A Question of Faith: A History of the Christian Pacifist Society* (Wellington, 2004), pp.18–27.
27 This information is gleaned from the Freedom League's Minute Books. See ATL, MS-Papers-2531-2 and MS-Papers-2531-4.
28 Algie would later become a cabinet minister in Sid Holland's National government in the 1950s.
29 All contemporary figures calculated using the Reserve Bank's Inflation Calculator, http://www.rbnz.govt.nz.
30 Baker, *King and Country*, p.78.
31 NZH, 2 November 1915, p.5. Baker, *King and Country*, p.77.
32 ATL, MS-Papers-2531-4, 'New Zealand Freedom League: Minute Books', 15 November 1915.
33 NZH, 2 November 1915, p.5.
34 Baker, *King and Country Call*, p.78.
35 *New Zealand Observer*, 29 April 1916, p.2.
36 Baker, 'New Zealanders, Conscription and the Great War' (PhD thesis, University of Auckland, 1986), p.157.
37 *Otago Daily Times*, 2 February 1918, p.10.
38 NZH, 2 February 1918, p.6. ATL, MS-Papers-2597-29/02, 'New Zealand Yearly Meeting of the Society of Friends', Eric J. Appleby to Friends, 31 January 1918.
39 ATL, MS-Papers-2597-29/02, 'New Zealand Yearly Meeting of the Society of Friends', Eric J. Appleby to Friends, 31 January 1918.
40 ATL, MS-Papers-2597-29/02, 'New Zealand Yearly Meeting of the Society of Friends', Alfred M. Naughton to Friends, 7 September 1918.
41 ATL, MS-Papers-2597-33/6/05b, 'New Zealand Yearly Meeting of the Society of Friends', Constance Gill to John Holdsworth, 1 August 1918. It was also noteworthy that his sentence was less than the one- or two-year prison sentences handed out to the bulk of conscientious objectors who failed, or ignored, their appeals against military service. Some objectors, of course, accepted non-combatant service, and served as stretcher bearers, medical orderlies or clerks at, or close to, the front line.
42 Two of McCullough's sons joined the Passive Resisters' Union and a third, Frank, edited its journal, *The Repeal*, for which he was fined and imprisoned. The war would break up the McCullough family. Frank left for the United States to escape victimisation as a conscientious objector. Another son, Jim, who had a fraught relationship with his father, volunteered for service in 1916 and was killed in France. Another son, Bill, was exempted on medical grounds; he worked in the railways

and was active in the Workers' Educational Association. Ron, the youngest and a farm labourer, spent three years on the run in the South Island after being called up. Melanie Nolan, 'McCullough, John Alexander', DNZB, www.teara.govt.nz/en/biographies/3m4/mccullough-john-alexander.

43 Baker, 'New Zealanders, Conscription and the Great War', p.152.

44 Baker, 'New Zealanders, Conscription and the Great War', p.152.

45 Grant, *Out in the Cold*, p.33.

46 Brocas later faced another torment when his son enlisted. He 'could not sleep at night for thinking of it'. Baker, 'New Zealanders, Conscription and the Great War', p.153.

47 He won 155 votes to his opponents' 83 and 69 votes respectively.

48 The Dargaville newspaper the *Wairoa Bell and Northern Advertiser* has a full transcript of the Magistrate's Court trial where Gregory refused to exhibit the National Reserve poster – and his subsequent disqualification as a borough councillor. *Wairoa Bell and Northern Advertiser*, 13 September 1916.

49 When his wife decided to contest his vacant council seat Gregory was further vilified as a man who not only would fail to defend her but would also hide behind her. She lost badly in the by-election. Baker, 'New Zealanders, Conscription and the Great War', pp.154–157.

50 Maurice Gee is James Chapple's grandson.

51 *Maoriland Worker* (MW), 8 December, 1915, p.6.

52 Geoff Chapple, 'Chapple, James Henry George', DNZB, www.teara.govt.nz/en/biographies/3c12/chapple-james-henry-george. Before he left for the United States, many Timaru people, he believed, thought he was a German. Baker, *King and Country*, pp.76, 168. Grant, *Field Punishment*, pp.27–28.

53 Grant, *Out in the Cold*, p.33.

54 Harry R. Urquhart, *Men and Marbles* (Auckland, 1917), p.4.

55 Grant, *Field Punishment*, p.27.

56 Along with Archibald Barrington, Burton formed the Christian Pacifist Society in 1936.

57 Megan Hutching, 'The Moloch of War: New Zealand Women who Opposed the War', in John Crawford and Ian McGibbon (eds), *New Zealand's Great War: New Zealand, the Allies and the First World War* (Auckland, 2007), p.87. See also Hutching, 'Mothers of the World: Women, Peace and Arbitration in Early Twentieth-Century New Zealand', NZJH, 27/2 (October 1993), pp.173–185.

58 'To the Women of New Zealand: A Plea for the Repeal of the Defence Act'. ATL, 82-213-02, 'Pacifism in New Zealand' Roth, Herbert Otto, Papers.

59 Weitzel, p.132.

60 For example see MW, 5 May 1915, p.1; MW, 15 December 1915, p.1; MW, 10, May 1916, p.3; MW, 12 January 1916, p.3.

61 Locke, p.51.

62 Locke, p.51.

63 Hutching, 'The Moloch of War', p.89.

64 These organisations were as much feminist as anti-militarist, with members wanting to advance women's solidarity and rights.

65 *Truth*, 27 May, 1916, p.4.

66 On her return to Melbourne, on 15 August 1917, she was arrested and sentenced to nine months' imprisonment for sedition after leading a crowd of several hundred women socialists to the Federal House of Parliament to try to force an entrance while the House was in session. The women shouted that they wanted work and

that the high price of food should be lowered. After a violent clash with police the women were arrested. EP, 16 August 1917, p.7; EP, 5 September 1917, p.7. In the 1930s, Adela changed her political views, becoming an outspoken anti-Communist. Hutching, 'The Moloch of War', pp.87–88.

67 See Graham Hucker, '"The Great Wave of Enthusiasm": New Zealand Reactions to the First World War in August 1914 – A Reassessment', NZJH, 43/1, (April 2009), pp.12–27.

Chapter Fourteen – 'We stand for the Protestant religion, the (Protestant) King and the Empire': The Rise of the Protestant Political Association in World War One

1 There has been no authoritative published account of the Protestant Political Association, but H.S. Moores, 'The Rise of the Protestant Political Association – Sectarianism in New Zealand Politics during World War I' (MA thesis, University of Auckland, 1966) is a source of much information that would otherwise be difficult to obtain. Max Satchell, 'Pulpit Politics – The Protestant Political Association in Dunedin from 1917 to 1922' (BA Hons, University of Otago, 1983) provides a unique local case study. Rory Sweetman, 'New Zealand Catholicism, War, Politics and the Irish Issue 1912–1922' (PhD thesis, University of Cambridge, 1990) offers valuable background from a Catholic perspective. Dickon John Milnes, 'The Church Militant: Dunedin Churches and Society during World War One' (PhD thesis, University of Otago, 2015) addresses issues concerning sectarianism and the PPA in Dunedin.

2 *New Zealand Herald* (NZH), 15 February 1918, p.4; *Wanganui Chronicle* (WC), 15 February 1918, p.5.

3 *Dominion*, 16 February 1918, p.8.

4 *Evening Post* (EP), 4 March 1918, p.6.

5 *Auckland Star* (AS), 18 May 1918, p.4.

6 P.S. O'Connor, 'Sectarian Conflict in New Zealand, 1911–1920', *Political Science* (PS), 19/1 (1967), pp.3–16; O'Connor, 'Protestants, Catholics and the New Zealand Government, 1916–18', in G.A. Wood and O'Connor (eds), *W.P. Morrell: A Tribute* (Dunedin, 1973), pp.185–202; Sweetman, 'New Zealand Catholicism and the Irish Issue, 1914–1922', in W.J. Shiels and Diana Wood (eds), *The Churches, Ireland and the Irish* (Oxford and New York, 1989), pp.375–384.

7 O'Connor, 'Protestants, Catholics and the New Zealand Government', p.185.

8 Jock Phillips and Terry Hearn, *Settlers: New Zealand Immigrants from England, Ireland and Scotland, 1800–1945* (Auckland, 2008); Hearn, 'The Origins of New Zealand's Irish Settlers, 1840–1945', in Brad Patterson (ed.), *The Irish in New Zealand: Historical Contexts & Perspectives* (Wellington, 2002), pp.15–34.

9 Richard S. Hill, *The Colonial Frontier Tamed: New Zealand Policing in Transition, 1867–1886* (Wellington, 1989), pp.156–161; Seán Brosnahan, 'The "Battle of the Borough" and the "Saige o Timaru": Sectarian Riot in Colonial Canterbury', *New Zealand Journal of History*, 28/1 (April 1994), pp.41–59.

10 Sweetman, 'Towards a History of Orangeism in New Zealand', in Patterson (ed.), *Ulster–New Zealand Migration and Cultural Transfers* (Dublin, 2006), pp.154–164; Gerard Horn, 'The Orange Order in Wellington 1874–1930: Class, Ethnicity and Politics', *Australasian Journal of Irish Studies*, 10 (2010), pp.55–80; P.J. Coleman, 'Transplanted Irish Institutions: Orangeism and Hibernianism in New Zealand 1877–1910' (MA thesis, University of Canterbury, 1994).

11 Patterson, '"We love one country, one queen, one flag": Loyalism in Early Colonial New Zealand, 1840–1880', in Allan Blackstock and Frank O'Gorman (eds), *Loyalism and the Formation of the British World 1775–1914* (Woodbridge, UK, 2014), pp.255–261.

12 Richard P. Davis, *Irish Issues in New Zealand Politics 1868–1922* (Dunedin, 1974), pp.71–98; Ian Breward, *Godless Schools? A Study of Protestant Reactions to the Education Act of 1877* (Christchurch, 1967), pp.21–36, 47–73.

13 Davis, *Irish Issues*, pp.78–79; Sweetman, *'A Fair and Just Solution?': A History of the Integration of Private Schools in New Zealand* (Palmerston North, 2002), pp.23–25.

14 Davis, *Irish Issues*, p.82.

15 Michael Bassett, *Sir Joseph Ward: A Political Biography* (Auckland, 1993), pp.141–155.

16 Moores, pp.24, 33; James Watson, 'Were Catholics Over-Represented in the Public Service during the Early Twentieth Century', PS, 42/2 (1990), pp.20–34.

17 Moores, p.33.

18 Davis, *Irish Issues*, pp.144–162.

19 O'Connor, 'Sectarian Conflict', pp.1–2; Donald Harman Akenson, *Half the World From Home: Perspectives on the Irish in New Zealand 1860–1950* (Wellington, 1990), pp.105–106.

20 Breward, pp.52–71; D.V. MacDonald, 'The New Zealand Bible in Schools League' (MA thesis, Victoria University of Wellington, 1964).

21 NZH, 10 December 1912, p.9.

22 Sweetman, *Faith and Fraternalism: A History of the Hibernian Society in New Zealand 1869–2000* (Wellington, 2002), pp.95–96.

23 EP, 8 January 1913, p.2.

24 Breward, pp.60–62.

25 *Manawatu Standard* (MS), 14 December 1914, p.5.

26 James Belich, *Paradise Reforged: A History of the New Zealanders from the 1880s to the Year 2000* (Auckland, 2001), p.98.

27 *New Zealand Tablet* (NZT), 20 August 1914; Hugh Laracy, 'Priests, People and Patriotism: New Zealand Catholics and the War, 1914–1918', *Australasian Catholic Record*, 70/1 (1993), p.19.

28 NZT, 10 September 1914, p.49; cited in Laracy, p.21.

29 EP, 18 February 1914, p.4; EP, 24 February 1915, p.3; EP, 12 July 1915, p.4.

30 EP, 24 February 1915, p.3.

31 Moores, p.52; EP, 25 August 1915, p.11; EP, 7 January 1916, p.4; AS, 20 January 1916, p.7.

32 *Feilding Star*, 8 September 1916, p.2; *Dominion*, 1 September 1916, p.6.

33 *Sun*, 19 May 1914, p.3; *Otago Daily Times* (ODT), 19 May 1914, p.6; EP, 24 February 1915, p.3; NZH, 19 November 1915, p.4; NZH, 3 December 1915, p.7; EP, 26 February 1916, p.2.

34 Moores, p.111.

35 C. Van der Krogt, 'Elliott, Howard Leslie', *Dictionary of New Zealand Biography, Te Ara – the Encyclopedia of New Zealand*, http://www.TeAra.govt.nz/en/biographies/3e5/elliott-howard-leslie; Moores, pp.87–90. A small collection of papers relating to Elliott, collected by Moores, is now held in the University of Auckland Library (an inventory is available).

36 *Australasian Christian Word*, Vol. 21, No. 1061, 27 July 1906; cited in Moores, p.88.

37 Breward, p.60; Moores, p.108. Elliott's proposed political party was to be a 'Christian Socialist Party', a counter to the 'atheistic, materialistic socialists' then

steering the Labour movement. In planning this party he flirted with rebel Liberal politician George Fowlds. Moores, p.103.

38 Moores, p.108.

39 Moores, p.86.

40 Moores, p.111. When researching his thesis, Moores had access to many involved individuals (29 interviewees), including H.S. Bilby and members of the Elliott family. He also had access to Orange Order records that are no longer locatable.

41 Moores, p.111.

42 Moores, pp.122–123.

43 NZH, 10 April 1916, p.7; NZH, 14 April 1916, p.7. Committee of Vigilance (Loyal Orange Lodge no. 70) *The Papal Delegate and the Mayor* (Auckland, 1916).

44 Moores, p.116.

45 NZH, 20 April 1916, p.8.

46 EP, 22 April 1916, p.6; *Dominion*, 24 April 1916, p.9; *Report of Proceedings of Eighth Annual Session of the Grand Orange Lodge of New Zealand* (Christchurch, 1916), pp.14–18.

47 Moores, p.124.

48 Moores, p.128. All contemporary figures calculated using the Reserve Bank's Inflation Calculator, http://www.rbnz.govt.nz.

49 G.E. Horn, 'The Irish Revolution and Protestant Politics in New Zealand 1916–22', unpublished paper delivered to 'The Irish Diaspora and Revolution' Conference, NUI Maynooth, November 2012, p.4.

50 In spite of a courtesy visit by Prime Minister Massey, there is no evidence that he was party to the plan. Moores, p.129.

51 Moores, pp.131–135.

52 Regular flows of donations are recorded in the Minute Book of the Orange Hall Trustees, Auckland, 1915–32, cited in Moores, p.134. The Secretary of the Trustees was J.J. Carnahan, influential historian of the New Zealand Orange movement.

53 Published by Free Press Print (Wm Richardson) Auckland; *Marlborough Express*, 20 August 1917, p.8; Moores, p.145.

54 *Appendix to the Journals of the House of Representatives* (AJHR), 1917, F-8, 'Auckland Post Office Inquiry', p.105. See also Alex Frame, *Salmond: Southern Jurist* (Wellington, 1995), pp.175–178.

55 Moores, p.153.

56 Moores, p.153; EP, 27 January 1917, p.3; *Eltham Argus*, 25 January, 1917, p.4.

57 Cited in Moores, p.154; *Truth*, 17 February 1917, p.1.

58 NZH, 1 March 1917, p.6; AS, 1 March 1917, p.4.

59 NZH, 1 March 1917, p.6.

60 NZT, 15 March 1917, p.31.

61 *New Zealand Baptist*, May 1917, p.76.

62 Moores, p.159.

63 ODT, 9 April 1916, p.6; ODT, 10 April 1917, p.6. *Report of Proceedings of Ninth Annual Session of the Grand Orange Lodge of New Zealand* (Wellington, 1917), pp.22–24.

64 H.S. Bilby interview, 2 June 1965; cited in Moores, pp.165, 168.

65 *Nation*, 10 July 1917, p.10.

66 NZH, 12 July 1917, p.6.

67 NZH, 12 July 1917, p.6.

68 AJHR, 1917, F-8, 'Auckland Post Office Inquiry'; Moores, pp.174–207, focusses fully on the Post Office Inquiry.

69 *New Zealand Parliamentary Debates* (NZPD), Vol.180, 13 September 1917, pp.108–109, 133.
70 *Dominion*, 16 October 1917, p.5; *Maoriland Worker*, 24 October 1917, p.4.
71 NZH, 3 November 1917, p.8; *Press*, 3 November 1917, p.8.
72 *Truth*, 10 November 1917, p.1.
73 EP, 12 December 1917, p.3.
74 *Colonist*, 16 April 1919, p.1.
75 *Press*, 20 August 1920, p.8.
76 The lack of primary documentation precludes precise determination of just what sort of people made up PPA membership. That they were Protestants is axiomatic, indications being that Methodists, Baptists and other nonconformist churches were most strongly represented. Moores, pp.221–223.
77 Moores, pp.209–212.
78 *Nation*, 10 September 1917, p.4, *Nation*, 10 October 1917, pp.12–13.
79 *Nation*, 10 October 1917, p.10; EP, 12 December 1917, p.3; *Ellesmere Guardian* (EG), 20 March 1918, p.3; *Otautau Standard and Wallace County Chronicle* (Otautau SWCC), 4 March 1919, p.3. The 225 branches by mid-1919 ranged in size from over 4,000 to less than 50 members, almost all having exhibited significant growth from mid-1917. By early 1918 it had become readily apparent that an increasing proportion of the PPA membership was drawn from outside the ranks of the lodges, and that an adjustment was required in the relationship with the Loyal Orange Institution. When attempts to paper over the differences were unsuccessful, it was agreed at the April 1918 meeting of the Grand Lodge that separation was inevitable. EP, 18 June 1919, p.6; *Report of Proceedings of Tenth Annual Session of the Grand Orange Lodge of New Zealand* (Wellington, 1918), p.9; Moores, pp.241–246.
80 *Press*, 21 September 1917, p.5.
81 *Wairarapa Age* (WA), 20 February 1918, p.4.
82 *Dominion*, 24 April 1918, p.6.
83 NZH, 28 August 1918, p.9.
84 NZH, 28 August 1918, p.9.
85 Sweetman, '"Who Fears to Speak of Easter Week?" Antipodean Irish Catholic Responses to the 1916 Rising', in Ruan O'Donnell (ed.), *The Impact of the 1916 Rising: Among the Nations* (Dublin, 2008), pp.74–77.
86 NZT, 4 May 1916; Cited in Sweetman, 'Antipodean Irish Catholic Responses', p.76.
87 *Taranaki Daily News* (TDN), 12 February 1918, p.5.
88 NZH, 12 July 1917, p.6.
89 O'Connor, 'Storm over the Clergy – New Zealand 1917', *Journal of Religious History*, 4/2 (1966), pp.129–148; Paul Baker, *King and Country Call: New Zealanders, Conscription and the Great War* (Auckland, 1988).
90 EP, 11 December 1916, p.8; Laracy, pp.21–22.
91 NZH, 27 February 1917, p.6.
92 *Dominion*, 22 February 1917, p.6; O'Connor, 'Storm over the Clergy', pp.132–135.
93 WC, 18 July 1917, p.5.
94 *Press*, 21 September 1917, p.5.
95 Bassett, pp.229–230.
96 EP, 12 December 1917, p.3; AS, 28 August 1918, p.6.
97 O'Connor, 'Sectarian Conflict in New Zealand', p.9.
98 *Timaru Herald* (TH), 9 May 1918, p.2.
99 EP, 11 December 1916, p.8.
100 NZH, 17 September 1917, p.6.

101 AJHR, 1917, H-19D, 'Return Showing the Number of Adherents of Each Religious Denomination Embarked on Active Service to and Including the 28th Reinforcements'.
102 AJHR, 1917, H-19K, 'Defaulters from Military Service Not Found by Police up to 17 October 1917'.
103 Otautau SWCC, 4 March 1919, p.3.
104 ODT, 7 May 1918, p.7.
105 Brosnahan, '"Shaming the Shoneens": The *Green Ray* and the Maoriland Irish Society in Dunedin, 1916–22', in Lyndon Fraser (ed.), *A Distant Shore: Irish Migration & New Zealand Settlement* (Dunedin, 2000), pp.117–134.
106 Sweetman, 'Antipodean Irish Catholic Responses', pp.81–86; see also Sweetman, 'Kelly, James Joseph', *Dictionary of New Zealand Biography, Te Ara – the Encyclopedia of New Zealand*, http://www.teara.govt.nz/en/biographies/3k6/kelly-james-joseph.
107 Sweetman, 'Antipodean Irish Catholic Responses', p.82.
108 Laracy, pp.21–24; Moores, pp.218–219.
109 Barry Gustafson, *Labour's Path to Political Independence: the Origins and Establishment of the New Zealand Labour Party 1900–19* (Auckland, 1980), pp.89–94.
110 WC, 18 July 1917, p.5.
111 EP, 25 April 1918, p.4.
112 EP, 15 December 1917, p.4; EP, 1 January 1918, p.2.
113 EP, 1 January 1918, p.2.
114 While no formal alliance was brokered, the evidence suggests that between 1916 and 1919 the bulk of Irish Catholics did indeed transfer their allegiance from the Liberals to Labour. Catholic confidence in Ward had been severely eroded because of his failure to advance state aid for denominational schools, his inability to secure exempting legislation for conscripted clergy, and his relative silence on Irish issues. Labour also came to win the support of the Catholic bishops concerned at the economic and social problems confronting working-class Catholics. However, the Labour leadership, while including a sprinkle of practising Catholics, had as many or more who were committed Protestants or claimed no religion at all. Moores, p.273; R.P. Davis, 'The New Zealand Labour Party's "Irish Campaign", 1916–1921', PS, 19/2 (1967), pp.13–23. Gustafson, p.120.
115 Moores, p.216.
116 EP, 26 September 1917, p.3; *Truth*, 6 October 1917, p.1.
117 Moores, p.251. *Dominion*, 24 April 1918, p.3; *Hawera & Normanby Star*, 17 August 1918, p.5.
118 Moores, pp.287–310; Bassett & Michael King, *Tomorrow Comes the Song: A Life of Peter Fraser* (Auckland, 2000), pp.82–86; *Truth*, 28 September 1918, p.1.
119 EP, 28 September 1918, p.3.
120 *Dominion*, 4 October 1918, p.6.
121 *Nation*, October 1918, pp.2–3.
122 *Hastings Standard*, 31 January 1919, p.6.
123 *Truth*, 17 January 1920, p.5; *Dominion*, 25 February 1920, p.5; Bassett, pp.246–249.
124 TDN, 22 December 1919, p.5, TDN, 3 January 1919, p.11.
125 TDN, 5 June 1920, p.4.
126 *Dominion*, 13 May 1920, p.8; *Press*, 4 August 1920, p.6; EP, 8 September 1920, p.8; *Press*, 14 September 1920, p.6; *Press*, 18 September 1920, p.8; O'Connor, 'Mr Massey and the PPA – a Suspicion Confirmed', *Journal of Public Administration*, 28/2 (March 1966), pp.69–74.
127 NZH, 6 February 1929, p.12.

Chapter Fifteen – 'Bundling out the Hun': The Women's Anti-German League during the First World War

1 The Hawke's Bay league, under the presidency of Colonel J.L. Wheeler, was later incorporated into the New Zealand branch of the British Empire Union. The Parnell organisation operated under the presidency of a person named Chamberlain. Another league in Wanganui, under the presidency of F.M. Gifford Moore, was later presided over by John Jones in 1918.

2 For further analysis of this phenomenon see Steven Loveridge, 'A German is Always a German? Representations of Enemies, Germans and Race in New Zealand towards and during the First World War', *New Zealand Journal of History* (NZJH), 48/1 (2014), pp.51–77.

3 *New Zealand Gazette* (NZG), 10 November 1914, p.4022.

4 For scholarship on other examples see Andrew D. Trlin, *Now Respected, Once Despised: Yugoslavs in New Zealand* (Palmerston North, 1980), pp.99–134 and Judith Bassett, 'Colonial Justice: The Treatment of Dalmatians in New Zealand During the First World War', NZJH, 33/2 (1999), pp.155–179.

5 *Auckland Weekly News* (AWN), 21 October 1915, p.14.

6 For further scholarship on the riots see Andrew Francis, *'To Be Truly British We Must Be Anti-German': New Zealand, Enemy Aliens and the Great War Experience, 1914–1918* (New York, 2012).

7 David French, 'Spy Fever in Britain: 1900–1915', *Historical Journal*, 21/2 (1978), p.370.

8 *Feilding Star* (FS), 23 October 1914, p.2.

9 AWN, 3 September 1914, p.56.

10 AWN, 25 February 1915, p.14. Archives New Zealand (ANZ), R22430591-AAYS-8638-AD1-776-24/21/28, 'Personnel – Aliens – Enemy – Resolutions urging Government to take Additional precautions'.

11 See for example *New Zealand Parliamentary Debates* (NZPD), Vol.170, 9 October 1914, p.595; NZPD, Vol.171, 23 October 1914, p.309; FS, 23 October 1914, p.2.

12 ANZ, R21371954-AAAB-478-10/r, 'Signalling, Hutt and Belmont'.

13 ANZ, R21371954-AAAB-478-10/r, 'Signalling, Hutt and Belmont'.

14 ANZ, R21371956-AAAB-478/10t, 'Signalling, Karori'.

15 Peter Rees, *The Other Anzacs: Nurses at War, 1914–1918* (Crows Nest, 2008).

16 Loveridge, *Calls to Arms: New Zealand Society and Commitment to the Great War* (Wellington, 2014) pp.171–204.

17 *Evening Post*, 11 January 1916, p.9.

18 Simon Johnson, 'The Home Front: Aspects of Civilian Patriotism in New Zealand during the First World War' (MA thesis, Massey University, 1975), p.114.

19 *New Zealand Observer*, 1 April 1916, p.8.

20 Raewyn Dalziel, 'Stout, Anna Paterson', *Dictionary of New Zealand Biography, Te Ara – the Encyclopedia of New Zealand*, http://www.teara.govt.nz/en/biographies/2s47/stout-anna-paterson.

21 *Manawatu Standard*, 26 April 1916, p.5.

22 Bill Francis, *Tom Lowry: Leader in a Thousand* (Wellington, 2010), pp.23, 26–27.

23 *New Zealand Times* (NZT), 20 January 1916, p.9. All contemporary figures calculated using the Reserve Bank's Inflation Calculator, http://www.rbnz.govt.nz.

24 Women's Anti-German Manifesto cited in Johnson, p.113.

25 *Auckland Star*, 23 March 1916, p.2.

26 NZT, 9 February 1916, p.8; NZT, 29 July 1916, p.10; *Truth*, 5 February 1916, p.7; ANZ, R22434297-AAYS-8638-AD1-1030-59/86, 'Chaplains; Prisoners of War; Reservists – Aliens – Enemy – Correspondence with anti-German League'.
27 NZT, 2 May 1916, p.2.
28 ANZ, R22434297-AAYS-8638-AD1-1030-59/86, 'Chaplains; Prisoners of War; Reservists – Aliens – Enemy – Correspondence with anti-German League'.
29 NZT, 7 February 1916, p.2.
30 NZT, 27 July 1916, p.5.
31 NZPD, Vol.175, 17 May 1916, p.184.
32 ANZ, R21371766-AAAB-478-6e, 'Lights suspicious'.
33 ANZ, R21371629-AAAB-478-5/a, 'German celebrations, Auckland'.
34 NZT, 23 June 1916, p.4.
35 ANZ, R21371513-AAAB-478-1/ao, 'Boeufve, Madame'; *Dominion*, 20 March 1916, p.6.
36 *Hawke's Bay Herald*, 18 April 1916, p.5.
37 *Manawatu Daily Times* (MDT), 25 April 1916, p.5.
38 MDT, 25 April 1916, p.5.
39 MDT, 26 April 1916, p.4.
40 Details in this section are taken from MDT, 26 April 1916, p.4.
41 MDT, 26 April 1916, p.4.
42 NZT, 20 May 1916, p.4; *Dominion*, 20 May 1916, p.11.
43 *Dominion*, 10 July 1917, p.3; *Dominion*, 14 June 1918, p.2.
44 *Population Census*, 1911, p.xi.
45 NZG, 19 July 1915, p.2474.
46 *New Zealand Statutes*, 1917, No.8, pp.22–23.
47 ANZ, R22430591-AAYS-8638-AD1-776-24/21/28, 'Personnel – Aliens – Enemy – Resolutions urging Government to take Additional precautions'.
48 ANZ, R22431326, AAYS-8638-AD1-778-24/64, 'Personnel – Aliens (enemy) interned'.
49 *Appendices to the Journals of the House of Representatives*, 1919, H-33, 'Prisoners of War at Somes Island', p.2.
50 ANZ, R22431326, AAYS-8638-AD1-778-24/64, 'Personnel – Aliens (enemy) interned'. For further scholarship on internees see Francis, 'From "proven worthy settlers" to "lawless Hunnish brutes": Germans in New Zealand during the Great War', in Panikos Panayi (ed.), *Germans as Minorities during the First World War* (Surrey, 2014), pp.289–310.
51 ANZ, R22431326, AAYS-8638-AD1-778-24/64, 'Personnel – Aliens (enemy) interned'. For further analysis on recommendations concerning Yugoslavs see Bassett; Trlin.
52 ANZ, R22431326, AAYS-8638-AD1-778-24/64, 'Personnel – Aliens (enemy) interned'.
53 The caveat that this retention required prior permission from the German authorities seems to have been less well understood. Alfred Michael Boll, *Multiple Nationality and International Law* (Leiden, 2007), p.186.
54 NZT, 23 June 1916, p.4.
55 NZT, 23 June 1916, p.4.
56 See ANZ, R22431354-AAYS-8638-AD1-779-24/140, 'Personnel – Aliens at Gore – Alleged celebrations loss ships'. The file holds newspaper clippings and letters but no conclusive evidence that the disturbance was pro-German.
57 NZT, 13 March 1916, p.3.

58 *Te Puke Times*, 28 April 1916, p.2.
59 *Dominion*, 15 December 1917, p.8.
60 NZT, 23 June 1916, p.4.
61 NZT, 23 June 1916, p.4.
62 NZT, 12 May 1916, p.6.
63 ANZ, R21371462-AAAB-478-12/ac, 'W.A.G.L. Resolution'.
64 *Dominion*, 10 July 1917, p.3.
65 ANZ, R22430591-AAYS-8638-AD1-776-24/21/28, 'Personnel – Aliens – Enemy – Resolutions urging Government to take Additional precautions'.
66 ANZ, R22430591-AAYS-8638-AD1-776-24/21/28, 'Personnel – Aliens – Enemy – Resolutions urging Government to take Additional precautions'.
67 ANZ, R22434297-AAYS-8638-AD1-1030-59/86, 'Chaplains; Prisoners of War; Reservists – Aliens – Enemy – Correspondence with anti-German League'.
68 *New Zealand Herald*, 23 June 1916, p.7.
69 ANZ, R22431326, AAYS-8638-AD1-778-24/64, 'Personnel – Aliens (enemy) interned'.
70 ANZ, R22434297-AAYS-8638-AD1-1030-59/86, 'Chaplains; Prisoners of War; Reservists – Aliens – Enemy – Correspondence with anti-German League'.
71 ANZ, R22434297-AAYS-8638-AD1-1030-59/86, 'Chaplains; Prisoners of War; Reservists – Aliens – Enemy – Correspondence with anti-German League'.
72 *New Zealand Philistine* (NZP), 1/4 (1916), p.1.
73 *The Truth about the Grierson Inquiry* (Wellington: New Zealand Times Office, 1916?), p.4.
74 *The Truth about the Grierson Inquiry*, p.2.
75 *Press*, 5 May 1916, p.6.
76 MDT, 4 May 1916, p.6.
77 NZPD, Vol.175, 12 May 1916, p.102.
78 NZPD, Vol.173, 25 August 1915, p.132.
79 WAGL Broadsheet, *The German Menace* (Auckland, 1918).
80 *The German Menace.*
81 NZP, 1/4 (1916), pp.2–3.
82 ANZ, R22434297-AAYS-8638-AD1-1030-59/86, 'Chaplains; Prisoners of War; Reservists – Aliens – Enemy – Correspondence with anti-German League'.
83 *Colonist*, 25 October, 1918, p.7.
84 Beatrice Day had received the medal the previous year. See *Truth*, 5 January 1918, p.6.
85 *Dominion*, 12 July 1919, p.4.
86 *Dominion*, 12 July 1919, p.4.
87 *The Empire's Task: The Story of the Menace of German Trade* (Christchurch, 1918), p.10.
88 French, p.365.
89 For analysis of the emotional forces backing commitment see Loveridge, *Calls to Arms.*
90 C. Haste, *Keep the Home Fires Burning* (London, 1977), p.138.

Chapter Sixteen – When Neighbours Became Alien Enemies: Germans in New Zealand during World War One

1 Andrew Francis, 'From "Proven Worthy Settlers" to "Lawless Hunnish Brutes": Germans in New Zealand during the Great War', in Panayi Panikos (ed.), *Germans as Minorities during the First World War: A Global Comparative Perspective* (Surrey, 2014), pp.289–310.

2 Facets of German-speaking Europe in nineteenth-century New Zealand are considered in various essays within James Bade (ed.), *The German Connection: New Zealand and German-speaking Europe in the Nineteenth Century* (Auckland, 1993).
3 Francis, 'From Proven', p.290.
4 *Evening Post* (EP), 12 August 1914, p.6.
5 *Colonist*, 6, August 1914, p.7.
6 *Colonist*, 14 August 1914, p.7. Similar resolutions and declarations of loyalty were voiced by other German communities, as well as the Lutheran church. For an example see *Wanganui Chronicle*, 11 August 1914, p.5.
7 *Colonist*, 25 August 1914, p.7.
8 For further analysis see Judith Bassett, 'Colonial Justice: The Treatment of Dalmatians in New Zealand during the First World War', *New Zealand Journal of History* (NZJH), 33/2 (October 1999), pp.155–179; Steve Marti, 'Frenemy Aliens: The National and Transnational Considerations of Independent Contingents in Australia, Canada, and New Zealand, 1914–1918', *Itinerario*, 38/3 (December 2014), pp.119–38. For Croatian and Dalmatian assurances of loyalty see *Colonist*, 12 August 1914, p.7.
9 Eli Nathans, *The Politics of Citizenship in Germany: Ethnicity, Utility and Nationalism* (New York, 2004), pp.155, 170, 176–179.
10 Samantha Owens, '"Unmistakeable Sauerkrauts": Local Perceptions of Itinerant German Musicians in New Zealand, 1850–1920', forthcoming in *Nineteenth-Century Music Review*, 13.
11 Jürgen Tampke (ed.), *'Ruthless Warfare': German Military Planning and Surveillance in the Australia–New Zealand Region before the Great War* (Canberra, 1998), pp.90, 101.
12 *Colonist*, 19 May 1915, p.7; J.W. Pobóg-Jaworowski, *History of the Polish Settlers in New Zealand, 1776–1987* (Warsaw, 1988), p.93.
13 For further analysis see Natalie J. Wright, 'Beyond the Pale of Human Recognition: The Image of the Enemy as Portrayed in the Otago/Southland Press during World War One: Attitudes towards British Propaganda and Censorship' (MA thesis, University of Otago, 1996); Simon Johnson, 'The Home Front: Aspects of Civilian Patriotism in New Zealand during the First World War' (MA thesis, Massey University, 1975), pp.85–107.
14 *Colonist*, 20 August 1914, p.3
15 *Colonist*, 25 August 1914, p.7.
16 *New Zealand Parliamentary Debates*, Vol.171, 20 October 1914, pp.139–140.
17 *Colonist*, 21 January 1915, p.6.
18 *Colonist*, 19 May 1915, p.5
19 Francis, *'To Be Truly British We Must Be Anti-German': New Zealand Enemy Aliens and the Great War Experience, 1914–1919* (New York, 2012).
20 Steven Loveridge, 'A German is *Always* a German?: Representations of Enemies, Germans and Race in New Zealand, c. 1890–1918', NZJH, 48/1 (April 2014), pp.51–71.
21 *Colonist*, 12 November 1915, p.3.
22 *Otago Daily Times*, 13 May 1915, p.4; *Colonist*, 13 May 1915, p.4.
23 For further analysis see Jean King, 'Anti-German Hysteria during World War I', in James Bade (ed.), *Out of the Shadow of War: The German Connection with New Zealand in the Twentieth Century* (Auckland, 1998), pp.19–24; Val Burr, *German-ating the Seed of Anger: The Great War's Impact on Germans in Manawatu and Rangitikei, New Zealand* (BA Hons, Massey University, 1996); Burr, 'Enemies Within: A Study of New Zealand's Home Front during the First World War' available at http://www.oocities.org/somesprisonersnz/germanating/ger0.html, accessed 18 February 2015 (a

revised edition of Burr's BA Hons is also available at this site).

24 Marti, p.122.

25 Alexander Turnbull Library (ATL), MS-Papers-5969-1, 'Mr and Mrs Langguth (paper)', p.4.

26 For additional details see Christopher Pugsley, *On the Fringe of Hell: New Zealanders and Military Discipline in the First World War* (Auckland, 1991), pp.77–90; Archives New Zealand (ANZ), R3885217-AAYS-8647-AD10-2-5/4, 'Pte [Private] WP Nimot, deserter, August 1916 – November 1919'.

27 For a wider consideration of the dynamic see Brigitte Bönisch-Brednich, *Keeping A Low Profile: An Oral History of German Immigration to New Zealand* (Wellington, 2002).

28 For examples see EP, 8 December 1915, p.2; EP, 3 May 1916 p.3; EP, 17 January 1918, p.6.

29 *Colonist*, 1 June 1915, p.4.

30 *Ashburton Guardian*, 5 January 1916, p.4.

31 *Population Census*, 1911, p.xi; *Population Census*, 1916, p.14.

32 ATL, MS-Papers-5477, 'Murie, David fl 1995–1996 A life of Henry Joosten', p.2. For other examples of donations see *Dominion*, 2 December 1915, p.4; EP, 3 December 1915, p.2. All contemporary figures calculated using the Reserve Bank's Inflation Calculator, http://www.rbnz.govt.nz.

33 EP, 15 December 1914, p.2. Later Wolter developed his argument of naturalisation as the foundation of loyalty and pondered the contradictions the opposing position entailed: 'A naturalized British subject is, by the very fact of being a British subject, an enemy of those countries with whom Great Britain is at war, and calling him an "enemy in New Zealand", is, therefore, equal to supposing him to be an enemy of himself – a very difficult "alien".' EP, 19 January 1915, p.3.

34 ATL, MS-Papers-5981-2, 'Wolter the Learned', p.9.

35 *New Zealand Free Lance* (NZFL), 23 December 1919, p.24.

36 NZFL, 23 December 1919, p.24.

37 Jacob Joseph bequeathed two scholarships to Victoria College in 1903 with an annual value of £60 each. This sum was paid in two instalments.

38 EP, 27 January 1915, p.10.

39 *New Zealand Gazette*, 10 November 1914, p.4022.

40 *New Zealand Statutes* (NZS), 1917, No.8, pp.22–23.

41 Loveridge, 'A German is *Always* a German?', p.54.

42 *Press*, 10 August 1914, p.8; *Colonist*, 10 August 1914, p.3.

43 EP, 13 August 1914, p.8.

44 David McGill, *Island of Secrets: Matiu/Somes Island in Wellington Harbour* (Wellington, 2001), p.44.

45 ANZ, R21371869-AAAB-478-8/bc, 'Prisoners of war: letters for'.

46 Burr, 'Enemies Within'.

47 *New Zealand Herald* (NZH), 26 September 1914, p.6.

48 ATL, MS-Papers-5969-1, 'Mr and Mrs Langguth (paper)', p.2.

49 See Nelson Wattie, 'George von Zedlitz', in *Out of the Shadow of War*, pp.137–141.

50 Tim Beaglehole, 'Zedlitz, George William Edward Ernest von', *Dictionary of New Zealand Biography, Te Ara – the Encyclopedia of New Zealand*, www.teara.govt.nz/en/biographies/3z1/zedlitz-george-william-edward-ernest-von.

51 Francis, *To Be Truly British*, pp.153–154. See also Francis, 'Anti-Alienism in New Zealand during the Great War: The von Zedlitz Affair', *Immigrants & Minorities*, 24/3 (2006), pp.251–271.

52 NZFL, 15 August 1914, p.6. For further commentary see *Manawatu Times* (MT), 13 August 1914, p.4 and *Truth*, 15 August 1914, p.3.

53 *Colonist*, 30 October 1914, p.4.

54 An alleged history of mental illness in Rottmann's family may have also been a factor.

55 For further analysis of public perceptions and commentary on the German military's conduct see John Horne and Alan Kramer, *German Atrocities, 1914: A History of Denial* (New Haven, 2001), pp.227–261.

56 EP, 2 January 1915, p.3; ANZ, R24209573-ACGO-8333-IA1-1451-20/1/725, 'Naturalisation – Application – Wohnsiedler, Friedrich'.

57 MT, 25 January 1915, p.4. Another example at Mangawhare saw Frank Pavlovich, a native of Herzegovina, die from a self-inflicted gunshot to his left lung in an action said to reflect enmity against aliens. *Waikato Argus*, 30 November 1914, p.3.

58 Burr, *German-ating the Seeds of Anger*, concluding remarks.

59 ANZ, R21371462-AAAB-478-12/ac, 'W.A.G.L. Resolution'. The Grierson affair forms a major example of such cases and is considered in Loveridge, 'A German is *Always* a German?', p.68. See also chapter 15, this volume.

60 NZS, 1917, No.12, pp.64–66.

61 ATL, MS-Papers-5969-1, p.1.

62 EP, 5 February 1916, p.4.

63 ATL, MS-Papers-2071, 'Somes Island internees' statements'.

64 AJHR, 1919, H-33, 'Prisoners of War at Somes Island', p.2.

65 Sarah Wright, 'Moral Panics as Enacted Melodramas', *British Journal of Criminology*, 55 (2015), pp.1246–1247.

66 NZFL, 13 August 1915, p.6.

67 Francis, *To Be Truly British*, p.178.

68 *New Zealand Observer*, 4 September 1915, p.2.

69 NZS, 1915, No.67, pp.361–362.

70 Francis, pp.153–154. See also Francis, 'Anti-Alienism in New Zealand during the Great War: The von Zedlitz Affair', *Immigrants & Minorities*, 24/3 (2006), pp.251–271.

71 Bernard John Foster, 'Zedlitz (-Neukirk), George William Edward Ernest von', *Te Ara, The Encyclopedia of New Zealand*, Vol.3, 1966. www.teara.govt.nz/en/1966/zedlitz.

72 Beaglehole, 'Zedlitz, George William Edward Ernest von'.

73 Rachel Barrowman (ed.), *Victoria University of Wellington 1899–1999: A History* (Wellington, 1999), pp.35–36.

74 George William von Zedlitz, *The Search for a Country: The Autobiography of G.W. von Zedlitz* (Hamilton, 1963).

75 ATL, fMS-Papers-1651-1, 'papers', pp.8, 304, 502, 508.

76 The *Feilding Star* condemned the one-hundred-to-one odds as 'unBritish', 'especially when the one is a German'. *Feilding Star*, 20 November 1915, p.3.

77 Albert Gudopp and Dorothy Strauch, *St Martin's Lutheran Church, Marton: 1877–1977 Centennial* (Marton, 1977), p.17.

78 Burr, *German-ating the Seed of Anger*; *Dominion*, 7 August 1918, p.4.

79 For a wider consideration of New Zealand responses to the sinking of the *Lusitania* see Paul Diamond, 'The heart-breaking calamity that has befallen us all', 7 May 2015, https://natlib.govt.nz/blog/posts/the-heart-breaking-calamity-that-has-befallen-us-all.

80 NZH, 17 May 1915, p.6.

81 Nicola F. Gullace: 'Friends, Aliens, and Enemies: Fictive communities and the Lusitania riots of 1915', *Journal of Social History*, 39/2 (2005) p.346; Tilman Dedering, '"Avenge the Lusitania": The Anti-German Riots in South Africa in 1915', *Immigrants & Minorities* (2013), pp.1–33.

82 McGill, p.64.

83 McGill, pp.43–76.

84 Examples are displayed within the Museum of New Zealand Te Papa Tongarewa collections and are available online at http://collections.tepapa.govt.nz/object/709988 and http://collections.tepapa.govt.nz/object/1295164. See also examples in McGill, p.67 and Kate Hunter and Kirstie Ross, *Holding on to Home: New Zealand Stories and Objects of the First World War* (Wellington, 2014), pp.178–179.

85 ANZ, R21371053-AAAB-482-W291-38/b-346, 'Hansen, (Sautag) Hans'.

86 Francis, 'From Proven', p.302.

87 See for example NZFL, 8 August 1918, p.8.

88 Collections of internees' accounts are available in ATL, MS-Papers-2071, 'Somes Island internees' statements' and ANZ, R3796234-ACHK-16602-G47-1, 'Copies of letters to and from Dr. Schultz and others'. For the 1918 parliamentary inquiry see AJHR, 1919, H-33, *Prisoners of War at Somes Island*. See also Rolf W. Brednich, 'Enemy Aliens: Internierungslager für Deutsche in den beiden Weltkriegen. Eine Problemskizze am Beispiel Neuseelands', in Thomas Hengartner and Brigitta Schmidt-Lauber (eds), *Leben – Erzählen. Beiträge zur Erzähl- und Biographieforschung* (Berlin and Hamburg, 2004), pp.249–276.

89 Motuihi Island, New Zealand's other major internment site, is generally considered to have operated under a less antagonistic air. This subject, and possible explanations, are considered in Francis, 'From Proven', p.302 and further explored in Francis, *To Be Truly British*, pp.123–129.

90 McGill, p.49.

91 McGill, pp.51, 60, 67. For von Luckner's encounters with New Zealand see James Bade, 'Count Felix von Luckner', in *Out of the Shadow of War*, pp.37–49.

92 McGill, p.64.

93 ATL, MS-Papers-5981-2, pp.5–6.

94 *Hawera & Normanby Star*, 20 May 1915, p.4.

95 L.H. Barber, 'The Twenties: New Zealand's Xenophobic Years', *The New Zealand Law Journal*, 4 (1976), pp.95–96.

96 Francis, *To Be Truly British*, p.261. The 1919 passage of the Undesirable Immigrants Exclusion Act similarly reflected the restrictive disposition.

97 McGill, p.69.

98 ATL, MS-Papers-5477, pp. 4, 6–9.

99 ANZ, R24209573-ACGO-8333-IA1-1451-20/1/725, 'Naturalisation – Application – Wohnsiedler, Friedrich'.

100 Beaglehole, 'Zedlitz, George William Edward Ernest von'.

101 *Dominion*, 7 June 1918, p.4.

102 *New Zealand Gazette*, 25 January 1923, pp.204–205.

103 EP, 16 June 1922, p.8.

104 Some relief came by way of conducting classes for the study of French, German, Italian and Spanish language and literature and from the Victoria College Council, which elected to pay him a second instalment of the Jacob Joseph Scholarship. *Maoriland Worker*, 30 June 1920, p.8; *Dominion*, 12 February 1920, p.5.

105 For New Zealanders' rules of social interaction see Bönisch-Brednich, 'Watching the Kiwis: New Zealanders' rules of social interaction', *Journal of New Zealand*

Studies, 6–7 (2007–2008) pp.3–15.
106 Barber, p.96.
107 *Press*, 21 March 1921, p.10.
108 W. J. Gardner, 'Bell, Francis Henry Dillon', *Dictionary of New Zealand Biography, Te Ara – the Encyclopedia of New Zealand*, http://www.teara.govt.nz/en/biographies/2b16/bell-francis-henry-dillon. For Wolter's correspondence to Gibb see ATL, Ms-Papers-2053-45, 'Correspondence – F F Wolter's case', pp.1–7.

Chapter Seventeen – Turangawaewae: Maori Relationships with the Great War

1 It is worth noting that Maori offer the major but not the only example on this front. For further examples of non-Pakeha engagement with New Zealand's war effort see Jane McCabe, '"An Ideal Life": Anglo-Indians in the New Zealand Expeditionary Force', in David Monger, Sarah Murray and Katie Pickles (eds), *Endurance and the First World War: Experiences and Legacies in New Zealand and Australia* (Newcastle upon Tyne, 2014), pp.196–214; Christine Liava'a, *Le Fitafita Mai Samoa: The Force from Samoa: Soldiers from the Samoan Islands in the Great War* (Auckland: 2013); Margaret Pointer and Kalaisi Folau, *Tagi Tote A Loto Haaku: My Heart is Crying a Little: Niue Involvement in the Great War, 1914–1918* (Alofi, 2000).
2 For introductory accounts of the 'imperial turn' in First World War scholarship see John H. Morrow, *The Great War: An Imperial History* (New York, 2004); Andrew Tait Jarboe and Richard S. Fogarty (eds), *Empires in World War I: Shifting Frontiers and Imperial Dynamics in a Global Conflict* (London, 2014); and Robert Gerwarth and Erez Manela (eds), *Empires at War 1911–1923* (Oxford, 2014).
3 J.G.A. Pocock, *The Discovery of Islands: Essays in British History* (Cambridge, 2005), p.190; Steven Loveridge, *Calls to Arms: New Zealand Society and Commitment to the Great War* (Wellington, 2014), pp.28–68.
4 Vincent O'Malley, *The Meeting Place: Maori and Pakeha Encounters, 1642–1840* (Auckland, 2012). For further analysis of Maori adoption of European culture see James Belich, *Making Peoples: A History of the New Zealanders from Polynesian Settlement to the End of the Nineteenth Century* (Auckland, 1996), pp.148–155; Hugh Douglas Morrison (eds), *Mana Maori and Christianity* (Wellington, 2012); Matthew Wright, *Guns and Utu: A Short History of the Musket Wars* (Auckland, 2011); Lachy Paterson, *Colonial Discourses: Niupepa Maori 1855–1863* (Dunedin, 2006).
5 Hazel Petrie, *Chiefs of Industry: Maori Tribal Enterprise in Early Colonial New Zealand* (Auckland, 2006).
6 Ian Pool, *Te Iwi Maori* (Auckland, 1991), p.76. For some of the debates on Maori population and its nineteenth-century decline see Belich *Making Peoples*, pp.173–178.
7 Richard Boast and Richard Hill, *Raupatu: The Confiscation of Maori Land* (Wellington, 2009).
8 *Appendix to the Journals of the House of Representatives*, 1917 Session I, H-39a, 'Census of the Maori Population', p.1.
9 Michael King, *Maori: A Photographic and Social History* (Auckland, 1983), p.200.
10 King, 'Between Two Worlds', in W.H. Oliver (ed.) *The Oxford History of New Zealand* (Wellington, 1981), pp.279–301.
11 John Barrington, *Separate but Equal?: Maori Schools and the Crown 1867–1969* (Wellington, 2008), pp.14–16; Derek A. Dow, *Maori Health and Government Policy: 1840–1940* (Wellington, 1999); Belich, *Making Peoples*, pp.265–266.

12 Tony Ballantyne, *Entanglements of Empire: Missionaries, Maori and Questions of the Body* (Auckland, 2014).
13 Ian F. W. Beckett, *The Great War: 1914–1918* (London, 2014), p.9.
14 Ian McGibbon, *The Path to Gallipoli: Defending New Zealand 1840–1915* (Wellington, 1991), p.200.
15 Monty Soutar, 'E te Iwi, Whitiki! Whiti! Whiti! E! Call to arms: the formation of the Maori Contingent in the First World War', *Turnbull Library Record*, 46 (2014), p.9.
16 Belich, *Paradise Reforged: A History of the New Zealanders from the 1880s to the Year 2000* (Auckland, 2001), pp.206–215.
17 Paul Diamond, *Makereti: Taking Maori to the World* (Auckland, 2007).
18 Belich, *Paradise Reforged*, pp.194–215.
19 Hill, *State Authority, Indigenous Autonomy: Crown–Maori Relations in New Zealand/ Aotearoa* (Wellington, 2004), p.44. Emphasis in original.
20 For the broader dynamics of local collaboration in the British Empire see David Cannadine, *Ornamentalism: How the British Saw Their Empire* (London, 2001) and John Darwin, *Unfinished Empire: The Global Expansion of Britain* (New York, 2012), pp.10–11. For a consideration in regard to New Zealand see Belich, *The New Zealand Wars and the Victorian Interpretation of Racial Conflict* (Auckland, 1988), pp.211–213.
21 Ranginui Walker, *Ka Whawhai tonu Matou: Struggle without End* (Auckland, 2004), pp.112–114.
22 Judith Binney, Gillian Chaplin and Craig Wallace, *Mihaia: The Prophet Rua Kenana and His Community at Maungapohatu* (New York, 1979).
23 O'Malley, '"Recording the Incident with a Monument": The Waikato War in Historical Memory', *Journal of New Zealand Studies*, 19 (2015), p.81.
24 Apirana Ngata and a number of important Ngati Porou rangatira visited King Te Rata attempting, unsuccessfully, to convince Te Rata and Taingakawa to halt this plan. *Te Kopara*, April 1914, pp.5, 8, 9.
25 Belich, 'Myth, Race, and Identity in New Zealand', *New Zealand Journal of History*, 31/1 (April 1997), pp.9–22.
26 *School Journal*, 3/4 (May 1909), p.116. For further analysis of the notion of Maori as equals see James Bennett, 'Maori as Honorary Members of the White Tribe', *Journal of Imperial and Commonwealth History*, 29/3 (2001), pp.33–54. For school lessons see Colin McGeorge, 'Race, Empire and the Maori in the New Zealand Primary School Curriculum 1880–1940', in J.A. Mangan (ed.), *The Imperial Curriculum: Racial Images and Education in the British Colonial Experience* (London, 1993), pp.64–78.
27 *New Zealand Herald* (NZH), 7 June 1906, p.4. For further analysis of the notion of Maori as an antitype of thrift and industry see Petrie, 'The "Lazy Maori": Pakeha Representations of a Maori Work Ethic 1890–1940' (MA thesis, University of Auckland, 1998).
28 *Manawatu Standard*, 22 June 1916, p.5; *Truth*, 24 June 1916, p.6.
29 *Otago Daily Times*, 4 August 1914, p.5.
30 *Northern Advocate*, 21 August 1914, p.5.
31 Soutar, 'E te Iwi, Whitiki! Whiti! Whiti! E!', p.10; Soutar, 'Te Hokowhitu-A-Tui: A Coming of Age?' in John Crawford and Ian McGibbon (eds), *New Zealand's Great War New Zealand, The Allies and The First World War*, (Auckland, 2007), pp.99–100.
32 *Evening Post* (EP), 29 September 1914, p.3.
33 Ashley Gould, '"Different Race, Same Queen": Maori and the War', in John Crawford and Ian McGibbon (eds), *One Flag, One Queen, One Tongue: New Zealand, The British Empire and the South African War 1899–1902* (Auckland, 2003), p.123.

34 One of them was Hami Grace: http://www.aucklandmuseum.com/war-memorial/online-cenotaph/record/C5756.
35 *Auckland Star* (AS), 7 August 1914, p.6.
36 P.S. O'Connor, 'The Recruitment of Maori Soldiers, 1914–18', *Political Science*, 19/2 (December 1967), pp.51–52; Soutar, 'E te Iwi, Whitiki! Whiti! Whiti! E!', p.12. Under this system Northern Maori were to recruit 100 men, Western Maori 180, Eastern Maori 180, and Southern Maori 40. If one district could not fill its quota then others would make it up. Archives New Zealand (ANZ), R22429031-AAYS-8638-AD1-707 9/32/1, 'Expeditionary Force – Maori Contingents N.Z.E.F'.
37 Soutar, 'E te Iwi, Whitiki! Whiti! Whiti! E!', p.13.
38 Franchesca Walker, '"Descendants of a Warrior Race": The Maori Contingent, New Zealand Pioneer Battalion, and Martial Race Myth, 1914–19', *War and Society*, 31/1 (March 2012), pp.1–21; Christopher Pugsley, 'Images of Te Hokowhitu a Tu in the First World War', in Santanu Das (ed.), *Race, Empire and First World War Writing* (Cambridge, 2011), pp.194–210. For the mobilisation of notions of past European warrior traditions see Goebel Stefan, *The Great War and Medieval Memory: War and Remembrance in Britain and Germany, 1914–1940* (Cambridge, 2006).
39 Rikihana Carkeek, *Home Little Maori Home: A Memoir of the Maori Contingent* (Wellington, 2003), p.9.
40 For further examples of political rhetoric on commitment see EP, 4 September 1915, p.3.
41 *Dominion*, 15 February 1915, p.6.
42 NZH, 7 January 1915, p.6.
43 EP, 20 October 1914, p.6.
44 *New Zealand Parliamentary Debates* (NZPD), Vol.169, 1 September 1914, pp.661–662.
45 Pugsley, *Te Hokowhitu a Tu: the Maori Pioneer Battalion in the First World War* (Auckland, 1995), p.30.
46 O'Connor, p.51.
47 The most recent account of this episode is available in Soutar, 'Kua Whewhe Matou! Breaking up the Maori Contingent and the ordering home of its four officers', in Charles Ferrall and Harry Ricketts (eds), *How We Remember: New Zealanders and the First World War* (Wellington, 2014), pp.49–79.
48 ANZ, R24048325-ACID-25038-WA252-1/[2], '[Correspondence between] General Sir Alexander Godley [Commander New Zealand Expeditionary Force] and Colonel Hon. [Honourable] Sir James Allen, Minister of Defence, 2 April – 18 December 1915'.
49 ANZ, R24048326, ACID-25038-WA252-1/[3], '[Correspondence between] General Sir Alexander Godley [Commander New Zealand Expeditionary Force] and Colonel Hon. [Honourable] Sir James Allen, Minister of Defence, 4 January – 29 December 1916'. During this impasse Cook Islanders and Niueans were first recruited. O'Connor, pp.60–61.
50 On South Island Maori volunteering see NZH, 19 February 1918, p.4.
51 *Te Kopara*, 12 September 1918, p.12. On Tuhoe soldiers see http://www.aucklandmuseum.com/war-memorial/online-cenotaph/record/C74537.
52 *Te Paki o Matariki*, 12 July 1915 p.1.
53 The report made a number of other observations. Firstly, it noted that, under the Treaty of Waitangi, Queen Victoria had promised to protect Maori and noted that enlistment threatened this protection. Secondly, it cited Tawhiao's 1881 declaration that warfare should be banished. Thirdly, Te Rata proclaimed that

Maori should not search for war but should abstain from fighting until conflict came to New Zealand.

54 King, *Te Puea: A Life* (Auckland, 1977), p.78.

55 ANZ, R18874768-ADTO-18998-STATS1-32-23/1/96, 'Military Service Act, 1916 – Military Service registration and calling up of Maoris in Waikato-Maniapoto district'.

56 ANZ, R22436335-AAYS-8638-AD1-1046-66/11, 'Conscription – Maoris under Military Service Act – Correspondence'.

57 J.C., Fussell, *Letters from Private Henare Tikitanu* (Auckland, 1917), p.5; Fussell, *Corporal Tikitanu, V.C.* (Auckland, 1918). For further examples see *Chronicles of the NZEF*, 30 May 1917, p.151; 12 December 1917, pp.204–205; 16 August 1918, pp.32–33; *Countess of Liverpool Gift Book of Art and Literature* (Christchurch, 1915), pp.70–72; and numerous examples throughout *New Zealand at the Front* (London, 1917). On 'stage Maori' see Shaun F.D. Hughes, 'Was there ever a "Maori English"?', *World Englishes*, 23/4 (2004), pp.565–584.

58 Fussell, *Letters from Private Henare Tikitanu*.

59 Fussell, *Corporal Tikitanu*, pp.51–52.

60 *New Zealand Observer* (NZO), 6 October 1917, p.3.

61 Gould, 'Maori and the First World War' in Ian McGibbon (ed.), *The Oxford Companion To New Zealand Military History* (Auckland, 2000), p.297. Note that the discrepancy between the 477 cited in this source and the 497 cited here reflects recent findings which have revised the number of New Zealanders deployed at Gallipoli. These findings are available at http://www.mch.govt.nz/sites/default/files/ENUMERATING%20NEW%20ZEALAND%20EXPEDITIONARY%20FORCE%20SERVICE%20INTERIM%20REPORT%20MARCH%202016%20(D-0651931).PDF.

62 On the frontline experiences of the Maori Contingent see James Cowan, *The Maoris in the Great War: A History of the New Zealand Native Contingent and Pioneer Battalion: Gallipoli 1915, France and Flanders 1916–1918* (Auckland, 1926); Pugsley, *Te Hokowhitu a Tu*; Tania Simpson, *The Last Maopo: The Life and First World War Sacrifice of Wiremu Maopo* (Auckland, 2014).

63 O'Connor, p.53. For discussion of the imperial context and implication behind this development see Timothy C. Winegard, *Indigenous Peoples of the British Dominions and the First World War* (New York, 2012), pp.97–99.

64 ANZ, R10075086-AAYS-8698-AD82-5-11/1/2, 'General file, June 1917 – October 1918'; ANZ, R3885537-AAYS-8647-AD10-17-30/3, 'Recruiting Maoris, March–April'; R22429222-AAYS-8638-AD1-719-9/276-1, 'Expeditionary Force – Maori contingent active service'; R22429223-AAYS-8638-AD1-719-9/276-2, 'Expeditionary Force – Maori contingent active service'.

65 O'Connor, p.53.

66 ANZ, R24048325-ACID-25038-WA252-1/[2], 'Correspondence between] General Sir Alexander Godley [Commander New Zealand Expeditionary Force] and Colonel Hon. [Honourable] Sir James Allen, Minister of Defence, 2 April – 18 December 1915'.

67 *New Zealand Official Year Book*, 1919, p.257; 1925, pp.77, 105.

68 John Horne, 'Remobilizing for "Total War": France and Britain, 1917–1918', in John Horne (ed.), *State, Society and Mobilization in Europe during the First World War* (Cambridge, 1997), pp.195–211.

69 NZPD, Vol.175, 1 June 1916, p.610.

70 Winegard, p.5.

71 Some accounts emphasise the limits of those operating from the Pakeha world; Pomare, for example, has been noted as taking on 'Anglophile values to such an extent' that he 'alienated himself from his people.' Ranginui Walker, p.180.
72 ANZ, R10075086-AAYS-8698-AD82-5-11/1/2, 'General file, June 1917 – October 1918'.
73 *Te Kopara*, September 1918, p.31.
74 AS, 25 November 1916, p10.
75 NZH, 5 July 1917, p.6.
76 Cowan, pp.19–20.
77 Alexander Turnbull Library (ATL), MS-Papers-6919-0234, '040 – Papers re Maori in the Second World War'.
78 NZH, 5 July 1917, p.6.
79 It did not help that Maniapoto had a higher per capita rate of enlistment than Pomare's own Taranaki. King, *Te Puea*, p.85.
80 King, *Te Puea*, p.92.
81 Hill, p.107.
82 ANZ, R24048326, ACID-25038-WA252-1/[3], '[Correspondence between] General Sir Alexander Godley [Commander New Zealand Expeditionary Force] and Colonel Hon. [Honourable] Sir James Allen, Minister of Defence, 4 January – 29 December 1916'.
83 The most detailed account of this episode is in Binney, Chaplin and Wallace, pp.81–134.
84 Paul Baker, *King and Country Call: New Zealanders, Conscription and the Great War* (Auckland, 1988), pp.214–217; Mark Derby, *The Prophet and the Policeman: The Story of Rua Kenana and John Cullen* (Wellington, 2009); Hill, p.92; Peter Webster, *Rua and the Maori Millennium* (Wellington, 1979), p.261; Binney, Chaplin and Wallace, p.82.
85 AS, 19 February 1916, p.19.
86 Kenana was released in April 1918 (ten months early) seemingly in exchange for a pledge to encourage recruitment. Though he did produce volunteers, they were evidently unfit, very old or too young, and none saw service. Kenana himself noted 'the government won't take them . . . It won't be long. No more war; all the people will come back.' Athol Anderson, Judith Binney and Aroha Harris, *Tangata Whenua: An Illustrated History* (Wellington, 2014), p.344.
87 Baker, p.217. All contemporary figures calculated using the Reserve Bank's Inflation Calculator, http://www.rbnz.govt.nz.
88 *Wairarapa Daily Times*, 4 August 1916, p.4.
89 *New Zealand Gazette*, 26 June 1917, pp.2509–2510. This brought some complaints from Te Arawa, and Maori in Hauraki and Thames, who petitioned not to be included in the Waikato-Maniapoto District and asked to be exempt from conscription. ANZ, R10075086-AAYS-8698-AD82-5-11/1/2, 'General file, June 1917 – October 1918'; ANZ, R22436335-AAYS-8638-AD1-1046-66/11, 'Conscription – Maoris under Military Service Act – Correspondence'.
90 For Australia see Joan Beaumont, 'The Politics of a Divided Society', in Joan Beaumont (ed.), *Australia's War, 1914–18* (St Leonards, 1995), pp.35–63; for Russia see Norman Stone, *The Eastern Front, 1914–1917* (London, 1975), p.214; for Canada see Martin F. Auger, 'On the Brink of Civil War: The Canadian Government and the Suppression of the 1918 Quebec Easter Riots', *Canadian Historical Review*, 89/4 (2008), pp.503–540; for Ireland see Alan J. Ward, 'Lloyd George and the 1918 Irish Conscription Crisis', *The Historical Journal*, 17/1 (March 1974), pp.107–129.

91 ANZ, R18874766-ADTO-18998-STATS1-31-23/1/63, 'Military Service Act, 1916 – Enrolling Maori Expeditionary Force Reserve'.
92 O'Connor, pp.67–68.
93 ANZ, R18874766-ADTO-18998-STATS1-31-23/1/63, 'Military Service Act, 1916 – Enrolling Maori Expeditionary Force Reserve'.
94 ANZ, R18874766-ADTO-18998-STATS1-31-23/1/63, 'Military Service Act, 1916 – Enrolling Maori Expeditionary Force Reserve'.
95 ANZ, R18874766-ADTO-18998-STATS1-31-23/1/63, 'Military Service Act, 1916 – Enrolling Maori Expeditionary Force Reserve'.
96 NZO, 3 February 1917, p.16.
97 ANZ, R18874766-ADTO-18998-STATS1-31-23/1/63, 'Military Service Act, 1916 – Enrolling Maori Expeditionary Force Reserve'.
98 ANZ, R18874768-ADTO-18998-STATS1-32-23/1/96, 'Military Service Act, 1916 – Military Service registration and calling up of Maoris in Waikato-Maniapoto district'.
99 ANZ, R10075086-AAYS-8698-AD82-5-11/1/2, 'General file, June 1917 – October 1918'.
100 King, *Te Puea*, p.90.
101 O'Connor, p.77.
102 King, *Te Puea*, p.90.
103 ANZ, R10075086-AAYS-8698-AD82-5-11/1/2, 'General file, June 1917 – October 1918'.
104 *Te Kopara*, 31 August 1917, p.4.
105 Baker, p.220.
106 ATL, MS-Papers-6919-0234.
107 O'Connor, p.80.
108 Jock Phillips and Chris Maclean, *The Sorrow and the Pride New Zealand War Memorials* (Wellington, 1990), pp.86–88.
109 Geoffrey W. Rice, *Black November: The 1918 Influenza Pandemic in New Zealand* (Christchurch, 2005), p.17; Belich, *Paradise Reforged*, pp.112–113, 193.
110 Gould, 'Maori and the First World War', pp.298–299; Gould, 'From taiaha to ko: repatriation and land settlement for Maori settlers in New Zealand after World War I', in James Watson and Lachy Paterson (eds), *A Great New Zealand Prime Minister? Reappraising William Ferguson Massey* (Dunedin, 2011), pp.97–120.
111 Cowan, pp.ix–x.
112 ATL, MS-Papers-6919-0234.
113 Keith Newman, *Ratana: The Prophet* (Auckland, 2009), p.36.
114 King, *Te Puea*, pp.98–126.
115 *Wanganui Chronicle*, 24 May 1919, p.5.
116 Malcolm Mulholland, 'Māori rugby – whutupaoro - Rugby union, 1910s to 1930s', Te Ara - the Encyclopedia of New Zealand, updated 2-Aug-13, http://www.teara.govt.nz/en/photograph/39619/parekura-tureia.
117 Ranginui Walker, pp.183–184.
118 Soutar, 'Te Hokowhitu-a-Tu: What Did They Come Home To?', *Turnbull Library Record*, 42 (2009), pp.39–41.
119 M.P.K. Sorrenson (ed.), *Na to Hoa Aroha, From Your Dear Friend: The Correspondence between Sir Apirana Ngata and Sir Peter Buck, 1925–50*, Vol. 1 (Auckland, 1986), pp.30–31.
120 King, *Te Puea*, pp.201–216.

Chapter Eighteen – Enduring Mystery: New Zealand Children and the Great War

1 Jeanine Graham, 'Children and the New Zealand Wars: An Exploration', in James Marten (ed.), *Children and War: A Historical Anthology* (New York, 2002), pp.216–226. The 21 essays in this international volume provide many comparative perspectives on children's experiences of war.

2 Dorothy Butler, 'Born to Read', in Michael Gifkins (ed.), *Through the Looking Glass: Recollections of Childhood from 20 Prominent New Zealanders* (Auckland, 1988), p.9.

3 Cited in Steven Loveridge, '"Sentimental Equipment": New Zealand, the Great War and Cultural Mobilisation' (PhD thesis, Victoria University of Wellington, 2013), p.262, footnote 1043, *New Zealand Herald*, 8 August 1914, supplement, p.1.

4 See Margaret Tennant, *Paupers & Providers: Charitable Aid in New Zealand* (Wellington, 1989), passim. For Aubert's work with infants and children in need of care see Jessie Munro, *The Story of Suzanne Aubert* (Auckland, 1996), pp.208–231 (Hiruharama), 302–319 (Wellington) and 320–338 (Auckland).

5 Raeburn Lange, *May the People Live: A History of Maori Health Development 1900–1920*, (Auckland, 1999), pp.147–188 for the work of the Native Health Officers and registered Maori nurses; Geoffrey Rice with assistance from Lynda Bryder, *Black November: The 1918 influenza pandemic in New Zealand*, 2nd ed. (Christchurch, 2005), pp.159–183 for specific discussion of the pandemic's effect on Maori communities.

6 Charlotte Bennett, '"Now the war is over, we have something else to worry us": New Zealand Children's Responses to Crises, 1914–1918', *Journal of the History of Childhood and Youth*, 7/1 (2014), pp.19–41. This article draws on an extensive investigation of publicly available oral history collections and analysis of 'Dot's Little Folk' letters, published in the *Otago Witness*, 1914–1918. Bennett's MA thesis, of the same title (Victoria University of Wellington, 2012), discusses both 'younger' and 'older' children, defining the latter as up to 20 years of age.

7 Ian Pool, *Te Iwi Maori* (Auckland, 1991), pp.59–129.

8 For children's correspondence to the *Otago Witness* see Keith Scott, *Dear Dot, I must tell you: A Personal History of Young New Zealanders* (Auckland, 2011). Examples of graduate research using both letters and recorded interviews include Deborah Challinor, 'Children and War: A Study of the Impact of the First World War on New Zealand Children' (MA dissertation, University of Waikato, 1993) and Rosemary Goodyear, 'Black Boots and Pinafores: Childhood in Otago 1900–1920' (MA thesis, University of Otago, 1992).

9 Graham, 'Child Employment in New Zealand', *New Zealand Journal of History* (NZJH), 21/2 (October, 1987), pp.62–78.

10 As an example of the legislative inconsistency, girls could marry at 12 and boys at 14, a situation unchanged until 1933 when the minimum age for both was raised to 16, the age of female consent for sexual liaison as established in 1896.

11 Colin McGeorge, 'Childhood's Sole Serious Business: The Long Haul to Full School Attendance,' NZJH, 40/1 (April, 2006), pp.25–38.

12 Graham, *'My brother and I': Glimpses of Childhood in our Colonial Past* (Dunedin, 1992). This 1991 Hocken Lecture drew extensively on interviews recorded for an oral history project which involved 160 New Zealanders born before 1903. See Graham and Sally Maclean, 'The Colonial Childhoods Oral History Project: a report on progress', *Oral History in New Zealand*, 2 (1989), pp.31–36. All CCOHP tapes and copyright are in the author's possession.

13 See Claire Toynbee, *Her Work and His: Family, Kin and Community in New Zealand 1900–1930* (Wellington, 1995); and Rosemary Goodyear, 'Overworked Children? Child Labour in New Zealand, 1919–1939', NZJH, 40/1 (April, 2006), pp.75–90 for the interwar period.

14 For an example of contrasting experiences, see 'Two Wellington Childhoods', the Radio New Zealand interviews with Marjorie Lees and George Davies, in Alwyn Owen and Jack Perkins, *Speaking for Ourselves: Echoes from New Zealand's Past from the Award Winning 'Spectrum' Radio Series* (Auckland, 1986), pp.93–104. The interview was first broadcast in 1972.

15 Sally Maclean, 'Child Cruelty or Reasonable Punishment? A case study in the operation of the law and the courts, 1883–1893', NZJH, 40/1 (April, 2006), pp.7–24.

16 Philip Ridge (ed.), *The [Auckland] Weekly News: Those Were the Days: 1900–1919* (Auckland, 1989), p.138, 13 July 1915 for a composite of images showing children engaged in the war effort. More images are accessible online at http://www.aucklandlibraries.govt.nz/EN/heritage/usingnewspapereresources/Pages/aucklandweeklynewsimages.aspx, accessed 23 May 2015.

17 For examples, see Sandy Callister, *The Face of War: New Zealand's Great War Photography* (Auckland, 2008), particularly pp.103–121.

18 Melanie Nolan, '"Keeping New Zealand Home Fires Burning": Gender, Welfare and the First World War', in John Crawford and Ian McGibbon (eds), *New Zealand's Great War: New Zealand, the Allies and the First World War* (Auckland, 2007), p.501.

19 Malcolm McKinnon (ed.), *New Zealand Historical Atlas* (Auckland, 1997), Plate 78, 'The Great War: Patriotism and memory' for regional differences in recruitment and details on the social effects of the war. Note especially the graphic showing soldier casualties from households in Invercargill as an example of the scale of mourning within neighbourhoods.

20 E.P. Malone, 'The New Zealand School Journal and The Imperial Ideology', NZJH, 7/1 (April, 1973), pp.12–27; and see Roger Openshaw, 'Patriotism and the New Zealand primary school: the decisive years of the twenties' (DPhil thesis, University of Waikato, 1978), passim, for the link between patriotism and the curriculum.

21 Scott, p.422.

22 Graham, 'Young New Zealanders and the Great War: exploring the impact and legacy of the First World War, 1914–2014', *Paedagogica Historica*, 44/4, (2008), pp.429–444. The four paragraphs following draw on evidence cited in this article.

23 See Denise Van Patten, 'Top Five German Antique Doll Brands', http://collectdolls.about.com/od/germanantiques/tp/Top-German-Antique-Doll-Brands.htm for bisque dolls, and BBC Schools – World War One, 'What did children do for fun?', http://www.bbc.co.uk/schools/0/ww1/25183931 for teddy bears, accessed 21 April 2015. For an evocative example of how a German-made doll became the target of unwanted adult attention, and a child's agency in resolving the situation, see 'A ruddy little Hun', excerpt from Mary Drake, *The Trees Were Green* (Sydney, 1984), pp.42–43, reproduced in Gwyn Dow and June Factor (eds), *Australian Childhood: An Anthology* (Ringwood, 1991), pp.160–161.

24 This information is drawn from Dylan Owen's panel on the Foxton School piano, as featured in the National Library's exhibition, 'World War One – A Contemporary Conversation', on display in Wellington, 16 October 2014 – 3 October 2015, viewed 3 February 2015.

25 Graham, 'Young New Zealanders', footnotes 55 and 56.

26 Lauris Edmond with Carolyn Milward (eds), *Women in Wartime* (Wellington, 1986), pp.134–135; and Judith Bassett, 'Colonial Justice: The Treatment of Dalmatians in

New Zealand During the First World War', NZJH, 33/2 (October, 1999), pp.155–179. An insightful Australian example of a similar situation, David Gleason's memoir, 'At first I thought it was the most wonderful adventure', in Jacqueline Kent (ed.), *In the Half Light: Reminiscences of Growing Up in Australia 1900–1970* (Moorebank, NSW, 1991), pp.47–64, describes a young boy's exposure to wartime bigotry and a parent's determined stand against it.

27 See Scott, pp.413–451.

28 Exhibit 16 in 'A Child's War: Words and Pictures from World War 1', Turnbull Gallery, National Library, Wellington, 24 November 2014 – 27 February 2015, viewed 3–4 February 2015. Some material from the exhibition is available at https://natlib.govt.nz/events/a-child-s-war-opens, accessed 22 May 2015. Norah was the daughter from Colonel William Malone's first marriage, which ended in 1904 when his wife died in childbirth; Malone also wrote to Denis, Barney and Molly, the young children from his second marriage in 1905. I am most grateful to the exhibition's curator, Mary Skarott, Research Librarian, Children's Literature, for her generosity in discussing the exhibits and in facilitating my use of the display materials.

29 Edmond and Milward, p.238.

30 Auckland War Memorial Museum Library (AWMML), MS2004/16, 'Henry (Harry) Thomas Norton Letters, 1900–1938', Folder 3, Harry Norton to Leonard Norton, 27 March 1916.

31 For a selection of Smith's letters and family photographs see Jock Phillips, Nicholas Boyack and E.P. Malone (eds), *The Great Adventure: New Zealand Soldiers Describe the First World War* (Wellington, 1988), pp.195–228.

32 See AWMML, MS2004/16, 'Harry Norton Letters', Folder 5 – Letters July–August 1916 and Folder 6 Letters September–December 1916 for correspondence by Leonard (Lennie) and his sister Jean (Lottie) to their father.

33 This image and others from the family collection are reproduced in Callister, pp.114–116. They can also be viewed online at http://www.aucklandmuseum.com/war-memorial/online-cenotaph/search/?n=henry+thomas+norton&w=World+War+I%2c+1914-1918, accessed 21 May 2015.

34 Miles Spencer interview with Jim Sullivan, 'Sounds Historical' programme, first broadcast 3 October 2004, Radio New Zealand National. For comparative insights into the ongoing effects of absence and demobilisation in children's lives see William Tuttle, *'Daddy's Gone to War': The Second World War in the Lives of America's Children* (New York, 1993).

35 Examples of contemporary literature used in the 'Child's War' exhibition include: Harold Golding (ed.), *The Wonder Book of Empire* (London, 1915); Elphinstone Thorpe, illustrated by G.A. Stevens, *Nursery Rhymes for Fighting Times* (London, 1915); Percy Westerman, illustrated by Wal Paget, *A Lively Bit of the Front: A Tale of the New Zealand Rifles on the Western Front* (London, 1918); Thomas Kehoe, illustrated by Christopher Clarke, *The Fighting Mascot: The True Story of a Boy Soldier* (London, 1919); Bessie Marchant, illustrated by Wal Paget, *A Transport Girl in France* (London, 1919), all of which are held within the National Library's Dorothy Neal White children's literature collection. For examples of soldiers who did not talk about the war after their return see Nicholas Boyack and Jane Tolerton (eds.), *In the Shadow of War: New Zealand Soldiers Talk About World War One and Their Lives* (Auckland, 1990).

36 Sam Neill with Owen Hughes (producer), *Anzac: Tides of Blood*, screened on Maori Television, 25 April 2015. Additional footage and a study guide are available at https://www.maoritelevision.com/tv/shows/anzac-2015/sam-neills-extras, accessed 20 May 2015.

37 For this term and its context see Raymond Evans, 'The lowest common denominator: loyalism and schoolchildren in war torn Australia 1914/1918', *Queensland Review*, 3/2 (1996), pp.100–115, 154–158, passim. There are significant parallels with New Zealand children's experiences.

38 See 'Part III: Mourning', in Stephane Audoin-Rouzeau and Annette Becker, translated by Catherine Temersen, *14–18: Understanding the Great War* (New York, 2002), especially pp.203–225.

39 Edmond and Milward, pp.250–251. Emphasis as in the original.

40 See Chris Maclean and Jock Phillips, *The Sorrow and the Pride: New Zealand War Memorials* (Wellington, 1990), for examples from throughout the country.

41 Ruth Park, *A Fence Around the Cuckoo* (Ringwood, 1992), pp.14–17.

42 Graham, 'World Contexts', in Joseph Hawes and N. Ray Hiner (eds), *A Cultural History of Childhood and Family: Volume 6: In the Modern Age* (New York, 2010), pp.195–212.

43 Dugald McDonald provides the social policy framework for viewing the changing status of children, from chattel to social capital to psychological being and then to citizen. See McDonald, 'Children and Young Persons in New Zealand Society', in Peggy Koopman-Boyden (ed.), *Families in New Zealand Society* (Wellington, 1978), pp.44–56. See also Claire Breen, 'From Paternalism to (Partial) Autonomy: The Evolution of Children's Rights in New Zealand', NZJH, 40/1 (April 2006), pp.91–101.

44 For a summary of the child-saving movement, see Caroline Hinkle McCamant, 'Child Saving', in Paula Fass (ed.), *Encyclopedia of Children and Childhood*, Vol. 1 (New York, 2004), pp.195–197.

45 Linda Bryder, *A Voice for Mothers: The Plunket Society and Infant Welfare 1907–2000* (Auckland, 2003), p.x for infant death rates and reductions in family size. See Nolan, pp.504–515 for a case study of the Otago Soldiers' and Dependants' Welfare Committee (OSDWC) and the changing attitudes of those who visited families in need.

46 For child-related health and welfare initiatives see Margaret Tennant, *Children's Health, The Nation's Wealth: A History of Children's Health Camps* (Wellington, 1994); Bronwyn Dalley, *Family Matters: Child Welfare in Twentieth-Century New Zealand* (Auckland, 1998); Derek Dow, *Maori Health and Government Policy 1840–1940* (Wellington, 1999); Margaret McClure, *A Civilised Community: A History of Social Security in New Zealand 1898–1998* (Auckland, 1998).

Index